Edward Griffiths was born in Zimbabwe and educated in England. He was a sportswriter with *Business Day*, and was sports editor of the *Sunday Times* until 1993. He became the first chief executive of the South African Rugby Football Union in 1995, and later worked as general manager of SABC television sport, a consultant to each of SA's major events bids (Cape Town 2004, FIFA 2006, RWC 2011 and FIFA 2010) and as chief executive of Saracens rugby club in England. He has written biographies of Naas Botha, Kepler Wessels, Kitch Christie, Jonty Rhodes and Joost van der Westhuizen, and collaborated with François Pienaar and Gary Teichmann in the writing of their autobiographies.

Stephen Nell is one of South Africa's most experienced rugby writers, having started his career at the *Daily Dispatch* in 1994. An award-winning journalist and prolific writer in both English and Afrikaans, he works as a specialist rugby writer at *Die Burger*. He was previously employed by the South African Press Association and the *Cape Times*. Nell is also the author of the books *Springbok Glory* and *Bokspronge*. He has covered international rugby since 1995 and been on numerous Springbok tours. During his career he has developed close relationships with players, coaches and key rugby stakeholders.

To Bridget

EDWARD GRIFFITHS & STEPHEN NELL

THE
SPRINGBOK
CAPTAINS

The men who shaped South African rugby

JONATHAN BALL PUBLISHERS
Johannesburg & Cape Town

Originally published in hard cover and trade paperback as *The Captains* in 2001 by
JONATHAN BALL PUBLISHERS
A division of Media24 Limited
PO Box 33977
Jeppestown
2043

Second edition published in 2006.
This revised and updated edition published in 2015.

ISBN 978-1-86842-670-6
ebook ISBN 978-1-86842-671-3

Cover design and photo sections by MR Design
Cover photos by Gallo Images/Steve Haag (Victor Matfield), Gallo Images/Getty Images/
David Rogers (Jean de Villiers) and Gallo Images/Steve Haag (Fourie du Preez)
Typesetting and reproduction of text by Alinea Studio, Cape Town
Set in 11.5 on 14 pt Bembo

Printed by **paarlmedia**, a division of Novus Holdings

*Every effort has been made to trace the copyright holders and to obtain their permission for the use of
copyright material. The publishers apologise for any errors or omissions and would be grateful to be
notified of any corrections that should be incorporated in future editions of this book.*

CONTENTS

ACKNOWLEDGEMENTS

In the first instance, I am grateful to the Springbok captains themselves, for their time and, in almost every case, their searing honesty. In every face there is so much experience, emotion and wisdom. I hope I have managed to condense at least some of these precious resources into these pages.

I am also profoundly indebted to Jonathan Ball, the publisher, who handed me the concept and gave me the opportunity to put it into words, and to every member of his staff, who have relentlessly contributed to the project, particularly to Francine Blum for her patience and understanding.

Owen Hendry has proved a gifted, knowledgeable and sensitive editor, for whose skill and application I am profoundly grateful.

It is also correct that I should acknowledge debt to two other people who enabled me to enter, and then work within, the Springbok world.

First, Hugh Eley – as sports editor of *Business Day*, it was his decision in 1986 that the naïve, probably brash 23-year-old reporter should be assigned to writing about the tumultuous series between the Springboks and the New Zealand Cavaliers. Through those four Test matches, of enormous, impassioned crowds and rugby of rare intensity and drama, a seed was sown.

Second, Louis Luyt – as the president of the South African Rugby Football Union, it was he who asked me to work as media liaison officer with the squad on tour to Wales, Scotland and Ireland in 1994, and then to serve as the first Chief Executive of SARFU, from March 1995 until the following year.

During the past 11 years, I have also relished the opportunity to produce either the biography or autobiography of four individual Springbok captains: Naas Botha, Joost van der Westhuizen, François Pienaar and Gary Teichmann. During many hours in their company, I have grown familiar with the pressures and the work, with the essence and spirit of being the Springbok captain.

In compiling this book, I have drawn primarily on the personal recollections of the Springbok captains themselves, and on the memories of those who played with and against them. However, in reconstructing the eras of those captains who have passed away, I have discovered an invaluable source of fact and anecdote in *Springbok Saga*, the authoritative history first published by Don Nelson in 1997, written by the late, passionate and respected Chris Greyvenstein.

Lastly, I am grateful for the tolerance, understanding and forbearance of Bridget, David, Kate, Harry and, of course, the eight ducks.

Edward Griffiths
February 2006

For this third edition I am grateful to Jean de Villiers, Victor Matfield, John Smit and Bob Skinstad, the Springbok greats who were generous with their time in allowing me to update Edward Griffiths' splendid book. I am also indebted to Heyneke Meyer, Gert Smal, Swys de Bruin, Louise and André de Villiers, Pine Pienaar and De Jongh Borchardt. As if putting up with my usual eccentricities isn't enough, my partner, Adele, was a rock in tolerating the late nights a project of this magnitude inevitably demands. I am most grateful to Edward for entrusting me with "polishing the Mona Lisa". If I have done justice to his high standards, it owes much to my editor, Alfred LeMaitre. Thank you also to my publisher, Jeremy Boraine.

Stephen Nell
September 2015

PREFACE

Through 110 eventful and passionate years, the Springbok rugby captain has represented many things to many South Africans.

For generations of enthusiastic schoolboys excitedly pinning pictures to their bedroom walls, he has been a hero. For many others of his compatriots, he has been an indifferent figure, removed from their lives.

For millions of white South Africans during the 20th Century, he has been a positive, strong symbol of the courage and strength they believe are so integral to their principles and way of life; yet for millions of black South Africans, he has been a visible face of minority breast-beating and arrogance.

He has united, and he has divided. He has thrilled, he has disappointed. He has inspired, he has depressed. He has triumphed, he has failed.

He has always, always had an impact. He has never been less than a profoundly significant presence in public life, enjoying much greater bearing than mere sportsmen in many other parts of the planet.

Who has most regularly filled the newspaper columns? Who has been the subject of discussion at the Sunday braai and in the office on Monday morning? The Springbok captain, the President ... usually in that order.

Where else in the world would two sporting captains not simply popularise but actually create a brand new Christian name in their country? Since 1975, two Bok captains have demonstrated precisely this influence.

When the newborn Morné du Plessis was named after his father's brother in 1949, he became only the second Morné in South Africa.

His profile during six celebrated seasons as Springbok captain, between 1975 and 1980, caused the boy's name to become one of the most popular in the country.

David Jacobus Serfontein was christened after his paternal grandfather, following the Afrikaner custom that first-born sons should carry the family names. His mother was content to maintain tradition, but, creative by nature, she sensed David was simply too regular for her son. She started to play with the name. She reversed the letters, and produced Divad. She tried it for a week, but it sounded odd. What about if she changed the last "d" for an "n" … Divan. She liked the name, and the name stuck.

Relatives may have raised their eyebrows as the years passed, and there were certainly no other Divans at his school. Yet, by the time the young boy had become a renowned scrumhalf, led Western Province to three successive Currie Cup titles and captained South Africa in 1984, little Divans were being born week after week. Today, Divan is an established name in South Africa.

As it was with triumphant generals in ancient Rome, so it has been with popular Springbok captains in South Africa during the 20th Century.

When William Shakespeare wrote, at the start of the 17th Century, "uneasy lies the head that wears a crown", he might have been referring to England's King Henry IV rather than the succession of gentlemen who have carried the mantle of the Springbok captaincy, but the words are appropriate.

The title has ever been an honour, and a burden.

It is difficult to find a Springbok captain, past or present, who confesses to having keenly sought the role. Without exception, this select band of men reflects upon the weight of responsibility and, notably in recent years, the demands to fill airwaves and columns with quotes … and the need to win.

To be Springbok captain is to live under pressure.

"We happen to live in a country where the national rugby team is expected to win every time they take the field," notes André Vos, who led 16 times from 1999 before being relieved of the duty in 2001. "That is the scale on which we compete. There is no point complaining about it, saying it is unfair or pointing out that the world has changed.

"The fact is we have a proud, winning rugby history, and every Springbok team is expected to maintain the standard. If you win, you are only doing what is expected. If you lose, you must expect the public appetite for someone to blame. As captain, you swiftly learn that whatever you do will provoke a strong reaction, whether it is congratulations in victory or criticism in defeat."

It was ever thus.

Felix du Plessis captained the 1949 Springboks to victory over the All Blacks in the first Test, victory in the second Test, victory in the third Test and was then dropped, without explanation, for the fourth Test, forever.

When Stephen Fry led his Springbok team to Port Elizabeth, needing to win the fourth and final Test to square the series against the 1955 Lions, he did so following threats that he would be murdered if he did not resign.

Abie Malan captained South Africa to a record victory over Wales in 1964 and was dropped, again without explanation, for the next match.

Tradition has rumbled through the decades, ruthless and proud. The most appropriate analogy for Springbok rugby is of a great river, sourced as a trickling stream in the minds of a few sporting gentlemen at the close of the 19th Century, developing genuine momentum between the two World Wars.

The flow was guided and nurtured above all by Danie Craven, scrumhalf in 1931, captain in 1937, coach and selector many times thereafter, president of the Board from 1956 until 1993; onward and onward, the river current gathered strength and power through the 1950s and 1960s, coursing through the veins of public life during the 1960s and 1970s, rolling along.

Mere men were plucked from the crowd, hoisted high on the crest of the wave as Springbok captain, each eventually to be submerged again.

Their names thunder through South African history: Johan Claassen, Avril Malan, Dawie de Villiers, Hannes Marais, Morné du Plessis, Wynand Claassen, Naas Botha, François Pienaar, Gary Teichmann, Joost van der Westhuizen, John Smit, Jean de Villiers and others. Each one was at some stage eulogised as a hero; each one was, in degrees, treated in a harsh, and sometimes downright cruel, manner.

South African rugby has evolved as a world of glory and honour, but it is a world that very few manage to leave without regret or rancour. In many ways, the system offers an incredible ride, and then spits the rider out. Yet, yet ... through most of the past hundred years, through the crisis and trauma, the chicanery and politics, it is the glory that has prevailed.

This book tells the story of the Springbok captains, the men who have led the team in green-and-gold, the small group of men who understand how it feels to lead the South African side on to the field in a Test match, into the deafening roar summoned from the depths of a nation's soul, history and heart.

It is a simple fact of history that these men have all been white. It is also a simple fact that generations of black South Africans were denied the opportunity even to play Springbok rugby, let alone captain the team. They were denied by a lack of coaching, a lack of facilities, a lack of funds. They were denied. That was wrong. That was unacceptable. But that is also another story.

This is the story of those men who, right or wrong, captained South Africa on the rugby field. It is neither endorsed nor justified. It is simply told.

Here follows the Springbok captains' story,
From humble origins to the crowning glory.

Edward Griffiths
September 2015

1 THE CROWNING GLORY

It was 24 June 1995.

For more than a hundred years, those black and coloured South Africans who had showed any interest in rugby enthusiastically supported whatever team was playing against the Springboks: Lions, All Blacks, Wallabies, France, Wales, England, Scotland or Ireland; it did not matter. For many millions, the foreigners would be heroes if they could defeat the team in green-and-gold.

No Springbok captain had ever been recognised as a role model in every community of his sadly divided nation; no Springbok team had ever played with the united support of all South Africans.

It was 24 June 1995, and everything changed.

Before 65 000 fortunate spectators watching in the stadium, an estimated worldwide television audience of more than two billion and, surely, many rows of sepia faces gazing down proudly from above, South African rugby lived through an experience, a moment, an image of staggering proportions.

The powerful river of Springbok rugby, relentless yet ever restricted by the rigid banks of South Africa's social and political reality, finally flowed into the wide and open ocean where the team would not only be cheered by all South Africans but would also earn effusive praise in every corner of the globe.

And magazine posters of the Springbok captain would be enthusiastically pinned to bedroom walls in the township of Soweto ...

It was 24 June 1995, and grown men wept.

1

Rugby, so long regarded as the defiant, breast-beating drum of apartheid, was suddenly producing a sweet symphony for the new South Africa, the young, liberated democracy inaugurated barely 12 months earlier; and the Springbok captain seemed a relevant, recognised leader across the nation.

Ellis Park Stadium was bathed in warm, slanting winter sunshine, and an eerie glow had descended upon the arena. Amid thousands of flags, wide smiles and tears, South Africa had somehow won the Rugby World Cup final, defeating odds-on favourites New Zealand by 15-12 after extra time.

The eyes of this occasionally fragile nation, so earnestly desperate to be a success, were focused on a podium that had been wheeled onto the field in front of the main stand for the trophy presentation.

In this place, at this time, two South Africans arrived from opposite ends of the country's social spectrum and stood together, side by side, wearing identical Springbok jerseys, emblazoned with No. 6 on the back.

President Nelson Mandela and François Pienaar.

Mandela, the global icon who had committed his entire life to the liberation of South Africa, had emerged in 1990 from 27 years of imprisonment to inspire and drive a miraculously peaceful negotiated revolution. As he was inaugurated the first president of democratic South Africa, his country was transformed from a polecat nation into a shining example of peace and reconciliation.

His experiences of rugby had been limited to watching impromptu games played by his fellow prisoners on Robben Island, but he had taken care to attend the first Test match played during his presidency, against England in Pretoria on 4 June 1994. A stunning, unexpected defeat prompted Mandela to express the hope to the then president of the South African Rugby Football Union, Louis Luyt, that the Springbok team would improve for the 1995 World Cup.

Prior to the opening match of the tournament, he visited the Springboks at their training ground, playfully placed Hennie le Roux's

Bok cap on his head as he was introduced to the players, and, in that one gesture, guaranteed a future for the team's proud emblem that had been threatened by leaders in the National Sports Council who felt it should be abandoned as a symbol of the past.

Part of Mandela's genius was to take elements that had once represented bitter division, and transform them into vehicles for national unity. As May became June in 1995, his endorsement meant that Springbok caps were soon being worn by aware, fashion-conscious young men in the townships.

On the morning of 24 June 1995, the president went a step further. Only five hours before the World Cup final was due to start, Mary Mxadana, from the president's office, contacted Russell Mulholland, liaison officer with the team, at the Sandton Sun Hotel, and asked whether a spare Bok jersey was available.

Every player had been provided with two green jerseys for the match, one to wear and one to swap with their opposite number, each specially embroidered with the words "RWC Final 1995" beneath the Bok emblem. Mulholland took one of the No. 6 jerseys prepared for Pienaar, and, confident of finding a replacement jersey for the captain in due course, happily handed it over to Mxadana when they met at eleven o'clock that morning in the foyer of the Sandton Sun.

And so Mandela strode out onto the field at Ellis Park to hear the national anthems and be introduced to both teams, wearing not only the green Springbok cap but also the No. 6 Springbok jersey. Immediately, the capacity crowd roared its approval of this remarkable gesture. Many heads of state would have looked ridiculous in similar circumstances; Mandela looked magnificent.

"Nel-son!"

"Nel-son!"

"Nel-son!"

The bellowing stadium began to chant in unison. Heavyweight Afrikaners, born-and-bred rugby men who for so long would have condemned Mandela as a terrorist, suddenly found themselves chanting his name. "My father was a serious far right supporter," says one young man, who was sitting in the East stand, "and he was certainly no fan of the new South Africa. But, when he saw Mandela walk onto the field in the Springbok jersey, he leaped to his feet and started cheering. I could not believe my eyes. I think it is accurate to say that moment affected my father's entire outlook on life. It was an incredible gesture."

Amid such emotions, moments after the final whistle, President Mandela stood on the podium on the field at Ellis Park, beaming.

The other man wearing a Springbok No. 6 jersey at Ellis Park on 24 June 1995 was the oldest son of a steel worker from the Transvaal hinterland. His first meaningful interaction with a black compatriot had been when, at the age of nine, he gashed his hand as a man tried to snatch from him a plastic carrier bag full of empty bottles. Young François Pienaar ran all the way home.

Through high school and his years at the Rand Afrikaans University, he was brought up in the traditional mould of white Afrikaans-speaking South Africans: brave and bold, God-fearing, fiercely loyal, inherently colour-suspicious.

In June 1993, at the age of 26, he was selected to play flanker for South Africa, and named as captain. Surviving series defeats in Australia that year and in New Zealand in 1994, his squad started to thrive under the skilful guidance of his hugely respected friend and mentor, coach Kitch Christie.

Broadly written off before the 1995 World Cup, Pienaar's Springboks won their group safely, and heroically triumphed in a colossal, waterlogged semi-final against France at King's Park in Durban. Although the popular consensus held that the South Africans would be overrun by Jonah Lomu and the All Blacks in the final, yet again they prevailed by sheer force of will.

Pienaar, well spoken and sensitive in public, led his Springboks in every possible respect. With the countenance of a Roman general, he laid his body on the line at the apex of the fiercest drives and the roughest mauls; and he earned the absolute respect of his players and, in most cases, real affection.

During the brief interval between the first and second halves of extra time in the World Cup final, the captain had gathered his tiring players around, in the middle of Ellis Park, and emotionally asked them to look at the new "united South Africa" flags being waved in every corner of the stadium.

"Come on guys, we have to pull it through for these people," he said, as he knelt on one knee, stressing every word with a sweep of his hand. "We have to do it for our country. We need this. We all need this."

And Joel Stransky kicked the decisive drop goal, and referee Ed Morrison blew the final whistle, and, again, Pienaar called his players into a huddle. At the moment when most sportsmen would have embarked upon an orgy of unbridled and self-indulgent celebrations, this captain gave thanks.

A photograph of the newly crowned rugby world champions kneeling in prayer was later framed and presented by manager Morné du Plessis to Pope John Paul II when the squad visited the Vatican City five months later, during the preparations for their Test match against Italy in Rome.

As 65 000 people pinched themselves to make sure it was all true, rubbed their eyes in wonder, and waved their flags, the exultant Springbok captain made his way across the field and eventually reached the podium.

Pienaar looked up through the throng, and saw Mandela.

He had first met the President before the ill-fated Test against England in 1994, shaken hands and nodded. He met him again during preparations before the opening match of the World Cup, and shortly before that match. To his great surprise and pleasure, the captain was phoned by Mandela on several occasions as the tournament ran its course, off the cuff, mobile to mobile.

"Hello?" Pienaar was answering his mobile telephone while swigging from a water bottle during a tough training session before the semi-final.

"François, how are you?"

"Er, Mr President, how are you?"

"Fine, fine ... how is the team looking?"

"Very well, thank you. Very well ..."

Barely 20 minutes before the World Cup final, amid the bristling nerves of the changing room, the captain was pulling his green socks over his ankles when he suddenly became aware of a visitor standing over him. He looked up and saw Mandela, wearing his own No. 6 Springbok jersey. The President wished him well and, in a blurred instant, was whisked back to his suite.

More than two spell-binding hours later, the two men were standing face-to-face once again, this time as many millions looked on.

Pienaar stepped onto the podium, glanced briefly at the gleaming golden Webb Ellis trophy, and then looked into the President's still-smiling face.

"François, thank you for what you have done for this country."

"No, Mr Mandela, thank you for what you have done."

And with these words, as bedlam erupted around the stadium and in bars and living rooms across the Republic, the trophy passed from the hands of the President into the hands of the captain. The President clenched his hands and punched the air in double-fisted delight, the captain, jersey darkened by sweat, squeezed his eyes shut and raised the trophy to the skies.

A volley of camera flashes spectacularly illuminated the scene, and the image was broadcast around the world, destined to appear in newspapers and magazines, on television and on book covers *ad infinitum*.

The photograph conveyed one overwhelming message: that the newly united South Africa was a winning country, a winning combination that could take on the world and emerge in triumph. The shared joy of the black President and the white Springbok captain broadcast every ounce of the optimism, hope and success embedded in the nation's miracle reconciliation.

And, remarkably, the Springbok captain stood at the centre of national unity; a traditional idol and champion of white South Africa was suddenly earning the enthusiastic approval and support of black South Africa.

For more than a century, he had been at best ignored, at worst hated as a symbol of the oppressors. No longer, it seemed. Mandela's sheer delight opened a door of opportunity that had seemed to be locked forever. The Springboks had become Amabokoboko; Pienaar had become a national hero.

On 24 June 1995 it appeared as if everything had changed, almost as if a beautiful butterfly was triumphantly emerging from its cocoon. The day seemed to be the crowning glory for a sporting phenomenon that had often strayed, often erred, but was now being welcomed into the mainstream. For so long a source of division, the Springboks were now heroes of unity.

They had always been proud, always been brave, had earned renown as the outstanding rugby team in the world, but now, in this crowning moment, they had united all compatriots as nothing had ever united them.

Would the image of the president and the captain turn out to have been the first exciting glimpse of a prosperous future for rugby as a genuinely national sport, played and supported by all South Africans?

Or would the evident harmony between Mandela and Pienaar eventually be exposed as an illusion, nothing more than a tantalising and false suggestion that the entire code could be transformed so dramatically from something that had been so long, so ruthlessly restricted?

Time would tell.

Would historians one day look back upon the occasion of the 1995 Rugby World Cup final as merely the end of the beginning for Springbok rugby, or would the day ultimately be regarded as the crowning glory of an extraordinary sporting saga, after which would follow stagnation and painful decline?

Would Springbok captains of the future enjoy the same national profile as François Pienaar, or would they slink back to a white trench?

Again, time would tell.

Perhaps the clue to the future lay buried in the past.

To understand how the game would respond to this amazing, possibly quite undeserved opportunity, it is necessary to dissolve into the mists of time, to reflect on the origins of Springbok rugby, to drift back more than a hundred years and settle upon the very first South African captain.

2 THE PIONEERS

When François Pienaar stepped onto the podium to collect the Webb Ellis trophy at Ellis Park on 24 June 1995, he was collecting the absolutely deserved reward for his Springboks who had worked so hard to win the World Cup.

And yet he was also carrying the torch borne by every Springbok captain who had passed before. The World Cup success was the culmination, not simply of two months' preparation, but of 104 years of noble history.

Pienaar was carrying the torch lit at St George's Park in Port Elizabeth on Thursday 30 July 1891, when Herbert Hayton Castens led a South African rugby team out to play for the first time. Here the spark was struck.

These were exciting times in South Africa. Just five years before this historic first test, gold had been discovered on a farm that would quickly develop into the great city of Johannesburg. Twenty years earlier a pebble found at Hopetown had sparked the diamond rush in and around Kimberley that created the great De Beers mining company, and turned wild prospectors into millionaires overnight. Gold- and diamond-hungry diggers flocked to South Africa from all over the world, as the poor, agricultural, remote colonial backwater at the foot of the continent became suddenly a fountain of untapped riches.

Rugby had been played in South Africa since the 1860s, enjoyed as the favoured winter game of those mannered English gentlemen who arrived to rule, and probably exploit, the colony. These were hearty, robust, enthusiastic chaps, living out their lives in confident concurrence with Cecil John Rhodes's characteristically humble suggestion that "to be born British is to win first prize in the lottery of life". Just as they had relished a spot of "rugger" on the fields of their public schools at home, so they would in the Cape.

Settlers of Dutch descent took to the vigorous outdoor game with genuine enthusiasm, and the sport began to grow in popularity. During the late 1880s in Cape Town, it would have been possible to stroll around Table Mountain and find games of rugger being played on the lush, clodded, green fields that rolled down uninterrupted from the rocky slopes to the so-called "new lands".

And the gentlemen would dress in tight-fitting, long-sleeved, round-necked shirts, often drawn in colourful horizontal stripes. Matching striped long socks and close-fitting long trousers completed the dashing outfit. This was clearly a game for gents, and, throughout history, the most important rule of being a gentleman has generally been, at the very least, to look like a gentleman.

The South African Rugby Board was founded in 1889 and, within two years, T.B. Herold and W.V. Simkins, respectively secretary and president of the Western Province Rugby Union, were telegraphing the esteemed mandarins at the Rugby Football Union in Twickenham to enquire whether the mother country would not agree to dispatch a team to tour South Africa.

Rhodes, then prime minister of the Cape Colony, agreed to underwrite the costs of the tour, and the invitation was eagerly accepted. It was July 1891, and yet again eager Victorian gentlemen were establishing another lasting tradition. It was an era for bright innovation, for giving everything a go. Apathy was absent from the minds of this wide-eyed, occasionally wacky generation.

A week before the British squad was due to arrive in Cape Town aboard the *Dunottar Castle*, Herold and Simkins suddenly realised with some alarm that they had made no arrangements for the selection of a South African team. Hasty plans were laid for a trial, but the event was a failure. Many of the invited players failed to turn up for the match largely on account of, according to the *Cape Times* report, "the doubtful aspect of the weather and the arrival of the Mail".

Of those who did perform in the trial, Herbert Castens created the greatest impression, kicking out of his hands efficiently and proving extraordinarily expert in the most fashionable strategy of the day: dribbling the ball upfield in front of a mass of rampaging forwards. A strong, square-jawed, square-faced man with his hair swept back over his temple, piercing eyes, and the obligatory moustache of the time, Castens also featured in a second trials game, this time provoking loud laughter among the spectators when, during another charge upfield, he collided with a team-mate, and both men tumbled head over heels.

Undaunted, he played up and played the game.

Castens was born in Pearston in the Eastern Cape on 23 November 1864, but was very much the British gentleman, having been appropriately educated at Rugby school before going up to Oxford University, where he won his "rugby blue" in the traditional Varsity match against Cambridge in 1886, a feat he repeated the following year. His sporting prowess extended to the cricket field, where he represented both Middlesex and the south of England.

Castens eventually settled in Cape Town, joined the Villagers club, and soon started coaching at the Diocesan College.

In 1891, he was presented with an opportunity of playing for a South African team against a touring side from England, the country he had left only four years earlier. This contest would not be so much a full-blooded Test between fiercely independent nations as a courteous gentleman's challenge between mother country and colony.

At any rate, Castens looked forward to again meeting two of his contemporaries from Oxford who had been included in the England team. It would be good to see them again, and to show them life in Africa. The 20-strong tour party docked in Cape Town and, amid great excitement, were serenaded by brass bands as they strolled to their lodgings at the Royal Hotel. Castens was among the first to visit his old friends from Britain, and welcome them to Africa.

The first match of the tour was scheduled against a Cape Town Clubs XV and, to his great delight, Castens was invited to referee the match. Officials had reasoned that he knew well many of the players on both sides and was therefore ideally qualified for the role. Everyone was happy with the choice, and Castens was delighted as he blew the first whistle of an historic tour.

He emerged unscathed from the British team's 15-1 victory, a result that enhanced the reputations of tour captain W.E. (Bill) Maclagen, resplendent with both ends of his luxuriant moustache waxed into sharp points; "Baby" Hancock, a 6' 5" (1,96 metres) tower in the lineout; and R.L. Aston, the greatest centre of his era.

Castens had taken great pleasure in awarding the local team's only try to Charles "Hasie" Versfeld, one of four much respected rugby-playing brothers, one of whom, Loftus, would eventually give his name to the stadium in Pretoria. Little did any of the eager spectators know then that Versfeld's try would be the only score conceded by the Britons during 20 matches. In reply, they would score no fewer than 224 points and hand the colonials a ruthless drubbing.

Two days after refereeing the opening tour match, Castens was taking his place in the Western Province team to play the visitors, and his performance at the forefront of the drives and mauls, and what the Cape Times described as the "grand rushes", was greatly admired on all sides. Province were defeated 6-0, but Castens was touted as a possible South African captain.

It had been decided that local officials in each venue would be responsible for selecting each South African team, and Castens was delighted when the Eastern Province administrators invited him to captain the home side against the tourists in the first Test in Port Elizabeth.

On a blustery day at St George's Park, as the wind whipped off Algoa Bay, a crowd of eight thousand stood up to three or four deep round the touchline as South Africa formally entered the international rugby arena. The vast majority of spectators wore sober suits and bowler hats: that has changed today. And the overwhelming majority of spectators were men: that has not.

The home side trailed 4-0 at half time, but Castens reorganised his team as he passed around the lemons during the interval, and truly excelled in leading them through a scoreless second half. Defeat had always been anticipated, and the score was quite satisfactory for the Test debutants. In modern parlance, Castens would have said his team were on "a learning curve".

Such sentiments did not, however, keep him in the side for the second Test, to be played in Kimberley. The administrators from the Griqualand West Rugby Union now charged with the task of selecting the South African team for the match to be played in their home town were simply not familiar with the front row forward from Cape Town. In these early days of national selection, continuity was an unknown currency, regarded as worthless.

Instead, the Griquas men unashamedly appointed as captain one of their own Griqualand West players. In later years, national selectors would be no less partisan in their decisions, but marginally more discreet. Castens ended up playing the infamous "two" Tests, his first and last.

In bizarre circumstances, Castens later accepted an invitation to referee the third Test against Maclagen's team. Captain of South Africa for the first Test, referee in the third: he holds a record that will never be matched.

Castens's contribution to South African sport was not yet complete. He was selected as captain of the first South African cricket side to tour England, where they won 12 out of 25 matches during 1894. This included an 11-run victory over an MCC side in which W.G. Grace played, but the matches were denied first-class status since the South Africans were of unknown quality.

This was Herbert Castens's fate. He blazed a trail for others to follow but was generally denied the status and honour he deserved. He eventually returned to England, and died in London on 18 October 1929. His name, however, stands immortal as the first man to lead the South African rugby team.

The local hero selected to lead the team in the second Test at Kimberley was R.C. Snedden, known to friend and foe as Bob. A stocky man, distinguished by a thick mop of hair, precisely parted on the left, and the handlebar moustache of the day, he had been drawn to Kimberley by the diamond rush, and he stayed to become a well-known and respected figure in the town.

He bravely roused another scratch combination, in which only Duff, Vigne, Richards, Marthinus Versfeld and Japie Louw were retained from the first Test, and succeeded in preventing the tourists from scoring a try. The British team won the second Test 3-0, by virtue of a drop goal, a novelty in South Africa.

The third Test of the series brought a third South African captain, and this time the honour was bestowed upon Alf Richards, the Western Province halfback, as recognition for his outstanding performances in the first two internationals. Fast and incisive, he had earned the visitors' respect and was a popular choice to lead South Africa in the first international match ever to be played at Newlands, appropriately his home ground.

The *Cape Times* praised the South African captain for his "dodgy runs and long punts", but the touring team won 4-0, completing a clean sweep of the three-match series. Richards, 23, was set for a fine career, but he did not play another match for South Africa and died at the age of 36.

By any measure, however, the first rugby tour to South Africa had been an enormous success. Maclagen's side were feted as guests of honour at a farewell dance before their departure on the *Garth Castle*. They had arrived in a country with no sense of international rugby; six weeks later, they were leaving a country that was thirsting to see the South African team in action again.

Nonetheless, there were other priorities during the 1890s, like getting rich. Diamonds were being reaped in Kimberley, and the cut-throat tented settlement on the Witwatersrand, increasingly known as Johannesburg, was growing as hundreds upon thousands of men arrived to join the rush for gold. If Barney Barnato could do it, the fortune hunters told themselves, so could they.

Thus, five years passed until another British tour was arranged, although even this invitation was accepted with reservations. Barely a year before, a plan conceived by Rhodes to capture Johannesburg from the Boers and "give us the African continent" had failed. The Jameson Raid ended with Dr Leander Starr Jameson being led away in tears to gaol in Pretoria. Afrikaner-dominated northern regions were still uneasy and restless, and anti-British sentiment ran high.

Nonetheless, even then strong elements within the Rugby Football Union seemed to feel war and rugby should be kept apart, and they agreed to dispatch a touring squad composed solely of players from England and Ireland, to be led by Johnny Hammond, vice-captain of the 1891 touring side. The visitors arrived at Cape Town docks and, once again, were marched in a colourful, loud parade to the same Royal Hotel. South Africa was already becoming renowned in the rugby world as much for its lavish hospitality as for its hard grounds.

The undoubted star of the 1896 tourists was Tommy Crean, a charismatic and talented Irishman. He drew gasps of admiration for his all-round performance in the opening match of the tour, but these were strange times. Barely three years later, Crean was winning more praise for his efforts against South Africans but in an altogether more serious arena: the Anglo-Boer War.

In 1896, the hail-and-well-met Irishman was instructing his teammates not to drink more than four tumblers of champagne during an official lunch reception at the Cape prime minister's residence, Groote Schuur. In 1899, he was awarded the Victoria Cross, Britain's highest military honour, for leading a defiant bayonet charge against the Boer forces at Elandslaagte.

Fitzmaurice Thomas Drake Aston, known as Ferdie, was selected as South Africa's captain for the first Test against Hammond's team and, as the value of continuity became recognised, he would be retained for the second and third Tests. His emergence presented another example of the essentially small sporting community turning in upon itself to sustain and develop tradition and strength.

Aston was an Englishman, the younger brother of Robert Aston, who had been admired as an outstanding centre in the 1891 British touring squad. As a young man, he had listened keenly to his older brother's exciting tales of South Africa and, upon graduating from Cambridge University, he sought out for himself the next Castle Line ship to the Cape. Ferdie Aston arrived in Cape Town, but swiftly found his way to the hustle and bustle of the Rand, where he played rugby and became a valuable player in the Transvaal team.

As in 1891, the 1896 tour could be characterised as a noble challenge between gentlemen rather than a bitter conflict between rival nations, yet there was no doubting the improvement in local standards since 1891. Early in the tour, South African supporters were hugely encouraged when Western Province managed to hold the tourists to a 0-0 draw at Newlands.

A punishing schedule took Hammond's squad up and down the country. At one stage, they took two days to travel in a convoy of horse-drawn carts from Grahamstown to King William's Town and, at the halfway point, they were asked to sleep five men to a bed. Despite such obstacles, the Britons rallied to defeat South Africa 8-0 in the first Test match at Port Elizabeth.

Aston and his fellow backs were disappointed by the inability of the South African forwards to provide them with any possession, although the captain was careful not to be too critical of the large men up front. The newspapers did the job for him, one castigating Barry Heatlie as "worse than useless". Even in 1896, the South African press angrily hunted for scapegoats in defeat. Heatlie, a hero in the Western Province, was consequently not invited to play again.

For the second Test Aston took his team to Johannesburg, an infant city that had grown in ten years from a tent-camp of hopeful gold-diggers into a wealthy, decadent boom town of elegant multi-storey Victorian buildings and high-spending, hard-living opportunists. Again the tourists prevailed, but they were flattered by the 17-8 margin of victory and, more significantly for Aston and his players, and for the wildly excited home crowd, South Africa scored their first points in international rugby, two tries and a conversion.

Aston was instrumental in creating both tries, the first by breaking clear and hard for the British line before distributing the ball out wide left, the second by drawing two defenders before delivering a scoring pass to the wing. On both occasions, it was Theo Samuels who was able to touch down. A fullback from Griqualand, he was playing only because F. Maxwell had withdrawn at the last moment through injury, but he seized both chances and wrote his name in history.

Each time he scored, the Johannesburg crowd indulged in a response that could be described as the "Mexican Wave" of its time: a mass hurling of hats and walking sticks in the air. Quite how anyone recovered their property afterwards is unclear, and many might have sustained light injury from the shower of wood, but the effect was exhilarating. South Africa had scored! Hoorah!

Davey Cope happily converted the second of the tries, and the home team headed for the third Test in Kimberley defeated but now believing victory over the British side, so long unthinkable, was within their reach.

Aston again rallied his team, relying heavily upon players such as George St Leger Devenish and Percy Twentyman Jones, star names of the day. "Come on chaps, get stuck in," he would urge, repeating again and again the essential strategy of the day. Shift defences and the like lay in the future.

When Twentyman Jones sniped over for a first-half try, South Africa for the first time found themselves leading at half time of a Test match, but again Crean and the British forwards eked out dominance after the interval and prevailed 9-3. Aston had battled, but this halfback, like all others, needed the ball.

As the fourth and final Test at Newlands approached, the popular cry for Barry Heatlie to be recalled to the team grew deafening, and the selectors were moved to action. The folk hero was recalled not only to the heart of the pack but also as captain of the team. Aston was retained as halfback. Not for the last time in South African rugby, the hero of the north found himself in competition with the totem from the Cape for the right to captain the national side.

One of nine brothers born in the district of Worcester, in the heart of the Cape winelands, Heatlie only started to play rugby at the age of 17, but nonetheless captained Western Province while a student at the

Diocesan College, and was first selected to play for South Africa at the age of 20. He was confident, strong, and a natural ball-player. Forceful by nature, Heatlie swiftly assumed control of the team.

In the six previous international matches, the South African team had worn whatever jerseys came to hand. Sometimes they had been light, on another day they had been dark. Nobody had minded very much. Heatlie, no shrinking violet by nature (even if his popular nickname was "Fairy"), decided he would take the issue of the team jersey into his own hands, and he provided his squad with a set of jerseys from the Old Diocesan club.

The jerseys were myrtle green; and, after some interruptions, myrtle green they would remain, to be recognised wherever rugby is played.

Newlands was ablaze with excitement, and an enclosure had even been created for the ladies who had come to see the match. They were the beautiful creatures of Cape society, colourfully dressed to the nines. All was set and, as a strong crosswind billowed from the south, Alf Richards sounded the first whistle. South Africa's captain from the third Test of 1891 had now returned as a referee. In the meantime, he had also played cricket for South Africa.

Heatlie here, Heatlie there, Heatlie everywhere. Inspired by their captain, the South African forwards set about the tourists with vigour, hurling the Britons back on desperate defence. Aston used the unaccustomed wealth of possession intelligently and, in one fine move, led the charge upfield.

From a lineout Byrne, playing for the tourists, was tackled to ground and Biddy Anderson took the ball and sprinted clear. Anderson drew the fullback and passed to Alf Larard, who scored beneath the posts.

"Penalty please, Mr Referee," proclaimed Hammond, indicating that Anderson had taken the ball illegally.

Alf Richards shook his head.

"Excuse me! Penalty please, Mr Referee," Hammond repeated.

Richards shook his head again.

Amid bedlam around the field, even in the Ladies' Enclosure,

Hepburn's conversion soared to give South Africa a 5-0 lead, albeit in the most controversial of circumstances.

Hammond stood, hands on hips, shaking his head, and the touring team threw themselves forward for the remainder of the first half and into the second period, but Heatlie continued to rally his players and, gallantly heroic in defence, the home side withstood wave upon wave of British pressure.

Finally, as darkness crept over the mountain, Richards sounded the final whistle, confirming South Africa's first victory in a Test match. Heatlie was carried shoulder high from the field, instantly installed as a national hero. Some people nicknamed him "Ox", many more knew him as "Fairy", but, by any name, Heatlie became the focus for thousands of schoolboy ambitions.

Through the debates that followed, even some South Africans appeared unable to accept a result that appeared to threaten the natural order: the colony had defeated the motherland. It had not happened before; and it was Larard, scorer of the winning try, who bore the brunt of this indignation.

"It was a pity that the match should have been decided by what was after all a piece of sharp practice," said the Cape Times, perhaps influenced by the wrath of the incensed British tourists. "A player less inclined than Anderson to take every advantage he can get, lawful or unlawful, would have left Byrne in charge of the ball and allowed a scrum to be formed in that place."

Heatlie brushed such remarks aside. The touring squad, Anglophiles and several pressmen may have grumbled, but the overwhelming majority of elated supporters at Newlands were jubilant. They gathered outside the changing room to cheer their heroes, and escort them happily home.

The British might have won the series 3-1, but South Africa had earned its long-cherished first victory, and its self-respect. The country might still have been politically divided as two British colonies and Boer republics, but the earliest buds of national unity, among whites at least, appeared on the rugby field.

This said, the presence of a British touring rugby side scarcely concealed the frost in general relations between the Boer republics and Britain. Jan Smuts would recall: "Jameson's Raid was the real declaration of war in the Anglo-Boer conflict. In the four years of truce that followed, the aggressors consolidated their alliance and the defenders grimly prepared for the inevitable."

In such tense and uncertain circumstances, it was remarkable that both English-speaking and Afrikaans-speaking South Africans alike should have enthusiastically admired Fairy Heatlie, the rugby hero.

Britain was desperate to gain control of the precious Witwatersrand gold fields. President Paul Kruger was equally determined to protect the threatened independence of his Afrikaner South African Republic and, on 11 October 1899, the Boers formally declared war. Britain believed the conflict would be over within months, but their dated tactics foundered on the Boers' defence. Only after almost three years of resistance, and the deaths of at least 22 000 British soldiers and 25 000 Afrikaners, did the Boer generals gather in Vereeniging and propose to their delegates that Kitchener's terms for peace should be accepted. The Boer leaders would act as leaders of the government of South Africa, but they would pledge loyalty to King Edward VII. The generals had no means to continue the war, and no food to feed the women and children. The surrender, with honour and dignity, was agreed.

The war left scars, not only between British and South Africans, between those who had fought with the Crown and those who had fought with the Boers, but also between those Afrikaners who had fought until the bitter end and those who had lost heart in the struggle long before the final treaty.

When a British rugby team agreed to tour South Africa in 1903, no more than a year after the war ended, they did so primarily in a spirit of reconciliation but also in the hope that South Africa's splintered people would be joined once again by the spectacle of their rugby team in action. After he had been the last to sign the Treaty of Vereeniging, Lord Kitchener had broken an awkward silence by declaring: "Now, we can all be friends again." The 1903

British rugby tourists, led by Mark Morrison, were expected to justify his optimism.

South Africa's post-war gloom, reflected in thousands of ruined farms and a destroyed infrastructure, was in part lifted by the emergence of the nation's first rugby superstar, a character who prompted a broad range of opinions and never failed to provoke some kind of reaction. Fairy Heatlie had been the focus of public affection, but no South African player had generated as much debate and discussion as Japie Krige, a genius and maverick centre.

Angelic in appearance, wonderfully agile, and so quick that he once came a close second to future Olympic sprint champion Reggie Walker, Krige emerged at the Victoria College at Stellenbosch under the admiring eye of the celebrated coach A.F. Markötter. His ideally matched midfield partner both at Stellenbosch and for Western Province was Bob Loubser, and Krige's familiar trademark became the cry of "Come, Bob!" as he set off through another defence. Wherever he played, crowds flocked through the turnstiles. Krige was box office.

The son of a Dutch Reformed Church minister, Krige was not backward in coming forward and appeared keenly aware of his own gift, yet he also inspired genuine affection, from none more than coach Markötter who intensely admired the dazzling player he christened his "witkoppie" (blondie). Krige made his provincial debut at the age of 17, and represented Western Province from 1886 until 1906. During this period, remarkably, he never played on the losing side.

Krige was the first name written on the South African team sheet ahead of the first Test, to be played in Johannesburg against Morrison's tourists. It was clear to everyone that the primary challenge for the home side's captain would be to bring out the best in this match-winning centre.

It was expected this challenge would fall to Barry Heatlie, who knew Krige from playing for Western Province; and the hero of 1896 was indeed named in the team but the captaincy was awarded to a serious and sober Scot, Dr Alex Frew, a disciplined, organised man used to his ways and means.

Frew was a front row forward who had been capped by Scotland before deserting the frozen north and settling in Johannesburg. Perhaps the officials of the Transvaal Rugby Union, who selected the team for this first Test, believed his experience would prove useful in what was almost a team of debutants.

Frew was not the kind of man who would blithely make allowances for the mercurial magician in midfield. If Krige wanted special treatment, he would seek in vain from the dour Scot.

The result was a disaster. South Africa had selected the Griqualand West pair of halfbacks, Uncle Dobbin and Jackie Powell, and, with Frew's blessing, they pursued a tight, restrictive strategy whereby they held possession among the forwards for long periods of the game. Dobbin and Frew both scored tries, but South Africa was probably flattered by a 10-10 draw.

Krige was enraged. He had hardly touched the ball, and declared he would not be available to play in the second Test at Kimberley "because Dobbin and Powell won't let me see the ball". Was he right in insisting his talents should be used? Was he putting himself ahead of the team? Everyone had a view as South African rugby wallowed in its first full-blown rash of internal strife.

Officials of the Griqualand West Rugby Union, selectors of the team for the second Test, appointed Powell, their local man, as captain. Krige remained in Cape Town, and, compounding the loss, Heatlie was unavailable because, unfashionably at the time, he wanted to be present at the birth of his second son.

In these circumstances, the South Africans were content to draw 0-0 with a British team that many sensed was there for the taking. Morrison's touring squad was evidently not as strong as its predecessors, and the home supporters anticipated the third Test at Newlands with confidence.

The Western Province Rugby Union, were the hosts for the match, so Heatlie, Jones and Anderson sat together to select the side. Their meeting lasted scarcely an hour before they emerged with a team that appeared more accurately to reflect the considerable playing talent available at the time.

Using his role as convenor of selectors to good effect, Heatlie announced that he himself would captain the side. The halfbacks, Dobbin and Powell, were briskly replaced by Tommy Hobson and Hugh Ferris, a move that persuaded the elusive Japie Krige to emerge from self-exile and take his place in the team. Bob Loubser was included as well. South Africa was at full strength.

Much to Heatlie's disappointment, South Africa had not donned their myrle green jerseys in the first two Tests of the series, so he retraced his steps to the very same outfitter where he had found the full set of Old Diocesan club jerseys before the fourth Test in 1896. He travelled much more in hope than expectation, because this particular rugby club had ceased to exist.

To his relief, the shopkeeper had one set remaining. Heatlie was thrilled, and presented each of his team-mates with a myrtle green jersey with white collar, and a pair of black shorts. He also gained permission from Villagers for the South African team to wear the club's trademark bright-red socks.

Seven years on from South Africa's first victory in a Test match, Newlands primed itself to host another historic landmark: the match that would give South Africa its first victory in a series. The old field where the spectators had packed around the touchline, held back by stakes and rope, had now been transformed into a distinguished sporting stadium. The main stand provided no fewer than 25 rows of fashionably stepped seating, and the roar that greeted the arrival on the field of Heatlie and his team resonated in 23 000 throats.

Expectations were high, and none was disappointed. Playing in his last Test match, Heatlie proved a tower of strength among the forwards and, happy to see the ball, Krige and Loubser tormented the British defence. In truth, the result was scarcely ever in doubt, and South Africa triumphed 8-0. Once again, the hats and walking sticks were sent flying as the country rejoiced in victory.

Above all, this was Heatlie's day. The veteran forward had played his last Test match, bringing to a close a remarkable Test career. Despite the infamous vagaries of the home town selection process, he had played in six of the first ten international matches contested by South Africa, and had captained the national side on two occasions … and some occasions they were: the country's first Test victory, and the triumph that had secured the team's first-ever series win.

In 1905, finding himself in awkward personal circumstances, Heatlie left South Africa and settled in Argentina, where he rose to be general manager of a large sugar company and involved himself in the establishment of rugby among the Argentine people. Aged 49, he finally retired from the game.

He returned to South Africa in 1925 and lived quietly until, in April 1951, he was knocked down by a car on his way to an Old Diocesan dinner. The sepia rugby hero never wholly recovered, and died on 19 August of that year. He lies in the cemetery at Plumstead, one of rugby's most noble pioneers.

Heatlie's most enduring legacy to South African rugby is the myrtle green colour of the jersey. On the two occasions when he captained the team, he had unilaterally insisted this colour be worn, and his preference was confirmed at a meeting of the Board on 12 September 1906. On this day, myrtle green was finally adopted as the official colours of the national team.

By then, members of the Board were already contemplating a new horizon for South African rugby: the country's first overseas tour. The South African team had been invited to tour Britain, and the Board eagerly accepted.

In this period, the Currie Cup was contested as a series of matches played in one venue and, in 1906, the event doubled as trials. The squad was named at the Grand Hotel in Cape Town, after which the players gathered to select their tour captain. The virtually unanimous choice was Paul Roos, 25.

As a ten-year-old, Roos had stood beside his father and seen Maclagen's British team play against Stellenbosch in 1891, and his searing passion for rugby grew through his education at Victoria College and his career as a steady and sober schoolmaster. Tall and well built, distinguished by the three thick, dark bushes of eyebrows and moustache on his face, Roos emerged as a determined and steadfast leader.

As a Christian, he would not travel or indulge himself in any way on a Sunday. As a teacher, he did not spare the rod.

Upon his election by his peers as tour captain, surely the most democratic and emphatic mandate, the man known to all as "Polla" addressed his players in a distinctive, heavy voice: "As a teacher, I am within the law if I cane my lads, but the law will not permit me to cane you. Therefore I can only lead willing men, and I would like to make absolutely clear at the outset we are not English-speaking or Afrikaans-speaking, but a band of happy South Africans."

Roos was intelligently aware of the divisions within his squad, the majority of which were Afrikaners. Sommie Morkel, for example, had been among the four thousand prisoners taken after the Battle of Paardeberg when the Boer general, Piet Cronjé, surrendered to Lord Roberts. Morkel was incarcerated on the island of St Helena where he organised prison rugby. Four years later, as a member of the 1906/07 squad, he lunched in the House of Commons.

Two of Morkel's team-mates, Billy Millar and Rajah Martheze, had actually fought against him in the Boer War as members of the "loyal" Cape and Natal forces who opposed the Boer republics of Transvaal and Orange Free State. In 1906, South Africa still comprised four separate governments, and it would not be until 1910 that these were merged into one country. "South Africa is disunited about every subject under the sun, but in hearty agreement when supporting our rugby team," wrote Vere Stent, editor of the Pretoria News.

Roos would return to the theme of bringing unity to South Africa through rugby in a post-match speech at Swansea: "There is something much deeper than football beneath this tour," he would say, speaking slowly and emotionally, "and that is wiping out memories of our divided past."

Before departure, the full squad was divided into two teams, both of which played against the Rest of Western Province. Both sides were soundly defeated. Duly humbled, the players boarded S.S. Gascon and sailed north.

Their team manager was John Cecil Carden, a Scot by birth, known within the squad, almost unbelievably, as "Daddy". In seasons to come, national players would often require essentially paternal care from the team manager, but none would bring themselves actually to call him "Daddy".

"Daddy" was not happy when a group of players, grown bored on the voyage, started to pass the time by throwing overboard all the ship's deckchairs except one; and this remaining chair they labelled "J.C. Carden". Roos was not at all troubled by such pranks. In 1906, this was good, clean fun. Ninety years later, in an age when rugby players and managers took themselves far more seriously, the offenders would probably have been sent home.

Upon arrival in England, Roos was asked by the press whether his team had a nickname, as the All Blacks had recently required theirs. After some false starts, the name "Springbokken" was decided on.

Springbokken eventually evolved into Springboks.

And the name stuck.

The South Africans came to an England in the throes of social revolution. The relaxed reign of popular King Edward VII had already lifted his country out of the oppressive gloom of the last years of the Victorian age, and the intense battle for women's suffrage was gathering strength. The visitors found themselves received like circus animals by media intrigued by these "men from Africa". Their Afrikaans was mistaken for Zulu, their lineout calls were mistaken for exclamations of delight as a spear pierced the enemy's flesh, but the players accepted the guiltless errors in good heart and soon became tremendously popular visitors.

Roos responded to the mood magnificently. At one stage, according to a report in London, he led his team for a stroll down the Old Kent Road and joined locals in an impromptu singsong outside the Bermondsey Arms. According to the reporter, Roos sang "with a slight Dutch accent but in perfect tune".

Matches against various club and composite teams packed the first seven weeks of the tour, in preparation for the first of the four international matches, to be played against Scotland at Hampden Park.

Roos led a strong, hardened pack of forwards, and was confident in the ability of his halfbacks, Uncle Dobbin and the tour vice-captain, Paddy Carolin. The greatest strength of these first Springboks, however, lay in a quartet of three-quarters from Stellenbosch that was revered in rugby circles as the legendary Thin Red Line. Bob Loubser, Japie Krige, Boy de Villiers and Antonie Stegmann combined speed and rare skill.

The fates decreed not only that they would play together only in one Test match, the first international match of the 1906/07 tour, against Scotland, but also that the weather should be so appalling that afternoon in Glasgow that any brand of constructive backline play was almost impossible.

Instead, the Scottish forwards relished the waterlogged surface as perfect conditions for their favourite kicking, dribbling and chasing game. South Africa's preparations had been further disrupted when Roos was forced to withdraw with a knee injury scarcely two days before the match.

Harold Carolin, known to all as Paddy, assumed the captaincy for the Test against Scotland. His parents had emigrated from Ireland to South Africa in 1876, and young Paddy had earned acclaim as a superb all-round sportsman at Cape Town's Diocesan College, winning the famous Jameson Victor Ludorum trophy. On the fringe of selection for the national cricket team in 1905, he had already qualified as a lawyer (and would practise for the remainder of his life), but he was hugely enthused by the challenge of joining Roos's tour squad to Britain, and honoured, at the tender age of 24, to be named as vice-captain. To lead his countrymen out at Hampden Park was a privilege beyond his boyhood dreams.

"Feet, Scotland! Feet!"

Through a frantic, occasionally desperate afternoon, the South Africans literally threw their bodies into the mud before the Scots' kicking charge. Arthur Marsberg, the tall, angular fullback from Kimberley who had emerged as one of the successes on tour, was stretchered unconscious from the field; Dietlof Maré, originally selected as a halfback but playing as a forward, winced as two of his fingers were crushed by rampaging Scottish studs. Far from home, in appalling conditions, Carolin's team performed heroically and only lost 6-0.

"The ground was in terrible condition," Carolin recalled. "And we scarcely enjoyed our first experience of trying to play football in mud up to our ankles with a ball as heavy as lead and as slippery as an eel."

Roos was restored to lead his team for the international match against Ireland at the Balmoral ground in Belfast, and the Springbok captain was relieved when match day dawned dull and overcast, but dry. Loubser and Krige, the gifted backs from Stellenbosch, combined to give the tourists a 12-3 lead at half time. Loubser scored two tries within the space of three minutes, the first after an elusive run past four defenders, and Krige wrestled over for the third try as the dominant South Africans appeared set for victory.

Ireland fought back well in the second half, drawing level before Stegmann sped down the touchline to score the decisive try in a thrilling match. For a frozen moment, it seemed as if Stegmann had put a foot in touch and that the winning try would be disallowed. The touch judge had raised his flag.

In this era, it was customary for each of the two teams to provide a touch judge, and it so happened that the man running the line on Stegmann's side was Klondike Raaff, a player in the South African squad. Roos stood stock still as the referee jogged over to ask Raaff why he had raised his flag.

"Did he put a foot in touch?" the referee asked.

"No, sir, I am afraid I was just excited and I raised my hand when I saw that Anton was going to score beneath the posts," Raaff replied.

The referee smiled, and awarded the try. South Africa won 15-12, and the sporting Irish crowd applauded generously as the tourists trooped off the field. In this moment of glory, Roos would reflect, his team came of age. He was pleased, for he knew the most daunting match of the tour was imminent.

Wales had beaten the inaugural, all-conquering New Zealand All Blacks the previous year, and the celebrated centre Gwyn

Nicholls had been persuaded to postpone his retirement and play against the Springboks. As the match drew near, the contest between Nicholls and Krige to prove who was the outstanding centre in world rugby intrigued the media and supporters. "We all know you are the best," Roos told Krige privately. "Just show these people as well."

Ever willing to learn, the captain had noted during earlier matches against Glamorgan and Newport how the Springbok scrum had struggled against Welsh opponents, and he devised two strategies to use in the Test. The first was simply to copy Wales's bright innovation of only putting the ball into their scrum from the side where the loosehead prop was packing down. The second was to pack in a revolutionary 4-3-1 formation when the Welsh had the put-in.

Both strategies enabled the Springboks to dominate at forward, and give their star-studded three-quarters the opportunity to win the Test. One smooth and skilful passing movement sent Stevie Joubert running clear to score and, several minutes later, Krige hoisted a clever high kick. The forwards chased and hacked ahead. Loubser collected the loose ball and scampered over.

Roos applauded both his try-scorers by trotting over and placing his firm, congratulatory palm on their shoulder blades. Klondike Raaff, by now seizing his chance on the field, added a third try after half time. The tourists triumphed 11-0, a result so stunning that 45 000 stood in silence as the team left the field. Paddy Carolin reflected with wry humour: "The Welshmen gave our men a really warm congratulation by observing the most dreadful silence."

Japie Krige had dominated Nicholls, the local hero, throughout the match, never letting him past, and often outwitting him on attack. This would be the last Test match played by the Stellenbosch genius. He underwent an appendicitis operation soon afterwards, and did not play another match on tour. At least, his Springbok career had ended at the very pinnacle of the game.

Roos began to recognise his players were tiring and, showing a sensitivity lacking in many of his successors, the captain suggested to "Daddy" Carden that preparations for the concluding international, against England, should not be too strenuous. In fact, Roos proposed, they should be positively fun.

It was arranged that the squad would visit the seaside resort of Margate for three days, enjoying the fresh air and amusements, their minds far from the rugby challenge that lay ahead. Soon after ten o'clock on the Friday, they caught the train from the Kent resort to London. That afternoon, the touring party visited the House of Commons at Westminster where they sought autographs from any Members of Parliament who passed by. The players finally strode into the public gallery, from where they listened to a lively debate in the chamber.

Only on Saturday morning, Roos gathered his men at breakfast and told them casually: "Now, manne, we are playing England today."

The heavy rain that had fallen over London for three days had reduced the Crystal Palace field to a swamp, and the forwards utterly dominated the contest. The tourists took a 3-0 lead when the wonderfully unpredictable Marsberg kicked a high ball deep into opposition territory. England's fullback fumbled the ball and Billy Millar, the youngest member of the South African squad, excelling in his Test debut, snapped up possession and dived over for the try.

Freddie Brooks managed an equalising score after the interval and, having lost the influential Sommie Morkel to injury, the visitors were eventually content with a 3-3 draw. Roos told the assembled players and officials afterwards: "We have enjoyed great hospitality on this tour and, I hope, we have produced football that was entertaining for you."

The groundbreaking tour was over. Or maybe not?

Some dignitaries at the cocktail party following the 3-3 draw suggested a replay between England and the South Africans. Among the supporters of this proposal was Winston Churchill, the young politician and hero of the Anglo-Boer War, who declared his great admiration for the pluck and ability of the Springboks. "Their visit will increase the goodwill happily now existing between the South African colonies and the Motherland," he declared.

Roos was not keen on the prospect of a rematch, and his firm response that the tourists accepted the draw ended the discussion.

On behalf of his team, he did seek permission to play one match in France before returning home. This was granted, and the Springboks scored 13 tries in beating an unofficial French team by 55-13. The match was not given official status, which was a pity for Dietlof Maré who compiled a personal tally of 22 points. If the match had been official, he would have retained for 69 years the record for most points scored by a South African in a Test.

The one-sided nature of the match had disappointed Roos and, reverting to his schoolmaster's tone, he admonished the French afterwards, saying: "You should all remember that, in rugby, it is a matter of all for the team, and not each one for himself." His advice would apply for decades to come.

Roos was welcomed as a hero when he returned to South Africa, but he did not play international rugby again. He turned back to teaching and was soon appointed principal of Stellenbosch Boys' High School, a respected establishment that would eventually be named in his honour. Towards the end of his life, Roos stood and was elected as a Member of Parliament.

Now a forthright and sturdy figure, he remained respected across the land. On 22 September 1948, Roos delivered a speech calling for more funds to be directed towards improved housing for underprivileged South Africans. Barely two hours later, at home in Stellenbosch, he collapsed and died.

Roos left a legacy of dignity, sensitivity and integrity. He had earned not only the respect of his players but the admiration of his hosts. The first Springbok captain had established exceptionally high standards for the position, and it would be the fate of his successors to stand or fall in comparison.

In the seasons that followed the inaugural Springbok tour to Britain, South African rugby returned its attention to the Currie Cup, the domestic competition that continued to be dominated by the "invincible" Western Province team, led in these years by William Alexander Millar, widely known as Billy.

This compact and combative loose forward had squeezed into the 1906/7 tour squad when a rival was forced to withdraw, but took his chance and crowned his growing reputation by scoring the crucial try against England. Season upon season, he captained Western Province to domestic success and, by the time it had been arranged for Dr Tom Smyth's British team to tour South Africa in 1910, he had become the obvious choice as Springbok captain.

Castens, Heatlie, Roos and now Millar: South African rugby, developing apace, had identified the next colossus to take the game forward.

Originally from Bedford in the Eastern Cape, Millar was educated at South African College School (SACS) in Cape Town, and, at the age of 17, his restless and enthusiastic spirit moved him to leave his school desk and enlist in the Cape Cycle Corps, loyal to Britain and fighting against the Boers.

Wounded near Three Sisters during the Anglo-Boer War, he proved his loyalty to Britain again during the First World War, sustaining a serious arm injury at the Battle of the Somme. Despite his first wound, Millar was the consumate sportsman. He maintained an unbeaten record as the Western Province amateur heavyweight boxing champion, and whittled his golf handicap down to three. In 1903, he was picked for the Western Province rugby team and developed his own legend in the blue-and-white-striped jersey for the remainder of the decade.

Broad and sturdy, Millar parted his thick black hair in the centre and oiled both sides down flat and neat. In these increasingly fashion-conscious times, he was regarded as something of a trendsetter in and around Cape Town, whether appearing on the rugby field for Western Province or being seen near the docks, where he had taken a well-paid job with a trading company.

The arrival of Smyth's British team in 1910 presented Millar with a golden opportunity further to enhance his reputation. With the first Test in Johannesburg imminent, the Springbok captain-in-waiting was aghast to be firmly informed by his employer that a large consignment was expected in Cape Town and that he could not travel to the Highveld. He would be required at work. Millar was not the first or the last to discover there was no legitimate choice between his livelihood and his rugby, and he informed the Board accordingly.

In Millar's absence, the captaincy for the first Test was awarded to Duggie Morkel, a formidable and uncompromising front row forward from Transvaal who had played two Tests during the 1906/7 tour to Britain. Even if his hairline was fast receding, Morkel was an imposing presence on the field and, in terms of the captaincy, was regarded as a safe pair of hands.

Born in 1886, he had grown up in Kimberley but moved to Johannesburg where he played for the Witwatersrand team against the 1903 British tourists. He was selected to join the 1906/7 tour to Britain, and was capped in two Tests not only for his imposing presence among the forwards but also for his astonishingly reliable placekicking. Three steps and a clattering thud with the toe of his boot was usually enough to propel the ball between the uprights.

Duggie Morkel was a member of what, over a period of 25 years, would become recognised as the virtual royal family of South African rugby. In total, no fewer than ten members of the Morkel family earned Springbok colours between 1903 and 1928, a collective feat that will surely never be matched. Altogether, in the 1910 season, there were no fewer than 22 Morkels playing provincial rugby. It was little wonder that Sir Abe Bailey, a philanthropist of the age, contemplated the project of taking a Morkel XV on tour to Britain.

In 1910, South Africa were inspired to a 14-0 victory in the first Test by a new generation of talented three-quarters, including "Hudie" Hahn, Freddie Luyt and the skilful Dirkie de Villiers. Millar was excited by this potential and, finally given leave from work, looked forward to clinching the series when he returned to lead the Springbok side in the second Test at Port Elizabeth.

His plans were destroyed by the performance of Cherry Pillman, the tall, slender English forward who single-handedly carried the touring team to a shock 8-3 victory. Millar would later reflect: "My memories of this game are dwarfed by Pillman's brilliance. I confidently assert that if ever a man can have been said to have won an international match through his own unorthodox and loose-handed efforts it can be said of the inspired, black-haired Pillman that I played against at the Crusaders' ground in Port Elizabeth on August 27, 1910."

Just as in 1896 and 1903, the 1910 series would end with an exhilarating contest at Newlands in Cape Town. Before a large and partisan crowd, the Boks hurled themselves into the contest and began to adopt a demonstrably physical approach against the tourists. "In the excitement of the day," the captain wrote later, with admirable candour, "and when our blood was rather heated from the virile nature of play, a few of us lost our heads."

Future South African teams would employ the same strategy of softening up British opposition ... with great success, at least until 1974.

The prime casualty of the early Springbok onslaught was, not completely by coincidence, the highly rated British fullback Stanley Williams. He was helped off the field after ten minutes. Now playing against only 14 men in this age before substitutes were permitted, the home side seized control. Tries by Gideon Roos, younger brother of the former captain, and Percy Allport helped Millar's team to an ultimately comfortable, but no less joyous, 21-5 triumph.

Amid the celebrations, Millar and his players looked forward with renewed excitement to their next tour of Britain, which had already been scheduled for the northern hemisphere winter of 1912/13. This was a young group of players who, barring disaster, would reach their prime on that tour.

Smyth's British team bade farewell to a country newly proclaimed as the Union of South Africa – but the political unity did not necessarily bridge many of the old cultural divides, as Millar would discover.

Rumours had started to circulate some months earlier, and the Springbok captain was not completely surprised when he was told in August 1912 by a top official of the Western Province Rugby Union that a majority of the national selectors, who would pick the touring squad, would pick him as a forward but did not support his retention as captain in Britain.

No formal reason was given, but it was suggested that several Afrikaner selectors still harboured a grudge against Millar for fighting against the Boers in 1899, and believed the Cape hero had grown too big for the game. These views were clearly conveyed to the South African Rugby Board, and emphatically and finally rebuffed by the then president.

A curt message was drafted, and dispatched from the union: "Selectors, please be informed that William Alexander Millar will captain the Springboks on tour to Great Britain and France later this year. Thank you."

That was the end of the matter and Millar, apparently unconcerned by the politicking in the boardroom, duly resumed his duties as captain. He encountered no trouble in blending the squad together, not simply because many of them had played against Smyth's touring side two years earlier, but also because so many of this 1912/13 tour party happened to be related to one another.

South African rugby was becoming a family affair. Richard, Freddie and John Luyt were brothers; Gerhard and Jackie Morkel were brothers, Boy Morkel was their first cousin and Duggie Morkel was also related; Jan Stegmann's brother Antonie had toured with Paul Roos in 1906; Willie Krige was the brother of the legendary Japie; Wally Mills and Japie Louw were first cousins.

"Many of you know each other already," Millar told the squad, to general laughter, prior to their departure from Cape Town. Max Honnet, an amiable team manager, stood, smiling and distinguished, in quiet support.

The South Africans arrived in Britain to find news dominated by enquiries, on both sides of the Atlantic, into the sinking of the S.S. *Titanic* on 15 April. Europe was in wild and frantic mood: the navies of France, Britain and Germany were growing ominously and the continent seemed to be moving inexorably through a period of skirmishes and treaties towards the great conflict of 1914.

Amid this discernible tension, the South African tour began with six successive victories followed by a surprise defeat against Newport and an exhilarating encounter against Llanelli, in which Millar took his turn as touch judge and ran the line.

"That wonderful Welsh crowd on the popular side gave me a roasting," the Springbok captain recalled later. "At length, a hoarse voice shouted to me clearly above the din: 'What do you think of Llanelli now?' Rather foolishly, I responded by shouting back: 'Play the whole damn lot for Wales!'

"I instantly became a favourite of the crowd and was applauded loudly for everything I did. As a matter of fact, when Jackie Morkel scored our second try, the crowd encroached on to the field of play and I was forced to hit one fervent Welsh objector over the head with my flagstick. My dramatic action immediately met with universal approval for now I could do nothing wrong!"

The tour followed a pattern of gentle training, formal function, match day, formal function, official visit and maybe some more practice; and the Springboks produced occasionally outstanding rugby, although their frustrating inconsistency prompted unfavourable comparison with the 1906 squad.

When Millar was injured in a depressing 10-8 defeat against London, the squad approached the Test against Scotland as underdogs. Uncle Dobbin, the veteran halfback from Kimberley first capped in 1903, was widely ranked as the world's outstanding player in his position and, as the tour vice-captain, assumed the captaincy in Edinburgh. At the age of 31, he was renowned for his remarkable durability and his accurate pass.

A survivor of the waterlogged, bone-crushing 6-0 defeat in 1906, Dobbin was relieved to arrive at the Inverleith ground and find firm conditions on a bright autumn day. It was instantly clear to the halfback that, this time, the Scots would not be able to prevail by feet alone. They would have to play.

Recalling the manner of victory at Newlands in 1910, Millar had implored the touring forwards to yet again get among the Scots, and the imposing Duggie Morkel set the tone by thundering into the opening maul. The captain had asked his backs to be patient "until we have softened up the Scots". Only then, he had said, would the ball be released to Fred Luyt and his mates.

Millar's strategy worked impeccably and, their minds full of exacting sweet revenge for the defeat in 1906, the tourists began to dominate the match. Early in the second half, they scored one of the most magnificent tries of any era, lovingly recalled and described by Millar afterwards.

"Right on top of our game, our backs were handling the ball in a way that defied the Scots," Millar recalled. "Once again the ball crossed the whole backline and reached Stegmann on the right. The winger gave an inside pass, and away went the ball to McHardy on the left. The Free Stater found the way blocked – he could not get through. But Dobbin was lying handy, so 'Mac' threw the ball to the little halfback. 'Uncle' put in a short, snappy sprint, sidestepped an opponent – an old trick of his – and then cross-kicked. It was a dainty touch. Duggie Morkel was there to snap up the ball and he sent out to Boy Morkel. He set off on a thrilling 25-yard dash to the line, crowning one of the most brilliant movements ever. The ball, in this one memorable movement, had passed three times across the field, and not one of our players had been tackled in possession!"

With this whole-hearted 16-0 victory over Scotland in their sails, Millar's Springboks travelled west and ruthlessly overwhelmed Ireland in Dublin. The tour captain had recovered from injury to lead the side at Lansdowne Road in what was then the most one-sided Test ever played.

On a bitterly cold day, playing on a pitch hardened by frost, Ireland started strongly and seemed set to score as their rampaging forwards dribbled the ball to the visitors' line. Then, with the swooping movement of a natural sportsman, Fred Luyt literally scooped the ball off an Irish boot, wheeled behind his line at a sprint, and launched the most audacious, dazzling of counter-attacks. The ball passed to Jackie Morkel, to Dick Luyt, and then to Jan Stegmann who sprinted 55 metres up the touchline and scored the try that broke Irish spirits.

The deluge followed. McHardy and Stegmann each scored three tries, Morkel scored two, and Joe Francis and, appropriately, Millar also crossed the bewildered Irishmen's line. The final score stood at 38-0.

As the stunned, suited crowd filed away into the quiet streets of Dublin, someone suggested that, at least, they had witnessed a magnificent exhibition of rugby. "Bedad, me bhoy," replied his friend. "That wasn't rugby. At least, if it was, I don't know what we have being playing these last few years."

Almost 21 years after entering the international arena, South Africa was finally being respected as one of the finest teams in the world.

Inevitably, the 1912/13 Springboks' good fortune with the weather ended when they woke on the morning of the international against Wales. Cardiff was covered in thick grey clouds, and steady rain had turned the streets outside the hotel into shallow lakes. The players' spirits sank. The match would be played as another sodden battle of muscle and grit among the forwards.

As kick-off neared, a gale-force wind had started to blow across the newly opened Cardiff Arms Park. Conditions were truly appalling and, when the visitors won a penalty thirty metres out and to the right of the posts, Millar was not certain whether Duggie Morkel should even attempt to kick at posts.

"Go on, skipper, set it up. I will give it a try," Morkel said. "But I think you're going to have to hold the ball for me. The wind is so strong."

Millar took the ball, dug a shallow hole in the mud and lay down flat on his stomach, his right hand reaching out to the top of the ball, holding it straight. And Morkel took his familiar three steps before channelling all the power in his titanic frame through the metal toecap of his right boot, and the ball soared towards the posts, up and over. The flags were raised. South Africa led 3-0.

The captain could hardly believe his eyes. "Wonderful, Duggie, wonderful," he declared as he jogged back to join his team-mates downfield.

The match developed into an energy-sapping wrestling match in the mud and, after 15 minutes, both the red jerseys of Wales and the myrtle green jerseys of South Africa had been reduced to an indistinguishable sodden brown. It was a wonder that either the referee or the supporters could distinguish the players, yet the game progressed; and still South Africa clung to a 3-0 lead.

With time running out, Wales were awarded a penalty directly in front of the South African posts, barely ten metres out. Millar, ever the realist, turned and reconciled himself to the match ending in a draw. F.W. Birt, reputed to be among the finest place-kickers in Britain, lined up the equalising kick and, to the horror of the crowd, skewed the ball so badly that Stegmann caught it near the corner flag, advanced ten metres and then punted the ball deep into touch.

The final whistle heralded South Africa's third successive Test victory. The tour was becoming a significant triumph for Millar and his squad, and reporters started to assess the tourists' chances of completing the Grand Slam by beating England at the recently established Twickenham ground.

Millar assembled his players again, and implored them to produce one last effort at the end of an exhausting five-month tour. In truth, the idea of the Grand Slam was too new to mean much to the South Africans, but their natural urge to defeat England on their home ground was great enough.

The South Africans were initially set back on their heels when the England centre, Ronnie Poulton, sliced through the touring defence to score a memorable solo try. Minutes later, the same inspired player grabbed possession and set off on another impressive run, skipping past defenders at will. As most of the crowd rose to their feet, the powerful centre appeared unstoppable.

Boetie McHardy, a 22-year-old champion athlete from Bloemfontein, was South Africa's last line of defence. Educated at Grey College, he had thrived on tour and was now sprinting across the field in cover defence. A spectacular dive propelled him forward, and he heroically bundled Poulton into touch.

This remarkable tackle proved the turning point of the match. Millar's pack of forwards gained control soon afterwards. Jackie Morkel's try levelled the score and, once again, the tourists were grateful for the consistency of Duggie Morkel's placekicking. His brace of second-half penalties, the second of which was kicked from inside the halfway line and was even applauded by English spectators, gave the Springboks victory by 9-3, and clinched the Grand Slam.

Once again, the tour ended with a concluding match in France, won 38-5 by South Africa, and once again Morkel's remarkable goal-kicking left the deepest impression on the spectators. At one stage, the referee awarded South Africa a penalty that Millar felt was unjustified. He told the referee.

"OK, Dougie," Millar told his kicker, "just punt it back to the full-back and let him clear the ball. We do not deserve this penalty."

Morkel, however, was enjoying himself too much to waste the kick and, in a carefree moment of indulgence, he dropkicked the ball from a distance where he would have considered it impossible to convert the goal. Yet the ball soared unerringly between the uprights for another four points.

Even the French players, grinning beneath the crossbar, applauded the South African kicker and shouted out "Bravo! Bravo!"

Millar's Springboks were welcomed home as heroes. They had triumphed in all four international matches, and lost only three games on tour – to Newport, London Counties and Swansea. For the first time in history, and certainly not the last time, it was possible to make a powerful case that the Springboks of South Africa were the strongest rugby team in the world.

Barely a year later, this same world would be distorted by the First World War, and rugby, like every other area of society, would suffer its own losses. Both Poulton and Jackie Morkel, the opposing try scorers on that thrilling afternoon at Twickenham in 1913, gave their lives on the battlefields of France. As the conflict raged, the Springboks did not play for eight seasons.

By 1914, however, it was widely accepted not only that rugby had been successfully launched in South Africa, but also that the game owed an enormous debt to three distinguished captains. Their names stand immortal.

Barry Heatlie had given the team its jersey.

Paul Roos had given the team its name.

And, in leading the 1912/13 Grand Slammers, Billy Millar had established the Springboks among the very strongest teams in the world.

Thus, the legend was born.

3 THE GENTLEMEN

The first man to lead a Springbok squad to New Zealand was, inevitably, the first man to discover that South African rugby coaches and captains rarely return from that part of the world with any real credit or public sympathy. The land of the long white cloud has buried many green-and-gold reputations.

History decreed it would be the long-suffering Theodorus Barend Pienaar who first set forth with soaring hopes and yet returned in acrimony. He blazed the bittersweet trail that so many Springbok captains would follow.

New Zealand and South Africa had embarked upon inaugural rugby tours to Great Britain in 1905 and 1906 respectively, but the two southern hemisphere countries did not meet until after the First World War.

A New Zealand Armed Forces team toured South Africa in 1919, winning ten and drawing one of their 14 matches, and impressing all observers with their robust manner of play, but it was not until the 1921 season that the New Zealand Rugby Union finally issued an invitation to the Springboks. The South African Rugby Board accepted eagerly, and also agreed to the Springboks playing four matches in Australia on their way to New Zealand.

The unknown and unfathomable prospect of these new opponents appears to have prompted an attack of nerves among the national selectors. It was true that eight years without Test rugby compelled them to select a squad from scratch, but the panel took almost every observer by surprise when they named Theo Pienaar to captain the touring squad. The veteran forward was only a few months short of his 33rd birthday, and it was difficult to imagine how, on merit, he could ever secure a place in the Test team.

The most likely explanation was that Pienaar, a popular Western Province stalwart, had been appointed for his exceptional leadership skills. Since the Boks were heading into uncharted waters, perhaps the selectors resolved to provide mature and strong support for H.C. Bennett, the manager.

In this role, Pienaar rose to the challenge. As the son of a Dutch Reformed Church minister, he understood the importance of self-discipline and order; and as one of eight boisterous sporting brothers, he had also learned how to control and manage a high-spirited group of young athletes.

The concept of appointing a captain primarily for his ability to direct, guide and encourage his players has been more common in cricket than rugby, but the selectors' confidence in Pienaar for the 1921 tour was inspired. When the players boarded S.S. Aeneas for the 17-day voyage, it was towards the steady, solid and dependable captain that they looked for reassurance.

Rugby in Australia was so embryonic that the opposition in the first match on tour had needed to advertise in the local newspaper to raise 15 players. In the event, the Victorian XV was thumped 51-0, but Pienaar cautioned his players to expect a sterner challenge from New South Wales, the state team that would be their opponents in all three of their remaining fixtures in Australia.

He was right. South Africa did manage to emerge from the mini-series with three hard-fought wins, but no fewer than eight members of the squad sustained significant injuries against New South Wales. A cloud of despair settled upon the tour party as they boarded S.S. Mararoa and set their course for New Zealand. The challenge ahead had always been great. With more than a third of the squad unavailable, and no sign of substitutes, it was now daunting.

Theo Pienaar ached among the wounded. He had suffered an accidental elbow to the side of his head, and been severely concussed. Whether or not the selectors had ever intended for him to play against

New Zealand, it had become clear that, in any case, he would not be fit to lead the team.

These pioneer South Africans were not the last to be overwhelmed by the hospitality of the New Zealand people. The cheering crowds at every venue, the brass bands and pipers marching in the streets: few touring squads can have felt so welcome as the 1921 Springboks. "It seems as if the entire country has come out to welcome us with all their hearts," Pienaar noted.

When first-choice flyhalf Sas de Kock broke his ankle against Wellington and was ruled out of the rest of the tour, spirits dipped again, but the tourists battled on and managed to win their matches against provincial opposition, except for a defeat against Canterbury and a draw against Taranaki.

As the first-ever international against the All Blacks approached, Pienaar was effectively acting as an assistant manager. The honour, and the burden, of leading South Africa at Carisbook, Dunedin, would fall to a 35-year-old front row forward who had been summoned out of semi-retirement to tour.

William Henry Morkel, known as Boy, was ideal material for the brand of romanticised Springbok legend that has always been so popular in South Africa. Indeed, if Wagner had been a South African, it is easy to conceive Morkel as the hero of a grand opera.

Boy Morkel, a thickset, resourceful and powerful man who tied his shorts with a piece of cord, was a farmer in the Western Transvaal. He had played for South Africa in the third Test against the 1910 British tourists, and then excelled in all five international matches on the 1912/13 tour. With his sheer strength and determination, he had earned a reputation as a great forward.

By 1921, this stalwart was playing only an occasional match for Western Transvaal. His 36th birthday was approaching, and he was much more concerned with harvesting his maize than rampaging up and down a rugby field. One day at work in the fields, he heard the fabled call of the selectors.

"Boy, we are playing New Zealand," they said. "They are a fearsome side. We need players of strength and experience. We need you!"

And Morkel literally left his plough in the soil, rejoined the squad, and once again pulled the familiar green jersey over his head. His country needed him; and as the vice-captain of the touring squad, he was now being asked to step forward and lead South Africa at Carisbrook on 13 August 1921.

Pienaar, ever a sober gentleman in his dark three-piece suit and tie, was accorded the honour of leading his players out onto the field, albeit at a walking pace, and it was the tour captain who waited at the head as the South Africans formed a line for the presentations before the match. Morkel stood beside him, a right arm draped over Pienaar's shoulder in support.

Nerves on both sides paralysed the opening phases, but South Africa led 5-0 at half time following a try by wing Attie van Heerden, who would compete in the 100 metres at the Olympic Games, and Gerhard Morkel's conversion. This lead served only to provoke the All Black forwards, however, and the touring team were ruthlessly swept away by three second-half tries as the New Zealanders romped to a thoroughly deserved 13-5 victory.

Morkel, who had played the match with the crudest of shin pads strapped to his left knee, was hugely impressed by what he had seen, and made a point of shaking every single All Black by the hand afterwards. For him, defeat was not so much a disaster as an absolutely unforgettable experience.

The second Test drew a capacity crowd of 40 000 to Eden Park, Auckland, and the dry, firm surface proved more conducive to a convincing performance by the Springbok forwards. Yet again the tourists established an early lead, this time when the diminutive Billy Sendin scampered through to score; once again, the All Blacks struck back, drawing level before half time.

One moment of individual brilliance decided the match. Gerhard Morkel, a cousin of the captain, had scarcely erred at fullback and, early in the second half, he scooped up a ball that the driving New Zealanders had carelessly hacked too far ahead. Just inside his own half and a few metres from touch, Morkel ran three paces and then kicked a 60-metre drop goal that, even today, would be hailed as one of the greatest feats in the entire history of the game.

Drop goals were rated four points in 1921, and Morkel's effort was worth every one of them. The Auckland rugby authorities, in total awe, were moved to present the Springbok with a gold medal to commemorate his goal. South Africa triumphed 9-5, and the series was level with one to play.

Both teams were primed for the third Test in Wellington, but every plan to play constructive rugby was rendered worthless on a day of driving rain and gale-force winds that swept the squalls across the sodden ground. After 80 minutes of heroic and courageous defence on both sides in the most unpleasant conditions, both nations had to settle for a 0-0 draw, and a shared series.

Honours even.

Phil Mostert, the Springbok forward, graphically recalled how the pack had grown used to hearing, somewhere behind them, the sound of a wet ball slap into the safe hands of Gerhard Morkel, followed by an even louder thud as the fullback cleared the ball upfield and away from his line: "It was raining so heavily that we could scarcely see each other," Mostert said. "Gerhard was like a ghostly shadow at the back of us, and he certainly saved us from defeat."

Pienaar, the tour captain, and Boy Morkel, captain on the field, stood sure in the knowledge that the 1921 Springboks had achieved something remarkable in travelling to the other side of the globe for the first time and holding the strong All Blacks to a drawn series. Their squad had been disrupted by injuries from the outset, but they had stuck resolutely and bravely to their task.

They deserved to be cheered on their return home; instead, they found themselves embroiled in a public debate about their tactics in New Zealand. Boy Morkel shrugged his shoulders and returned to his farm, but Theo Pienaar would not stand by while his players were unfairly criticised.

He was motivated to take the unprecedented step of writing a newspaper article in defence of the 1921 squad, in which he rebuffed the prime charge that his team had played dour, defensive rugby rather than attacking.

"True, we may not have done much that was sensational," Pienaar wrote, "but let me stress this point: there is neither time nor space for the sensational in New Zealand rugby … To all our critics I say: 'Go out there yourselves and fight a New Zealand team on its own soil, a team that is filled with consciousness of its own prowess and flushed with its great achievements of the past.' And if you do not eat humble pie on your return home, well … I shall."

While Theo Pienaar argued with the critics at home, the Herald newspaper in New Zealand put forward its own post mortem of the tour. Pointing out that the South Africans had conceded only 13 tries in 19 matches, the editorial closed by hailing "the greatest defensive team we have ever seen".

For the first, but certainly not the last, time, a Springbok rugby squad had battled bravely in New Zealand and been wrongly maligned on their return home. Many Springbok captains in years to come would share the solemn sentiments of Theo Pienaar, this indisputably mild and decent man, that "South Africans show a sad lack of loyalty towards their own chosen gladiators".

From its earliest days, South African rugby had shown a curious tendency to raise very decent men on a pedestal of fame, to bathe them in glory; and then, sooner or later, ruthlessly and mercilessly to cast them aside.

The game thrived because the very decent men kept coming.

Pierre Kuyper Albertyn, known since childhood as "P.K.", was ushered into rugby union by no less a man than Paul Roos, former Springbok captain and the headmaster at Stellenbosch Boys' High. Mrs Albertyn had been reluctant, but her fears had been rationalised and, by the age of 17, P.K. was playing senior rugby and catching the eye of A.F. Markötter, the revered rugby coach at the University of Stellenbosch. The master had discovered his protégé.

Tall, strong, and possessed of the most devastating sidestep, Albertyn was ranked by his coach alongside the famous Japie Krige and Bob Loubser. "These three are my world-beaters," Markotter would declare.

Early in 1919, Albertyn scored no fewer than six tries for Stellenbosch in the opening 15 minutes of a match against Villagers, a club for whom Markötter had always felt great affection. The coach could not bear the slaughter, and sent a message to his forwards that they should not give the ball to Albertyn any more. The salvage strategy worked. Albertyn scored just one more try, and Villagers were spared a truly embarrassing defeat.

Three weeks later, the team photograph was taken of a Western Province Universities side picked to play against the touring New Zealand Armed Services team. Markötter himself, wiry, suited and moustached, sat in the front row beside Albertyn, 22, wonderfully gifted, neatly blazered, elegant in a white silk scarf. The coach sat in the middle of the row but with his entire frame turned toward his star player. The bond between the men was evident to all. At that happy moment, the future stretched ahead, the rugby world spread at their feet.

Disaster struck.

As Albertyn danced towards the New Zealand line, two soldiers tackled him at the same time, one falling heavily upon his trapped leg. Every ligament in the winger's knee was ripped. In hospital that night, internal bleeding turned his leg black. Doctors declared the young man's career was over.

Markötter, however, would not give up hope, and advised Albertyn to meet a well-known homeopath, Clifford Seven. Following six weeks of serious therapy and massage, the player returned to the rugby field wearing a guard constructed from rubber bands, crepe bandage and elastic. Playing for Stellenbosch against Somerset West, he marked his return by scoring five tries.

Albertyn looked fine but, in his heart, he knew he didn't feel the same. He had lost speed and sharpness; he felt he could not turn without pain. By the end of 1919, he considered his rugby career had essentially finished, and he decided to leave South Africa to study dentistry at Guy's Hospital in London.

And yet he never quite managed to throw away his boots. The soft fields in England were gentler on his knee, and he started playing for the hospital, and even accepted an invitation to play for the Barbarians. As he rediscovered some of his best form, he was even invited to take part in official trials for the England team, but he declined. "I am a South African," he responded.

He returned home later in 1923, opened a dental practice in George and, still only 26, appeared in a few friendly matches for the town team. He harboured no further ambitions in the game yet, far away in Stellenbosch, Markötter, now a Springbok selector, had not forgotten about his "world beater".

In April 1924, Springbok trials were held ahead of a tour by a British team, and a squad of 17 players was announced. Albertyn read about such events with passing interest, then checked his list of patients for the day.

Out of the blue, he received a message from Markötter, instructing him to attend an additional trials match to be played in Durban, and to bring his boots. In deference to his old coach, Albertyn did as he was asked. "Now, please don't go and make a fool of yourself out there," Markötter implored the three-quarter just before the match. If the coach was suffering a moment of doubt that his instinct may have been misplaced, he need not have worried.

Albertyn rolled back the years and dazzled once again.

To the amazement of most South Africans, Albertyn was soon afterwards appointed Springbok captain for the series against Ronald Cove-Smith's touring British squad in 1924. He had been so far away, despaired so often, yet now he had reached the pinnacle of the game. With the enduring confidence of a coach, and a little natural talent, Albertyn proved anything is possible.

The new captain looked around curiously as his team assembled, having heard of many of his players, but seen few of them in action. Yet, with a calm and quiet assurance, he established his authority and prepared his Springboks for the three Tests against a British team already ravaged by withdrawals and injury. If ever a team was disrupted by misfortune upon misfortune, it was the 1924 Lions, as the British touring team was now starting to be known.

South Africa won the first Test in Durban 7-3, the difference between the sides being a dropped goal magnificently struck by the home team's 23-year-old flyhalf, Bennie Osler.

"Now I know why the Maties are so scared of you," Albertyn told the young player as he thumped him on the back. The Springbok captain had been in England during the period when Osler, playing for the University of Cape Town, emerged as the scourge of Stellenbosch University in the close-fought annual inter-varsity matches. Now, he was seeing for himself the prodigious talent that would dominate South African rugby for the next decade. The Bennie Osler era had been launched.

Albertyn was playing at centre, displaying guile and great intelligence as he drifted into dangerous positions and timed passes perfectly to create alluring gaps for his younger and more fleet-footed teammates. Provided ample ball by a combative pack led by Phil Mostert, the three-quarters thrived during the second Test in Johannesburg, scoring four tries without reply in a 17-0 victory.

The team deserved to be retained for the third Test in Port Elizabeth, but, inexplicably, Dauncey Devine, from Transvaal, replaced the clever Pally Truter at scrumhalf. Osler was unnecessarily unsettled, and South Africa were fortunate to escape with a 3-3 draw from a dour match played in miserable weather. "Don't worry," Albertyn consoled Osler afterwards. "You have a wonderful career ahead of you, and I, for one, will enjoy watching you from the stands."

South Africa rediscovered better form for the final Test at Newlands and, even in the mud and driving rain, ran home four tries, two of which were scored by Kenny Starke, who added a drop goal. The 17-9 victory properly reflected the superiority of the resurgent captain and his players.

His knee familiarly bandaged, Albertyn continued to play club rugby in the South Western Districts for four more seasons and, in 1928, was even implored by Markötter to attend Springbok trials before the visit of the All Blacks. This was a bridge too far. Albertyn would later reflect: "On the Monday, I played badly; on Tuesday I was worse, and on Wednesday I was terrible."

Almost ten seasons after suffering the severe injury that was supposed to have ended his career, P.K. Albertyn retired from the game, and began to devote his time to maintaining the teeth of the good citizens of George. He had inscribed another gallant chapter in the history of Springbok rugby.

As the first All Black tour of South Africa approached, the selectors were again looking for a formidable and inspiring captain. The New Zealand team had toured Britain and France in 1925 without losing a single match, being christened by the British press "The Invincibles". South Africa prepared with apprehension and excitement for the long-awaited arrival of the All Blacks.

The selectors were looking for a senior member of the side, a brawny and resolute personality; and they settled upon Phil Mostert, a man blessed not only with physical presence but also the most delicate of skills.

Mostert was born in Krugersdorp, but he lost his father at an early age, and moved with his mother to live in Somerset West. In his teenage years, his natural affinity for rugby was nurtured at the town's rugby club, one of the strongest sides in the country. Even as a young man, he was revered for his power on the drive, but this mightily built man relished nothing more than to demonstrate his ability to dropkick for goal. In one provincial game, he refused to pass the ball to the great Bennie Osler, kicked the drop goal himself and joked: "You see, Bennie, you are not the only one who can do that sort of thing, eh?"

Having led the Springbok forwards with distinction through all three Tests against New Zealand in 1921, and played three of the four Tests versus the 1924 Lions, Mostert knew his way around international rugby. By 1928, he was amply qualified to take the team under his wing, and particularly to cultivate and cherish the greatest match-winning talent in the country, Bennie Osler.

Now at the age of 27, the flyhalf was at the peak of his powers. His talent lay in a remarkable ability to kick the ball, both between the posts and for position, but his exceptional gift lay in a talent to read the game and exploit weaknesses in the opposition more quickly than anyone had ever done before.

Bennie would enjoy most of the attention; Mostert accepted that. Osler would win most of the praise; Mostert knew that as well. Osler would be given almost all the credit; Mostert acknowledged the reality. Osler presented South Africa's best chance of winning the series; Mostert liked that best of all.

The All Blacks arrived in South Africa wearing woollen scarves to keep out the early winter cold, but they were accorded the warmest of welcomes, including a personal greeting from General Jan Smuts. The tourists' "Invincible" tag did not, however, survive even the opening fortnight of the tour. Before they had settled, the New Zealanders had lost two of their first four matches.

This was partly because the All Blacks discovered that their favourite scrumming formation of 3-2-3 had been overtaken by the South African standard of 3-4-1. Eased back in the set pieces, the tourists never moved forward. But the South African Rugby Board had also displayed the gentle gamesmanship of the age by scheduling disguised fixtures at the start of the tour.

For example, the All Blacks may have anticipated a fixture against a Cape Town Clubs XV would present a reasonable warm-up, until they saw the nominal club side would include Springbok captain Mostert, Bennie Osler and his talented brother Stanley, and at least ten other internationals. A packed Newlands thrilled to the ritual softening up of the vaunted tourists. New Zealand was defeated 7-3, and after a long train journey lost again, 6-0 to Transvaal.

Throughout this baptism of fire, the All Black captain, Maurice Brownlie, remained the perfect gentleman, never complaining about the long and arduous travelling as his side criss-crossed the country by train, and never questioning the clear loading of the early opposition. In adversity, his team retained dignity and earned the public's respect and affection.

Amid growing South African optimism, the first Test attracted a large and boisterous crowd to the old Kingsmead stadium in Durban. It was 30 June 1928, and the Springboks would finally play against the All Blacks on home soil. On this most historic and exciting occasion, the opening exchanges were not much less than profoundly embarrassing for the players in green.

Mostert's team had spent some time discussing the famous All

Black ritual of performing the "haka" on the field before kick-off, and they had agreed that this traditional Maori ritual of laying down a challenge could not pass by without some kind of response. A pre-match Springbok dance was hastily conceived and even rehearsed before its world premiere on the field at Kingsmead.

Once the spectators had applauded the compelling All Black haka, the Springboks formed their own semi-circle around their captain, Phil Mostert. Even the most ardent South African supporter would have conceded these men were not blessed with natural rhythm, and this was proven beyond doubt as the leaden rugby players trundled through a laborious, halting routine, chanting a mixture of Zulu and gibberish as they slapped their thighs and hips.

The referee, Boet Neser, offered relief, blew his whistle and began the first Test, a game that would become known simply as "Osler's Match".

A neat drop goal by the flyhalf enabled South Africa to reach half time with a 4-0 lead, but the home team had been far from convincing. During the interval, it was decided centre Bernard Duffy was concussed and unable to continue. As Mostert contemplated playing the second half with 14 men, he saw the figure of Markötter, a national selector, striding across the turf towards him.

"What are you going to do now, Osler?" Markötter barked.

"I don't know, Mr Mark. Phil is the captain."

Both men looked towards Mostert. He said nothing. Markötter was content to leave his question hanging in the silence. This was his style. He preferred not to instruct his players, but to help them think for themselves.

After an interminable minute had passed, Osler replied: "From some of the scrums in the midfield, I will use Stanley on the blindside. For the rest of the time I will use the touchline as long as Phil and the forwards stay on top."

Markötter nodded. He wanted variety. "That's it," he said, and he turned on his heel and briskly returned to his seat in the grandstand.

Osler kicked a second drop goal early in the second half and, within two minutes, added a penalty. Mostert was slapping his flyhalf on the back, happy to have established a commanding 11-0 lead. Then Osler began to probe the blind side, seeking to release his brother Stanley: first time, the wing dropped the ball on the line; second time, Jack Slater scored and the Test was won. By the end, Osler had scored 14 points in South Africa's 17-0 victory.

Mostert's team was hailed as "world champions" in the jubilant aftermath of the Durban success and, as the captain later conceded, some of his players may have started to take the laudatory headlines to heart.

General Hertzog, the prime minister, joined a capacity crowd of 38 000 for the second Test in Johannesburg, anticipating more of the same, but the national selectors once again inexplicably tampered with a winning side. Just as they had done for the third Test against the Lions four years earlier, they drafted scrumhalf Dauncey Devine into the team; just as he had been four years earlier, Osler was unsettled by his new partner. On that occasion, the Springboks had escaped with a draw. This time, the effects of a disrupted team combined with a general mood of complacency, and 80 frenzied minutes later the All Blacks had won 7-6 and, against every expectation, squared the rubber at 1-1.

Mostert was grim afterwards, his heavy brow bowed and all but obscuring his eyes. "Their forwards carried the day," he accepted sadly.

To their credit, the selectors remedied their mistake before the third Test in Port Elizabeth, restoring scrumhalf Pierre de Villiers to rejoin Osler as one of six changes. Mostert was satisfied, now leading a Springbok team that included no fewer than ten of his Western Province team-mates.

Another record-breaking crowd enjoyed a far stronger performance by the Springbok forwards, and Osler was able to take control in the second half. Time and again, the maestro drove the All Blacks deep into their own half with soaring touch kicks, and intelligently released his backs to strike for the line. In spite of his occasional critics, the flyhalf's rare gift reached far beyond his bootlaces, and South Africa scored three tries in an open 11-6 victory.

Mostert approached the fourth and final Test of the series, to be played in Cape Town, with quiet confidence. After all, South Africa had never lost a Test at Newlands, the scene of so many memorable home victories. Even the persistent rain that fell throughout the day, and ensured the occasion would ever be known as the "Umbrella Test", failed to douse the local optimists.

To their dismay, however, the All Black forwards produced an almighty performance in the heavy conditions, and new flyhalf Mark Nicholls kicked two penalties and a drop goal as the tourists dramatically squared the series. The contest frequently strayed over the dividing line between robust and violent, and referee Neser twice called New Zealanders to one side and administered a stern warning.

Mostert battled gallantly to urge his team-mates forward, but they had met their match, and few denied New Zealand deserved not only the 13-5 victory but also to return home with credit in the 2-2 drawn series.

Some South African supporters would claim Mostert had lacked tactical acumen, but his resolve was beyond doubt, and the indefatigable totem retained his place in the touring squad for the 1931/32 tour to Britain. By then, however, the Springbok selectors had decided to confirm in rank and title what so many believed had long been the case in practice: that Osler was the inspiration, the director and, indeed, the leader of the Springbok side.

The legendary flyhalf was only a few months short of his 30th birthday and perhaps past his prime, yet he remained a huge influence, and now Bennie Osler was formally appointed to lead South Africa on tour to Britain.

He had reached the pinnacle of the game, something he had appeared destined to achieve since his early steps at Western Province Prep School, on to Rondebosch Boys' High, and finally at Kingswood College in Grahamstown. Osler himself would maintain he played the finest rugby of his life during the five years he spent studying law at the University of Cape Town.

The flyhalf was settled in the Western Province team by the age of 20, and had set about establishing a record of winning that would only be matched, five decades later, by a blonde flyhalf from Pretoria named Naas Botha. With Osler at flyhalf, South Africa never lost a single Test series. With Osler at flyhalf, Western Province never lost the Currie Cup. With Osler at flyhalf, the University of Cape Town, Hamiltons and Villagers all won the Grand Challenge, in that order as the peerless pivot moved from one club to the other.

Osler won, and won, and won. Such success prompted jealousy and bitter criticism, usually in that order, yet he remained resolute and utterly assured that his strategy of kicking for position and using the backs to strike from short range was completely vindicated by his amazing run of success.

Some people said he was autocratic on the field; and they were probably right. Perhaps the sheer weight of his achievement earned him the right to get his own way. The statistics tend to weigh in his favour.

Under his direction, the Springboks would employ the same strategy in the British Isles that had succeeded against the 1928 All Blacks: grind the opposition among the forwards, and allow Osler to kick for victory. It was not extravagant; it was not daring; more often than not, it was not entertaining.

And the critics were not slow to voice their opinions, hurling adjectives like stodgy, cautious and conservative at the 1931/32 team.

Osler countered: "We play to our strength, and it would be foolish to adopt any other approach. We have a magnificent pack of forwards, and our strategy ideally suits the heavy fields that we will encounter in Britain." The captain had decreed it would be so and, without further discussion, so it was.

On the eve of his squad's departure, Osler was pleased when his tactics were publicly endorsed by the three men who had previously led South African tours overseas: Paul Roos, Billy Millar and Theo Pienaar.

Pienaar had been appointed team manager for the 1931/32 tour, another clever appointment that maintained continuity, developed tradition and upheld the highest standards within Springbok rugby. The legend would be solidly founded on perhaps a dozen personalities, who gave their entire lives to the colours – as player, coach, manager, national selector and, in many cases, president of a provincial union and member of the Executive.

"Oom Theo," as he was known, wasted no time in imposing discipline on the touring squad. He assembled the players on their very first day aboard the *Windsor Castle*, and delivered a solemn speech outlining the great responsibility of representing South Africa. His gentle suggestion that the players make use of the ship's gymnasium to stay fit was noted only by the younger players, and the manager's plans to conduct handling practices on deck were scrapped when no fewer than three new rugby balls were lost overboard.

Jock van Niekerk, the team's outstanding wing, had been vainly trying to save one of the lost balls when he damaged his knee and sustained an injury that would ultimately compel him to retire from the game. The farcical loss of his primary strike weapon disappointed Osler greatly.

His squad appeared strong on paper, combining the experience of players like Phil Mostert, now 33, and Jackie Tindall with the relatively young talents of such as Gerry Brand, Phil Nel, Boy Louw and George Daneel fast emerging. In many ways, these Boks were the product of Markötter's fertile mind: it was the widely revered coach who had one day instructed André McDonald to buy a scrumcap, turning him from a mediocre centre into a fine eighthman; it was the coach who plucked Jimmy White from the backwaters of Queenstown to become one of the most devastating crash-tacklers in the squad; and it was he who spotted Ferdie Bergh meandering in the leagues at Stellenbosch University and turned him into one of the country's most formidable lock forwards. It was also Markötter who had discovered a talented scrumhalf called Danie Craven.

Osler arrived in Britain, every inch the gentleman, every inch the titan of the game. He would be seen in the fashionable dress of the day: a tweed jacket, thick knitted plus fours, polished brogues. And the Springbok captain started to look the part on the field as well, leading his side through several combative early games against the celebrated clubs of Wales. Daneel, a Dutch Reformed Church minister, implored one opponent in Swansea: "Look, kick if you must; punch if you must; but please would you stop swearing."

Victory followed upon victory, until the Springboks performed poorly in the 13th match of the tour, against Midland Counties. They trailed 24-6 with little time left, battled back strongly, but were ultimately defeated 30-21. No South African national team had ever conceded so many points in one match.

Hurt and maybe even humiliated, Osler was even more ruthless then ever in guiding his team to victories over Cardiff, Llanelli, Neath and Aberavon. Every tactical kick was measured, every possible point was reaped. As the Test against Wales approached, the tour was set firmly back on track.

Cardiff was ablaze with red and, moments before kick-off, Osler called his team together in the changing room. Standing with one foot perched on a small bench, the captain began: "Boys, we are all feeling a little scared. It is a feeling we all share. It is right that we should feel like that because the entire honour of our country is at stake today ..."

As he spoke, the room was suddenly filled with noise. Outside, in the wind and driving rain, the famous Arms Park erupted into song as a brass band led the gathered thousands through the opening lines of the Welsh anthem, Land of My Fathers. The Springboks knew the song well since it had been sung before each of their matches in Wales, and they listened with pleasure, appearing equally as inspired by the soaring emotion as the home team.

Following the closing chord, a roar summoned from the very depths of the Welsh nation seemed to shake the foundations of the ground. Down in the South African changing room, Osler smiled gently and ended his speech: "Boys, please remember this. We will try to handle the ball. We want the ball. But if we find we can't handle the wet ball, I will tell you what to do. Good luck."

Within 15 saturated minutes, Osler was issuing new instructions. He saw how the Welsh scrumhalf was struggling to control the ball, and told his forwards not to contest either the Welsh lineouts or scrums but to concentrate on following through powerfully and seizing upon any slithering loose ball.

Then he turned to Craven, imploring his young scrumhalf: "If the ball does come your way, kick high ones, low rolling ones or touch kicks, or, if you have not enough time, pass the ball to me, so that I can do it." Either way, every ball would be kicked deep into Welsh territory, and the Boks would chase.

Wales scored the first try, but the Springbok tactics paid dividends midway through the second half when Osler's clever chip kick was dropped by the Wales fullback, and Daneel dived through the mud to score. Osler converted safely, and the Test was eventually won 8-3. He might not have been playing the best rugby of his life, but the Springbok captain was still a winner.

The flyhalf was also influential in the Test win over Ireland, executing what had become the trademark move of the 1931/32 tour. Osler would take the ball and manufacture a perfect punt over the opposition defence, landing the ball into the path of Maurice Zimmerman. And Osler would cry: "Run, Zimmie, run!" And, more often than not, another Springbok try would follow.

Again, South Africa had trailed at half time, but Zimmerman levelled with his familiar brand of try, and the day was won when Osler dashed on the blind side and created enough space for Waring to scramble over Ireland's line. The final scoreline, 8-3, understated an emphatic Springbok victory.

The tour was unfolding as a success but, within days, it was interrupted by an incident more significant than any try or drop goal. Fullback Jackie Tindall was heavily tackled during the game against the London Division, and left lying still on the field. He was rushed to hospital where an emergency operation on his throat and chest was followed by a prolonged, anxious stay in hospital.

Osler was shattered. Several times during the weeks that followed, he left the touring squad to continue their schedule and spent time at the bedside of his friend, who remained in critical condition. In tandem with manager Theo Pienaar, the captain had already informed his players that the squad would cancel all their remaining matches and return home if Tindall died.

As he sat in the London hospital, waiting for an improvement, Osler's mind drifted back to the Springbok trials that had been staged before the tour, when an evidently concerned Jackie Tindall had approached him and asked the flyhalf to leave out the dangerous kicks into space that afternoon. The friends were playing on opposite sides that day, and Tindall was eager to impress.

"What kicks, Jackie?" Osler teased, innocently.

Soon after kick-off, the flyhalf launched his first kick into the opposing half and Tindall knocked on. Moments later, he launched another punt, but this time the fullback swooped forward, collected cleanly, dodged past a fast-approaching forward and punted the ball back over Osler's head.

At half time, Osler walked past his friend, smiling broadly, and said: "You see, Jackie. I did you a favour by kicking on you because I knew you would have the spirit to get across and overcome your weakness". And Tindall had deserved his place in the touring squad; now, in hospital far from home, he would require that same fighting spirit again to recover from his injuries.

Springbok minds were understandably elsewhere when they ran out to play England at Twickenham, and an unremarkable Test was decided only in the closing seconds when Gerry Brand caught the ball out on the touchline and five yards inside his own half, and turned around to kick a drop goal that was officially measured later that evening at 62 metres. South Africa won 7-0, but neither the captain nor any of his players was in a mood to celebrate.

Osler returned to Tindall immediately after the match, and continued what had become a ritual of reading telegrams extending good wishes that had arrived from South Africa. At last, the fullback's condition began to improve, to the extent that he was able to send a note to the team wishing them luck in the fourth and final international of their tour, the Test against Scotland.

This letter in his blazer pocket, Osler hurried north to Edinburgh, where he led his team in preparations for the match at Murrayfield. Once again, match day dawned grey, miserable and wet, and for the third time in four internationals the tourists found themselves trailing at the interval, this time 3-0.

More than 74 000 people had squeezed onto the wide-open terraces that surrounded the famous stadium and, amid the skirl of bagpipes on the wind, it seemed as if the South African tour would end in defeat. In the approaching crisis, the Springboks were again rescued by their captain.

Osler later witnessed that the icy northern wind had turned his hands a shade of blue, but he proved alert enough to capitalise on a misunderstanding between the Scottish halfbacks and score an opportunist try for himself. The conversion attempt could have been struck from wide on the left, but the strength of the gale was such that Osler judged any attempt would be a waste of time.

Scotland enjoyed more than a fair share of possession, but the Springbok defence stood firm. Bergh managed a remarkable try-saving tackle after Brand's attempted clearance had been charged down and Mostert, above all, appeared a glorious and majestic figure as he played through the last Test of a distinguished career. Tall, strong, indomitable and craggy, he reflected all the finest qualities in the sport he had graced at international level since 1921.

The match was decided by a moment of inspiration from the Springbok scrumhalf. After watching his forwards suck in the Scottish flankers, Craven took the ball, skipped through a gap, and scored under the posts. Even though the gale blew the ball over and spoiled what should have been an easy conversion for Brand, the South Africans battled through to win 6-3.

Of greater importance to the tour captain, he learned after the game that the doctors would allow Jackie Tindall to travel with his team-mates on the Castle ship home to South Africa. The fullback made a full recovery.

Like Billy Millar before him, Osler had captained South Africa to a Grand Slam of international victories on tour to Britain. Some of his compatriots would carp about the conservative strategies, but, in the mind of Osler and his legion of admirers, the triumphant end more than justified the means.

Yet the debate raged on and, when it was confirmed that Australia would make their first full tour of South Africa in 1933, it appeared as if the old maestro was being turned by the continuing clamour to spin the ball down the line against what most South Africans believed would be weak opposition.

"The object of the game is to win, and we have played winning rugby," he declared. "Some people maintain there are more entertaining ways to win. Well, the Australians' visit may give us an opportunity to find out. I am not especially happy with changing something that works, but we will see."

For no sound reason, opinion seemed to be turning against Osler. Maybe he was suffering from the pitiable phenomenon that invariably affects great men who have dominated their area of life for many years. Perhaps the public grow tired of their faces; perhaps they fall victim to common jealousy; perhaps officials will always strive to cut down players who grow strong.

Whatever the cause, a recurring theme of this saga – that Springbok rugby elevates decent men, then spits them out – would be played out again, on this occasion in the foyer of a drab hotel in Cape Town.

The Australians had arrived from a country still smarting from the loss of the Ashes to England's cricketers and their controversial "bodyline" tactics. Despite losing four of their nine matches before the first Test, they swept away any South African complacency by playing an open, exhilarating brand of rugby. Their forwards were so light they may not have had any option but, at stages of their tour, they ran much heavier forwards around the field until the big men stood panting, spent. In more ways than one, the first Australian tourists brought a deep breath of fresh air.

Springbok trials were staged through a wet week at Newlands, with more than 120 players summoned from all over the country and accommodated for the five days at a mediocre, medium-range hotel in Sea Point. These were hard times. The 1929 Wall Street crash had caused an economic slump throughout the western world, and South Africa was also affected. Wool and maize prices fell dramatically, and bankruptcy and unemployment soared. To make matters worse, during 1932 and 1933 the country suffered through a severe drought, and poverty spread like a plague. The excitement generated by the imminent rugby Test matches brought much-needed cheer amid the gloom.

It was almost midday on Sunday morning after the final trial, and several players were speckled around the foyer in hushed conversation. Suddenly, Bill Schreiner, one of the national selectors, walked in and pinned a sheet of paper on the wooden notice board. He greeted nobody, said nothing, and immediately disappeared back up the stairs from where he had come.

In an instant, everyone knew this was the South African team to play in the first Test against Australia. Careful not to appear too excited, players moved towards the board and scanned the list of names.

Phil Nel, a gentle farmer from Greytown, Natal, who had appeared in each Test played by South Africa since 1928, was relieved to find his own name on the list, and then astonished to find the word "captain" clearly typed alongside. Bennie Osler, the icon of his generation, was retained in the side as flyhalf, but had been unceremoniously dropped as captain.

Within minutes, a receptionist was calling across the foyer: "Excuse me, is there a Mr Philip Nel here? We have a telephone call for Mr Nel."

The powerfully built farmer took the telephone. It was Bennie Osler, calling from his room upstairs where he had been informed of the decision. He offered Nel his sincere congratulations and pledged his support to the new captain. Even amid great disappointment, he remained the perfect gentleman.

"I regretted very much that Bennie had been deposed as captain after our winning tour to Britain," Nel reflected later. "On hearing the news, I felt that some kind of injustice had been done to him. His telephone call was as fine a sporting gesture as I have come across. Bennie and I always remained great friends and I admired his strategic approach to the game tremendously."

The entire team seemed to share these sentiments, and if the selectors had hoped the change in captain would provoke a change in strategy for the first Test, they would be disappointed by events at Newlands. Perhaps in defiance, perhaps in solidarity with Osler, the Springboks pursued the same strategy that had served them so well in 1928 and on tour to Britain.

The tight forwards subdued and pressed forward, and Osler's intelligent tactical kicking bewildered the Wallabies. Craven scored before half time, Bergh scored twice during the second half and, appropriately, Osler dashed through a gap to complete an emphatic 17-3 victory for South Africa.

It appeared that the players had been psychologically spurred into action, but spirits ran wild and loose within the Springbok camp, with the players finding themselves set against the national selectors and the Board in a frankly suicidal struggle to determine how the team would play on the field.

Shortly after the first Test, an official of the South African Rugby Board was quoted in a newspaper expressing the hope that, "for the good of the game", the Springbok team would adopt the same open strategy as the Australians in the remainder of this marathon five-Test series.

Osler read the article and was enraged. Ironically, with Nel injured, the veteran flyhalf had to be restored as captain for the second match of the series in Durban. Fine, he thought, he would teach his critics a lesson.

In an angry atmosphere of mutiny among the Springboks, Osler gathered his players and outlined to them how he had grown sick and tired of the constant carping since the tour to Britain, and that he had decided the team would play the kind of inherently risky open rugby the clamour demanded.

A frenetic, untidy and largely disorganised encounter followed. The heavy Springbok forwards, who had become so accustomed to moving forward beneath Osler's ranging punts, now found themselves run ragged as the error-ridden play switched from one side of the field to the other, then back again. The forwards' exhaustion combined with a general lack of commitment to the strategy and the occasion, and the Wallabies seized their opportunity.

At the last whistle, Osler walked slowly from the field, sad, shattered, but strangely vindicated by the scoreboard: South Africa 6, Australia 21. His players had conceded four tries and made Australia look like the world champions. This would remain South Africa's heaviest Test defeat until 1965.

Nel returned as captain for the third Test, and his calm authority restored some kind of normality to the squad, but the players' resolve and, to an extent, their interest in the series had been largely dissolved. Osler's drop goal secured a 12-3 victory for South Africa in the third Test at Johannesburg, but again the performance had lacked the passion and hunger for glory that had characterised the team at home to New Zealand and on tour in Britain.

Another lacklustre match followed in Port Elizabeth, when the Wallabies seemed to focus so greatly on countering Osler's effect that they failed to play their own open rugby and reduced their threat. The Springboks won 11-0, securing a winning 3-1 lead in the series with one Test still to play.

Both teams headed to Bloemfontein when they would have preferred to be heading to their respective homes and, amid an almost carefree atmosphere, the Springboks attended a series of convivial social gatherings with hospitable Free Staters during the days before the Test. One group of players were seen sipping champagne late on the night before the match. More than 50 years later, James Small would be dropped for doing the same thing, but he was sipping a soft drink and it was only the Thursday night before the Test.

On the day, the Australians performed poorly, and the home team played much worse as they produced what would become recognised for many years as the worst-ever performance by a Springbok team. At times, the players appeared uninterested. This was not surprising. They were uninterested. For those people who cared, and there were not many in evidence, the Wallabies won the fifth Test by a margin of 15-4, scoring three tries without reply.

Out of this shambles, the South African Rugby Board learned the salutary lesson that home series should not exceed four Test matches, and they may also have recognised that rugby remained an amateur game founded on the spirit and whole-hearted commitment of the players. When such qualities were undermined by official interference and meddling, the game suffered.

The Board may have recognised this fact, but the evidence of the next 60 years does not provide conclusive proof that they acted accordingly.

Without doubt, the greatest sadness of the spoiled 1933 series against the first Wallabies was the reality that Bennie Osler, one of the all-time giants of the game, would retire on such a discordant and disappointing note. The flyhalf had deserved to be carried shoulder-high from the field after his final Test, and not to slink away from a defeat in which his team had barely competed.

Other great Springboks would suffer a similar fate.

Just a week after the Test in Bloemfontein, the Australians played the concluding match of their tour against a Cape Town Clubs XV at Newlands. Osler was selected to play what would be his last match against an international side on the ground where he was loved and revered as "Baas Bennie". The final score reflected a 4-0 victory for the Cape Town clubs, with a typical Osler drop goal proving decisive.

And, amid scenes of considerable emotion and excitement, the flyhalf was carried shoulder high from the field, the departure he deserved.

4 THE GRANDEST OAK

There are people who commit themselves to an enterprise for ten years, and are revered for their long service. There are people who serve the same company for 25 years and are hailed, and rewarded with a gold watch. There are even people who dedicate 40 years to their rise from post boy to chairman.

Danie Craven lived, plotted, inspired and dreamed Springbok rugby not for only ten or 25 years, not for 40 or even 50 years. As a Test debutant in 1931, as captain in 1937, as coach, as manager, as selector and as president of the South African Rugby Board from 1956 until his death in 1993, this formidable bulldog of a man devoted himself to the game for more than 60 seasons.

Through thousands of training sessions and matches, selection sessions and Board meetings, through so many tours and traumas, through the politicking and crisis, for the University of Stellenbosch, for Western Province and for South Africa, it is difficult to conceive the titanic scale of his devotion.

Craven has been rightly eulogised for his law innovations, his leading role within the International Rugby Board, his enthusiasm, his wisdom and his usually expert management of the fierce political winds that howled through the game in the 1960s, 70s and 80s. He was known globally as "Mr Rugby".

And yet, perhaps the most accurate method of measuring his enormous contribution to the game is to assess, firstly, the regard in which he was held by his players and, secondly, his personal status at the end.

Ask Hansie Brewis, Springbok flyhalf against the 1949 All Blacks, what Craven represented to him. "He meant everything to me," he replies, eyes alight with emotion. "He meant everything to me. He made me."

Put the same question to Abie Malan, the extrovert hooker who captained South Africa during the early 1960s, and his dancing voice suddenly slows, and the broad Upington farmer clearly speaks from the depths of his heart. "Doc was like a second father to me," he says quietly.

And ask the question a third time, of Divan Serfontein, Springbok captain and scrumhalf of the early 1980s, and he will reply directly, repeating exactly the same words chosen by a Springbok three decades his senior. "Dr Craven meant everything to me. I respected him so much. We all did."

Craven was unashamedly loved by literally hundreds of Springboks, as profoundly respected and revered by those who were readmitted to Test rugby in 1992 as by their predecessors who toured the British Isles in 1951; and many of these brave, formidable, imposing men wept softly at his funeral.

The second measure of the man's greatness is the relatively humble and simple environment in which he died. It might be presumed that a leader who had so emphatically reigned over such a wealthy, profitable sport for 37 years would own a gleaming Mercedes. Craven drove a Toyota.

Gate receipts from enormous crowds, and rising revenues from television rights, ensured millions of rands rolled into the amateur sport, but these resources were channelled into youth development and the construction of the finest rugby stadiums in the world. Dr Craven sought no personal fortune. For him, his work was inspired by a pure love of the game. That was all, and that was enough. His urge was not for material gain, but to see rugby thrive.

He would be infinitely more excited to discover a young Maties wing take flight at Coetzenberg than to sign another sponsorship deal. Throughout his life, it may be said that he showed a healthy disdain for money.

There were occasions in his latter years when this commercial lack of interest was ridiculed by men whose involvement in the game was motivated by a more mercenary spirit; and Dr Craven would shudder to hear the present-day officials of South African rugby coldly refer to the game as a business ... for him, it was a consuming passion; he would be horrified when they described the Springbok team as "the product" ... to him, they were truly beloved.

Of course, he had faults. He was intrinsically manipulative in maintaining his grip on authority and control, and there were times when he would prefer to compromise with what he knew was wrong, such as the Broederbond's sporadic elitist control of election and selection, rather than stand against what he knew, deep down in his fine soul, to be hugely damaging. In his declining years, to the detriment of the game, he could be astonishingly stubborn, often seeming quite unable to appreciate any opinion other than his own.

Yet, through 60 years, he inspired heartfelt affection among generations of players at all levels, and he was motivated by the purest of intentions. Among the flowers, trees and shrubs that adorned the garden of Springbok rugby as season followed upon season, Dr Danie Craven was the grandest oak.

He was born in Lindley, a small farming town in the picturesque landscape of the eastern Free State, and his parents were archetype Afrikaners from their faith to their love of the land. His father was a prosperous farmer; his mother was a talented teacher who had been imprisoned during the Boer War, held by British troops in the concentration camp at Kroonstad. The third of eight children, one of seven sons, Daniël Hartman was brought up as a typical plaasjapie (country bumpkin), resourceful, getting into scrapes, bright, combative, brave, lively.

As farmers, the Cravens thrived when the crop thrived. If the maize and wheat was safely harvested, the family were wealthy. If the crop was ruined by a hailstorm, as happened one year, there was no income at all.

Craven's grandfather was British. He left south Yorkshire, home of the most blunt, awkward and brave of Englishmen, eventually came to South Africa in 1862, and bought more than 600 acres in the Free State. He named his new farm "Steeton" after the Tyke village where his parents remained. His first son, James, eventually inherited the farm; and it was James who signalled the change in the family's identity and loyalties by becoming known around Lindley as "Jan". While Danie Craven was reared and bred as a proud and distinguished Afrikaner, the fact remains that he qualified for a British passport.

This heritage was exposed in the family's passion for soccer. Indeed, a full-size soccer pitch had been established on Steeton, and young Danie would lie awake at night looking forward to the soccer matches played by his father, his brothers and the labourers from the farm. Yet the main sport at Lindley Primary School had always been rugby union and, as the young boy showed an aptitude for the oval ball game, so his enthusiasm increased.

July 1921 was a frozen month in the eastern Free State, and it was bitterly early on a Tuesday morning when Danie was summoned by his father and older brother, John, to assist in the most miserable chore on the farm: rescuing sheep that had been trapped by the overnight snow storm. The three woollen figures set out, scouring the bleak, white fields, their breath freezing on the air.

"Pa, what do you think went wrong?" John asked his father.

Jan Craven shook his head, saying nothing.

Danie wondered what on earth could have so upset his father and brother. They had been morose ever since they had read The Friend, the newspaper that had arrived from Bloemfontein the previous afternoon.

John asked again: "Are New Zealand too strong for us?"

"No, of course not," his father replied. "It was just a bad day."

It was soon evident the pair had been plunged into this gloom by news of the All Black victory over the touring Springbok side in the first Test at Dunedin. As they dragged shivering sheep out of gullies and snow shifts, conversation did not stray from the latest crisis for South African rugby.

Danie had just started to participate in the debate when he was interrupted by a sharp pain in the sole of his foot. There might have been thick snow lying on the ground, but the young boy only wore boots on special occasions, and a day spent locating sheep in the snow was never special. The offending twig was not all that got beneath his skin that day; rugby seeped in as well.

Progress was swift: at the age of 13, Craven was playing scrumhalf beside 18-year-olds in the senior school side, and the following season he was selected to play in the town's senior club team. By his 18th birthday he was respected and recognised wherever he went in Lindley, a small-town hero. Soon he was moving on, leaving to continue his studies at the University of Stellenbosch. There, amid the classic whitewashed Cape Dutch buildings gently cradled in the Helderberg mountains, Craven seemed just another face in the crowd.

The farm boy stood still, alone, in awe as he surveyed the green fields that stretched away into the mountainous distance, side by side, one upon the other, distinguished by neat white lines and so many posts. This was the famous home of Stellenbosch rugby, and it would soon be his home forever.

Craven attended the trials for the Stellenbosch under-19 team on the opening day of the 1929 rugby season; he started in the B side, but was moved to the A team by the imposing coach on the touchline, a man he would know as "Oubaas" Markötter. It was raining heavily, but the scrumhalf from Lindley, out of the platteland (country areas) wilderness, created an instant impression.

He returned to the rugby fields the next day to practise on his own, but he was aware that the university senior team trials were being held on an adjacent field. As he kicked and fetched, Craven kept a close eye on the trial, and he saw the B team scrumhalf fall after a heavy tackle. He quickly looked away, pretending not to have noticed, but his 18-year-old heart was racing now.

"Craven! Come over here!"

Markötter had noticed the rookie scrumhalf, and summoned him to fill in as a replacement for the B side. Craven seized his chance again, and, according to legend, prompted Markötter to inform fellow selectors on the touchline: "That is our Springbok scrumhalf for the 1931/32 tour to Britain."

The revered old coach thus launched another great rugby career. Craven would always be grateful, later reflecting: "Mr Mark taught me how to think rugby. Whenever he picked me out for something, I asked him what I should have done, and he always replied: 'Think it out for yourself.'"

Later that year, with Craven established in the university side, the coach approached his scrumhalf moments before a club game against the University of Cape Town. Without six top players, Maties were underdogs.

"Danie," the coach said, "what's it to be today?"

"Our best, Mr Mark," the scrumhalf answered.

"You silly fool! As if that will see you through! You'll need much more than that. Do you think they are not going to give their best?"

Craven mumbled something about trying to use his forwards. The coach grumbled about common sense and wandered away. Hoping his ordeal was now over, the player took his kit and headed for the changing room.

Barely five minutes later, Markötter was bearing down on him once again, threatening and angry: "Have you got the answer?" he barked.

Craven was stunned, silent.

"Don't you know mathematics?"

"Well, yes, a little, Mr Mark."

"Look," the coach said, exasperated, "you must learn to think things out for yourself. Your forwards are much heavier, so you can play with seven men in the scrum. The opposition will all go for you. Don't let them. Use your eighthman. Let him stand shoulder to shoulder to you for scrums. Let him take the ball on the blind side while you are being tackled. Next time, they will all go for him, and you can find space on the open side. Use your coconut and you'll win."

Needless to say, the strategy worked and Stellenbosch recorded a famous and quite unexpected victory. Markötter stood quiet amid the celebrations in the changing room, taking care only to approach Craven and whisper in his ear: "And Danie, you must remember ... I only shout at players I like."

"Yes, Mr Mark. Thank you, Mr Mark." Saturday by Saturday, the affection and mutual respect grew stronger between master and pupil.

In 1931, at the insistence of Markötter, Craven was named as one of two Springbok scrumhalves to tour Britain. Remarkably, the talented 20-year-old had still not made his provincial debut for Western Province.

Craven was travelling on the golden highway between Stellenbosch and the Springbok team. Much to the resentment of many in the north, he was not the first to do so and he was certainly not the last. That said, he utterly vindicated his selection on tour, displacing Pierre de Villiers as the first-choice scrumhalf, and playing in the Tests against Wales, Scotland and Ireland.

He retained his place through the 1933 series against the Wallabies, built his reputation as an influential provincial scrumhalf, and arrived at 1937 as one of the first names to be pencilled in for the Springbok touring squad to Australia and New Zealand. Fit and decisive, Craven was at his peak.

Markötter surveyed the progress of his protégé with pride, and confidently anticipated the Maties scrumhalf would be appointed as captain of the 1937 Springboks. This view was not, however, shared by his fellow national selector Bill Schreiner, the highly influential and powerful convenor.

"Uncle Bill" had been appointed as a Springbok selector at the age of 26, while still a player, and was in his 16th season on the panel. He had reservations about Craven's leadership qualities, and produced an alternative by persuading Philip Nel, captain of the 1933 Springboks, to come out of virtual retirement on a cattle farm in the Natal Midlands, and lead the team once again.

At 34, Nel was reluctant, but was soon persuaded.

The oldest son of a farmer and a product of Maritzburg College, he did not watch a rugby match until he was 15, and he was initially prevented from playing the game by his parents because one of his cousins had developed cancer after breaking his hip on the field. Yet the tall young man persisted, won permission, started impressing as an imposing forward, made his provincial debut for Natal while still at school, and developed a distinguished career.

He had essentially grown tired of rugby by 1933, wearied of the travelling from his farm to club matches in Pietermaritzburg. This involved riding his horse for 30 miles to a point where, together with three team-mates, he caught a taxi to the field. The effort, let alone the expense, had taken its toll; and his round-trips to provincial matches in Durban were even more arduous.

Yet he had continued to play sporadically for Natal and, early in 1937, like Boy Morkel 16 years before, he was summoned from his plough to lead the Springbok rugby team. This was a call rarely declined.

Nel assumed control, and immediately sought to draw a line beneath the Bennie Osler era. The ritual of successive Springbok captains indulging in frank criticism of each other is sometimes regarded as a modern phenomenon, yet it has roots that extend far back into the 20th Century.

"It is goodbye to dullness and safety-first methods," declared Nel boldly in 1937. "Our followers must delve many years back to recall international football of which they can be truly proud. Our aim on this tour is finally to rid our game of the cloak of dullness it has worn in the years since the War."

The same man had not been so frank while Osler remained in the squad, but he was certainly not the first Springbok captain resolved to mark out his own territory, even if it meant denigrating the giants of the past.

A Springbok trial had been held in October 1936, amazingly eight months before the opening match of the tour was scheduled, but the selectors delayed naming their squad until after a second series of trials, to be played at Newlands during April 1937. No fewer than 97 hopeful players were invited; and two of the players who would emerge as heroes in New Zealand, Flappie Lochner and Tony Harris, started the week in the lowest-ranked Team F.

At the conclusion of the trials, the selectors retreated to the Civil Service Club for their deliberations, and the players were left to endure a five-hour wait at the Metropole Hotel in Long Street, Cape Town. Nel, Craven, Gerry Brand, Fanie Louw and Boy Louw sat together, quiet and smiling, sharing in the knowledge of their selection. Markötter had already given them the nod.

It was past 11 o'clock at night when Schreiner arrived at the Metropole to announce 29 names. Since more than three thousand supporters had gathered in the street outside, it had been skilfully arranged that the convenor of selectors would read out the names of the touring party from a particular first floor balcony, enabling him not only to inform the nervy players in the room but also to address the excited crowds in the street. This was pure theatre.

Loud cheers greeted the announcement of each name, and Nel concluded proceedings by declaring: "I think these players will mould into the greatest side I have ever known." Markötter was more guarded in his reaction, warning the Bok captain, "Your pack is good, but I am not sure about the backs."

Paul Roos, captain of the 1906/07 Springboks and a figure of tremendous authority, travelled to Durban to address the touring squad before their departure on the ship Ulysses. Broad-shouldered, distinguished by a thick moustache and heavy black spectacles, his voice thundered across the players as he emotionally outlined the ethos of what it meant to be a Springbok. At such meetings, the solid foundations of this sporting dynasty were mightily enforced.

"You have a clear duty to perform first to your hosts, who have invited you there, and secondly to your own country, which is sending you overseas as true ambassadors of good sport and friendship," Roos declared.

"Let your spirit be the spirit of the Charge of the Light Brigade. Yours is not to reason why, yours is but to do or die. Go forth, my boys, win your spurs." It is not clear whether any of the players were aware of what actually happened to the Light Brigade, but they heartily cheered Roos and sailed east.

The issue of how best to keep fit aboard ship dramatically divided the tour party when Harry Martin, prop forward and SA Air Force pilot, decided to conduct classes in developing muscles while Louis Strachan, veteran of the 1931/32 tour to Britain and a detective sergeant in the police force, organised drills in jumping and running on the opposite side of the main deck. Nel responded to this delicate situation by telling his players they could make up their own minds and train on whichever side of the deck they wanted.

The captain carefully established ground rules for the tour, notably that if any player became drunk at any stage, his team-mates nearby would accept the responsibility and ensure that he was carried back to his room. Comfortably bilingual, Nel made a point of speaking privately to all 28 of his players, making sure each man knew precisely what was expected of him.

Hours were whittled away by games until the ship's supply of cricket and rugby balls had travelled past outstretched fingers into the ocean. After two hard weeks at sea, the Springboks finally disembarked at Fremantle, near Perth, late on 30 June 1937, eager to set about the 11 matches in Australia, including two Tests, which would be followed by 17 games in New Zealand.

Emphatic victories over largely bewildered opponents in their opening four matches were followed by a stunning 17-6 defeat against New South Wales. The tourists conceded five tries in ankle-deep slush and driving rain at the Sydney Cricket Ground, and, a week before the first Test against the Wallabies, the early optimism was being washed away by waves of self-doubt.

A visit to Sydney Zoo was arranged to lift the spirits, but the players were further disheartened when two springboks on display turned their backs on the South African rugby players. The beautiful gazelles pointedly remained facing the back of their enclosure, ignoring increasingly frantic encouragement. "We all felt terrible for several hours afterwards," Craven recalled.

The team's unease was further exacerbated by the Board decision before the tour that Percy Day, the manager, should not sit on the selection committee. The result was that five players, four of whom were not widely regarded as being certain selections, would choose the team for the first Test.

While the manager was reduced to issuing stern warnings that the players should smoke less and rise earlier in the morning, upsetting many of the squad in the process, the tour selection committee of Nel,

Strachan, Brand, Boy Louw and Craven found themselves in a highly compromised situation. One after the other, they recused themselves from discussion of their respective positions.

A team was finally produced on the day of the match in which Craven had been moved to flyhalf, Nel to the front row and Boy Louw to eighthman, and the Springboks set to work against Australia on the selfsame Sydney Cricket Ground where, in summer, Don Bradman was establishing his own legend.

Inspired by Jimmy White's aggressive midfield tackling, the tourists carried the match to the Australians and, for all Nel's lofty pre-tour ambitions, reverted to the classic Bennie Osler strategy of kicking for position. This pragmatism suited the appalling conditions and laid the foundation for a 9-5 triumph, but sections of a 33 000 crowd booed ironically every time Craven kicked for touch. The flyhalf played under strict instructions and achieved his captain's goal.

The Springboks scored no fewer than 45 tries during their next four games as they reverted to their expansive approach; and not even a severe injury crisis among the forwards, that forced Craven to play eighthman, prevented the tourists from carrying their much-improved form into the second Test.

Nel was delighted to see his team take control of an international match by dominating the set phases and spinning the ball wide at every opportunity. By the half time break, the tourists had run the Wallabies ragged, scoring no fewer than six tries, and established a commanding 26-6 lead. "We'll need Bradman to catch this lot now," remarked an Australian wit in the crowd.

There, the rugby stopped and the street brawl began. The second Test at Sydney in 1934 would quickly become renowned throughout the rugby world as the most dirty international match ever played. Nel stood by, bewildered, pitiably disappointed by the turn of events and unable to instil peace as his fellow South Africans responded violently to intense provocation.

In the most excessive exchanges, scrumhalf Pierre de Villiers was hacked in the head while lying on the ground. He was carried off the field in the arms of Boy Louw, and although he did return later, succeeded only in persistently asking the score and getting in the way of his team-mates. Harry Martin and Wallaby Aub Hodgson at least fought to the Queensbury rules, exchanging a flurry of cultured blows in classic fighting pose before the main stand.

Mr Kilner, the referee from Sydney, was presumably as disappointed by the incessant brawl as all the other spectators in the ground. Asked to comment on the match afterwards, Nel only shook his head and walked away. The South Africans had won the series 2-0, but resolved to leave acrimony behind and start anew as they sailed across the sea to New Zealand.

Their official welcome at the Auckland Town Hall was remarkable, more enthusiastic and energized than anything the Springboks had experienced in Britain, Australia or even at home; and the consensus among the hundreds of eager New Zealanders thronging the event was that South Africa should expect to lose four matches during their tour, maybe more.

"Be careful. The All Blacks are riding high," a councillor told Nel.

"Excellent," the captain replied. "That is why we are here."

After his unselfish exploits at flyhalf and eighthman, Craven was restored to the scrumhalf position for the match against Auckland, and he began to deploy his innovative long dive-pass to feed new flyhalf Tony Harris and deliver the ball beyond the reach of home loose forwards. To the South African's surprise, most of the capacity crowd started to roar with laughter.

"It was unnerving," he recalled later. "I became suspicious, felt if my pants were torn, but found they could not be the cause of the laughter. This continued and it was only after the game I discovered my dive-pass had been the cause of the laughter, it being seldom or never used in New Zealand."

Craven's dive-pass became the primary talking point around the tour as, against predictions, the Springboks set off on a potent winning streak, defeating team after team by spinning the ball out to the wings as swiftly as possible. Five successive victories, and 22 tries in the process, doused any All Black optimism ahead of the first Test match, to be played in Wellington.

However, the tourists insanely conceded their momentum during the days before the Test. Perhaps unnerved by the rain and promise of sodden conditions, the five players on the selection panel decided by a 3-2 vote that the team would revert to a kicking strategy. Only Craven and Nel had wanted to keep faith in the open game. During the selection, once again, one by one, each player recused himself from the discussion of his own particular position.

The result was muddle and shambles. Craven, who had been so effective at scrumhalf, was restored to flyhalf and instructed to kick. When the discussion turned to the forwards, Nel duly left the room, returning in due course to discover that, to his great disappointment, he had been completely dropped from the side. Strachan would lead the forwards, and Craven would be captain.

His appointment to lead the Springboks against New Zealand should have been a moment of great joy for Craven, the fulfilment of a dream nurtured back in his Lindley childhood. On the contrary, he was despondent and depressed by the selection panel that had lost its direction. The two leading personalities in the tour walked away from the meeting together, united in shock.

"Daantjie, what on earth have we done?" Nel asked incredulously. "I can't speak about my own position, but it appeared obvious to me that we should have played you and Tony Harris at halfback."

Craven agreed, adding sadly: "We're going to miss your leadership on the field, Phil. I am sorry. We will not win with this team."

His fears were realised as the home forwards, all fire and brimstone on the rampage, took control. An early injury did reduce the All Blacks to 14 men, in this age before substitutes, but they still proved strong enough to secure an emphatic 13-7 victory. Even in celebration, the local newspapers united in suggesting the South Africans would not blunder as seriously in selection again.

It was Harris who hauled the tour back on track, masterminding a superb performance that overwhelmed Canterbury 23-8, inflicting upon the home side a first-ever defeat against a touring team. The flyhalf's exploits secured his place in the team for the second Test, Craven was returned to the base of the scrum, and Nel, ever dignified, was invited back to lead his team.

The Springboks had been vivacious and boisterous, even cracking jokes, in their changing room before the first Test, to a point where this was later cited as a reason for their defeat. It was thereafter agreed that near-silence should be maintained during the journey to the ground and in the last few minutes before a Test, enabling each player to concentrate. This tradition, introduced ahead of the second Test in Christchurch, 1937, is still observed today.

In spite of their apparently stronger selection, the tourists began nervously and were thrust back when Harris's stray pass near his own line was pounced upon by an All Black forward, who scored the try. Only two minutes later, now on the attack, Harris fired a pass towards Babrow, only to watch in horror as a New Zealand centre, Jack Sullivan, intercepted, dashed clear, chipped over the head of fullback Gerry Brand, and touched down for a devastating try.

South Africa trailed 6-0 at half time, and the series appeared to be slipping from their grasp. Nel gathered his players around and urged them to have faith in their ability to fight back from the precipice of defeat. Freddie Turner struck the spark. Released by Harris, the left wing sidestepped two challenges on the blind side, wrong-footed another defender, and scored. Gerry Brand's calm conversion reduced New Zealand's lead to 6-5, and battle was joined.

Craven later wrote: "Backwards and forwards, left and right, field side and blind side, swerve, sidestep, dummy: we tried everything to secure the vital score but the New Zealand defence was equal to the attack. Then there was a whistle! What for? It was a penalty! For whom? It was ours, but a long way off and there was a reasonably strong breeze blowing across the field.

"As Gerry Brand placed the ball, his hands were trembling. He was biting his under lip. The crowd was as silent as a graveyard, and only the breeze bore any witness of life. Gerry placed the ball, and took one last look at the ball whilst sitting on his haunches behind it. He repositioned himself. This was to be South Africa's most important kick at goal for 16 years.

"Bang! The sound seemed all right. The ball travelled straight and like a bullet. Dead centre! It was over. We were leading. Our whole world had suddenly changed into something that was worthwhile after all. Howard Watt, one of our men sitting on the grandstand, jumped out of his seat for sheer joy and fell to the ground so awkwardly that he sprained his ankle."

South Africa led 8-6.

Ebbo Bastard and Boy Louw had been gamely trading fists with the All Black forwards, and both played on through serious concussion in this era when no one was aware of the dangers. It was the famously named Bastard who took the ball in the closing seconds to score the clinching try. Brand converted again, and the most momentous Springbok comeback was complete.

The series was level at 1-1 and, of equal importance, Nel and Craven had been vindicated within the tour selection panel. Outvoted in Wellington, they had got their way before the second Test and won the debate. At the behest of these two men, the 1937 South Africans would play an open game. Springbok captains have very rarely been granted their wishes as a right. They have generally had to argue, cajole, debate, negotiate and plot. It was ever thus.

As four more fine provincial victories gave the tourists confidence ahead of the third Test in Auckland, Craven was earning repute as a player of world class. Aggressive and always involved, his ability to improvise attacks from unpromising situations made him a constant threat. He had become most renowned, however, for the dive pass that New Zealanders were starting to fear.

Mindful of his growing reputation, Craven devised a plan for the third Test, in which, before feeding a scrum, he would ostentatiously call Harris to stand yet further away to receive another long pass. Craven intended the All Black flyhalf, in response, to drift out to mark his opposite number. He would certainly have read the newspapers and be aware of the long pass threat.

Then, instead of passing long, Craven would pop a short pass to left wing Freddie Turner, looping around from the blind side, who would then burst through the gap left by the All Black flyhalf. This was the plan, and the Springboks went so far as faking the end of their training sessions to practise it.

Craven recalls: "Our practices were always well attended, but we wanted to rehearse this move in private. So, at one point, we arranged for all the players to return to the changing room as if the practice was over. Only when the media and several other observers had left for home, we re-emerged and practised this move until everything was clicking together like clockwork."

As the third Test drew near, the enthusiasm of the people and the tension among the players reached unprecedented levels. International rugby union had always been a gentlemen's challenge and Nel, for one, began to ask whether the game was starting to be taken too seriously for its own good.

Newspapers were breathlessly pointing out that both the 1921 and 1928 series between the two countries had been shared, and that this decisive Test in 1937 would thus decide the true world championship of rugby.

Nel resolutely declined to join the pre-match vibe, declaring to journalists at the team hotel: "The game will suffer if far more importance is attached to the result than to the manner in which it is achieved. The shared goal of both teams must be to produce a compelling spectacle. If these international series are going to encourage the mad hunger for victory that we are seeing around us now, then I must question whether they are worthwhile any longer.

"Of course, we would like to win. We intend to scrum the All Blacks hard on Saturday, but we will keep everything in perspective."

Upstairs in his room, Craven was running through the moves he intended would see South Africa hailed as world champions. To his astonishment, he and Nel had faced another lengthy debate in the selection committee on the question of whether Harris should play flyhalf. Common sense had prevailed insofar as it was agreed Harris would play if the weather was dry, but Daantjie van de Vyver was placed on reserve, ready to play if the day dawned wet.

Once again, Craven and Nel were aghast, left to rely on the weather. It was with considerable relief that the two men woke on 25 September 1937 to find overcast but dry skies over Auckland. Harris would play. Ironically, a slight drizzle did start around noon, but by then the team was final.

Nel signalled his intentions within the opening minute, stilling the 55 000 crowd by opting to take a scrum rather a lineout. The Natal farmer had resolved his team would take control of the game in the front row, then spin the ball out to Harris who would set the backline free to win the match.

When the All Black eight were edged perceptibly backwards, the captain glanced towards Craven and said: "Danie, this is our day." Babrow's darting try after only eight minutes seemed to affirm this conviction, and the gifted medical student created a second try when his cross kick was collected by Ferdie Bergh, who plunged over. Brand converted and South Africa led 8-0.

However, an All Black penalty reduced the advantage, and the match was still in the balance at the interval. It was a few minutes after the break that South Africa won an attacking scrum, and Craven decided this was the moment to use his meticulously planned move, and maybe win the day.

"Further, Tony, further," he shouted at his flyhalf. "Go on, man, a few more yards. Get further out. Go on, man, further."

As Harris moved out, the All Black flyhalf, Trevathan, appeared to hesitate. He wanted to cover his man, but seemed to sense something was afoot. Step by step, he did edge out until he stood directly opposite Harris.

Craven fed the scrum, Jan Lotz hooked cleanly, Craven gathered the ball at the back of the scrum and fed Turner, on the loop. At speed, the wing sprinted through the gap. He drew the fullback, looped a pass to Lochner, who whipped the ball wide for Babrow to score in the corner. What a try!

The All Blacks never recovered from the shock, and conceded another try soon afterwards when Dai Williams beat three men to score. The scintillating Babrow was still not finished, creating a further try for Turner. Thousands of young New Zealanders had travelled to Eden Park to see their first-ever Test match, and they were left silent and saddened by a final score of 6-17. Their All Blacks had been well beaten at forward, and overrun in the backline.

In contrast, the South Africans celebrated, singing in their changing room for an hour after the match. The plans carefully laid by Nel and Craven had been impeccably pursued by the players, and A.H. Carman, writing for the Wellington Sporting Paper, neatly summed up the tourists' victory as having been won "not in mere man-power, but by their superior brainpower".

Nel and Craven have been rightly praised ever since. Percy Day, the team manager, had rarely been more than a peripheral figure, and had in fact departed for home a week before the third Test. In these circumstances, the two men had accepted additional responsibility and led the squad with distinction. It is almost inconceivable that any modern player would have been able to shoulder so calmly the burdens of playing, captaincy, coaching and management.

True to his word, Nel found much more pleasure in the style of his side's success than in any claim to be world champions. Victory in the decisive Test by five tries to nil was more than he had ever dreamed possible. In 28 matches, his team had won 26 and lost two, scoring 184 tries and conceding 30, scoring 855 points and conceding only 180. Nel had said they would play an open, expansive style of rugby, and they had generally done nothing less.

The captain recalled: "It was an honour to captain this team, that not only played rugby football in the best traditions of the game but also proved that bright football is not necessarily losing football. The 1933 Wallabies reminded us of the thrills of open football and, while we have endeavoured not to play with the same degree of recklessness, we have followed their lead. In so doing, I hope we have persuaded everyone that there is no need to tinker with the laws of the game, or to seek special amendments to make the game attractive."

It was true that the 1937 Springboks had encountered better weather than Theo Pienaar's sodden squad in 1921; this was their good luck. New Zealanders have also claimed the South Africans were fortunate to find the All Blacks at low ebb, but nobody was saying that when the tourists arrived.

In truth, the 1937 Springboks were heroes, absolutely deserving the title they would soon be given: the "Invincibles". Their fate is to stand alone in history as the only South African side ever to win a series in New Zealand. Furthermore, since the traditional Test series between South Africa and New Zealand seem to have been abandoned following the introduction of the annual Tri-Nations series in 1996, they may stand alone for the rest of time as well.

Nel will forever be recalled as the man of integrity who led this squad. He finally returned to his farm in Natal, having signalled his total retirement from the game in decisive and spectacular fashion, hurling his rugby boots into the ocean during the voyage back home from New Zealand.

His capable vice-captain, Danie Craven, was not finished with South African rugby; in fact, would not be finished for another 56 years. Within only five months of arriving back in Cape Town, the irrepressible scrumhalf was preparing to face a strong British Lions squad, led by Irishman Sam Walker.

Walker's side sailed from an unsettled country that had barely recovered from the shock of its king's abdication in 1936, and now hovered on the brink of war. Hitler's Germany was aggressively on the move in Europe, and despite the optimism of prime minister Neville Chamberlain many in Britain already recognised a violent confrontation with Nazi Germany as being inevitable. The spirit in South Africa was more optimistic: over the past five years the country had enjoyed a spectacular economic recovery, driven by increases in the gold price and led by the gold mining industry. The countrywide optimism would soon be shattered by South Africa's involvement in the war in Europe, but Walker's Lions arrived in a country still buoyed by a level of affluence and security such as South Africans – at least white South Africans – had never previously known.

Craven had completed his studies at the University of Stellenbosch, and taken up a teaching position at St Andrew's School in Grahamstown. Early in 1938, however, he accepted an appointment as a director of physical education in the South African Defence Force. This necessitated a move to Pretoria, where he began to play for Northern Transvaal, a new provincial union that had claimed its "independence" from Transvaal at the start of 1938.

Chirpy and dapper, Craven appeared to strut as the perky personification of South African rugby's newly declared world dominance. Already respected for his talent to think broadly and to innovate, he was
recognised and cheered at every ground in the country. His legend was
up and running.

The confidence billowing through Springbok rugby in the wake
of the 1937 triumph in New Zealand was such that the national selectors declared trials were not necessary before the Lions tour. A gentle
warm-up match was instead played at the Wanderers. Only Louis Babrow, who was continuing his medical studies in London, was not available to retain his place in the team.

To general surprise, the Lions had demonstrated considerable talents and physical courage during their early matches, recording a notable 20-12 win over a Northern Transvaal team that had included
six Springboks, among them Bergh, Roger Sheriff and Craven. This
result was welcomed because all South African supporters wanted the
Springboks to be fully stretched in the three-Test series. Defeat was not
even mentioned as a remote possibility.

South African rugby was beginning to display the self-assurance
and blunt confidence that would often be interpreted, and usually resented, in many parts of the rugby world as the most boorish form of
arrogance.

The first signs of complacent administration, another long-term
trend, were also emerging. First the players had been offended by a
telegram from the South African Rugby Board in which they were
warned that anyone found guilty of dirty play would be severely punished. Secondly, the selectors named the team for the first Test against
the Lions without bothering to appoint a captain.

It was broadly anticipated that Craven would be elevated to this
position following Nel's retirement, but the scrumhalf only received
formal confirmation of his appointment by reading a newspaper during the train journey from Pretoria to Johannesburg on the day before
the match. World champions on the field, South Africa may have been;
world champions off the field, maybe not.

One advantage of this general optimism was that everyone wanted to see the heroes of 1937. So many thousands of people turned up to watch the first Test against the Lions at Ellis Park, Johannesburg, that the authorities suddenly became concerned by the increasingly frantic crush outside the ground and, half an hour before kick-off, decided to open the gates.

The result was that the two sides eventually took the field to find that every inch of space had been occupied by a spectator. There was not a gangway, not a step to be seen, and the crowd heaved together, held back scarcely a metre from the touchline on either side. The Boks were box office.

Nobody went home disappointed from a match that included re-markable goalkicking by Vivian Jenkins, of Wales and the Lions, and by the revered Gerry Brand, playing what would turn out to be his last Test. South Africa scored a try when Craven cheekily called the same move that had worked at Eden Park, first waving Harris out, then bringing Turner round on the loop, but Jenkins continued to kick penalty goals, and the Lions led 9-8 after half an hour.

Clever work by Craven on the fringes of an attacking scrum ena-bled Fanie Louw to barge over from close range, but the Springboks reached half time fully aware that they were involved in a hard match. The anticipated parade of heroes had been abandoned. Defeat was sud-denly a possibility.

Inspiration was provided by Brand who, at Craven's insistence, agreed to attempt a penalty goal from the touchline. The angle was dif-ficult enough, but the kick was uniquely awkward because spectators were packed barely a metre from the line. To widespread amusement, the legendary fullback managed to wrestle his way into the crowd, ek-ing out the bare minimum run-up.

"Gerry was asking the people to make a gap," Craven recalls, "and it was my task to dig the hole for the ball. That meant removing all the burning cigarette ends from the turf. As Gerry stood between the legs of one spectator who had to lean back, I teased him that I would buy him a farm if he got the kick over. He just smiled and started his run-up. It was a great kick. It went over, and the two of us left that group of spectators with smiles on their faces."

Subsequent tries by the alert Harris and Williams secured a 26-12 victory, and Craven took his team to Port Elizabeth for what he would call the "Tropical Test" because it was played in harsh sun and soaring heat. Craven derived huge pleasure from a sense of participating in history, of being at the centre of major events and, in some ways, he contributed to his own legend by giving nicknames to memorable Tests, ensuring they would not be forgotten. This was not cynical in any way, merely another expression of his enthusiasm.

As players flagged under the sun, Craven implored his team to score early in each half when they would be feeling relatively fresh, and then to hold firm for the rest of the match. Always thinking, always planning, he seemed able to make a plan for any situation at any time against any opposition.

Ben du Toit and Flappie Lochner scored within the opening ten minutes.

Johnny Bester scored immediately after the interval, and, according to plan, South Africa won 19-3, taking an unassailable 2-0 lead in the series and heading for the third Test in Cape Town with nothing more than pride at stake.

In their wisdom, the South African Rugby Board then enraged their team by arranging for them to stay at a small hotel far outside Cape Town. On behalf of his players, Craven asked that they move to a hotel nearer the city. At first, his request was declined. It was only when he suggested the team would not play the Test match against the Lions if they were treated so shabbily that the Board grimly agreed to move the team to appropriate accommodation.

These angry exchanges took place on the Friday before the match, and soured the mood of a Springbok team that was already struggling to overcome a sense of complacency in this "dead" Test. Craven desperately urged his players to channel their anger into an efficient performance, and it seemed as though he had been successful as his team stormed into a 13-3 lead.

However, the Lions were determined to end their tour on a high note and, turning to play with a strong wind at their backs in the second half, they exploited a rash of injuries to the home side and led

21–16 with several minutes left to play. Craven was by now animated and annoyed, shouting and snapping at his pack, urging them forward somehow to salvage the Test.

Johnny Bester took the ball from an attacking scrum, and burst clear before sending a pass to Williams who seemed to score a try beneath the uprights that would enable the Springboks to draw the match. It was not to be, as the referee ruled the pass forward. The Lions' consolation victory was safe.

At the final whistle, even in his disappointment, Craven called his forwards together and requested them to hoist Sam Walker, the Lions captain, up on their shoulders and to carry him from the field. The Springboks may have lost, but the least Craven would do was ensure the game was the winner.

Those words would become a cliché in South African rugby as provincial union presidents without number would write in programme notes, expressing the hope that "rugby would be the winner". By the 1980s, the phrase was rendered almost meaningless by overuse but, for Craven in 1938, it was sincere, and reflected the true protective affection he felt for the game.

It is difficult to know what Craven's Springbok team might have achieved during the 1940s. We shall never know, because the advent of the Second World War ensured South Africa would not play for another 11 years.

Much has been written about the unfulfilled potential of players who were not able to play during the partial isolation of Springbok rugby during the 1970s and 1980s, but it is also true that many genuinely great careers were brought to an unfortunate and premature conclusion by war in 1939.

Unbeknown to anyone, Newlands 1938 would be the final Test match for men such as Craven, who was effectively retired at 27, Tony Harris who was still only 22, Freddie Turner and Flappie Lochner, both 24, Ebbo Bastard at 26, Ben du Toit at 25 and the renowned hooker, Jan Lotz, at 27.

Craven, however, wasted no time cursing events beyond his control. He had embarked upon an extensive overseas trip, researching the most recent methods of physical education training around the world, and his itinerary took him to Nazi Germany at the time when Adolf Hitler provoked the war.

This eyewitness experience motivated Craven to become one of the most vocal Afrikaans-speaking champions of South Africa's support of the Allies, and he started to travel around the country recruiting men to join the forces. As ever, he developed a strategy, specifically to deploy popular Springbok rugby players in a kind of road show that urged young men into uniform.

He returned to Stellenbosch after the war, where he eventually secured no fewer than three doctorates, in anthropology, psychology and physical education. Throughout, he continued to coach and administer rugby, emerging as by far the most dominant figure in the game. In thousands of small remarks, in thousands of major decisions, he ruled as a benign dictator; and he had a profound impact on many people's lives, invariably a most positive impact.

It may be true that he derived the greatest pleasure from his work with the University of Stellenbosch rugby club, the Maties, where he became a man who earned both absolute respect and affection. Young students would arrive at his *koshuis* (boarding hostel), "Wilgenhof", and would remember the first time they addressed him for the remainder of their lives. Craven was not prone to idle chat, and he could be devastatingly blunt, but he was always relevant. He would become a familiar figure on the fields at Coetzenburg, walking his loyal dog, Bliksem, a seemingly omniscient presence, still recalled today in a striking statue.

If Stellenbosch was his passion, then Springbok rugby was Dr Craven's mission. He dedicated season upon season to establishing South Africa as one of the leading rugby nations in the world. A champion of the smaller unions, many of which he created to secure his position, he administered the domestic game as a kind of power broker between them and the larger provinces.

He remained close to the Springbok team throughout his life, serving as national selector, manager and coach on many occasions. Even as president of the Board, it was often hard to believe he strayed far from the selection process. At all times, he acted honourably, in the interests of the team.

The third strand of his life's work was largely conducted within the realm of the East India Club, on St James' Square in the West End of London. It was from this civilised and elite establishment that the International Rugby Board presided over their amateur game. They tinkered with the laws, arranged tours, and always set the game higher than any national or individual need.

These were gentlemen, old friends who in most cases had played against one another on the field; and Dr Craven became universally respected as a man whose understanding of the game was profound, and whose opinion of the laws was ranked as highly as any opinion expressed anywhere.

South Africa's political isolation placed Dr Craven in an awkward position with his friends, and his personal contacts undoubtedly sustained the Springboks in international rugby when other sports were isolated. It is remarkable to ponder that the country was expelled from the IOC in 1960 and from FIFA in 1963, yet played official rugby Test matches in 1965, 67, 68, 69, 70, 71, 72, 74, 77, 80, 82 and even in 1984, before normal relations were resumed in 1992. Rightly or wrongly, other countries continued to play the Boks because of Craven.

At all times, in every meeting, he remained a fierce advocate of rugby as an amateur game simply because he believed money would corrupt the special quality of comradeship that, for so many, sets the code apart.

He was a pragmatist insofar as he turned a blind eye to the sheaf of brown envelopes filled with cash being passed around during the 1980s, and he should probably share responsibility for the IRB's failure to manage efficiently and wisely the game's inevitable transition to professionalism, but these errors were born of a most pure, sincerely held belief in the amateur ethos.

It was perhaps a blessing that Dr Craven died in 1993, two years before the IRB announced, suddenly and without planning, that the game was professional. It is likely that he would have found the effect of hard-nosed commercialism on the sport, at every level, profoundly distressing and pitiable.

At all times, he was controversial: criticised in 1940 for supporting the war, repeatedly criticised by right-wing and left-wing politicians alike, criticised at the IRB for striving to sustain links between the rest of the world and his country that legislated apartheid, accused in northern provinces of being partisan towards any player from Stellenbosch or Western Province, resented by strong presidents of provincial unions for his iron control over the game, et cetera. If there was ever a storm in rugby, Dr Craven was invariably standing at the eye.

And yet, despite the decades of conflict, it is impossible to find a single critic or opponent who does not reflect on Dr Craven as a remarkable man who fought courageously for his beliefs, who sought no material gain from the game for himself, and who inspired the affection of thousands.

Yes, he made mistakes. Yes, he was stubborn and unbending in the last years of his life. Yes, he may never have clearly understood the needs of many black rugby communities in South Africa, although he could not be accused of lacking real commitment to broadening the base of the game – he resigned as a professor at Stellenbosch in 1982 to concentrate on development of the game. Yes, he may have been autocratic, insistent that his way was the only way. Yes, he may sometimes have been wrong. Yes, he may have failed to contemplate, let alone arrange, a smooth succession. Yes, he was mortal.

But …

When asked how he would defeat his enemies, Craven once replied with characteristic candour: "I will outlive them."

In medical and physical terms, not even he could deny mortality. In terms of reputation and influence, however, he has certainly succeeded.

This book seeks to tell the story of the Springbok captains. In a sense, it is the story of a family, and the father of that family is Dr Craven. There could have been no more caring, passionate and devoted father than "Doc".

This was a great man.

He was, and remains, the grandest oak.

5 THE GIANTS

These men were giants in ways that modern rugby players, for all their five-star wealth, could scarcely imagine. When these men arrived at a hotel on tour, three thousand people would gather in the street outside to glimpse them. When these men played a Test match, people would travel hundreds of miles, by train, by car and on foot, to sleep the night in the streets outside the stadium just to guarantee themselves a ticket and be part of the capacity crowd.

These men were giants.

Television had not yet arrived to strip away their mystique, and journalists remained generally deferential and polite. Contact with millions of admirers was maintained only through excited radio commentaries, listened to in silence, and eyewitness accounts of the lucky few who had "been there".

These men were giants.

The Springboks had been hailed as world champions before the outbreak of the Second World War and, from 1949 until 1955, these men would ensure the crown remained firmly on South Africa's head. They whitewashed the All Blacks 4-0 in 1949, won 30 out of 31 matches on tour to Britain two years later, beat the Australians in 1953, and shared the series with the Lions in 1955.

These men were giants.

Decades later, their names would still be instantly recalled, with awe and affection, by grandfathers and grandmothers, by millions of South Africans born before 1940. Nostalgia would be everything it used to be ...

He sits in a large office, secretaries attendant, surrounded by trappings of power and wealth, but he pauses a moment and reflects. The frown of pressure and responsibility evaporates, replaced by the bright eyes and enthusiasm of his youth: "I can still see them now … Fonnie du Toit, Hannes Brewis, Tjol Lategan, Ryk van Schoor, Chum Ochse, Paul Johnstone and Johnny Buchler – and there they go. You don't find a backline moving like that any more," he says.

And he sits back and smiles, the image of sheer pleasure and satisfaction as he recalls the men who illuminated his boyhood. He grew up to be an admired Springbok captain himself, then a minister in three governments, yet his memory of the giants remains as keen and reverent as it was on the day his father first took him to see the Springboks, the second Test against the 1953 Wallabies at Newlands in Cape Town. His name is Dawie de Villiers.

In the record books, in the manner of their triumphs, in the misting minds of many millions, this generation of Springboks remain giants.

Amid the grim post-War haze, the South African Rugby Board had invited New Zealand to tour in 1947, but various arrangements had proved impossible to conclude within time. In 1948, they had all tried again but the proposed tour was postponed due to "transport difficulties". By then, the National Party had moved into government after winning the 1948 general election but the apartheid laws enforcing racial segregation had not been introduced by the time, in May 1949, when, at last, Fred Allen's All Black squad arrived in South Africa.

To say this squad was welcomed by local rugby supporters would be a major understatement. Eleven years without Test rugby had left South Africans in a slavering state to see their Springboks take the field once again, and the man chosen to lead the team in the first Test at Newlands was Felix du Plessis, a tall, dignified gentleman who had served in the Air Force.

A nephew of Nic du Plessis, who had toured New Zealand with the South African squad in 1921, Felix du Plessis was brought up on a sheep farm known as Brookspruit, situated between the small, quiet Karoo towns of Steynsburg and Burgersdorp. His father could trace his family back to Jean-Pierre du Plessis, an ardent Protestant who had fled Catholic persecution by leaving Poitiers, France, in 1688 and setting sail to start a new life in the Cape.

Life was simple on the farm, and young Felix was reared on the stories of Osler and Craven as they excelled through his teens. These images sprang to life in 1938 when, as a callow but talented 19-year-old, he played alongside Craven in the Northern Transvaal team. Upon the outbreak of war, however, Du Plessis joined the South African Air Force and trained as a navigator.

After helping Craven in his recruitment road show around the country, Du Plessis headed north and joined a significant number of renowned rugby players among the 15 000 South Africans based in Italy during the hot summer of 1944. Most had originally been based in Egypt and, in essence, their military task was now to join the Allied forces in driving the Germans north.

A young medical orderly named Cecil Moss was there, and Louis Babrow; the talented twin brothers from Somerset West, Alec and Stephen Fry, were there with the Sixth Division, and many others; and the concept grew in the mind of Bombardier Boy Louw that a rugby match should be played in Italy between a South African Armed Forces XV and their New Zealand counterparts.

With typical bravado, the extrovert Louw found out where top players were stationed, and dispatched a fleet of army ambulances to bring them to the ground just outside Rome where the match would be played. Du Plessis dominated the line-outs in a match narrowly won by the South Africans.

Further north, at an increasingly dismal prisoner-of-war camp situated near the village of Thorn in Poland, more South African and New Zealand servicemen lifted their sagging spirits by dividing themselves into two rugby teams and renewing the special rivalry between their countries. Bill Payn, a Springbok in the 1924 series against the Lions, marked out yellow clay lines on the sandy parade ground. The man of the match, beyond doubt, was a powerful 22-year-old Jewish front ranker from Johannesburg named Okey Geffin.

Du Plessis returned home safely from the war, and briefly worked with a bank until, like many leading rugby players at the time, he accepted a position as a sales representative with the South African Breweries. These were ferociously amateur days, but SAB were renowned as sympathetic employers who would not stand between a young man and the demands of his rugby.

They certainly offered no objection when Du Plessis, now aged 30, asked permission to attend a full week of Springbok trials to be played in Pretoria soon after the All Blacks had arrived in the country. The national selection panel, while still chaired by Bill Schreiner, now included Danie Craven, who, it was soon agreed, would assist in the preparation of the team. The word "coach" was not in general usage at this time. Craven would simply assist.

More than 120 players attended the trials, and a prospective group of 32 players was announced at the end of the week. The most notable omission was the elegant Pretoria policeman and flyhalf, Hannes Brewis, to the benefit of Henry Joffe. In the end, Joffe fell by the wayside, Brewis played, and the rest is heroic history. It had become custom that every round of trials should uncover a new and previously unknown talent; in 1949, the selectors proudly settled upon a young fullback from Griqualand West, Jack van der Schyff.

"The whole trials system was cock-eyed," remembers Cecil Moss, captain of Natal at the time, a centre who had been invited to play wing at the trials. "The selectors had a tough task in choosing a team of debutants but I believe anyone needed a bit of luck to end up in the 1949 team. In the end, it was the strength of Dr Craven's personality that welded the side together."

It was widely anticipated that Du Plessis would be named as captain but, in what was fast becoming tradition, the selectors would retire for their reflective deliberations and eventually hand over the team to the radio service of the South African Broadcasting Corporation. On the appointed Saturday evening, millions of people would sit close to their radios, waiting for the words that would become so familiar ... "*Die Springbokspan is soos volg ...*" ("The Springbok team is as follows ...")

This Saturday in 1949, Du Plessis sat alongside his radio and was startled soon after eight in the evening when it was announced that normal programming would be interrupted by a news flash. Was this the moment? In solemn tones, it was declared that Bobby Locke, South Africa's outstanding golfer, had won the Open Championship in Britain. Du Plessis was happy, but his wait continued. An hour later, the team was announced, and he was captain.

He was a popular choice. The dominant lineout jumper in the country, this was an imposing man who combed his hair soberly to one side each morning. By nature, he commanded immediate respect. He would lead the team, but Craven would take responsibility for developing a strategy.

Still smarting from their defeat in 1937, the New Zealanders had set their hopes on a heavyweight pack of forwards, none of whom weighed less than 90 kilograms. Craven responded by building his strategy on the lightning speed of the tearaway Transvaal flank forward, Hennie Muller. As his team trained at Groote Schuur, Craven gave Muller the nickname "Windhond" ("Greyhound").

It would become a name that resonates in the annals of the game. In the coach's mind, Muller would snap at the vulnerable All Black halfbacks, maintain a breathless pace through the game, and inspire victory.

As the first Test at Newlands approached, the All Blacks were concerned by problems within their scrum, which they believed were rooted in the way local referees interpreted the laws of hooking. Controversy was brewing, and the New Zealand team manager, Jim Parker, took the innovative step of inviting Craven to address the All Black players on the subject of the scrum. The Springbok selector and, in truth, coach, duly arrived at the touring squad's hotel.

New Zealanders like Bob Scott and Kevin Skinner recall what followed as a discussion to clarify different law interpretations, while Craven would later relate how he, himself, had effectively coached the touring team. "Their scrum was very much below our standards," he wrote, "and I found myself in a tight corner when they asked me to assist them. My first inclination was to decline, but I was finally swayed by the fact that rugby is only a game, not a form of war."

Whether through the implementation of Craven's wisdom, or through their own skill, the All Black front row of Skinner, Simpson and Catley seized control of the scrums, and this trio became legend in their own country.

During the last minutes before the first Test, Du Plessis took upon himself the task of calming his players, many of whom had deteriorated into hopeless bundles of nerves and tension. Brewis recalls being so terrified by the scale of the event and the roar of the crowd that when he finally ran out to play, to his great embarrassment, he collided with a flag post on the halfway line.

The All Blacks established an early 8-0 lead, and young Van der Schyff missed two penalty attempts at goal. When South Africa were awarded another kickable penalty, the dead ball happened to rest at the feet of Okey Geffin, who looked at the ball and then looked across quizzically to Du Plessis. The captain simply nodded, thus making his most crucial decision of the day.

Geffin, who had famously rehearsed his kicking in the grisly war camps of Poland, strode up and calmly kicked the first of what would be a record-breaking five penalty goals as the Springboks prevailed 15-11. Bob Scott, the celebrated All Black fullback, was fated to miss a penalty attempt when his side trailed 12-11 with two minutes remaining. His kick grazed the upright.

"If that had gone over," the New Zealander reflects, "I am certain we would have held on to win the Test, and the series would have taken a completely new course because the South Africans, in defeat, would surely have made changes to their team. History would take differing views of these two sides. In Test series between South Africa and New Zealand down the years, the lines between glory and ignominy have generally been remarkably thin."

As Du Plessis celebrated Geffin's kicking heroics and a fortunate victory, the tourists complained bitterly about the refereeing decisions of Eddie Hofmeyr. One All Black had wanted to punch the official at the end of the game, only to be restrained by his team-mates, and the touring captain, Fred Allen, later reflected how he had been on the point of taking his team off the field in angry protest at the stream of penalties awarded against them. Relations between the two teams would be sour and fraught for the remainder of the series.

Du Plessis's response was to suggest to the media that Hofmeyr had given a sound performance and that, if they could perform near their potential, his team would defeat the tourists by a considerable margin. These remarks were not well received amid the indignation in Auckland and Wellington.

These sharp verbal exchanges fermented feverish excitement among the 74 000 spectators who packed Ellis Park for the second Test. Du Plessis urged his forwards to greater efforts, confidently assuring them: "If we can win our share of the ball, our three-quarters will certainly win the day."

The captain's view was soon vindicated when Brewis took the ball from a scrum near the grandstand touchline and shaped to drop kick for goal. Instead, he wrong-footed the All Black defence and darted around the scrum on the blind side. More than 70 000 people rose to their feet in breathless anticipation, among them Craven, who later recalled: "Brewis darted forward but, finding his path was blocked, he took the ball in two hands to kick it. Again, the defence hesitated and again he shot forward. For the third time, he found his way blocked, and this time he was ready to give an inside pass. The reaction of his opponent was the same. He hesitated. Brewis ran on and scored a brilliant try."

In 12 seconds, Brewis had carved his own name in legend with a score that the admired South African sports writer, Chris Greyvenstein, would later describe as the most exhilarating moment he ever witnessed in sport.

Tjol Lategan scored a second try, South Africa won 12-6, and Du Plessis's side had established an unassailable 2-0 lead in the series. At the final whistle, the captain took care to jog across the field, reaching Brewis and quietly patting him on the back. The flyhalf turned and beamed.

"Felix was a wonderful man," Brewis reflects. "Doc Craven always used to say a captain should be able to know his players and get the most out of them. You do get identical twins, but there is still a difference between everyone. As a captain, you must know how to get the most out of each individual player. This was exactly what Felix did for us during the 1949 series."

If the All Blacks looked forward to a period of recovery following the Test at Ellis Park, they were quickly disappointed. Fred Allen would later reflect upon the travel itinerary as "great fun but absolutely exhausting".

Sunday morning: board the train in Johannesburg. Tuesday early evening: arrive in Salisbury, capital of Southern Rhodesia. Wednesday: play Rhodesia, a match the All Blacks lost. Wednesday evening: board the train once again. Friday night: arrive back in Johannesburg. Saturday: play in Pretoria. The tourists spent five out of six nights sleeping on the rattling rails.

The third Test in Durban unfolded as an anti-climax, as the rigours of their tour appeared to sap the All Black forwards, and the Springboks suffered from the decision to field forwards with injuries, among them Du Plessis with a sore neck. South Africa managed to extract a 9-3 victory from the tedium, setting up a clear possibility of dealing the New Zealanders a 4-0 series defeat.

In these circumstances, following three successive victories, any selection panel might have been expected swiftly to retain the same side and to wish them well as they bid to complete the clean sweep. The Springbok selection panel was not, however, any ordinary group. They dropped the captain.

Du Plessis was omitted from the team for the fourth and final Test against the All Blacks in Port Elizabeth; worse, not one of the selectors, not even his old wartime friend Craven, offered him any explanation for their decision. Yet another eminently decent man in Springbok history had been lifted on a pedestal of glory only to be ruthlessly cut down without apparent reason.

In his searing disappointment, Du Plessis said nothing, made no public comment, accepted his fate, and quietly retired from the game at the end of the year. It must surely have been tremendously hard for him to disappear from the side on the brink of a glorious 4-0 victory, doubly so when he appeared to have been so successful in moulding a team from scratch.

The consensus at the time murmured that, at the age of 30, Du Plessis was considered too old for the 1951/52 tour, and that the selectors were looking to the future. Is it credible that a winning captain should be dropped because he would be too old for a tour that was still 18 months away?

Basil Kenyon was named to lead South Africa in the fourth Test. Perhaps the panel were simply swept away by the public enthusiasm for this charismatic captain who had led Border to a celebrated victory against the tourists, and who was identified as a man for the future. "Basil was hot property," Cecil Moss recalls, "and people were eager to give him a chance, but it was a surprise that Felix was dropped. He was one of the giants at the time and, as vice-captain in the second and third Tests, I was in awe of him."

Three decades later, Moss would serve both as a Springbok selector and as coach, and if ever Craven chided him over one decision or another, would take great pleasure in replying: "Come on, Doc, leave me alone! At least I didn't drop the captain when we were three-nil up in the series."

Du Plessis retreated from rugby to run a bottle store in Stilfontein, west of Johannesburg. A proud South African, a resolved follower of Jan Smuts and the United Party, he never relinquished his dignity. It would subsequently be evident that, in 1949, this decent man had given much more to Springbok rugby than just a 3-0 lead in the series against the All Blacks. In that same year, he had celebrated the birth of a son, Morné du Plessis.

Kenyon led the South African team through an open, intense match in Port Elizabeth, and the All Blacks scored two fine tries in their desperate attempt to avoid a whitewash, yet their efforts proved in vain. Fonnie du Toit scored a try, Brewis kicked a superb drop goal, and the irrepressible Geffin kicked a conversion and a penalty, securing an 11-8 victory and the 4-0 series win.

Geffin had scored a remarkable 32 points in the series. While South Africa had scored only three tries in four Tests, they had been propelled to this historic series triumph by the front row forward's huge, swinging boot.

Bob Scott wept in the changing room at Port Elizabeth, aghast at how his kicking form had deserted him on tour, and perhaps aware how harshly the 1949 All Blacks would be criticised at home. They had conceded only eight tries in 24 matches, but had been defeated seven times, in four Tests and in the provincial matches against Rhodesia, Border and Eastern Transvaal.

Most South Africans were too delighted to comfort the vanquished, too busy celebrating their continued reign on the throne of world rugby. By general consent, they had only truly played near their potential in the second Test, yet they had defeated opponents hailed at the start of the tour as "the finest New Zealand team ever". For this triumph, a considerable debt was owed to the man who had bonded the talents of Geffin, Brewis, Muller and others into a team. Regrettably, this debt was never properly repaid to Felix du Plessis.

The future, it seemed, belonged to Basil Kenyon. With his luxuriant, dark eyebrows and film star looks, he swiftly established his authority within the game through 1950 and, by the middle of 1951, was regarded as a certainty to captain the Springboks on tour to the British Isles at the end of the year.

He sailed through the week of trials in Cape Town, and was confirmed as captain when the ubiquitous Bill Schreiner, still serving as convenor of selectors, emerged at the Muizenberg Pavilion soon after midnight to announce the touring squad. In honoured tradition, each name was roundly cheered.

The election of the tour management team was proving more contentious, with the emergence inside the Board of a group, led by president Sport Pienaar, apparently resolved to clip Craven's wings. Perhaps they resented his increasing pre-eminence within the game; perhaps they sought to demonstrate that he was not, in fact, the fountain of all rugby knowledge. Whatever their motives, they put forward Bert Kipling to oppose Craven in the election for the position of assistant manager, essentially team coach. Three times, the Executive Committee voted; and three times the result was declared as a dead heat.

Craven finally prevailed on the fourth vote, but an enraged Pienaar turned upon his Executive and delivered strict instructions that under no circumstances should the assistant manager be permitted to coach the team. His role would be to assist the manager, Frank Mellish, and that was all.

These official divisions presented the unabashed Kenyon with an inviting opportunity to stamp his own authority on the tour. His squad was united in their desire for Craven to coach the squad and, barely two days into the voyage north, the captain requested a meeting with the manager.

"We would like Danie Craven to coach the team," Kenyon declared.

"Well, you are aware of what the president said," responded Mellish, an intelligent and pragmatic man.

"Yes, I am," Kenyon said, "but Craven must coach and, with the greatest of respect, Mr Manager, that is that."

That was that. This particular incident may have explained why, for many years afterwards, Craven would rate Basil Kenyon as the most admired of Springbok captains. This had been an early example of "player power".

Craven assumed control and, just as he did en route to New Zealand in 1937, he determined to use the long voyage to lay down parameters for the tour. He told the players they did not compare as individuals to the 1937 squad, and they would have to develop their strength as a unit. Kenyon added that they should concentrate their minds on playing "good, correct rugby".

For the captain, however, active participation in the tour would be pitifully brief. He had damaged his right eye during the war when a rifle kicked back into his face, but this generally concealed susceptibility had not affected his rugby, nor did so until the fifth match on the 1951/52 tour, against Pontypool, when a stray, but unintended, Welsh finger lodged in his eye. That evening, the popular tour captain was diagnosed as suffering a detached retina.

Only an operation at a London hospital on Christmas Eve 1952 saved his sight. When Kenyon awoke from his anaesthetic on Christmas morning, he found Mellish, Craven and all 29 of his players standing round his bed, singing the carol "Silent Night". As Johnny Buchler, the religious young fullback, read prayers, each man present at this intimate and private ritual recognised the reality that their tour captain would never take the field to play rugby again.

Amid this solemn mood, Hennie Muller stepped forward and assumed the position of Springbok captain. Widely recognised as the outstanding talent in the side, he now shouldered the added responsibility of leadership. In adversity, this giant of a man rose to the magnificence of the challenge.

Hendrik Scholtz Vosloo Muller had been born into adversity. The youngest of five brothers, his mother died barely a month after he was born and his father died five months later. Left alone, it was inevitable that the five orphans would be split up and, as the baby, Hennie was taken in by his mother's sister, Isabelle Fourie, who was married to Chris Fourie, a police sergeant, living blamelessly in the quiet eastern Free State town of Ficksburg.

The boy grew up to attend the local schools, played rugby barefoot and, from the age of 12, would regularly guide the oxen as they ploughed the fields. To this rigorous, healthy outdoor life Muller would later attribute his terrific stamina and mobility. Soon after his 16th birthday, the Fouries moved to Empangeni, and the young man decided he would go to Johannesburg. With no distinguished qualifications, he started work at the ERPM gold mine, east of the city.

His greatest ambition was to wear the famous red-and-black jersey of the Boksburg club team, and with this goal in mind he would spend hour upon hour running up and down the mine dumps. He had applied to join the army no fewer than four times, but on each occasion had been declined on the grounds that he was working in an essential occupation in the mines. During the war, Muller and his colleagues worked 12-hour shifts, seven days a week.

Peace enabled him to focus his energy on the rugby field, and he swiftly became renowned as perhaps the fastest loose forward ever to play the game. In the blink of an eye, he would ruthlessly swoop on any halfbacks in possession, or relentlessly chase three-quarters across the field. "Speed was my most effective weapon," he recalled humbly, "and I tried to use it."

Cecil Moss is in no doubt that Muller would have emerged as a dominant player, indeed a genius, in any generation of players. "In those days, there was no 15-metre restriction on the length of the lineout, so Hennie was able to stand opposite the inside centre if he wanted," Moss recalls. "Over and again, he would appear out of nowhere and take the ball from the opponents.

"I saw him burst from the back of a lineout, force the flyhalf to pass to the inside centre, make the first centre pass to the second, make the second centre pass to the wing, and still be able to tackle the wing to the ground, collect the ball and take the ball forward. In 50 years of watching rugby around the world, I have never seen anyone else do that. He was a great player, faster than any back and more intimidating than any forward. He just mowed people down."

Muller started to play provincial rugby for Transvaal, but in 1952 moved south to play for Western Province, and became a folk hero in the Cape. "Daar kom Baas Hennie, die windhond" ("There comes 'boss' Hennie, the greyhound"), Cape Coloureds in the Newlands crowd would shout as their hero set off on another exhilarating 50-metre dash clear of a flailing defence.

The loose forward led by example rather than intellect, almost challenging his team-mates to match his physical efforts, unbending courage and powerful sense of right and wrong. With Craven at his side, Muller stepped into Kenyon's role and proved an exemplary captain as the tour advanced.

This Springbok squad was patently happy, among the happiest of all; at every opportunity they laughed together and sang together. They trained hard, gave their all in every match, and never forgot their duty as ambassadors for their country. One evening in Belfast, the squad attended the theatre and returned to their hotel to learn that a newspaper advertisement that day had proclaimed they would be attending a certain dance. Most Springbok squads would have laughed off the confusion of dates and headed either for their rooms or for the bar, united in the belief that this was not their problem at all.

The 1951/52 tourists were, however, a different breed. Concerned that nobody should have attended the function hoping to see the Springboks, and then been disappointed, the players turned on their heels and headed out to the dance. Most of them did not return to their hotel until after five o'clock in the morning, but this did not deter Craven from insisting that training would go ahead as planned at ten o'clock. However, the management recognised the circumstances, and the session was abandoned after only ten minutes, enabling grateful players to return to sleep in their rooms. On this tour, as on any tour, the genuinely happy team turned out to be the team that performs at its potential.

On Saturday 24 November they produced the complete performance for which they would be remembered by generations to come. The opening Test of the tour was to be played against Scotland at Murrayfield. Early on match day morning Craven pulled Muller out of breakfast and said he wanted the two of them to wander down to the stadium and assess conditions.

Coach and captain were pleased to discover a firm ground, ideal for their strong scrum which looked faster than any they had fielded on tour to date. As he stood and gazed across Murrayfield's green acres, Craven's eyes misted over as he pointed out to Muller exactly where he had scampered over and scored a try during South Africa's victory twenty years earlier. Once again, players of the present were drawing inspiration from the past. "On a day like this," Muller mused to Craven, "we can beat any team by double figures."

He was almost right.

Scotland ... 0, South Africa ... 44

Muller had led his team out, his hair parted at the centre and slicked back, shoulders braced, boots laced under and around the ankle, seizing the ball in his right hand, expecting a battle; and yet, from the moment Chris Koch scored a try in the fourth minute, the hapless Scots were swept aside by an irrepressible tide of rampaging forwards combining sweetly with incisive backs.

Nine tries, seven conversions and a drop goal without reply represented the largest margin of victory in international rugby at that time. There were some mitigating factors in the Scots' humiliating defeat – they had not played trials, and had been caught totally unprepared, but the rout was complete.

Midway through the second half, Muller had ceased to enjoy the one-sided nature of the match and, during a break in play, he approached Angus Cameron, Scotland's young captain, suggesting the home forwards should be bound more tightly around the edges of the scrum. "Angus just gazed back at me," the South African recalled later. "He seemed bewildered by what was happening. It showed me yet again that it is always folly to appoint a back as a captain."

At the final whistle, scarcely able to believe the scoreboard himself, Muller was hoisted high on Scottish shoulders and borne off the field.

Mellish described the Springbok performance as being "as near perfect as one is likely to get", and Fry recalls an astonishing afternoon when everything went right for the touring side and everything went wrong for the Scots. "But we did have some damn good moves," the flanker recalls. "We used to run through and memorise our moves before breakfast every morning."

Watched by capacity crowds wherever they played, the Springboks were proving hugely popular tourists, and another chapter was inscribed in their legend when they played Ireland before 42 000 wildly enthusiastic supporters in Dublin. On this afternoon, Ryk van Schoor was the name in lights.

With barely five minutes played, the famed crash-tackling centre mistimed a challenge, and was knocked unconscious and carried from the field. Three doctors treated him in the changing room, and each agreed he would not play any further role in the game. By this time, Van Schoor had come round and he asked for an opportunity to speak with his manager. Mellish was summoned from his seat in the stand and, after several minutes, emerged to declare that if the centre felt he was able to play, then he could return to the fray. The manager added that he would take full responsibility for whatever happened.

Muller was astonished to glance towards the touchline and see the centre limbering up, preparing to return. Modern medical wisdom confirms Van Schoor's actions as being foolhardy in the extreme, but, back in 1951, they were regarded as the heroics of an exceptionally courageous man. "When we saw Ryk back in his place, we all felt inspired," the captain recalls.

Chum Ochse scored in the corner, Brewis kicked another of his trademark drop goals, and victory was finally secured when Van Schoor, clearly dazed but still on his feet, cut inside two defenders, ran around a third and then sidestepped the fullback before plunging heroically over the line. South Africa won the Test at Lansdowne Road, and the centre, blurred but glorious, spent the next two days in bed, recovering from his exertions. These men were giants.

Muller was relishing every minute of the tour on the field, but his formal responsibilities off the field remained a burden. The day's captain was expected to address a cocktail party after almost every match, and the Springbok loathed public speaking. Ever resourceful, he found salvation.

"We were in the cinema," he recalled, "and the feature film was preceded by a newsreel in which President Eisenhower told how Winston Churchill wanted him to speak at a particular function. 'About what?' Eisenhower had asked, and the British prime minister replied: 'Oh, about a minute.'

"I thought this was quite humorous, so I switched Eisenhower for myself and Churchill for the team manager, and used the story several times during the tour. The audience usually laughed, and I was able to get by."

If he barely got by on the podium, Muller was not less than majestic on the field where he was combining with Stephen Fry and Basie van Wyk in a melodious loose trio that was favourably compared with anything in the game. They seized control of many matches during the tour, but were perhaps never more dominant and impressive than in the Test against Wales in Cardiff.

Time and again, the Springbok back row would throw a defensive blanket around the fringes of the scrum and, in the blink of an eye, hurtle across the field to tackle an opponent into touch. Swift to the point of breakdown and ruthless in the tackle, they proved instrumental in restricting a strong Welsh team to scoring only three points all afternoon. Ochse dashed to score another try in the corner, Brewis kicked another precise drop goal and, by the end of a ferocious struggle, South Africa had squeezed past Wales, 6-3.

The demands of a marathon six-month tour were starting to take their toll on the players and, at Muller's specific request, Craven agreed to scale down the intensity of the training sessions. One drill, where players pulled their chins up to the crossbar, was completely set aside, much to the relief of the host unions who had grown weary of replacing crossbars snapped in two.

Success bred confidence within the ranks, and Muller introduced his team to the Duke of Edinburgh before the Test against England at Twickenham in no doubt that his players would prove equal to the challenge. Their talents were now beyond question, and Craven's psychological skills ensured that the players took the field in the correct frame of mind. It occasionally happens in sport that everything runs smoothly, whatever; and so it happened in 1951/52.

Midway through the first half against England, the touring team suddenly found itself in a goal-kicking crisis. The recognised kickers were either injured or out of touch, but there was no panic. Everything kept going right. Muller himself casually accepted the responsibility, safely kicking a penalty and a conversion in what unfolded as an otherwise uninspired 8-3 victory.

The fifth and final international of the tour was contested in Paris, and the Springboks proved far too strong for the French team, literally walking the scrum down the field almost at will and scoring a clear 25-3 victory.

By now, the 1951/52 Springboks had secured their honourable berth as one of the truly great teams in the history of the game. Their glory lay not only in the statistical fact that they had won 30 of their 31 matches on tour, scoring 562 points and conceding only 157, but also in their general conduct. Even amid the disappointment of their solitary defeat, suffered against London Counties in the gloom at Twickenham, the touring South Africans were so gracious and gallant that they themselves were heartily cheered from the field.

"We were so moved by the crowd's response," Muller reflected, "that we were almost happy to have lost and experienced their warmth. The spectators were not just being generous. They were really applauding us. That afternoon in London, it dawned upon me that, in sport, there is almost as much pleasure in an honourable defeat as there is in even the greatest victory."

The players reflected upon their achievements during the voyage home, and Craven started work on his latest book. The *Carnarvon Castle* finally docked at Cape Town on 22 March 1952, and was cheered by several thousand supporters on the quayside. These Springboks had left as world champions, and they returned home as world champions.

Several suited Board members had also gathered to welcome the squad home, and they lined up to shake each player by the hand as he walked down the gangway to the dock. The cordiality did not last long. Within minutes a group of players was engaged in an animated discussion with Board officials. Muller, as captain, was talking most. Voices were raised, tempers frayed. Mellish saw what was happening and strode briskly towards his captain.

"What's the matter, Hennie?" the manager enquired.

"Look at this," the captain exclaimed, showing the manager the rail ticket to Johannesburg he had just been handed by a Board official. "We have been on tour for six months, we have given everything, and now we just want to see our families. Don't you think it should be possible for those of us who live in the north to fly to Johannesburg, rather than have to travel by rail?"

"Well, that's a Board decision …"

"I know," Muller interrupted, "and it's a very poor decision."

In anger, the captain hailed four taxis and led the group of players directly to Cape Town airport. He bought one-way tickets to Johannesburg and asked the South African Airways staff to send the bill to the Board.

This was duly done. In South Africa, a winning Springbok captain usually gets what he wants. No more was said. The Board paid.

In word and deed, Muller had identified himself as a players' captain, quite unmoved by the trappings and status of his position, far more concerned that his team should be treated fairly. He harboured no desire to be paid; indeed, during the 1949 series with the All Blacks, he had rejected an offer to turn professional and play rugby league in

Britain. He simply believed his players should be neither out-of-pocket nor taken for granted within an amateur code.

In response, many of his players revered him and, upon arriving home in 1952, one of the Springboks was moved to write a letter to Florrie Muller in praise of her husband. "He has given us inspired leadership," the player wrote. "On and off the field, your husband's mode of life has been such that he has given all of us a grand example. Hennie has told us that he owes much to you for your loyal and unfailing support in everything that he does. As a result, we, as a team, are aware that we owe a great deal to you that we could have had as our leader such a kind, devoted and unselfish friend."

Muller was deeply touched, carefully folding the letter away and keeping it safe among his most prized and personal possessions.

Notwithstanding his principled stand at the Cape Town docks, Muller's fine form for Western Province during the 1952 season and the early months of 1953 ensured that there was no need for debate regarding who would captain South Africa against the touring Australians in 1953. He might have lost a yard of pace as he passed his 30th birthday, but Windhond remained an enormous influence on every match he played, and commanded complete respect.

In Muller's mind, rugby remained a simple game in which you physically confronted your opponent among the forwards, ran the opposition ragged in loose phases, and spread the ball wide at every opportunity. Through 60 years of history, South Africa had developed a forward-orientated mode of play. Critics complained the approach was restrictive and tedious, placing too much emphasis on brute power and not enough on flair. They may have been right, but the pattern was justified in South Africa because it patently worked for South Africa.

The Wallabies had arrived in 1933, preaching an open strategy where the scrums and lineouts were reduced to mere methods of restarting the game, where the ball was thrown around the field with carefree abandon. The insecure, fickle South African public had been seduced into believing the planned, tighter, kicking approach of Bennie Osler was an aberration in comparison, and the result was a most shambolic, ill-disciplined and unsatisfactory series.

Twenty years on, more Wallabies arrived in South Africa with precisely the same strategy of talking up the open game and sowing doubts within their hosts' minds about how rugby should be played. John Solomon's team included a couple of dangerous wingers, but their unimpressive forwards seemed no match for the heroes of South Africa's 1951/52 tour to Britain.

When the tourists had been beaten by Natal, Griquas, Transvaal, Northern Transvaal and Free State, and drawn with Rhodesia, all before the first Test, Muller appeared justified in believing the Test matches would be one-sided. With public support for the champion Springboks growing season upon season, the grounds would be packed by many thousands, all thirsting for a rout.

Ryk van Schoor set the tone with a bone-crunching tackle in the very first minute of the opening Test at Ellis Park, throwing up an eerie cloud of chalk and brown grass. Ninety minutes later, it was Muller who, pinning back his ears, ran through a tiring defence and set the seal on a solid 25-3 victory.

All seemed well until the Springbok captain arrived at breakfast the next morning. He could hardly believe his eyes. Almost without exception, the Sunday newspapers roundly criticised his team for playing through the forwards, for not spreading the ball wide, for not playing "open" rugby.

The articles might have been written by the Australian tour management, and they appeared to have had the desired effect when, to the amazement of his team-mates, Brewis was dropped for the second Test at Newlands. Just as South African rugby had been rattled in 1933, so the foundations were being rattled in precisely the same manner two decades later. Muller tended not to speak much as a rule but, upon hearing of Brewis's omission, his silence was thunderous. The gifted flyhalf would never play international rugby again.

Nonetheless, it seemed as though the Wallabies were so poor that even perverse Springbok selection could not reduce the home side's superiority. When Basie van Wyk went over for a try early in the second half at Newlands, South Africa led 14-3 and appeared set for another decisive victory.

Then, as the packs prepared for a scrum, Solomon, the Australian captain, instructed one of his eight forwards to leave the scrum and rove loose among the backline. Leaning against his lock, Muller lifted his experienced head and tried to fathom what his opponent was doing. It seemed bizarre.

"What do you think?" he asked Van Wyk.

The loose forward shrugged his shoulders, looking perplexed.

Confronted by such unorthodox tactics, Muller decided he would stick to his strategy, maintain his eight forwards intact and play on, but his team started to lose focus and, as he later conceded, "too many of us wanted to show up our critics by showing we could play open rugby if we wanted".

Where once there was discipline and a plan, now the ball was tossed from one side of the field to the other. The Australians gained heart, and two converted tries suddenly brought them to within a point of the home team.

Progressively grim-faced, Muller persisted with his strategy, but too many of his players were indulging in individual dashes for glory. Van Wyk, Chris Koch and Buks Marais might all have scored match-winning tries, but the opportunities went begging. In the first minute of injury time, the Wallabies launched an attack from their own try line and created an overlap for Garth Jones.

As the tall, square-jawed winger sprinted down the touchline, the familiar figure of Muller started to gather speed in cover defence. Pace for pace, the wing and the loose forward matched each other, and the gap appeared neither to grow wider nor to close. As his home crowd roared him on, Muller pounded on and on, desperately trying to get close enough to launch himself in a match-saving tackle. Arms pumping, chest heaving, Muller seemed to be gaining.

The Springbok captain ran out of metres.

Jones reached the line, promptly collapsing beneath the posts, exhausted, and Muller was left, standing alone, bent double, his hands on his knees, a tragic figure as he contemplated Test defeat for the first time. After ten successive Test wins in the Springbok jersey, he could hardly believe what had happened. There was only time remaining for the conversion and, contrary to every prediction, the Australians had won the Test 18-14 and levelled the series.

Muller sat disconsolate in the changing room for an hour after the match, his eyes dark and sunk, strange bubbles of white foam appearing at the corner of his mouth. The post mortem that followed predictably held Muller responsible for the shock defeat, primarily for not reacting to Solomon's tactics. Yesterday's hero can become today's villain in any field – such is human nature – but this dramatic transformation has been perfected in Springbok rugby.

Public criticism drained his confidence, and he was soon beating a path to Danie Craven's door in Stellenbosch. The two men spoke for several hours, first agreeing to shoulder any blame together and secondly resolving that a Springbok team would never again allow themselves to be influenced by the strategy of the opposition. South Africa would play in the South African style.

Muller felt revived by his meeting with Craven, and he drove back towards Cape Town freshly resolved to rout the Wallabies in the third and fourth Tests of the series. He drilled his team ruthlessly, instructing the new flyhalf, Natie Rens, to kick for touch from within his own half; and Australia were duly overwhelmed 18-8 at Kingsmead in Durban, and then 22-9 in Port Elizabeth.

These victories ensured that a series of great Springbok careers ended on a properly triumphant note. Ryk van Schoor, Tjol Lategan and Chum Ochse would not play for South Africa again; and Windhond had run his last.

"It had not been an easy series in many ways," Muller reflected later, "and I had found myself feeling more tired than usual after the matches. Danie Craven told me I looked like an old man when I left the field after the fourth Test, and he also said the foam around my mouth was a concern. Finally, he put his hand on my shoulder and said: 'No, Hennie, I really think you should stop at the end of the season.' Doc was right. It was time for me to retire from rugby." Muller had played a total of 107 provincial matches, initially in the colours of Transvaal and latterly for Western Province. He had worn the Springbok No. 8 jersey in all 13 Test matches played since the war, and he captained the team in nine international matches, beating Philip Nel's record by one.

Hennie Muller stands forever on the top rung of legendary Springboks; more than five decades after he played his last Test, his name is still mentioned in deferential tones. He would not scale the same heights as either the coach or manager of the South African team in later years, but his reputation in the game would be undiminished. Windhond stands immortal.

The gaps left by the simultaneous retirement of so many leading players combined with the growing reputation of British rugby to prompt real concern in South Africa that the 1955 Lions would prove too strong for a Springbok squad that was necessarily inexperienced and vulnerable.

However, when some of Danie Craven's friends warned him, to safeguard his reputation, not to have anything to do with the national team, the foremost thinker in the game briskly ushered them out of his house. No matter how dark the sky, he would stand at the forefront of resistance.

Craven set about persuading his fellow national selectors that Stephen Fry should be appointed Springbok captain for the series. The fair Western Province flanker, a veteran of the 1951/52 tour to Britain, had initially been regarded as an awkward character, perhaps too tricky to lead the side; but midway through the British tour, Craven and Fry happened to take tea together.

"You know, people warned me about you," Craven began. "They told me you would be one of the players who would give me trouble, but I must tell you, that has not been the case at all. I think you are committed and reasonable."

Fry smiled, replying: "That's strange, Danie, because people told me you were a difficult customer as well, but I think you're all right too."

They began to trust each other, and grew to like each other. With Craven's enthusiastic support Fry was appointed Springbok captain to meet the Lions. Together, the two men would live through a remarkable series.

When Winston Churchill became British prime minister in the

early days of the Second World War, he reflected how he sensed his entire life had been but a preparation for this moment. In many ways, the same thoughts might have struck Fry when he was elevated to lead South Africa against the Lions.

The loose forward emerged as one of five gifted sporting brothers, reared in Somerset West, outside Cape Town. Anthony, the oldest, had been shot down over Holland in 1941; then there was Robert, followed by the twins, Stephen and Alec, with Dennis as the youngest. The boys would thrive on the rugby field, with Stephen and Dennis both growing up to represent their country. As brothers, they competed, and ran, and extended each other to the limit.

Their father worked as chief engineer at the town's explosives works, and each Christmas holiday would pay his sons three pence for each box of grapes they picked from the vines growing on the family's 12 hectares. Fry was educated at Bishop's and the University of Cape Town before signing up for the Sixth Division and fighting in Italy during the war. He returned in 1946, and resumed his studies at UCT, playing rugby for Varsity and Western Province.

"The game seemed so simple in those days," Fry reflected. "We played to a basic strategy: the loose ball would go straight to the wing, tight ball would go no further than the flyhalf. Of course, it was not an absolute rule, but this was how we planned."

Fry emerged as the antithesis of the "maak sag" ("soften up") strategy that dominated rugby thinking in the north of the country. His instinct was to play fast, disciplined, positive rugby, moving the ball around the field. Ceaselessly thinking about the game, he would not hesitate to share his opinions with his team-mates, whether his views were flattering or otherwise.

It was perhaps this tendency to speak his mind that moved people such as Hennie Muller to note how "it takes times to get to know Stephen".

Fry was announced as Springbok captain, appropriately for a man with an appreciation for the finer things in life, at the conclusion of an elegant Springbok dance held after the second series of trials had been played in Durban. "It was a fantastic experience," he recalls. "I enjoyed captaincy and had led the Springboks twice before, against Combined Services on Boxing Day in 1951 and, later during that tour, against Bordeaux, but I suspect that was only because I spoke French and would be able to get through the post-match speech."

He was happy with his team, which, though inexperienced, included young prospects such as Theunis Briers, a farmer from Paarl, Johan Claassen, a strong lock from Potchefstroom, and Daan Retief, a tall eighthman from Pretoria; yet the perception throughout South Africa was that, no matter what Springbok team was selected, the lauded 1955 Lions would sweep all before them.

Robin Thompson, Ulsterman, captained a gifted squad that was founded on the two large, powerful centres from England, Phil Davies and Jeff Butterfield; the try-scoring panache of the flame-haired Irish wing Tony O'Reilly; the tactical skill of Cliff Morgan at flyhalf; and the constant presence of hooker Bryn Meredith, the latter two players both from Wales. For the first time, the Lions had arrived in South Africa wearing the blazing red jerseys with the composite badge of England, Scotland, Ireland and Wales.

British sport, and with it British morale, was riding high: Roger Bannister had recently run the first sub-four-minute mile in history, Donald Campbell was driving his hydroplane "Bluebird" over the water at amazing speeds, and England's cricketers had retained the Ashes in Australia.

The days of the motherland kindly dispatching some chaps to play a spot of rugger with teams in the colony were over. This was serious: serious rugby on the field and serious fun off the field. When the squad arrived at Johannesburg airport, the first tourists to arrive by air, they stood on the tarmac for 30 minutes singing their repertoire of songs for the newsreel cameras.

Naturally the South African Rugby Board had planned a cordial welcome for the Lions, sending them to Potchefstroom where they would open their tour against a physical Western Transvaal side on the hard, scorched, winter-brown field at Olën Park. South African tactics against the Lions have always been to soften up the pallid British, and 1955 would be no exception.

The tourists knew what was coming. After watching barely ten minutes of a Currie Cup match between Northern Transvaal and Western Province at Loftus Versfeld, before heading to the bright lights of Potchefstroom, O'Reilly sprung up from his seat in the stand and shouted across to Jack Siggins. "I'll have my return ticket now please, Mr Manager. It all looks rather too fierce for me." In the event, the 19-year-old would score 16 tries in 15 matches.

Yet, to great relief around South Africa, the Lions lost their opening match against Western Transvaal when Jack van der Schyff, the gifted fullback who had played against the 1949 All Blacks and fallen by the wayside since, caught a long clearance by Morgan in one hand on his own 10-metre line. In one movement, he turned and kicked an astonishing 65-metre drop goal. Western Transvaal won 9-6, and Van der Schyff, who had spent two of his wilderness years working as a crocodile hunter in Zambia, was recalled to the Test side.

It would be misleading to suggest the crowd control before the first Test at Ellis Park, Johannesburg, was inadequate, for this would be to presume that there was any meaningful crowd control at all. The doors were hurled open 30 minutes before kick-off, to ease the crush outside the ground, and the people flooded in to occupy every seat and space, every ledge and perch with a view of the field. It is estimated the match was attended by between 95 000 and 100 000 people. This would remain the largest crowd for a rugby Test until Australia and New Zealand played before 110 000 at Sydney's Olympic Stadium in 2000.

There must be some doubt, however, whether any atmosphere can have matched the bedlam that erupted around Ellis Park when Ernie Michie, kilted and playing the bagpipes, led the Lions onto the field. The gentle Scot from Aberdeen strained and reddened as he blew every ounce of breath into the instrument, heralding his team-mates amid the hometown hysteria.

Fry, as ever dapper and focused on the task at hand, emerged into a wall of noise at the head of his Springbok team, a bellowing roar so deep and strong it seemed to resonate from the very soul of South Africa.

The captain was, however, anxious. He was eager to maintain discipline in his side, and he had been alarmed to see several younger players brashly playing the fool and eating too much food at the pre-match meal. Fry had walked over to the culprits, and warned them to concentrate on the match.

Worse was to follow. Two players were inexplicably late for the team bus, delaying departure by ten minutes; and then, on their way to the stadium, the bus was held up by a wedding party emerging from church. To the captain's absolute horror, three players leaped off the bus and posed for photographs with the bridal couple, amusing their teammates. Arriving in the changing room, Fry angrily told his side to stop the laughter and think about the game.

"Craven always said the team that sings before a Test weeps afterwards," Fry recalls wistfully, "but we just had too many debutants in our side who did not understand the magnitude of the challenge that lay ahead."

The Test started and quickly established a thrilling momentum, as play swung from one end of the field to the other. This was not carefree, casual rugby but the intoxicating spectacle of two high-quality sides probing each other, down either flank and around the scrum, searching out weakness.

South Africa led 11-8 at half time, but the Lions launched the second half in a blur and, twice in nine minutes, tentative kicks ahead bounced unkindly for Van der Schyff, the Springbok fullback. The tourists capitalised on their good fortune and stormed into what appeared to be a winning 23-11 lead.

An opportunist Springbok score reduced the Lions' lead midway through the half, but Chris Koch's gallant driving try in the 79th minute appeared to be no more than a consolation. Van der Schyff converted efficiently, but the Lions were still leading 23-19 as the match moved deep into injury time.

"How much time left, Mr Referee?" Fry asked.

"Not much," came the reply.

Morgan kicked off, and the growling Springbok forwards started to make ground, mauling up field. When the ball popped loose, Fry swooped and sent an intelligent, crucial pass wide right to Briers, who took possession at speed. The temporary grandstands swayed alarmingly as thousands of spectators stood and cheered the Springbok wing to the line. Inside, outside, he surged, and scored. It was the greatest comeback of all time! Ellis Park roared.

The operator in the outsized scoreboard beside the Quinn's Bread sign, as excited as anyone, removed the second figure of South Africa's score as 100 000 eyes focused on Van der Schyff preparing the conversion.

The scoreboard read:

BRITISH ISLES 23
SUID-AFRIKA 2

If Van der Schyff kicked the conversion, the Springboks would win 24-23. If not, the Lions would win 23-22. Like the operator in the scoreboard, holding the "2" and "4" anxiously in sweating palms, everyone knew this would be the last kick of the game. This was death or glory, nothing less.

As Van der Schyff started to scuff a trench in the turf, he noticed Fry, his captain, standing ten metres behind him, his hands on hips.

"Don't you want to take this one, skipper?"

In fact, Fry did take the long kicks for goal for Western Province, with his brother Dennis taking the shorter ones, but this was not his moment. "No, it's all right, Jack," he replied. "You have been kicking superbly today."

Van der Schyff had completed the trench, and was propping the ball in its vertical position, but he seemed restless and unsettled. Out of the corner of his eye he saw Johan Claassen, his Western Transvaal team-mate and friend, yet another Springbok with genuine goal-kicking experience.

"Claassie, you should be taking this kick."

The lock forward grinned, assuming his colleague was joking, and took up a position directly behind Van der Schyff. Tommy Gentles, the scrumhalf, lay on the ground, holding the ball in position with his right hand.

A moment of silence. Van der Schyff kicked, toe first, and Claassen's first reaction was that the kick was perfect, heading for dead centre, but the ball began to swing left, and left, and left, and it passed by the upright; and the final whistle sounded. Van der Schyff stood, alone among thousands, his head bowed, chin on his chest, his shoulders collapsed in disappointment. Ivor Hanes snapped the photograph and captured the moment for the rest of time.

Fry ran straight to his fullback, throwing an arm around his shoulders and telling him not to worry about the kick. It was simply a game. Around the country, disappointed South Africans would not be so charitable. Van der Schyff scarcely slept that night, enduring a kind of anguish that few can imagine. His roommate, Johan Claassen, could but sit on his bed and sympathise.

It had been arranged that the two squads would gather for a post-match dinner at the Carlton Hotel and, in conversation with Craven and Philip Nel, the former Springbok captain, Fry suggested that a one-point defeat in the opening Test was by no means a disaster for his largely untried team. The captain was heartened when both men wholeheartedly agreed with him.

Soon after nine o'clock, however, the Springbok captain was becoming distinctly agitated. Almost half the Lions squad had not turned up for the dinner and, as Robin Thompson proposed a toast to the South African team, scarcely ten of the tourists were on hand to raise their glasses. To Fry and many others, this behaviour was nothing less than rank bad manners.

The Springboks had taken the trouble to arrange a post-dinner party at their hotel, where a band had been booked and a few beers were provided, and Fry invited those Lions players he could find to join them. It was not long, however, before someone was tugging persistently at his blazer.

"Come on, Stephen, this is a waste of time," said Angus Cameron, the Scot who had led his country in the 44-0 defeat four years before and was now the Lions vice-captain. "We'll have a party at our hotel."

It had been a long day. Fry had had almost enough, telling Cameron he could do exactly as he wished. Where the Springboks enjoyed a fine band and some dancing, he sensed the Lions simply wanted to drink. It was no problem. As he glided across the polished floor, Fry was satisfied to know that he would see his anti-social British friends again at Newlands.

The selectors made six changes for the second Test, with the unfortunate Van der Schyff among those dropped. As the squad gathered in Cape Town, the Springbok captain seized tighter control of his team, demanding that his players should be in the right place at precisely the right time, and insisting that the tight ball should be cleared upfield and not shovelled dangerously down the line as it had been at Ellis Park. "We'll play my way," he told his team.

Fry was determined the big Lions centres, Butterfield and Davies, should be contained, and he held major reservations over the choice of Wilf Rosenberg and Des Sinclair, two relatively small men, in the Springbok midfield, but he accepted this as a fact of life. The jokes of Johannesburg were consigned to the past, and the South Africans started to focus: telephone calls and visitors were banned at the team hotel. Quiet and purposeful team talks were conducted daily as each player was thoroughly briefed on what was expected.

Absolute silence reigned in the Springbok changing room as the minutes ticked away before kick-off, and Craven implored the players to concentrate on what they had practised all week. For him, for the team, for every South African, it was utterly unthinkable that the Lions should be permitted to take a 2-0 lead in the four-match series. A solid victory was imperative.

"No mistakes, lads," Fry urged. "No mistakes, please."

If the South African captain could have scripted the game, he would not have been able to improve on what unfolded. The Springbok forwards started to dominate from the outset, and the home side led 5-3 at half time. As confidence spread through the ranks, the South Africans cut loose during the second half, running in no fewer than six tries. Tom van Vollenhoven scored an unforgettable hat trick, Rosenberg touched down after Sinclair had darted between Butterfield and Davies, fullback Roy Dryburgh cut the line sweetly to score, and both Briers and Ackermann crossed the line to complete the rout.

With their backs to the wall, and a nation of critics snapping at their heels, the Springboks had defeated a fine Lions side 25-9. Fry looked emotional in the changing room afterwards and, propelled by a sense of honour, made his way to where Sinclair and Rosenberg were sitting. The two young centres had thrived in attack and, more importantly, remained solid in defence.

"I owe you chaps an apology," Fry said, humbly. "I didn't think you could cope with Butterfield and Davies today and, to be honest, I still don't quite know how you did it, but you proved me wrong. Well done."

Once again, the teams were invited to a post-Test dinner, this time at the Rotunda in Cape Town, and once again when the night was still young, Fry felt a tugging at his blazer. Once again, it was Angus Cameron.

"Come on, Stephen," the Scot said. "This is very dull."

"Look, Angus, with the greatest of respect, do whatever you want. You can take your bloody team back to Britain if you want."

Several Lions later apologised to Fry, but relations between the two teams were never better than cordial. They would improve dramatically in years to come when O'Reilly shared the benefits of a prosperous business career to host a series of highly successful, much enjoyed reunions.

The villains of Ellis Park had become the heroes of Newlands and, as fans milled around the team hotel on the Sunday morning, Van Vollenhoven found his autograph had suddenly become a valuable commodity. After almost an hour of obliging eager supporters, he began to decline invitations.

Johan Claassen was standing nearby, enjoying the merry scene, when a stranger pushed some paper towards him and asked if he would kindly arrange for Van Vollenhoven to sign. Claassen agreed, and persuaded his roommate to scrawl his name once again. The stranger was delighted.

"Where is your bank account?" he asked the lock forward.

"At Barclays in Potchefstroom," Claassen replied, and thought no more of the incident until his bank manager called, two days later, and informed him that a Mr Morton, from the Stock Exchange, had deposited 25 pounds in his account as a token of appreciation. The lock decided to spend this unexpected windfall to buy a Springbok blazer. These garments were handed out to touring squads, but players selected at home had to buy their own.

Fry recalls: "Our daily allowance during the series against the Lions was 50 cents per day. This was intended to be used to buy your opposite number a drink after the game, but it was hardly enough for that. It didn't really matter. We would have accepted whatever the Board gave. It might sound strange now, but we only played the game because we enjoyed the game."

Flushed with success, the Springboks tried to sustain the intensity of their preparations before the third Test in Pretoria, but succeeded only in exhausting the players. When the team arrived for their first training session on the Thursday morning, they discovered Craven laying out rows of large tackling bags. Ever the innovator, he declared his intention to build their stamina.

They sweated through another demanding session on the Friday morning and, that evening, were seen practising their lineout drills on the Zwartkops golf course, near Pretoria. Almost unbelievably, the team was summoned to a further training session on the Saturday morning, five hours before kick-off. The exertion took its toll on Daan Retief, who withdrew at the eleventh hour.

Completely over-trained, the South Africans could barely raise a gallop during the Test and were ultimately defeated more comprehensively than the final score of 9-6 suggests. "We did not perform at all," Fry recalls, "and we would have lost heavily if the Lions had not adopted conservative tactics. Cliff Morgan was a fine flyhalf, but he probably kicked too often. Most of us believed that if he spread the ball to the wings, we would have been in serious trouble."

Defeat brought the critics to the fore once again: it was said there were too many English-speaking players in the side; Craven was criticised for training the players too hard; Fry was blamed for adopting the wrong tactics. To their credit, the selectors turned deaf ears to the chorus and entrusted essentially the same team to win in Port Elizabeth and square the series at 2-2.

Public concern reached terrifying proportions when Fry received a letter warning him that his life would be in danger if he dared travel to the Eastern Cape to lead South Africa in the fourth Test. "That sort of thing went with the territory," he recalls, smiling, "but I did keep an eye open whenever I was walking around town before that Test, though I didn't take the threats too seriously."

Before another capacity crowd, amid breathless tension, the Lions took control of the first half, but the Springboks were running on sheer desire, and fine tries from Briers either side of the interval decisively turned the tide. There have been many occasions during the past hundred years when any careful analysis of the situation suggested a South African defeat was inevitable, yet, somehow, an extraordinary Springbok gees (spirit) has defied the odds.

This was such an occasion. The Lions should have won, and become the first tourists to win a series in South Africa for 61 years, but they were beaten. In a startling display of controlled desperation, Ulyate, Van Vollenhoven and Retief all scored tries, and the home side celebrated a 22-8 victory.

O'Reilly had scored a consolation try in the last minute, and been heavily tackled, possibly late, as he grounded the ball. In some agony, the Irishman was borne back to the changing room on a stretcher.

Many years later, the Springbok wing that day, Theunis Briers, arranged a meeting with O'Reilly to seek investment in a possible business venture. As the conversation turned to the good old days of 1955, the Irishman recalled the final Test and casually mentioned how he had never discovered which South African had tackled him so brutally, so unfairly, so late in the last game of the tour, and, even worse, had rubbed his face in the chalk of the touchline.

Briers shrugged his shoulders, mumbling how it was a long time ago and he could not remember. If O'Reilly did not know who had tackled him, Briers was certainly not going to tell him ... for it had been Briers himself!

Thus, the honours were shared. In four Tests, South Africa had scored a remarkable 16 tries and conceded 10. The total of 26 tries added credence to the suggestion made many times since that the

1955 series between the Springboks and the Lions was one of the most entertaining ever contested. A mediocre third Test aside, the standard of rugby had been consistently high.

Relieved that his team had drawn the series, Fry decided the end of the tour represented an appropriate moment to retire. "I was not looking forward to touring New Zealand in 1956," he recalls, "and I was really struggling to take the knocks. I was 31, and I had simply had enough.

"Throughout my career, I used to work on my stamina by running up and down the hills near Somerset West and, when that started to feel like hard work, I realised my body was telling me to call it a day."

Fry retired from the game with the same elegance with which he had graced it, and never emerged thereafter in any coaching or management capacity. "I had to start working," he laughs. "It was all right for those chaps who worked for the breweries, but I had to start making a decent living."

As South Africa celebrated Christmas 1955, Felix du Plessis was running his bottle store in Stilfontein, Hennie Muller was working hard in Cape Town, and Stephen Fry was considering a business opportunity in Northern Rhodesia. Each former Springbok captain had settled comfortably and quietly back into the crowd that had cheered them, back into the routine of daily life.

They were ordinary men again. Dressed in green-and-gold, however, they had been titans, the adored and admired giants of a golden age.

6 THE BROTHERS

The theory is simple. The Broederbond was a secret organisation established in 1918 to sustain Afrikaner culture and society by ensuring its 12 000-odd members were placed in positions of influence around South Africa. *Broeders*, or brothers, were found within the National Party government, the Dutch Reformed Church, the armed forces, education structures ... and rugby.

Their activities were not always sinister, at least no more sinister than the activities of any organisation concerned solely to safeguard a way of life from the perceived threat of outsiders. That said, it is beyond dispute that, within the world of South African rugby during the late 1950s and 1960s, it was doubly difficult to become president of a provincial union unless you were a *broeder*, doubly hard to be a member of an executive committee or a selector; and it was doubly hard to become Springbok captain – unless you were a *broeder*.

This manifestation of Afrikaner nationalism was encouraged in 1924 by the election of a new government that had campaigned on an Afrikaner-dominated "White South Africa first" platform. Foundations were being established for a general state of mind that would reverberate through every aspect of South African life, including rugby, for decades to come.

Of the eight men who led South Africa onto the rugby field between 1956 and 1965, it is conceivable that only two were not *broeders*, and they captained the side for a mere three Test matches between them. The suggestion has been made that, during this period, outstand-

126

ing leaders such as Doug Hopwood were overlooked patently because they were not *broeders*; this suggestion cannot be proven, but neither has it ever been remotely refuted.

Both the game and the position were tainted by suspicion.

It would be unfair to question the credentials of those who did captain the national team during this period, all of whom did so with true honour and courage in the traditions of the game, but it would also be wrong not to acknowledge those who might have led the Springboks, but were denied the chance.

The influence of the Broederbond in South African rugby was, for three decades, the influence that dared not speak its name. When Chris Laidlaw, the All Black scrumhalf, mentioned the issue in his book *Mud in your Eye*, he was widely vilified in South Africa. When Wynand Claassen addressed the subject in his autobiography in 1985, he was replaced as a national selector.

Under challenge, *broeders* most often refute all accusations of bias and abuse by pointing to the continuing dominance within the game of Danie Craven, who was famously not a member of their organisation. However, every indication is that the Broederbond had no choice but to tolerate Craven as president of the South African Rugby Board from his election in 1956 onwards. His status within the game, at home and abroad, made him almost untouchable.

Equally, it seems that Craven was compelled to accept the influence of the Broederbond as a fact of his own life. In essence, the powerful man and the most powerful organisation learned to function alongside each other in an early form of a condition that France during the 1990s, governed by a socialist prime minister and a right-wing president, would identify as *cohabitation*.

This understanding was struck before his election as president in 1956, when Craven accepted the *broeders'* endorsement on condition that, if they ever wanted him to leave, he would be given the opportunity to resign rather than be unceremoniously sacked. This was a peculiar condition, and seemed to confirm the extent of the Broederbond's influence over the game. Craven might not have been a member of the organisation, but neither was he a threat.

While not minimising the Broederbond factor in any way, it should also not be exaggerated. When more than 120 provincial players were assembled to play the national trials ahead of the 1956 Springbok tour to New Zealand, people were not assessing their chances by working out who was a *broeder* and who was not. The issue was not burning at the forefront of every mind.

There were other more appealing topics of gossip, such as the astonishing rumour that spread through the corridors of the Avalon Hotel, Cape Town, on the last night of trials. It was said that Jan Pickard, the formidable Western Province lock forward, had suffered a broken nose, angrily checked out of this hotel where all the players were staying, and left for home.

Hushed groups of players gathered in animated conversation around the hotel, and the suggestion quickly spread that the punch had been thrown by none other than Salty du Randt, the admired Northern Transvaal forward widely expected to be named as the new Springbok captain.

Danie Craven, newly elected president of the South African Rugby Board, arrived at the hotel soon after ten o'clock that night, striding straight past a group of players in the foyer, brow furrowed by the latest turn of events. The trials had passed off well, raising hopes that a powerful squad could be chosen, and Du Randt had impressed everyone with his leadership and authority.

Early the following morning, the players were summoned to a meeting in the hotel's ballroom. Craven started by referring to an unfortunate event that had taken place the previous evening; he then invited Du Randt to speak. In scarcely audible tones, head bowed, the Northern Transvaler mumbled an apology and asked to be forgiven. Craven then declared the matter closed, and requested that the incident be immediately forgotten and set to one side.

If his request had been realised, perhaps the 1956 Springboks would not have emerged as such a divided, unhappy squad; there again, it may have been fanciful for anyone to hope that the incident would not leave scars.

The immediate consequence was that Du Randt was officially

ruled out of contention for the captaincy; and, to widespread astonishment, Basie Viviers was elevated to lead the squad to New Zealand. The Free State fullback did not ask to be appointed and yet, from the outset and ever since, he has been mercilessly dismissed as an inappropriate choice. People said he was past his peak on the field, people said he did not command the respect of his team. Viviers had been placed in an invidious, impossible position, and Craven hardly delivered a ringing vote of confidence when he grumbled grimly: "What is done is done. Our task is to make the best of the squad that has been chosen."

Both Pickard and Du Randt, the seething, wounded bulls of this saga, were included in the tour party and, almost from the day of selection, the players were more or less divided between the two totems. Those from the Cape tended to look to Pickard for leadership, and those from the north sensed Du Randt held the moral authority of a captain. Viviers, through no fault of his own, found himself caught in the middle, his reputation peppered by crossfire.

Inevitably, each side clung to its own version of exactly what had taken place that fateful night at the Avalon Hotel in Cape Town.

What is beyond any dispute is that the players had returned to their rooms after a gruelling day of trials, and Du Randt was lying on his bed, stomach down, talking about the day's events with a few teammates. The door was open, and Pickard happened to be strolling down the corridor.

An abrupt conversation followed: some say Pickard suggested Du Randt's captaincy that afternoon had been ineffective, others say Du Randt scoffed at the Capetonian for not being a true Afrikaner because he played for a predominantly English-speaking club, Hamiltons. Du Randt had suffered an unpleasant cut over his eye that morning; perhaps he was irritable and unsettled.

Whatever the reason, he leaped to his feet and delivered a ramrod punch into Pickard's startled face. The Western Province forward stayed on his feet, but staggered away, his pride evidently as broken as his nose.

When Craven arrived at the hotel later that night, his original intention had been to resolve the matter internally but, it was alleged, this option was ruled out when Pickard called in his lawyer and threatened a civil action. With great regret, the president realised Du Randt could no longer be captain.

The selectors turned to Viviers because he was from the Free State, thus neither from the north nor the south, and, as a veteran of the 1951/52 tour to Britain, he understood the particular challenge of touring overseas.

Almost teetotal and resolutely religious, Viviers appeared to embody the kind of Springbok spirit that Craven so admired. Back in 1951, his son had been born on a Friday and baptised on a Saturday, enabling the young father to join his team-mates and board the ship to Britain on the Sunday. A talented baritone, he had proved a popular tourist, ever bursting into song.

When Viviers heard he had been included in the squad for New Zealand, he was seen to place his head in his hands. When he then heard the convenor of selectors add the word "captain", he began to weep openly.

Pitiably, his captaincy appears to have been undermined by the reality that he was not a fullback of genuine international standard. The nearest he came to a Test cap on the 1951/52 tour was when he was asked to be touch judge in one of the internationals, and he had not been selected since. Anyone who does not earn respect as a player struggles to be respected as a captain.

As the squad finally boarded the flight to Australia, it was evident that Du Randt and Pickard were not speaking to each other, and were refusing even to acknowledge each other's presence, but this ongoing quarrel was not the limit of Craven's problems. He had been unanimously elected manager and, effectively, coach to the Springbok team, but the Board had then proceeded to appoint Dan de Villiers as assistant manager. The two men did not get along from the outset and, as the weeks drew into months, the South African management team would prove to be as profoundly divided as their players.

It didn't rain, but it poured.

During their brief stay in Australia, Viviers's beleaguered players suffered blow upon blow. First, news arrived that Bertus van der

Merwe's young son had died suddenly; then, it was learned that Ian Kirkpatrick's father had passed away; then Basie van Wyk, the revered veteran flank, freakishly broke his leg during the warm-up before a match; finally, Brian Pfaff's brilliant form was suddenly interrupted when injury ruled him out of action for weeks.

The South Africans won all their matches in Australia, including two Tests against the Wallabies, but their spirits remained low as they headed to Auckland, to a country stirred into a frenzy unknown before or since.

New Zealand may be a small country, almost tumbling off the edge of the world and generally overshadowed by Australia. In so many ways, it has been an observer of events, almost irrelevant to the mainstream. And yet this country has found definition and identity in rugby union, and earned global acclaim for the All Blacks, the most visible and powerful symbol of the nation.

Tom Pearce, a councillor on the New Zealand Rugby Union, set the tone in 1956 when he declared it would be crucial for the All Blacks to "have hatred in their hearts" when they played the South Africans, and it often felt as if every man, woman and child invested their self-esteem in this series.

The message was clear: win and New Zealanders would stand tall, lose and they may as well topple off the edge of the map. The Springboks arrived to discover enormous, seething crowds wherever they went and a degree of public fascination in them, as the deadly foe, that was almost frightening. Every single New Zealander seemed possessed by this need to win.

This national desire was partly explained by a thirst for revenge for the All Blacks' 4-0 series defeat in 1949, but the significance of the 1956 series against the Springboks seems to have run far deeper into the national psyche, entering the realm of defining what it meant to be a New Zealander, of what this country would represent. Years later, books would be published assessing the impact of this particular tour on this small but spirited land.

"We all went a little mad," an All Black selector would reflect.

Viviers responded to this astonishing atmosphere as the most genial and appreciative of guests. When the team arrived in Dunedin, he led his players to the town hall, discovered an organ in the street and led the squad in an hour of hearty community singing with more than 1 500 New Zealanders. Asked to try a local drink or wear Maori dress, he always obliged with a smile.

If the captain offered the velvet glove, the manager's reaction was to show an iron fist. Craven was never less than an autocrat, certain of his own ways and intolerant of alternatives, but he was never stricter or more ferocious than on this tour to New Zealand in 1956. Perhaps he did not believe in the ability of his team to defeat the All Blacks; perhaps he concluded that extraordinary measures were required to give the Springboks even the slightest chance. Whatever the reason, the coach's training methods could at best be described as unusual. Viviers, still lacking clout and authority, meekly followed instructions when more established captains might have at least challenged and queried.

Craven ran rampant. Ever an innovator, he resembled a professor at play with his experiments. In 1956, the Springboks were his guinea pigs.

First, he instructed players to train with strips of lead placed in the soles of their boots because he wanted to simulate the heavy, muddy conditions typical of New Zealand. The result was a series of pulled hamstrings.

On other occasions, he would make the players hop the length of the field on one leg or endlessly piggy-back each other through the mud and rain; and, all the while, Craven would stand on the touchline, ears tucked beneath a motorbike cap, trousers folded into his woollen socks, barking orders.

He introduced one drill where Chris Koch and Jaap Bekker were asked to place the ball beneath a sack full of wet sawdust, and then to lie on the sack. The idea was for the rest of the forwards to charge into this obstacle and, by whatever means, release the ball. The result of the bone-crunching, full-speed collision that followed was that Koch and Bekker required medical treatment.

Another day, the coach handed each of his players a rugby ball and asked them to sit quietly in a chair. Each Springbok was instructed to stare at the ball for a period of 30 minutes, apparently to improve concentration. "Hell, if someone told me to do that," All Black Tiny White said, upon learning of the South African training methods, "I would have thrown the ball back at them."

Yet the Springboks respected Craven, and did as Craven asked. There was no argument and no dissension. That was that. Viviers, as captain, sat and stared at his rugby ball; so did Pickard and so did Du Randt.

This had not suddenly become a poor or inadequate Springbok team. It still included many talented players, but the captaincy and management conflicts ensured that the whole amounted to much less than the sum of its parts. Any team requires a conducive environment to play at its potential, and the 1956 Springbok team was denied a conducive environment.

The tourists were drowned in the pandemonium of their first match in New Zealand, against a powerful Waikato side at Hamilton. More than 40 bright floats had joined a pre-match parade down the city's main street, and a young fullback named Don Clarke ensured the carnival continued by kicking eight points as the home side burst into an 11-0 half-time lead and won 14-10.

Pickard, ironically, had captained the team in this opening defeat, but it was Viviers who managed a sporting smile as he handed the mounted springbok head, the traditional trophy for the first provincial team to defeat the tourists, to the Waikato coach, Dick Everest. A long tour stretched ahead.

It seemed poetic justice that, following an injury to Viviers, the selectors decided Du Randt should be called to lead the team in the first Test at Dunedin, and the hoary old forward delivered an impassioned speech before the match, imploring his pack to stop the All Blacks in their tracks.

Yet the die was already cast. The Springboks lacked cohesion, order and discipline; and they also lacked luck as the All Black wing Ron Jarden intercepted a Springbok blind-side attack, scampering through to score a decisive try in what became a rapturously received All Black victory, by 10-6. Du Randt, at least, had left a positive impression. "He was the only captain who always took trouble to walk up and check if an injured opponent was all right," recalls Terry McLean, the doyen of New Zealand rugby writers. "He was a gentleman."

When Canterbury defeated the tourists soon afterwards, Craven declared his side were literally paying the penalty for the poor refereeing the All Blacks felt contributed to their defeat in 1949. "They think we crooked them then," the coach said, "and now they are using their referees to crook us."

At this point, a creative newspaper in New Zealand started a column that was dedicated to counting and listing the excuses offered by Craven for a South African defeat. By the end of the tour, the list had reached 18.

Viviers returned to lead the Springboks in the second Test and, although the All Blacks ruthlessly exploited his hesitance under a high ball, the Springboks rallied to secure a completely unexpected victory. Frank McAtamney was popped out of the very first scrum, and the tourists founded an 8-3 victory on the strength and power of Chris Koch and Jaap Bekker in the front row.

New Zealanders read how Bekker would practise his scrumming against goalposts, often snapping them in two, and, with the series at 1-1, the All Black selectors took emergency measures to challenge the Springbok front row. Kevin Skinner was chosen for the third Test, as the terminator.

He thumped Koch at the first lineout, then swapped sides at half time and ploughed into Bekker during the first scrum of the second half. "I'd have been a mug to have missed," Skinner, a boxing champion, said later. "Those guys were bigger than me. My attitude was that if there's going to be a donnybrook, let's do it in front of the referee. He was always going to warn before sending anyone off, and it would make him watch play closely. That was fine. It basically stopped the Boks from intimidating our guys, and we could play rugby."

Don Clarke, playing his Test debut, kicked another eight points and the All Blacks left the field with a 17-10 victory; Bekker left with a grotesquely engorged and bloodied face; Skinner left the field with a grin. Viviers, detached at fullback, had been more than 30 metres from the heat of the battle.

Suddenly, the South Africans were contemplating the unthinkable: a first series defeat for 60 years ... not six matches, not six months, not even six years. It bears repeating: the Springboks had not lost any series for 60 years and, since 1931, had grown used to being hailed as world champions. Defeat was palpably not feared. It was scarcely contemplated. It was unknown.

Yet, if the tourists were desperate to preserve their long unbeaten record by squaring the series with victory in the fourth Test at Eden Park, Auckland, it is probably true the All Blacks were twice as desperate to win. In this most raw and emotional of series, the stronger heart would prevail.

Saturday 1 September 1956 dawned as the day of reckoning.

As ever, the teams tore into each other from the kick-off. The players may not have been especially muscular or imposing by modern standards; they knew nothing of protein diets and weight training, but the tackles thudded into rib cages with an intensity that shuddered through the grandstands.

Don Clarke kicked a long-range penalty, then a second, and New Zealand led 6-0 when the decisive moment of the series unfolded. Out of scrappy play, All Black eighthman Paul Jones hacked the ball ahead and sprinted on towards the static Viviers. Instead of tackling the man, the Springbok fullback flapped both his hands at the ball, missed completely, and Jones was clear, dashing over the line as the crowd erupted, shaking his fist in the air, screaming delight.

For the Springboks, there was no return, even if an opportunist late try did bring some respectability in the 11-5 defeat. The series was lost, and the misery was complete for the Springbok captain. Viviers had endured so much, but cruel fate decreed it would be him who was crucially found wanting. Silence reigned in the stunned Springbok changing room. "The younger players could not believe it, the older players would not believe it," Du Randt reflected.

Outside, New Zealand celebrated national victory and redemption. Jones famously announced to radio listeners that he was "absolutely buggered", and, to his credit, Craven left the desolation of the visitors' changing room and agreed to address the overjoyed, hollering Eden

Park crowd from the microphone installed on a platform in the middle of the main grandstand.

"It's all yours, New Zealand," Craven declared.

The South African rugby chief would not reflect happily on the 1956 tour to New Zealand, later suggesting he had never truly believed the Springboks would be successful once their morale and leadership structure had been shattered by the punch thrown at the Avalon Hotel, Cape Town.

Inevitably, the team were judged harshly at home. Indeed, sections of the Ellis Park crowd hissed the Springboks when they played a Rest of South Africa XV three weeks after their return from New Zealand. Viviers could not believe his ears: South Africans were booing the team in green-and-gold.

The gentle Free Stater quietly retired from the game, the unwitting victim of unexpected events. He had not asked Du Randt to strike Pickard, not asked to be captain of a divided team against wildly motivated opponents, yet he seemed unable to come to terms with what had happened. The years passed but they did not heal. When former Springboks gathered at a function, Viviers would typically not turn up, and his old team-mates would shake their heads sadly, hearing tales of heavy drinking, of how their captain had become reclusive.

Aged 60, Viviers hit the headlines again, in tragic circumstances, when he was prosecuted and fined the sum of R1 000 following a motor accident in Long Street, Bloemfontein, in which a 26-year-old man had died. For Basie Viviers, the Springbok captaincy turned out to be a poisoned chalice.

In 1958, South Africa was preparing for an inaugural tour by the French squad, and the national selectors eagerly sought a safe pair of hands for the Springbok captaincy. There appeared to be none safer than those belonging to Johan Claassen, the powerful, talented lock forward from Western Transvaal, and he was duly appointed to lead the side against France.

Springbok rugby has been well served by a handful of men who, in many ways, have devoted their lives to the cause. Craven stands first among this elite, but Claassen, strong in jaw and principle, follows close behind. As a player, then coach, selector, manager, union president and Executive Committee member, he would serve at the heart of the game for more than 40 seasons.

Folklore maintains that the greatest Springbok rugby players emerge from the platteland, God-fearing men reared under wide African skies, developing strength as they work the land, durability as they farm in harsh conditions, and fierce pride as they create wealth for their kin and country.

Claassen sustains the legend, the third of seven children born to a farmer in the Karoo, in the district of Prins Albert, at the foot of the Swartberg Mountains. When the ostrich market collapsed during the early-1930s depression, the family moved to the Christiana region, south-west of Potchefstroom.

He thrived through school, trained as a teacher, and soon became a pillar of authority at the University of Potchefstroom. He played his debut for Western Transvaal at the age of 20, and made 105 appearances for the province during the course of 13 seasons. "That used to be the record," he reflects wistfully, "but they pass that number in three years now." It might be calculated that the modern equivalent of Claassen's career would be more than 350 games.

The lock forward won Springbok colours against the 1955 Lions. "Jack van der Schyff was my roommate during the trials week, and we were together when we were both named in the side for the first Test," he remembers. "Jack was very emotional, even though he had made his debut in 1949. I was not so emotional. There have been times in my life when I wish I could have been emotional, but I have not always found it easy to express my feelings."

Neither Claassen, nor South African rugby in general, knew what to expect from the French squad, but nobody anticipated a great threat to the Springboks. In spite of the fact that many leading players had retired following the 1956 tour, the national selectors were content to hold a solitary trial and hand Claassen a relatively untried, inexperienced team.

Mickey Gerber was among those playing their Springbok debut, and the fullback vividly recalls the anxious moments before the first

Test at Newlands, when the imposing captain addressed his team one last time: "Johan Claassen looked around at all of us," Gerber remembers, "and he said, '*Manne* (Guys), it will be a national disaster if we lose'. It was spine-chilling stuff."

Such a crisis was averted, narrowly. To general incredulity, France earned a 3–3 draw when their gifted scrumhalf, Pierre Danos, kicked a sweet drop goal, which was cancelled by Butch Lochner's try. Claassen had tried manfully to goad his players, offering encouragement at every opportunity, but the players appeared unable to establish any kind of rhythm against unpredictable opponents.

The French tourists attached little significance to their midweek matches, and did not seem unduly disturbed when they conceded more than 40 points to a combined Western Province, South-Western Districts and Boland XV only a few days before the second and final Test in Johannesburg.

In contrast, the South African selectors saw this game and believed they had discovered the secret of playing France. They drafted no fewer than eight of this scratch Cape XV into the Springbok side for the second Test. Maybe their minds were not completely focused on their task; maybe the French had caught South African rugby drifting in a daydream of complacency.

"It was remarkable," Claassen recalls. "I arrived at the team hotel on the Thursday before the second Test and was confronted by players I had never met before. We were starting from scratch. I had no say in selection of the team. In those days, you just accepted what you were given.

"But it was very difficult. At that time, there was no coach for home Test matches. Dr Craven was usually around, but his influence was not as great as it would have been on tour. It was left to me, as captain. I had 48 hours to mould this diverse group of players into an international side."

When centre Jeremy Nel executed a scintillating break early in the game, sending Lofty Fourie through to score, it appeared as if Claassen had remarkably forged a worthy performance from the bizarre selection, but the French forwards would not subside and the impulsive, wild flair of the touring back line continued to trouble the hesitant and uncertain Springboks.

The contest lost shape, the French began to gain in confidence, and dread seized the South Africans. Claassen worked relentlessly, wheeling in broad arcs to lineouts and scrums as he implored his players to greater efforts, but two more drop goals and a penalty carried France to a stunning victory.

Once again, the Springbok dressing room fell silent in defeat. "It was very disappointing," Claassen recalls. "If we had just stayed calm and chosen roughly the same team in both Tests, we would have won the series comfortably, but we were complacent in so many ways and we paid the price."

To be more accurate, it was the Springbok captain who paid the price. In the absence of any other scapegoat, Claassen was held entirely responsible for this catastrophe and he was savagely criticised. The lock accepted his unjust fate with stoicism but, amid the crazed attacks, he did make himself one private and resolute promise: he would not retire from the game until he had led South Africa on the rugby field again, and proved his critics wrong.

Springbok rugby seemed to be losing its focus through the late 1950s. Perhaps this was simply the unstoppable cycle of sporting success and failure in motion. Maybe the administration of the game was being diverted by questions of who knew whom, and who was a member of what, rather than simply who would be the best player in his position on the day of the match.

The golden years of the post-war era had been replaced by a mish-mash of bewildering selection decisions. As 1960 dawned, there was no room for error. The All Blacks were coming to South Africa, and the Board, in their desperation to develop a new Springbok team, finally pulled itself together.

Scotland were invited to undertake a brief tour, playing one Test against the Springboks in Port Elizabeth. The match had been scheduled as a warm-up before the series against the New Zealanders, but the selectors again sprung a surprise by appointing Des van Jaarsveldt as captain.

The loose forward was 32 years old, and approaching the end of a career that many believed should have been decorated with Springbok colours several years before. Van Jaarsveldt was reared in Bulawayo, Rhodesia, and emerged as a talented 18-year-old wing in 1947. He had featured strongly in the Springbok trials of 1951 and 1956, on both occasions reaching the final match.

"But I missed out on both tours," he recalls. "I was playing as a wing in the trial before the 1951/52 tour to Britain, and I had moved to eighthman by 1956 when the Springboks toured New Zealand. It was frustrating. I was a Rhodesian and I was English speaking. Those were the hard facts. I reckoned my face and my language didn't fit. There is no doubt politics and the Broederbond had a lot to do with selection of the Springbok team in those days. That was the plain reality, and there was not much any of us could do about it."

By 1960, Van Jaarsveldt assumed his chances of realising his Springbok ambition had faded, but he produced an outstanding performance in leading a South African XV to victory over a Junior Springbok side in what served as a trial match, and suddenly found himself appointed as the new Springbok captain.

"I knew most of the players very well," recalls Van Jaarsveldt, who spoke no Afrikaans but understood the bare essentials, "and I can recall Danie Craven telling me at breakfast on the Thursday that the team was my responsibility and I should decide how we played. In any event, there was not much we could do in the couple of practices we fitted in before playing Scotland."

South Africa won the Test 18-10, with Van Jaarsveldt running clear from halfway to score the winning try. Even so, wizened rugby men sitting at the bar in the Salisbury Sports Club surveyed the situation and began to conclude that Craven, racked by guilt for so long overlooking Van Jaarsveldt's strong Springbok claims, had tossed the Rhodesian a consolation prize of the captaincy in what had been a relatively low-key international against the Scots.

This theory gained credence when Van Jaarsveldt was abruptly discarded, and not included in any Springbok team against the All Blacks later that year. "I was very disappointed," he recalls, "but I was getting on by then. The real missed opportunities of my career were in 1951 and 1956."

Nonetheless his elevation, albeit belated, did serve to encourage rugby in Rhodesia, and this respected man continued playing for Matabeleland until 1967. He later coached his country's national team, and then served as president of the union when Zimbabwe was granted independence in 1980.

Van Jaarsveldt had joined the elite club of Springbok rugby captains, yet the persistent suspicion remains that this most talented Rhodesian was denied a fine international career because he was not a *broeder*. Selection is not an exact science and nothing is proven; yet the suspicion remains.

If Van Jaarsveldt would not lead South Africa against the 1960 All Blacks, then who would? The national selectors launched themselves into an exhaustive search, summoning the country's 120 finest players to a week of trials at a place near Bloemfontein called Maselspoort. It was deep mid-winter in the Free State, and bitterly cold, but the players were accommodated in tents. If they are going to be hard enough to beat the All Blacks, the officials reasoned, then the players should be able to withstand a shivering night or three.

The general standard of play was heartening and, when the selectors met to choose a side at the end of the week, they included six debutants, six players with minimal Test experience, three veterans, but still no obvious captain.

The selection meeting continued deep into the Bloemfontein night, and it was eventually agreed that the captain would have to come from the three more experienced players. When Claassen and Koch were deemed inappropriate, the panel was left with Roy Dryburgh, the Natal fullback. Talented and skilful he might have been, a signed-up *broeder* he was not.

Perhaps in desperation, one of the selectors mentioned the name of Avril Malan, the earnest, promising, profoundly Afrikaans 23-year-old lock forward who had been picked to make his debut in the first Test. Could he lead the side? The question was asked. No, it was agreed, Malan was not quite ready.

Decision was reached in the early hours of the morning: Dryburgh would be Springbok captain, and Malan would be vice-captain. Anyone concerned that an English-speaking player would lead the side might have been consoled by the emergence of Malan as a prospective captain of the very near future.

Dryburgh was not appointed with conviction, and one of the New Zealand rugby writers following the 1960 All Blacks around South Africa, Terry McLean, recalls a whispering campaign against the new Springbok captain: "Roy was an absolute gentleman, but he seemed to be another victim of the Afrikaner-English split. The Afrikaners have memories like elephants, and people kept on talking about a time when Dryburgh missed a catch against Timaru on the 1956 tour to New Zealand. It was being held against him four years later.

"There is no doubt," McLean reflects. "There were people in South Africa who were not happy unless the Springbok captain was an Afrikaner."

In marked contrast, the touring All Black captain enjoyed the whole-hearted support of his union and players, and was admired on all sides.

Wilson Whineray was only 14 years old when his father dragged him and his four brothers out of bed at two o'clock one morning. The boys were laid together on the sitting room floor, wrapped in warm blankets, to listen to radio commentary of a Test match between the Springboks and the All Blacks. That was 1949. Seven seasons later, the young front ranker had played twice against the touring South Africans, coming face to come to with Chris Koch. "I still remember looking into his eyes," Whineray says. "He was a big man in my life."

Led by the fair-haired front row forward, the 1960 All Blacks campaigned across a tense country living in an official State of Emergency, declared after the Sharpeville killings of 21 March. The visitors applied themselves single-mindedly to their rugby challenge, however, and approached the first Test of 1960 as favourites, but Dryburgh, bravely undaunted by rumour, applied himself to the task at hand. He invited the legendary Hennie Muller to coach the team and, with the ubiquitous Craven adding his thoughts, a powerful Springbok side rose from the shambles of the warped selection process.

Keith Oxlee directed play at flyhalf, John Gainsford ruled the midfield, and Martin Pelser, a one-eyed flanker, magnificently scurried and scampered around the fringes of the scrum. Dryburgh worked hard to communicate with his players, ensuring everyone understood his role in the team, and soon earned the respect of each of his men, irrespective of their home language.

In the event, the All Blacks were swept aside in the first Test at Ellis Park, rocked back in the fourth minute when South Africa brought the blind-side wing across to create an overlap that Hennie van Zyl gleefully exploited. The tall and powerfully built wing galloped across the line to score.

Among the delighted South Africans who rose to their feet in that corner of the ground was a small boy from the town of Middelburg, watching his first Test at his father's side. The spectacle of the gold numbers on green jerseys and the white numbers on black jerseys thrilled him beyond words. He watched in awe as the match unfolded. One day, he told himself, he would be part of all this, would be part of this special rivalry. His name was Wynand Claassen.

South Africa won 13-0, and a delighted Dryburgh sensed Springbok rugby had recovered from the traumas of 1956 and 1958, but the longed-for revival did not last. Don Clarke, the All Black fullback, produced what he later described as the finest performance of his career in the second Test at Newlands, driving the home side back with spiralling punts for touch, and kicking eight points through a penalty, a drop goal and the conversion of Colin Meads's try.

Dryburgh could do nothing but watch his team slip to an 11-3 defeat, and the fullback visibly limped as he left the field. He had been struggling with a knee injury for two seasons and, in the course of a long, anguished discussion with the selectors later that evening, it was mutually agreed that the fullback would step aside for the remaining two Test matches of the series.

Avril Malan was named as the new Springbok captain.

As different in nature and personality from Dryburgh as night from day, the resolute young lock took the responsibility in his stride. Brave and humble, strict and firm, disciplined and straightforward, he seemed the crew-cut personification of what every dutiful Afrikaner father would hope for in his son.

Malan was born and raised in the Moot, the working-class area of Pretoria that would in later years produce Naas Botha and Uli Schmidt. His father was a professor at the national veterinary college, and little interested in sport, and his brother was seven years older, so young Avril would travel to Loftus Versfeld, sit alone in the open stand, and watch the likes of Brewis in action.

He played rugby through school in Pretoria before heading south to the University of Stellenbosch where, he dearly hoped, he would have the chance to play under the wise eye of Danie Craven. "I had bought a book he had written," Malan remembers. "It was called Draers van die Groen en Goud (Wearers of the Green and Gold), and I found his stories about what happened to the Springboks very interesting."

As an under-19 player at Stellenbosch, Malan was summoned by Craven, who told him decisively that forwards do not kick the ball: "They kick and chase in the north," Craven said, "but we prefer to keep the ball in the hand here, to pass and run across the field." Malan took every word to heart, and prospered to play three successful seasons for Western Province from 1957.

He returned to Johannesburg early in 1960, found a post with Union Steel, and started to play for Transvaal. His selection as Springbok vice-captain for the first Test against the All Blacks had taken him by surprise, and he was relieved to be accepted by senior players such as Claassen and Koch.

Now, suddenly, he was the captain.

For Avril Malan, this elevation did not bring gushing honour and glory so much as a heavy burden of responsibility. This was a man who never strutted or boasted, who never regarded himself as any more important than anyone else. He accepted the challenge of leading South Africa with a serious, solemn nod of the head rather than any euphoric, thrilled punch in the air.

Named as the new captain in Cape Town on Saturday, he travelled home to Johannesburg on the Sunday and was to be found back behind his desk at the Union Steel offices on the Monday morning.

Some of his fellow trainees had read the daily newspaper, and they offered their congratulations. Malan said thank you briskly, and modestly suggested they all resume work.

These were amateur days, and he did not particularly dwell upon rugby as the week took its course. He was, however, grateful to the management at Union Steel for allowing him Thursday and Friday off work, enabling him to travel down to Bloemfontein and gather with what was now his Springbok team.

A fervent advocate of systems and clear structures, Malan spoke strongly at an early team meeting, setting out exactly what he wanted to happen. He was scarcely 23 years old, the youngest Springbok captain in history.

The Free State Stadium, a vast scaffolding bowl filled with 60 000 people, grew merrier and merrier as the third Test unfolded. Many people had travelled great distances to attend the match. They cooked big slabs of steak on open fires outside the ground, emptied their bottles of brandy; and, with only six minutes left of an uncompromising contest, were preparing to celebrate victory. South Africa led 11-3, and Malan seemed to have made a winning start.

Don Clarke was not finished. Nicknamed "Thunderboots", the All Black first kicked an immense penalty from 65 metres, reducing the deficit to five points. With one minute remaining, the tourists kicked ahead and McMullen won the chase to score in the corner. Silence fell upon the stadium.

Clarke lined up a touchline conversion that would salvage an improbable draw for the New Zealanders. Malan stood, his hands on his knees, beneath his posts, calmly accepting his fate, whatever it would be. Kel Tremain, the All Black flank, wished the fullback good luck as he handed him the ball. "Don't worry, Kel," came Clarke's assured reply. "She'll be all right."

The All Black kicked and, after a hanging pause, the touch judges, one of whom strangely was Clarke's brother, Ian, raised the flags. It finished 11-11, and the teams headed to Port Elizabeth for the fourth and decisive Test.

"We were lucky to get off the hook in Bloemfontein," Whineray recalls, "but the series had been close from the start. There was never much between the two teams. Our problem was that our guys were exhausted. The travel was extremely tiring, and we were being confronted twice a week by an unending supply of big, tough, physical men storming at us. This barrage was taking its toll. All of us had painful grazes from the hard fields, but I remember telling the guys over and over again before the last Test that we were one game away from making history. No All Black side had won a series in South Africa. That was the big dream of every New Zealander, and that was what kept us going."

The All Black captain had been waging his own war during the series in a one-on-one contest with the renowned and feared Springbok front ranker, Piet du Toit. "Our policy in the scrummage was to get the ball out and away as quickly as possible," Whineray recalls. "If we couldn't get the ball away, I would collapse the scrum and we would start all over again.

"Piet du Toit was a very strong prop, and his party trick was to scrum at an angle that would buckle his opposite number. That tactic was illegal in 1960, and it is absolutely illegal now because it is so dangerous. I was not surprised to hear later that when Piet had tried the same thing against Oxford University on tour to Britain, the Oxford prop walked straight off the field, saying that kind of game was not rugby and that, if it was, he wasn't interested."

Malan recalls the fourth Test in Port Elizabeth as an anti-climax in terms of the rugby played, but it was a huge relief for South Africa. "Hennie Muller was still coaching our team and, together, we decided we would confront the All Blacks up front," he remembers. "It was very tense in our changing room before kick-off. Everyone knew we could not fail. We simply had to win."

The young captain won the toss, decided to play against the wind, and felt his team had secured an advantage when they reached half time at 3-3. The day was won soon afterwards when Martin Pelser, most people's player of the series, managed to scramble heroically over the line from close range.

By then, however, another name had been added to the long list of

New Zealanders who felt they had been unjustly denied their moment of glory on South African soil. Frank McMullen had sprinted clear and been ankle-tapped by Oxlee as he approached the Springbok line at full speed.

Did he then illegally move the ball over the line in a double movement, or did his own momentum drive him over for the try? The referee, Ralph Burmeister, looked long and hard but finally signalled a penalty to South Africa.

Forty years on, Malan reflects upon the incident with serenity. "I was in a perfect position and, at the time, I was convinced the referee had made a good decision. In my heart, however, I believe McMullen was not properly held in the tackle as he bounced across the line. It was a fair try."

By such tiny margins, heroes are born and losers condemned. Such is the game. Refereeing decisions, good and bad, must be accepted. It is notably odd, however, that matches between South Africa and New Zealand should so often have hung upon one man's interpretation of one incident.

When Malan returned to his work at Union Steel on the Monday morning, even the company managers were beating a path to the trainee, eager to congratulate the young captain on defeating the All Blacks. Again, he thanked them for their kind words, and turned back to his paperwork.

To the world, and his colleagues, Malan presented a firm face, apparently in control of every situation. Beneath this iron façade, however, he was as ridden with self-doubt and uncertainty as any other 23-year-old.

Only six weeks after the All Blacks returned home, the Springboks were scheduled to sail north and undertake a full tour of Britain. For the young Malan, the prospect and the challenge suddenly appeared too daunting. "Everything was happening so quickly," he recalls, "so I decided I would sit down and write a letter to Baas Frank Mellish, convenor of the national selectors, and explain to him that I believed Roy Dryburgh should captain the team to Britain. He had played well in the All Black Tests, and he was recovered from his injury."

Mellish responded firmly.

"We have not reached this decision lightly. You are our captain."

Malan said nothing further.

He learned soon afterwards that Boy Louw had been appointed as coach and Ferdie Bergh would be the manager of the 1960/61 Springboks. Craven, as president, would join the squad later in the tour. Malan overcame his own doubts by developing a fitness regime for his players on board ship.

He would get on with the job.

"We worked hard during the voyage," Malan recalls, "but most of us will remember that trip for the afternoon we spent together as we approached British waters. We all gathered in the lounge, and we sat staring at this peculiar small box on the table. It was a television. At first, there was only the test signal on the screen but we still sat and watched the colour bars for at least 30 minutes. We sat in silence. It was all so new to us. When the picture and sound came through, we were absolutely entranced. It was incredible."

The Springboks arrived in Britain, and were further intrigued to find three or four people standing outside their hotel, holding a board and seeming to shout in their direction. "Somebody asked if they were shouting at us," Malan recalls. "I didn't know. If they were, I could not imagine what they might be shouting about. I really had no idea. We were sportsmen. I knew nothing about politics. We didn't discuss the issue. We didn't even know if there was an issue."

Malan led a squad, forged and welded in the series against the All Blacks, and commanding enough talent to leave players such as a young Frik du Preez, Mof Myburgh, Piet Uys and Mannetjies Roux in the B team. They would remain unbeaten until the last match on tour, against the Barbarians, and yet this was a team that would be denied widespread admiration.

The 1960/61 Springboks were cast in the image of their captain. He might have been young, but Malan was clear of thought and firm of purpose. He would work hard and long, he would not try to cut corners, he would be honest in his endeavours, he would be quick to work, perhaps slow to laugh.

The captain was eager that his players should mix freely, breaking down any remnant cliques from the All Black series. A more relaxed, instinctive leader might have mentioned the issue at a team meeting and moved on, but that was not enough for Malan. He meticulously kept a notebook, maintaining a record of who roomed with whom at each stop of the tour, and he ensured that he, and he alone, would draw up the squad's rooming list at each hotel.

That was his system, his manner.

It was neither right nor wrong. Some players felt comfortable in such controlled, highly disciplined circumstances, others felt restricted by a manner of management that occasionally seemed more appropriate to a school trip. Their British hosts occasionally noted the tourists appeared introverted, a little unwilling to loosen their ties and relax. This was the tone of the tour.

An internal disciplinary committee was formed, under the chairmanship of the senior player, Johan Claassen, and it became commonplace for anyone who was late for the bus or for a function to be made to bend over while every other member of the squad lined up and thumped his backside. No exceptions would be tolerated. Again, some enjoyed the ritual; others loathed it. Some shrugged off the punishment, others were reduced to tears by the beating.

On the field, this inherent conservatism was translated into a safety-first approach where the ball was retained among the forwards and ploughed upfield in an uncompromising, arm-wrestling struggle. Under pressure, perhaps Malan opted to revert to the kick-and-chase approach of his Pretorian youth rather than keep faith with the open game he found at Stellenbosch. In fairness, the British winter of 1960/61 unfolded as the coldest, wettest for decades, and the conditions often ruled out any bright intention of spinning the ball wide.

Match after match, the Springbok backline would stand and shiver in the wind and rain, at times so eager to keep warm that, during a break in play, they would run and huddle close to a group of steaming forwards.

It is substantially to the credit of the captain and the resolute spirit that he managed to instil within his squad that the players accepted the conditions as a fact of life, resisted the temptation to moan and wish they were back at home in the sun, and maintained such a high standard of rugby that, match after match, they may have shivered but they also won and won.

The weather was never more brutal than on 3 December, the day of the Test against Wales in Cardiff. The Arms Park was effectively flooded by the adjacent River Taff, but local officials gave no thought at all to postponing the match, and 62 000 supporters filled the open, drenched stands to see a contest not so much of skill or strategy, but of sheer desire.

As the Welsh singing soared into the dark heavens, and driving rain fell in the opposite direction, Malan led his team into every grinding ruck and maul, to every sliding scrum and slithering lineout. With Doug Hopwood heroic at the back of the scrum, Oxlee managed to kick the sodden ball over the crossbar once and South Africa emerged from the swamp with a 3-0 victory.

"Conditions were so bad," the captain recalls, "that we would win a penalty on Wales's 25-metre line, and I would ask Lionel Wilson to kick for touch because there was obviously no chance of anyone kicking the goal."

The South Africans ground on and on. Hopwood scored the crucial try in an ill-tempered victory over England. "People criticised us for playing dour rugby at Twickenham," Malan recalls, "but the English were at home and they adopted the same approach. We had to play skop-rugby (kicking rugby) to beat them. In any event, it is wrong to say that we followed pre-determined, dull tactics.

"Players made the decisions on the field. The scrumhalf decided where we would throw the ball at the lineout, and, if we won possession, the flyhalf decided whether we would kick or run. That was their job."

Hopwood scored two further tries in a more entertaining win over Scotland at Murrayfield, but it was the Springbok captain who emerged with credit from an anxious match against Ireland in Dublin. The Test moved into injury time with the score still at 3-3, and South Africa won an attacking scrum.

Malan instructed his forwards to apply a wheel. The Springbok scrum took one small step forward, heaved as one, twisted to the right, powered over the line, and it was Hugo van Zyl who fell on the ball to score. Lockyear converted, and the cherished Grand Slam was secure. Under tremendous pressure, far from home, the captain had cleared his mind, hatched the plan and prevailed.

The South Africans' 30th and last fixture in Britain brought the solitary loss of the tour, a 6-0 defeat against the Barbarians in Cardiff. The tourists had been depleted by 'flu to an extent where manager Ferdie Bergh had asked if the match could be postponed, but this request was declined. The closely contested match that followed was primarily remarkable for a shuddering tackle on the Springbok captain by Baabaas substitute Haydn Mainwaring.

Vivian Jenkins, the British rugby writer, reported: "When the two men met there was a thud like a comet burying itself into earth, and it was Malan, hit with the full force of Mainwaring's shoulder, who hurtled backwards and sideways into touch, to remain semi-conscious for several minutes."

There were no hard feelings, however. Malan recovered his composure, played on, and was carried from the field at the final whistle on the shoulders of several Barbarian players, among them Mainwaring. The Springbok captain's sense of order was more disturbed when, seven days later, his side managed no more than a 0-0 draw against lowly rated France in Paris.

Against his better judgement, Malan had agreed the players could set out with liaison officers and visit the Louvre museum on the Friday afternoon before the match. As they wandered between works of art, the South Africans began to grow tired and Malan, who had joined this trip, persuaded those players involved in the Test to return to the hotel and rest their legs.

"The damage was done," he recalls. "We were not properly prepared, and the match was unsatisfactory in many ways. There were several incidents of dirty play and, by the end, we had to be content with the draw."

The 1960/61 Springboks to Britain may not be remembered with the same affection as their lavishly celebrated predecessors in 1951/52, but their excellent record stands comparison with any. Moreover, by his method and discipline, the young captain had guided the recovery of Springbok rugby from true disarray at the start of 1960 to victories over the All Blacks and the Home Unions, and renewed status as unofficial world champions 15 months later.

Still short of his 25th birthday, his authority seemingly unchallenged at the head of a strong and developing team, Avril Malan held the future in his hands. However, the captain damaged his knee early in the 1961 season and was ruled out of the early Test against a touring Ireland team.

The selectors were cast back to square one, and their gaze fastened upon the universally revered figure of Johan Claassen. He had thrived against the All Blacks and, to his enormous satisfaction, the big lock forward was named to lead South Africa against Ireland at Newlands. "It meant a lot," Claassen recalls. "In my mind, the appointment showed I had restored my dignity after being dropped as captain following the 1958 series against the French."

By such twists of muscle, this saga turns.

Malan was injured, Claassen was vindicated, and the fates would decree Claassen remained as Springbok captain even after Malan's return to full fitness, leading South Africa in two Test matches against the touring Wallabies in 1961 and then in all four internationals against the Lions in 1962. Not for the first time, one man's injury became another man's opportunity.

Claassen was a big man with a big heart, and he was a *broeder*.

His renown throughout the rugby world as a towering lock without doubt enhanced his capacity to lead. When he asked, players obliged. When he spoke, they listened. When he clapped his huge hands and implored them to dig deep into their reserves, they breathed hard and did precisely that.

Ireland arrived having made the unorthodox request to play the Test as the first game of their tour. This was agreed, and the Springboks merrily continued where they had left off in Britain, running in five superb tries and winning 24-8. Amid the cheers at Newlands, it was clear Claassen had slipped smoothly into the driver's seat vacated by Malan. The Springbok motor was roaring.

Fathers brought up on the feats of Osler, Craven and Nel could once again assure their eager sons: "Don't worry. The Springboks don't lose."

It was the misfortune of Ken Catchpole, a 21-year-old captain, to lead his hopeful Australian team into this cauldron of Springbok confidence and form. The first Test would be played at Ellis Park in Johannesburg.

"We had played three pretty decent warm-up Tests against Fiji," Catchpole recalls, "and we knew we could give the Springboks a run for their money. There was a fantastic buzz outside the ground when we arrived, and I will never forget the roar that greeted us when we ran out onto the field. It was deafening. I recall thinking it was great. The South African crowds really like us.

"Moments later, Johan Claassen ran out at the head of his Springbok side, and the whole stadium was literally shaken to its foundations. I have never heard any noise quite like it. It shook you; it really shook you. I thought to myself, 'What on earth are we doing here?' It was genuinely awe-inspiring."

Catchpole's worst fears were realised, and the Wallabies were overrun by an inspired Springbok team, which rushed in eight tries and triumphed 28-3. Ellis Park bellowed its pleasure, and Claassen heartily thumped each of his players on the back as they left the field. It had been a day to remember.

The sated Springboks predictably failed to maintain the same standards in the second Test at Port Elizabeth, winning 23-11 as the Wallabies gallantly stood their man among the forwards and were left to rue a refereeing decision, where a knock-on had been controversially called, that might have brought the scores yet closer. Yet, such thoughts did not temper the celebrations.

"Of course, it was fun," Claassen recalls, eyes bright. "We had become a very strong side, and we were respected again. I did not particularly enjoy being Springbok captain, and I think I played much better when I was not captain, but the honour was important to me. Throughout 1961, I kept thinking back to what had happened against

France in 1958. The same people who had criticised me then were congratulating me now. I smiled, but I knew."

Malan had recovered his fitness by the start of the 1962 season, but the national selectors were not going to tamper with the winning formula that spread such joy the previous season. Trials were staged, and Claassen was retained as captain for the Tests against the Lions, led by Arthur Smith, a mathematician and scholar of note. This was to be professor versus professor.

"I was not particularly disappointed," Malan recalls. "My main focus was on getting into the team because competition for places in the second row was very tough. In the end, I was chosen for the first Test but then dropped for the second Test. That was my own fault. I was not playing well enough."

Claassen remained in charge, dominant in the team and dominant in the lineouts. "Johan Claassen's ball was always Johan Claassen's ball," remembers Abie Malan, hooker in the first Test, "finish and klaar (and that was that)!"

The Lions' hopes of winning the first Test were acutely reduced when their playmaker flyhalf, Richard Sharp, was injured during the match against Northern Transvaal. "There was an incident involving Mannetjies Roux," Claassen recalls, "and several Britons believed Richard had been deliberately assaulted. That was nonsense. South Africans did not approach the game in that way. Of course, it was true we wanted to win, but not at any price."

In the event, the opening Test finished in a 3-3 draw, as John Gainsford's spectacular try was cancelled out by a Lions penalty late in the game. Claassen was generally satisfied, but concerned when the selectors shuffled the team for the second international. Malan was among those dropped, a bullocking young forward from Pretoria called Frik du Preez was switched from flank to the second row, and a perilously young, diminutive scrumhalf was plucked from obscurity at Stellenbosch University. The captain's fears would prove unfounded. It may not have been apparent, but a new Springbok era was dawning.

"Good afternoon, who are you?" Claassen enquired politely when he saw a young man checking in to the Springbok team's hotel.

"De Villiers," came the reply. "Dawie de Villiers."

The second Test would prove pivotal, and controversial. Once again there was little to choose between two organised and powerful packs, once again both defences held firm against every scheme and plan. When Oxlee kicked a penalty with barely eight minutes remaining, it seemed as if South Africa would prevail by the most slender of margins, but the Lions surged back.

As time ebbed away, the British pack laid siege to the Springbok line, and the tourists seemed to have snatched dramatic victory when their forwards rolled a maul from a five-yard scrum. Keith Rowlands, the red-haired Welsh lock, stood up last from the pile of bodies and clearly claimed to have grounded the ball. Like Frank McMullen two years before, he would be denied the glory.

Ken Carlson, the referee, was well positioned. If he awarded the try, the relatively straightforward conversion would surely give the Lions a 5-3 victory. He looked long and hard, and decided he could not be sure. He signalled no try, and moments later blew the final whistle on a 3-0 Springbok win. The Lions slumped to their knees in disappointment. Rowlands trudged from King's Park with tears of anger and frustration welling in his eyes. More than an hour later, he was still to be found in the changing room, too emotional to speak. The Springbok captain was notably quiet, relieved to have escaped with victory.

More than 30 seasons later, Claassen and Rowlands found themselves at the same function. The South African and the Welshman greeted each other, and conversation soon turned to the Durban Test of 1962.

"You know, Keith, one of our players fell close to the ball."

"Yes?"

"But I think you scored the try, fair and square."

Rowlands stared wide-eyed, eyebrows raised in evident surprise.

"Yes, Keith," Claassen repeated. "You scored a fair try."

"Well, it's a bit bloody late for that now, isn't it?"

On that note, the conversation ended.

The Springboks clinched the series against the luckless 1962 Lions with an 8-3 victory in the third Test at Newlands. The tourists may have dominated the tight phases, but the South African loose trio of Hannes Botha, Doug Hopwood and Hugo van Zyl competed relentlessly, and Oxlee delivered another decisive contribution. He kicked a first-half penalty before converting his own try after the interval. A record crowd in Cape Town roared its approval. Claassen, every inch the hoary warhorse, raised his hands to acknowledge the cheers.

Perhaps believing their luck had to change, the Lions threw caution to the wind in the fourth Test at Bloemfontein, and bravely held their own until half time. At that point, however, Claassen's Springboks erupted, producing their finest 40 minutes of international rugby in a decade. Oxlee twinkled brightly, Van Zyl and Hopwood were magnificent, Gainsford and Roux drifted magically through every midfield gap, and Engelbrecht blitzed down the wing.

Even Claassen scored a try. South Africa won 34-14, the sun shone, and the Springbok captain left the field at the Free State Stadium, happy in the warm knowledge that he could retire at the pinnacle of the game. His team had won the series 3-1; his legend had been indelibly engraved.

"I didn't say anything to anyone," Claassen recalls, "but I had decided to retire after the series. It was the Saturday before the fourth Test, and I was playing in a club match at Lichtenberg. You often have to travel extremely long distances in Western Transvaal club rugby and, for the first time, I didn't feel any excitement when I took my car out of the garage to travel to the game. My wife had come out to see me off, and I remember saying to her there and then that it was now time to stop. I simply was not enjoying the game anymore."

Not for the first time, Craven sought to persuade a great Springbok to play another season and, even three years later, the Board president was still trying to lure Claassen out of retirement to boost the South African scrum. But the forward would not be persuaded, and he moved seamlessly from the second row into the selection committee and then to the Executive Committee room, where he would continue to serve the game with integrity and dedication.

Claassen's retirement prompted chaos. Springbok rugby has known many difficult, disappointing times, but it has rarely experienced the kind of bewildering disarray that unfolded when Australia toured South Africa during 1963. If any of the Test venues had been big tents or the referees dressed as ringmasters, few would have noticed anything wrong. Wild, unfathomable selections reduced the institution of Springbok rugby to not much more than a circus.

Following the triumphs of 1960, 1961 and 1962, it was wholly predictable that South Africans in general should underestimate the Wallabies. The likeable John Thornett led the tourists, but their headline player remained their elusive scrumhalf, Ken Catchpole, now 23 years old. With hardened forwards and swift backs, Thornett and his 1963 Wallaby squad would be cast as Hannibal and the Carthaginians, with complacent South Africa as ancient Rome.

Abie Malan was appointed as the 30th man since Herbert Castens to lead South Africa in a Test match, and the extrovert hooker winning his 11th cap was broadly regarded as a compromise choice between the two leading personalities of the era, Avril Malan, the Transvaal captain, and Doug Hopwood, the captain of Western Province. Yet again, Springbok selection contrived a diplomatic balance between the respective powers of the north and the south.

Malan, no relation to Avril, was the only son of a sheep farmer settled near Upington in the northern Cape. He was not the first Springbok who emerged from the platteland, nor was he the first to study at the University of Stellenbosch, and nor was he the first to be personally inspired by Danie Craven.

"Rugby was everything to me," Malan remembers, "even though I did not have a chance to see the Springboks in action until the second Test against the 1955 Lions when Tom van Vollenhoven scored three tries at Newlands. I studied two subjects at Stellenbosch: agriculture and rugby. And Craven became a huge influence in my life. He was like a second father to me."

First spotted by an ageing Oubaas Mark Markötter in the famed under-19 trials at Stellenbosch, Malan moved through the ranks and was selected to make his Springbok debut against France in 1958. He had become a senior player by the start of 1963, even if his experience of captaincy in senior rugby was limited to a handful of matches with Transvaal. "I was surprised to be named captain," he recalls, "and it was an awkward situation because Avril and I had been close friends since we were in the same *koshuis* (boarding hostel) at Stellenbosch. Fortunately, we both decided selection issues would not affect our friendship.

"In those days, we didn't really know who the selectors were. As players, we never spoke to them. We just accepted whatever they decided."

Malan was alarmed when his team's preparations for the opening Test at Loftus Versfeld were disrupted by the withdrawal on match-day morning of the injured wing, Jannie Engelbrecht. In confusion, the selectors contacted the Natal wing, Trix Truter, and summoned him to fly north from Durban. He arrived at the stadium 30 minutes before kick-off, unaware of prepared moves and calls he was supposed to recognise when throwing the ball in at the lineouts.

Despite this frantic activity, the Springboks settled to their task, took their chances, and emerged from an even contest with a 14-3 victory. Catchpole was disappointed. "But I recovered by the second beer," the Australian recalls. "The South Africans were a strong side. They lacked the rucking technique of the All Blacks, but we regarded them as the top team in the world.

"Abie Malan was a very competitive hooker, and the Springbok scrum was obviously an important part of their game. Whenever I presented the ball for the put-in, the entire crowd would be hushed. The first time it happened, I stood up and looked around because I thought something must be wrong. I thought there had been an incident somewhere else in the stadium. It was almost as if 65 000 people were studying the foot position of the props. South Africans regarded this phase of the game as something that was almost sacred.

"As far as we were concerned, we just wanted to get the ball in and out as fast as possible, and constantly move their pack around the field. Our scrumming was diabolical, but we won our share of ball in the lineouts.

"We had a fantastic time on tour, travelling all over southern Africa, up to what is now Zambia and Zimbabwe, visiting game parks.

Some of the guys were very uncomfortable about what they saw of apartheid, but we were guests in the country and we generally kept our views to ourselves."

Abie Malan had not been entirely happy with the first-Test performance and, when the team assembled for the second Test in Cape Town, the captain suggested to George van Reenen, convenor of selectors, that he would like to switch Keith Oxlee and Mannetjies Roux, flyhalf and wing respectively, if things were not going well at any stage. The convenor shrugged. If that was what the captain wanted, then the captain would take responsibility.

With his team trailing 6-5 in another tightly competitive match, Malan was to be seen gesturing for the switch to be made. Oxlee, clearly disappointed, took heed and wandered to the wing, while Roux took up his position at flyhalf. Malan had, boldly and unmistakeably, placed his head on the block.

The plan flopped. The crowd groaned as Roux knocked-on several times, and the Springboks were repeatedly pinned back by Catchpole's superb tactical kicking from the base of the scrum. Australia levelled the series with a 9-5 victory and, within hours, Abie Malan had been dropped as captain.

"People made a fuss about the flyhalf switch," Malan recalls, "but that was not the real problem. We lost the Test because scrumhalf Piet Uys dislocated his shoulder and we had no decent replacement. I found out later that Tom Bedford had played scrumhalf at school, but he never said anything on the field. To me, the flyhalf situation was irrelevant, but I was the scapegoat."

He was one of many.

The stunned selectors panicked, and the unfortunate captain was among seven Springbok players dropped from the side for the third Test at Ellis Park. In crisis, the panel found comfort in an often repeated, but unsubstantiated, mantra that the players had become slack and ill disciplined. Stalwarts like Hopwood, Oxlee and Roux were discarded, and Avril Malan, the reputed authoritarian, was installed as captain, ostensibly to restore order and discipline.

"Abie was unlucky," his namesake recalls, "but there was nothing that we, as players, could do about the situation. We had no negotiating power. You could moan to your friend about the selectors, or about the R1 daily allowance that we were paid whenever we gathered for home Tests, but any public statement at all would have resulted in the end of your rugby career.

"We were getting some benefits. Representatives of a cigarette company would give cigarettes to the players. They would meet you in the hotel and ask if you smoked. Even if you didn't smoke, you would say you did so you could take the packet of 20 and give them to your friends. But that was all."

Mindful of previous Wallaby tours to South Africa, Avril Malan believed the Australians would be effectively put in their place by a concerted forward effort in the third Test and, on the Thursday afternoon, he arranged for his pack to scrum relentlessly against the highly motivated forwards of the Diggers club team at the Roodepoort field. Time and again, prop crashed against prop.

"Again," Malan demanded. "Again."

Yet he was not satisfied. He felt the pack was not working as a unit.

"Again," the captain demanded. By now, the Diggers pack was taking great delight in moving the Springboks backwards. Malan was frustrated, and determined to continue training until he was satisfied.

"Er, Avril, I think we must stop now."

It was the team manager speaking.

"But, Meneer (Mister) Bosman, I am not happy. We need to carry on."

"No, we must stop."

"Why?"

"We are scheduled to meet the Australians at the Jamie Uys film studios. It has been arranged. We have an obligation to be on time."

"We have only been training for an hour," Malan protested.

"I am sorry."

"*Meneer!*"

"I am sorry."

Angry and troubled, the captain decided his side's only chance of victory was to play a tight game, and he repeatedly urged Norman Riley, the new flyhalf, to pursue a disciplined ten-man strategy. In essence, this was the time-honoured option of Springboks in adversity ... *maak sag* (soften up).

Certain members of the team were appalled by the authoritarian approach and conservative strategy. John Gainsford, the admired centre, has related how, after barely 20 minutes at Ellis Park, Dave Stewart, his fellow Western Province back line player, ran across the field and actually pleaded with Avril Malan to let the ball move past the flyhalf. "We had been told we would not run the ball in our own half, under any circumstances," Gainsford wrote. "At one stage, Riley broke clear, saw a clear overlap outside him but, in a moment of panic, remembered his instructions and kicked the ball directly into touch."

Nelie Smith, making his debut at scrumhalf, kicked three penalties, but the Springbok pack failed to exert the pressure Malan had intended, and, with barely three minutes remaining, South Africa were trailing 11-9.

Australia were awarded a scrum on their own 25-metre line and, aware how both the 1960 All Blacks and 1962 Lions had been denied by highly controversial refereeing decisions at crucial moments, Catchpole called Wallaby hooker, Peter Johnson, to one side before the front rows packed down.

"Peter, we have to be very careful," Catchpole said. "We can't give the ref any chance to award a penalty against us. He'll be watching."

"What do you think?"

"Well, I don't think you should strike for the ball. I will lob it in really slowly, and you should just leave it. If you strike, he'll penalise us."

The scrum was joined, and Catchpole lobbed the ball impeccably beneath the front rows. Meanwhile, Springbok hooker Ronnie Hill had been thinking along similar lines, that if he did not strike out for the ball he would win the penalty. As a result, to the embarrassment of all concerned, the ball just sat there, left alone on the ground for what seemed to be an eternal ten seconds.

Finally, a Springbok foot hacked the ball forward; Catchpole collected the ball at the back of the scrum, and passed to Phil Hawthorne, who punted the ball into touch. The final whistle followed, and the Wallabies had won.

The Springboks magnanimously gathered to congratulate the Australians in their changing room afterwards, but the sense of injured pride was acute. Now trailing 2-1 in the four-match series, the selectors reacted in predictable fashion, wielded the sword, and made seven changes for the fourth Test.

Their process had become a farce. Avril Malan was dropped completely from the side, and Abie Malan, apparently cast into the wilderness after the defeat at Newlands, was recalled to captain the team in Port Elizabeth. For the first time in 60 years, the Springbok captaincy, so long a title bestowed and removed with the most meticulous care, was being carelessly tossed to and fro.

Players literally did not know whether they were coming or going. A strong young prop forward called Hannes Marais had been chosen to make his debut at Ellis Park, but was then dropped for the next Test. "Everyone was fighting to stay in the side," Marais recalls. "It was chaotic. One minute, Avril was captain. Then, it was Abie again. It was embarrassing for me. When I was selected for the third Test, my fellow students at Stellenbosch congratulated me. Then, a week later, I was back in class, having been dropped, and they didn't know what to say. There was no real team spirit. Everyone was focused on survival."

Combative and mischievous by nature, Abie Malan arrived promptly at the Springbok Hotel in Port Elizabeth as if he had never been away. Inherently jovial, he wore no laden expression of gloom. For him, rugby remained a game, a game he was desperate to win, but a game nonetheless.

On this Thursday afternoon, it had been arranged that the Springbok pack would scrum against the Port Elizabeth Police forwards. Once again, the practice was unfolding as a humiliating shambles when Abie Malan suddenly called a halt and pulled his battered, panting players into a circle.

"Manne, this is what we're going to do," the captain said. "We are going to have three more scrums here. If they go well, that is fine. If they don't go well, we know we're going to struggle. Whatever happens, after only three more scrums, we are going to finish and go back to the hotel."

Three times in succession, the Police pack was pushed into reverse, and the Springbok forwards were grinning as they headed for their bus. Malan's high risk strategy seemed to have restored their self-confidence.

"I told the guys we should relax and play our normal game," Abie Malan recalls. "There was no point getting tense about the fact that we might lose the series. We had some great players in our team, and the simple challenge was to calm down and perform near our potential on the day."

Hennie Muller had served as coach during the entire series, but appeared an almost peripheral figure amid the general turmoil. In Port Elizabeth, however, encouraged by Malan, the old Springbok produced a stirring and emotional team talk on the morning of the Test. At last, the South African team ran onto the field in something approaching the right frame of mind.

The Wallabies were equally well prepared and, ten minutes after half time, the tourists were leading 6-3. Oxlee, rightly recalled to the team, kicked a penalty to bring the scores level, and the teams appeared implacably locked together. As the warm sun beat down, the sweating tension on the field was matched only by growing discomfort among spectators in the open stands.

Midway through the second half, Malan was distracted by a disturbance in the south-west corner of the Boet Erasmus Stadium, around the stand traditionally reserved for "coloured" spectators. South African sports venues were segregated at the time, and it was generally recognised that the "non-white" spectators would support whoever was playing against the Springboks.

The sun beat down.

Tempers started to fray.

Coloured supporters became progressively more excited by the prospect of a series victory for the Wallabies; white Springbok supporters in adjacent stands became progressively irritated. The situation swiftly became a racial tinderbox, and beer bottles started to be hurled across the dividing fence.

When black and white spectators spilled out from the stands and sporadic fist fights broke out on the field, the referee stopped the game and the Wallabies gathered together beneath their posts. "It was scary," Catchpole recalls. "People were fighting and bottles were flying around. We were ready to head for the exits, but the situation did calm down after 15 minutes or so."

The Test resumed, and the series came down to the wire. Amid the drama, Abie Malan dared to strike out and clinch the day. He urged his halfbacks to spin every ball wide. Thus, the captain diced with death or glory.

He was rewarded with glory. Oxlee kicked a penalty before Tiny Naudé, Malan and Gainsford scored tries in lightning succession and, in what felt like the blink of an eye, South Africa had won the Test by 22-6. The series was drawn at 2-2 and, amid intense relief, South African pride was salvaged.

The Wallabies were left to wonder why Catchpole and Johnson had been penalised so often, the former for feeding the scrum and the latter for striking too soon. To the most neutral observers, the local referee had seemed to impose a different interpretation of the laws from what had applied in the first three Tests. Again, a touring team left South African shores convinced that South African referees had contributed significantly to the Springbok victory.

This most physically and emotionally exhausting of series prompted a rare period of introspection within Springbok rugby, perhaps unequalled since Osler's tactics were scrutinised after the inaugural Wallaby tour of 1933. In essence, the status quo was challenged by the proposition that South African rugby was being restricted and ruined by the ultra-disciplined, authoritarian approach to the game identified with the views of the omnipotent Danie Craven. The alternative was to be found in the rugby being played during this era by Natal, under the visionary and imaginative guidance of coach Izak van Heerden.

A philosophical debate took place, yet Craven's authority over the sport was such that there was only ever going to be one verdict. Most of the Springbok captains through the 1960s had completed their rugby education at Stellenbosch, under the Doctor's wise guidance.

As the Springbok captains were reared at his knee, so their Springbok teams would follow his thinking. The Craven way would emphatically remain the Springbok way.

Nonetheless, there were alternative views.

Tom Bedford, the youngster who had been the only Springbok forward to play in all four Tests against the Wallabies, had surveyed the tactical chaos and wondered if the pattern he played at Natal did not present more exciting options for the abundant natural rugby talent within the Springbok squad. He respected Craven absolutely, but he was inspired by the Natal coach.

"Izak van Heerden was streets ahead of his time," Bedford recalls. "Natal had no star players in those days. We could not poach talent like Northerns, Transvaal or Western Province, and we had no real executive power to protect our interests, but we did have a genius as the coach.

"He sought players with two great qualities: an ability to think, and the flair to make decisions on the field; and he created an environment where players of this type could enjoy themselves and play some great rugby. Izak van Heerden was a teacher at Durban High School, and he coached the under-15 team along the same lines as he coached the Natal provincial side; and both teams played this instinctive, fantastic, expressive brand of rugby."

Bedford recalls how the coach would arrive at training with diagrams of various moves, and present them not as cast-iron instructions but as ideas that could be worked into the game. Players would take the diagrams home, coming back to propose their own amendments and suggestions.

"He always challenged us to think. His great philosophy was that the ball was the advantage. He taught us to treat every piece of possession like a nugget and, he would say, no one kicks a nugget away. In his mind, the most important thing was not to cross the advantage line but to keep the ball. Sometimes we had to go backwards before we went forward. That was the game."

Around the country, coaches taught players you kick and grind your way down the field, but only regularly spun the ball wide when you were within striking distance of the opponents' line. Bedford continues: "Izak van Heerden looked at the game in a different way. He said that a team on its own try line is in a superb attacking position because it has 100 metres of field to exploit. When you are on the opposition's 25-metre line, there is not so much room because 30 players are squeezed into roughly one third of the playing area.

"One Currie Cup afternoon in Bloemfontein, we scored a try against Free State by running the ball from a scrum on our own line. It was fantastic rugby, but the approach was so revolutionary rugby people around the country did not really consider it as an option. They thought Natal were a bit strange."

The 1963 Wallabies may have posed several new questions for Springbok rugby, but the answers remained essentially the same. Natal apart, a consensus remained that you scrum the opposition into the ground, work the game into the opponents' half, and only then release the ball to the wings.

In two words … maak sag.

The qualifications to be considered eligible to become Springbok captain were becoming tighter and tighter: not only would your claim be strengthened by sound Afrikaner pedigree and Broederbond potential, but a strong empathy with Dr Craven's perspective on the game also seemed helpful.

Abie Malan qualified on both counts, and was duly retained as captain for the one-off Test against Wales in Durban early in the 1964 season. The Welsh had never defeated South Africa, but they arrived with a talented team hoping to find Malan's Springboks in rusty and vulnerable condition.

The Springbok preparations had been scant, amounting to not much more than a handful of lineout drills on the bowling lawn behind the Edward Hotel, and the South Africans were relieved to reach half time at 3-3. The match turned with 20 minutes to play when Lionel Wilson kicked a 65-metre drop goal that was as outrageous as it was out of character. Marais, Hopwood and Smith each scored tries in the last quarter. When Oxlee converted all four and added a penalty, the Springboks were celebrating a record 24-3 win over Wales.

With two decisive victories to his credit, Abie Malan may have assumed he was beginning to establish himself as Springbok captain. A strong character with a wise perspective on the game, he was settling into the role and looked forward with confidence to the formal announcement of the Springbok side to play France at Springs in a one-off Test at the end of the 1964 season.

"And the team will be captained by ... Nelie Smith."

What? Who? Abie Malan had been dropped from the Springbok team. "I was not given a reason," he recalls. "I was very surprised and very disappointed but there was not much I could do. I enjoyed being the captain, although the motto of the team used to be that everyone was the captain in their position. All of a sudden, I was out of the side. Nobody ever explained anything to me."

With Avril Malan injured, the selectors turned to the 30-year-old Free State scrumhalf selected to play in his fourth successive Test.

The son of a worker on the South African Railways, Smith had been born and bred in Bloemfontein, first catching the eye as a talented scrumhalf when he played for Central Universities against the 1955 Lions. He proved pivotal in Free State's emergence as a consistent force in the Currie Cup, and captained both his province and the Junior Springboks against the 1963 Wallabies. He was also regarded as entirely compatible with the Broederbond.

"It was a total surprise to be named captain," Smith recalls, "but there was not much time to prepare the Test side. South Africa had hosted a series of three matches where Springboks mixed with leading overseas players to celebrate the 75th anniversary of the Board, and it was hard to get the players focused back on the proper discipline required for hard international rugby."

The advent of a French side should have concentrated minds, particularly since South Africa had drawn two and lost one of their last three matches against France, but the Springbok preparations before this late-season Test match in the Eastern Transvaal town of Springs were almost comical.

Training seemed aimless and inconsequential, and the team hotel proved inadequate in every respect. There were not enough rooms, and two players were forced to sleep on a sofa in the sitting room of the owner's flat. When the players gathered for their customary private pre-match meal three hours before kick-off, they were astonished to find themselves forced to queue for their food and then sit among ogling, star-struck members of the public.

Smith looked around in vain for someone to correct the situation, but much worse was to follow. The Springbok bus was delayed in a traffic jam and arrived more than 20 minutes late at the austere PAM Brink Stadium. When the players eventually made their way into the venue, they were amazed to realise that their Springbok changing room was occupied by one of the local club teams that had just left the field after playing in an early curtain-raiser.

The captain was aghast as his players spent almost 30 minutes hanging around in a cramped, dark corridor. Distracted, confused and irritated, the team was evidently in no condition to perform near its potential.

Michel Crauste led the apparently untroubled tourists out to play, and the South Africans appeared ineffective from the outset. Smith had hoped the team would establish some kind of rhythm, and rediscover the form they had shown in the early Test against Wales, but he found only chaos in Springs.

A precarious temporary scaffolding stand had been built behind the main grandstand, but it was constructed at such an angle that whenever spectators at the front rose to their feet in excitement, they entirely blocked the view of people sitting behind them. Time and again, the ball would be kicked into the crowd, and the irritated spectators on the scaffolding seats refused to return the ball until the people in front sat down. Arguments flared; time was wasted.

Christian Darrouy scored a try, Pierre "Monsieur Drop" Albaledejo added a penalty and a conversion, and, despite Stewart's try and penalty, the Springboks were once again caught cold by their French jinx. Smith tried hard, but it seemed as if a greater power had decreed everything would go wrong for South Africa on this bizarre afternoon in Springs. France won 8-6, and the match was consigned to history as one of the poorest Springbok performances ever.

"It was chaos," Smith recalls plainly.

Optimists might have hoped the prospect of a tour to New Zealand would snap Springbok rugby back to form, as it had done five years before, and a warm-up tour to Scotland and Ireland was arranged for March 1965. It was perilously early in the season, but the intention was to nurture a strong squad.

The national selectors contemplated their options for the captaincy and, after much debate, decided Doug Hopwood should be given what many felt was a long overdue opportunity to lead the side. The eighthman had played 19 Tests and emerged as a fine Currie Cup captain for Western Province.

According to custom, the captain's name was passed on for the official sanction of the Board. This procedure had always been a formality but, on this occasion, the Board sensationally vetoed Hopwood's appointment.

Rumours ran wild.

Some referred to a perception that the eighthman enjoyed a party and was therefore regarded as an inappropriate ambassador for the nation abroad. Others were adamant, and remain adamant to this day, that Hopwood was rejected only because he spoke English as a first language and was not a *broeder*. Almost 40 years on, players of the day recall the saga and their eyes fire with anger at what still seems to have been a blatant example of discrimination.

It is peculiar, of course, to allege discrimination against English-speaking players in a team that, for 70 years, had effectively been restricted to whites, yet the continuing denial of black and coloured players does not minimise the injustice done to others. For all the glory and courage that runs through this tale, the ugly stain of discrimination rarely escapes from view.

Through the 1960s, the authorities scarcely tried to conceal it.

With Hopwood rejected as captain but permitted to take his place in the side, the selectors were requested to think again, and they swiftly fell back upon an unequivocally "acceptable" figure, Avril Malan, to lead the side on the short 1965 tour to Scotland and Ireland. Malan, this overwhelmingly earnest, decent and sincere man, had been handed an almost impossible task. The Hopwood saga had irretrievably poisoned the entire tour.

"I did not know why the Board were not content for Doug to captain the side," Malan remembers, "and I didn't want to know. There were plenty of stories running around at the time. So far as I was concerned, I had been asked to lead the side on tour to Britain and that was what I tried to do.

"But it was too early in the season. Our players were not fit, and we had no time to develop as a unit. Boy Louw was named to coach the side, but it became clear before long that this particular tour would be a fiasco."

To his credit, Malan attempted to clear the air at the first meeting prior to the squad's departure for Britain. He addressed Hopwood directly.

"Doug, I am sorry for what has happened," he said, "but the selectors have asked me to captain this side and all that you or I can do is try our very hardest to make the best of these extremely difficult circumstances."

It should be emphasised that while Avril Malan was sometimes perceived as a prime beneficiary of the Broederbond's influence on the game, he invariably retained the respect and affection of all his players. He may have been stern, and he may have been serious, but he was straightforward and unselfish, and he set the goals and welfare of his players before everything else.

Dawie de Villiers, scrumhalf on the tour to Scotland and Ireland, recalls: "I respected Avril tremendously. There were times when he might have been too inflexible. If he didn't think the players should go for a walk, he would tell them in no uncertain terms, and some of them would resent that. But, above all, he was a very genuine and supportive person, a very good friend."

Despite Malan's best efforts, the tour unfolded as a disaster. South Africa lost every game, including both Test matches. The Springboks were beaten 8-5 by Scotland at Murrayfield, and then 9-6 by Ireland at Lansdowne Road. On any other day, either match might have been won, but the players were not prepared for the tour, physically or psychologically, and the famed *gees* (spirit) did not materialise to pull them through tight situations as it had done before.

Responsibility for the disaster lay squarely on the shoulders of the short-sighted officials who had allowed their political prejudice to affect the selection of the squad, but these faceless suits were far from public view as the team arrived back in South Africa. Avril Malan, an upright pillar of integrity, was left to shoulder the burden of criticism that was showered upon his team.

The captain reflects: "Even before the tour, I had virtually decided to retire from Test rugby. I had recently been promoted at work, and it was going to be hard to take three months' leave for the tour to New Zealand later in 1965. The events in Britain left me mentally exhausted, and served only to affirm my decision. I was not enjoying the game. I wanted to stop. The tour had been a very disappointing experience. I played one more match after we returned home, and that was that. I then announced my complete retirement from the game."

Malan focused his energies within the steel industry and later accepted a post as Director of Development at the Transvaal Rugby Union, where his talent for devising and implementing structures and systems established a solid, if still small, base for rugby in the immense township of Soweto.

"I enjoyed my rugby career," reflects Malan, now retired in Pretoria. "It was a privilege to have played 16 Tests for South Africa, but you have to keep things in perspective. The truth is that most people forget you after a week. They might have known you when you played, but that doesn't last long.

"Not long ago, someone stopped me in a supermarket and said he knew my face. This man was shopping with his son and, after a moment, he asked if I had been Springbok captain. I said that was correct, but it was obvious none of this meant anything to his son. People who attach too much significance to what happened in the past are usually disappointed in the long run."

Malan left a significant gap and, by May 1965, Springbok rugby seemed at a low ebb. The squad was scheduled to set off for New

Zealand three weeks later, yet the captain had retired and the team lacked spirit.

One moment, the game was scaling the heights of ecstasy.

The next, it was sinking to the depths of despair.

Understatement has rarely been rife within South African rugby.

To stand back is to see that the game had been riding a rollercoaster ever since 1956, first plunging to defeat in New Zealand and at home against France, then soaring to victory over the 1960 All Blacks, 1961 Wallabies and 1962 Lions (with a little help from one or two referees), before flirting with calamity against the 1963 Wallabies, staggering through the disjointed schedule in 1964, and then being humiliated in Scotland and Ireland at the start of 1965.

Such chronic instability contrasts with the more sedate, stable experience of the years preceding and following the Second World War, and it was primarily caused by the disruptive, souring influence of the Broederbond.

Des van Jaarsveldt, Roy Dryburgh and Doug Hopwood were three leading players whose careers seemed to have been notably affected, but this prejudice developed as a malignant cancer, blighting the lives of many men throughout the game. The game was shadowed by suspicion and resentment.

As the selection focus shifted from discovering not simply who was the best player to finding out who was the best player and a *broeder*, instability and insecurity set the game on the queasy rollercoaster ride. Inherently decent men such as Johan Claassen and Avril Malan sustained traditionally high standards of integrity, honesty and courage within the four walls of the changing room, but the game at large had become seriously infected and damaged.

And yet ... this was only prejudice within a much greater prejudice.

Rugby union in South Africa, a country afflicted by institutionalised racism, remained an exclusively white game. And still, by 1965, hardly anybody either on the South African Rugby Board or at the International Rugby Board had raised a clear voice against the exclusion of black and coloured players.

That would soon change.

Rugby administrators, at home and abroad, insulated themselves from the growing international condemnation that resulted in South Africa's expulsion from FIFA, the world governing body of soccer, and the Olympic movement, during the early 1960s, and the tours would continue ... but the yelling voices and marching feet would soon be heard at the door of Springbok rugby.

From 1956 until 1965, the *broeders* had effectively seized control of rugby in South Africa. These faceless men might not always have achieved their goals, though they almost always achieved them in the end. Their influence would remain considerable, but the party was drawing to a close. Opposition, both within South Africa and around the world, was starting to assemble.

Meanwhile, there were Test matches to be won ... and, in May 1965, in this hour of need, the Springbok team was seized by a talented man who brought new dimensions of diplomacy and understanding to the game. He was appointed to lead the side on tour to New Zealand, and he would bring priceless stability by remaining as Springbok captain for the following six seasons.

He was, inevitably, a *broeder*, but he also heralded the start of a bold new era, and he eventually cleared a way for a much happier, more equitable future in which any South African could captain the national rugby team. In May 1965, the Springbok spotlight was turned upon the fair head of Dawie de Villiers.

7 THE DOMINEE

Perhaps the clue lies in his eyes. They sparkle, dart this way and that, miss so little, notice so much. Are they clever? Are they shrewd?

He has presence. He enters a room and commands awareness. He speaks to you, and awards you his undivided attention. He appears anchored by his principles and faith, incessantly motivated by his mission, and still his eyes go left and then right, then left again, missing nothing.

And he smiles, comfortably, and he motivates, and he leads.

Dawie de Villiers was born in Burgersdorp, deep in the Karoo, the oldest son of a committed and decent Afrikaans family. His father worked on the South African Railways and, when his son was five, moved to Cape Town to take up a position as a full-time organiser for the National Party.

It was 1945. Within three years the NP had defeated Jan Smuts's United Party and launched itself into a legislative programme that the world would soon recognise as apartheid. The De Villiers family would live and breathe politics; in years to come, son would follow father into parliament.

Such thoughts were far from the mind of the flaxen-haired boy who settled into the family's new home in Bellville, one of the recently established, affordable suburbs of Cape Town. He walked barefoot to school, only agreeing to pull on his shoes on the coldest of winter mornings, and he lived for the hours when he could join his friends and play touch rugby on an unused area of sand.

In 1949, he had sat in silence with his parents and younger sister as they listened to radio commentary of the Test matches between South Africa and Bob Scott's All Blacks; four years later, amid gasping excitement, he and his father had watched the Springboks play Australia at Newlands.

"It was a great day," De Villiers recalls, "but I was a bit disappointed when the Springboks ran out in white jerseys to avoid a clash with the colours of the Wallabies. I had desperately wanted to see the green-and-gold jerseys."

Newlands became a frequent and favourite destination for the teenager. Saturday after Saturday, he would cycle to the station at Bellville and chain his bicycle to the railings before catching a train into Cape Town. There, he would leap aboard another train to Rondebosch, then walk to wherever his age-group team was playing that morning. The boys changed on the touchline, kicked off at nine, played the game, then rushed to the stadium at Newlands where the day's rugby programme would start soon after eleven.

They would watch the under-19's, the B-team game and the main game, entranced by the spectacle, whether it was a provincial fixture or a club match. It didn't matter. And, as the sun sank behind Table Mountain, they would drag their weary bodies back to the station, catch two trains and finally get home soon after seven in the evening. These were carefree, golden days.

"Every generation needs its idols," De Villiers reflects. "Today, youngsters go with musicians and movie stars. In my day, we followed rugby players. I loved watching them play and I never missed the radio commentary of a Test match. I knew them all: Brewis, Tjol Lategan, Chum Ochse, Chris Koch. It was wonderful for me when I was able to meet these men later in life, but it was different. They were not on a pedestal then. When I was 11, they were heroes.

"And we were influenced and inspired by our teachers. We had a maths teacher at Bellville High School named Amy Gonnin, who played for Western Province. He was a wonderful man, and a role model.

"Every Monday morning, at the school assembly, the headmaster would read aloud the rugby scores from the weekend, occasionally adding a remark about who had played well or scored a try. Bellville was a mixed school, and there used to be no greater thrill for me than to be mentioned on a Monday morning in front of all the girls. It felt great. The modern trend is to downplay sport in schools, and that is a pity. I believe the youngsters miss a lot."

De Villiers advanced to study theology at his local university, only 20 miles up the road in Stellenbosch. He had keenly followed Maties rugby for many years, even pasting a newspaper photograph of James Starke on the cover of his scrapbook. By 1958, the Stellenbosch captain was his team-mate.

Quick and decisive, with excellent hands, De Villiers was a central member of a powerful Maties under-19 side that became assured and confident as they overwhelmed all opposition. Shortly before one match, the young players were exchanging jokes, teasing, laughing and shouting.

The door of the changing room swung open.

"What is going on in here?" a suited bulldog of a man wanted to know. "Do you think it is a joke to represent Stellenbosch University? You believe you don't have to take the game seriously? Do you know what jersey you are wearing? Do you know what players have worn that jersey in the past?

"You're a disgrace. You think you're special, but you're not. In fact, I don't want anything more to do with you. That's it. I'm finished with you."

The man stormed out of the changing room, and the callow students fell stone silent, shamed and stunned. Nobody laughed, nobody scoffed. De Villiers had several times greeted the renowned Dr Danie Craven around the University, but this was the first time he had seen him in action.

Needless to say, the Stellenbosch University under-19 side trounced their opponents that particular day. Craven's psychology worked again. As he moved through the ranks, De Villiers started to develop a profound relationship with the man whom he still refers to, respectfully, as "Doctor". The student recognised rare wisdom in the coach; the coach saw raw courage in the student.

"As far as we were concerned, Doctor knew everything about rugby," De Villiers reflects. "He was utterly respected. He always wanted to try something new. At one point, he decided the Maties captain should pick the University team on his own, asking only that he retain the right of approval.

"On one occasion, before a big intervarsity match, I went to hand in my team at his office, and Doctor called me in to discuss the side. He encouraged me to argue my case, but he didn't really enjoy the process.

"After a long debate, he pushed the piece of paper back across the table and said, 'Dawie, there are a lot of players in your team who I regard as drawing room furniture – they're good to look at but they're no use in an intervarsity. But it is your team, so you must go and play with them on Saturday.'

"I stuck to my guns and, thankfully, we managed to win that game, but the Doctor was a truly remarkable and gifted man. He had a significant impact on my perception of so many things. He was a character."

It had been Craven who, one Tuesday afternoon during the 1961 season, had summoned a then unknown De Villiers from a third team training session to run over the hill and join the Stellenbosch first team practice. The awed student had been playing centre at the time, but Craven ordered him to slot in at the base of the scrum. "Yes, that's right, scrumhalf! Go on!" he barked.

De Villiers survived, trained again on the Wednesday, and made his debut in the maroon Maties No. 9 jersey on the Saturday afternoon. Thrown in at the deep end, the young scrumhalf thrived, and Stellenbosch handed Villagers one of the heaviest defeats in their history. Within three weeks, he was selected to play his provincial debut for Western Province, aged 21.

This swift progress was interrupted at the start of the 1962 season when the WP selectors preferred Aubrey Luck at scrumhalf, but the situation became an issue of public debate and the rumour spread that De Villiers, who had excelled on a Junior Springbok tour to Southern Rhodesia, could yet be named in the Springbok Test team against the touring Lions, even if he was not first choice for his province. In the event, Piet Uys was selected to play in the first Test, and the rumours appeared to have been unfounded.

When the national selectors were gathering to choose their team for the second Test, De Villiers was taking his girlfriend to the cinema in Cape Town. He drove her back to her parents' house later that night, and bashfully agreed to step in and listen to the SABC radio news at 11 o'clock, just in case.

"*Die Springbokspan is soos volg ...*" ("The Springbok team is as follows ...")

He heard his name announced and, in a moment of joy, realised his boyhood dream. He telephoned his parents. He was a Springbok.

Several days later, De Villiers was thrilled to receive out of the blue a hand-written letter from Pierre de Villiers, the famous Springbok scrumhalf of the 1930s, offering his congratulations and good wishes.

"It felt as though I was being welcomed into a family," De Villiers recalls. "It was very special. In those days, older players reached out to younger players, and the younger players in turn respected their predecessors.

"It was a family with particular customs and standards, and everyone was always supporting and encouraging everyone else. In a sense, nobody ever stopped being a Springbok. I don't believe the same is true now. Today, you tend to play your last Test match, say goodbye and disappear."

De Villiers played in the second and third Test victories over the Lions, but missed the final Test through injury. By the end of the 1962 season, he was even established in the Western Province side. Posters of the blond, boyish scrumhalf were pinned to thousands of walls, and a bright future beckoned. He appeared to represent an acceptable and admirable face of South Africa.

One wet day early in 1963, he was playing against a combined Oxford and Cambridge team. He deftly skipped past a challenge, but was heavily tackled just below the left knee. His leg buckled, and the crowd fell eerily silent as the referee called for a stretcher. Everybody could see this was serious.

The doctors were agreed: De Villiers would not play rugby again, and only the Heidelberg operation, in which muscles from the right side of his knee would be strapped to support the left side, would restore mobility. The young scrumhalf accepted his fate with equanimity. That was that. He would focus his attention on completing his degree in theology and advancing towards his long-held goal of becoming a *dominee* (minister) in the Dutch Reformed Church.

"It was a disappointment for me," he recalls, "but my religion was a huge part of my life, and I was able to move in another direction."

As the months passed, he enjoyed coaching junior teams at Stellenbosch and gradually started to exercise again, jogging gently among the hills around the university. Craven never stopped watching, and he eventually asked the question that had also crossed De Villiers's mind: could he play again?

"Dr Craven believed medical doctors were all sissies who did not understand rugby, so he sent me to see a retired Scottish orthopaedic surgeon," De Villiers recalls. "This man declared my knee was strong, and told me there was nothing to lose in trying to play rugby again. He said that if water developed on the knee after a game, I would know it was not possible to resume my career. If it didn't, then there was no problem. It was a green light."

The scrumhalf telephoned Craven with the verdict. "Excellent," the reply snapped down the line. "I want you to play on Saturday."

"Doc!"

"What's the problem? You've been running in the mountains. You're as fit as anyone in the team. What do you want to wait for?"

De Villiers returned to action, and his knee withstood the strain. Five weeks later, at the end of the 1964 season, the national selectors staged a week of Springbok trials in preparation for the tour to Scotland and Ireland scheduled for the start of the following year. Days before the trials, the panel announced De Villiers would be a late addition to the list of players already named. "There is no question," the player says gratefully, "I owed that break to Dr Craven."

The scrumhalf struggled through the week of intensive rugby. Each night he would soak in a hot bath, and each night his wife would rub his aching limbs. In these days before physiotherapy, simple guts had to suffice.

A further trial game was held at the start of 1965, after which De Villiers's remarkable recovery from a career-ending injury was completed by his inclusion in the tour squad, as vice-captain to the experienced Avril Malan.

"It was a disastrous tour," he recalls. "Not much went right for us, and we lost four matches and drew the fifth. When we arrived home, Avril said he would not be available to tour New Zealand, and I assumed Doug Hopwood would be named to lead the squad. He was my captain at Western Province, and he was an outstanding leader. I had never even captained Province. To me, it seemed like a relatively straightforward decision.

"In fact, the selectors said they wanted me to captain South Africa. I could not believe it. To be frank, I thought they were making a huge mistake. I was only 24 years old and, I felt, very inexperienced. I was amazed. It was a huge honour and I was extremely proud, but everything seemed so big. I remember not knowing quite where to start."

De Villiers could hardly have been handed the captaincy in less promising circumstances. The Board's unexplained veto of Hopwood's selection as captain in March had irrevocably soured the season, and any confidence that remained in the team had dissolved during the demoralising tour to Britain.

That was the sympathetic view. In cynical quarters, the young captain was immediately dismissed as the latest model to roll off the same old production line: pure Afrikanerdom, Stellenbosch University, Craven, etc.

The scrumhalf assembled his squad with enthusiasm and determination, but he brought no magic wand. A dark, dank cloud of depression had settled over the 1965 season, and it was unreasonable to expect it would be lifted by a young captain tossed in at the deep end of international rugby.

His squad did not lack talent. Jannie Engelbrecht, John Gainsford, Lionel Wilson and Mannetjies Roux were widely regarded as world-class backs, and the pack was founded upon the talents of Frik du

Preez, the enduring Abie Malan, Tiny Naudé and Hopwood. Like their unfortunate predecessors nine years earlier, however, the 1965 Springbok touring squad to Australia and New Zealand would eventually add up to much less than the sum of its parts.

De Villiers's hopes of asserting his authority were not helped when he suffered an injury shortly before departure that ruled him out of both Tests in Australia. Nelie Smith, unusually selected as both reserve scrumhalf and the vice-captain, was promoted to lead South Africa on the field again. "Dawie and I were big rivals for the No. 9 jersey," the combative Free Stater recalls, "but we were great friends as well. There was no problem."

Disaster followed upon disaster. The Springboks were defeated 18-11 in Sydney and then 12-8 in Brisbane, losing a series against Australia for the first time. "We had huge problems with the referees," Smith reflects. "The Wallabies felt hard done by when they toured South Africa in 1963, and we suffered two years later. Our forwards were repeatedly penalised at the rucks."

It might be assumed that a series victory over the Springboks represented an hour of glory for the Australians, but scrumhalf Ken Catchpole reflects upon the 1965 series without enthusiasm. "Both Test matches were flat," the legendary Wallaby recalls. "We didn't play particularly well, but the Springboks were worse. They were obviously a team without unity, and they played as individuals. They were poor, and they seemed to play without real purpose."

Catchpole adds: "I could see Nelie was doing his best. He was a strong scrumhalf in the mould of Sid Going. In fact, I reckon he would have been highly effective behind an All Black pack, but there was not much he could do in 1965. Something was seriously wrong in that Springbok team."

Heads bowed, mentally prepared for the worst, the South Africans travelled to New Zealand. The team had now lost five successive Test matches. Such a desperate record was previously unimagined and unthinkable for a nation grown accustomed to being respected, even feared, as unbeatable.

It is often said that winning teams have great spirit and losing teams have no spirit, but this simplistic approach overlooks the role that alert and perceptive management plays in a successful side. It would be easy to reflect upon the 1965 Springboks and assert that they were miserable because they were defeated so often, but perhaps they lost precisely because they were so miserable. This was a team whose balance and morale were incessantly disturbed by politics.

The effects of the Hopwood saga, and the enduring influence on rugby of the Broederbond, were awkward, but worse followed. The first example of direct interference in rugby by the South African government erupted during this tour to New Zealand. With arrogance and idiocy, they blundered forth.

As the Springboks prepared to play the All Blacks, the South African prime minister of the day, Hendrik Verwoerd, delivered a speech to an Afrikaner youth group at Loskop Dam, east of Johannesburg, in which he declared that Maoris would not be welcome in any future All Black team to tour South Africa.

The impact of his statement was devastating. It was immediately assumed that New Zealand's scheduled visit to South Africa in 1967 would be cancelled; it was further concluded that this government policy signalled nothing less than the end of all rugby competition between the two countries.

Craven was ironically flying to join the Springboks in New Zealand when Verwoerd rose to speak, and the Board president was horrified to read a text of the speech upon his arrival in Christchurch. When the media sought a response, he said he hoped the Prime Minister had been misquoted. In private, Craven was devastated, humiliated before his long-standing Maori friends, though such bonds would prove strong enough to survive political storms.

The players scarcely knew what to make of these developments, and De Villiers resolutely sought to maintain his squad's focus on the rugby challenge at hand, but this proved impossible. Amid the screaming headlines, the bewildered Springboks started to feel like leaves being swirled in the wind.

Confusion reigned. These were young men, most of whom had been born and bred in a fiercely disciplined environment where government policy was seen as beyond dispute. Two weeks earlier, they had played against the Maori team, and enjoyed the most generous hospitality after the match. Now, their own prime minister was saying they should not mix with these people.

How should they react? What should they do? Hell, they didn't understand politics. They wanted to ignore these issues and just play rugby.

The All Blacks, at least, were ready.

"We were on a high," recalls Wilson Whineray, the captain who had briefly rested from the game in 1964 but been recalled to lead his country against South Africa in 1965. "If you rate our results against major rugby nations, statistics show the 1960s was the most successful decade in All Black history.

"The South Africans had battled in Australia, but we were not complacent. We knew they would be tough. They're always tough."

Battered 23-6 by Wellington, De Villiers's side approached the first Test at Athletic Park more in hope than in expectation, but the South Africans were hardly blown away in the gale-force wind. They scampered and scrapped, but could not win enough ball and eventually succumbed to a 6-3 defeat.

A great All Black pack of forwards was seizing the Test series by the scruff of the neck. Whineray and Ken Gray were the props, the Meads brothers were at lock, Kel Tremain and Brian Lochore in the back row: these men were all farmers by trade, heroes by nature, rugby legends by popular acclaim. New Zealand moved up a gear in the mud at Dunedin, cruising to a 13-0 victory in the second Test.

De Villiers had watched this defeat from the main stand at Carisbrook, yet again ruled out by a nagging injury, leaving Smith to step forward and deputise as captain. The All Black forwards seemed unstoppable. Trailing 2-0 in the four-match series and now burdened by a record of seven consecutive Test defeats, the South Africans sat solemn in their changing room.

"It was very hard to know what to say," De Villiers recalls. "Everyone had tried hard, but it seemed as though we were caught in a downward spiral. Losing was becoming a habit, and I was an extremely young captain."

In the deepest trough of adversity, this apparently bewildered Springbok captain and his downcast, forlorn players reached deep into the reservoir of gees that has so often sustained this team through the years and, against every prediction, they produced one of the great comebacks of all time.

It was half time during the third Test of 1965, played at Lancaster Park in Christchurch, and the Springboks were trailing 16-5.

They were surely dead and buried, surely heading for South Africa's heaviest Test defeat ever, surely plumbing new depths of despair.

De Villiers disagreed.

Small but strong, his animated blonde head bobbing above the larger men encircling him during the break, the captain believed he had finally glimpsed light at the end of the tunnel. He urged his players: "I know it looks bad, but we can win this Test. The surface is slippery, but the ground is firm. This is the first time we've had decent conditions in the series. We must run the ball."

De Villiers's hopes had been raised by the spectacle of John Gainsford, the genius centre, jinking through the All Black defence, dancing right, then left, right, then left again before diving across the line to score. "If we can win enough ball," he implored, "our backs can cut this lot to pieces.

"Come on, come on. Let's believe in ourselves. We can do this."

Flyhalf Jannie Barnard kicked off the second half, and the ball was neatly marked by Ken Gray. Several of the All Blacks burst out laughing at the prospect of the front row forward having to punt the ball down the field. De Villiers noticed this unusual flippancy among traditionally grim-faced opponents. "They think they have won already," he told a team-mate. "They're complacent."

Two minutes later, Gainsford took the ball again, drifted outside his man, and fed Mannetjies Roux who set Gertjie Brynard dashing clear to the corner. As the All Blacks gathered beneath their posts, nobody in black was laughing. Another eight minutes passed, and De Villiers was driving his men forward again. The ball was whipped down the three-quarters to Brynard. This time the wing cut inside, wrong-footing three All Blacks, and swallow-dived over the line.

The South Africans now trailed only 13-16. De Villiers, bustling and bright, crouched to feed another scrum, and tidily whipped the ball right to Barnard, who popped a short pass to Gainsford at speed. The centre was clear again, swerving outside Williment to score his second thrilling try. Colin Meads would later recall: "Dawie was right. The Springbok backs did cut us to pieces."

Scores level at 16-16, the All Blacks were stung into attack, but the green-and-gold jerseys, now caked in mud, stood firm. With three minutes to play, the referee's whistle pierced the frenzied buzz around the ground. Meads was ruled offside. Penalty to South Africa. Brynard eagerly suggested they tap a short one and dash for the line. De Villiers said no, taking the swollen, misshapen ball and tossing it to Tiny Naudé. "We'll kick for goal," he ruled.

Naudé, the tall lock forward, wiped the ball on Brynard's jersey. Suddenly the responsibility for securing South Africa's first win in eight Tests weighed down on his shoulders. He kicked, kept his head down. The ball travelled straight and low, and over the crossbar. Springbok hands were raised.

Some of the Christchurch crowd groaned, some applauded the Springbok heroics, most of those present cheered, thrilled to have witnessed a match that would become known as the Miracle at Lancaster Park. South Africa won 19-16. On this magical day, De Villiers had emerged as a Test captain.

There was no fairy-tale conclusion to the series. Whineray primed his All Blacks for the fourth Test, and the home team scored five tries without reply at Eden Park, Auckland. Three times, the New Zealanders pounced upon errors as the Springboks tried to run the ball from deep inside their half. "We might have got a little carried away with our expansive approach," De Villiers reflects. The record 20-3 defeat was not received sympathetically at home.

Defeated by three Tests to one, the 1965 Springboks were widely condemned as a team that under-performed. "That is a fair verdict," the captain concedes. "We had deficiencies in our team, and these were exposed by a strong All Black side. The third Test was a wonderful occasion, but I was disappointed with my own personal performances.

At stages, I wished I could just concentrate on my own game without worrying about the captaincy."

The 1965 season ended quietly, swiftly consigned to the history books as the least successful year in Springbok rugby. De Villiers had not transformed the team's fortunes, but he had survived with his reputation intact and was regarded as part of the solution rather than part of the problem. In 1966, he captained a South African Gazelles squad on tour to Argentina, where a blend of young talent and experienced players augured well for a brighter future.

Early in 1967, De Villiers was ordained as a minister and he started work at the Dutch Reformed Church in Wellington, a little more than an hour's drive out of Cape Town. In years to come, leading sportsmen would not hesitate to parade their faith, to the point where it became fashionable, but the Springbok captain of the late 1960s chose not to wear his cross on his sleeve.

He would eagerly accept any invitation to address a church congregation, he enthusiastically welcomed any opportunity to discuss his convictions, and he assumed a leading role when his team-mates organised prayer meetings, but De Villiers took care never to trivialise his beliefs or force his views upon anyone else. His principles were neither concealed, nor cosmetic.

"There was never any real conflict between my religion and my rugby," he reflects. "It was true that I did not drink heavily and I believed strongly that it was not correct to use God's name in vain, but, as a student, I had learned to accept different views and lifestyles. I don't think I was intolerant.

"As captain, I tried to establish a code of conduct that matched everyone's lifestyle, and, inevitably, there were times on the field when I also used language that would not be described as civilised. That was the game."

Nonetheless, Springboks of the time were unavoidably aware of being captained by a minister, and most would generally refrain from swearing when he was within earshot. "It was not a major problem," recalls Piet Greyling, who would come into the team during 1967. "If anyone did swear, Dawie didn't bat an eyelid, but you just didn't feel like swearing when there was a guy like that around. You could say he had a positive influence on the rest of us."

The Springboks' primary task in 1967 was to avenge the defeats suffered against France in 1958 and 1964; and De Villiers was routinely confirmed as captain soon after Christian Darrouy arrived with a talented French squad, the reigning Five Nations champions, on South African soil.

"It was a crucial series," the captain remembers. "There was a new panel of national selectors, with Flappie Lochner as convenor, and they named eight players to make their debut in the first Test. Everything seemed new. Either we were going to win and launch a brave new era, or we would fall by the wayside. Our supporters were desperate for something to cheer."

The public was hardly enthused with confidence by the announcement of such an "unknown" team for the opening Test, but De Villiers, imbued with the confidence and authority that only experience can bring, hurled himself into the challenge, setting a disciplined example off the field and sparking a vibrant display within the four white lines.

By the end of a frenetic afternoon at King's Park, South Africa had won the first Test by 26-3, and a fickle nation was hailing a new generation of heroes: Piet Greyling and Jan Ellis had thrived as flanks, H.O. de Villiers had thrilled as a true counter-attacking fullback, wings Corra Dirksen and Jannie Engelbrecht, centres Gainsford and Eben Olivier, and halfbacks Piet Visagie and De Villiers had moved the ball with pace and skill. The Springbok was leaping again.

De Villiers's team was held for long periods of the second Test at the Free State Stadium in Bloemfontein, but Olivier, Dirksen and Engelbrecht each scored in the second half and the long-awaited South African revival was sustained with a 16-3 win. As De Villiers smiled, so the happy hordes smiled with him.

"Our instinct was to play attacking rugby," the captain reflects, "and France were also playing an expansive game that gave us space and opportunity to move the ball out to the wings. However, when they fell 2-0 behind in the series, they changed their approach and adopted spoiling tactics in the third and fourth Tests. The matches suffered as a result."

Guy Cambérabéro kicked 10 points in France's surprise 19-14 victory at Ellis Park, and the fourth Test at Newlands deteriorated into an untidy contest in which De Villiers, so bright and dominant at the start of the series, was afforded no protection, but left to scavenge and scrap for the ball. The Test was drawn 6-6, although Frik du Preez secured a victory of sorts when he settled the combative Alain Plantefol with a grotesque, bulging black eye.

The captain reflects: "In some ways, it was like taking two steps forwards and one step backwards. We had performed so well at the start of the series, but then been hassled out of our stride, and in the closing minutes of the fourth Test we were hanging on to win the series. This was frustrating, but we had made progress. The selectors had been patient, using only 17 players in the entire series, and that policy encouraged confidence and stability."

This was the captain's view but, despite his outstanding form in provincial rugby, De Villiers remained a target for dissatisfied critics, many of whom lived in Pretoria and steadfastly maintained Piet Uys, the Northern Transvaal scrumhalf, had a stronger claim to wear the green-and-gold No. 9 jersey.

History repeats, and repeats. The scrumhalf debate became another spat in the classic north-south divide. And, yet again, an apparently settled incumbent Springbok captain would find himself the focus of raging controversy, compelled to prove himself all over again. It was never a quiet job.

It was 1968, and the Lions had arrived in the country. Full Springbok trials were being held in Pretoria, culminating in the final match, to be played at Loftus Versfeld between the A team, captained by De Villiers, and the B side, led by Tom Bedford with Uys at scrumhalf. The event had stirred public interest in the city, and more than 52 000 enthusiastic supporters packed the stands, fervently supporting Uys, the local hero, in his bid for selection.

De Villiers accepted the challenge manfully, leading his side onto the field amid boos and whistles. The atmosphere crackled with tension.

Freeze the frame.

How often would this scene be played out, in any other sport, in any other country? The established national captain was effectively being made to run the gauntlet of a lynch mob, being forced to defend his position amid the most ardent antipathy, being thrown if not to the lions, certainly to the bulls. The answer must be "hardly ever". Once again, in terms of its intensity, in terms of its ruthlessness, in terms of its searing passion, Springbok rugby stood apart.

Loftus was buzzing. De Villiers and his A team huddled together amid the mounting bedlam. The captain sensed a heavy palm rest on his shoulder. "Don't worry about the crowd, Dawie. Play your usual game, and you'll be all right." The timely words of encouragement were offered by Frik du Preez, a Pretoria hero in his own right and a friend of Uys. De Villiers was profoundly grateful.

Across the field, the B side were preparing for battle. They bound into a circle and listened warily as one of the national selectors earnestly promised that every one of them could yet be included in the Test side. As soon as the official had strolled out of earshot, the highly motivated Bedford rasped: "That is total nonsense. The A side is basically the Springbok team and the fact is none of us have any chance at all unless we win this afternoon."

The scene was set, and the team with everything to gain eagerly swarmed over the team with everything to lose. Twice, Uys caught De Villiers with the ball; twice, the Loftus crowd roared with delight, taunting its prey.

There was little to choose between the teams, even after the selectors had taken the unusual step of switching the in-form B team flyhalf Jannie Barnard into the A side; and De Villiers's side was ultimately relieved to escape from a fraught 80 minutes with a narrow and unconvincing victory.

South Africa's team for the first Test against the 1968 Lions was due to be announced at the official function later that evening, and speculation focused on whether Uys would displace De Villiers at scrumhalf. It was generally agreed the Northern Transvaler had performed effectively during the trial.

"Scrumhalf ... Dawie de Villiers, captain."

189

The declaration prompted a sudden chorus of boos around a hall packed with Northern Transvaal officials and supporters. The Springbok captain, and still the Springbok captain, held his head high as he stared resolutely at the convenor of selectors, who read out the rest of the team at the podium. Neutral bystanders cringed in embarrassment at the barefaced dissent.

"It was a difficult day," De Villiers recalls. "It felt like a rejection, but I had the backing of senior players like Frik du Preez, and I was certain I would retain that support. I also understood the criticism would disappear like mist before the sun if we played well and were successful against the Lions."

The 1968 Lions appeared a powerful team, constructed on the emerging talents of the young Welsh halfbacks, Gareth Edwards and Barry John, coached by the distinguished Ronnie Dawson, but their ambitions were dealt a cruel blow when John broke his collarbone early in the first Test in Pretoria.

Piet Greyling, Tom Bedford and Jan Ellis had been selected together as a redoubtable Springbok loose forward combination, and this trio conceived a trap where they would offer the young flyhalf an inside gap. John sprinted at the bait, but Ellis was waiting and tackled him heavily to the ground. The Lion was carried off the field, provoking accusations among the touring media that this influential player had been deliberately eliminated. "That is not true," Bedford reflects. "Jan was so strong. The injury was just an unfortunate accident."

De Villiers goaded his team forward, determined to win the important first Test of the series. Minute-by-minute, choosing his options wisely, directing an impressive Springbok display, the scrumhalf started to earn the respect of the same Loftus Versfeld crowd that had jeered him in the trial. At the end of a 25-20 victory that was more emphatic than the score suggests, the captain ran from the field, right hand raised humbly to acknowledge the applause.

"Frik du Preez had scored a great try, brushing aside several Lions as he stormed over the line, and I was very pleased with the performance," De Villiers recalls. "Our scrum was solid and the dry ground suited our intentions to run the ball. At last, we were on top of our game.

"In some ways, I sympathised with the Lions. They suffered many injuries and had a tough time. Twice a week every week, they were confronted by strong, physical provincial teams who had trained months and months for that one game. Wherever they went, they were physically hammered and this battering inevitably took its toll. I think the Lions have traditionally found touring South Africa as hard as we always find touring New Zealand. Every match you play feels like a Test, with a large crowd and opponents bursting to cause an upset."

An undistinguished second Test was drawn 6-6 in Port Elizabeth, and South Africa clinched the series with a decisive 11-6 victory at Newlands. Increasingly praised for his calm leadership of a consistent, resolved side, De Villiers had delivered another neat, efficient performance.

Gareth Edwards joined the chorus. "I was very young in 1968 and in awe of everything about South African rugby," the Welshman recalls, "and Dawie was a huge factor in their side, a real handful and very shrewd. Personally, I learned a lot from his tactical approach to the game."

The Springboks played their most fluent rugby of the series in the fourth Test at Ellis Park, scoring four tries without reply in a 19-6 triumph. With Bedford and Du Preez outstanding, the forwards again established a strong platform and De Villiers was able to release regular possession to a potent backline, in which Piet Visagie sparkled at fly-half, the veteran Roux dazzled in the midfield, and Syd Nomis contributed genuine pace and courage on the wing.

As the public basked in the celebration of a decisive 3-0 series victory, De Villiers had been vindicated. The critics had indeed disappeared like mist before the sun, and the despair of 1965 in New Zealand was a distant memory. Three seasons of sensible selection and stability later, De Villiers stood at the head of a happy Springbok team that once again rivalled any in the world.

The momentum was sustained when the captain led his team on a happy and triumphant six-match tour to France at the end of the 1968 season. Perhaps De Villiers's enduring success as Springbok captain was the product of his ability to harness and sustain strong-minded personalities in one harmonious squad. Intelligent, alert and sensitive, he typically said the right thing at the right time. In this respect, his rugby career provided ideal preparation for later political life.

Powerful men such as Mof Myburgh, Gys Pitzer and Frik du Preez did not suffer fools lightly, and the likes of Piet Greyling and Tom Bedford were not slow to express fervent opinions, yet they all appeared content to follow De Villiers as captain. Where the dominee led, they were happy to follow.

This is not to say their conduct was always exemplary, naturally. After securing a narrow victory in their opening match in France, the Springboks were guests of honour at an elegant cocktail party in Marseilles where, to their horror, only wine and champagne were served as refreshments. The players reluctantly started to drink the bubbles, and more bubbles and more bubbles. By midnight, the party was being unanimously slurred as the best ever.

De Villiers joined in the spirit, if not the substance, of the festivities, but he had returned to his room by the time Johan Claassen, the former Springbok captain and now team coach, discovered three players raiding the hotel kitchens for food. This remained a fiercely disciplined environment, and Claassen did not hesitate mercilessly to run the miscreants into the ground during practice the next morning. If they wanted to drink hard, they could also train hard.

Visagie emerged as the tourists' hero of the first Test in Bordeaux, kicking four penalties in the 12-9 victory. France had scored three tries without reply and, aggrieved to have lost in such circumstances, resolved the South Africans would reap "le whirlwind" during the second Test in Paris.

"That match was a classic," De Villiers recalls. "I do not possess a single video tape of any match that I played in, unlike the players of today who all seem to have libraries of their own. But, if I could choose to own the tape of one match, it would be the second Test in Paris, back in 1968."

South Africa weathered the initial French onslaught and, playing into a strong wind, reached half time just 6-3 in arrears. De Villiers gathered his players during the interval, recalled the progress they had made during the year, and said they were 40 good minutes away from an unbeaten season.

Jannie Engelbrecht, revelling in his prime, swerved inside and outside on his way to the French line; then De Villiers himself sprinted clear from a scrum and accelerated away to score; most memorably, Nomis dribbled a loose ball into the goal area and appeared set to score a simple try when cramp seized his right leg and every staggering step forward towards the ball became agony. As French defenders closed in, the Springbok heroically plunged to score.

The Test was thus won 16-11, the series was won 2-0, and De Villiers and his team were feted upon their return to South Africa. "Everything was going well for the team," the captain reflects, "but I was already starting to focus my mind on the planned All Black tour to South Africa in 1970.

"I was desperate to beat New Zealand, partly because the 1965 tour had been such a disappointment, both for the team and for me personally, and partly because I had tentatively worked out that a victory in that series would be a neat and satisfying way to end my Springbok career."

First, there were other battles to be won, on and off the field.

Greg Davis led the Wallabies on tour to South Africa during 1969, but the touring pack were steamrollered by the Springbok forwards. Once De Villiers had led his team on a gleeful rout at Ellis Park, winning the first Test by 30-11, the joy ebbed away and the series ran its course. Any sport depends upon the essence of competition to entertain, and, for all their efforts, the Australians lacked the power and presence to withstand Hannes Marais, Myburgh and Pitzer in the front row or the thriving back-row triumvirate of Ellis, Greyling and Bedford.

A great Springbok team was emerging, and De Villiers was frustrated to suffer an injury that ruled him out of the second and third Tests. Established as vice-captain, Tom Bedford was automatically elevated to lead the side.

If this era of Springbok rugby had ever been depicted in a film, there is no doubt De Villiers would have been cast in the leading role, but the name of Tom Bedford would also have featured prominently in the publicity, and most probably been displayed in neon above the cinema entrance as well.

As scrumhalf and eighthman, the two men stood at the heart of the team on the field and, by the strength of their personalities, they rarely strayed from the core of the squad's psychology and mood as well.

They were very different in many respects.

De Villiers was generally perceived as the darling of the South African establishment, talented, clever, a minister in the Dutch Reformed Church, closely connected to the National Party. Bedford was the forthright, impassioned, gifted, free-thinking Rhodes scholar who had emerged from relatively liberal Natal and studied for three years at Oxford University in England.

Yet they were united by their talent for rugby, their undying patriotism and their determination for the Springboks to be successful. They did not always agree, but they respected each other and functioned impressively together.

At times, their Springbok team-mates would relish the exchanges between these two highly principled and intelligent men. "There were many discussions in changing rooms and at airports, on various tours and between Tests," Greyling recalls. "Tommy and Dawie had very different outlooks on life, and they were not afraid to talk about politics. It was always very interesting."

Bedford was born in Bloemfontein and reared initially in the small Free State town of Dealesville, and latterly Welkom, as his father took up appointments as headmaster of various schools. At the age of five, speaking Afrikaans as his first language, managing only broken English at best, he enrolled as a boarder at the renowned Christian Brothers' College in Kimberley.

He advanced to study architecture at Natal University and, under the eye of the admired coach Izak van Heerden, was propelled into the Natal team at the age of 19. His progress as an outstanding loose forward was such that, aged 21, he was named in the Springbok side to play the 1963 Wallabies.

"A lot of my friends had decided to leave South Africa after the massacre at Sharpeville," Bedford recalls, "but I decided to stay. My professor thought that was the right thing for me to do, and I also believed that rugby might take me somewhere interesting. I had no desire to emigrate."

He kept his eyes wide open. At school, he had studied alongside Chinese and coloured colleagues; at home, he was richly influenced by the thinking of his mother's brother, the celebrated writer Laurens van der Post; and, at university, he watched intently when the police bulldozed squatters living in shacks following riots at Cato Manor, and again when the army occupied the campus.

"Rugby appeared to be played in a parallel world to these events," he recalls, "but I went along with the game and took it very seriously. It was not too long before anti-apartheid demonstrations started whenever the Springboks toured overseas, and these two worlds started to converge."

Touring Ireland early in 1965, Bedford was intrigued to discover a group of anti-apartheid protesters gathered outside the Sherbourne Hotel in Dublin. The post-Test cocktail party was being held on the first floor, and several laughing Irish players began to hurl eggs at the demonstrators below. Bedford stood in a group of Springboks looking on in silence, and wonder.

He noticed more pockets of protesters when the Springboks played in Australia en route to New Zealand in 1965, and was soon afterwards depressed to read newspaper reports of Verwoerd's speech at Loskop Dam. It had been the same Verwoerd who, as prime minister, had presented the young Bedford with his first Springbok cap at Loftus Versfeld in 1963.

"Once Verwoerd had said Maoris would not be welcome in South Africa, we started to see more demonstrators on tour," Bedford recalls, "and there was one occasion in Canterbury when I confronted some of these guys outside the team bus, and tried to make them understand the situation was more complex than they assumed. At least, I was doing something. As a player, I was becoming frustrated with the management because they did not reply to the protesters at all. They said nothing and, as a result, looked guilty."

Three weeks after returning from New Zealand, Bedford left South Africa to take up a prized Rhodes scholarship at Oxford University. He had prevailed in an exhaustive selection process, and was keen to broaden his horizons. There was, he had concluded, more to life than playing rugby.

"Britain was very wild in the late 1960s," he recalls. "There were marches and riots about the situation in Rhodesia and the war in Vietnam, and there was the Ban the Bomb campaign. I watched situations unfold in Hyde Park that were both frightening and fascinating. I also played rugby for the Richmond club, and we were on tour in Paris during the time of the student riots."

By the time he returned to South Africa in June 1968, Bedford had seen a great deal and, inevitably, had changed as a person. Within scarcely two weeks, however, he was excelling in the final trials and was included in the Springbok team for the first Test against the Lions at Loftus Versfeld.

"Hello, Tom. Long time, no see."

"Hello, Dawie, how are you?"

He played throughout the series and on tour to France, but issues within South African rugby that had simply intrigued him before he spent three years in Europe were now starting to cause him serious concern.

In his mind, Transvaal rugby had always maintained a delicate balance between Afrikaans and English speakers, but the province now appeared to be dominated by the fierce Afrikaner elite of Jannie le Roux, the provincial union president. Similarly, he sensed the Springbok side was dominated by Afrikaans-speaking players to a far greater degree than had ever been the case before. He asked why.

Appointed captain of Natal, he started to become convinced many gifted English-speaking players were not being equitably considered for selection in the Springbok team; ever more urgently, he asked why.

Strangely, at precisely the time when he was starting seriously to question the integrity of the whole system, De Villiers's injury during the 1969 series against Australia propelled Bedford to the pinnacle of that system.

At the age of 27 he was the Springbok captain, leading out the national team to play the second Test against Australia at King's Park, Durban, his home ground. "It was a proud day," he recalls. "The team was very important to me, but there were other things going around in my head as well."

The Springboks cantered to a 16-9 victory, and Bedford also led the team to a comfortable 11-3 win in the third Test at Newlands. Strong and clever, an imposing presence around the field, the eighthman had proved a natural captain in his own right, but this was not his era. Without undue fuss or debate, De Villiers regained fitness, resumed the captaincy, and led the team to a solid 19-8 success in the fourth and final Test at the Free State Stadium.

"Well played, Dawie."

"Well played, Tom."

Encouraged by the 4-0 series sweep over the Wallabies, every Springbok looked forward to the full tour of Britain and Ireland that had been planned for the 1969/70 season in the northern hemisphere. However, only one Springbok knew what lay ahead, and that was the man who the previous year had been standing behind police lines in Hyde Park and on the streets of Paris.

The selectors announced a tour squad founded upon the nucleus of players that had first emerged against the French in 1967 and, under De Villiers's alert leadership, had matured into such a consistent force. As usual, the players assembled in Johannesburg prior to departure and, on this occasion, they would attend a farewell function at the Casa Mia Hotel in Hillbrow. The room was full of optimism, and officials from the Transvaal Provincial Council.

Excited players gathered in groups, discussing the merits of the R3 daily allowance they would receive during the tour and exploring rumours that the four Transvaal players on tour had each been given the princely sum of R400 by their union president, Jannie le Roux. "They're lucky," grumbled a Northern Transvaler. "Our union gave us a tie and a beer tankard."

Soon the speeches started, and various civic dignitaries, weighed down more by the burden of their official chains than by any worldly wisdom, stepped forward to express their confidence that the Springboks would again overwhelm all opposition in Britain and return home with a Grand Slam.

After 45 minutes of such brash enthusiasm, the master of ceremonies asked the tour vice-captain if he would like to speak. Tom

Bedford nodded, and purposefully approached the podium. He had something to say.

"It is wonderful that we have so many people here tonight who believe we will succeed on this tour," Bedford began. "We have heard how well we are going to do in Britain, and how we shall overcome, but I wonder if we will.

"Many of you understand the obstacles of a long overseas tour, but this tour will be even tougher. Quite apart from the challenge of playing in the British winter, I am sure no Springbok squad has ever faced the scale of demonstrations that lie ahead for us. I do not know what is going to happen when we arrive but, if we do not achieve the wonderful results that you all anticipate, please remember there may very well have been unusual circumstances."

Amid virtual silence, most people sipped at their drinks. Avril Malan, the former Springbok captain who had been appointed to coach the squad, stepped forward to address the function. Striving to resurrect the mood of optimism, he urged the players never to be negative, and expressed his complete confidence that, whatever lay ahead, the Springboks would prevail.

Everyone felt better. Applause rippled around the room.

For his part, the captain was preparing for a rugby tour. His father might have been a member of parliament, but De Villiers was not particularly focused on any political implications. He was far more concerned with ensuring his team performed to their potential in Britain, and had been absolutely astonished when, upon his arrival in Johannesburg, he had been greeted by Malan and told there was a possibility the tour would have to be cancelled.

"Why on earth would they do that?" the captain had asked.

Within their own cocoon, most of the players knew there was a climate of protest and demonstration in Britain at the time, but they did not understand quite why anyone should want to protest against South Africa, and they assumed the rugby people would stand their ground and ensure a happy tour. The Springboks did not want to fight anyone. They wanted to play the game. After all, the refrain would run for 20 years, this was about sport, not politics.

Naïve? Certainly.

Earnest? Absolutely.

The tone of the tour was established from the moment the squad landed at Heathrow Airport in London, where the Springboks were met by a bus on the runway and driven to an isolated golf course hotel that had closed for the winter but been specially reopened and secured for the South Africans. Some players headed for the restaurant and something to eat, others gazed out of their rooms at the bleak landscape and wondered what lay ahead.

Their arrival in Britain had felt more appropriate to criminals awaiting trial than to one of the great rugby teams of the world. Was this the kind of welcome that the British people would accord to the mighty Springboks?

What was going on?

Nobody seemed to know.

The next morning, the South Africans were informed that the opening game of the tour, against Oxford University, had been switched from Iffley Road in Oxford to the "more secure surroundings of Twickenham".

More secure?

Why?

When a policeman arrived at their hotel on the evening before the match and suggested the Springboks should plan to arrive at the stadium not later than 12h30, fully two-and-a-half hours before kick-off, more players began to ask what on earth was happening. They usually arrived at the ground only an hour before the game. Clearly, there would be nothing usual about this tour.

De Villiers recalls: "The main problem was we never knew what to expect at any moment. It was impossible to plan. As our bus arrived at Twickenham, we saw hundreds of police. We were rushed through to the changing room and told to wait there. We just sat around. It was difficult for everyone.

"When we did finally run out to play, there was this general mood of chaos and conflict between the spectators who wanted to watch the match and a vocal minority who wanted to protest. Individuals persistently ran across the field during the game, and it was extremely difficult to concentrate."

As the weeks passed, the tour slipped into a routine of players advised to remain in their hotel, players being rushed onto secure buses, players spending hours in changing rooms, players trying to concentrate when the field was ringed with coils of barbed wire, players kept awake at night by demonstrators standing outside the hotel, players ceaselessly under pressure.

Inevitably, different players reacted in different ways.

Many Springboks stood firm, resolved to accept any incident or imposition with calm and, often, a deflating sense of humour. If the authorities wanted them to stay in the changing room for two hours, they would ask why not three hours. If they were confronted by shouting protesters, they would dismiss them as hippies, and crack jokes. Such players believed the tour was being disrupted by no more than Rent-a-Mob and that, as soon as it was over, the same hooligans would be moving anywhere else to protest about anything else.

"We would rather have died than admit the demos affected us in any way," recalls Hannes Marais, the prop. "Our challenge was to press on regardless and, after a while, we learned how to cope. In Swansea, we were walking around the field before the game when someone threw a brass tap that landed on the grass at my feet. It could have killed one of us, but nobody panicked. We just decided we would not walk around any field before matches again."

Piet Greyling, the admired loose forward, was another genuinely amazed by what he saw: "We were playing one match," he recalls, "and, early in the first half, three long-haired guys ran on the field. I just stood still but one of them ran up to me and spat in my face. I was astonished. As Springboks, we thought we were quite important. We were heroes at home, and we thought we were doing a great job. Now this guy was spitting in my face and I just could not imagine why. It seemed so strange. I was more amazed than angry."

Other members of the squad could not handle the relentless pressure, just could not cope with the experience of sitting in a changing room while protesters shouted obscenities from the street right outside the window. They would run onto the field with glazed expressions and fail to perform. In one match, several players were shocked to watch a team-mate's knees visibly shaking as he waited to field an up-and-under. He didn't even touch the ball.

As captain, De Villiers recognised his responsibility to assist any member of his squad suffering such trauma. "It was not pleasant," he reflects, "and there were players who became depressed and just did not want to go on. They would tell me how they played the game for fun and that it was no longer a pleasure to play under such conditions. They would say the rugby did not mean a thing, and ask me for permission to return home immediately.

"I told them that we had to see the tour through to the end. In a sense, our goals had changed. When we arrived in Britain, we set out to win every game but that altered as time moved on. We still wanted to perform well and win, but the overriding aim became to complete the tour. Yes, I wanted to beat our opponents on the field, but it was equally important to beat the demos."

So De Villiers would sit down with unhappy players, and explain how they would be letting down not only themselves and their families but the whole squad if they left the tour. He said people at home would not understand, and would say they had run away. Whatever happened, he would conclude, the players needed to stick together and see the tour through to the last match.

Throughout this turmoil, through the bomb hoaxes and threats, the fears and constantly altered schedule, De Villiers remained steadfast and calm. He did not retreat to his room, nor did he lose his nerve. In many ways, on almost every day, the captain succeeded in holding the tour together.

His paramount rule was no matter how great the provocation might be, no Springbok should ever retaliate against a protester. The squad had arrived with their dignity, he would stress, and we will return home with our dignity. Late in the tour, Mannetjies Roux failed to resist making passing contact with a demonstrator who had run onto the field, and the player was reprimanded.

Corrie Bornman, the team manager, played his part in maintaining morale but, once again, several players grew frustrated by the blunt reluctance of South African officials to stand their ground and state their case.

Bedford recalls: "I tried to engage protesters in conversation whenever it was possible. My point was not that we should try and defend apartheid or the policies of the South African government, but that we should defend the right of the Springbok rugby team to accept an invitation to tour Britain. Nobody wanted to stand up and explain why we were there. They said nothing.

"Of course, it was difficult talking to the demonstrators and I started to hate Peter Hain, who led many of the marches, not because of what he was saying but because of the restrictions his campaign imposed on our players. I knew from experience how travel broadens the mind, and that should have been the case on this tour, but most of our players were scarcely able to leave the hotel. As a result, people who could have started to understand other points of view became stuck in their rooms and entrenched in their opinions."

And there was also some rugby ...

Inevitably, the 1969/70 Springboks rarely played to their potential, and the tour record of played 24, won 15, drawn 4 and lost 5 does not stand comparison with previous tours to Britain; yet, under extraordinary circumstances, De Villiers's players emerged with great credit and the respect of their opponents. "We didn't understand what the South Africans were going through until afterwards," reflects Gareth Edwards, "but they showed real character in adversity."

To the captain's enduring disappointment, however, the touring side failed to win any of the four close-fought international matches, losing by three points to both Scotland and England and then drawing against Ireland and Wales, on both occasions conceding equalising scores deep in injury time.

A try only twelve minutes from time gave the Scots a scrappy 6-3 victory at Murrayfield; then, a controversial late score by John Pullin enabled England to eke out an 11-8 triumph at Twickenham. De Villiers was loath to seek excuses in defeat, but he was at a loss to explain his side's persistent bad luck. Towards the end of the England Test, the scrumhalf seemed to have saved the day when he prodded a perfect chip into the path of Andy van der Watt, but a bizarre bounce took the ball away into English hands and the Test was lost.

The Springbok forwards produced a much-improved performance against Ireland, and South Africa should have extended their lead far beyond the slender 8-5 margin they took into injury time at the end of the second half; and yet even that should have been sufficient. It wasn't. In the eighth and last minute of added time, an Irish interception resulted in a straightforward penalty goal for the home team and the Test was drawn. Once again, De Villiers returned to a sad, sombre changing room. Would anything ever go right on this tour?

For long periods at Cardiff Arms Park, it seemed as though Wales would suffer a Springbok backlash, and when the irrepressible Jan Ellis had created a try for Nomis, the tourists held a thoroughly deserved 6-3 lead at the end of full time. Surely the Springboks would this time hold firm to win.

Three minutes into injury time, Barry John kicked deep into the visitors' half, the Welsh forwards pounded into the ruck, and the ball popped cleanly into the hands of Gareth Edwards, who dived to score. The scrumhalf proceeded to miss an awkward conversion, and the match was drawn 6-6.

"I felt sorry for the players," De Villiers recalls. "We had endured so much off the field, I felt we were entitled to an ounce of luck in the Tests, but we didn't get that. At least, we had contributed to what, with the exception of the Scotland match, had been positive advertisements for rugby. With all the negative publicity around the tour, it was important to entertain the crowds."

Such considerations cut no ice among critics at home, and the defeats provoked disparagement of Avril Malan. This was unfair. The coach had worked hard to introduce an attractive brand of attacking rugby, and the problem seemed to lie not so much with his plan as with the plain fact that his players struggled to focus their minds amid the chaotic circumstances of the tour.

When Malan himself captained the Springboks to Britain in 1960/61, the tourists had approached the traditional end-of-tour match against the Barbarians lightly, but the festival game assumed special significance for De Villiers and his squad precisely because it was their 24th and last match.

"I had repeatedly told the players that we would show we had overcome the demonstrations if we finished the tour on a high note, and that meant we had to beat the Barbarians," the captain recalls. "We had suffered many tough times, lost four players to injury, survived smoke bombs, tacks in the grass, everything, but we were resolved to complete the tour still standing."

The Springboks would finish where they had started, beneath the green grandstands at Twickenham, and they were initially rocked back as the dynamic Edwards created early Barbarian scores for Arneil and Duckham, but De Villiers courageously inspired his team into the match, taking over the goal-kicking from H.O. de Villiers, the fullback who had won widespread praise for his outstanding performances on tour. This day, the captain took charge.

When the influential Ellis scored in the corner, his captain converted from near the touchline and the visitors reached half time trailing 9-8. "This is our last chance to salvage our pride," De Villiers implored his players. "I know you're tired but this is our opportunity. We need to play our best rugby of the tour."

As ever under pressure, as ever still together, as ever displaying bravery in crisis, the players rallied to their captain's call. At last, the Springbok forwards rediscovered the relentless rhythm that had overcome the Lions and France in 1968, and crushed Australia. Frik du Preez, playing his 72nd match in green-and-gold, stoked the engines, and the tourists drove forward.

Mike Lawless kicked a drop goal, Van der Watt touched down a second try, and Ellis brought the crowd to its feet when he seized upon a loose ball, sold two dummies and beat J.P.R. Williams before scoring. De Villiers kicked the conversion, and the exultant tourists had established an unassailable lead.

As the final whistle confirmed the 21-12 victory, the South African captain was hoisted on the shoulders of Gareth Edwards and Mike Gibson, the luminary Irish centre, and carried from the field with the applause and cheers of the crowd ringing in his ears. Protesters may have pursued the Springboks throughout the tour, but it was the roar of rugby supporters that endured.

"It was a happy day," De Villiers reflects. "Nobody could ever describe the 1969/70 tour to Britain as a success, but we had found ourselves in an extremely difficult position, and I was proud of the fact we had prevailed."

Brigadier Glyn Hughes, the fourth president of the Barbarians and a man of stature decorated in both World Wars, spoke at the formal post-match dinner, bestowed honorary membership of the club on De Villiers, and then reflected the opinions of many millions of Britons who had been embarrassed and appalled by the manner in which the Springboks had been treated.

"Politics has no place in the realm of amateur sport," the feisty 78-year-old thundered. "A player should be free to play with whom and against whomsoever he chooses, and nobody has the authority to withdraw that right."

The Springboks applauded, and finally relaxed. The conduct of this group of young South Africans in the face of ceaseless pressure and bitter provocation had been exemplary. Later that night, the players emerged from the hotel where the Barbarian dinner had been held, and found no protesters in sight. After three arduous and challenging months, their trial was over.

De Villiers arrived home in the first week of February 1970, but there was no respite. The All Blacks were scheduled to arrive in June, and his active mind immediately shifted to the immense challenge ahead. His experiences in Britain had confirmed his intention to retire at the end of the season, but he desperately wanted to end his Test career with victory over New Zealand.

"It had become an obsession," he remembers. "People always said you did not rate as a Springbok unless you had played in a team that defeated the All Blacks, and I realised this would be my last opportunity.

"We were underdogs in 1970. While we had been struggling in Britain, the New Zealanders had extended their unbeaten record into a fifth season, and they started their South African tour in style, sweeping through their provincial fixtures like a great wave. Most people thought we had no chance."

The All Blacks had not been defeated in 37 matches under the leadership of eighthman Brian Lochore, and they had extended this remarkable run to 47 by the time they started to prepare for the first Test at Loftus Versfeld. Some people would later suggest this team had passed its peak in 1967, but nobody held that view when Lochore's tourists blitzed through the country, looking for all the world as though they were destined to become the first New Zealand team to win a series on South African soil. History was beckoning.

At home in Johannesburg, where he had moved in 1969 and was now playing for Transvaal, De Villiers contemplated the prospect.

"We had to break up the momentum of the All Black forwards," he reflects. "That was the key. They just seemed to roll over their opponents. We developed a plan where we would leave what looked like gaps in our defence, draw the New Zealanders to attack down these channels, and then cut them off. If was clear we would have to tackle relentlessly if we were to survive."

Most assumed the established and admired Springbok loose forward trio, Greyling, Bedford and Ellis, would play an integral role within this defensive plan, but the selectors had other ideas. Bedford was dropped. He would play no role during the entire 1970 series against the All Blacks.

The official explanation for this ostensibly bizarre decision was that South Africa required additional height at the back of the lineout to counter the threat of the All Black captain, Lochore. Thus Albie Bates was chosen as eighthman, and the bitterly disappointed Bedford was left to point out in vain that he had held his own against the giant French lock, Dauga, 12 months before.

This logic was accepted in some quarters, but not in others. Rumours ran wild that Bedford had been abruptly removed from the Springbok team because he had started openly to express his views on South African rugby. In essence, the theory ran, he had become just too hot to handle. Was this the Broederbond exerting its influence, or were the liberals seeing ghosts?

The eighthman had been injured towards the end of the tour to Britain, and later received a letter from Flappie Lochner, convenor of selectors, asking about his recovery. The Natal team doctor had replied that Bedford's injury was healing satisfactorily, and that he would be fit to play in the final trials.

By coincidence Frik du Preez was also recovering from injury as the trials approached and, while Bedford proved his fitness by playing two club matches in Durban, the tremendously popular lock forward joined a less-than-serious tour of Southern Rhodesia with the University of Pretoria team.

Both Springboks were ready for the Springbok trials.

Not quite. What was good for the goose was not good for the gander. Du Preez was selected. Bedford was cast aside.

That was that.

If the selectors had actually dropped Bedford for a rugby reason, such as the need for height at the back of the lineout, they would surely still have invited the 28-year-old hero of 23 Tests to the trial. Instead, he was completely ignored. Perhaps his presence at the trials was regarded as too much of a risk. Perhaps, horror of horrors, he would have outjumped Bates.

"I was disappointed not to make the trial," Bedford reflects. "I genuinely do not know what happened. It was true I had started to talk about problems facing South African rugby, even wondering in one speech if Peter Hain may have had a point: perhaps it was time for us all to change. Maybe someone did not think it was proper for a Springbok to express such views."

Towards the end of the All Black tour, the national selectors attended the tourists' match against Natal in Durban, and they were standing by as, following tradition, the home captain stepped forward to speak at the post-game function. Bedford cleared his throat, and seized the opportunity.

He first expressed his regret that so many talented Natal players had been overlooked by the national selectors, and then hinted at the growing perception in Durban that the predominantly English-speaking province was becoming isolated within the increasingly

Afrikaans-speaking game when he greeted the panel with the words: "Welcome to the last outpost of the British Empire."

De Villiers had surveyed Bedford's tribulations from a distance, and with genuine regret. The two great Springboks would never play another Test match together. Their long and distinguished alliance was over.

The captain reflects: "I have always had great respect and admiration for Tommy. In some ways, he was responsible for stimulating an awakening in me. We used to have many long discussions about South Africa and, while I argued with him on many points, he always made me think, and consider another view, and maybe eventually accept a different perspective.

"As a vice-captain, he was always supportive and positive, and we shared many great occasions together. We might not have agreed on everything, but the key to our successful relationship was that we were always open with each other. Little was left unsaid. We kept in contact for many years after we retired from the game but, unfortunately, we have lost touch recently."

It is hard for modern rugby supporters, who watch the leading players from New Zealand and Australia perform in South Africa two or three times every year, to imagine the enormous impact of an All Black tour in 1970. It was only the third visit by a New Zealand team since the Second World War, and the first since the departure of Wilson Whineray's squad a full decade earlier.

A Test series between the All Blacks and the Springboks was so rare and special that it would prove a seminal moment in hundreds of thousands of lives. Many South African men aged between 50 and 60 today might struggle to recall results from last year's Tri-Nations Series, but they will still remember incidents and events from the four titanic Tests played during 1970.

It was a time when white South Africans had begun to feel the icy winds of isolation, a time when it seemed ever more important that the Springboks should defeat the All Blacks and claim the unofficial title of world champions. For many, the idea that the rest of the world could impose boycotts and sanctions "but they still can't beat us at rugby" was profoundly comforting.

Perhaps it was this need to play, and win, that persuaded the government to relax the ban on Maori players imposed by Verwoerd, for it was only this slight loosening of the racial noose that enabled the tour to go ahead.

Loftus Versfeld was packed beyond its capacity for the first Test, although few of those crammed together on the scaffolding stands held out much hope of a Springbok triumph. South Africans customarily either eulogised or berated their own players, depending entirely on the Test result, but they appeared to set the New Zealanders on a different level. The men in black were revered as genuine giants of the game, admired as mythical heroes who only played in South Africa once every ten years, to be cherished and appreciated.

Hannes Marais, the Springbok prop, recalls: "I organised some tickets to the first Test for some friends and, when they came to collect the envelope, one of them explained to me how he had travelled a long way to see the match so he would be very grateful if we would try and keep the score down. That was all. He was dead serious. Our own supporters didn't give us a chance."

Professor Johan Claassen, still the coach, and De Villiers intelligently used the low expectations to positive effect. Springbok history has known many stirring team talks, but few to compare with Loftus Versfeld in 1970.

Amid silence and frowns of deep concentration, the big men changed from blazers into jerseys. Claassen snapped the group together.

"Let me make one thing clear," declared this imposing man, speaking with all the knowledge and authority of his own 28 Tests in green-and-gold. "If there is anyone in this changing room who does not sincerely believe we can beat the All Blacks today, then he must please leave now."

There followed a pause for effect, as when a minister asks the congregation if they know of any reason why the bride and groom cannot be married. Claassen looked around the room in a steady arc, his wide eyes challenging.

Nobody moved.

"I am quite serious," the coach continued. "If you are scared of these All Blacks, then we don't need you here. Please leave."

Still nobody moved.

De Villiers picked up the theme. "Each of us knows what we must do, and we all understand what lies ahead," the captain said. "It is going to be very tough, but I want each of you to take a moment and concentrate on doing something on the field today that will be an inspiration to your team-mates."

Within minutes, the players were high-stepping into bedlam, picking a path through hordes of people on the field as the stadium erupted in noise and colour. From the brave souls perched precariously at the top of the grandstands down to the keen rows of cross-legged schoolboys squeezed together, two metres from the touchline, Loftus was buzzing. This was not so much the biggest rugby day of the year in Pretoria as the biggest rugby day for an entire generation.

And, as visible in the midst of this feverish excitement as Napoleon on his white horse at the battle of Waterloo, the distinctive blonde head of the Springbok captain bobbed up and down. He clapped his hands, urged here, goaded there, in his element, in charge, every inch the leader of his team.

With the benefit of hindsight, it is possible to argue that the series was decided within the opening ten minutes of the first Test, for that is exactly how long it took for the home side to be transformed from a team that eagerly wanted to believe it could win into a side actually convinced that it would prevail.

After three minutes, the Springbok front row prepared to scrum down ten metres from the New Zealand line. Marais and hooker Piston van Wyk gathered and agreed to try a ploy that had worked effectively for Stellenbosch University. Instead of hooking the ball, Van Wyk would kick it forward through the All Black scrum, giving the tourists' scrumhalf Chris Laidlaw uncontrolled possession. As the packs locked together, Marais warned both De Villiers and Greyling, on the flank, to be aware of what was being planned.

The scrum was set, and the ball duly squirted clear at the back of the New Zealand scrum. With Laidlaw wrong-footed, De Villiers managed to hack the ball forward. The tourists were turned, panicking. Greyling dashed off the flank, and side-footed the ball over the

All Black line. De Villiers led the frantic chase for the touchdown, and, bringing the crowd to their feet, dramatically dived to score the try with his outstretched right hand. The plan had worked.

From the restart, New Zealand recycled possession, and the flyhalf Wayne Cottrell confidently drifted in search of a gap on the blind side. Joggie Jansen, a resolute Free State centre playing his debut Test, had not stopped thinking about his captain's words: "Do something that will inspire your team-mates". And he moved across field to shadow Cottrell, focusing, bracing, closing in.

Jansen's shoulder crashed into Cottrell's chest, leaving the All Black flyhalf lying flat on his back with the ball seemingly buried in his stomach. Thirty years on, Springbok forwards sparkle as they recall the audible thud of bone on flesh. With one perfectly timed, crunching tackle, Jansen had engraved his name in rugby history and, more importantly, inspired his team.

De Villiers recalls: "I can honestly say that, after that start to the Test, we never looked back in the series. We started as underdogs, and suddenly we had proved to ourselves and everyone else that we could disrupt the All Blacks, and knock them backwards. Joggie Jansen's tackle was an important moment, but it was only one of many outstanding tackles we made that day."

Confidence flooded through the home side.

Piet Visagie snapped a neat drop goal, Ian McCallum kicked a magnificent 55-metre penalty, and Syd Nomis, all buzz and pace on the wing, scored a second Springbok try. Not even a spectacular solo try by wing Bryan Williams could save the "unbeatable" All Blacks from a stunning 17-6 defeat.

De Villiers sat quietly in the changing room afterwards, savouring the taste of a special triumph. While young players tend to wolf down the spirit of a vintage win, the veterans generally take care to enjoy every drop.

The Springbok captain did not believe for a moment the rest of the series would be comfortable. Test matches between South Africa and New Zealand are almost always fierce and closely contested, but the mood had changed. If the All Blacks were to achieve their dream of winning a Test series in South Africa, they would now have to win three Test matches in a row.

History suggested this would be an almighty task.

New Zealand came out fighting in the second Test at Newlands, literally, and the Springboks were swift to retaliate. Another enormous crowd witnessed a match of extraordinary physical intensity in this era when men were men, and the spectacle of two grown men standing toe-to-toe and exchanging brutal punches was regarded as being part of this gentleman's game. Only sly blows, delivered from behind, were regarded as being beyond the pale.

When Alan Sutherland launched a mighty fist into Van Wyk's face, the bloodied Springbok hooker was led from the field; and the All Black's punishment was imposed not by the referee but by Marais, who hovered around the fringes of the next maul and seized his chance to land the revenge punch.

The prop recalls: "It was embarrassing for me because a newspaper, Die Landstem, published a sequence of photographs showing my punch. A friend of mine telephoned early the next morning and said I should quickly go out and buy every copy of the paper to protect my reputation."

De Villiers understood the physical dimension of the sport, and was keen that his players should not be intimidated, but the pattern of the game was lost at Newlands and, although South Africa led until the 72nd minute, the New Zealand fullback Fergie McCormick kicked a late penalty and, suddenly, the tourists were celebrating a 9-8 victory, and the series was level at 1-1.

The captain ensured defeat did not prompt panic in Springbok ranks, and he worked hard to restore confidence ahead of the third Test in Port Elizabeth. It is hard to exaggerate the authority with which De Villiers led his side during this series. In everything he did and said, he managed to convey steady confidence that, whatever the odds, his team would emerge in triumph.

Apart from his clever, sensitive leadership, the captain had also emerged as a match-winner. It had been his alert opportunism that struck the initial spark in the opening minutes of the first Test at Loftus

Versfeld and now, with the series back in the melting pot, it was once again the scrumhalf who immediately stamped his mark on the third Test in Port Elizabeth.

Collecting the ball from a ruck, De Villiers dashed past the loose forwards and was suddenly sprinting into open prairie, clear of the All Black defence. His impeccable pass to Gert Muller enabled the winger to score an opening try, and his Springboks started to believe all over again. Deep in the second half, Roux created a second try for Muller, and the 16-3 win was sealed.

The Springboks may have been flattered by that margin of victory, but De Villiers was thrilled beyond words. Whatever happened in the fourth Test at Ellis Park, his team could not lose the series. Along the corridor under the main stand at the Boet Erasmus Stadium, the All Blacks sat silent.

Lochore still feels the sense of disappointment. "It will bug me for the rest of my life," the All Black captain reflects, "that, in 1970, we produced our worst performances of the tour in the Test matches.

"We made far too many mistakes, but Dawie and his team deserved a lot of credit. The Springboks were good planners, pugnacious, determined; and they pulled together with unshakeable pride in what they represented. I believe that, in 1970, they were even more determined than us to win."

In trying to explain the stunning defeats, New Zealanders criticised the initial selection of Laidlaw ahead of Sid Going at scrumhalf, and the unexplained decisions to drop Sutherland and move Williams to centre for the third Test; and there was the normal grumbling about arguable refereeing decisions, but nothing so clear that it could be said to have affected the results.

The fourth Test started in a blur as, for the third time in the series, the Springboks leaped out of the blocks and never looked back. After only five minutes, Piet Visagie broke through the tourists' defence and scored a scintillating try. "Piet was a formidable flyhalf," De Villiers recalls. "We played 17 Test matches together, and, in many ways, he was the general."

The Ellis Park crowd were treated to a richly entertaining contest, with the ball being moved around at pace and the rival packs of forwards holding nothing in reserve. Ian McCallum and Gerald Kember traded enormous penalties, but the match turned late in the second half when Kember lost the ball under challenge from Jansen, and Roux sent Muller storming over the line.

South Africa thus extended their lead to 20-14, and an outstanding late try by Bryan Williams, New Zealand's player of the series, only served to reduce the final deficit. By this stage, Williams's popularity among South Africans had grown to a point where he had received more than 1 600 fan letters.

The irony of his fame was that the Samoan-born winger was one of those New Zealanders who, back in 1965, Verwoerd had said would not be welcome in South Africa. It seemed the Prime Minister had been mistaken.

The final whistle confirmed South Africa's 20-17 win in the fourth Test, and their victory in the series by three Tests to one. In this moment of achievement, in this instant of realised ambition, as the curtain fell on his great career, De Villiers permitted himself the slightest of happy skips. He was then engulfed by delighted team-mates, and carried shoulder-high from the field at Ellis Park.

"Everywhere you looked, people were smiling," he recalls. "You only had to see the faces to understand what the victory meant to so many South Africans. We had worked very hard and, I think, we deserved to win."

Thus the Dawie de Villiers era, which had begun so inauspiciously with the miserable 1965 defeat in New Zealand, ended in the glory of a series victory over the "unbeatable" All Blacks. The South African captain had decided to retire and, just past his 30th birthday, he would not be dissuaded.

"I was eager to get on with my studies and the rest of my life," he recalls, "and, moreover, the prospects for Springbok rugby were not good. The squad was scheduled to visit Australia in 1971, and I told Dr Craven that tour would be a disaster. So far as I could predict, there were only going to be more and more demonstrations, and I didn't want to be any part of that.

"It had a been a tremendous honour to lead South Africa in 22 Tests, and it was wonderful to be carried off the field, but I made great sacrifices as well, and I believed it was time to focus on something else."

Neatly, the scrumhalf played the very last match of his career as part of the Rugby Football Union's Centenary celebrations early in 1971 at Twickenham, scene of one of his great days, the Barbarians game in 1969.

For the fair scrumhalf, of course, there had been many great days.

The Miracle at Lancaster Park in 1965, the rout of the Lions at Ellis Park in 1968, the valedictory victory over the Barbarians at the end of the demo tour, and the opening ten minutes of the first Test against the 1970 All Blacks: the images of courage and memories of leadership were not only his to take into retirement, but were bequeathed to cheer and inspire millions.

The end of his rugby career was, however, very far from the end of Dawie de Villiers. By 1972 he had followed his father into parliament and been elected as the member for Johannesburg West. Initially eager to focus his energies on sport, he soon found himself embroiled in controversy.

Marais Viljoen, the Minister of Home Affairs, had delivered a speech in Alberton declaring "black and white will never pack down in the same scrum", and a wide-awake journalist decided to telephone the former Springbok captain and new National Party member of parliament to hear his response to the speech.

"Well," De Villiers replied, "who am I to repudiate the minister? However, I would say this, that we should never say never."

That was all, but that was enough. De Villiers was severely criticised by right-wing politicians for what they interpreted as his call for mixed sport, and his reputation as a verligte (enlightened) Afrikaner was enhanced. Within two years, he had made a stand and publicly declared his firm support for merit selection in representative teams, regardless of race or colour.

However, he soon grew weary of sport, of annual policy reviews and very little progress, and started to devote more time to issues such as housing, trade and industry. His career advanced in 1979, when he was appointed to serve as South Africa's ambassador in London, where his memories of the 1969/70 tour were daily rekindled by the protests, 24 hours every day, seven days every week, outside the Embassy's iron gates in Trafalgar Square.

He returned to South Africa after 20 months and, following a gentle chat with P.W. Botha, the state president, agreed to return to parliament. He eventually became the member for the Piketberg constituency on the coast north of Cape Town. Viewed as one of the bright young men in the National Party, De Villiers joined the cabinet and served as Minister of Trade, Industry and Tourism until 1987.

He had switched portfolios, to become Minister of Mineral Energy Affairs and Public Enterprises, just before F.W. de Klerk took over as state president, and during the following seven years he also worked as Minister for Administration and Privatisation, and latterly as Minister of Environmental Affairs and Tourism.

Now recognised as a strong liberal influence over the National Party in the Cape, De Villiers played a significant role in the delicate negotiations with leaders of the African National Congress, attending bosberade and conferences on the road to South Africa's negotiated revolution and the final transition to democracy in 1994. Bright and clever, he proved charming and constructive.

And still he prevailed, serving under President Mandela as the Minister of Environmental Affairs and Tourism in the Government of National Unity. In 1996, he joined the en bloc National Party resignation from the government but, within a year, with South African government approval, De Villiers was seconded to join the World Tourism Organisation in Madrid.

Many Springbok captains have discovered there is a worthwhile life after their days of glory and fame in green-and-gold, but De Villiers stands unique as a man who has consistently held high office beyond his playing days. "I have been very fortunate," he reflects, "and made friends all around the world. That is what matters to me. The prestige and the positions are not important at all. Sooner or later, we will all be gone. It's the relationships that matter."

And still the De Villiers eyes sparkle, dart this way and that, miss so little, notice so much. Are they shrewd?

It is inevitable that a man who has achieved so much should also have attracted criticism, and it has frequently been claimed that De Villiers is more of a politician than a dominee, adept at plots and planning, more concerned with how things look and reflect upon him than with any moral principle.

Team-mates were sometimes intimidated by his intelligence, and political colleagues have occasionally appeared suspicious of his uncanny ability to back the winning horse. In both cases, the implication is that the bright, boyish looks generally conceal a far more complex and calculating nature.

Such criticism is unsupported by fact and record, and it may be instructive to provide a final, objective assessment of this man from Sam Ramsamy, former leader of the anti-apartheid sports movement in London, a long-time adversary of De Villiers in many capacities and situations, president of the National Olympic Committee of South Africa and a member of the IOC.

"In all dealings with him," says Ramsamy, "I always felt Dawie de Villiers was a sincere man, and I have never wavered from that view."

Yes, De Villiers was anointed as a Springbok captain by the Broederbond, an organisation he would later join, but the fact remains that, through his bravery and outstanding leadership on the field, he earned the total respect and affection of rugby players and supporters from all walks of life.

Yes, De Villiers entered parliament under the National Party banner, but he proved a diligent and successful minister and ultimately played an important role in South Africa's momentous transition to democracy.

Dawie de Villiers was born into an Afrikaner family that loved rugby and supported the National Party. Those were his circumstances, and this was the starting point of his life's journey. Through 60 years of ceaseless commitment to a broad variety of causes, it is possible to reflect that he served his country with distinction and integrity in both rugby and politics. Ranking among the shortest of Springbok captains, he stands tall as a man of true distinction.

8 THE BESIEGED

For the Springboks, the world was becoming a smaller place.

Governments around the planet had discovered there were few forms of sanction more visible, uncomplicated and, for them, comparatively painless, than to end sporting contact with the Republic. South Africans earnestly enquired why they were being isolated when the international community happily continued to play against countries such as China and the Soviet Union, but their words were lost on the wind. Apartheid would no longer be tolerated, and the sporting boycott was identified as a legitimate means of protest.

FIFA, the world governing body of soccer, and the International Olympic Committee had switched off the lights on South Africa in the early 1960s, and by 1971 even the old games of the British Empire, rugby and cricket, were starting to sway with the prevailing political winds.

Danie Craven was still welcome whenever the International Rugby Board gathered at the East India Club in London, of course, but the once amicable and civilised discussion to determine the calendar of international tours had become fraught and uncomfortable. Life was becoming complicated.

The blazered leaders of the game, many of whom had played against the South African Rugby Board president, upheld the principle that politicians should not interfere in sport, and dearly wanted to oblige Craven's pleas; but the tide was turning against South Africa, and against its national rugby team.

Through 40 seasons, the Springboks had established themselves among the leading rugby nations in the world; now, they would learn to wait alone in the wilderness, gratefully seizing upon what scraps of international competition were slipped through the political net by their old rugby friends.

From 1971 until 1979, the team would tour overseas only twice, and host six visiting international sides: two from France, two from Great Britain, one from New Zealand, and a World XV. Even this trickle of competition provoked extreme anger worldwide: the 1976 All Black tour of South Africa prompted many African nations to withdraw from the summer Olympic Games in Montreal.

"And we just wanted to play rugby ..."

It may have been naïve for members of the whites-only rugby team, from a country where whites were legally privileged at the expense of a black majority, to expect their traditional rivals would continue to turn up and play the game, yet the overwhelming majority of white players and supporters seemed unable to fathom why they were being isolated. Initially, at least, the boycott served only to harden white opinion, and was received with fury and indignation.

Whenever the Springboks did find someone to play, the occasion seemed even greater, public support even more passionate, and the white breast-beating even more intense. The team had always been driven by national pride, but their sporadic performances through the 1970s appeared to be spurred by defiance, a deep-seated need to show the rest of the world that, no matter what they banned or boycotted, they could not beat South Africa at rugby.

Norman Sanson, a reflective Scot, was appointed to referee the 1975 Test between South Africa and France, and recalls "the most intimidating atmosphere that I have ever experienced". For many white South Africans, every rugby Test represented a rare opportunity to be seen and heard.

The players adapted to isolation. If there was to be no jam, they would eat bread and butter. If there was to be no butter, they would make do with a piece of bread. Some did shrug their shoulders, pack away their boots and do something else with their spare time, but the vast majority trained harder, became even more resolved to win every time they had the chance to play.

Their spirits were raised in 1971 when confirmation was received that the French team would tour South Africa, and rugby people were temporarily able to overlook isolation and discuss who should succeed Dawie de Villiers as captain and lead the Boks in two Tests against the tourists.

The choice appeared to rest between a popular prop, Hannes Marais, and an experienced eighthman, Tom Bedford. Not for the first time, lines were drawn between an Afrikaans-speaker and an English-speaker, between a man brought up within the establishment and a leader who had become increasingly critical of the game's administration, between two decent, principled men.

A week before the Springbok trials, where the captaincy debate would be resolved, the telephone rang at Bedford's house in Durban.

"Hello."

"Hello, Tom?"

"Yes, it's Tom Bedford speaking."

The Natal captain was being contacted out of the blue by a senior figure in South African rugby, and the player listened intently.

"Tom, I am calling you because I want you to understand what is going on. You should not expect too much at the trials in Cape Town. By rights, you should be the next Springbok captain but, from what I have heard, I don't know if you will even be in the team. I am a member of the Broederbond and it has been decided the next Springbok captain must be one of us. I am sorry, but that is the situation, and I thought it was only fair you should be aware."

Bedford replied: "Look, I only play the game for enjoyment, so I am not too worried about what happens at the trials, but I appreciate your call. Certain things in and around the Springbok team have upset me in the past few seasons, and you have helped me make sense of what has happened."

"All right, but, please, I never spoke to you, OK?"

Bedford arrived in Cape Town to find himself starting the week as captain of only the C team, but he sustained his superb form for

Natal and reached what was beginning to look like his glass ceiling in Springbok rugby. He was named as vice-captain of the team to play against France.

The new Springbok captain was Hannes Marais, a proud, emotional and brave man known to thousands as *Ons Hannes* (Our Hannes).

Born in Somerset East, in the Eastern Cape, he was raised on the family farm cradled majestically in the hills near the small town of Cookhouse. This was not a pampered life of luxury and wealth. Among the sheep and cattle, there was always work for the small boy and his older brother; and, in every available hour, they set about their tasks, looked after the animals, developed their own area of the garden, worked with their hands, and grew strong.

Young Hannes played rugby at school, listened to Test commentaries on the radio and, in 1955, perched on empty brandy bottles to watch the Springboks play against the Lions in Port Elizabeth. "Theunis Briers made his great tackle on Tony O'Reilly in front of us," he recalls. "I was 14 and, when we walked out of St George's Park at the end, I was literally lifted off my feet."

Harbouring ambitions to become a veterinarian, Marais enrolled to study agriculture at the University of Stellenbosch but he didn't forget his rugby boots. In 1962, he was spotted by Danie Craven and hurled into the Maties first team to play against Collegians, the Bloemfontein club. That day the debutant prop was assisted through his senior club debut by his front row opponent, Slang van Zyl, who offered pertinent pieces of advice during breaks in play.

Marais relished Stellenbosch, but he lived for the weeks between terms when he could return home to the hills around Cookhouse, to the beautiful, bare and bleak landscape of bush and rocks that he called home.

The young man would stand on the *stoep* (verandah) of the family house and gaze up the steep hill towards one particular aloe, a tall plant clearly visible at the summit, etched against the sky. And he would run, up the hill to the aloe, then back down the hill to the house. Every afternoon, in searing heat, or in driving rain, he would run and run. Supreme fitness would become his greatest asset.

Almost 40 years on, Marais stands on the same stoep and gazes up at the same aloe, clearly visible on the same horizon. The farm has now passed into his care, but nothing else has changed. "My best time was twelve-and-a-half minutes up to the aloe," he muses, drifting back to the days of his heroic youth, "and nine-and-a-half minutes down. One time, some friends from Stellenbosch came to the farm, and one of them was an excellent runner who thought he could improve my record. He got very near to the aloe in about seven minutes but then lost his way and took 14 minutes. He lacked local knowledge, you know.

"In those days, I used to run and run."

And the old Springbok's words trail away ...

Marais made his Test debut during the frenzied series against Australia in 1963 and, although he never slipped far from the reckoning, did not become an automatic choice until the start of 1968. By the time of his appointment as captain in 1971, however, he had propped the Springbok scrum in 18 consecutive Tests and earned a proud reputation wherever rugby was played.

A roguish, upright and intelligent man, he completed his Master's degree in agriculture and, after a spell playing provincial rugby for North-eastern Cape, eventually settled in the colours of Eastern Province. He was strong in the scrum but his name was founded upon his speed and strength in the loose. Sideburned and moustached, Marais cut a dashing figure.

"I had been vice-captain in 1970, so it was not a complete surprise when I was named to lead the Springboks in 1971," he remembers. "Tom Bedford had his supporters. We were due to tour Australia after the Tests against France, and people said Tom would be able to handle the press on that tour better than me, and they were probably right, but there are always dissenting opinions. That is part of the game. I was just pleased to be made captain."

Marais was encouraged by the support of senior players such as Frik du Preez and Jan Ellis, and adopted a personable approach to the captaincy, taking care to spend time with the players in the squad whom he had not met before. The skills of leadership did not come easily to an experienced player who had grown accustomed to sitting in the back row of the bus and disrupting team songs, but the prop forward emerged as an effective, modest captain.

He did not indulge in extravagant gestures on the field, concentrating on organising his side rather than being seen to organise his side, and he resolutely stood by his players in every situation. He recalls: "The worst part of the job was having to think of something original to say in all the team talks."

Christian Carrere led a French side remarkable for the fact that it included Roger Bourgarel, the first black member of a touring squad to South Africa. The country that had so long declared players of colour were not welcome in touring teams embraced the winger, and the crowd cheered as he twice tackled Frik du Preez during the first Test in Bloemfontein. However, it was Ian McCallum who scored the points that counted, and South Africa won 22-9.

Marais was satisfied with the performance, but his hopes of a repeat at King's Park in Durban were dashed when the second Test unfolded as an untidy scramble of flailing fists and repeated foul play. Contrary to popular legend, the Springbok captain did not enjoy such exchanges, although that is not to say he could not deal with threatening opponents. If he needed to get his retaliation in first, as the saying goes, then he did exactly that.

"It was a pretty rough afternoon," the captain recalls, "but we certainly did not look for trouble. Our policy was that we would only strike back under the most severe provocation and, midway through the second half, Frik du Preez came to me and said he was getting fed up with one of the French locks who was repeatedly kicking our blokes when they were on the ground.

"I asked him what he wanted to do, and he replied that the next time we were awarded a penalty we should just 'put it up'. That was all. We would kick the ball in the air so the offending lock would have to catch it. The idea was that he would catch Frik in full flight as well; and so it happened."

The second Test was drawn 8-8, but Marais's Springbok side had won the series 1-0, boosting confidence before the full tour to Australia.

Once again the South African rugby players would find themselves in a position where they were generally welcomed by the sporting public of their host country, and yet were incessantly dogged by demonstrators. Australia permitted the Springbok rugby visit to proceed but, later in 1971, a proposed South African cricket tour was abruptly cancelled, and there would be no further sporting contact between the two countries, in either code, for two decades.

Marais hardly discussed the protests with his players. There was nothing to be said. Many of the squad had been hardened by their experiences on tour to Britain during 1969/70, and they accepted with equanimity the siege conditions at their hotels and around the stadiums, the barracking and chanting.

When they ran out to play in Melbourne, they found mounted police trying to drive protesters off the field. Unconcerned, the Springboks casually jogged to the opposite end of the stadium and serenely started their warm-up exercises. In many ways, the players had become immune to demonstrations.

"It was a difficult tour," recalls Morné du Plessis, the young loose forward enjoying his first series, "but Hannes Marais was a mischievous kind of captain who managed to keep the mood light, even in the tensest situations. He was an extrovert character, always ready to smile and laugh."

Since commercial flights and hotels were considered security risks, the South African players grew accustomed to travelling in chartered airplanes and staying in private homes. Midway through the tour, Marais and Bedford, as the captain and vice-captain, were billeted to stay with Mr and Mrs Cowper, whose son Bob had played cricket for Australia with distinction.

The Cowpers noticed how much their Springbok guests enjoyed watching television each evening, and Cowper was moved to ask Marais why television had not been introduced in South Africa.

"Well, er," the Springbok captain replied, "we're waiting for the Americans and Germans to perfect their technology for colour television. There is not much point starting with black-and-white television now."

Cowper smiled. "That's a good story," he said, "but I don't buy it. Perhaps the real reason is that, if you did have television, you South Africans would not be able to separate the black from the white!" Marais and Bedford laughed. In fact, South Africans had been denied TV because the government feared too much open information would unleash dangerous influences.

The 1971 Springboks coped ... not only with the protesters off the field but also with the Wallabies in the three-Test series. Coached by Johan Claassen, the team played open rugby and scored many excellent tries, not least when Marais dashed 30 yards to touch down against New South Wales. Such a turn of speed in a burly prop forward regularly flummoxed the opposition.

South Africa eased to a 19-12 first-Test victory in Sydney by taking control among the forwards, and they secured the series by winning the second Test at Brisbane by 14-6. This team's remarkable ability to perform at its potential under the most enormous pressure was testament to its captain's gift for maintaining a nimble balance between impish humour and grim resolve.

Marais also displayed a dexterous touch when he invited Frik du Preez to lead the team onto the field before the third Test, back in Sydney. The veteran lock forward had announced his intention to retire from international rugby after playing this, his 38th and final Test match for South Africa, and he appreciated the gesture from the increasingly admired captain.

Where many had predicted disaster, Marais emerged in triumph. His side returned home as the first Springboks ever to remain unbeaten on any overseas tour. In 13 matches, they had scored 396 points and conceded only 112, scored 76 tries and conceded 11. The two thousand people who turned up to greet the players at Jan Smuts airport in Johannesburg roared their approval when Marais appeared first in the international arrivals hall. With his boots hanging around his neck, the Eastern Cape farmer wore the broadest of smiles.

"It was not an easy tour," he told the assembled press, "but the guys were determined to get the job done, and I am proud of them all."

The Springboks appeared to be surviving in isolation. They had won four of five Tests during 1971 and drawn the other, but Marais and his players were disappointed to discover their only international action in 1972 would be a solitary Test against a touring England team in Johannesburg; and the Bok captain was further dismayed when doctors ruled that the delayed effects of a detached retina meant he would not be fit to lead the side at Ellis Park.

Throughout the 1970s and 1980s, this pattern would become increasingly familiar. Inactivity and injury would combine to deny the Springboks momentum, any opportunity to build and develop. The team would virtually have to start from scratch every time they assembled to play a Test.

In Marais's absence, the selectors invited the experienced and admired flank forward, Piet Greyling, to lead South Africa against England. Approaching the end of a distinguished career, he accepted the challenge.

"It was an honour," Greyling recalls, "but I knew it was going to be difficult because so many guys had retired at the end of 1971. It would have been ideal to develop a new team on a tour, but we just had this one Test at Ellis Park. Even so, we felt we would win. Jan Ellis and I had just been to Edinburgh to play in the Centenary match of the Scottish Rugby Union, and we had seen some of the top English players there. We felt reasonably confident."

Born at Zastron in the Free State, Greyling spent the happiest days of his childhood running around his father's tobacco farm, at a place called Hartley, 50 kilometres south of Salisbury, capital of Southern Rhodesia. When he turned 14, however, his father believed he was becoming "too much of an Englishman" and decided the boy should be sent back to South Africa to continue his education at the staunchly Afrikaans Sentraal Hoërskool in Bloemfontein.

"My favourite sport was soccer," Greyling recalls, "and I told the teachers at Sentraal that I wanted to play soccer and cricket. They laughed and said they were very sorry, but there was no choice: Sentraal played rugby and athletics. I hardly touched a rugby ball until I was 15 years old."

He started making up for lost time, representing Free State schools within two years and playing for the Western Transvaal under-19 team when he moved on to study at the University of Potchefstroom. But Greyling was a Rhodesian at heart, and he excitedly returned home to start farming in Hartley. Before long, he was thriving at the back of the Mashonaland scrum.

The 20-year-old was selected to replace the legendary Des van Jaarsveldt as eighthman in the Rhodesian team, and the following season he was invited to Springbok trials. Greyling was becoming renowned for his speed over 15 metres, harassing flyhalves into errors. He would tirelessly develop his pace by leaning against a tree as if it were the side of the scrum and then launching himself like a missile on a 15-metre sprint to the point of breakdown.

Day after day.

Excellence was earned not by luck, but in sweat.

In 1964, restrictions placed on tobacco production in Rhodesia persuaded him reluctantly to leave the farm and head south once again. He began work as a sales rep for South African Breweries, a typical rugby player's job of the day, and played two seasons for Northern Transvaal. In 1967, he was transferred to work in Bloemfontein where he started to represent Free State.

By general consent, his Springbok debut against France in 1967 was long overdue: "Many people thought I was too skinny for international rugby," Greyling recalls, "and that is why I missed the 1965 tour to New Zealand. But in 1967 the loose forward combination was Jan Ellis, Tom Bedford and me and we clicked as a trio. Tom was the crafty player with plenty of ability, Jan was the attacking guy, a master of running with the ball, and I was the quick defender."

Ellis, Bedford and Greyling became renowned and admired wherever the game was played. "They were golden years," he recalls. "Jan Ellis and I played 24 Tests together but we never once played against each other."

Greyling was never dropped in his rugby career, not once. He missed three Test matches in 1968 after breaking his collarbone but, aside from this interlude, had not missed a single international match from his debut in 1967 through to the one-off Test against England at Ellis Park in 1972. Then aged 30, the new captain had long since earned the respect of his team-mates.

Hooker John Pullin captained what appeared a mediocre England touring team widely dismissed as also-rans. However, on the other side of Johannesburg at the Holiday Inn, the home team was also in disarray.

Greyling looked across the foyer at a tall man in a tracksuit. He could see this was a player, one of his team-mates, but the captain had no idea who it was, where he came from, or what position he played. Such awkward situations would become familiar in a team that played so infrequently.

The captain introduced himself. "Hello, I'm Piet Greyling."

"Er, hello, I'm Piet du Plessis."

"Oh, all right … the Northern Transvaal lock?"

"That's right."

"Good to meet you. We're training this afternoon, OK?"

"Fine."

The Springbok team bore the hallmarks of selectors with too much time on their hands, resolved to make the most of an increasingly rare chance actually to pick a national side and unequivocally demonstrate their wisdom. Ray Carlson, a centre, was inexplicably switched with Tonie Roux, a fullback, and Dawie Snyman was chosen as flyhalf in a team that raised eyebrows.

"We trained on the Thursday," Greyling recalls, "and we were pushed all over the field by the Diggers scrum. In 24 Tests, I had learned how to recognise when things were wrong, and things were very, very wrong. We were a bunch of strangers who had been thrown together with no preparation. Everyone said we would hammer England, but I knew we were in trouble."

The captain's fears were realised on the Saturday afternoon at Ellis Park when, to general astonishment, England scored the only try of a scrappy contest and emerged with an 18-9 victory. Dawie Snyman had kicked three penalties for the home side, but the team had failed to function as a unit. Defeat was startling and unexpected, but the Springboks had few complaints.

Greyling reflects ruefully: "In modern rugby, it is the coach who is criticised when the team loses, but, in our day, it was the captain who copped the flak and I copped it second to none after we lost to England. The selectors had picked the side but people still criticised me for not switching the centre and fullback back to their proper positions. I found that very interesting.

"It was very hard. We all played badly. With so much going wrong, it was hard for me to see exactly where our problems began. I could sense the alarm bells were starting to ring for South African rugby. The supporters were becoming frustrated with sporadic, brief tours and even then, it seemed as if the Springboks were too rusty and disorganised to win. It was depressing."

South Africa were scheduled to visit New Zealand in 1973 but, when that tour was cancelled, the celebrated flanker started to acknowledge his career had reached a natural conclusion. He would have preferred to end his last Test in far happier circumstances than the defeat against England, but Greyling duly retired from the game amid sustained and heartfelt praise.

"I had had my share," he recalls.

He has remained a popular, admired figure in and around the game ever since, supporting the regular reunions held to honour former players, maintaining and enjoying the cherished camaraderie of rugby. During the 1995 Rugby World Cup, Greyling was surprised to discover a tall Frenchman arriving unannounced at his house in Johannesburg. It was Benoit Dauga, the lock and his opponent in 1967 and 1968. The pair spent the following week together.

The aborted 1973 tour to New Zealand sent new waves of defiance and anger rippling through the South African rugby community, but the indefatigable Bedford continued to raise his voice of reason. He had been invited to play in New Zealand as an individual and, following discussions with Colin Meads and others, proposed that the top South African players would be able to continue playing international matches if they temporarily shed their national status as the Springboks and played under the colours of the Barbarians.

His creative and proactive initiative was prompted not by a selfish desire to play international rugby, but out of his conviction that the rugby players could serve as forces for reconciliation in South Africa and abroad.

"There was support for the idea around the rugby world," Bedford recalls, "and I proposed the concept in a memo to Dr Craven, but he was not concerned about isolation at the time because the Lions had confirmed they were coming to South Africa in 1974. I was frustrated. There was no real appetite to address the sports boycott in an open-minded way and find a solution. The public consensus was that we were doing nothing wrong, and we should just plough on regardless of anyone else, stubbornly insisting it was business as usual."

While Bedford was growing infuriated in Durban, 750 kilometres down the coast Hannes Marais was drifting away from the game in Port Elizabeth. His eye injury had ruled him out of most of the 1973 Currie Cup season and, as inactive month followed inactive month, he had started to focus his attention on studying for a PhD at the University of Port Elizabeth. With few regrets, he was beginning to accept his rugby career had drifted gently to a conclusion.

Then the telephone rang.

"Hannes, how are you feeling?"

It was Johan Claassen, the former Springbok captain and now a national selector, on the line once again.

"I'm OK."

"Don't forget, we're going to need you against the Lions. Experience will be crucial, and we need you to lead the team."

"Well, we will see."

Call by call, the warhorse prop was cajoled to start training again, to start running up the hill to the aloe on the horizon, and to prepare himself to lead the Springboks against the Lions. Marais was not too concerned by the prospect of the 1974 series. "We thought the Lions would be just another bunch of typical Engelse (English) who tried their best at the start but would be too soft and crack under the physical pressure of a tour to South Africa," he recalls. "That happened in 1968, and we assumed it would happen again."

Marais was aware how Willie-John McBride's Lions team had defeated the All Blacks in New Zealand in 1971; and, two years later, he had sat in a cinema and watched the same British players wear Barbarian jerseys and produce some of the finest rugby of all time against New Zealand in Cardiff.

And yet, he told himself, the Engelse were still the Engelse.

Soft.

What Marais and his compatriots did not realise was that the 1974 Lions would be built around two tremendously impressive men who had suffered at the hands of Springbok teams in 1962 and 1968, and resolved to learn the lessons of the Lions' generally undistinguished record in South Africa.

Willie-John McBride and Syd Millar originated from the same rugby club, Ballymena RFC in Northern Ireland, and they burned with the same raw desire to win a series in South Africa. Millar had toured the Republic three times and been converted to the local creed that set the scrum apart as the most important phase of the game. As the Lions coach, he understood that if his team were to upset the Springboks, they would first have to beat them in the scrums.

"We will be dedicated, rugged and well prepared," Millar told the British media before the team's departure, "but we are under no illusion about the size of this task. No touring squad has won a four-Test series in South Africa for 68 years. Indeed, I would rate playing the Springboks in South Africa as being much harder than playing the All Blacks in New Zealand."

Millar's respectful opinions were published in Johannesburg, Cape Town and Durban, and they succeeded in flattering most Springbok supporters into a false sense of security. Amid widespread delight that the Lions were coming at all, the country prepared for another momentous victory.

McBride was touring South Africa for the fifth time, and his approach was more blunt and uncompromising. In essence, he had had enough sand kicked in his face. In 1974, he and his tremendously talented team would play fine rugby and, when the need arose, they would also kick sand.

"We do not plan to be messed around," the captain announced

upon his arrival at Johannesburg airport; and he smiled broadly as he slipped two tablets of slow sodium into his mouth, the medicine that had been distributed to the tour squad to counter the effects of unaccustomed sweating.

In every way, the Lions were ready.

South Africans watched the early matches of the tour with great interest, and growing apprehension. A Test team of impressive proportions was starting to emerge from Millar's painstakingly planned selections. Ian McLauchlan, the Scot known as "Mighty Mouse", Bobby Windsor from Wales and the Englishman Fran Cotton combined as a formidable front row; Gordon Brown, the smiling, convivial Scot known as "Broon from Troon", and McBride locked the scrum; and the loose forward combination of Fergus Slattery of Ireland, Roger Uttley of England and Mervyn Davies of Wales assumed a lean and hungry look.

"That was a decent pack," Marais recalls, grinning at his understatement. By the end of the tour, the Lions had become legends.

Gareth Edwards and Phil Bennett presented a Welsh halfback pairing of impish skill, redoubtable bravery and plenty of common sense. Ian McGeechan and Dick Milliken held their own in midfield, and the "back three" were showered with golden praise. J.P.R. Williams of Wales towered at fullback, while J.J. Williams of Wales on the left and Andy Irvine of Scotland on the right needed no second invitation to carry the ball and run like the wind.

The mere recollection of these players will warm many hearts throughout the British Isles and Ireland, but the names resonate no less loudly in Benoni and Bloemfontein, in Pretoria or Potgietersrus, in Cape Town or Clocolan. The 1974 Lions arrived in South Africa as just Engelse but, in many ways, they never left. Even today, these men are recalled with awe and respect.

If it is possible to identify one day when South Africa awoke to the power of this touring team, then it was 25 May 1974, when the Lions played Eastern Province at the Boet Erasmus Stadium. With Marais leading his province against the tourists, the softening-up process was expected to begin.

As the Lions spread the ball wide from the second lineout of the game, an Eastern Province forward charged into Edwards, roughly knocking the scrumhalf to the ground. Three minutes later, the Welshman was heavily challenged, again without the ball. Edwards appealed to Van der Vyfer, the referee, and then to Marais, protesting at the foul play. Shoulders shrugged.

Cotton looked at Brown, Brown looked at McLauchlan. They all looked at McBride and the now-infamous call "99" was audibly uttered. At the next lineout, the Lions forgot about the ball and ran amok, throwing punches in all directions, laying into their South African opponents, standing firm. They had waited for this moment to demonstrate, emphatically, they would not be "softened".

Calm was restored and Edwards played the remainder of the match with concussion, but the Lions had made their point and won comfortably; and South Africans realised this nut would not be so easy to crack.

"I was not aware of any special '99' call," Marais recalls. "When the Lions started punching, I just assumed one of our guys had done something stupid to make them so angry. That sometimes happened in the EP side. We always had one or two forwards who tended to play on the edge.

"The '99' call is a good story, and it has been told again and again, but it soon became clear to us the Lions had decided they would not come second in the physical exchanges. In this respect, they were different to the British teams we had known before. The first time I scrummed down against Ian McLauchlan, he took me roof high. He clearly meant business."

It is hard to exaggerate the level of anticipation ahead of the first Test in Cape Town. Through the week before the Saturday, it seemed as if nothing else mattered to white South Africans. Newspaper columnists and radio announcers analysed every aspect of an event whose significance clearly reached beyond the boundaries of mere sport. This was about isolated white South Africa putting its prestige, its self-esteem and its reputation on the line.

Isolated she certainly was. A succession of Olympic Games, the long and tedious Watergate scandal in the U.S.A., a fierce war in the Middle East were all distant noises in a world far removed from a lonely African country that was now widely condemned for her intractable, oppressive politics.

Victory on the rugby field would set white spirits soaring, and all would be well in the world. Defeat would prompt deep and dark depression.

The Test match even dominated the breakfast table conversation across the water from the city, at the prison on Robben Island where Nelson Mandela, Steve Tshwete and other leaders of the African liberation struggle were serving life sentences. The prisoners fervently supported the Lions.

As nerves frayed and the pressure increased, Danie Craven drew closer to the Springbok team and the process to determine strategy. As president of the Board, he had no official role in such matters but, as the doyen of Springbok rugby, he was eminently qualified to seize the reins.

The weather forecast predicted rain, and Craven powerfully advocated a "horses for courses" selection policy in which the panel chose a Springbok team suited to playing in wet weather. Marais was not entirely happy, believing that if a player was good enough to play for South Africa, he was good enough to play in any conditions. Inevitably, Craven's opinion prevailed.

Further discussions took place on the morning of the match. Jan Boland Coetzee, a Springbok who farmed in the Cape, studied the weather and claimed the wind was going to change direction at around four o'clock. Craven listened to the flanker and decided that, if Marais won the toss, South Africa should play with the wind in the first half because it would change at half time.

Once again, the Springbok captain sat silent. Throughout his long career, he had played into the wind in the first half, preferring to set his team against the elements when they were fresh. Just before kick-off, Marais did win the toss and, against his better judgement, he indicated to the referee that South Africa would play with the wind in the first half, as Craven wanted.

Marais recalls: "It was unsettling because we were doing the little things differently to the way we had always done them. Everyone seemed quite happy with the team that had been selected, but it appeared as if the Lions' form in the early part of the tour was rattling us out of our routine. We thought we would win the Test, but these niggling issues started to sow doubts."

Down the corridor at Newlands, the Lions were preparing for an almighty struggle. The opening match is pivotal in any four-Test series, and Willie-John McBride implored his players to focus on the stated goal of their tour: to become the first Lions to win a series in South Africa since 1908.

"This is where it counts," the mountainous Ulsterman roared.

Gareth Edwards, eyes aflame, picked up the theme.

"Listen, boys," he said. "I remember when we were in exactly this position in 1968. When we run onto the field, you will hear the most deafening roar in the world. It will hit you straight in the face and go right to your knees. But when the Boks run out, it will be like an atomic explosion. You will feel like fainting. You will wonder if we can ever beat them. We can. We are better equipped; we have the ability and the belief. Say that to yourself when they run out. Get them down to their true size, otherwise they will be all over us. Remember the planning and the coaching, and stick to the methods you know."

Marais led his team out with his head held high and, for long periods of a ferocious encounter, the Springboks held their own, to such an extent that it was hard to believe Millar's subsequently reported claim that he had known the Lions would win the series after only 10 minutes because their front row controlled the scrums. Twenty-twenty hindsight is a perfect science, but many observers who were at Newlands maintain the first Test could have gone either way.

The Lions won 12-3, with three Bennett penalties and a neat drop goal by Edwards outweighing Snyman's drop goal. In the dressing room afterwards, the Springbok captain was too disappointed and exhausted to mention that the wind had not, in point of fact, changed direction at half time.

"Defeat was not the end of the world," Marais remembers, "but we needed to stay calm and build upon what had been a respectable performance for a team that had not played a Test in two years. There is no doubt in my mind that, if we had kept that group of players together, we would have improved with every Test and matched the Lions by the end of the tour. I don't say we would have won the series, but we would have won one Test, maybe two."

The captain made his plea for calm and stability, but the selectors followed the populist logic that if the Springboks had lost, there must be something wrong, and if something is wrong, it must be put right. The revolutionary concept that the opposition might just be a better team than the Springboks was hitherto unknown in South African rugby. Thus, changes were imperative.

As captain, Marais was disappointed not to be consulted by the selectors when they were pondering the side for the second Test. As the veteran prop, he was doubly disappointed that his view was not sought before the panel reached a decision to discard the hooker, Piston van Wyk.

Spray-gun selection undermined his efforts to build confidence, spirit and stability within the squad. The Springboks gathered in Bloemfontein, riddled with uncertainty and self-doubt, burdened by the expectations of supporters who still expected them to recover and win the series.

In stark contrast, the Lions were relaxed and focused. McBride and Millar would habitually sit by the hotel swimming pool, enjoying the South African sun while they plotted the humiliation of the South African rugby team. The Irishmen would alternately frown in deep discussion and laugh uproariously. At one stage, McBride would strike out and rip Millar's shirt. Millar would respond by tearing at the captain's shirt; and the two men would both be left bare-chested, indulging in the tomfoolery of happy chaps enjoying the time of their lives.

Marais sweated through training, tried everything he knew, cracked jokes to relieve the pressure, offered encouragement wherever he could, but he knew he was whistling in the storm. He would glance at his players as they trained, as they ate meals, as they signed autographs, and he recognised fear in their faces, fear of defeat, fear of being dropped, fear of being mocked.

By five o'clock on that warm Saturday afternoon in Bloemfontein, even the captain's worst fears had been exceeded by the horrible reality writ large across the scoreboard at the Free State Stadium: SUID-AFRIKA 9 LIONS 28. His team had collapsed, suffering the largest Test defeat in Springbok history. Marais sat silent, stunned and sad in the changing room, as Craven and the selectors stood by, distraught. The atmosphere was desperate, grim and funereal.

Five tries to nil.

There was nothing to say.

The selectors reacted in predictable fashion, dropping no fewer than 11 players from the side humiliated in Bloemfontein. They also staged a mini-trial in search of a brand new scrumhalf, from which it emerged that Gerrie Sonnekus, an eighthman for his province, would wear the No. 9 jersey.

Roy McCullum and Paul Bayvel were both injured, but there were several other Currie Cup scrumhalves available. The Sonnekus selection would become the symbol of the Springbok selection chaos of 1974, the trademark decision of a panel who, in their desperation to win, lost their way.

No fewer than 33 players would represent South Africa in the four Tests; of these, 22 were making their debut. These young men were as infantry, hurled into battle by careless generals without a plan, meagre Lion fodder. The tourists used a grand total of 17 players during the four Tests.

Marais recalls: "We had made changes after the first Test, and now there were more changes after the second Test. It felt as if we were playing a scratch team of debutants for the third match in a row. It was impossible to combine as a unit or to develop any understanding. We were in trouble."

The Springbok captain banked on some respite when he returned to play for Eastern Province between the second and third Tests against the Lions, but was bemused to discover the provincial selectors had taken a decision to relieve him of the Eastern Province captaincy. They said they wanted to ease pressure on Marais, but they had never discussed the move with him.

With friends like these, Marais didn't need enemies. "It was a neat vote of confidence in me at a difficult time," he remembers dryly, and he suddenly swats away the memories with a sweep of his hand. "It was a difficult time in my life, but it is water under the bridge now." He looks up, smiles thinly.

So the 1974 Springboks had reached a point of no return. Two down with two to play, they needed to win the third Test in Port Elizabeth or be remembered as the first South African team to lose a major series at home since 1908. Marais led his players out at his home ground, hoping against hope that the traditional gees would somehow prove his team's salvation.

Moaner van Heerden and Johan de Bruyn had been chosen to bring steel into the Springbok second row, and they held the Lions in check for much of the first half. De Bruyn made an impact not least when his glass eye was dislodged, found on the turf and shoved back into its socket. His opposite number, Gordon Brown, dined out on the story for many years to come.

Yet, as the Springboks began to tire, the Lions calmly seized control and eased to a 26-9 victory. Sheer class and planning had overpowered sheer desire, and the series was won. McBride raised his hands in triumph, acknowledging his joy at what he ranked as "the greatest victory of my career".

Marais walked slowly from the field, glancing briefly over his left shoulder towards the stand reserved for coloured supporters. While white South Africans were coming to terms with a desperate disappointment, their brown compatriots were stepping up the celebrations. "Through all my playing years, I never saw the people of colour supporting the Springboks," the captain recalls with a measure of understanding rather than resentment. "They always supported the opposition, and, obviously, the 1974 Lions were their greatest heroes."

He reached the changing room, showered silently and quietly headed for the post-match reception where, as Springbok captain, he delivered a gracious speech, congratulating the Lions on their series victory and expressing his hope that his players would redeem themselves in the final Test.

His official duties discharged, Marais left the function, threw his kitbag into the back seat of his car and was soon accelerating away from the Boet Erasmus Stadium towards the N2 highway. He reached Cookhouse within two hours, and night was falling by the time he approached the farm.

At last alone, at last far from the peering eyes and criticism, he sat briefly on the stoep and gazed up at the aloe etched black on the twilight horizon at the top of the hill. He had needed to get away, to escape from the pressure and the ignominy of defeat. Alone with his thoughts, he sat for several hours.

It was past one o'clock in the morning by the time he tried to sleep but he had damaged his neck during the second half, and the pain meant he could not relax or think properly. He sat again. Soon dawn was creeping over the hill, and another day was starting all around him. He would survive. By Monday evening, he was ready to stand up and face the world again.

South Africans were generally outraged by the thumping defeats. People acknowledged the Lions had proved far stronger than anyone expected, and yet they continued to focus on the shortcomings of the home side. This sense of fury was particularly acute in Durban, where the tourists arrived to play against Natal on the Saturday before the fourth Test. In wielding their spray gun, the selectors had not called upon a single player from Natal ranks.

Tommy Bedford captained this provincial team with a point to prove, and led from the front, at one stage brawling with J.P.R. Williams. The fiery Welshman incensed the King's Park crowd by showering punches on their local hero, but the tourists eventually recovered their composure and pulled clear in the final quarter to preserve their cherished unbeaten record on tour.

Proud of his team's performance, Bedford approached the podium at the post-match function with purpose. To the discomfort of the Natal Rugby Union, he had bravely continued to raise his voice against the status quo within South African rugby, and he was clearly not going to waste this opportunity to address an audience that included the five national selectors.

"Ladies and gentlemen," Bedford began, echoing his words of four years earlier, during the All Black tour in 1970, "allow me first of all to welcome the five Springbok selectors to the Last Outpost of the British Empire."

To general laughter, he then proceeded to show five extravagant V signs around the room as he swung his right hand in five wide arcs, "Welcome to you! And you! And you! And you! And you!" To nobody's great surprise, the eighthman was not included in the Springbok team for the fourth Test.

"It may have been crude but I was angry," Bedford recalls. "Nobody in the game was saying anything about what was going wrong with our rugby, and that seemed the only way I could express what I felt."

Bedford played two more seasons for Natal and eventually coached their Currie Cup side before drifting away from the game. He clung to his hopes for a better future for South African rugby, arranging two tours by mixed teams to the United States during the 1980s; and he later proved instrumental in facilitating a series of meetings between Craven's South African Rugby Board and the African National Congress. He has lived in London since 1990.

For more than 20 years since his return from Oxford in 1968, Bedford had been perhaps the only Springbok rugby player who consistently, fearlessly spoke out against racism at the heart of the game. While most were content to toe the official line and be cocooned from reality, Bedford seemed driven to address the problems of his era. Whether engaging demonstrators in debate, or meeting with representatives of the South African Rugby Association (for black players) and the South African Rugby Federation (for coloured players), he never gave up his belief that creative and innovative solutions were possible.

As reward, he has often been labelled as "bitter". This is a gross injustice. The B in Bedford stands for brave, not bitter. Who else cared so passionately for the future of Springbok rugby that he was prepared to jeopardise his career and his popularity by speaking out for justice and dialogue?

Nobody.

In this history of Springbok captains, Tom Bedford stands alone ...

Hannes Marais avidly read the newspaper reports of the Lions' unseemly struggle against Natal, and was encouraged by the suggestions the tourists may be losing their edge. He was further emboldened when lock John Williams and hooker Piston van Wyk were recalled to the side to play the fourth Test.

For the first time in the series, the captain sensed a positive mood as the team gathered at their hotel in Johannesburg. "The series was lost," he recalls, "and I suppose the pressure drained away, but we were still desperate to avoid the 4-0 whitewash. The atmosphere was very positive."

At Ellis Park, at last, the Springbok front row put the wheel on the Lions eight and began to apply pressure on Edwards at scrumhalf, thereby denying the tourists the momentum that had enabled them to run riot in the second and third Tests. The 75 000 spectators sighed with relief: at least, this fourth Test was a contest, and the match appeared to be heading for an honourable 13-13 draw when, in the last minute, Fergus Slattery took a pass from J.P.R. Williams, dashed for glory, and appeared to score the winning try.

No try! Referee Max Baise ruled the ball was not grounded, awarded a five-metre scrum and, moments later, blew the final whistle. The official departed the field with enraged Lions shouting insults at his back.

Slattery did score a fair try, but the angry Lions conveniently overlooked the fact that, as photographs later proved, Uttley's try earlier in the game should not have been awarded. One referee's error had cancelled out another, as it so often does, and the draw was a fair conclusion to the series.

An element of Springbok pride had been salvaged at Ellis Park, but this crushing series defeat destroyed for all time the team's aura of invincibility when playing at home. Winners by three Tests to nil and 10 tries to one, the 1974 Lions had left an indelible scar on the face of South African rugby.

Yet Marais had survived. Throughout this turbulent series, the Springbok captain had maintained his dignity, declined to make excuses, refused to assign blame, and never stopped trying. These chivalrous qualities were appreciated not only by his beleaguered team-mates, but also by the Lions.

"Of all the Springboks, we felt sorry for Hannes," Gareth Edwards recalls. "He was one of the world's outstanding props and personally played very well in the series, but he was never given a settled side. The press were fiercely critical of him because he was on the losing side. The Lions got better and better while the great hero of many a Springbok victory grew visibly smaller.

"Only when the final Test was shared did Hannes receive any credit. He deserved better because he was not only a great player, he was a gentleman. His defeats were bitter and hard to swallow, but he was invariably the first in our changing room with a can of beer after the match. Hannes Marais was not used to losing Test matches, but he knew how to do it with honour."

Many years on, Marais clearly does not enjoy recalling the events of 1974. His recollections are punctuated by glances to the floor, sighs, wry smiles. Again and again he says: "It's all water under the bridge now." The wounds have healed long ago, of course, but some of the pain lingers.

"Many people have told me I should not have come out of what was virtual retirement to play against the Lions," he says. "They say someone like Morné du Plessis should have captained the team because he was more enterprising than me, but I have always disagreed with that view.

"I don't believe any captain could have made a difference to the result and I was perfectly happy that it was me, a veteran at the end of his career, who took the criticism that followed the defeats. If Morné had captained the team, the 1974 Lions could have ruined him. He would have had to carry that stigma for the rest of his career, and he might never have been allowed the time to develop into the exceptional Springbok captain that he later became. For that reason alone, I am pleased that I led the side against the Lions in 1974."

Marais had played in Springbok teams that defeated the Lions in 1968, the All Blacks and Australia, but the irony is that none of these triumphs brought him as many opportunities later in his life as the defeat in 1974. He and his wife have been invited to travel to Britain to attend no fewer than three 1974 reunions; and, on each occasion, he would sit and smile graciously as the heroes regaled one another with tales of their triumphant tour to South Africa.

It was during one of these dinners that Stuart McKinney, one of the Lions, walked over to Marais and told the old Springbok that he felt so bad because he had to sit and listen to all these old stories. "I want you to have my Lions blazer," said McKinney, pulling the blazer off his shoulders as he spoke. "Go on, take it, Hannes. You have earned it by listening to all of us."

Like the rider who falls off his horse but is determined to get back into the saddle as soon as possible, the Springboks were grateful for the opportunity to tour France eight weeks after their defeat against the Lions. The team urgently needed to win again, to regain confidence and restore their reputations. Marais accepted the invitation to lead his country one more time.

In ordinary circumstances, the 33-year-old captain of a team so severely defeated would have been asked to step aside, but Marais was not regarded as an ordinary captain. He remained the senior player, a pillar of the squad, and his standing among his team-mates was undiminished by defeat.

French rugby was suffering its own difficulties at the time, and the South Africans were grateful to win their first three matches and establish a victorious momentum, yet the two Tests presented the core challenge and, once again, the captain summoned a supreme effort to inspire his side.

After 19 minutes of the first Test in Toulouse, Marais chased a kick ahead and sprinted to reach the breakdown point, where he flattened a French defender in a memorable tackle and heroically secured possession that was spun wide for Willem Stapelberg to pin back his ears and score in the corner.

South Africa won the match 13-4 and, two weeks later, secured the series with a close-fought 10-8 second-Test win in Paris. The Springboks had returned to basics, concentrating on the scrums and lineouts, letting the ball down the line within striking distance of the try line, playing the percentages.

A solitary, narrow, careless midweek defeat against the West of France in Angouleme denied Marais the unique distinction of once again leading his team home from an overseas tour with an unbeaten record. In the face of occasional bouts of anti-apartheid protesters and sustained rough play on the field, he again proved himself an exceptional leader in adversity.

Marais consistently rose to the challenge. When coach Johan Claassen fell seriously ill midway through the tour, Ian Kirkpatrick was summoned to take over the coaching role, but he would only arrive eight days later. With the minimum of fuss, the captain took the coaching responsibilities in his stride.

From his initial appointment as Springbok captain in 1971 through to the tour of France in 1974, Marais had grown accustomed to adversity. His players had been dogged by demonstrators on tour and by fierce critics when playing at home, but his unwavering capacity to be honest and straightforward in word and deed enabled him to emerge with everyone's respect.

He announced his retirement from international rugby upon his return to South Africa, amid widespread gratification that this most illustrious career should have closed on a winning note. "It was the end of the road for me," he reflects. "There was not the slightest doubt in my mind."

Marais continued to turn out for his residence XV in the University of Port Elizabeth league for five more seasons until, during a match against Despatch, he tore his hamstring, damaged his ankle and collapsed to the ground. "People were laughing at me," he recalls. "That was the final straw."

He finally retired just short of his 40th birthday, but remained close

1. Bennie Osler (right) with his brother, Stan *(Sunday Times)*
2. Felix du Plessis *(Harold Strange Library)* | 3. Basie Viviers *(Harold Strange Library)*
4. Hennie Muller *(Sunday Times)* | 5. Danie Craven *(Sunday Times)*

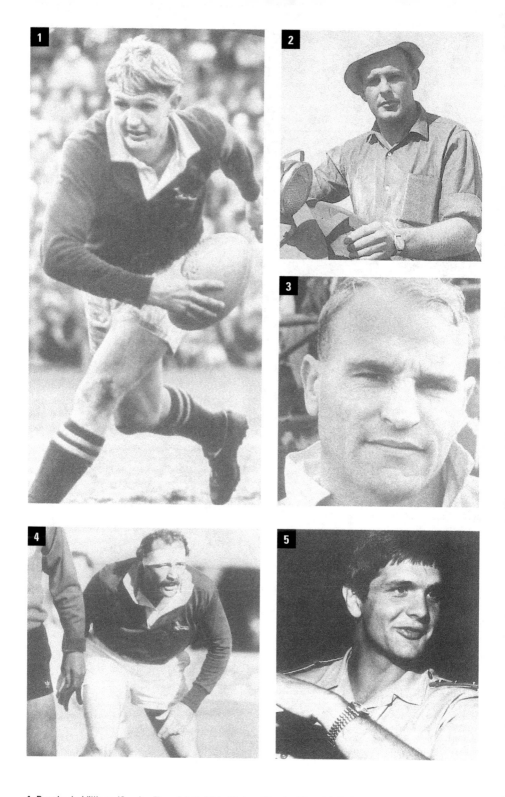

1. Dawie de Villiers *(Sunday Times)* | **2.** Abie Malan *(Sunday Times)* | **3.** Nelie Smith *(Sunday Times)*
4. Wynand Claassen *(Sunday Times)* | **5.** Theuns Stofberg *(Sunday Times)*

6. André Vos *(Sunday Times)* | **7.** Stephen Fry *(private collection)* | **8.** Johan Claassen *(private collection)* | **9.** Gary Teichmann *(Sunday Times)* | **10.** Corné Krige *(private collection)*

1. Avril Malan (centre) rises high *(private collection)* | **2.** Morné du Plessis (right) *(private collection)* | **3.** Hannes Marais (right) *(private collection)*

to the heartbeat of South African rugby, using his knowledge and experience variously as coach of both the University of Port Elizabeth and Eastern Province under-20 teams and, briefly, assistant coach to the Eastern Province side.

First appointed to serve as a Springbok selector from 1982 until 1986, he was then recalled to the national panel for a second term from 1993 through to the Rugby World Cup in 1995. "Prof Marais", as he had become respectfully known throughout the game, could always, always be relied upon to offer a straightforward, sincere and honest opinion. Nothing less.

Hannes Marais was fated to lead South Africa during a period when the Springbok team was relentlessly besieged but, through every trial, he proved himself physically and emotionally equipped to withstand any adversity. This prop, farmer and academic may have been besieged, but he was never broken.

9 THE MODERN TOTEM

The tall, angular boy was sitting comfortably as the veteran teacher ran through the names of the new boys in his class. It was the opening day of term at one of South Africa's foremost schools, Grey College, Bloemfontein.

"Ah, Retief. I remember your father."

Ewie Cronjé, Afrikaans teacher, had lived and worked for many decades in and around the sporting and education communities of the Free State capital, developing an encyclopaedic knowledge of who was who. Universally admired, he took gentle pleasure in recognising the new intake.

"Yes, Retief ... your father opened the bowling for Old Greys, didn't he? I remember he also played a few matches for Free State."

"Yes, sir."

The teacher moved down the list, recalling that Potgieter's father had played scrumhalf for the University of Free State team, the Shimlas, and how Strydom's father had scored a superb century for Grey against Queen's College. And still the tall, angular boy sat comfortably, and now expectantly because his name appeared next on the list.

"Du Plessis?"

Mr Cronje paused for dramatic effect.

"Er ... and who is your dad?"

The smile disappeared from the boy's face as an audible snigger rippled around the classroom. He was aghast, suddenly humiliated. Cronje's kindly face slowly creased into a playful smile.

"It's all right, Morné," he said finally. "I know your dad."

Everyone knew his dad. Felix du Plessis had captained the Springboks to three consecutive Test victories against New Zealand in 1949, securing a special place in the affections of South African supporters. Unbeknown to anyone in that Grey College classroom, the boy would grow up to follow in his father's footsteps. Morné du Plessis would also become a great Springbok captain.

When the 26-year-old eighthman was appointed to succeed the legendary Hannes Marais and lead South Africa in two home Tests against France in 1975, he was regarded as a potentially exceptional leader. By the time he retired six seasons later in the wake of victories against the South American Jaguars, the Lions and France, his qualities were recognised worldwide.

Danie Craven often espoused the theory that rugby talent is carried in the genes, that Springboks somehow breed Springboks, and he would cheerfully cite the example of the Du Plessis family as his evidence.

Morné du Plessis was born in Vereeniging on 21 October 1949, several months after his father had led South Africa against the All Blacks, but this was not the extent of his remarkable sporting pedigree: his mother, Pat, captained the South African women's hockey side, and his uncle, Horace Smethurst, led the South African soccer team. Sport ran hard in the family, but Du Plessis insists he grew up with neither a sense of burden nor a sense of destiny.

"There were only two sporting photographs on the wall in our house," he reflects, "one of my mother in the hockey team and one of the 1949 Springboks with my father as captain. That was all, and I don't think we ever spent much time talking about what my parents had achieved in sport.

"Perhaps the greatest legacy my father left me was the way he handled that situation. Everyone knew I was Felix du Plessis's son, but he was always very quiet and humble. I hope I have been the same with my son."

Du Plessis attracted attention as an all-round sporting talent at Klerksdorp Primary School, but he started to focus on rugby and cricket soon after his arrival at Grey College. Under the adept guidance of cricket teachers Ewie Cronjé and Des Schonegevel, he developed into a gifted fast bowler, becoming only the third boy from the Free State to play in the South African Schools XI.

"I owe a huge debt to Ewie Cronjé," he recalls. "He was a great teaser in the classroom, and that incident in my very first class at Grey when he pretended not to know my father was the start of an exceptional pupil-teacher relationship that extended through my school days. Des Schonegevel also gave me a love for cricket. At my first cricket practice, he told me in a very soft voice that it was not possible to be a cricketer without looking like a cricketer. It was important to him that sportsmen dressed properly. I took that on board."

Grey College, source of so many Springboks across so many codes, was turning another sparkling model off the production line.

Felix du Plessis owned a bottle store in Stilfontein on the West Rand and, as respite after the busy Christmas period, every Boxing Day he would take his son Morné to Johannesburg to watch cricket at the Wanderers. Year after year, father and son would set off on what became a cherished ritual.

Up early in the morning, they would stop on the way to eat a full breakfast at a place called Drie Riviere, drive on to the northern suburbs of Johannesburg, and park outside the house of a family friend, Ted Sceales, before walking down the hill to the stadium. Their seats, organised by contacts at South African Breweries, would be ideal, in the main stand, behind the bowler's arm.

And they would sit together and watch the cricket, most often the opening day of a Test match. Travelling to Johannesburg was a big event for the young man. Joining a huge crowd to marvel at the likes of Graeme Pollock and Denis Lindsay would always rank among the highlights of his year ... and he would sit beside his father, and watch, and wonder, and dream.

Inspired by his heroes, Du Plessis successfully pursued his cricket career to a point where he played three provincial matches for Western Province before, while he was at university, the demands of training forced him to choose between cricket and rugby. With regret, he decided to fold away his flannels.

He had initially struggled on the rugby field at Grey, first being moved from flyhalf to centre because everyone in the school recognised a young man named Dawie Snyman was the most gifted No. 10; then, at senior level, being shunted to fullback because he was considered too slow to play centre.

His fortunes suddenly changed at training one solemn Tuesday afternoon after Grey had been defeated by their great rivals, Queen's College. The admired school rugby coach, Stoney Steenkamp, gathered the downhearted team together and declared wisely: "We lost the game in the lineouts."

As he spoke, the coach slowly ran an outstretched finger along the players that surrounded him. "You," he said, pointing directly at Du Plessis. "Yes, you, come … slot (lock)." Thus admitted to the pack, he swiftly solved the team's lineout problems and thrived as a clever, mobile forward.

In the young student's mind, Stellenbosch stood apart as the most exciting and awe-inspiring university in the country, and when he matriculated from Grey he made his way to the whitewashed haven outside Cape Town. Du Plessis had not secured a place in a hostel when he arrived on campus, but a telephone call from his father to his old rugby friend, Danie Craven, warden at Wilgenhof, yielded a room in this preferred koshuis for promising and gifted sportsmen.

He was soon accelerating on a golden highway from Grey through Maties, where he was switched to the back of the scrum, and on towards the pinnacle of the game. In 1970, at the age of 21, he was selected to make his début for Western Province against Griqualand West. The following season, the lanky eighthman was elevated again, invited to attend a full week of Springbok trials ahead of the imminent tour to Australia.

Everything was happening so quickly, and, as the top 80 rugby players in South Africa assembled at a Cape Town hotel, Du Plessis took the opportunity to secure a seat in the foyer and enjoy the passing parade. He found it hard to believe he had been included in this company.

"Morné, I would like you to captain the E team."

Johan Claassen, the formidable national selector, interrupted the rookie's wide-eyed sightseeing. "This is your team for tomorrow," announced the former Springbok captain, presenting a list. "Please arrange a team meeting tonight, so I can come and watch how you give the team talk."

Du Plessis scanned the team sheet, recognising the names of established players with many years of Currie Cup experience. Why should they listen to him, a mere laaitie (lightweight)? He swallowed hard, headed for the hotel reception to find out the room numbers, and was soon walking the corridors, list in hand, knocking on doors and inviting his players to the team meeting.

Room 212 … Peter Cronje and Peter Swanson.

He knocked on the door.

"Yes?"

"Er, hello, I'm Morné du Plessis."

"Yes?"

"Well, I am captain of the E team tomorrow, and, umm, you are both in the team, and please come to a meeting downstairs at seven."

The two experienced players gazed at the gibbering youngster standing in their doorway, and burst out laughing. "It was embarrassing," Du Plessis reflects. "Peter Cronje became a great mate of mine and, many years later, he took great pleasure in telling me how I looked such an idiot with my list."

Recovering from this blow to his morale, the young Stellenbosch captain eventually managed to hold the meeting as requested and delivered his team talk, with Claassen sitting in the corner of the room. He played well, his team won the game, and on the Saturday night he was selected as the eighthman understudy to Tom Bedford in the 1971 Springbok squad to tour Australia.

Du Plessis had emerged from his pure pedigree to establish a remarkable track record of honours and achievement, and his education at international level was enhanced by the management decision that the young eighthman setting out on his first tour should room in Australia with Frik du Preez, the great lock playing his last Springbok tour. The torch was being passed.

"I kept my eye on Morné," recalls Johan Claassen, who was coaching the South African side, "and there were times during that tour when I was worried he was developing a loose and undisciplined attitude. I called him aside and told him he should leave behind that carefree student approach if he wanted to realise his tremendous potential and become a great player.

"I had known Morné since he was a child because his father, Felix, used to be manager of the Western Transvaal team, and he would often bring his son with him. I admired Morné very much, but some people saw me talking to him in Australia and deduced I had something against him. That was not true. In fact, I spoke to him because I was so keen he should succeed."

Du Plessis thrived on tour, seizing his opportunity when Bedford suffered an injury in the opening match and establishing himself in the Test team for three Tests against the Wallabies. He relished international rugby, and was astonished rather than upset by the persistent demonstrations. "I was genuinely surprised so many people could be so vociferously opposed to our country. I began to wonder how we could have angered these people so much," he recalls, "but it would be untrue to say I was preoccupied. I was young and keen, and desperate to retain my place in the Test side. The rugby was everything."

Named as a reserve for the Test against England in 1972, Du Plessis was recalled to the Springbok team for the series against the Lions, but then became one of 11 players dropped after the catastrophic second-Test defeat. Critics had started to suggest the eighthman tended to play too loose and failed to meet the physical challenge of Test rugby because he was too soft.

When he was overlooked as captain of the South African Gazelles team, a young squad of emerging talent, to tour Argentina in 1974, some observers were tempted to suggest the Du Plessis magic was wearing thin.

"It became an issue of controversy," he reflects. "My father had steadfastly declined to be involved in my rugby career, to the point of scarcely ever watching me play at school and university, but he was incensed by the Gazelles selection. He was adamant the Broederbond were trying to block my career."

Felix du Plessis complained to Craven, and also approached the convenor of the Gazelles selection committee, inevitably Johan Claassen. "Felix was very angry with me," the professor reflects, "but I told him Morné would certainly be Springbok captain one day. He asked about the Gazelles. I told him not to worry about that, but I realised we had made a mistake."

Du Plessis was reinstated in the Springbok squad for the tour to France at the end of 1974, played in both Tests, and appeared to be in pole position to succeed Hannes Marais as Springbok captain when the French team visited South Africa early in 1975. Weathered by his share of trauma and tribulations, the Western Province eighthman seemed ready to lead his country.

The trials were held in Potchefstroom and, on a hard field baked by a hot sun, the Springbok captain-elect found himself being tugged and prodded by the talented B-team eighthman, Kleintjie Grobler. Renowned for his even temper, Du Plessis snapped and punched Grobler at a lineout. Moments later, he landed a blow on Boland Coetzee's face. Spectators were on their feet in the grandstand, shouting abuse, waving their fists. Not for the first time, this equitable man had impulsively placed himself in the midst of crazed chaos.

Tempers were soothed when Grobler was deservedly included as a flank in the team to play France and, following everyone's prediction, Du Plessis was confirmed as captain for the first Test at the Free State Stadium, Bloemfontein. His father was among the very first to offer his congratulations, with a firm shake of the hand, a proud gaze to the eye and a firm, disciplined "well done".

"I could see my father was tremendously proud," Du Plessis recalls, "but I sensed he was equally aware of the pressures the job would bring. He knew the Springbok captaincy was at once an honour and a burden. He was tremendously supportive of me, but we were not massively close. That was typical of the time. Father-son relationships are more like friendships today."

While cricket's first World Cup tournament was taking place in

England, with South African absent, the French squad arrived in the Republic without many leading players, all withdrawn citing pressure at work, but their novel concept of appointing Jacques Fouroux and Richard Astre as joint captains succeeded in welding a youthful side that performed above the generally modest expectations.

Du Plessis led a team fuelled by Moaner van Heerden and Kevin de Klerk in the second row, and sparked by Paul Bayvel, Peter Whipp and Dawie Snyman in the back line, all supported by the kicking talents of Gerald Bosch; and after an hour of the first Test at the Free State Stadium, South Africa led 35-9. However a courageous, stirring French fightback in the fourth quarter took the gloss from the home team's victory, eventually banked at 38-25.

The tourists adopted an overtly physical approach for the second Test at Loftus Versfeld and, amid the fists and hacks, Du Plessis demonstrated his rare talent for leadership by ensuring his players remained calm in the face of blatant provocation. Scotsman Norman Sanson, the first neutral referee to handle a series in South Africa, penalised the foul play, Gerald Bosch kicked a record 22 points, and the home team emerged with a 33-18 victory.

Du Plessis had made a victorious start as Springbok captain, and he also brought an enlightened vision to the role. From the start of his tenure, the young captain associated himself with campaigns to develop and expand South African rugby beyond its introverted white base. He excitedly led the first mixed team to play a touring side when he captained a South African Invitation XV, including two black players, two coloured players and 11 whites, to a ground-breaking and emotional 18-3 win over the French at Newlands.

Thoughtful by nature, imbued with a strong sense of right and wrong, Du Plessis rose to the occasion when called to stand for his principles, even if he incurred establishment displeasure in the process. He held no connections at all with the Broederbond. He was unequivocally his own man.

How then had he become Springbok captain? He had been appointed to lead the side simply because his claim was so overwhelming, his capacity to lead so far beyond dispute, that other considerations were swept aside. His prominent status may have caused some unease in the shadows, but Du Plessis only used his position to become a potent force for good in the game.

Through six seasons as the dominant player in South African rugby, this Springbok captain emerged as the antithesis of the uncouth arrogance and bleak insensitivity for which the squad was from time to time resented. In speeches and at media conferences, his inclination was to be open and welcoming, humble and empathetic. Quiet and occasionally diffident by nature, he did not seek conflict or confrontation; yet, once challenged, he would not back down.

"I just wanted to do my best," Du Plessis recalls. "Even today, I am in awe of the position, of being the Springbok captain. I still wake up and think, hell, was that really me? It is something that I have never taken for granted. I was carefree and almost irresponsible as a youngster, but the captaincy meant I was suddenly responsible for something important. It changed me. I have often wondered what might have happened if I had not been made captain."

On the farms and in the *dorps* (small towns), in the suburbs and the cities, South African supporters had been consoled by away and home victories against France, but it was generally accepted that the lingering shame of humiliation against the Lions in 1974 would only be cleansed by a major series victory.

Du Plessis was set a clear challenge.

Beat the All Blacks in 1976.

Andy Leslie led the New Zealand squad to South Africa through a chorus of international protest – but it was this rugby tour, and not the Olympic Games in Montreal, that mattered in the tiny corners of the sporting globe occupied by New Zealanders and white South Africans. African countries registered their protest by deciding to boycott the Olympics in 1976, declining to compete with athletes from New Zealand, the country that played with apartheid.

South African rugby supporters shrugged their shoulders at the disruption of mainstream international sport. It wasn't their problem, but the Olympic boycott dragged the Springbok name further into disrepute. Whatever the history and the talents of the players, a global consensus was tiring of the constant controversy, starting to wish the Springboks would simply disappear.

For Du Plessis and his players this was unfortunate, but they were still the Springboks, still ranked among the leading rugby teams in the world, and still bred to strain every sinew for victory; and millions of their compatriots were still stirred into a frenzy of excitement by the imminent arrival of the All Blacks.

Leslie's squad was driven to South Africa, through the political gauntlet, by the irresistible urge to scale the peak that none of their All Black predecessors had conquered: to defeat the Springboks on their own soil. New Zealanders had failed in 1928, 1949, 1960 and 1970, but the 1976 tour party ardently believed in their ability to win in South Africa, and they were prepared to endure worldwide condemnation in defending their right to try.

The All Blacks were not oblivious to apartheid, and they justified their tour by advocating communication rather than isolation. Bryan Williams, the admired Maori winger, felt the pressure acutely. "It is not a very nice thought knowing that I would be in the same situation as the blacks if I lived here," he said shortly after his arrival in South Africa, "and I do get depressed, but if you fight the problem by boycotting, by bullying people, you just get resented. If you go there and discuss it with people, you communicate and that is healthy."

Du Plessis acknowledged these issues, but he was merely a rugby player and, in 1976, rugby players were not in a position to transform the country. Times would have changed by 1995, and by then he would have been appointed as the Springbok team manager, but that is another story.

When he arrived at King's Park to play the first Test against the All Blacks in 1976, the Springbok captain focused solely on winning the game. The strength of his team lay in an uncompromising, powerful pack of forwards, and the reliable goal kicking of Gerald Bosch. Like Bennie Osler before and Naas Botha to come, Bosch was criticised for kicking too much and starving his three-quarters, but he learned to keep his critics at bay by kicking accurately – in four Tests versus the 1976 All Blacks, he would kick 33 of South Africa's 55 points.

Both camps believed the opening Test of the series would be pivotal and, to his horror, Du Plessis seemed to have committed a critical error when his wild pass in the early seconds of the second half was intercepted by Grant Batty. The All Black dashed clear, and created the try for Lyn Jaffray. South Africa's captain trudged back towards his posts, bewildered and shaken.

"Sorry, boys."

The Springboks were staring down the barrel of a 7–3 deficit, but their rally began when Gerrie Germishuys found a fifth gear on the left wing and literally ran around the All Black defence to score a famous try. Edrich Krantz then followed a break by Paul Bayvel to seize a second try, and Ian Robertson's drop goal limped over the bar to clinch the 16–7 victory. Under beautiful blue skies, the capacity Durban crowd and the South African captain shared a sigh of relief.

Du Plessis had recovered from his own personal calamity, settled his team to the task at hand, and repeatedly led the Springbok charge around the fringes of the scrum, carrying the ball forward, maintaining momentum. For lengthy periods of the second half, the upright captain resembled nothing so much as the tallest ship in a fleet at battle on the seas. Constantly visible at the heart of the struggle, relentlessly surging forward, he led with distinction.

Terry McLean, most admired among New Zealand rugby writers, had sat in wonder. "I have seen Springbok captains come and go since 1937," he recalls, "but Morné du Plessis ranks as the greatest of them all. He was a fine player and an absolute gentleman. The All Blacks admired him tremendously."

The tourists approached the second Test in Bloemfontein knowing that nothing less than victory would sustain their hopes of winning the series, and they played in that perfect state that is found somewhere near the brink of desperation. Peter Whiting and Ian Kirkpatrick bossed the forwards and, with Sid Going directing at the base of the scrum, the All Blacks powered to a 15–9 victory.

Thousands of fans streamed onto the field after the final whistle, and Du Plessis headed sadly towards the changing rooms, finding a way through hordes of Grey College boys, distinctive in their black-

and-white-striped blazers. Young hands patted his back in consolation, but the captain had struggled to impose his presence on the game. Rumours ran loose that he would be replaced for the next match, but the national selectors ultimately stood by their captain.

In the third Test at Newlands, Du Plessis banished forever any suggestion that he could not meet the physical challenge of international rugby. With his side trailing 7-3 and half time approaching, the Springbok captain charged into a ruck, twice kicked an All Black who was lying on the wrong side of the ball, and sparked a mass bout of pawing and pushing between rival forwards.

"There goes Du Plessis, kicking violently," trilled the commentator from the New Zealand Broadcasting Corporation. "This bloke has done it before, and now he is doing it again. This sort of thing should not be allowed."

The All Blacks relied heavily on their capacity physically to intimidate their opposition, on prompting brief moments of hesitation that would prove decisive in the 50/50 challenges. Blatantly and bravely, Du Plessis had shown he would not be overcome, and his players took heart from his example.

Rampie Stander, Piston van Wyk and Johan Strauss stabilised the front row, Kevin de Klerk and Moaner van Heerden emerged as leviathans at lock, and the captain was vigorously supported in the loose phases by Jan Boland Coetzee and Theuns Stofberg, a 21-year-old flanker who had been selected to replace Jan Ellis after the first Test. Ellis had played 38 Tests since his debut in 1965, and he shared with Frik du Preez the distinction of being the most capped Springbok at that time, but a new team was emerging.

Urged on by the passionate Cape Town crowd, South Africa trailed 7-6 at half time, but eased ahead when Johan Oosthuizen intercepted an All Black pass and sprinted clear. Bosch converted, and the Springboks were clinging perilously to a 12-10 lead as the minutes slipped away, one by one.

Any missed tackle, any conceded penalty might have lost the Test, but the home team maintained its discipline and Dawie Snyman eventually sealed victory by kicking a late drop goal. Du Plessis allowed himself a raised hand to salute the final whistle; South Africa could no longer lose the series.

In defeat, the New Zealanders blamed the referee, Gert Bezuidenhout, for his handling of the scrums and a series of marginal decisions. Leaving aside their praise of the same official after his display in the second Test, the tourists should have directed any anger towards their own officials. The South African Board had proposed neutral referees for all the Tests, but this sensible suggestion had been inexplicably rejected by the New Zealand Rugby Union.

To their credit, the All Blacks again raised the tempo in the fourth Test at Ellis Park and, for long periods before a vast crowd, the tourists looked the more gifted and creative team; yet they continued to concede careless penalties, and the imperious Bosch continued to kick magnificently. Amid bludgeoning, bruising exchanges, neither side could establish a clear advantage.

The tension crackled. Du Plessis ceaselessly implored his team to remain calm and focused, to minimise their mistakes. Twice the All Blacks declared their centre, Bruce Robertson, had been obstructed as he bore down on the Springbok line, and twice referee Bezuidenhout shook his head. The decisions were certainly not clear-cut. Tempers started to fray.

Still New Zealand led 14-12 with nine minutes to play. An obvious barge at the front of the lineout then presented Bosch with a further penalty chance, and the flyhalf sent the ball soaring between the uprights. This tightly contested series was going down to the wire, and South Africa prevailed 15-14.

The Test had been close, might have gone either way; and the series had also been close, might also have gone either way, but the tourists, who had sadly failed to control their anger after the third Test, now unleashed remarkable volleys of vitriol and bitterness upon their bewildered hosts.

Batty, the pugnacious wing, sniped: "We endured a lot to come to South Africa because we wanted a sporting chance, but we were denied that chance by the worst refereeing I have ever seen. The best thing about the All Black tour to South Africa in 1976 was undoubtedly the trip home." J.J. Stewart, the manager, oozed resentment when he summed up the series with the words: "We outplayed South Africa, South Africa outkicked us. Goodbye, rugby!"

Perhaps, on reflection, the New Zealanders would concede they were the architects of their own downfall insofar as they had rejected neutral referees and they failed to select a placekicker as reliable as Bosch.

Somebody once noted that there are two certainties about an All Black team in South Africa: first they wear black jerseys with a silver fern, second they complain about the referees. History suggests that somebody was right.

The touring squad's intemperate outbursts soured the Springbok victory, and moved a disappointed Du Plessis to respond: "Sure, we enjoyed our share of luck, but I have often played in matches where the opposition was lucky. It's part of the game. We should all be able to accept that." The 1976 All Blacks were a fine team but, when the one great scorer comes to mark against their name, they may regret that they so casually hurled the blame.

As passing time dulled the whingeing, the hard fact remained that the 3-1 series victory over New Zealand had largely restored South Africa's credibility in international rugby, and Du Plessis's talented team should have advanced to win further honours. Instead they were frozen by the icy grip of isolation.

The Gleneagles Agreement of June 1977 called on Commonwealth countries to suspend all sporting ties with South Africa, and the General Assembly of the United Nations Organisation, in the same year, called on UN member countries to stop all sporting contact. Yet the South African government remained committed to the ideologies of grand apartheid: Steve Biko died in detention, and the country's new leader, P.W. Botha, introduced a "Total Strategy" to secure the country for white domination. As pawns in the game, the Springboks were destined to play one solitary Test during the next three seasons.

And even that was not a genuine international. In 1977, the bold Northern Transvaal Rugby Union decided to celebrate the rebuilding of the Loftus Versfeld stadium in Pretoria by inviting leading players from around the globe to combine and play one game against the Springboks. This formidable World XV was led by Willie-John McBride and included Andy Haden, Ian Kirkpatrick, Gareth Edwards, Jean-Pierre Rives, Gerald Davies and J.P.R. Williams.

Du Plessis was named to lead a team that, the Board had decreed, would be awarded full colours, and an open, exciting 45-24 win was illuminated when Hermanus Potgieter, the Free State winger, dashed along the touchline to score a thrilling try. The players celebrated, the crowd cheered, the opposition retreated to await the conversion beneath their posts ... but this was not the real deal. This was not the red-blooded, thunderous Test rugby of lore.

Isolation was starting to hurt.

Du Plessis folded away his green-and-gold jersey, and focused his efforts on captaining Western Province in the Currie Cup. Their fiercest rival during the late 1970s was proving to be a Northern Transvaal side built around a powerful pack of forwards and an extraordinary flyhalf, Naas Botha.

On 30 July 1977 the eighthman led his side in their most important match of the season, against the Blue Bulls in Pretoria. South Africans were learning to cope with the lack of real Tests by behaving as though premier provincial fixtures such as this were indeed full internationals: the media build-up was extreme, and Loftus Versfeld buzzed with 52 000 fans. In reality, isolation did not diminish the public appetite for rugby; it loaded everything on the Currie Cup.

With Western Province leading 13-12 into the final quarter, Botha took a pass and, almost simultaneously, was pole-axed by Du Plessis's challenge. Loftus erupted in outrage. Pretoria's golden son was stretchered off the field and, again, the captain stood alone, surrounded by fury in the stands.

Referee Ian Gourlay awarded a penalty that won the game for Northerns, and at the final whistle Du Plessis required a police escort to help him reach the sanctuary of the visitors' changing room. The controversy over "the tackle" raged for several weeks – in spite of Botha's own acknowledgement that the challenge had been fair, and Du Plessis's conciliatory telephone call.

The row was certainly fuelled by the fact that Du Plessis was unpopular in the generally conservative city of Pretoria, not only because he was the Western Province captain but also because of his reputation as a verligte (enlightened) white man and the widespread perception of his liberal views.

In this country at this time, the accepted white consensus held that Nelson Mandela was a convicted terrorist who deserved to be in prison, that apartheid was necessary to maintain order in at least one country of an otherwise chaotic continent, that the police service and defence force heroically guarded and maintained the princely lifestyle enjoyed by most whites, and that the *broeders* should be supported ... shhhhhhh, they're supposed to be secret.

In 1977, more than 90% of provincial rugby players in South Africa would have wholeheartedly agreed with all four of these statements. Du Plessis clearly did not. He rarely sought confrontation with the authorities, but his enthusiasm for communication and conciliation had been widely noted. To hold such views as an ordinary citizen required nerve; to hold them as the Springbok captain demanded substantial courage. This leader did not follow; he led.

The Springboks did not play during 1978 and 1979, but Dr Danie Craven continued to attend meetings of the International Rugby Board, arguing cogently that rugby was a power for reconciliation among different races and deserved to be encouraged in this role. A South African Barbarian tour to Britain in 1979, by a squad that included eight whites, eight blacks and eight coloureds, thoughtfully managed by the urbane Chick Henderson, succeeded in proving to the watching world that South Africans could unite on the rugby field.

Patiently and skilfully, Craven was regaining support.

The president of the South African Rugby Board was rewarded by a series of announcements that effectively signalled the Springboks' unexpected return to international competition. Against every other trend, arrangements were made for the South African team to play nine Tests during 1980.

After the famine, the harvest: two home Tests against a South American Jaguars side would provide the perfect warm-up before a four-Test series against Bill Beaumont's Lions, followed by a tour to South America including two Tests against the Jaguars, and finally a summer Test against France at Loftus Versfeld in November. Rugby supporters, aged from 5 to 90, rejoiced.

Du Plessis was an entirely automatic and uncontested choice to captain the Springbok team. The thrilling prospect of playing Tests again had rallied even the rump of Pretoria to his side and, more popular than ever, more admired than ever, the eighthman eagerly assembled with his players.

"Morné was an outstanding captain," recalls Stofberg. "He understood his players and never needed to shout to impose his authority." Divan Serfontein, an emerging scrumhalf who would make his debut against the Lions, regarded the captain as irreplaceable: "I can very clearly remember thinking to myself that we would be lost if anything happened to Morné," Serfontein says. "He was a quiet type of person, and guys would not casually go to his room for a chat, but he did convey a sense of being able to handle any situation, and of being able to do the right thing at the right time. He inspired tremendous confidence."

Nelie Smith, the former Springbok scrumhalf and captain, was appointed to coach the squad, and he arrived to discover Du Plessis established not only as the most capped player, with 14 Tests behind him, but also as the overwhelming personality and influence in the squad. To his credit, Smith opted to complement the revered captain, and add value in his own way.

Sixteen years later, another new Springbok coach would find an equally esteemed captain in place, but feel threatened and take a different course. He tried to impose his will by dropping the icon, but succeeded only in transforming world champions into a side beaten at home by the All Blacks.

In 1980, however, Smith resolved to enhance rather than destroy. "Morné was instrumental in ensuring the essential human relationships in the squad were sound," the coach recalls. "He was thoughtful, and succeeded in building a great team spirit out of the fierce provincial rivalries that existed at that time. Everyone respected him because he was determined and very fair."

Du Plessis is characteristically modest in assessing his own achievements with the 1980 Springboks. "There was certainly a tension between players from the north and the south, but everyone knew we were in a battle together, and that knocked the hell out of any petty tensions within the team.

"But I was aware of the situation. My nature is to avoid conflicts. If there is a problem, I prefer to have it resolved and out of the way, and it was important for me that I earned the respect of the key players from Northern Transvaal, people like Moaner van Heerden and Louis Moolman. The old division between English and Afrikaans speakers was another issue, but if you push South Africans in the same direction, they usually get along with each other."

All but four of the 26 members of the South American Jaguars tour group hailed from Argentina, and these Pumas-in-disguise immediately found their feet in South Africa, scoring 18 tries in their four tour matches prior to the first Test in Johannesburg, to be played at the Wanderers cricket ground while Ellis Park was being flattened and rebuilt. Encouraged by recent drawn Tests against Australia, England and France, the Jaguars were riding high.

The South African selectors responded by giving Du Plessis the heaviest pack of Springbok forwards ever assembled, averaging 102 kilograms per man, and summoning Naas Botha for his Test debut alongside his halfback partner at Northern Transvaal, the protective Tommy du Plessis.

"People had warned me to be careful of Naas," the captain reflects. "They said he was an individualist, but I sat down and ran through our basic game plan with him. We agreed he would kick all the bad ball downfield, and allow the good ball down the line, and he did exactly that. There was no problem. In fact, I found him to be an exemplary team man throughout 1980."

South Africa won the first Test 24-9, with Du Plessis emerging as a force in the loose, constantly tidying, recycling and feeding, but the home side failed to dominate a Jaguars team that held their own in the scrums and lineouts and, in Hugo Porta, fielded a dangerous and creative playmaker. Worst of all, the South Africans had conceded a pushover try, recalling the most horrifying memories of the front row havoc wreaked by the Lions in 1974.

Smith recalls: "That try was an embarrassment for Springbok rugby, and an embarrassment for me as coach. The Lions were on their way to South Africa and I made a solemn promise to myself we would not concede another pushover try during the time I was working with the team, and we didn't."

The home forwards also failed to impose themselves on the second Test at King's Park, Durban, and only Du Plessis's close-range try and a trio of Botha drop goals enabled South Africa to eke out an 18-9 win. The captain was carried shoulder high from the field by three delighted supporters, but the newspapers were not so enthusiastic about South African prospects. NOT GOOD ENOUGH BOKS declared the following day's headlines. "No-one should talk until we have played against the Lions," Craven responded defiantly.

In the minds of the Springbok selectors, in the minds of Du Plessis and his players, in the minds of millions of South African rugby supporters, the challenge of the series versus the 1980 Lions was simply to avenge the humiliation inflicted upon the Springboks by McBride's team six years earlier.

Even Bill Beaumont, the affable Lions captain who arrived in South Africa fresh from guiding England to a Five Nations grand slam, sympathised with the predicament of his Springbok counterpart. "It was obvious that Morné was under enormous pressure to deliver the result that all South Africans wanted," reflects the Lancastrian lock. "Everywhere we went, people were talking about what had happened in 1974. They were obsessed with settling the score, and it was clear there would be no excuses if the Springboks did not win."

Beaumont's Lions were facing their own difficulties. Cleverly managed by Syd Millar and passionately coached by Noel Murphy, the touring squad was only assembled at the last moment to evade anti-tour demonstrators, and thus denied any productive preparation before their departure. Once arrived, the tour squad was incessantly disrupted by injury… and yet the players never gave up, hardly complained, and emerged from the tour with credit.

Both captains recognised the crucial importance of winning the first Test of the series in Cape Town, and Du Plessis worked tirelessly to insulate his players from the wild expectations swirling around the country. As he sat in the changing room at Newlands, intently passing the last minutes before kick-off, the captain glanced across at Botha and saw the 22-year-old flyhalf playfully trying on one of the paper sun-visors that were being distributed free to the crowd. The absence of nerves was amazing; the totem sensed all was well.

After only 10 seconds, the Springbok captain was seen to stagger away from a rolling maul. He had been brutally elbowed in the face by Derek Quinnell, the Lions eighthman, in what appeared a pre-meditated assault. Du Plessis's eye started to swell alarmingly, but he strongly forbade any retaliation. If the tourists hoped to rattle the Boks, they would be disappointed.

"Forget about it," the captain urged. "Just play, just play."

And his team played: Gysie Pienaar chipped ahead, creating a try for Rob Louw; Botha chipped, Willie du Plessis gathered the bounce and scored; Moaner van Heerden thundered over the Lions line. Three tries in 12 minutes helped the Springboks establish a 16-9 lead by half time, but Tony Ward's goal kicking kept the Lions in touch as this classic Test weaved towards its conclusion.

Graham Price barged over for the Lions; Gerrie Germishuys launched a counter-attack from deep inside his own half, and finished the move by taking a pass high above his head and diving to score. As the Test moved into injury time, the teams were locked level at 22-22. The series, and perhaps even Du Plessis's entire reputation as a captain, was hanging in the balance.

Botha ran the ball from deep inside his own half, Ray Mordt sprinted clear, and Rob Louw set up a ruck on the Lions line. Locks Van Heerden and Moolman simultaneously thundered into the wrestling maul, and Louw popped the ball out for Serfontein to dive over the line. The Newlands crowd bawled its approval as South Africa claimed a truly dramatic 26-22 victory.

"Mon Dieu," exclaimed François Palmade, the French referee, catching his breath afterwards, "that was a Test match for supermen."

As he conducted a round of post-match interviews, Du Plessis was asked about his grotesquely swollen eye: "Oh, that's nothing," said the captain, smiling broadly. "It really doesn't hurt when I look at the scoreboard."

Three metres down the corridor, Beaumont accepted the result, keeping private his suspicion that two Springboks had strayed offside before Serfontein's try. The Lions captain was preoccupied by the unending series of serious injuries that would force more than a third of the squad to return home early. "We had to use eight different halfback combinations in the first eight matches," Beaumont reflects ruefully. "We reckoned our pack was far superior to the Springboks, but we didn't have much luck at crucial stages of the tour."

The number of penalties conceded by his side at Newlands concerned Du Plessis, but the strategy remained unchanged for the second Test before another immense crowd at the Free State Stadium in Bloemfontein. The home side would swing the ball wide, away from the Lions forwards, and rely upon their swift loose forwards to retain possession at the points of breakdown.

Just as they had at Newlands, the Springboks established a 16-9 lead by half time, but the tourists gradually ground their way back into the match. Under a sweltering sun on the familiarly parched-white field, the Lions kicked one penalty, then another, and missed a third. As time ebbed away, Du Plessis seemed in his element, upright and prominent in every forward exchange, intelligently directing the defence, cajoling his players to dig deep and prevail. Once again he provided consummate leadership under nerve-shredding pressure.

South Africa were desperately defending their 16-15 lead with two minutes remaining. Then the wonderfully in-form Gysie Pienaar stepped forward: first he chipped perfectly into Germishuys's path, and the winger scored; then he collected a loose ball and dashed down the left touchline to score himself. The Free State fullback raised the ball high in the air, an enduring image of sheer joy amidst the applause of his home crowd. There was still time for another Lions try, but in the twinkling of their fullback's feet, the Springboks had won 26-19.

With one side jubilant and the other despondent, the post-match cocktail party started uneasily and rapidly deteriorated. Butch Lochner, convenor of the South African selectors, attacked the Lions during his speech: "You thought too much of yourselves, and too little of us," he said. "That is why you are 2-0 down. It is the result of your own arrogance and over-confidence."

Amid unconcealed animosity, Syd Millar approached the microphone and demanded that Lochner apologise and withdraw his remarks. Beaumont and his players stood, drinks in hand, seething. Every one had endured virulent criticism for joining this tour, many had lost their jobs and would return home to uncertain futures. In the hour of defeat, battered by unrelenting injuries, they certainly did not need to be harangued by a triumphal administrator.

Du Plessis saw the anger among the touring squad, and the situation was hurtling out of control when he, as captain of South Africa, was invited to address the function. If ever his calm and graceful diplomacy was required, it was at this fraught moment of deep embarrassment for Springbok rugby.

"I would like to thank the Lions for another hard match," the Springbok declared. "They are a great side who have encountered an incredible series of obstacles on this tour and, as one group of players to another, we are extremely grateful that they have been able to participate in this series. I want everyone to know that we have nothing but respect for this team."

His speech directly soothed British sensibilities, and Millar was moved to grumble in Lochner's direction: "Your captain is a great man."

When the morning of the third Test dawned overcast, wet and cold in Port Elizabeth, many observers assumed the British players would prosper in familiar conditions and keep the series alive. They should have felt at home: the rain had become so severe by kick-off that drenched spectators sitting in the open stands had decided to return home and watch the match on television.

The impressive Lions forwards did establish control as Ollie Campbell, the tourists' third flyhalf in three Tests, kicked an early penalty, and Bruce Hay scored after collecting a stray fly-hack. Du Plessis worked hard to revive his side, but the Springboks were struggling up front and their dangerous three-quarters shivered in the rain, denied possession and opportunity. The Lions were leading 7-3 at the interval and, once a second Campbell penalty had cancelled out Botha's magical drop goal, they were coasting to victory at 10-6.

Barely six minutes remained. Du Plessis had started to ponder a losing speech for the post-match function. His side had not subsided, but they had been outplayed from the start and could have no complaint.

Botha directed a clever punt across field into touch. Clive Woodward, the Lions wing, footed the ball over the line; and as he checked his position, Germishuys took a quick throw to Stofberg. The flanker instantly returned the pass, and the wing was suddenly crossing the line in the corner. As rain pelted his back, Botha prepared to attempt what looked an almost unattainable touchline conversion. He struck the ball low, but straight and true. The flags were raised; Lions' heads were bowed.

South Africa had won 12-10, and secured the series. Du Plessis's shares had reached an all-time high, and again the captain was carried off the field. His team had followed victory over the All Blacks in 1976 with a resounding triumph over the Lions, yet the captain remained unassuming and modest at a time when others would have boasted and basked in glory.

"We know we played a match today where Lady Luck played a great role," Du Plessis declared in his speech at the post-Test function in Port Elizabeth. "We have won the series but, please believe me, any of the three Test matches might have gone the other way. I know how close they have been."

The remainder of the Lions tour was conducted in something approaching a carnival atmosphere, with celebrities such as Porta and Rives arriving to join a South African Barbarian side that played first the tourists in Durban, and then the Junior Springboks as a curtain-raiser before the fourth Test.

Du Plessis dutifully prepared his team to complete a 4-0 series win, but with the rubber decided it was hard to instil the same frantic craving to win, and the team's soft mental state was scarcely bolstered when

Craven arrived in the home changing room and openly predicted the Lions would win.

Meanwhile Beaumont stirred his team to avoid the ignominy of becoming the first British tourists to be whitewashed in South Africa, and his players reacted in formidable fashion. They led 7–3 at half time and, despite a Springbok surge in the second half, scored tries through Irvine and O'Driscoll to secure a thoroughly deserved 17–13 victory. The Springbok captain, and the overwhelming majority of South African supporters, were content that justice had been done.

Gracious in victory and comfortable in defeat, Du Plessis had imposed his dignified, even noble personality on the series. The bitter aftermath of the second Test was forgotten, and the Lions flew home amid a consensus that the tour had been successful in every respect. "Morné was obviously a towering influence on the game in South Africa," Beaumont recalls. "He was always calm and decisive, and emphatically fair in his approach. He was easy to respect.

"On a personal level I got along as well with him as with any captain I ever played against. He was, and remains, a credit to the game."

For Du Plessis, victory over the Lions fleetingly seemed less like a comma in his Springbok career, and more like a full stop. He was absolutely determined to retire at the top of the sport and, in one discussion with the national selectors, he wondered whether they might like to blood a new captain during the imminent tour to South America. It seemed, he said, like an option.

"No, thank you."

"But I am starting to feel tired," the eighthman persisted.

"Look, Morné," Lochner replied, "you are our captain. Please won't you at least agree to lead the team until the end of the season?"

Du Plessis nodded.

There was no such thing as a free Saturday during 1980 for South Africa's leading players, and the Springboks returned to their provincial squads to resume the intensely physical Currie Cup competition. The risk of injury was obvious and, to national alarm and distress, it was Du Plessis who hurt his shoulder playing for Western Province against Eastern Province in Port Elizabeth.

News that he would miss both the Currie Cup final against Northerns and the opening fortnight of the tour to South America was conveyed to an anxious nation at the top of the television news bulletin and on front pages. A household name, Du Plessis was cherished like a national treasure.

The tour to South America was shrouded in mystery and intrigue until the day of departure when it was disclosed that, having been refused entry visas to Argentina, the Springboks would play two matches in Paraguay, two in Uruguay and two in Chile. Their schedule included two Test matches against the Jaguars, the Argentine national team in everything but name.

Nine years after his first Springbok tour overseas, Du Plessis led a happy and confident squad across the ocean, but his powers of leadership were soon to be tested. Hannes Pretorius, the Western Province president and tour manager, discovered somebody had ordered a bottle of whisky at the hotel and signed the R80 bill with his name and room number. Such behaviour would not be tolerated, and the manager asked the captain to deal with the matter.

A team meeting was called.

"Boys, everyone knows what has happened," said Du Plessis, calmly and purposefully, "but I don't think we want a witch-hunt. Let's face this situation like a squad, and let's pay the bill as a squad. Everyone chips in their share, and that is the end of the matter. Is that OK? Are you happy with that?"

Nervous frowns morphed into broad smiles. The captain had in fact known very well the identity of the guilty players, but he had decided to turn an awkward situation into a vehicle for bonding his players more tightly together. The episode had neatly exemplified his captaincy, his legend.

Naas Botha was converted. "I played for many captains during my career," the flyhalf recalls, "and Morné du Plessis was the best. Personally, I always felt absolutely confident when he was in charge of the team."

Welcome to Asuncion! Perhaps the strongest rugby team in the world had been driven to this unlikely destination in their desperate quest for opposition, but the opening match of the tour proved less than satisfying. The Springboks barely broke sweat in an 84-6 victory, the referee had worn white slacks, the match was restricted to 30 minutes each half and, worst of all, only 220 people turned up to watch. In many respects, the occasion was demeaning.

The players were not at fault and, stirred by the enthusiasm of debutants like Errol Tobias, the first coloured South African to become a Springbok, and an explosive young centre named Danie Gerber, the tourists continued ruthlessly to dismantle their opposition. At least, Hugo Porta's Jaguars side was preparing to provide a genuine Test, both by name and by nature.

With Du Plessis still ruled out by injury, Theuns Stofberg had emerged as an obvious choice to lead the Springboks in the first Test, to be played on a small soccer field in Montevideo, the capital of Uruguay; and his team emerged from a generally uninspiring afternoon with a 22-13 victory. Though clearly stronger and more talented, the tourists had struggled to establish a rhythm.

Several of the South Africans reluctantly started to question the validity of their victory. "The Argentinian guys were playing on a neutral venue in a strange jersey," Botha reflects, "and I just wondered how much the Tests meant to them. They would have been much tougher if they were playing as the Pumas in front of their own crowd in Buenos Aires, but that was not possible."

Du Plessis returned to captain the tourists in the second Test in Santiago, capital of Chile, and he urged his players to forget their surroundings, forget the opposition, and start to focus on playing to their potential. The result was greater continuity between forwards and backs, a surfeit of possession, and two tries for each Springbok wing, Gerrie Germishuys and Ray Mordt. If anything, the 30-16 result did not adequately reflect the visitors' domination.

The players were acclaimed upon their return to South Africa. So far as their fervent supporters were concerned, the team had scored 66 tries in winning six matches out of six, but the statistics could not tell the whole story. The squad had travelled unnoticed through three countries with little interest in rugby, been disappointed by small crowds and the lack of match-day atmosphere throughout, and twice defeated Test opposition of dubious quality.

Du Plessis graciously accepted the eager congratulations, yet it is hard to believe this intelligent, perceptive man had not recognised the inglorious poverty of Springbok rugby during isolation. Beggars could not be choosers, but the days of being mobbed by adoring crowds in New Zealand and through the British Isles belonged to a different era. Once there had been parades and packed stadiums, now there was secrecy and the echoing cheers of a few hundred.

Far from reversing the captain's continuing inclination towards retirement, this strange tour to South America moved him to request a meeting with Dr Danie Craven, president of the South African Rugby Board.

Du Plessis reflects: "I did not think the tour had been a waste of time. You only had to see the enthusiasm of the young players to realise that, from a rugby point of view, any kind of opposition was better than no opposition; but I wanted to discuss the long-term strategy with Doc. It appeared as though we were trying to busk our way through isolation when I felt we should have been conceding our problems and taking a positive line to put our house in order."

The president and captain engaged in earnest discussion. In his youth, the eighthman had cowered in awe of Craven, scared to be in the same room as the revered ruler of the game, but the passing seasons with Stellenbosch, Western Province and South Africa had brought a sense of affection and mutual respect to the relationship. "I became close to Dr Craven towards the end of my career," Du Plessis recalls, "and that had a lot to do with the politics of the game. He was seriously committed to change, and was looking for allies."

Sitting in the Board president's office, the Springbok captain proceeded to advocate nothing less than a revolution in South African rugby.

"Doc, let's hit it one time," he implored. "We need to start all over again and get everyone together. We can't continue with the whites playing under the Board, the coloureds staying in the Federation, the blacks playing in SARA, and SARU being out on their own. It is time to start afresh."

Craven listened.

"We must seize the initiative," the captain continued. "Let's announce that we will disband the South African Rugby Board and launch discussions with the aim of forming one united rugby organisation."

The President replied: "I agree with you, Morné, but the time is not right at the moment. We can't change everything overnight."

The captain deferred, respectfully. In evoking the sentiments expressed by Tom Bedford a full decade earlier, Du Plessis proved to be still another ten years ahead of his time. Craven and his Board would remain defiant before seriously pursuing the goal of rugby unity during the late 1980s.

If rugby administrators of the day had embraced the wisdom advocated by Bedford and latterly Du Plessis, who can fathom what role their sport would have played in the reconciliation and transformation of South Africa?

Such matters could not have been further from the minds of the Springbok supporters who excitedly gathered at Loftus Versfeld on 8 November for the last Test of this long and successful season. Their team had started 1980 under a cloud of uncertainty after three inactive seasons, but seven wins in eight Tests had restored the Boks' reputation as one of the world's top teams.

These were happy days in rugby's cocoon. Impromptu braais (barbeques) were being set along the pavements around the Pretoria stadium, and the rugby songs of Leon Schuster reverberated from car stereo systems. What more could anyone want? The Springboks were playing Tests, and winning, and the latest reports predicted a South African tour to New Zealand would go ahead in 1981. If this was isolation, people smirked, what was the problem?

France would provide the opposition on this sunny summer's day. Led by the charismatic blonde flanker, Jean-Pierre Rives, the tourists had landed in fear of being overwhelmed by what the Paris daily newspaper France Soir had described as "the greatest rugby war machine in the world". Yet the French had rallied from behind to win their first three matches, and had shown sufficient ability to concentrate the minds of Du Plessis and his squad.

The Springbok captain was determined to finish the season on a victorious note, and the players sensed a serious tone in his voice as he gathered the team in the Loftus changing room and ran through some calls.

"Finally," he declared. "We have become a very close team this year, and I think many of you know I have been thinking about retirement. Well, I have made my decision, and I wanted you to be the first to know. This will be my last Test for South Africa. That's all. Now let's go and enjoy it! Good luck!"

With these words ringing in their ears, the Springboks stomped out of their changing room, pounded along the corridor beneath the main stand, turned left again, and high-stepped into a bright summer's evening. They would play this Test for Morné; they would not be denied; they would win.

Gysie Pienaar, brimming with confidence, perhaps the player of the year, sparked a world-class team performance, breaking on the blind side to score the first try. Germishuys soon blitzed over near the corner to score his ninth Test try, establishing a new South African record. The Pretoria crowd was basking in the warm sunshine, and the Springboks led 13-0 at half time.

Into the second half, Serfontein's try completed another spectacular, fluent move, before the enterprising Botha nudged a soft grubber kick into Stofberg's path and the flanker galloped across the line. As he charged from lineout to ruck, Du Plessis willed himself to savour every moment of what was now unfolding as the most perfect, fitting and downright joyful send-off.

The French played their full part in the spectacle, most notably the gallant Rives, who suffered a severe gash on his forehead, and left the field but returned to the fray with his head dramatically bandaged ... and still the blood streamed down his porcelain-white face, clotting in his blazing blonde hair. John West, the referee, asked the French captain to leave the field again. Staggering to and fro, scarcely able to stand, Rives argued. He would not leave his team.

So he stayed, and he rampaged through the loose, creating a fine try and winning the admiration of South African rugby supporters.

Du Plessis was thrilled by the courage of his French counterpart, seeing in Rives the most wonderful, selfless, audacious spirit of the game. Perhaps these two rugby men recognised something of themselves in each other, for they would remain close friends for many years to come. Indeed, Du Plessis would name his son Jean-Pierre in honour of his most admired opponent.

"Morné is a great gentleman," Rives reflects. "Everyone can see that he is an admired ambassador not just for the game of rugby, but also for South Africa. He is calm, fair, and modest, a great man in so many ways.

"For me, he is much more than that. He is an extraordinary friend. We talk about anything together. Maybe we were team-mates in a past life. To be honest, I don't remember much about the matches I played in my rugby career but I have incredible memories about the people, people like Morné."

The 37-15 victory over France in Pretoria completed a superb year for the Springboks, in which they not only won eight Tests out of nine but also unearthed a new generation of remarkable talent. Young players such as Naas Botha, Ray Mordt and Danie Gerber would sustain the game for a decade.

This general sense of wellbeing served to affirm Du Plessis's intuition that the time was right for him to retire, but the captain soon found himself the object of an intense campaign to make him change his mind. Nelie Smith tried on three occasions, several players pleaded. Craven arranged a meeting.

"Morné, I know how you feel," the Board president said, "but it seems the tour to New Zealand will go ahead next year, and we need you to lead the side. I don't know how to put it any other way. We need you."

Du Plessis had listened, round eyes alert, face set.

"Doc, I am sorry. I have switched the engines off. That's it."

"Morné, no, I can't accept that."

"Doc, please, I am looking you in the eye and telling you I have enjoyed every minute of my career, but I have had enough. It is time to stop."

"You don't mean that."

"I do."

"You don't. You will change your mind."

Du Plessis had risen from his seat and started to walk backwards out of Craven's office, step by step, like a medieval knight leaving his king. He kept his eyes fixed on Craven, but kept walking, step by step.

"Doc, I am sorry."

"You will come back."

"Doc, I have said my piece."

And he left.

The captain had pledged to give his final decision to retire as an exclusive story to A.C. Parker from *The Argus*, one of the most gentle and respected rugby writers of the era. So, on the morning of 29 January 1981, he gave notice of his retirement to officials from his club, Villagers, the Western Province Rugby Union, and the South African Rugby Board, and Parker wrote the front-page story. Soon after half-past noon on the same day, the news exploded across the Western Cape and reverberated around the rugby world.

Du Plessis recalls: "It was the most beautiful thing in my life that I was able to carry through that resolution. I am not the most decisive person by nature, but that was such a decisive decision for me to make. I was adamant.

"It's the easiest thing in the world to change a rugby player's mind. Get 10 guys to tell him what a wonderful job he's doing, and he will usually agree to play one more match or one more season. But I wanted to stop. There was never one day when I did not want to be Springbok captain. I held the position in awe, and I loved the job. But, at the end of 1980, I wanted to stop."

He was physically tired, insofar as niggling injuries seemed to take longer to heal and he no longer looked forward to practices, but the emotional pressure of an exhausting 1980 season had also taken its toll. The boyish enthusiasm that lies at the heart of every sportsman had started to wane.

During August 1980, moreover, Du Plessis had led Western Province in a match against Free State, and seen the Province fullback, Chris Burger, suffer a severe neck injury on the field. Burger died later that night. With his team-mates, the captain established the Chris Burger Fund in memory of their friend, raising funds to support people severely injured playing rugby.

Many years on, he was still chairman of the management committee of the renamed Chris Burger/Petro Jackson Fund, which continues to support victims and has also launched a powerful preventative campaign.

For many years following his retirement at the pinnacle of the game, Du Plessis's active involvement in South African rugby did not extend beyond his role within the Chris Burger Fund. At stages, he seemed disenchanted with the petty politics of the game, unwilling to enter the scramble for blazers and preferential parking passes that so often characterised officialdom.

Headlines appeared sporadically, touting him as the ideal man to lead the game forward, to heal and unite, citing the esteem in which he is held among all the rugby communities, black, coloured and white, throughout South Africa, but such exciting suggestions tended to drift away on the wind.

As Du Plessis pursued a business career, a consensus started to emerge during the late 1980s and 1990s that this occasionally diffident man did not have the appetite for any struggle to take control of South African rugby. He preferred to watch a game at Newlands now and then, to spend time with his family. Even though the game missed him, he did not miss the game.

At last, in February 1995, he emerged from the wilderness and agreed to serve as manager of the Springbok team through the 1995 Rugby World Cup, a position he held until after the Tri-Nations series in 1996. As a player, Du Plessis had earned the enduring affection of the white nation; as a manager, he would guide a Springbok team that united all South Africans.

Today he continues to hover around the game, sitting on the board of Sail (South African Investments Limited), a company that owns a major stake in eight provincial rugby unions, and continuing to run the state-of-the-art Sports Science Institute of South Africa that he helped to launch in 1995.

And he remains special, unique, truly loved.

To say the words "Morné du Plessis" is immediately to conjure up the most acceptable and positive image of white South Africa. He is brave and passionate, respected and serene, reasonable, humble and reflective. His legend is engraved within the conscience of the nation: great captain, great man.

For many years after his retirement from the game, Du Plessis would be greeted at various functions by Dr Craven's wagging finger.

"Morné, jy het my gedrop," the president would chide, with an expression of disdain and a mischievous twinkle in his eye. Craven would never forget how the captain had declined to lead the 1981 tour to New Zealand.

"Morné, jy het my gedrop." (Morné, you dropped me.)

From his emergence at Grey and Stellenbosch, through his Test debut on tour to Australia in 1971, through his years of loyal service to the Villagers club in Cape Town, through 15 internationals as Springbok captain, of which only two were lost, through victories over the All Blacks, Lions and Jaguars, through his integrity and decency, through his example and outstanding leadership ...

Morné du Plessis has never dropped anyone.

He has been, every inch, the modern totem of Springbok rugby.

10 THE BOMBED

The roots of Springbok rugby reach, unseen and unhailed, through a network of rugby clubs across South Africa. Tomorrow's heroes emerge from plain grounds lost in green suburbs, from youth training sessions on Saturday mornings, from age-group teams coached by volunteers, from the fifth and fourth XVs, from the spirit in the clubhouse and even the spirits behind the bar, from the framed Test jersey on the wall, presented to the club in grateful appreciation ...

It is another busy Saturday night at the Collegians rugby club in Durban. The bar and restaurant are heaving with club members and their guests, sharing and belonging, recognising and greeting, discussing Natal's victory against Free State that afternoon, debating what the national selectors will do when, later that night, they announce their Springbok side to play Ireland.

Praise for the team's successes during 1980 has evolved into anticipation ahead of two home Tests against the touring Irish, arranged as a warm-up before the main event, the ultimate challenge, the 1981 Springbok tour to New Zealand. And everyone at Collegians this Saturday night wants to know if their man will be named to succeed Morné du Plessis as Springbok captain.

"Two Castles and a Lion, please."

"No, there's no news yet."

Soon after eight, Wynand Claassen and his wife, together with friends Pete Smith and his wife, arrive at the club. They have booked a table for four, and heads turn as they take their seats and order steaks.

One member congratulates the popular Natal captain for his perform-ance against Free State; another wishes him luck for later tonight. The bespectacled Claassen smiles, and eats.

He is hopeful, but not particularly optimistic. A newspaper claim-ing to have an inside track on the selectors' intentions had confidently predicted that Theuns Stofberg would be confirmed as the new cap-tain. Perhaps they were correct. The Northern Transvaal flanker had ca-pably led the team when an injured Du Plessis missed the first Test on tour to South America in 1980. He was experienced and guaranteed his place in the side. Claassen was uncapped.

"Wynand, the telephone is for you at the bar."

The eighthman took the call. It was a friend, phoning to say he had heard something about the Springbok team on the radio, but there was nothing certain. Grant Oxlee, son of Springbok flyhalf Keith, was standing by and asked whether there was any news. Claassen shook his head nervously.

Twenty minutes later there was another call to the club and, once again, Claassen was summoned to the telephone at the bar. It was Lappe Laubscher, the respected and well-connected rugby writer from Rapport, and now the news was confirmed: Claassen had been named Springbok captain.

In that instant, his Natal team-mate Gawie Visagie and Peter Pol-lock, the former Springbok fast bowler, led a delighted, cheering charge of club members into the bar. As the celebrations lasted until morning, Claassen began to savour the realisation of his boyhood dream.

He was destined to lead South Africa for only two seasons, but these were two of the most dramatic seasons in Springbok history. He would overcome bitter opposition from within and without, and he would become the first captain to lead the Boks while an airplane flew above, dropping flour bombs.

Fated to be measured against the successes of his predecessor, bombed and battered along the way, Claassen proved an emotional, committed leader of a team that, almost without exception, grew to adore him.

The youngest of three sons, Wynand Claassen was reared in Middelburg, an industrial town east of Johannesburg, where his father worked as headmaster of the Middelburg High School. George Claassen had played rugby for Western Transvaal in his youth, but he captured the imagination of the sporting public when, at the age of 44, he won the 1961 Comrades Marathon. He had only run his first marathon five years earlier, and he proved an inspiration to many.

Encouraged by a sporting father, brought up within a school where hearts rarely beat faster than on the day of the annual derby fixture against Middelburg Technical High School, and inspired by watching the Springboks in action against the 1960 All Blacks, Claassen seemed to emerge from the archetype mould of South African youth: athletic, strong, brave, obsessed by sport.

Yet there was much more to this individual. His sharp, focused eyes hinted at an intense, sometimes troubled and unpredictably creative nature. By the time he had enrolled to study architecture at the University of Pretoria, he was reading poetry, listening to classical music, and counting painting among his pastimes. This man had clearly not run off any production line. He had emerged from his own mould.

Sensitive and delicate with a brush, he nonetheless developed as a robust eighthman at Tukkies (the University of Pretoria) and advanced to play his provincial debut for Northern Transvaal in 1973. Through the seven seasons that followed, he appeared no fewer than 61 times in the famous light-blue jersey, but his Springbok ambitions appeared to be constantly blocked by the established figure of Morné du Plessis, South Africa's captain and eighthman. Through the 1970s, Claassen played in the shadow of the totem.

He missed most of the 1978 season with a serious eye injury and, while struggling to regain his place in the Northerns team the following year, he started to be attracted by an option of relocating to Durban, where he would be given the captaincy and challenged to inspire a revival in the fortunes of the Natal team. At the end of 1979, he took the plunge, moved to the coast and joined Collegians.

"I desperately wanted to be a Springbok," Claassen recalls. "Some people reckoned I had missed the boat, but I hoped the move to Natal would improve my chances of impressing the selectors. I was obsessed about it. I suppose I was a bit nuts. I wanted to be a Springbok more than anything."

Even the bumper international season of 1980 did not yield the opportunity he craved. The eighthman captained the Junior Springboks against the touring Lions and also led a South African XV against Bill Beaumont's side, but later in the year he was massively disappointed to be omitted from the Springbok squad to tour South America.

As a specialist eighthman, he knew he lacked the versatility required to be a reserve in the home Test matches, but now it seemed he could not even win a place on a rare overseas tour. His optimism began to wane. Then on 29 January 1981 Claassen bought a newspaper on the way home and read about Du Plessis's decision to retire. That evening, just two weeks past his 30th birthday, he was at the gym, training harder than ever.

Natal started the 1981 season powerfully and, in tandem with Welsh coach Roger Gardner, the captain started to reap the dividends of bringing a dose of Northern Transvaal discipline to the natural talents in the Natal squad. His reputation soared, and he could hardly wait for three days of Springbok trials, to be held at Stellenbosch before two home Tests against Ireland.

This was his chance, perhaps his last chance.

He performed well on the Monday, and was satisfied with his efforts on the Tuesday, but he was left under no illusion about the size of his task when the teams were announced for the Wednesday, the final day. Theuns Stofberg was named to captain the A team, in pole position to be Springbok captain, with Thys Burger selected as eighthman. Claassen would lead the B side.

If ever, he needed to perform; if ever, he did perform. Claassen played as though his life depended on the outcome (in rugby terms, it did), and his B team swarmed all over the shadow Springboks, scoring five tries to one. On this critical day, he had produced one of the most compelling performances of his career, evidence even the most obdurate selector could not ignore.

Claassen returned to the players' hotel, excited by the day's events.

He switched on the television in his room, and happened to watch an interview with Butch Lochner during the main evening news. "It was an interesting trial match," the convenor of selectors opined, "but I believe we would be foolish to make too many changes from our original plans."

Here we go again, the eighthman sighed. Soon afterwards, he saw the report claiming to have been told Stofberg would be named captain and Burger would play eighthman against the Irish. He sighed again. It seemed as though his efforts had been in vain, as if his dream would remain a dream.

Far away in the fabled smoke-filled room, the selectors were split on the issue of the captaincy. Lochner and Nelie Smith, the Springbok coach, evidently favoured Stofberg, but it appeared as though Daan Swiegers, Dougie Dyers and Brian Irvine would vote for Claassen. This particular scenario would explain both the ultimately inaccurate "leak" to the media that raised and dashed Stofberg's hopes, and the subsequent announcement that prompted the delighted celebrations throughout the night at the Collegians club in Durban.

In any event, Claassen was confirmed as the new Springbok captain. However, like any captain, he required the unequivocal support and confidence of both the coach and the convenor of selectors. Would Lochner and Smith accept the majority decision and give him that support, or would they sense he had been imposed upon them, resent his emergence, and contribute towards an unsettled atmosphere within the team? The answer to this question would determine the mood and tone of his tenure as captain of South Africa.

"I didn't know how Butch and Nelie would react," he reflects. "It was not an issue in my mind at that time. I was very nervous because I was about to play my first Test as captain of what was an established and extremely successful team. I was replacing Morné. That was a daunting prospect."

His position was eased because he was well known to most of the leading Springboks at the time. He had played alongside Naas Botha and Louis Moolman in Pretoria, had always got on well with Gysie Pienaar, and had been to high school with Tommy du Plessis in

Middelburg. He had also nurtured a particularly close friendship with Divan Serfontein ever since they had played together in an invitation team against the 1976 All Blacks.

Amid the torrent of congratulations showered upon Claassen that Sunday after his appointment, Serfontein called and invited the new captain to fly down to Cape Town a few days early, stay with him and his wife in their Newlands flat, around the corner from where the first Test against Ireland would be played, and run through some moves and issues. Claassen eagerly accepted.

The team eventually assembled on the Thursday amid an unfortunate row over the inclusion of Errol Tobias ahead of Jannie Els as Danie Gerber's midfield partner. Els had excelled at the trials, but Tobias was now set to become the first coloured man to play Test rugby for South Africa. The controversy was evidently tinged with racial prejudice, and Claassen pointedly welcomed Tobias into the team. Enlightened by nature and conviction, far removed from the *broeders*, he resolved to ensure the trailblazer would feel comfortable in every way.

Ireland had arrived without a dozen leading players, notably Hugo McNeil and Tony Ward who both refused to tour on principle, and Mike Gibson who had been told he would lose his job if he toured; but the Irish Rugby Football Union remained adamant that, firstly, no country was clear of all injustice (they pointed out how Ireland had recently played soccer against Argentina, ruled by a military junta) and, second, that South African rugby's ostensibly genuine efforts to integrate the game among all races deserved to be encouraged and supported by their old rugby friends.

The tourists' early matches revealed a competitive tight five, a world-class loose forward combination of Fergus Slattery, Willie Duggan and John O'Driscoll, and a young backline with the desire and talent to dash hard and free. The day of the first Test dawned sunny and warm in the Cape, and Claassen prepared his players for a rigorous challenge. His words carried weight. He had settled comfortably at the head of his team.

Perhaps a few South Africans recoiled at the sight of their new captain leading the team out to play at Newlands ... and not simply because the players were wearing their rarely-seen change kit of white jerseys with gold trims, black shorts, and black socks with white stripe. Far from complying with the traditional, neatly clipped image of a Springbok rugby captain, Claassen looked like a Bohemian: a slightly stooped figure, his hair receding at the front and, at the back, straggling loose down his neck from beneath an impromptu headband, apparently manufactured from a metre of broad white bandage.

Within moments of kick-off, his jersey was flapping outside his shorts and the eighthman set to work, keeping up with play, securing the ball, channelling possession, encouraging his team-mates, leading.

In the event, Ireland succeeded in disrupting the Springbok forwards for long periods of the game, and they were only beaten by the individual brilliance of Danie Gerber, who scored an unforgettable zig-zag-zig try in the first half, and a second after the break. On each occasion, Claassen had clambered to reach the try-scorer, backslapping warm congratulations as they jogged back to halfway. This habit would become a trademark.

South Africa edged to a 23-15 victory and, although his own performance had been sound, the team's strangely error-ridden display left the captain in no sort of mood to celebrate his long-awaited Test debut.

Seven days later, in the second Test at King's Park in Durban, Claassen's team again struggled to impose themselves on an Irish side that drew strength from Slattery's heroics, and only Naas Botha's masterly hat trick of drop goals carried the Springboks to a distinctly fortunate 12-10 victory. The home side had actually trailed with less than five minutes remaining, flirting with unimaginable disaster. "Naas pulled us out of the fire," the captain reflects. "That Irish team had given us a huge wake-up call."

There was, however, no danger of Claassen ever becoming complacent. The national selectors announced within days that they would hold another bout of Springbok trials before announcing the squad to tour New Zealand. The captain bought the *Daily News* in Durban the following day, and was astonished to read more purportedly well-informed predictions that he was going to be dropped from the team, and would be left at home.

So incessantly undermined by whispers in the media, lesser men would have buckled, but Claassen resolutely accepted whatever obstacle was placed in his path. Anxious and fearing the worst, he duly attended the Springbok trials in Pretoria, but injured his knee on the opening day. He was ruled out of any further participation, and left in the most tantalising limbo.

Once again, the selectors met. Again, they discussed the captaincy at length. Again, it appears Claassen prevailed by a narrow majority, with Lochner and Smith still preferring Stofberg. "I was genuinely surprised when I was named to lead the squad to New Zealand," the captain recalls. "After everything that had been written and said, it was an even bigger moment for me than my initial appointment before the series against Ireland. Back then, I had not been so aware that Butch Lochner and Nelie Smith didn't want me in the squad."

The bitter division between captain and coach became the weakest link for these 1981 Springboks. It lingered uncomfortably throughout the tour to New Zealand, and exploded into the public domain with the publication of Claassen's autobiography in 1985. The parties have since been reconciled, and neither Smith nor Claassen wishes to reopen any old wounds, but the essence of their differences lies at the heart of the captain's story.

Smith wanted Stofberg as captain because he had known him from his Free State days in the mid-1970s, trusted him completely, and appreciated his disciplined, determined approach. In contrast, he did not understand Claassen, appearing to resent his more relaxed attitude, his readiness to laugh and enjoy a party with his team-mates. Ask Smith even today what he seeks in his perfect captain, and he replies: "He must be a sober guy."

It was also relevant that, as a player, Smith had suffered a humiliating defeat with the 1965 Springboks in New Zealand and that, for him, the 1981 tour represented a once-only opportunity to restore his reputation at this level. He had spent many dedicated hours developing a game plan for victory, and he saw no reason to apologise that his plan required Stofberg as captain.

From Claassen's perspective, Smith was obviously entitled to his opinion, but he felt the coach should have accepted the majority decision of the panel and committed himself to working honestly and openly with the captain in the greater interests of the team. In his view, that sadly did not happen.

Harmonious sporting teams tend to be better equipped to deal with fierce opposition from external forces. If ever a squad needed internal harmony, it was the 1981 Springboks, for they would soon be subjected to angry demonstrations and incessant disruption far more severe than anything suffered on the 1969/70 tour to Britain and Ireland. Through seven traumatic weeks, their lives would be punctuated by shouting, threats, police cordons and barbed wire.

The tour was able to take place because a right-wing government happened to be in power in New Zealand and, while not publicly supporting the tour, Prime Minister Robert Muldoon had steadfastly refused to deny entry visas to the touring squad. All seemed well, but the South Africans arrived to find a usually tranquil country acrimoniously split down the middle between those who believed politics should not interfere with sport and those who argued their country must have no sporting contact with apartheid. Few sat on the fence.

A debate raged in the streets, in the media, in homes. The divisive issue of rugby links with South Africa would dominate New Zealand's agenda for many years to come. "We had no idea what to expect," Claassen recalls. "There had been no television in South Africa during the tour of 1969/70, and photographs in newspapers did not convey the intensity of the demonstrations at all.

"We also thought that the protests in a liberal place like Britain would not spread to a place like New Zealand, which was a rugby country far removed from mainstream politics. New Zealanders had always been our friends. We did not imagine there would be problems. At least, that was what we hoped."

Johan Claassen, the former Springbok captain, no relation to Wynand, had been appointed as manager of the team, and this distinguished man of rugby found himself hurled into the most volatile political spotlight. He had been given absolute instructions by the Board prior to departure firstly to complete the tour at all costs and secondly not to be drawn into any political debate.

This strategy directly resulted in a catastrophic opening press conference only hours after the Springboks' arrival in Gisborne. Flanked by his coach, Nelie Smith, and the assistant manager, Abe Williams, with his tour captain installed alongside, the grim-faced Claassen was mercilessly besieged by hostile questions concerning the political consequences of the tour.

Wynand Claassen sat silent, progressively concerned as the manager's responses became more abrupt and less satisfactory. By the time a sympathetic journalist asked the South Africans to outline the recent steps taken to integrate rugby among all races, offering a valuable opportunity for the panel to convey a far more positive image, the mood had turned sour. Johan Claassen angrily repeated that he would not talk about politics.

It is easy to proclaim the South African Rugby Board should have ensured the tour management was thoroughly prepared to answer such questions, but the scale and intensity of opposition to the tour caught everyone from Danie Craven to members of the public by surprise. Furthermore, the protesters proved so well organised and so utterly resolved that it is doubtful whether even the most astute of media managers could have improved the situation.

Johan Claassen, nicknamed "The Pope" by many of the squad because of his resemblance to John Paul II, stood firm and presented a steadfast, unapologetic front. This, he felt, was his patriotic duty. Alone in his room, however, this inherently decent man agonised in silence.

The embattled manager of the 1981 Springboks has now happily retired to the west coast town of Yzerfontein, from where he reflects softly: "It was not worth it. We were in an impossible situation at the time but, if I look back, I have to say no rugby tour is so important that it is worth that kind of conflict.

"Our arguments were sound in theory: we repeated that we had been invited to tour and that we had simply accepted that invitation, but the unavoidable reality was that our presence split a nation. The tour divided families against each other. One man came and told me how he had always been keen on rugby, but that his wife had moved from both table and bed because she supports the tour, and he does not. He went on to explain how his son had sided with his mother, and his daughter agreed with him.

"It may have been true that many of the protesters came along for the ride, and we even heard stories that they were being paid to march at the venues, but there is no point denying that, in practice, our tour seriously disrupted the lives of many decent New Zealanders. It was not worth it."

The second match of the tour, against Waikato at Hamilton, was cancelled when 200 demonstrators sat down, linked arms and could not be removed from the field. Amid the chaos and drama, Claassen telephoned Craven and asked whether the squad should come home. The Board president responded with an emphatic instruction that the Springboks must complete the tour.

"It had become more than just a question of right and wrong, because we had now become embroiled in a conflict," the manager recalls. "We were being urged by both the New Zealand rugby authorities and the police that, whatever happened, we must complete the schedule. They said anything else would be seen as a victory for the protesters.

"We were indebted to these people, so we resolved to carry on … but this does not alter the fact that the tour was not worth the disruption that it caused. As Springboks, we should not have been in that place at that time."

Keeping such personal views entirely and strictly to himself, Johan Claassen continued to appear on television and in newspapers blankly insisting that his squad had been invited to New Zealand and would complete the tour. He accepted the notion of discipline, and adhered strictly to his instructions.

Wynand Claassen, for his part, was so focused on his ambition of beating the All Blacks that he scarcely found the time to contemplate whether the tour should be abandoned or not. His mind was full of rugby, and the captain was pleased to see the overwhelming majority of his players accept the daily cycle of screaming protesters, barbed wire around the fields, and restrictions on leaving their barricaded hotel. Several Springboks were unsettled and did struggle to find their form but, for most, laughter was the best form of defence.

Naas Botha recalls: "Wynand was clearly relaxed about everything, and many of us took the lead from him. We dealt with the situation by laughing at the protests, turning everything into a joke. When people threw ink-injected eggs at the team bus, we were sitting inside and holding competitions to guess what colour would be the next to splatter over the window.

"One afternoon we were sitting around in our hotel rooms listening to the demonstrators chanting in the streets below, and Danie Gerber decided he would strip to the waist and stand in the window striking strange poses like some kind of body-builder. The protesters looked up and shouted: 'Paint him black and send him back'. The mood was light-hearted, and we all laughed."

On other occasions, there was nothing funny. One restaurant owner had to produce a gun to scare away a group of demonstrators who were threatening players during dinner. On another occasion, four South Africans had to leap for safety when a speeding car suddenly ramped the pavement where they were walking. On this tour, there was always a story to be told.

To their dismay, many All Blacks found they had also become targets of pressure and harassment in their own country. Both the outstanding centre Bruce Robertson and Graham Mourie, who had led New Zealand against Scotland earlier in the season, had already withdrawn from the series on moral grounds, but crank telephone calls and threatening letters served only to strengthen the resolve of men such as Andy Dalton, the Counties hooker soon to be confirmed as the new All Black captain for the series against South Africa.

Dalton recalls: "My father, Ray, had been vice-captain on the All Black tour to South Africa in 1949, and I was brought up to recognise that a Test series between New Zealand and South Africa was something special. I wanted to play against the Springboks in 1981, and I started to resent the hypocrisy that meant Kiwi yachtsmen who won a race that had stopped in Cape Town would be given a ticker-tape parade down Queens Street in Auckland – good luck to them – but it was a national crisis if we played rugby against the Springboks.

"We did feel sorry for the South Africans who had to endure something less than hospitable treatment from a vocal minority of New Zealanders, but that sympathy didn't make us any less desperate to win the series."

As the first Test at Christchurch neared, Wynand Claassen became less concerned about the demonstrators and more preoccupied with the conflict at the heart of the touring squad. He had been concerned when, as tour captain, he was not chosen to lead the side in the opening match of the tour, but Nelie Smith insisted there was nothing sinister in that team selection. Maybe the captain was being over-sensitive; maybe he wasn't.

Within days, Claassen realised his instincts were accurate. Small incidents at training and overheard remarks at the hotel combined to convince the touring captain that the coach intended to persist with his original plan to defeat New Zealand by naming Stofberg to lead the side in the first Test.

"The players all supported Wynand as captain," Stofberg recalls, "but the mood within the team did become extremely awkward when it became clear how Nelie was thinking. I did not ask for that to happen, but I had to accept it."

Claassen suffered the indignity of being asked to leave the tour selection meeting while his position was discussed, eventually being called back to hear that he had been dropped and that Stofberg would captain the side. In 1937, Danie Craven and Phil Nel had similarly been asked to leave a selection meeting in New Zealand, and been dropped. Forty-four years might have elapsed, but the consequences for South African rugby would be the same.

Johan Claassen had attended the meeting, and felt obliged to support the coach. "There have been so many inaccurate stories about the 1981 tour, I have often wondered whether I was actually there," he reflects. "The facts were that I was not a national selector at the time, but I had been on enough tours to know that, once the team leaves South Africa, the coach gets what he wants. I do not know if Nelie made the right decision between Theuns and Wynand, but he was the coach and he had the right to choose the side he wanted."

Most of the players were astonished to learn their captain had been left out of the team for the first Test; some hinted darkly at a Broederbond dimension in Smith's determination to elevate Stofberg, while others maintained this was a simple case of old Free Staters sticking together. Even today, however, the coach insists his decision was purely tactical.

Naas Botha reflects: "Wynand was the tour captain, and he should have led the side in Christchurch. The players all believed in him, and we were disrupted by his absence. That mistake proved crucial." Even the All Blacks were surprised. Dalton recalls: "We thought Wynand was a delightful fellow, and we all knew he should have been playing. I felt for him."

Claassen scarcely knew where to turn, where to look. Whatever anyone said to console him, he was not playing. When the Test team departed to spend the night before the match in the Linwood squash courts, following police advice to avoid confrontation with the demonstrators, the discarded tour captain was forced to stay behind with the rest of the non-playing squad members and be driven away to sleep in a private home. He felt empty inside and sad, deprived and angry. A profound sense of frustration burned within him.

One man's disappointment was another man's opportunity.

Theuns Stofberg had captained the Springboks once before, when he stood in for the injured Morné du Plessis in the first Test against the Jaguars at Montevideo in 1980, but now he was chosen to lead his country in his own right, against the All Blacks in Christchurch. The stakes rose no higher.

Some observers assumed that Stofberg's capacity to lead would be undermined by the fact that he stuttered, at times painfully. However, the occasional stumbling over words barely registered with his team-mates. To them, he was a tall, imposing man, an outstanding loose forward, and a loyal team-mate. Suggest the stutter was an issue, and they simply say it wasn't.

The fourth and youngest son of a minister of religion, Stofberg was born at Villiers, a town in the Free State, before his family moved to live on the Bluff, in Durban. Suckled on rugby and the Dutch Reformed Church, he was overjoyed one weekend in 1967 when Dawie de Villiers, the Springbok rugby captain, accepted an invitation to attend the Sunday evening service at his father's church.

On the Saturday, the young Stofberg attended his first Test at King's Park and watched De Villiers lead South Africa to a resounding victory over France; on the Sunday, he stood awe-struck in the aisle as the renowned scrumhalf signed his hymn book. Altogether inspired, he pursued his education at Grey College in Bloemfontein, before advancing to the University of the Free State where he played lock in a celebrated university under-20 team that included no fewer than nine future Springboks.

Nelie Smith, then the Free State coach, prompted the giant leap forward in 1976 when he switched the lock forward to flank and gave him his provincial debut. Two months later, Stofberg was named to replace his boyhood hero, Jan Ellis, on the side of the Springbok scrum and make his Test debut against the All Blacks in Bloemfontein.

Summoned to national service in Pretoria, most probably by generals who enthusiastically supported Northern Transvaal, he subsequently held a place in the dominant Blue Bulls pack through 1979. In the absence of an overseas tour at the end of that season, he blazed the trail as one of the first South Africans to fly north and play for a club in the emerging Italian league. He received expenses of R1 000 per month to rumble in the black jersey of Padua.

Stofberg returned home and consolidated his place in a famous Springbok back row alongside Rob Louw and Morné du Plessis through the nine Tests of 1980, all the while accepting an additional responsibility within the squad as a trained physiotherapist. In these days, the Board only made provision for a team doctor, and Stofberg found himself ceaselessly requested to relieve the aching muscles of pleading team-mates. Invariably, he obliged.

Reports that he would be appointed Springbok captain at the start of 1981 evaporated when Wynand Claassen was installed, but Stofberg insists he was not disappointed. "I was in the side. That was what I wanted," he recalls. "It was not important for me to be captain. The stutter was an issue for me, and I was genuinely happy to support Wynand. Everyone respected him."

Resolved to lead by example, Stofberg took his team onto Lancaster Park with confidence, but it quickly became clear that the heavy Springbok pack was struggling in the clogging mud. The All Blacks looked sharper and swifter, and they raced into a 10-3 half-time lead. The tourists continued to compete with evident desire, but Hennie Bekker's late try gave the final score of 14-9 a competitive gloss that was scarcely deserved. South Africa had planned to win the forward struggle, enabling Botha to kick New Zealand into submission, but the Springbok juggernaut had literally got stuck in the mud and, on this occasion, not even Botha could kick-start his team's performance.

Wynand Claassen had sat and suffered in the grandstand. "Our backline was maybe our greatest strength, but we hardly used them," he recalls. "The idea that we would be able to pressurise the All Blacks by playing 10-man rugby had failed, and we had given them control of the series."

The disgruntled Springboks immediately retreated to the west coast town of Greymouth, where a police decision to cancel their match against South Canterbury in Timaru (where they felt unable to secure the field) had created a welcome break of seven days for the tourists to revive, refocus and restructure. Wynand Claassen rose to the challenge and, for many of his players, his enduring reputation as an outstanding leader would forever be associated with these healing days in Greymouth.

Smith's credibility had been undermined by the first-Test defeat, and the tour captain sensed an opportunity to regain control of the power struggle at the heart of the tour; and, in this hour of need, he may have found an unlikely ally. "For the first time on tour, Johan Claassen gave me a virtually free hand in Greymouth," Claassen reflects, "and I was able to arrange a frank and honest meeting for the players in my hotel room. There were no officials present."

The captain pulled no punches ... there was no room for error, only the players could pull the tour back on track, they needed to be honest with one another, they needed to stand together, they needed to involve the back line and, as players, they needed to take command of the team strategy. "When that meeting drew to a close," Claassen reflects, "I sensed a new unity of purpose. We were a group of South Africans under incredible pressure a long way from home, and we decided we would not lose another match on tour. That was all. We simply decided we would not lose again."

Nelson's Bay suffered the impact of this resolution and were beaten 83-0 as Claassen's team – and, after Greymouth, it was Claassen's team once again – regained their rhythm. A consensus had emerged that the Springboks had lacked direction in Christchurch, and Smith, a pragmatist under pressure, accepted that Claassen's recall as eighthman would be one of seven changes made to the Test side ahead of the do-or-die second Test in Wellington.

The captaincy issue seemed settled at last, but a new controversy erupted around the decision to drop Rob Louw. Wynand Claassen and the rest of the tour selection committee had reached a conclusion that Burger Geldenhuys would be a stronger fetcher on the ground but, as ever among the troubled Springboks of 1981, some players sought dastardly motives in the decision.

Louw had been one of five South African players who did not return from a party given by Andy Haden, the All Black, until the Sunday morning after the first Test, and the fair flanker bristled against what he regarded as the schoolmasterly management's demand for an explanation. Relations between a significant group of Springboks and the tour officials were deteriorating.

The decision to omit Louw from the Test team struck a spark in the straw, and disaffected players started to propagate the story that the flank was actually being punished for attending Haden's party in Christchurch. They told how Johan Claassen and Smith did not like Louw because they were *broeders*, and he was English-speaking; and how they favoured disciplined, abstemious players while he liked to have a beer and let off steam after a match.

Perhaps this was true, or maybe the tour selectors actually did believe that Geldenhuys was a stronger fetcher on the ground. Who knows? What was clear was there were more sombre faces at the Springbok breakfast table, more angst and tension, more awkward moments within the squad.

Within any group of sports people at any time, there will always be some players who are satisfied, some who are disgruntled and some who are not even aware of the issue. It would be wrong to depict the 1981 Springboks as different except insofar as the unique circumstances of their tour did seem to ensure that every drama was rapidly escalated into a public crisis.

Wynand Claassen was fated to lead this stressed group of South Africans, and with confidence and status restored by his own Test recall he resolved to breech the chasm that had developed between certain players and management, and to carry the spirit of Greymouth into the second Test.

At least, the captain thought, he would try.

One day it was decided the players would conduct the training session on their own, so Wynand Claassen took the forwards and Divan Serfontein directed the backline. After two hours, the captain suggested the entire squad should run a few hills to maintain their stamina for the Test. Serfontein, a doctor, disagreed, saying it would be wrong to do endurance after sprints.

"You shouldn't do stamina after aerobic activity," the vibrant scrumhalf told his captain, his friend. "We can do it, but I don't agree with you."

"OK, fine, we'll leave it."

Claassen was upset, and he pointedly ignored Serfontein on the bus back to the hotel. That evening, the scrumhalf was knocking on his door.

"Look, Wynand, I am sorry but, physiologically, that is how it works. Don't be angry with me. You know you've always got my support. I know this tour has been difficult for you, but the guys are getting behind you now. Please don't make an issue of this. We're starting to get things right."

"No, I'm sorry," the captain replied. "I have been under a bit of stress over the past few days. It's been lonely, but I'm OK now. You were right."

The two Springboks went downstairs and settled in the hotel bar, where they spent the rest of the evening in the company of two policemen. Other players arrived in due course and, as their spirits started to pour and soar, the group took pleasure in composing an alternative haka to oppose the traditional All Black dance, just as Phil Mostert's team had done in 1928.

Claassen was a much happier man when he got to bed that night. With a little help from his friends, he would turn this tour around. He knew one thing: the Springbok revival would happen in the second Test at Athletic Park, Wellington, or it would not happen at all. His team would stand or fall.

"Everyone rallied together," the captain reflects. "When the police said we had to spend the night before the Test on bunks in a hall within the grandstand at Athletic Park, nobody complained. We arrived at the ground shortly after noon on the Friday, and we did not see any daylight again until we ran out to play at three on the Saturday afternoon, but none of that mattered. There was a snooker table in the hall to keep us busy, and we were so determined. After everything we had been through, nothing was going to stop us winning that match.

"In those days, we didn't stand in a straight line while the national anthems were played. We bound arms around each other's shoulders and formed a huddle; and I shall never forget the resolve in that circle. I looked at the faces. It was incredible. There was no way we would lose."

On the opposite side of the field, the All Blacks were caught cold, literally. They had been brought to Athletic Park early on the Saturday morning and been told to remain in the home team's changing room. While the Springboks watched videos, played snooker and relaxed in the centrally heated reception halls upstairs, the New Zealanders were wrapping themselves in three blankets and shivering in their icy dungeon. Dalton ruefully recalls that morning as being the worst build-up for any first-class match in his career.

South Africa led 12-0 after 11 minutes, and 18-3 at half time.

Botha was in breathtaking form, scraping a pass off his toes to spin the ball wide for Gerrie Germishuys's try, and kicking penalties with precision. Amid smoke bombs and an occasional ruckus in the stands, Claassen pounded around the field, imploring his men forward, heartily slapping them on the back. The crack policemen of the Red Brigade had positioned themselves behind the posts to prevent any crowd invasion from undercover protesters on the terraces.

Nothing would deny the tourists.

The All Blacks did warm up in the second half, and Allan Hewson started to chip away at the lead. One more score, Smith told himself in the stands, that's all we need. Botha kicked a drop goal into the teeth of the wind, and the Test was eventually won 24-12, the series levelled at 1-1.

Botha had scored 20 points, but every Springbok drank from the cup of joy and relief. As they celebrated this historic triumph in adversity, the South Africans sat in the visitors' changing room and sang like a choir:

The motto of the Springboks is come and drink with me.
The motto of the Springboks is come and drink with me.
The forwards made a scrum, the halfbacks put it in.
The halfbacks to the centres, the centres to the wing,
The wing scores a try, the All Blacks start to cry.
Hoorah! Hoorah! For we can sing and play,
For we can sing and play, for sporting men are we,
We never, never quarrel; we never disagree.

(At this point, ironic laughter broke out around the changing room.)

For the motto of the Springboks is come and drink with me.
The motto of the Springboks is come and drink with me.

And a shirtless Claassen sat and sang, this rugby-playing King Lear, this sweat-stained personification of triumph. After all the disappointments, the asides and humiliation, he had been unequivocally vindicated.

It was now more than 30 hours since the players had arrived at the ground, but nobody was in a hurry to leave the scene of such a memorable victory. The exhausted captain took his time, looking around the changing room, gazing at his players: at the prop forwards Ockie Oosthuizen and the 132 kg of Flippie van der Merwe, at the combative hooker Robert Cockrell, at locks Louis Moolman and De Villiers Visser, at Burger Geldenhuys, the young flanker who had played the debut of his wildest dreams, at the gallant Stofberg.

He looked across at Serfontein, who had snapped at All Black heels, and at Botha, the dedicated match-winner who had again demonstrated a rare ability to perform on the greatest occasions, and at Danie Gerber, the prodigy centre, at the creative Willie du Plessis, at the rampaging Ray Mordt on the right wing and the veteran Germishuys on the left, at the mercurial fullback, Gysie Pienaar. This was his team, and this had been his team's defining day.

Serfontein recalls: "Many years later, I visited Dr Craven when he was ill in hospital, and we started talking about the old days. He told me he rated the 1981 squad as one of the finest Springbok squads ever to leave our shore. The side in the second Test was strong, but we had fantastic strength in depth. Our midweek performances were excellent throughout the tour."

The challenge facing Claassen's players was to maintain their momentum and become only the second Springbok squad, following the Invincibles of 1937, to win a Test series in New Zealand; and the Saturday side's outstanding 39-12 destruction of Auckland at Eden Park inspired confidence ahead of the third Test to be played at the same ground only seven days later.

Team selection, for once, appeared to be a formality. In their enthusiasm to build on victory in Wellington, the Springbok management assumed injuries to Visser and Stofberg would resolve themselves by Saturday, and announced an unchanged team for the third Test. An opportunity to summon further players from South Africa was declined. They would soldier on.

Visser's condition suddenly deteriorated during the last training session and, on the Friday night, the lock was forced to withdraw. Smith responded quickly and decisively, moving Stofberg to lock and recalling Louw on the flank, but worse news was to follow.

As usual, the Test team were spending the Friday night before the Test at the stadium, sleeping in function rooms turned dormitories at Eden Park, and the players awoke on the Saturday morning to hear that Stofberg had been declared unfit. Smith was in trouble. His lock options were all but exhausted.

Hennie Bekker was carrying an injury himself, and he had spent the night at a private home believing his tour was over. It wasn't. There was no alternative. He would have to play. The towering lock was urgently summoned to join the Test team inside the stadium. "It was ridiculous," Botha says, reflecting upon an unsettling and chaotic 12 hours. "This was the most important match of our lives, and we did not even know the composition of our own team until a few hours before kick-off. Nobody knew what was happening."

Wynand Claassen cleared his mind, breathed hard. This was Saturday 12 September 1981, and he stood 80 minutes away from being ranked among the greatest Springbok captains. He was aware that his players had the ability to defeat the All Blacks and he was also aware that, whatever the result, the mere act of reaching the final match of this turbulent tour represented a monumental achievement for his squad. On an overcast, cool and strangely calm day in Auckland, rugby immortality wafted on the breeze.

As the morning dragged slowly into afternoon, his mind drifted back to that afternoon in his youth when he had first cast eyes upon the white numbers on the black jerseys and the gold numbers on the green jerseys, and been captivated by the beauty of the contest, the magic, the history and tradition, the sportsmanship and the glory; now, aged 30, he stood in the midst of it all.

Back home, in the freezing small hours of a winter morning, hundreds of thousands of excited fathers were shaking their dew-eyed sons out of bed, turning on kettles, pouring coffee and huddling together beneath blankets in front of the television. This was history. Everyone had to watch. As the pictures from Auckland flickered across the screen, many legions of South Africans prepared for an experience they would never forget.

Claassen delivered a last team talk, stressing how far the team had come and concluding they owed this ultimate victory to themselves. Along the corridor at Eden Park, as spectators edged through the turnstiles past rows of police and endlessly chanting demonstrators, Dalton was telling his All Blacks to prepare for nothing less than "the biggest match you will ever play".

The Test was only minutes old when players and spectators alike became eerily aware they were not alone. A white Cessna aircraft had started to buzz the stadium, flying in over the Number One stand, across the field and then soaring upwards, narrowly missing the uprights at the open terrace end before wheeling around and swooping, again and again, on the same flight path.

Players glanced anxiously at one another, then towards the sky. Claassen tried to focus on the match, but even the captain could not prevent himself from time after time checking the position of the plane. The pilot was dropping bags of flour and bundles of anti-tour pamphlets on Eden Park. If the engine had cut out, the plane would have crashed into the stand; if the plane had touched one of the uprights, it would have caused mayhem. And yet, in this surreal and dangerous atmosphere, this extraordinary Test ran its course.

The All Blacks bounced off the blocks, as winger Stu Wilson collected a pass above his head to score a fine try. When Gary Knight was allowed to score from close range after Frank Shelford had evidently knocked on, it seemed to be New Zealand's day, and the home side led 16–3 at half time.

Claassen swiftly gathered his players in a huddle and told them there was still hope. He explained the Springboks would now be playing with the wind, and stressed that one score would bring them back into the match. "I told the guys we simply had to turn things round," the captain recalls.

The Auckland crowd had started to celebrate, but their festival mood was quelled by a South African recovery that can be compared with the feat of Dawie de Villiers's team in the third Test of the 1965 tour, when the Springboks seized a 19–16 victory from a seemingly hopeless 5–16 half-time deficit. It had been done before, and Claassen believed it could be done once again.

Colin Beck, a substitute centre, chipped into the dead-ball zone and Mordt was suddenly dashing shoulder to shoulder with Hewson, the All Black fullback who, in the famous words of his team-mate Bernie Fraser, would this day swing from hero, to villain, to hero, to villain, to hero. Mordt won the race and gleefully scored the try, Botha converted neatly, and Claassen started clapping his hands together. At 16-9, the contest was alive again.

Mordt, the powerful Zimbabwean whose boyish enthusiasm was such that he habitually arrived an hour early for every practice, burst down the right wing, chipped infield, beat Hewson to the bounce, and scored again. Botha stroked the conversion and added a further penalty, but Doug Rollerson's drop goal gave the home side a 22-18 lead with the minutes ebbing away.

Still the Cessna buzzed above, still the flour bombs fell and, finally, at this crucial stage of the match, a flying bag of flour struck a player. Gary Knight, the New Zealand prop, was manifestly dazed. Referee Norling supplied a moment of humour to the trauma by suggesting to medical men who began sponging the All Black's face with cold water that they should be careful not to turn Knight into a pastry. In a more serious tone, the referee summoned the captains together and asked them directly: "Do you still want to play on?"

Dalton glanced at the scoreboard and said yes. Claassen responded: "We must get through this game. We must finish the series." Norling nodded, blew his whistle and restarted a contest that was beginning to fray at the edges. In these few remaining minutes, careers would be made and broken.

New Zealanders were shouting for the final whistle as the South Africans surged forward, but the All Black defence stood firm. Four minutes of injury time had elapsed when Botha gathered a loose ball, sprinted into a gap, slipped past two tackles, and managed to contrive a pass out to Mordt. The rampant wing was unstoppable seven yards from the line, and his third try of the second half brought the scores level at 22-22, with Botha's conversion to come.

Claassen could not believe his eyes.

Dizzy with delight, the captain threw his arms around the try-scorer as they jogged back towards the halfway line. Botha stood calm and watched as the Cessna swooped barely 15 metres above the spectators packed on the open terrace. He struck the conversion attempt cleanly, but the ball drifted away to the right of the posts. "It was strange," Claassen reflects, "but I didn't mind about that miss. I thought we had drawn the Test, and the series, and, after everything that had happened, it somehow seemed like the right result."

Standing out like a beacon in his red Welsh jersey, Norling gestured both teams back to the restart. "Come on, boys," he rasped. "Play on!"

Five minutes of injury time, six, seven … Norling waved play on, Claassen kept his head down, kept chasing, kept tackling. South Africa won the put-in to a scrum but, as Serfontein tried to manoeuvre the front rows squarely into line, the referee awarded a free kick to New Zealand, penalising the Springbok hooker for foot-up. What? The scrumhalf had not even presented the ball.

Claassen recalls: "It is basically impossible to award a free-kick for foot-up before the ball has been presented. I didn't see Clive Norling again until before a Test between Wales and South Africa in 2000. We chatted, and he said he would have awarded that same penalty all over again. I said the ball had not even been presented. He shrugged, and claimed he didn't even know the score at that stage of the game. To be honest, I found that very hard to believe."

It got worse. Donaldson tapped the free kick and darted forward. He passed to Rollerson who was tackled, it seemed, perfectly legally, but the referee sounded his whistle again. He proclaimed the Springboks had not retreated, and changed the free kick into a penalty. "Kick it," said Dalton, as he flicked the ball to Hewson. The fullback winked at his captain and, as the crowd hushed, kicked the penalty between the posts. New Zealand led 25-22.

There was still time for Botha to restart, for Gerber to chip ahead and for Mordt to bear down on Hewson once again, but the fullback cleared to touch and, at last, Norling blew his final whistle. Fifteen All Blacks raised their arms in delight, and fifteen Springboks plunged to the depths of despair.

"There was nothing we could do," Claassen recalls. "Everything ran away like water through our hands. It was over. After overcoming so many obstacles, it was incredibly tough to lose the series like that."

Botha wanted to "whack Norling's head off" as he left the field. "That man took a lifetime of pride away from 32 players just because, for whatever reason, he had decided they would not win," the flyhalf seethes, still. Serfontein recalls not so much a sense of disappointment, but of overwhelming despair and leaden exhaustion. Gerber's enduring memory of this dramatic day is the stunned, silent changing room. "Johan Claassen tried to say something," the centre recalls, "but his words just trailed away. There was nothing anybody could say."

The sense of outrage has scarcely subsided during the past 30 years. Ask any South African male over the age of 40 what they remember of the 1981 tour to New Zealand, and they are likely to spit out the name "Norling".

Ask Andy Dalton to concede that it is impossible to concede a free kick for foot-up before the ball is presented to the scrum, and the All Black captain smiles a knowing smile: "I must say I thought that was a really reasonable decision." No more words are necessary. The smile says everything.

It says hard luck; it says stop complaining. It says Frank McMullen scored a try that was wrongly disallowed in 1960. It says Bruce Robertson, Dalton's close friend, remains adamant that he was twice denied tries by obstruction in 1976. It says look at the history of Tests between South Africa and New Zealand, and be content to know the decisions have evened out over 80 years.

"Look, it was a very close series," Dalton adds. "If I was a South African, I would probably be on the same wavelength about the last penalty, but I'm a New Zealander and, for me, it was a good decision." He smiles again.

Claassen and his players were thus denied the crowning place in history for a series win in New Zealand, and yet posterity has set the 1981 Springboks apart in the history of South African rugby. They are admired for their courage under intense pressure, for their natural ability, and for the fact that they came within one referee's decision and one conversion of glory.

The bitter disappointment of Eden Park left the players looking forward to nothing so much as the flight home to normality, but the Board had committed the Springboks to play three matches in the United States, including a Test against the Eagles, on their way back to South Africa. It is perhaps amusing to reflect upon the almost unbelievable circumstances of this bizarre mini-tour, but the experience proved utterly demeaning for one of the leading sides in the world. In their desperate quest for Test opposition, the Board succeeded only in further devaluing the currency of Springbok rugby. The Springboks would probably have had to play against the North Pole, if the North Pole Rugby Union had agreed to pay the internal travel and accommodation bills.

Claassen led his team from the glare of a series that rated as an unofficial world championship of the game into circumstances that most club players would have deemed unacceptable. To the players' huge credit, they generally endured the Keystone Cops and maintained their own standards.

The opening match was played at an American gridiron field on the shores of Lake Michigan, and the second game only went ahead at the Bleeker Stadium in the town of Albany after Tom Selfridge, the larger-than-life chairman of the Eastern Rugby Union and the hero of this particular adventure, had secured a verdict at the US Supreme Court.

Selfridge then set himself up as a one-man security system, standing in an elevated position at the corner of the venue just to keep watch on demonstrators outside the main gate. "Please keep an eye on me during the game," he told the Springboks, by now open-mouthed in wonder, before kick-off. "If any protesters get into the ground, I will give you the signal to evacuate."

This was certainly a fresh style of rugby officialdom, but the circumstances of South Africa's first-ever Test match against the United States Eagles stretched even the most extravagant American imagination.

The match was scheduled for the Bleeker Stadium on Saturday afternoon, but security officials had become concerned about violent demonstrations, and a decision was taken to wake the South African Test team early on the Friday. The players were told to prepare for the Test, and ordered to say nothing even to the other members of their own squad, who were blissfully unaware of any change in plan and happily set off to visit the local baseball Hall of Fame. Meanwhile, the intrigued Test players travelled in private cars to the house of the ubiquitous Mr Selfridge where they changed into their playing kit.

Another short car journey carried the Springboks to a deserted polo field, where they were soon surprised to discover Thys Burger, the eighthman and their own team-mate, had been co-opted to help a group of local officials set up the posts. Claassen gave a team talk about focusing on the game and, although his side only led 6-4 at the interval, they turned to play downhill in the second half and powered to a 38-7 victory over a competitive and physical US Eagles team. Burger, for one, had thoroughly enjoyed the day: having successfully erected the posts, he ran the line as a touch judge, then ran onto the field as a second-half South African substitute, and ended up scoring a try.

The Test had been watched by 35 spectators, 19 policemen, a television crew and one journalist. David Chambers, president of the United States Rugby Football Association, Don Reardon, the originally nominated referee, and twelve travelling South African rugby writers were among those amazed to be told, later that Friday evening, that the Test had already been played.

On Thursday 1 October Claassen finally led his drained players into the international arrivals hall at Johannesburg airport, where they were surprised and lifted by the acclaim of a large crowd. With no barbed wire, no demonstrators and no Welsh referees in sight, they relaxed. Their adventure was over.

It would be uplifting to reflect how the sheer weight of shared experience on tour to New Zealand persuaded Smith, the coach, and Claassen, the captain, to set their differences to one side and move forward in harmony, but the world of Springbok rugby is not always an uplifting place.

The national selectors met in November and decided to stage Springbok trials during March 1982, in advance of an early season home series against the South American Jaguars. This seemed reasonable. It was, however, impossible to fathom why the panel should then have resolved to choose and announce the two trial teams almost six months before kick-off.

At best, the timing was just bizarre. At worst, the strategy was specifically devised to humiliate Wynand Claassen once again. The hero of the New Zealand tour was dramatically announced as captain of the B side.

Danie Craven was appalled by the decision and, as president of the Board, he told a television reporter: "That is no way to treat a Springbok captain." In such moments of blatant injustice, South African rugby could usually rely upon its benign dictator to step in, wield influence and impose justice.

The national selection committee was up for re-election at the Annual General Meeting of the Board early in 1982, and Craven appeared to be pulling the strings when Smith and Lochner were voted off the panel, to be replaced by Cecil Moss and Hannes Marais, the former Springbok captain.

No longer a selector, Smith could no longer coach the team. He insists he was ready to step aside, but his departure was regarded as uncomfortable at the time. It was certainly sad, and the unquestioned abilities of this dedicated coach should not be disregarded because he simply could not invest confidence in the captain most admired by his own Springbok players.

Professor Daan Swiegers was named as the new convenor and, following the convention that the coach must be chosen from within the selection committee, it was resolved that Moss would coach the Springboks against the Jaguars. There was no time to lose with the first Test in Pretoria barely a week away. Claassen had followed the dramatic boardroom developments with great interest. His prospects had been transformed literally overnight.

"Wynand was the automatic choice as captain," recalls Moss, soft-spoken and meticulous, the Springbok vice-captain against the 1949

All Blacks, a skilled surgeon by trade. "He was very well respected by the players."

The Jaguars once again materialised as an Argentine team under another name, yet they were ruthlessly destroyed at Loftus Versfeld by a Springbok team at the peak of its powers. Claassen cleverly prodded the sore memories of Eden Park to motivate his side. "Some people say we lost in New Zealand because we were not good enough," the captain had said in the changing room. "This is our chance to show them what sort of rugby we can play."

His words sparked a firework display.

Carel du Plessis launched his debut with a pedigree 50-metre sprint down the left touchline, creating a try for Ockie Oosthuizen. Claassen then gathered a loose ball deep inside his own half and set Gerber free down the right touchline. The young centre dashed 70 metres to score a thrilling try. The forwards mauled with power and conviction; the backs attacked with flair and speed.

Moss sat in the stand, purring as he pondered the potential of a dominant pack and world-class back-line talents such as Botha, Gerber, Du Plessis, Mordt and Heunis. His rampant team stormed to a 50-18 victory. No international team had ever scored a half-century of points in a Test.

Claassen's side had played so well in Pretoria that almost every observer predicted another stroll in the sunshine at the second Test in Bloemfontein just a week later. Despite lacking match fitness early in their season, the assured South Africans were satisfied to assemble late on the Thursday. No hassle. A lineout call here, a backline move there: where's the opposition?

Half an hour before kick-off, Professor Swiegers put his head around the door of the home changing room and asked: "Wynand, what do you need for the party tonight? Brandy, whisky, beer? What else?" The captain told the convenor they could deal with that later. Craven had also visited the Springboks while they warmed up, and he had been alarmed by an evident mood of complacency. The old man told the players to be very careful. They grinned.

By five o'clock, the hailed heroes of Pretoria had become the disgraced villains of Bloemfontein, beaten 21-12 in a result that stands comparison with the home defeats against France in 1958 and 1964, and England in 1972. On each of these notorious occasions, the Springbok team had tripped over its own pride and arrogance and lost to demonstrably weaker opponents.

Hugo Porta, the impresario Jaguars flyhalf, had scored all 21 points in his team's triumph, and embellished his reputation, but the South Africans had been unable to hold possession, to stay tight, to develop momentum.

"I was terribly disappointed," Claassen recalls. "Everything went wrong for us. Porta kicked almost every ball and controlled the game, and we could not find any kind of rhythm. I tried the big team talk at half time, but it didn't provoke much of a response. It was going to be just one of those days."

On this deeply unsatisfactory note, this gifted generation of Springboks was again forced off centre stage by the grim political realities of the age. In 1982, a Welsh tour was cancelled; a Five Nations XV arrived and marked the opening of the new Ellis Park by losing three matches in a row; and, striking right to the heart of white morale, Naas Botha announced he was going to leave South Africa in search of a better future as a specialist kicker in the professional world of American football. He joined the Dallas Cowboys.

Claassen was still leading Natal, but the realisation was starting to dawn upon him that he had already played his last Test. A respectable World XV did tour South Africa in 1983, to celebrate the centenary of the Western Province Rugby Union, but they were permitted to play against only a South African XV, not the Springboks, and the cherished green-and-gold jerseys remained folded and packed away through another grim and isolated season.

The eighthman eventually announced his retirement after leading Natal to the Currie Cup final in 1984, but he remained firmly in the public eye first when he was elected to become a Springbok selector, then when he wrote a controversial autobiography that led directly to his removal from the panel.

"It was a hectic period," he recalls. "The book caused a lot of problems. I do not regret writing a subjective account of what happened, but some episodes may have come out more harshly than I intended. The reaction was amazing. At times, I honestly didn't know who my friends were."

Claassen had offered his perspective on the role of the Broederbond in rugby, disclosing how it was usually necessary to be a *broeder* before you could be elected to either the executive or selection committees of most provincial rugby unions, and he gave a candid account of his association with Nelie Smith. Several months before publication, he had felt obliged to warn Craven that several leading figures within the game might be angered by the contents of his book. "Well, that's their problem," the Board president had replied, in typical fashion. "Whether they like it or not, they will just have to take it."

The captain may now reflect that, in the event, it was he who suffered most of the consequences of his printed honesty. He was essentially ostracised at a national level for several years before successfully returning to the code as the admired coach of a freethinking Natal University side.

Through the 1990s, Claassen proceeded to launch, run and edit a variety of rugby publications, and he proved instrumental in the founding of an official Springbok Supporters club. He remains close to the game, an eager travelling supporter of the national team wherever they play; and he is still "a bit nuts" about the Boks, still bold and impassioned, still creative and innovative, still a captain who will forever be admired for his courage in adversity.

South African rugby reverted to a purely domestic diet through 1982 and 1983, and vast crowds flocked to Currie Cup matches, but news from the Rugby Football Union in London that an England team would defy the powerful political consensus of the day and tour South Africa in 1984 was rapturously received by the palsied beggars at the gate of world rugby.

The national selectors reintroduced themselves to one another, and Moss proved successful in advocating Theuns Stofberg as Springbok captain for the two Test matches. "Stoffs was such a solid type of a guy," the coach recalls. "He was strong, fast and virile, and his mere presence in the changing room gave you the impression that everything would go well."

Stofberg, who had followed three years with Free State with three seasons in Northern Transvaal, had since moved again and established himself as a hero in the dominant Western Province team: "My experience with three top provinces made it easy for me to lead the Springbok side," he reflects. "There have always been divisions between north and south, but the sheer intensity of the Currie Cup competition during isolation was starting to create a more antagonistic element of provincialism among the players. I felt I could bridge the gaps."

Moss and Stofberg eagerly prepared an impressive Springbok team that included two coloured players: the gifted Errol Tobias at flyhalf, and Avril Williams on the wing. "They were both chosen on merit," Stofberg recalls, "and there was no problem within the team at all. There were no quotas in those days, and none of us doubted they were both genuine Test players."

The England squad had arrived in South Africa without 18 leading players, withdrawn because of injury, work commitments or principle, and even though John Scott's team performed respectably in their provincial matches, they were not expected to win the first Test in Port Elizabeth.

Stofberg needed only to mention the word "Porta" during his team talk, and the pride of South African rugby was soon stampeding out to play at the austere Boet Erasmus Stadium. Every player seemed to approach the match as though it was their last chance to wear the green-and-gold and, so far as any of them had any idea, that might easily have been the case. The players were desperate to succeed, to shine, to seize a headline – maybe too desperate.

Held 12-12 at half time, the Springboks pitched camp inside the England 22-metre line throughout the second half, eventually scoring three tries to nil and winning 33-15. Du Plessis, Gerber and Louw had all scored thrilling tries, but the overall performance had been too disjointed to allow any real sense of achievement in the home changing room afterwards.

Moss was relaxed, looking forward to the second Test, trusting his gifted players would fire on all cylinders at Ellis Park. His instincts were excellent. Few among the 74 000 spectators would be disappointed in Johannesburg.

In bright sunshine, Tobias set Carel du Plessis dipping and swerving down the left wing before Stofberg appeared on time to claim the inside pass and storm 15 metres for the opening try. The captain smiled, shyly.

As the Ellis Park crowd buzzed with excitement, Gerber proceeded to lift the game onto a different plane for 17 minutes. That is the exact amount of time the centre required to score three dazzling tries of his own and establish himself as, almost indisputably, the outstanding centre in the world. All power and grace, muscle and speed, talent and timing, this was Gerber *in excelsis*.

The second half yielded more memorable images when Tobias delivered a glorious hand-off before scoring jubilantly in the right corner: white policemen standing guard around the touchline stood and punched the air with delight, as the coloured man stood with his arms raised to the clear skies. It may not have been quite the Rainbow Nation, but the moment offered a tantalising shaft of rainbow light through the prism of Springbok rugby.

Gerrie Sonnekus, thriving as eighthman ten years after his odd selection as scrumhalf against the 1974 Lions, marked his long-awaited recall by scoring the sixth try on a day when every Springbok dream came true. "We had played truly exceptional rugby," Stofberg reflects. "Everything clicked, passes went to hand and the crowd responded. It was a very happy day."

South Africa won 32-9, and secured a 2-0 series win. For the quiet, calm Springbok captain, a noble Test career had ended on a high.

Injury kept Stofberg out of two Tests against the Jaguars in October 1984, and it was a persistent knee injury that ultimately forced his retirement from the game only a frustrating fortnight before the New Zealand Cavaliers arrived in April 1986.

"These were frustrating years for everyone," Stofberg reflects, "but I have no right to complain. In spite of the political problems, I had played against all the major rugby nations except Australia. That wasn't bad.

"It was a huge honour for me to be Springbok captain, but it is odd how life brings you back to earth. Soon after I retired, I was shopping at the OK Bazaars in Welkom when someone stopped me in the aisle. I was flattered. The man was clearly pleased to see me, and he called his wife.

"He asked her if she knew me. She stared long and hard at my face before declaring in triumph, 'Yes, you're Gerrie Coetzee!' I couldn't help laughing. That's how things go. People move on and the faces change."

Stofberg served briefly as a Western Province selector, and now runs his own business from his home in the northern suburbs of Cape Town. This still vast and imposing man may not have provoked many controversies or front-page headlines during his 21-Test career, but he had served the Springbok cause with a remarkable degree of calm courage and selfless integrity.

The loose forward's injury in 1984 compelled the Springbok selectors to find a new captain to lead the side against the Jaguars in October, and it seemed obvious that they should start their search in the Western Province team that had won the Currie Cup for the third year in succession.

"Come on, Doc, tell us who's the new captain."

National trials had been staged and Dr Moss was sitting quietly in the front seat of the bus carrying the trial players back to their hotel. The Springbok coach was aware that the voice booming from the seat behind him belonged to the mischievous Free State eighthman, Gerrie Sonnekus.

"Doc, please! You might as well tell us now. We need to know if it's Divan, so we can arrange to have a beer with him tonight."

Many national coaches, past and future, might have objected to such banter in the bus, but Moss could comfortably tell the difference between gentle fun and malicious disrespect. He had noticed Serfontein sitting quietly across the gangway and pretending to have heard nothing. Smiling gently, the coach turned and said: "Gerrie, I think you should have a beer with him."

That was that!

Serfontein beamed. He had played in 17 consecutive Tests since his try-scoring debut against the Lions in 1980; now he knew he would lead the side in what would turn out to be the two concluding internationals of his career. ·

This strong-minded man had sprung from Vanderbijlpark in the Transvaal and been weaned on rugby by his father, a bricklayer by profession, who happily took his oldest son to queue for tickets to watch South Africa play France at Ellis Park in 1967, and who didn't mind even when the persistent boy hung around the barber's shop in town where he and his friends would regularly meet and discuss the latest rugby news. Divan was content to listen and learn.

Serfontein had set his mind on becoming a medical doctor and, inspired by the images of the film *Matieland*, he eventually enrolled to study medicine at the University of Stellenbosch. However, the resolved Transvaler from Vanderbijl did not settle easily in the Cape. He grew lonely and increasingly frustrated to be playing rugby, apparently unnoticed, in the *koshuis* leagues.

One afternoon, Apies du Toit appeared on the touchline and the renowned coach spotted something about the physically small scrumhalf. Everything in his life changed. Noticed at last, he progressed swiftly through the age-group ranks, earning rave reviews in 1974 when playing for the Western Province under-20s against the Natal under-20s in a curtain-raiser before a Test against the Lions, becoming an established member of the Maties 1st XV, and playing his debut for Western Province in the tour match against the 1976 All Blacks.

Alert and determined, the sapling No. 9 was thriving beneath the wise old branches of the grandest oak of Springbok rugby, and Serfontein will never forget the debt he owes to Danie Craven. "Doc meant everything to me," he recalls. "He was an incredible man in so many ways. It went beyond rugby because he took an almost paternal interest in his Stellenbosch players."

Dr Serfontein's eyes fire again: "The thing about Doc was that he always had a plan, some new idea. Once, in 1978, he introduced a move where all seven backs would stand in a straight line directly behind the scrum and, upon the call, would play either to the open or blind side. I saw precisely the same move being used at the 1999 World Cup and everyone was saying how innovative it was. I think Doc would have enjoyed that. He was years ahead."

Serfontein emerged as a resourceful and dynamic scrumhalf. When critics said he was too small, he worked harder on his fitness. When they criticised the quality of his pass, he trained twice as often. By 1980, he was being touted as a possible Springbok. These were exciting times. He was buzzing.

Western Province had played Natal in Durban, and the South African team to play the first Test against the Lions was due to be announced later that same evening. It was shortly before eight o'clock and the scrumhalf was being driven to Umhlanga Rocks by his close friend, Wynand Claassen.

They switched on the radio to check whether there was any news. There was news. The team announcement headlined the bulletin, and Serfontein was in the side. Claassen immediately pulled over, applied the handbrake and produced two moderately cold cans of beer. The night was young.

The scrumhalf thrived through the 1980 season under Morné du Plessis, reliably supported Claassen through 1981 and 1982, and was perfectly happy to play under Stofberg against England. However, by October 1984 he had become established as an outstanding captain in his own right, set apart as the only man to lead his province to three consecutive Currie Cup titles.

In need of a new Springbok captain, the panel decided to look no further than the terrier who annually raised Sir Donald Currie's Cup.

Moss was pleased. Three seasons earlier, as convenor of the Western Province selection committee, he had appointed Serfontein as WP captain. "He was not particularly keen at first," the coach recalls, "and he had some awkward people in that Province side, but Divan was a natural leader. He is such a trier and he was never beaten. I had every confidence in him."

Particularly proud to become the eleventh Matie to captain South Africa, Serfontein settled comfortably into the role. The Springbok side for the first Test in Pretoria included six new caps, but the squad was packed with Western Province players and the new captain felt absolutely at ease.

"I was never going to be a captain like Morné du Plessis," he reflects. "My aim was to be more of a facilitator, trying to make life easier for the players. The team was full of seasoned Springboks. They knew what to do."

Hugo Porta was leading a Jaguars team on tour to South Africa for a third time, and the experienced flyhalf directed his composite team to a 12-10 lead at half time. A shimmer of concern rippled around Loftus Versfeld.

Danie Gerber had been given the goal-kicking duties after a magnificent exhibition during training on the Friday afternoon, but the centre had succeeded only in converting his own first-half try, and missed everything else. Serfontein calmly assessed the situation during the interval and took the decision to transfer the goal-kicking responsibilities to Errol Tobias.

As the flyhalf started to find the target, the Springboks settled and soon accelerated away to an emphatic 32-15 victory. Albeit against weak opposition, the captain had been examined, and emerged intact.

Nobody asked what drinks were required for any party before the second Test at Newlands and, with complacency banished by memories of Bloemfontein in 1982, the scrumhalf's diligent approach was reflected in a solid forward display that should have yielded more than a 22-13 triumph. Nonetheless, Carel du Plessis and Danie Gerber had both scored spectacular tries, as usual, and the Springbok team seemed to be enveloped in a warm glow of satisfaction as their 1984 season drew to a close.

The team may only have played against a weakened England team and a hotchpotch of Jaguars drawn from Argentina, Chile, Uruguay, Peru and even Spain, but at least they had played, winning four Tests out of four, scoring 18 tries to three, maintaining their reputation as giants of the sport.

Never mind, they said, Danie Craven was still welcome at meetings of the International Rugby Board, and the official tour schedule still indicated that the All Blacks would tour South Africa in 1985, and that the Lions would follow in 1986. Two major tours in two years, the optimists cried. What a feast!

Don't worry about the deteriorating political weather outside, they said. So the table was laid and Springbok rugby eagerly awaited the arrival of their guests as per schedule ... and the return home of a prodigal son.

11 THE BAAS

If Naas Botha had settled and remained in the United States, he would still have been remembered among the greatest Springbok flyhalves. He had won 17 caps, amassed more Test points than any other South African, and emerged as a huge force in the game, propelling Northern Transvaal to Currie Cup triumphs in five of six seasons between his debut in 1977 and his departure in 1982.

However, in March 1985 this extraordinary man did return, stronger, fitter, and more resolved than ever before. He would stand at the pinnacle of the game for a further seven years, claiming four more Currie Cups and eventually leading the Springboks back into regular Test competition. He would not so much rewrite the record books as produce his own personal edition.

Naas was Baas ("the Boss"), because of his natural ability to read the game, his skilful handling, his speed over 15 metres, his punts that spiralled 70 metres down each touchline, his relentlessly practised and consistent goal-kicking, his ability to land drop goals, his big-match temperament, his deep knowledge.

This was his era. This was his time.

He was just Naas. His surname became superfluous. His legend became woven into daily life. "Whether you're an expert or one of the millions who would not know the difference between a crêpe suzette and a conversion," wrote Jani Allan, the popular celebrity columnist in the *Sunday Times*, "when Naas runs on the field in that No. 10 jersey, it's pure electricity."

Hendrik Egnatius Botha was born in Breyten, a small town nestled in the south-eastern Transvaal, on 27 February 1958, but the family had moved to Pretoria by the end of the year. They settled in the Moot, a suburb east of the city centre that was home to men who worked in industry and on the railways, took their families to church on Sundays, and voted for the National Party.

His father, Hendrik Botha, worked as a boilerman, his mother, Jacomien, served behind the counter in the local chemist, and his brother, Darius, provided a constant source of fun and companionship through childhood.

"It was always rugby," Botha remembers. "We would get together with our cousins, the Krugers, and play literally from dawn to dusk."

The boys' imaginations ran riot. Test matches were played in the Krugers' garden because it was bigger, Currie Cup games would be played at the Bothas' house. The "visiting team" would first sit on arranged rows of chairs, rocking them as if they were actually on the team bus travelling to the stadium. Garden spades were tilted together to form a players' tunnel, hosepipes became touchlines, and Darius provided the match commentary. "We took these matches very seriously," he recalls. "The only time I ever lost my temper with Naas, and slapped him, was during one of these games. He always wanted to win."

In time to come, three of these boys would be playing for real. Naas and Darius both grew up to play for Northern Transvaal and for South Africa. Hendrik Kruger was destined to play 50 times for the Blue Bulls.

All that lay ahead. For now, they had their mothers' flowers for spectators, and nothing but the setting African sun for a final whistle.

By 1967, the group had started to show an interest in events taking place over the hill, at Loftus Versfeld. Darius learned all the Northern Transvaal players and statistics, while Naas was content to invent his own game, placing crayons in different formations on the carpet, but all the boys decided they wanted to watch the Blue Bulls play against France on Saturday 4 August.

There was a problem: they had no tickets. It was approaching six o'clock on the Friday evening. They would have to make a plan.

"How about this?" The small, slight, blonde boy was talking. "Why don't we walk to Loftus tonight? I know a place where it is easy to climb over the wall and get into the stadium. We can spend the night hiding in the toilets and then come out when the spectators start arriving tomorrow morning. We won't need tickets and we will be able to watch the match. Shall we do that?"

To his surprise, his friends replied: "Yes!"

Thus Naas Botha slept the night in the gents toilets underneath the north stand at Loftus Versfeld, but the discomfort was worthwhile. He and his friends saw two French players sent off as Northerns won 19-5.

Through Eben Swemmer Primary School and Hendrik Verwoerd High School, the young Botha scraped by in the classroom because he devoted most of his considerable energies to sport. He thrived in softball and baseball, to a point where he later won provincial colours in both codes, and he was becoming widely recognised as an enterprising schoolboy flyhalf.

His family assumed he would continue his education at the University of Pretoria but, ever prepared to try the unexpected, Botha sent an application form to Stellenbosch. He never received a reply, an oversight that Danie Craven later described as "a terrible, terrible mistake". It had been a close call. He might have become the hero, rather than the nemesis, of Western Province.

However he arrived at the University of Pretoria, started to make a name for himself in the Tukkies under-20 side and, in July 1976, played brilliantly as the Northern Transvaal under-20 team defeated their Natal counterparts 46-0 in the curtain-raiser before the first Test between South Africa and New Zealand. Many in the gathering crowd at King's Park noted his name. Even the All Blacks, sitting in the stand during the first half, checked their programmes.

Early in 1977, Botha felt the heavy hand of the Northern Transvaal coach land on his shoulder as he prepared for a Tukkies under-20 match. "I'm watching you today," said Brigadier Buurman van Zyl. "Don't let me down." The flyhalf did not disappoint and, two weeks later, was named as the new Northerns flyhalf. He was 19 years old, had not even played a senior club match.

The most significant relationship of his career had started. "Buurman van Zyl was unique," Botha recalls. "Everything in his manner, his approach, made me want to play for him, and never, never to disappoint him. I was maybe too young to play Currie Cup rugby in 1977, but Oom Buurman believed in me so much. He treated me like a son and took an interest in every aspect of my life. He protected me from critics, and he made everything work out for me."

Van Zyl planned to dominate South African rugby with Botha directing play from behind a powerful pack of forwards. This large, bald man ordered the flyhalf to resist any "diddly-daddly" inside his own 22-metre line and, without exception, to kick the ball downfield and play in the opposition's half. He forbade his young protégé to tackle, declaring: "I have 14 players who can tackle, and only one who can punt the ball 70 metres. You are no use to me at the bottom of a ruck. I need you in your place, ready to receive the ball."

Botha listened, and Botha obeyed.

This was the purest form of 10-man rugby, and it worked. Northerns won the Currie Cup in 1977 and 1978, shared the trophy with Western Province in 1979, and won it outright again in 1980 and 1981. Critics suggested Van Zyl wrapped Botha in cotton wool, suppressing his exceptional natural ability to run and pass but, in Pretoria at least, the ends justified the means.

With the Brigadier as coach and his "little general" at flyhalf, the Blue Bulls played 63 matches, and lost only six. As they won, and won, and won, the bond between coach and player grew stronger and stronger. Botha's commitment was such that he agreed to miss his grandmother's funeral because Van Zyl said he should spend the night before a match at the team hotel. For his part, the coach declared: "No side with Naas Botha at flyhalf should ever lose. If Northerns lose with Naas playing, I know it must have been my fault."

Van Zyl died suddenly in February 1982, after a heart attack. By then, Botha was established as the revered Northern Transvaal captain and Springbok flyhalf, one of the most influential rugby players in the world. However, the death of his mentor sapped his passion for the game, and within months he had made a decision to leave South Africa and strike out for America.

First and foremost, the 24-year-old yearned to become a professional, to devote himself to sport, to maximise both his playing potential and his earnings; and he believed he could succeed in American gridiron football, a sport that, he had been told, actually accommodated a specialist kicker.

If Botha wanted to do something, he did it. He was remorselessly positive and outrageously self-assured, almost willing events to fall in his favour. In early November 1982, he travelled secretly to America and managed to engineer an impromptu meeting with a coach from the Dallas Cowboys.

After brief introductions, he asked if they could go out to the playing field, and he proceeded to goal 14 successive place kicks from 50 metres. Two hours later, the South African stranger was sitting at the Cowboys headquarters with a three-year contract worth $250 000 on the table. He signed.

There was a catch. The Cowboys were still hedging their bets because the contract would only come into force if Botha proved himself during a seven-week pre-season camp, and secured a place on the Cowboys roster. It quickly became clear that the transition from Springbok rugby kingpin to gridiron kicker was more complex and challenging than he had ever imagined.

In Pretoria, he had kicked up-and-unders to land on the fullback. In Dallas, he was instructed to launch a kick that would travel precisely 48 metres with what an army of Cowboys coaches called a "hangtime" of 4,4 seconds. There was no margin for error. He punted, and punted, and punted. That was his job. Suddenly he began to appreciate the infinite variety of rugby union.

He responded to every demand, tried desperately to cram what amounted to 15 years of experience into seven weeks of training, and succeeded in earning the reserve place-kicker's berth in three pre-season friendlies, but he recognised the reality long before he was summoned to the office of the legendary Cowboys coach Tom Landry, and told that he would not be retained.

"Don't give up," Landry told him. "You just need more time to adapt to the demands of this game. Find another club. Give yourself a chance."

Botha thanked the coach and continued to train hard in Dallas, but by the time an offer arrived from the New England Patriots, he had been offered almost as much money to accept a public relations position in a company owned by the Pretoria businessman, Gerry Potgieter. The *Sunday Express* seemed to sum up the situation when it editorialised: "That's the way for Springbok rugby to combat professionalism – make sure the amateur game pays better."

He swallowed his pride, returned home and addressed the major obstacle preventing him from slipping back into the light-blue jersey. Needing to regain his amateur status after participating in a professional sport, Botha asked Professor Fritz Eloff, the soft-spoken president of the Northern Transvaal Rugby Union and delegate at the International Rugby Board, to put his case.

The laws of the game, no less, would have to be amended to permit an open gangway between rugby union and gridiron football, and when the IRB met in Paris on 21 March 1985 Eloff founded his argument on the premise that the American game presented no competitive threat to rugby.

"I was not confident at the outset," the gentle Eloff recalled, "but I finished my statement by explaining that Naas had tried to earn his living from gridiron but that it had not worked out, he had not earned any money, and he wanted to return to rugby union. I told them that he would become one of the greatest players, and I told them that we could not afford to waste Naas Botha."

The IRB voted, and the flyhalf became "amateur" again. Danie Craven, the other South African delegate at the IRB meeting, smiled broadly and leaned over towards his colleague. "Congratulations, Fritz," the president said. "You have just won the Currie Cup for Northern Transvaal."

All seemed well.

After the uncertainties of 1983 and 1984, Springbok rugby was regaining momentum: Botha was back, and the All Blacks were coming.

The New Zealand Rugby Union had formally accepted an invitation to tour South Africa, Andy Dalton was soon announced as captain of a powerful touring squad, Botha shone at the Springbok trials in Stellenbosch, and an eye-catching range of tour souvenirs started to appear in the shops.

Meanwhile in Auckland, two lawyers brought legal action against the New Zealand Rugby Union on the grounds that, by agreeing to tour South Africa, the union was not promoting the best interests of rugby, as it was obliged to do by its own constitution. The premise appeared feeble but the lawyers were sharp, and despite initially being dismissed in the High Court, they pursued their case to the Court of Appeal and secured a High Court hearing.

The dogs were loose. The rugby authorities became alarmed to find their legal team being outsmarted on technicalities, and their worst fears were realised when Judge J.P. Casey granted an injunction stating the tour could not go ahead until the case had been heard. That was enough to persuade the NZRU that, with a congested rugby calendar, the tour could not proceed. Amid outrage and anger in both countries, the All Blacks were forced to stay at home.

"I felt numb when I heard the news," Botha recalls.

The Board moved swiftly to fill the four empty Saturdays on the schedule, and arranged an internal tour for the squad that would have played against New Zealand, but full colours were not awarded and the four matches against regional Barbarian sides achieved nothing more than to confirm to players and spectators how much they would suffer during the years of isolation.

One moment, white South Africa was excitedly anticipating the All Blacks; within weeks, their entire world seemed to be falling apart.

A national state of emergency was declared to quell the rebellion raging in townships nationwide, State President P.W. Botha wagged his finger at the world and warned the international community not "to push us too far," and the value of the rand fell through the floor of the money markets.

South Africans suddenly appeared far more disturbed by the deepening economic and political crisis than by the frustrations of sporting isolation. It was getting serious. The Broederbond was more vexed by the schisms in Afrikaner politics than by the identity of the next Springbok captain.

Day by day, the issue of international rugby started to fade from the public conscience, effectively slipping from the news agenda. In clubs and bars, even in the school playground, South Africans sadly began to accept that the Springboks simply did not play any more. That was the reality.

In December 1985, Danie Craven and his Executive withdrew an invitation to the Lions to tour the next season, as he said, "to save our old friends from the embarrassment of having to say no". The Board president also confirmed that no further rugby tours, inward or outward, were scheduled.

The end credits were rolling, and people headed for the exits.

Divan Serfontein led a legion of players into retirement at the end of 1985. He would pursue his career as a doctor at the Panorama Hospital in Cape Town, and eventually drive the launch of veterans' rugby. In July 2000, at the age of 46, this indomitable scrumhalf would roll back the years and play remarkably well for an Invitation XV before 57 000 spectators at Ellis Park.

Rob Louw and Ray Mordt also departed, accepting lucrative offers to play professional rugby league in Wigan. Two dazzling Springboks would finish their careers not in triumph against the Lions or the All Blacks, but amid the mud, rain, sleet and mind-boggling tattoos of northern England.

Others remained at their posts.

In this darkest and most desperate hour, when the prospect of resumed tours appeared to be decades, if not generations, away, South African rugby was sustained by an exceptional group of leading players who raised the intensity and excitement of the Currie Cup to a level that could be compared with official Tests in other parts of the world. Saturday upon Saturday, they filled stadiums, thrilled the crowds, fuelled the buzz, and kept the game alive.

The Du Plessis brothers in Cape Town, Danie Gerber in the Eastern Province, Jannie Breedt and John Robbie in Johannesburg,

Johan Heunis, Uli Schmidt and Burger Geldenhuys in Pretoria, and many others: all played their part, but it would be hard to dispute that the individual who held the torch highest, who provoked the strongest emotions, who endlessly motivated, intrigued and stirred, was the genius playing at flyhalf for Northern Transvaal, Naas Botha.

He had slipped back into his berth as the Blue Bulls captain and the icon of Pretoria as if he had never been away, and his sparkling form during the 1985 season suggested his technical, scientific training in Dallas had left him mentally and technically stronger than ever. Through years to come, he would frequently resemble a professional playing in an amateur game.

"My entire philosophy when I returned to rugby was based on planning the next five minutes of the game in my head," Botha reflects. "I had to stay one step ahead of the opposition at all times. That meant calculating how they would react before I picked my option. For example, if I kicked towards a left-footed player in his right-hand corner of the field, I knew he would clear the ball up that touchline, so I would jog across into position and collect the ball there.

"The aim was always to reduce the opposition's options because this gave me a better chance of predicting what they would do. Elements like wind and rain could also help. People used to say I controlled the game, but all I did was work out how the play would unfold over the next five minutes. The Cowboys gave us lectures on this sort of thing, and it all made sense to me."

Botha scored 188 points in 10 Currie Cup matches during 1985, setting a new record for the competition, and although his young Northern Transvaal team lost the final against Western Province in Cape Town, the flyhalf finished his first season back in the saddle as South Africa's Player of the Year.

His profile had started to reach far beyond the touchlines. While his feats on the field dominated the back pages, every other aspect of his life was blazed across the front pages. The stories ranged from the personal, such as the painful failure of his marriage, to the trivial, such as an admiring businessman's plans to establish a life-size statue of the flyhalf in Naboomspruit.

This media obsession created a situation where millions of ordinary South Africans started to form intractable opinions about the rugby player. Some loved him, some hated him; very few remained indifferent. He became public property, alternately an object of total adoration and acid scorn.

Cheered in Pretoria, he would be booed when Northerns visited Ellis Park, King's Park and Newlands. As the home team kicked for goal, Botha would wait beneath the posts and have to stand in front of a touch judge to avoid the shower of naartjies and coins being hurled by local supporters.

At times Botha appeared to fuel the fury, relishing a psychological position whereby it was him against the world. He could be petulant, pushing or striking at any opponent who had the temerity to tackle him; he could be arrogant, shouting at team-mates who erred; and he could be thoroughly selfish, behaving as though the world of South African rugby revolved on his axis.

He made no apology, offered no concessions. People could love him or leave him; and, of course, the louder they booed, the better he played, driving his forwards 70 metres upfield, maintaining an 85% success rate in place-kicking to the posts, relentlessly keeping the scoreboard on the move by landing drop goals from every area of the field, clinically dictating the game.

Away from rugby, the constant critical scrutiny left him deeply suspicious of strangers, defensive to a fault, and trusting few beyond his family and a handful of friends. He tended to stay away from restaurants where he would invariably be confronted by an inebriated fool trying to impress his friends.

Team-mates sometimes found him aloof and anti-social, reluctant to join a post-match party and down a beer. Asked how he related to Botha, Divan Serfontein once famously replied: "Well, I wasn't that interested in ice cream and Coke." Maybe contemporary envy played a role, perhaps he did not always help himself, maybe the media's tendency to elevate him fomented jealousy among his peers. Whatever, it was clear Botha would stand apart.

Throughout, he remained unceasingly positive, treating every obstacle as an incentive to work harder and succeed. His response to what seemed a critical world was straightforward: to win, and win, and win again. He would not fail. One evening at his home, somebody produced a soccer ball and wondered how long the group would be able to juggle the ball with their feet.

"Let's get to 20," Botha enthused.

Almost an hour later, dripping in sweat, the three friends collapsed on the sofa. The task had been more difficult than any of them imagined, but Botha had refused to let anyone rest until they had completed 20 touches without the ball touching the ground. This was the essence of his legend. He simply refused to accept defeat, whether he was playing a Test against the All Blacks or fooling around in his living room. He craved victory, and was prepared to pay any price, to make any sacrifice required, to ensure he prevailed.

As the 1986 season approached, the flyhalf resolved simply to realise his potential as a rugby player and to make the most of every opportunity. If the fates decreed that meant only playing for Tukkies in the Carlton Cup and for Northerns in the Currie Cup, so be it. He would practise his kicking almost every afternoon, watch his diet, maintain his fitness, and embrace the reality.

Out of the blue, Botha received an invitation from the International Rugby Board to participate in two matches to celebrate the IRB centenary. An occasion of passing interest for the All Blacks, Australians and British players would rate as a career highlight for the five isolated Springboks on the list.

Together with Carel du Plessis, Schalk Burger, Flippie van der Merwe and Danie Gerber, Botha travelled to London and shone in the Southern Hemisphere team that overwhelmed a Five Nations side at Twickenham. Du Plessis scored a truly magnificent try, Gerber added two more, and Botha revealed a degree of flair and enterprise that belied his label as a kicking flyhalf.

The South Africans were enjoying themselves, but were also intrigued by the peculiar behaviour of the New Zealanders in their squad. Instead of jumping aboard the team bus after training, the All Blacks insisted on running back to the hotel. Botha asked Dalton what was going on, but the hooker shrugged and said nothing. Rumours had been circulating that a World XV would tour South Africa early in 1986, but that story was now starting to change.

Botha recalls: "A reporter contacted me when I was in London and said he had been told 30 top New Zealand players were preparing to tour South Africa as an unofficial group of individuals invited by the Transvaal Rugby Union. He said only David Kirk and John Kirwan out of the squad selected for the cancelled tour in 1985 had decided to stay home. I had no idea what to say, except that it was all news to me. It seemed too good to be true.

"There were so many stories flying around but I remember we telephoned Dr Moss from London and told him the All Blacks seemed very serious. He said he would start studying videos of their recent Tests."

Events became a blur. Craven and Eloff were attending a meeting of the IRB when news of the tour was released: they denied all knowledge of the plans, and promised to launch an enquiry. Both men remained convinced South Africa should remain patient within the official structures of the game, but they were also aware of the need for the Springboks to play again. After the disappointments of 1985, the Cavaliers tour appeared like an oasis in the desert.

Louis Luyt, the robust millionaire president of the Transvaal Rugby Union, took responsibility for welcoming the New Zealanders to South Africa, hosting a lunch for 250 people at his home in Johannesburg. The tourists certainly did not lack pedigree, with Ian Kirkpatrick as manager, Colin Meads as coach and Andy Dalton as captain, and they all seemed appropriately grim.

Everybody supposed the players were being paid (revelations eventually suggested amounts of up to NZ$100 000 per player were channelled through the company that owned Ellis Park Stadium), but nobody doubted the determination of this squad to vindicate their tour by winning the series.

Dalton reflects: "The idea to tour as individuals was floated in 1985, and we were resolved to get to South Africa. It was sad that we had to go behind the backs of the New Zealand Rugby Union to achieve our ambition.

"Our idea was to tour with the same squad originally selected in 1985 but, with hindsight, there is no doubt that the year's delay took its toll. We were at our peak in 1985, and there were a few of us hanging on at the end of our careers 12 months later. It was also sad that Brian Lochore, who would have been the coach in 1985, was unable to join us on the unofficial tour."

The Cavaliers repeatedly asked not to be called All Blacks, but their pleas were resolutely ignored by white South Africans who celebrated their arrival with blanket media coverage and unrestrained excitement.

South African cricket had pioneered the concept of "rebel tours", recruiting leading players to tour as "individuals" by offering sums of money large enough to compensate for any consequent ban. Squads from England, Sri Lanka, the West Indies and Australia had sold the idea to the white sporting public, and scarcely anyone batted an eyelid at the prospect of a first rugby tour hosted in South Africa outside the auspices of the IRB.

The consensus, shared by Botha and other leading players, was that there was little point staying a member of the IRB club if you were not allowed to share the benefits. If regular tours did not arrive through official routes, South Africans felt absolutely entitled to wield the wallet and recruit the rebels.

In April 1986, it must be recalled, the prospect that the country would soon be readmitted to the world was not so much remote as non-existent. P.W. Botha remained powerfully in control, and Nelson Mandela was still generally regarded as the correctly imprisoned leader of a terrorist organisation.

It is easy for people to revise history and reflect upon the Cavaliers tour as heavy-handed and shortsighted, but amid the gloom of 1986 there were very few who did not welcome the Cavaliers as the type of initiative that was essential to sustain the game through isolation.

During the flight home from the IRB centenary matches in London, Botha began to ponder who might be appointed to captain South Africa in the four Tests against the Cavaliers. He reckoned no-one could match his experience, in terms of playing 17 Tests and leading Northern Transvaal for four seasons, but he was also aware that some influential administrators believed he was too controversial to be captain, and still resented his American adventure.

Newspaper reports raised the name of Schalk Burger as a contender for the captaincy, and Botha braced for disappointment when the Western Province lock forward was named to lead the Probables against the Possibles in a single Springbok trial match, played in Bloemfontein.

The Cavaliers had boldly set about a daunting schedule, narrowly beating the Junior Springboks and Botha's Northern Transvaal side, but their plans were disrupted by the loss of Dalton, whose jaw had been broken in two places when he was punched from behind by Northerns flanker, Burger Geldenhuys. The New Zealand captain had played 36 minutes of rugby, harsh reward for his efforts in arranging the tour. "We knew we would have to face a physical challenge against the New Zealanders," Botha recalls, "and we were motivated for the contest, but Dalton's injury was very unfortunate, and very sad."

While the Cavaliers prepared for the first Test with a comfortable win over Free State, a narrow defeat against Transvaal and a strong victory over Western Province at Newlands, the Springbok selectors contemplated their options. It was eventually decided that the South African team, and its captain, would be announced in Cape Town on the Tuesday night before the Test.

Botha remained calm, prepared to accept any decision. That Tuesday in Pretoria, he had planned only to watch Tukkies play Teachers' Training College (NKP) in a Carlton Cup match on the Loftus B field, but he had become so frustrated by his club's display that, when a wing was injured midway through the second half, he pleaded to be allowed to run on as a replacement. The University had never lost against NKP, and he was not prepared to stand by and watch it happen. With 20 minutes remaining Tuks were trailing 18-6, but Botha took over at flyhalf, shouted a few instructions, and inspired a remarkable 24-21 victory.

"The points were later deducted because I was not a listed reserve," Botha recalls, "but at least we had kept our unbeaten record against NKP."

He drove home and, nearing eight o'clock on the evening of

Tuesday 5 May 1986, he leaned forward in his chair to watch the SABC television news. "And the headlines tonight … Naas Botha is the new Springbok captain." He rose to his feet, clenched his fists and vigorously punched the air twice.

The captaincy had not been a consuming issue in his mind. In any event, he often said, it is the flyhalf who makes decisions on the field, but he did like to feel in charge of the team, and he appreciated the honour. He scanned through the rest of the team as it rolled across the screen and was surprised only to see Geldenhuys had been left out. The Northerns flanker, he would learn, was being punished for his flash of temper in breaking Dalton's jaw.

Cecil Moss, the Springbok coach, remembers: "I was very happy with our choice of Naas as captain. In my opinion, he and Hennie Muller are the two finest players I have ever seen. Naas was completely two-footed and passed well on both sides; his distribution was fantastic, he was a magnificent kicker of the ball, and he had this unique ability to control the game. There were deficiencies, like his reluctance to tackle head-on, but we coped with these.

"In 1986 he was obviously going to play an enormous role in what was an inexperienced Springbok side, so he became a natural leader. We played Tests on four successive Saturdays, and his confidence rubbed off on everyone. Naas carried all the players with him; he almost took me with him."

The coach approached the series with concern. While the Cavaliers loose forwards boasted more than 100 Test caps between them, his own Springbok trio were all making their debut in the first Test at Newlands. Craven had taken Moss to one side and told him the series would be extremely tough. "Just try to win one of the four Tests," the president had said. "That will be fine."

Botha devised no special plan to transform himself from the most divisive presence in the Currie Cup into a unifying force as Springbok captain. He simply trained harder than anyone else, set down what he expected from the team, and assaulted the challenge. The simple magnitude of the occasion turned seething rivals into comrades, and the players followed his lead.

There were moments of tension. Jannie Breedt, a charismatic eighthman who had left Pretoria the previous year to become Transvaal captain, was named as Springbok vice-captain, but he arrived for the team photograph to find he was not to be seated beside the captain, but standing behind.

Several reporters leapt to the conclusion that Botha was making mischief: NAAS SNUBS JANNIE proclaimed the next day's headline. In reality, the coach had arranged the photograph, and Moss logically positioned Breedt in the second row because the eighthman was still uncapped.

Cape Town dawned wet and cold for the first Test, and the captain drew confidence from his acclaimed display in similarly appalling conditions during the Lion Cup semi-final at the same ground in 1985, but he needed the ball; and, as the first half wore on, the Cavaliers forwards took charge.

With six minutes remaining, the tourists led 15-12. Botha had kicked two penalties and two drop goals, magnificent connections soaring through the gloom and passing high above the uprights, but the tourists seemed to be running down the clock, using their experience, and maintaining their grip.

Soaked to the skin, Botha gesticulated wildly to his forwards. "We have to get into their half," he implored. "Please! We must get into their half."

The forwards responded, and another Springbok surge yielded a penalty. Botha made no mistake, and neatly levelled the Test at 15-15. With two minutes remaining, a buzz of expectation rumbled around the drenched stadium. Again, South Africa won the ball, again Botha pumped another punt downfield, and the torpedo kick skidded off the Cavalier fullback and into touch.

The rumble was becoming a roar. Botha had kept his team in contention through 75 minutes on the back foot, and now the flyhalf was suddenly in position to seize victory. On the right-hand side of the field, he called a scissors move in midfield to recycle possession in front of the posts and play from there.

Louis Moolman won the ball grandly in the lineout, but scrumhalf

Christo Ferreira's pass seemed too low and too far forward. Botha almost toppled over as he gathered the ball and then, acting upon an instinct called from the depths of his genius, contrived to execute a sumptuous punt, diagonal across the field, floating, rolling and scudding into the dead ball zone.

Carel du Plessis had taken flight on the left wing, somehow sure-footed in the sludge, chasing down the ball. He dived and scored. Newlands rose as one to acclaim the moment and, amid swirling wind and driving rain, time-honoured portents of momentous events, the Springbok captain made his way over to the left touchline and prepared to attempt the conversion.

The scene echoed his famous conversion to defeat the 1980 Lions in Port Elizabeth: the drenching rain, the heavy ball, the last minute, the sodden field, an almost impossible task. Again he kicked low, straight, and over.

South Africa had won 21-15. Sitting in the press box, Barry Glasspool was dictating his copy down the telephone: "Light the victory fires for Naas Botha and Springbok rugby," the admired Sunday Times sports editor shouted, struggling to make himself heard in the triumphal din. "The South African flyhalf out-generalled and out-kicked the All Blacks at Newlands yesterday …"

Back at the newspaper's offices in Main Street, Johannesburg, the editor, Tertius Myburgh, considered the headline to thunder across the front page of all editions the next morning: NAAS THE BAAS. He nodded.

The credibility of this bizarre tour scarcely crossed the minds of the South African rugby public, who simply treated the touring squad as the All Blacks with three yellow stripes on their shoulders and shorts, yet the rest of the rugby world looked upon the Cavaliers as an unfortunate aberration devoid of status and real significance, destined to be air-brushed from the annals.

Botha respected his opposition, but he was sober enough to recognise that the prime difference between an official squad and this unofficial group was the fact that the Cavaliers were answerable to nobody. When Andy Haden didn't like the referee's decisions against

Western Province, he threatened to lead his team off the field. When Natal players niggled and provoked, the New Zealanders reacted by resembling a teenage street mob lynching their rivals.

"We all wanted to believe this team was the All Blacks," Botha recalls, "but they didn't always conduct themselves like the All Blacks."

If the Cavaliers often lacked discipline, perhaps that was because the only structures available to impose discipline were the shadowy organisers of the tour, the paymasters, and they were not minded to intervene. Dalton's decision to stay with his squad, despite being unable to play again, certainly helped the situation, but the touring group remained generally sour and defensive.

They were destined to conduct their tour under relentless pressure, and in their own minds their only chance of salvation was to win the series. "People at home will laugh in our faces if we lose this one," said Grant Fox, the young flyhalf, as the Cavaliers prepared for the second Test in Durban. Jock Hobbs had taken over as captain from the combustible Haden.

Botha and his side maintained their basic strategy of holding the Cavaliers among the forwards and caning them with far superior backs, but for no particular reason the flyhalf abandoned his habitual custom of practising his goal kicking in the stadium on the afternoon before a major match.

Arriving at King's Park on the Saturday afternoon, he walked up the tunnel just an hour before kick-off and was alarmed to discover how recent construction work at the stadium had left gaps in the stands at the south-west and north-west corners of the ground. The result was a vicious, swirling wind.

Already stirred when Cavaliers centre Warwick Taylor charged down his clearing punt and scored an opening try, Botha stood amazed when his first penalty kick was blown wide of the posts. He attempted a drop goal soon afterwards, with the same result. He was aiming way to the right, and still missing to the left. The Springbok captain shook his head in disbelief.

The flyhalf proceeded to miss no fewer than 11 out of 16 attempts at the posts and yet, remarkably, moving into injury time, South Africa still trailed by just a single point. The Boks won a lineout two metres from the Cavaliers line. There would be one more chance to save the Test and, even at the end of this distinctly awkward afternoon, Botha did not shrink from the challenge. He was prepared to step forward, accept responsibility and strike out for victory.

Moolman took the ball two-handed at the front of the lineout, and Ferreira whipped the ball wide to Botha. His celebrity backline lined up on the outside, but he had put his team in this position, and he wanted to get them out of it. Barely eight metres from the posts, to the left, he sidestepped inside Fox, created a metre of space and dropped for goal … and missed again, the ball rebounding off the left-hand post and away. The Cavaliers had won 19-18, and Hobbs left the field with tears in his eyes. The series was back in the boiling pot.

The post-Test cocktail party was held at the Durban City Hall, and Botha accepted full responsibility for defeat. "Well played to the Cavaliers," he told the audience, "you scored two tries to one and deserved this victory. I must say hard luck to the Springboks. I know I didn't do my job today, and that is why we have lost, but we can all improve in the two remaining Tests."

Botha felt responsible for the three changes made to the South African side ahead of the third Test in Pretoria, saying, "If I had kicked one more penalty or drop goal, the three guys would not have been dropped," but he responded to the situation by practising his goal kicking for two hours on the Monday, another hour and a half on the Tuesday, and two hours on the Wednesday. Throughout his career, his success was bought in one currency: sweat.

Cecil Moss called. The coach asked to see his captain at the team's hotel in Pretoria before the rest of the Springboks arrived. The meeting was arranged for 10 o'clock on the Thursday morning; and Botha arrived on time, drenched in sweat. He had been practising his kicking since eight.

"I'm a winner, Doc, I want to put things right," he declared.

The coach was impressed by Botha's attitude, and the two men tweaked the team's strategy, resolving to introduce four-man lineouts to make any barging by the New Zealanders more obvious to the referee.

"There are a couple of other issues, Naas."

Moss had earned the affectionate nickname "Oumatjie" (Granny) among the Western Province players because of his particular attention to detail, but his manner was to address any awkward situation as it happened, to deal directly, to let nothing fester; and Botha listened respectfully.

They were not major issues, the coach said, but some players had been upset to see Botha's personal chiropractor, Ron Coetzee, travel to King's Park on the team bus. He understood that the flyhalf required treatment before the game, but he wanted Coetzee to make his own travel arrangements.

"Fine."

Second, there had been an incident before the second Test when Botha brought 50 small rugby balls to be signed by the entire team. Some players were wondering whether these balls were to be sold and, if so, who would receive the proceeds. The entire process may have been completely innocent, but this kind of incident was not helping to build morale.

"Fine."

Botha was encouraged by the straightforward nature of the meeting with a coach whom he unequivocally admired, but the captain was soon more concerned by another issue distracting his players in Pretoria: money.

Since 1891, the Springboks had been as amateur as their game, receiving only the IRB's daily allowance whenever they were assembled as a team. During the 1950s and 1960s nobody complained, and even through the 1970s and early 1980s the players were content to devote their time and energies to the national cause and the honour of the jersey.

Expenses were also paid by provinces, and in 1979 Botha had infamously stood up at a team meeting and asked officials of the Northern Transvaal Rugby Union if match expenses could rise from R10 to R15 each. The NTRU responded by deciding the players would receive R5 after the next match.

Times were changing in 1986. Soft jobs with large salaries, free houses and cars, even brown envelopes crammed with R50 notes, had become common practice in the provinces, and as South African rugby found a twilight "shamateur" world, the 1986 Springboks became the first to seek payment.

Their case was founded on two simple premises: first, the Cavaliers were being paid and it was indefensible for one team to receive so much and the other to receive nothing; second, the South African Rugby Board had clumsily raised the commercial stakes by allowing Toyota, the motor manufacturer, to place their logo on the green-and-gold Springbok jersey for the amazingly small investment of R50 000, and even this paltry sum was kept from the players.

Financially aware Springboks like Michael du Plessis and Schalk Burger felt insulted by the jersey fiasco, and murmuring around the team hotel in Durban had escalated to clandestine meetings before the Test in Pretoria.

Such players looked towards Botha to take a lead in these matters, but the captain stayed studiously clear of the discussions. A critical consensus grew that Botha was only interested in himself, that he already had his deal in Pretoria and so was not concerned about the other players. The captain insisted he could not lead any player movement because his rugby-related job as a sports organiser at the university left him vulnerable to official retribution. In contrast, he said, Burger and Du Plessis could fall back upon independent income.

Whatever the case, and the truth was probably to be found somewhere in between, once again Botha was cast as a man apart.

The money issue simmered unnervingly beneath Springbok preparations for the third Test at Loftus Versfeld, but the captain was satisfied by the quality of training and his team's resolve when the Cavaliers deliberately arrived to train on the Loftus field at a time allocated to the South Africans. On the brink of moving to accommodate the tourists, the Springboks had stood firm.

"It was an extremely tense situation," Moss recalls, "and I called Dr Craven immediately afterwards to tell him what had happened. He told me not to worry at all, saying the All Blacks had tried a similar ploy in 1937."

On Saturday 24 May 1986 Botha became the first home-grown Northern Transvaal player to lead South Africa at Loftus Versfeld, his Loftus, and he was thunderously welcomed by the crowd, his crowd. He had come a long way in the 19 years since the night he slept in the north stand toilets.

This pivotal third Test match hung precariously in the balance for an hour until, with the Cavaliers leading 15-12, these Springboks produced 20 minutes of rugby that would live long in the memory, 20 minutes of rugby when a genuinely imperious backline offered a glimpse of what standards they might have realised if they had been given the chance to play regular Test rugby.

There may well have been sound political reasons why the three-quarter line of Naas Botha, with Michael du Plessis and Danie Gerber at centre, Ray Mordt on the right wing, Carel du Plessis on the left, and Johan Heunis at fullback, was not permitted to thrill crowds throughout the world during the 1980s, but the denial of opportunities for them to play was, at the very least, a pity.

Botha started the euphoric rout at Loftus, chipping ahead with the outside of his foot, taking a kind bounce after Heunis's state-of-the-art offensive tackle on Murray Mexted, and sprinting clear, even allowing himself a swallow dive to score his first Test try under the posts at Loftus.

Minutes later, the maestro flyhalf gathered a pass off his toes and, in one seamless swing of his hips and arms, spread the ball wide to Gerber, all muscle and power straining on the leash. He strode six paces before feeding the artful, ingenious Michael du Plessis, who in turn sent an impeccable pass to the hip of his brother on the left wing. Carel du Plessis moved into sixth, a vision of speed, grace, strength, the beauty of movement personified.

He shimmied once, jinked inside, left Fox in his breeze. Gerber suddenly appeared at his shoulder, taunting the panicking New Zealanders. Would he go inside? Would he go outside? Du Plessis opted to feed to his left and Gerber was away, pumping legs, accelerating clear. He stormed over the line and, as Loftus roared, dived to score one of the greatest of all Springbok tries.

There was more. Uli Schmidt, the irrepressible hooker, seized upon a New Zealand error, darted blind and passed to Gerber, who set Jaco Reinach sprinting free down the right touchline. The champion athlete, an exceptional replacement for the absent Mordt, dashed from the halfway line to score.

Botha's touchline conversion soared straight and true, the last kick of what had become a resounding Springbok victory by 33-18. "It's difficult to explain my emotions during that last 20 minutes," the fly-half reflects. "Just thinking about the three tries gives me goose pimples down my arms. Everything slipped into place, and I felt so proud of what we had achieved for our country."

The All Blacks had never conceded 33 points in a Test; and, of course, the defeated team was not the All Blacks, but such technicalities did not in any sense diminish the delight writ large across the faces of the dazed, dazzled thousands who drifted happily homewards. Children and grandchildren as yet unborn would be regaled, again and again, with the story of this wondrous day at Loftus.

When the Springboks assembled again, on the Thursday before the fourth Test at Ellis Park, Botha soon realised that the short-term significance of the fireworks in Pretoria was to fuel the players' resolve to negotiate immediately some kind of payment for their efforts during the series.

High-powered attorneys were called to the team hotel to discuss strategy, but the meeting ended when Moss arrived and angrily instructed the legal men to leave or he would call the team manager. Both the coach and the captain remained adamant that the team should focus on securing the series win.

Yet the hawks among the squad were still talking about refusing to play in the fourth Test until Louis Luyt, an administrator trusted by the players, arrived at the hotel on the Friday night and promptly resolved the situation by promising the Springboks would be rewarded. Reports suggested the players later received the sum of R4 300 each. "It was seven on the Friday evening before the Test," Botha recalls, "and we were finally able to talk about rugby."

The Cavaliers launched the fourth Test in dramatic fashion when, for the first time on tour, they formed a crescent in the middle of the field and performed the *haka*, the war dance synonymous with the All Blacks. More than 72 000 fans packing Ellis Park Stadium roared with feverish excitement, perhaps recognising a confession of identity. Unconcerned, Botha continued to stretch.

Another bone-crunching forward struggle followed, with the New Zealand pack earning the kind of possession that could have starved the Springbok backs, won the game and levelled the series. Their failure to do so provoked bitter acrimony to match the moods of 1976 and 1981.

The New Zealand perception was that Ken Rowlands, the Welsh referee imported to handle all four Tests, had been fundamentally dishonest in penalising the tourists for marginal offences in the lineout and maul. Time and again, Hobbs demanded an explanation from the red-jerseyed official, and the Cavaliers raged as Botha transformed the stream of penalties into points.

At one stage, Rowlands marched the argumentative tourists 10 metres upfield for disputing his decision, then another 10 metres, and another 10 metres as the Test began to fray around the edges. "Our guys were becoming despondent," Dalton reflects. "Each time we got near the Springbok line, we conceded another penalty and the chance was lost. I think the final penalty count was 17-8 in South Africa's favour. That tells you all you need to know."

The Cavaliers captain produces his final piece of evidence: "After the Test, I went to see Mr Rowlands and asked him about some of his decisions. His reply to me was absolutely staggering. 'Come on, Andy,' he said seriously, 'I was more middle-of-the road in this Test than I was in the other three.' The Springboks did perform well in the series but, for us, it was a sad end to the tour."

In traditional style, South Africans took a different view. While conceding some decisions had gone against the Cavaliers, they maintained the tourists had yet again revealed their fatal flaw of indiscipline, screaming abuse at the referee during the game and even shoulder-charging him as he left the field. In essence, the New Zealanders lost their heads, and the series.

Botha did not doubt that verdict and, sustaining the excellent quality of his post-Test speeches throughout the series, he thanked the Cavaliers for making the decision to tour South Africa, before adding: "Please don't feel too bad about the referee. Now you know how we felt back in 1981 ... and remember we could have won the series then; you were only able to draw today."

The Cavaliers returned home to have their wrists slapped when the New Zealand Rugby Union imposed two-Test bans on the entire squad, but a general consensus would eventually emerge that, far from being the end of the world for All Black rugby, the unofficial 1986 tour to South Africa had served to create the nucleus of New Zealand's World Cup-winning squad in 1987.

Barely 12 months after being branded "liars and mercenaries" by their own prime minister, David Lange, the likes of Gary Whetton, Wayne Shelford, Grant Fox, Steve McDowell and others were hailed as heroes of the nation. Dalton was also included in the All Black World Cup squad but was again denied the chance to play, by injury. Calm and upright, he eventually returned to the official structure and served as president of the NZRU during 2000 and 2001.

For South African rugby, the Cavaliers tour proved to be not so much the light at the end of the tunnel as a tantalising solitary beam in the darkness, briefly illuminating a Springbok team that, given the opportunity to compete, would have mounted an almighty challenge for the World Cup in 1987.

Calm, diligent and sensitive at the helm of this squad, Moss had emerged from the series with enormous credit. "The quality of rugby in the four Tests was extremely high," the coach reflects. "The sadness was that we were never able to test ourselves on a major overseas tour. It was one thing to win at home, but we could not really tell our strength without playing away."

The coach continues: "Having said all that, there is no doubt that we could never have beaten the Cavaliers without Naas. We had started as a team lacking both confidence and real experience, but Naas led us from the front. Even today, with all the law changes, he would have proved equally effective."

Botha had scored an astonishing 69 points in the four Tests, failing by one point remarkably to double the previous points-scoring record for any individual in a series against New Zealand. Statistics are cold, and easily passed, but it does bear repeating that, playing in a relentlessly competitive, top-class series, Botha had contributed an average of 17,25 points per Test.

Victory over the Cavaliers carried Springbok rugby into a fool's paradise where it was widely assumed the Australians, French and Lions were jolly good rugby men who would by now be so desperate to play against the Boks that they would follow the New Zealanders and tour as "individuals".

This was romantic nonsense. Around the world, amateur rugby players basically smelt money in South Africa, but they would be frustrated. The South African Rugby Board eventually decided not to host further rebel tours for fear of jeopardising its full membership of the IRB.

In 1987, the full Australian squad let it be known that they would be happy to tour South Africa as "individuals" (at one stage, Wallaby captain Andrew Slack was literally waiting for his telephone to ring) but Danie Craven resolutely refused to sanction any payment or to allow any province to host a tour.

The Springboks did not play in 1987 or 1988. Botha and the country's top players were growing frustrated. "We should be organising unofficial tours," the Springbok captain declared. "We have the money, and players around the world are prepared to come if we make it worth their while. It's the obvious thing to do, unless we want our rugby to die a slow death in isolation.

"It's fine for the administrators to say we must wait for official tours to start again, but that won't happen until there's a black president sitting in Pretoria, and I reckon that could be some time. We need to act now."

It was December 1988: P.W. Botha still held sway as State President, and nobody with a sound mind was predicting the kind of dramatic developments that would soon prompt the country's swift transformation.

In the absence of international competition, Botha dedicated his efforts to restoring Northern Transvaal as the dominant provincial side in South Africa, and his form specifically during August and September 1987 may well have been the most devastating of his entire rugby career.

Gathering his strength at the end of a characteristically turbulent season when he had clashed with referees, been publicly criticised by colleagues jealous of his profile and commercial success, and been punched by Jannie Els, a Free State forward, in Bloemfontein, Botha led his rampant Blue Bulls on a run of form that secured their first Currie Cup title in six seasons.

On 15 August he kicked five penalties, four drop goals and a conversion in a 33-24 win over Transvaal at Loftus. Seven days later, playing in Port Elizabeth, Northerns were awarded a penalty near the touchline and Botha seemed to turn and take the ball back to attempt a kick for goal. The Eastern Province side were heading for their posts, but there had been no signal. In an instant, the flyhalf had tapped the penalty and, untouched, scampered over to score in the corner. The EP players stayed beneath the posts ... for the conversion.

Once Free State had been dismantled 47-6 in Pretoria, and Natal were overwhelmed 25-9 in Durban, Northerns prepared to play Transvaal in the 1987 Currie Cup final at Ellis Park. The home side started as favourites but, yet again thriving in the rain, Botha kicked four penalties and four astonishing drop goals to secure an extraordinary, career-defining 24-18 triumph.

In the last five highly competitive provincial matches of the season, Botha had scored a total of 114 points, averaging 23 points per game. He was setting standards of play that had not been equalled before and have certainly not been matched since. He often appeared to be playing his own game.

If Botha missed touch only once, the Loftus Versfeld crowd would audibly groan in disappointment. If he missed touch again, a consensus would grow that he was off form. If he missed touch three times, Monday's newspapers would be speculating what was wrong, proposing drastic measures.

He reflects: "I really enjoyed playing for Northerns but I was also starting to recognise that, at the age of 30, I needed to start making money. I respected the amateur traditions of the game, but I could not understand why I should not be allowed to make a living from my talent on the rugby field."

A solution emerged when he was offered a lucrative opportunity to spend the South African off-season playing for Rovigo in the Italian league. Exactly 24 hours after his Currie Cup-final heroics at Ellis Park in 1987, Botha took what was the first of many madcap dashes from South African to Italy where he played his debut in the red-and-blue-striped jersey of Rovigo.

Only 10 days later, he returned home to captain a shadow national team, playing as the South African Barbarians, to a 56-30 victory at Ellis Park against a composite team called the South Pacific Barbarians. That same evening, he was back on the flight to Italy, preparing for Rovigo's next game.

Botha would continue to juggle his commitments in South Africa and Italy as he played non-stop rugby for five consecutive years. On several occasions, he played for Northerns on the Saturday, then hurtled to the airport and arrived in time to lead Rovigo in an Italian league match on the Sunday afternoon.

Rugby officials in Pretoria instinctively reacted to this jet-set lifestyle like the rounding wife of a successful husband who has hired a glamorous secretary, and suggestions that the flyhalf was no longer completely committed to the light-blue cause prompted the Northern Transvaal coach John Williams sensationally to drop Botha from the provincial side during the 1988 season.

The legend responded by taking his medicine in the B team, returning to the senior side the next week and, six weeks later, leading Northerns to a second successive Currie Cup-final triumph, over Western Province at Loftus.

Everything he touched seemed to turn to gold.

Earlier in 1988 he had inspired Rovigo to become the club champions of Italy, scoring 301 points in 20 games and prompting a week of wild celebrations in the small town cradled 50 kilometres southwest of Venice.

And yet, despite these heroics, Botha remained a ghostly figure in world rugby: a name, a memory concealed by the pariah status of his country. When he might have been raising World Cups, his blonde head was recognised by only a few leading players and aficionados beyond South Africa.

One October day, Botha was just an anonymous face in the crowd as he arrived at Twickenham to watch an England XV play against Japan. He bought his own ticket, and quietly took his seat near halfway in the east stand. Not long after the start, England won a penalty 10 metres from the visitors' line and Stuart Barnes, the flyhalf, indicated to the referee he would kick for the posts.

"Run the ball, you fool," bellowed the well-fed, blazered gentleman seated directly behind Botha in the stand. "This is a running game."

The Springbok captain turned and suggested to his fellow spectator that, since this was a Test match, it was probably sensible to get points on the board, adding there would be time to run the ball later.

An expression of complete contempt crept across the English supporter's face as he exclaimed at Botha: "Oh, for goodness sake, please shut up. What do you know about rugby anyway … not very much, it seems."

Botha said nothing, stared directly ahead, eyes momentarily glazed. He shook his head so slightly that scarcely anybody noticed, then snapped his mind back to the Test match. If ever there was one moment that captured the profound sadness of his isolated, wasted prime, perhaps it was this particular exchange on an October day in the east stand at Twickenham.

By 1989, the International Rugby Board had agreed South Africa deserved to be rewarded for its restraint in declining to host any further unofficial tours, and promised to approve and help organise a star-studded World XV tour to mark the centenary of the South African Rugby Board.

The team, managed by Willie-John McBride, was imaginatively named the FNB International XV, after their bank sponsors, and scheduled to play two Tests against the Springboks, at Newlands and

Ellis Park. Botha keenly looked forward to representing his country again, but his complicated dual career in South Africa and Italy was predictably troubling the Springbok selectors.

The panel had also found an attractive alternative Springbok captain, the captivating and gifted Transvaal leader, Jannie Breedt.

"I voted against Naas as captain in 1989," Moss recalls. "He was still our automatic choice as flyhalf but he only arrived back from Italy in June that season and it did not seem right that he should lead the team. I explained the position to him and he accepted our decision like a good sport. Jannie was a very admired captain for Transvaal, and he was a very fine man."

There is no doubt that such public demotion injured Botha's pride, even if he insisted the only aspect of captaincy that he would miss was the single room to himself in the hotel. "The selectors wanted to cut me down to size," he reflects. "They said I was too controversial but it was not my fault that the media never left me alone. Anyway, I was relaxed. I didn't need to be captain."

In some respects, Botha had become the unwitting victim of his own high public profile, the target of a ludicrously infatuated media.

The flyhalf was once offered a life insurance policy worth a million rand. The story was broken on the Sunday, then regurgitated on the Monday to imply the money would be a gift. Tuesday's newspapers quoted officials threatening to remove Botha's amateur status if he accepted the gift, and Wednesday's papers confirmed that no, in fact, it was actually an insurance policy.

Desperate to keep the story moving, one newspaper printed a headline on the Thursday that proclaimed NAAS MUST DIE FOR A MILLION, as if the player was seriously considering the proposition. By Friday afternoon, this most hunted, hounded and high-profile of all Springbok captains had still not been contacted by anybody offering him any kind of life insurance policy at all.

The "controversy", like many others to hit the headlines during an era when Naas simply equalled News, amounted to nothing at all.

And yet the cumulative impression left on the man-in-the-street was of an arrogant, selfish man who considered himself bigger than the game. This image was clearly unfair, but even Botha was powerless to correct an impression that became so fixed in so many minds. In almost complete contrast, Breedt was cast as a beaming good guy, a big-hearted hero. The national selectors duly reflected the consensus, and Breedt was named Springbok captain.

The youngest of four sons, his father a factory worker, Breedt was born and bred in Kempton Park, near Johannesburg, and spent most of his childhood either playing rugby or listening to match commentaries on the radio. "Rugby was always there," he recalls. "We discussed the major issues endlessly, like whether Dawie de Villiers or Piet Uys should be Springbok scrumhalf."

During five years of service as a policeman, Breedt graduated through the ranks of Northern Transvaal rugby and made his debut for the Blue Bulls in 1981. Strong in the lineout and a natural ball-player, he remained in or around the team for four seasons, but his career took a leap forward in the middle of 1985 when he accepted an offer to become the new captain of Transvaal.

"People said I left Pretoria because Naas had come back as captain," the eighthman recalls, "but that was not true. I became frustrated because Northerns wanted me to play a much tighter game. I liked to take the ball at the back of the scrum and play from there, but I was instructed not to do that. The opportunity in Transvaal gave me more freedom, and it suited me to move."

Breedt's strong leadership qualities forged a happy unit from the disparate talents recruited by Louis Luyt and the TRU chequebook, and the team relished many days of triumph. The eighthman led Transvaal into the Currie Cup finals of 1986 and 1987 but, to his dismay, his team lost both.

Throughout this period of intense provincial rivalry, the respective captains of Northerns and Transvaal were increasingly cast as opposites. Botha, reigning king of Pretoria, versus Breedt, the disaffected prince who had fled and founded his own realm across the river: the poetry was perfect. The enmity was spiced by the reality that the two men didn't particularly like each other. There is no reason why they should have been best friends, but they were not.

They greeted each other briefly, co-existed and swiftly moved on.

In 1986, as Springbok captain and vice-captain, they had been united by the challenge of defeating the Cavaliers, but resentment remained: Breedt saw Botha as too selfish; Botha regarded Breedt as too loose. Now, in 1989, the two men returned to green-and-gold, but with the roles reversed.

Breedt recalls: "Naas was always around during my career, and I never had a problem with him at Northerns. There was one occasion when I heard him tell someone he didn't want me in the team, but that was OK. He was entitled to his opinion. After I had moved to Transvaal, everybody viewed us as huge rivals and I suppose there was an element of truth in that. Anyway, whatever anyone says about Naas, I have always maintained that I would much rather play in the same side as him than against him. He was a great player.

"And it was a huge honour for me to be Springbok captain. Leading the team out, into that amazing roar, was the highlight of my career."

For more than 80 years, the Springboks had been compatriots who also occasionally played against one another in provincial matches. However, the Test team assembled so rarely from 1984 onwards that the emphasis changed. South African players started to think of themselves first and foremost as Transvalers or Blue Bulls, Free Staters, Natalians or Western Province players.

The age of provincialism had dawned.

There had always been geographical divisions within the Springbok team, but they were as soft, grassy ditches compared to the mental Berlin Walls forged by the fury of Currie Cup combat during the late 1980s. Players who were hurled against one another Saturday after Saturday found it almost impossible to arrive at a hotel and transform deadly rivals into long-lost friends.

Each morning at their team hotel, the Springboks would drift down to have breakfast, collect the food from the buffet and choose where to sit. The inevitable result was the Transvaal players at one table, the Natalians at another, the Free Staters on their own, and the Western Province contingent together.

Successive Springbok captains would try to build bridges, and sigh. In the boardrooms, in selection committees, in Springbok squads, South Africans would invariably fail to set their deeply ingrained provincial loyalties aside and advance in the national cause, at least until the 1995 World Cup.

Thus, when the Springbok squad gathered in 1989, the Transvaal players warily greeted Botha, and several Northern Transvaal forwards felt such hostility towards Breedt that, as they later conceded, they had deliberately tried to make the eighthman look bad in a virtual trial earlier in the season. At least it was only their teeth, and not their fists, that were clenched.

The rugby public greeted the FNB International XV's arrival primarily as a pretext for the Springboks to play again; few expected serious opposition from a hopscotch squad, comprising mainly Welshmen and Frenchmen, who gathered from so many different countries and spoke so many languages that it appeared mere conversation, let alone top-class rugby, would be elusive.

In the event Robert Norster, the Welsh lock, inspired a powerful pack of forwards, and French centres Franck Mesnel and Philippe Sella brought flair and threat to the invitation team on attack. "Many South Africans underrated the FNB team," says Breedt. "They had some genuine world stars."

Newlands was packed for the first Test, but it swiftly became clear that the crowd's hopes for a Springbok rout would not be realised. Breedt marshalled his forwards effectively, but the home team could not seize control and was seriously disrupted when Botha was forced to leave the field with a damaged groin muscle. Heunis moved to flyhalf, and South Africa were decidedly relieved to escape from what had become an uncomfortable day with a 20-19 win.

Botha should not have played in the second Test at Ellis Park, but it is a measure of the flyhalf's determination to squeeze every possible drop of international rugby out of his career that he insisted he was fit, and arranged to have no fewer than six injections before kick-off to numb his entire abdomen.

"It was a foolish thing to do," Botha recalls but, heavily strapped and clearly restricted, he managed to play through the entire 80 minutes. An improved home performance yielded a 26-16 victory in Johannesburg, but this basically contrived series against a composite side had hardly thrilled the nation.

Breedt had proved an effective captain, leading the team with intelligence and passion. He was destined to play three more seasons in South Africa before, wearied by in-fighting in the game, he accepted an opportunity to play for Catania, an Italian second division club based in Sicily. With typical style and bravura, he became an admired icon among the local community, staying for seven seasons and guiding a modest team to third place in the league.

On the first Sunday in February 1990, Botha was lunching with friends in Pretoria, and watching avidly on television as Nelson Mandela walked free from prison. South Africans had not been allowed even to see this man's face for 27 years and, as curious as anyone, Botha stared at the screen.

The country was changing fast.

F.W. de Klerk had replaced P.W. Botha as State President, and daringly set a course of repealing apartheid legislation, unbanning the African National Congress and initiating negotiations towards full democracy. South Africans had embarked upon a roller coaster ride to a negotiated revolution.

There would be emotional highs ... days of unified sporting glory, touching days of reconciliation between people who for so long had lived side-by-side and yet so far apart, a clear "Yes" in the referendum, the Nobel Peace Prize; and there would be days when hope would fail ... massacres on trains, Boipatong, ongoing violence in Natal, the assassination of Chris Hani, moments of political stalemate, walkouts and threats, and the antics of the far-right.

Yet it became clear that Mandela's release had triggered an unstoppable reform process that would lead to South Africa's readmission to the international community and to the end of the sports boycott. The doors were suddenly being flung open, and South African sports codes were specifically instructed to achieve internal unity by bringing together the racially divided bodies that had sprouted under apartheid ... and only then to resume international competition.

To their credit, Danie Craven and Louis Luyt had already set out upon this road when they travelled to meet representatives of the ANC in Harare. That was in 1988, long before such excursions were fashionable, and the two rugby officials were widely criticised for talking to a banned organisation, branded as traitors by powerful members of the police force and also by the then minister of education with special responsibility for sport, a certain F.W. de Klerk.

The meeting was facilitated by Tom Bedford, the former Springbok captain who had developed extensive contacts and resolutely sustained his faith in what rugby could one day represent for all South Africans.

"There was preliminary contact in London and Frankfurt," Bedford recalls, "because the ANC people were not allowed into South Africa at the time – people were banned, people were under surveillance, phones were tapped. It was a long and difficult process. The rugby officials were motivated by the desire to get back into international competition. The ANC could assist in that aim, but for their part, they wanted to see the formation of a single non-racial governing body for rugby in South Africa. That was the basis of discussion in Harare."

Craven and Luyt returned from Zimbabwe with a clear understanding that the whites-only South African Rugby Board (and its associates the South African Rugby Federation, for coloureds, and the South African Rugby Association, for blacks) would have to merge with the anti-apartheid South African Rugby Union before the ANC would consent to a resumption of tours.

However the officials did not act upon this advice, and any benefit rugby may have earned by blazing a trail to the ANC was soon lost.

Past his 80th birthday, Craven seemed patently unable to accept the need to yield so much to an organisation such as SARU, which he believed was driven not so much by any love of rugby but by political ambition. This was not the case, but the Board president continued to insist the best vehicles for the development of black and coloured players were the Federation and SARA.

Botha followed these developments with interest, and continued to pursue his career in Rovigo and Pretoria. As the tortured negotiations between Craven's Board and SARU began, broke down, resumed, broke down and resumed again, the Springboks remained tactfully inactive during 1990 and 1991.

The blonde flyhalf continued to dominate the landscape of provincial rugby, leading Northern Transvaal to yet another Currie Cup final in 1990, only to suffer the indignity of a shock defeat at home to Natal. He recovered the following year, directing the Blue Bulls to a fourth title in five years when they defeated Breedt's Transvaal team in the 1991 Currie Cup final at Loftus.

He still read the game more accurately than anyone, his handling was still superb, his punts still spiralled, his place-kicking ratio remained above 80%, and his drop goals still soared. Entering his 34th year, Botha may have lost speed but he remained an enormous factor in every match he played.

Rugby's unity negotiations dragged on painstakingly, until Steve Tshwete, ANC spokesman on sport, emerged as an honest broker, knocked a few heads together and paved the way for the historic agreement that SARU would merge with the Board, Federation and SARA to form the South African Rugby Football Union, with Dr Danie Craven as co-president with Ebrahim Patel.

South Africa was already basking in the ecstasy of international sport. The country's cricket squad had toured India in November 1991 and, as dawn broke on Friday 20 March 1992, Kepler Wessels's team was preparing for a World Cup semi-final against England at the Sydney Cricket Ground.

That same March morning, Botha was in the town of Kimberley, attending the inaugural general meeting of the newly formed SARFU. Though not a man of searing political convictions, he understood the situation and had travelled 6 000 miles from Rovigo to be present at this historic occasion.

"It was exciting to be there," remembers the flyhalf, who earned additional praise for his performance when he led a Unity XV to a 38-31 victory in a special festival match on the Saturday. "Seeing everyone together made me think how stupid we had been to have wasted so many years apart."

The SARFU meeting reconfirmed green-and-gold as the national colours, and launched a series of discussions that would eventually lead to the Springbok emblem being supported by a semi-wreath of proteas on the jersey. Of particular interest to Botha, a schedule of forthcoming Tests was agreed.

He could scarcely believe his ears: a tour to Romania and Italy as careful preparation before a Test against the All Blacks at Ellis Park on 15 August, and a Test against the world champion Wallabies at Newlands just seven days later; a tour to France and England at the end of the 1992 season; a home series against France, a tour to Australia and a tour to Argentina in 1993; a home series against England, tours to New Zealand and the United Kingdom in 1994.

The chairman of SARFU's tours committee, Dr Nic Labuschagne, added that the 1995 Rugby World Cup would probably be held in South Africa, although that decision still needed to be confirmed at the IRB.

After the years of drought, this was Victoria Falls.

"It was amazing," Botha recalls. "My first reaction was to be thankful that I was still playing during this period of readmission, but I did spare a thought for all the players who had recently retired, and who missed out."

The proclamation of unity did not, however, soothe every concern, and the Springbok tour to Romania and Italy was cancelled at the behest of former SARU members who believed genuine structures to develop the game in coloured and black areas should be created before tours resumed.

The SARU contingent was concerned that most white administrators had embraced unity not out of any moral conviction to transform and grow the game, but because they were desperate for Test rugby. That suspicion would eventually be proven, but the result of the administrative wrangling was to place the Springbok players in an almost impossible situation.

A team that had played two low-key Tests in the past six years, and not even assembled for three seasons, would now have to face the All Blacks and the Wallabies on successive Saturdays with no warm-up.

Botha was alarmed: "The cancellation of the warm-up tour was a massive blow," he remembers. "People would say later that we were arrogant in believing we could return from isolation and beat New Zealand and Australia in the space of seven days, but that was never our original intention."

The flyhalf had learned the news while playing for a World XV against the All Blacks in Auckland, to mark the centenary of the NZRU. The same weekend, at the Test Unions day back home in Pretoria, François Pienaar led Transvaal to victory over Free State, Gary Teichmann scored two tries as Natal beat Eastern Province, and Joost van der Westhuizen played his second match for Northerns as they lost to Tiaan Strauss's Western Province side.

Perhaps the schedule was daunting but, for Springbok rugby, the horizon suddenly stretched far into the distance, and across the land strong young men were emerging to carry the game through the next decade.

Botha was running up the air miles again, leading Rovigo's march into the play-off stages of the Italian championships, returning home to play his part in the week of Springbok trials at Loftus Versfeld, then flying back to Italy the next night. "I had no option," he recalls. "I urgently wanted to keep my place in the Springbok team, but there was no way I could simply drop the people in Rovigo." Within this insane schedule, he maintained outstanding form.

On 17 May at Loftus Versfeld he kicked five drop goals and four penalties, scoring all Northern Transvaal's points in the 27-24 win over Natal. The next day, in Italy, he kicked three drop goals and four penalties, and added a try, scoring all Rovigo's points in the 25-18 semifinal win over San Dona.

Instead of celebrating this remarkable phenomenon (from being one great rugby player, Botha had effectively become two great rugby players) an inevitable core of small-minded critics claimed the flyhalf's absence in Italy demonstrated a lack of commitment, and suggested he should be shunned in favour of Hennie le Roux, Transvaal's dynamic and enterprising flyhalf.

A national debate ensued, as madly excited newspapers printed "probable" Springbok teams in virtually every edition. On Monday, Naas was in the team. On Tuesday, Naas was out. On Wednesday, he was definitely captain.

John Williams, the former Northern Transvaal coach, had been appointed to coach the Springboks during readmission, and the university professor was in no doubt that he needed Botha at flyhalf if his inexperienced and under-prepared team was to stand any chance against the All Blacks and Wallabies.

Botha's incessant travelling finally stopped in the second week of June; he was relaxed, in excellent form, and looking forward to the challenges ahead. His second marriage, to long-jump champion Karen Kruger, had brought stability and happiness to his personal life, and he had seen so many wild headlines and sour criticism over the years that he no longer took much notice.

He intensified his training programme, kicked for an extra half hour at the end of each practice, and soon it was the end of July.

Echoing the experience of so many predecessors, Botha learned of his appointment as Springbok captain by listening to an SABC radio news bulletin at home on a Saturday night. "John Williams had not said anything," he recalls, "but it was not a complete surprise. Jannie Breedt had been having a difficult time in Transvaal, and there were not many other options.

"I was obviously pleased to be captain but, above all, I was thrilled that Danie Gerber was included in the team. It felt as though we had both somehow survived the years of isolation; and it was nothing to do with emotion. Danie may have been 34, but he had scored two outstanding tries for Western Province the previous week. We had both been selected on merit."

The excited South Africans were not the only players preparing for one of the greatest days of their careers, not the only players who had been reconciled to the apparent reality that they would never have the opportunity to participate in an official Test between the Springboks and All Blacks.

Sean Fitzpatrick had grown up in Auckland, inspired by memories of lying on the living room floor, staying up late at night to watch television broadcasts of New Zealand playing South Africa in 1976. "The scorched grounds and the huge crowds: it left a vivid impression on me," he recalls, "but, with the political issues, I reckoned we would never go to Africa during my career."

However, on 26 July 1992 the combative hooker launched what would become an extreme personal relationship with South Africa when he led his All Black squad through the arrivals hall at Johannesburg airport. Grinding out solid wins against Natal, Free State, the Junior Springboks and a Central Unions XV, the revered black jerseys were joyfully cheered at every venue. For a generation of South Africans, this tour represented something completely new, a fresh dawn, the All Blacks! In many ways, it was 1928 all over again.

15 August dawned as the day of reckoning. Ellis Park Stadium might have been sold out three times over, and the roar that greeted Naas Botha at the head of his team conveyed a clear public expectation of victory. At that moment, it was hard not to be swept along by the tidal wave of optimism: Schmidt was the best hooker in the world, wasn't he? Breedt, Du Plessis, Gerber, they were all world-class, weren't they? And then, of course, there was Naas.

In the event, the All Blacks reduced 72 000 people to near silence. A team that had already played eight Test matches during 1992 proved far too organised and compact, too disciplined and ruthless for a side that had sweated through no more than four training sessions together. For all the Springboks' heart and gees, harsh reality splashed around the stadium like cold water.

New Zealand led 10-0 at the interval and 20-3 after 55 minutes. Botha had scarcely touched the ball and the stunned crowd was beginning to contemplate a defeat of humiliating proportions. There seemed no escape.

Breedt recalls: "We were following a basic Northern Transvaal game plan, grinding the opposition pack and playing for field position, and it obviously wasn't working. The All Blacks were strong up to inside centre, but we had their beating on the outside. I spoke to Naas early in the second half, and we agreed to start spreading the ball to the wings. Everything changed."

Gerber roused his team-mates and the crowd when he cut through the All Black defence to score; and, even though John Kirwan's try quickly restored the 17-point gap, the Springboks were gathering momentum. Pieter Muller, the bold Natal centre, rounded off another passing move with five minutes to go and, two minutes into injury time, Gerber powered over again.

When Sandy McNeill, the Australian referee, blew the last whistle after a frantic finale, South Africans looked at the scoreboard and saw they had lost this fast, unrelenting Test by only three points, 24-27. Botha recalls: "We came back really strongly in the last quarter, and I came off the field feeling quite frustrated. We had started so slowly, and yet we could easily have won."

The narrow margin of defeat focused the captain's mind on one incident when James Small, the young Transvaal wing playing his debut, had dropped the ball with the All Black try line at his mercy. "You can't blame one person," Botha recalls, "but that mistake was crucial. It could have happened to anyone. It could have happened to me, but that was how close we came."

As the dust settled, Springbok pride appeared precariously intact. The late comeback, several near misses and the three-point margin of defeat combined to persuade most South Africans that there was no real problem, and that the world champion Wallabies would reap the whirlwind a week later.

In fact, the Australians nearly went home.

By Sunday afternoon it was clear that the African National Congress was furious with SARFU for breaching each of three conditions upon which the ANC had granted its support for the tours. SARFU had accepted there would be no old South African flags at the Tests, but Ellis Park was awash with orange, white and blue; SARFU had promised a minute of silence would be observed in memory of the victims of the Boipatong massacre, but the silence had been interrupted; and most seriously, SARFU had promised that Die Stem, the national anthem, would not be played before the Test, but it was played.

Nick Farr-Jones, a lawyer by training, had captained Australia to victory at the 1991 Rugby World Cup and eagerly looked forward to this short tour in 1992 when his side could play the Springboks. However, at two o'clock on the Monday morning after the Ellis Park Test, the Wallaby captain was abruptly woken in his Port Elizabeth hotel room and called to an urgent meeting.

Joe French, president of the Australian Rugby Union, said he had been warned that, following events at Ellis Park, the ANC were likely to withdraw their support of the tour. "If that happens," French continued, "we are going to get you guys out of here tomorrow night. It could turn nasty."

In the event, the ANC leaders met and showed tolerance on the understanding that the three agreed conditions would certainly be enforced at Newlands.

Botha and Farr-Jones were equally relieved. The two men had met during the 1986 IRB centenary matches in London, and had become friends, joining forces to film an exercise video in Hawaii in 1987 and keeping contact by telephone. "I had a pretty clear understanding of Naas's situation," the Wallaby captain recalls, "and I knew how desperate he was to play well in these Tests.

"The Newlands match was important to us as well. We had all felt flat after the World Cup, a bit down because we had not won the final against England in style, so we wanted 1992 to be a big year. We had already beaten the All Blacks in the Bledisloe Cup before travelling to South Africa."

The Springbok selectors made only one enforced change to the team for Newlands, with Johan Styger replacing prop Heinrich Rodgers, and yet the mood within the camp had become tense and unsettled. Certain players from Transvaal and Western Province had started to rail against what they viewed as a Blue Bull axis between coach Williams and captain Botha, although the players did at least unite in their dismay at the outdated, insensitive management.

On a cold, dripping Friday afternoon before the Test, the entire Springbok squad had been instructed to board a bus, drive for 50 minutes to Constantia, get out at a café to drink a cup of tea and eat a scone, and spend 50 more minutes in the bus driving back to their hotel. Herbert Castens might well have enjoyed such a trip but, as one player noted, "this is 1992 not 1892".

The miserable weather had settled steadfastly over the Cape, promoting South African hopes that Botha would once again thrive in the wet conditions, as he had during the first Test against the Cavaliers and during the 1987 Currie Cup final. In both those matches, however, he received the ball.

Once the Newlands crowd had impeccably observed the minute's silence, the drilled and ordered world champions dominated the lineouts, scrums and loose phases, monopolised possession, and soon established such a grip on the Test that the Springboks hardly threatened the Wallaby line.

However, Botha's team gallantly tackled and chased, and trailed only 8-3 with 12 minutes remaining. There was still hope. The Springbok flyhalf attempted one long-range penalty, but missed, then he lined up another difficult penalty, but missed again. The margins of failure had been small, perhaps a metre here and a metre there, but evidently not much was falling into place.

The Australians showed no mercy. Clearly shifting up a gear in the last ten minutes of the Test, the world champions scored two tries and two penalties and, in the blink of an eye, condemned the South Africans to their heaviest Test defeat in history, eclipsing even the 28-9 loss to the Lions in 1974.

A closely contested match had suddenly become a rout, and as stunned spectators filed quietly homewards, the drops of rain on every roof and seat seemed like so many tears of disappointment. If the final score at Ellis Park had flattered the Springboks, the neon scoreboard shining through the gloom at Newlands did not adequately reflect their performance.

South Africa 3 Australia 26.

Botha was aghast.

He emerged from the steaming kit and eerie silence of the South African changing room to declare that he would decide within 24 hours whether to make himself available for the end-of-season tour to France and England.

"We had not played badly," he recalls. "That's the curious fact. People now look back on that Test at Newlands as a complete catastrophe but, if you look at the videotape, you see that we competed very well against the world champions for 70 minutes, but they cleaned us out in the last 10 minutes. There is no doubt that they were the stronger team, and deserved to win, but the final scoreline was an extremely harsh judgement on our performance."

Twenty metres down the corridor at Newlands, the Wallabies celebrated a sweet victory that unequivocally confirmed their status as world champions and, to their great delight, would silence the notably loud-mouthed and arrogant breed of South African who had relentlessly been prodding fat fingers in Wallaby chests and reciting: "You're not the champions till you beat the Boks."

No more. Michael Lynagh, the softly spoken record-breaking fly-half, sat in the corner of the changing room and noted: "The guys have been irritated by the South African attitude. Most people over here think their team is pretty good, but we showed them they're not as good as they think they are."

Farr-Jones sat, exhausted. He had emotionally informed his team before kick-off that this Test would be his last, and now he sat, content. Even in the glow of triumph, however, he spared a thought for his friend. "It had been an awkward afternoon for Naas," the Wallaby reflects. "He didn't get much ball and we put in place the same strategy against him that we always used for Grant Fox when we played New Zealand: getting our loose forwards to run down on him as much as possible. We realised Naas was the crucial factor for South Africa, and we knew how teams could unwind around their pivotal players.

"I think 1992 was very difficult for him. It was quite sad. I wish he had had a real opportunity to cement his place in world rugby. Oddly enough, just before the 1995 Rugby World Cup, I had the chance to play alongside Naas for a Danie Craven XV in a festival match at Stellenbosch and, even at the age of 37, he was unbelievably brilliant. He could have played in that tournament."

Botha returned home to Pretoria, to reflect upon the events of a frenzied eight days. This relentlessly positive man who had for so long and so often been a winner suddenly had to face not only the reality of successive Test defeats but, far worse, the prospect that even he would not be able to reverse the fortunes of what had been exposed as a naïve and divided Springbok squad. He sat at his kitchen table, and calmly assessed the situation.

What were the facts?

Challenged to emerge from total darkness into the blinding glare of Tests against the two strongest teams in the world on successive Saturdays, the South Africans had selected a heavy pack of forwards and, relying heavily on the flyhalf's skills, employed a conservative 10-man strategy. Despite being consistently penalised for lifting in the lineouts, an activity that local referees had long tolerated, the side had played well for long periods at Ellis Park and Newlands.

However, the facts remained that he had not received enough possession from the lineout or the loose phases to establish his authority on either occasion, and both matches were lost. The defeats had exposed both him, as captain, and the coach, John Williams, to widespread criticism, most significantly from a group of outspoken Transvaal players within the national squad.

Now he faced a major decision: should he retire from South African rugby, leave the new generation to their backstabbing and petty jealousies and return to Italy where he could trust his Rovigo teammates and enjoy the game? Or should he refuse to retire on the bitter memory of the Wallaby defeat, work with Williams to develop a stronger pack of forwards, face down his critics, and then retire after the last Test of the season, against England at Twickenham?

For Botha, this was no choice at all.

He would not walk away.

He resolved to retire on his own terms.

A week after losing to the Wallabies, Botha travelled to France to play in a farewell match for Serge Blanco in Biarritz and, his confidence restored by a fine performance among top-class players, he eventually returned to South Africa and announced he was available to tour France and England. He invited the critics to do their worst, and barked that he would do his best.

The 34-year-old flyhalf was duly appointed to lead South Africa's first tour since 1981, and he emerged as a relentlessly positive influence during a four-day training camp in Cape Town before the squad's departure. "We are going to tell each player what we expect from him," he told the media. "We are going to agree clear procedures and goals. Nothing will be left to chance."

Botha and Williams agreed that their team's best hope of survival against experienced and streetwise opposition, not to mention unpredictable referees, in Europe was to develop a commanding pack of forwards and play the game in the opposition's half. They would keep everything tight and organised, demonstrating discipline, discipline, discipline at all times. The coach and captain believed this strategy would maximise the potential of the playing resources at their disposal, and they knew that it worked: after all, this had been the blueprint for Northern Transvaal's domination of Currie Cup rugby since 1986.

Perhaps that was the problem. The print was light blue.

In the minds of too many Springboks, the team strategy was wrong simply because it originated in Pretoria. Certain players from Western Province, Natal and Transvaal, but far from all, would join the training ground huddle and appear to be listening to Botha's impassioned team talks ... but they were not prepared to commit themselves and make it work. In heart and mind, they seemed detached. In essence, they would be led to water but they would not drink.

And later, out of earshot, they would moan about outdated and outmoded tactics and they would amuse one another by denigrating Botha as being past his best and by demeaning Williams as a coaching dinosaur.

These eager, gifted young players signally failed to make the mental leap from seeing Botha as the Blue Bulls enemy who so regularly had eclipsed them on the field, to regarding him as their own captain, a motivated genius who would steer them to the top of international rugby. They simply did not like him, did not recognise his ability, and would not listen to him.

Botha looked into their eyes and saw everything: "I knew from the outset that the tour to France and England was going to be difficult," he says. "We were not getting through to a certain core of players. People said it was provincialism, but I cannot accept that as an excuse for that kind of behaviour."

He recalls: "There was a wider problem with the mentality of South African rugby: the players had been so spoiled and flattered in isolation that they thought they knew everything. They were not prepared to put in the effort required to step up and be successful in Test rugby. They were too clever.

"I had been shown time-coded photographs of some of the guys partying in a Cape Town nightclub at 02h45 on the Friday morning before the Test against Australia. It didn't bother me to be called the 'ice cream and Coke man of South African rugby' but it did bother me when Springboks neglected their responsibility towards their teammates, their supporters and their country.

"On my first Springbok tour, I hardly opened my mouth and did whatever Morné du Plessis wanted. Things had obviously changed."

Yes, his critics would exclaim, that is exactly the point. Botha lacked the kind of emollient personality, the ability to sit down with a player and talk through his problems, that distinguished Du Plessis as a great Springbok captain. This is a moot point. Literally hundreds of young players in Pretoria, and Rovigo, would disagree, describing the flyhalf as an inspiring mentor.

Ironically Abie Malan, the former Springbok captain appointed as the team manager, was soon telling journalists on tour: "Today's youngsters need heroes, like Tarzan or Batman or Naas Botha." The pity was that many of the youngsters within his own squad so obviously did not share his view.

Wherever the fault lay, the 1992 Springboks left South Africa as a deeply divided group; barely on speaking terms, neither faction was minded to seek any compromise. The emotional weather remained dismal.

Yet the tour ran its unsmiling course.

Defeat against an Espoirs de France team in the opening match raised the prospect of a long, wretched seven weeks ahead, but the

South Africans did rally and managed a trio of jittery victories over typically strong invitation teams before heading to Lyon, venue of the first Test against France.

Refusing to be depressed or downhearted by what had become a thinly disguised rebellion within his squad, Botha handled the situation by focussing all his energies and attention on the players who had shown they were prepared to work in the interests of the team, effectively the Test side, and ruthlessly ignored the rest, leaving them to flounder in the midweek team.

"It was not much fun, but there was no option," the captain recalls. "John and I had tried everything to get everyone on board, but certain guys did not want to respond. I didn't care about them. I wanted to win the Test."

His opening punt spiralled 70 metres down the left touchline at the Stade Gerland before bouncing left and into touch. He clipped his hip with his palm and jogged downfield, gently encouraging his forwards. The pack comprised no fewer than six Northern Transvaal players plus Tiaan Strauss and Wahl Bartmann, and it began to grind forward, prompting French mistakes.

If this was "outdated" rugby, it was also winning rugby.

Botha reaped a penalty and a drop goal from the pressure, and tries either side of half time, scored by Gerber and Muller, both from Garth Wright's delicate kicks, carried the Springboks into an unimagined 20-3 lead after 55 minutes. His players had followed the game plan, his players were maintaining discipline, and the flyhalf responded with another colossal performance.

Time and again, the French hurled themselves at the Springbok line, only for Strauss, Bartmann or Richter to make the tackle. The ball would be wrestled back to Wright, then to Botha who would launch another huge punt, driving the home team back into their own half. His side would not be denied.

Penaud did score one try and then another, reducing the deficit to 15-20 with four minutes plus six minutes of injury time to play. As the home supporters started to sense a dramatic victory, the royal blue jerseys again stormed forward, but driving forwards and dashing backs alike were courageously repelled ... and, with a thump of his boot, Botha sent them back 50 metres.

At last, the final whistle; at last, a Test victory. While the prophets of doom shuffled uncomfortably in the stands, most of the Springboks sank to the grass in exhaustion, relief and delight. There was no respite for their captain, whisked off as the Man of the Match to speak on French television.

"The 15 guys on the field did a fantastic job in Lyon," Botha reflects. "We were being written off by everyone before the match, but we got the points on the board and then managed to hold on in the closing stages."

The happy ending that Botha's 16-season career certainly deserved would have seen his Springboks charge to a second Test win in Paris to take the series win over France and then move on to a glorious and triumphant climax, defeating England at Twickenham, carrying their captain off the field.

It seemed unimaginable that a career studded with triumph should not end in victory against all the odds, victory to silence his critics again.

Yet there would be no happy ending.

The French forwards raised their game in Paris and, while the Springboks competed strongly before half time and trailed by only six points when the match moved into injury time, the tourists could not dispute the 29-16 defeat. They had not won enough possession, and the series was shared.

Botha's squad had not particularly enjoyed France: creative and pro-active team management had been non-existent, the players had complained about the food and a succession of grim suburban hotels, and they were then criticised for a unanimous decision, in a rare moment of unity, to leave a formal dinner after an hour because their French counterparts had still not appeared.

The captain recalls: "I was hoping the mood of the squad would improve for the last two weeks of the tour in England but, if anything, it got worse. Most of the Natal guys tended to follow Robert du Preez, who had become disaffected when he lost his place in the Test side. He got married while we were staying in London, and most of the players knew nothing about his plans. That is how far the squad had drifted apart. It was very disappointing.

"And, for some reason, Harry Viljoen was hanging around our hotel. He had recently resigned as the Transvaal coach, but he was always in discussion with his former players. One evening, I heard he held a meeting that was only for the Transvalers. It seemed he was undermining the tour."

It would be wrong to characterise this conflict as a mere personality clash between Botha and a handful of his squad. This was, plainly, the outright refusal of certain players to accept the authority of their coach and captain. Gerber had kept his eyes open and later reflected: "Several of the Transvaal guys would not take advice from experienced players. Remember, Naas and I had already played for the Springboks when they were still in primary school."

Yet the tour continued. Botha's team produced a happily enterprising and effective performance to beat the Midlands 32-9, earning a standing ovation from the Welford Road crowd in Leicester; and Jacques Olivier sprinted 50 metres to score a memorable try in a thrilling 20-16 win over England B.

All eyes turned to Twickenham.

"We all know what has happened on this tour," the captain told his team in the changing room moments before kick-off, "but all the negative things will fade away if we win today. If we can beat England, we will go home as heroes. This is our chance to put everything behind us and come out on top."

Botha then pulled a Springbok jersey over his blonde head for the last time and prepared to play the 28th and final Test match of his career. He had decided to retire from South African rugby three months before his 35th birthday. Eager to take his bow on the grandest stage, he had settled upon the occasion of leading his country out to play against England at Twickenham. Thus, a career so long in darkness would end under the brightest spotlight of all.

For 40 minutes, it seemed he would walk away in triumph. The flyhalf had kicked two long penalties, characteristically turning away as soon as he knew he had struck the ball straight and true, manufactured a trademark drop goal from an apparently scrappy "dead" situation, and smoothly converted Strauss's opportunist try. South Africa led 16-11 at half time, and deserved to lead.

Will Carling called his team together. "We were extremely concerned," the England captain recalls. "The Springbok forwards were winning a fair amount of possession, and Naas was starting to control the game. We had been warned to keep the ball away from him, but life does become difficult when you play against a flyhalf who keeps sending you back 50 metres."

Across the field, Botha emotionally implored his players to keep going, just to keep going for another 40 minutes. That was all he had left.

As the grisly gloom gathered on this overcoat, overcast day in London, the England forwards began to assert control and monopolise possession. Deprived of the ball, Botha could do nothing as the reigning Five Nations champions ran in three second-half tries without reply, and won 33-16.

The Springbok captain shook hands with players from both teams after the final whistle, and hurried quickly away to the sanctuary of the changing room. He had desperately wanted to finish as a winner. The reality of defeat combined with a sudden realisation that his Test career had ended, and it hurt.

"We were going backwards in the second half," he reflects. "Several of the tries we conceded may have been soft, but we couldn't really complain about the result. In 1992, we did not win enough possession to win Tests. The atmosphere within the squad, the total lack of preparation and warm-up fixtures, the standard of management, didn't help, but we did not win enough ball."

Some critics would later reflect upon the Test record of Naas Botha's 1992 Springboks (won one, lost four), and gleefully conclude that the celebrated flyhalf had finally been exposed as a worthless irrelevance unless his forwards provided him with the ball. This was tantamount to saying Don Bradman would never have won a Test for Australia if the bowlers hadn't taken wickets.

It is a statement of the sporting obvious. Botha never claimed to have won any game on his own. That statement was made so often not by him but by those few hundred coaches and few million supporters who recognised unique ability in this private, assured, self-oriented and driven individual.

His extraordinary talents, not only to kick the ball out of his hand and on the ground as it has rarely been kicked, but also to read the game, to inspire his team-mates, even occasionally to break and dash, probably set him apart as the outstanding player in the history of Springbok rugby, so far.

Consider the longevity of his career, how he played, lived and survived at the very highest level of South African rugby for no fewer than 16 seasons; and that, in this period, he guided Northerns to 12 Currie Cup finals, seven titles, two shared titles and two final defeats (one missed through injury).

Consider the sheer number of training sessions and team talks, the total dedication and resolve, the avalanche of drop goals and penalties, the number of times that somebody went to the rugby because he was playing, the excitement and enthusiasm that he generated Saturday upon Saturday, the way every head turned whenever he walked through the door, the tangible aura.

Consider all this and it is impossible to arrive at any conclusion other than that, ruling his era, Naas was not just the Baas ... he was pure class.

12 THE WORLD CHAMPION

Circumstances gave François Pienaar the opportunity to become the greatest of all Springbok captains, and he reached out with both hands.

No other Springbok captain had been afforded the prospect of winning the World Cup on home soil, before his own supporters; no other Springbok captain had found himself in an era when South Africans of every colour and creed were ready to unite in support of their national rugby team.

Yet opportunity is one thing.

Achievement is quite another.

François Pienaar achieved, and his reward was a degree of immortality in the hearts of his compatriots, an indelible association with one of the greatest days and one of the most enduring images in the history of South Africa: a World Cup final, a golden trophy, an applauding president, a united nation.

In many ways, he captained the Springbok side on a different plane, in a different world to that of his 40 predecessors. As he might have put it, his team played not for six million whites but for 42 million South Africans.

This fair, eloquent and principled man moved to the fore at the start of the 1993 season, a period when Springbok rugby cried out for new leadership. Naas Botha's retirement had left an enormous gap on the field, and Danie Craven, the game's grand leader, had passed away quietly in Stellenbosch.

All was not well. South African rugby was battling to implement the basic principles of unity and development, and the Springbok team had been ruthlessly exposed during its first year after readmission. Stung by adversity, a traditionally conservative establishment suddenly appeared ready to think the unthinkable, to break old conventions, to build a new union and a new team.

The mood within the game matched the mood within the country: perhaps change would be difficult, but change was absolutely necessary. Change would, however, require a leader, a man with personality and presence, with the bravery and charisma to carry the game forward through hard times and good times, who would motivate his teammates and inspire his country.

Like who?

Jan-Harm and Valerie Pienaar lived, worked and reared their four sons in the unforgiving industrial landscape south of Johannesburg. He typically worked night shifts at the local steelworks, and she would have her work cut out to keep the boys quiet while he slept through the afternoons. He had been the second of seven children, she had been the fifth of eleven: these were Afrikaners, and they worked from Monday to Friday, watched rugby on Saturday, and attended church on Sunday. They were not rich, but they were a family.

Their oldest son had been named François, after his paternal grandfather, and the small blonde boy soon showed signs of the quiet resolve that would carry him so far in life. Visiting his grandmother one Christmas, he arrived to discover his cousin had been given a radio-controlled car. Brimming with excitement, he opened his present, and found a small red bus. He felt sad and second-rate. That day, he promised himself he would never be second-rate again.

The incident stayed with him, motivated him to do whatever was required, to make whatever sacrifices were necessary to realise his goals. He would never drive a bus but, strangely, that small red bus would drive him.

And so he grew, studying a little and playing a lot. His days were filled with athletics, cricket and rugby, highly committed coaches, parched fields in dazzling sunshine, always outdoors: no inhibitions, no fear and no shoes.

During the school holidays, he used to catch the bus to Johannesburg and help out at his Uncle Kobus's garage, earning a little extra money. His first month's salary was enough to buy his mother an electric carving knife. He loved his Uncle Kobus, respected him. Uncle Kobus drove a Mercedes Benz.

Sport sustained the exuberant youngster through primary school and on to Transvalia High School in Vanderbijlpark. Rugby was fine, but cricket was better. As a medium-fast bowler and big-hitting lower-order batsman, he earned a place in the Country Districts high schools team to play at Nuffield Week in Cape Town. However, the experience of being struck around the ground by a Border batsman named Daryll Cullinan convinced the bristling young Pienaar that he was unlikely to play Test cricket; rugby soon seized his full attention.

His father's decision to change jobs took the family to the town of Witbank, east of Johannesburg, where the boy enrolled for one year at Patriot High School and started to climb the rugby ladder. He was tall and strong, and his hair was cut in the most fashionable style, every inch the school hero.

The Patriot 1st XV, the Eastern Transvaal side for the 1985 Craven Week, a place in the South African Schools team and a special recommendation from Danie Craven watching in the grandstand, large crowds, status, strutting to class, going out with pretty girls from rival schools: this was his life.

No fewer than three major universities offered him a bursary to continue his education, and play rugby. The Rand Afrikaans University, in Johannesburg, was determined to build a powerful team and offered R3 000 per year. Pienaar eagerly accepted, and arranged to read law.

He relished the order and authority of *koshuis* (hostel) life, the initiations, the pecking order, the rules and conventions, and he studied hard, juggling his rugby training with lectures to ensure he passed each year, but his student life soon revolved around big matches and bigger nights out.

Pienaar and his friends would typically turn out for RAU on the Saturday afternoon, then gather at the Alligators Bar near campus. As

1. Tommy Bedford on the charge *(private collection)*
2. Naas Botha was prolific with the boot *(private collection)*

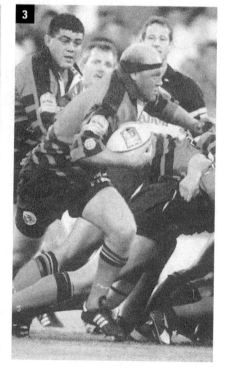

1. Divan Serfontein clears his line *(private collection)*
2. Tiaan Strauss offloads skilfully *(private collection)*
3. Adriaan Richter, a World Cup captain in 1995 *(private collection)*

4. Jannie Breedt in action against the New Zealand Cavaliers in 1986 *(private collection)*
5. Rassie Erasmus had a brief cameo as captain, against Australia in 1999 *(private collection)*
6. Joost van der Westhuizen, revered as a scrumhalf, in full cry *(private collection)*

1. François Pienaar (left) and dropgoal hero Joel Stransky *(private collection)*
2. François Pienaar, holding the Webb Ellis Cup, 1995 *(Sunday Times)*
3. Gary Teichmann raises the Tri-Nations Trophy, 1998 *(private collection)*

the night drew on, they would head for the bright lights of Hillbrow, to drink some more, laugh and fight. Once provoked, they excitedly raised their fists.

The easily recognisable rugby player quickly earned a reputation, and a succession of daring young bloods would deliberately bump his shoulder as they walked past his table in the bar, or swear at one of his friends. The consequent brawl usually ended with just a black eye or a broken chair. Sometimes, the night would lead to sober Sunday morning stitches in hospital.

Moving steadily through under-20 ranks, his ambition was to win a place in the Transvaal side. On weekday evenings, Pienaar would wander down to Eben Cuyler Park, near RAU, and stand silent in the shadows while the provincial team trained. He would use a stopwatch to time the first-choice flankers, Pieterse and Bartmann, as they ran their sprints; and the following day, he would return alone to the same field, and desperately try to better their times.

He broke into the Transvaal team at the end of the 1989 season, but only started to prompt headlines when Harry Viljoen arrived as coach. Through 1991 and 1992, Pienaar felt merrily liberated by an enterprising game plan in which the flyhalf would run at the advantage line, popping passes to flanks on the charge, and yet both seasons ended in Currie Cup-final defeats.

The Transvaal flank had made an impact, but there was no certainty that he would reach the highest levels of the game. He had featured powerfully in the Springbok trials of 1992, but then failed to make the team for the Tests against New Zealand and Australia and, to his great disappointment, he had been left out of the end-of-season Springbok tour to France and England.

Exclusion did not dampen his enthusiasm. He sat in the stands and sang Die Stem before the Test against the All Blacks, and then travelled with a group of friends to watch South Africa play the Wallabies at Newlands, being asked in a restaurant before the game to fold away his South African flag.

He had not felt like going out that dismal night in Cape Town, following the Springboks' 26-3 defeat, but his friends dragged him to a bar and, around one in the morning, he was excited to find himself in the same Long Street nightclub as David Campese and several other Australian players. He stood and watched the world champion rugby players being serenaded like movie stars. "That looks fun," he thought to himself. "I want to be like them one day."

So he kept working, kept sweating at the gym, kept bulking so much that mischievous rumours suggested he was taking drugs (he wasn't). His resolve to be successful was such that, until shortly before, he had been working part-time at the steelworks, scraping the stubborn grime from the kilns to earn a few rands. He wanted to be wealthy and respected, to be a Springbok; and every waking hour, every ounce of energy was channelled towards these goals.

Impatience simmered. While South Africa was defeating France in Lyon, he was playing golf in Swaziland. Most of the players interrupted their rounds to watch the Test on TV, but Pienaar decided to keep playing. His solo round was punctuated by cheers from the clubhouse, but he was in his own world, working out what was wrong and what he needed to do to succeed.

He need not have worried. The final piece of his jigsaw had been pushed into place two weeks before when Viljoen was succeeded as Transvaal coach by a strong, decent, loyal and disciplined man named Kitch Christie. By far the most significant relationship of Pienaar's career had started.

Just as so many Springbok captains had been inspired by Danie Craven, as Tom Bedford was enthused by Izak van Heerden, as Naas Botha was guided by Buurman van Zyl, so Pienaar would be stirred by Christie. Behind every great captain, there has generally been a much-loved coach.

Christie and Pienaar would form a classic partnership, trusting each other absolutely, admiring each other without reservation, each instilling self-confidence and self-esteem in the other on a daily basis. As coach and captain of Transvaal, and subsequently as coach and captain of South Africa, they would bring out the best in each other and emerge as a world champion combination.

"From the start, I respected François as a very intelligent man of integrity," Christie recalled, "and I admired his courage and talent. The basic coach-captain relationship is crucial to any team, and I felt extremely privileged that I was able to work for three seasons with such an exceptional individual."

Those words are classic Christie, redolent of his Scots stock, clinical and taciturn, as close to emotional as this privately emotional man dared. Pienaar is able to reflect more precisely upon a relationship that became something closer to father-son than coach-captain. "I knew Kitch supported me," he recalls. "And I knew he cared for me and would never let me down."

The captain continues: "I listened to his advice. I implemented his game plan. I learned from him how to conduct business, how to invest in property, how to be professional and disciplined. When I started to work with Kitch, selling gas braais imported from America, we spent virtually all day, every day together, and became very close. He was the teacher; I was the student."

Christie prepared for the 1993 campaign by recruiting five players rejected by Northerns. He literally plucked Uli Schmidt, Rudolf Straeuli, Hannes Strydom, Johan Roux and Gavin Johnson from the scrapheap of the game, and retreaded them to emerge as Currie Cup champions and Springboks.

The coach affirmed Pienaar as captain, trained his squad relentlessly, and declared Transvaal ready to win the Super 10, a new competition involving the four leading South African provincial sides, four top provinces from New Zealand, and Queensland and New South Wales from Australia. "Kitch kept saying we had to be super fit," Pienaar says, "and he was right. The fitness gave us confidence, and we were transformed from a talented team that didn't know how to win into a super-confident squad that never contemplated defeat."

Transvaal blitzed through the group stages of the Super 10 and advanced to beat Sean Fitzpatrick's Auckland team in the inaugural final at Ellis Park. After the numb disappointments of 1992, South African rugby felt able to raise its head again; and, when it did raise its head, it found the young Pienaar lifting the trophy for the top provincial side in the southern hemisphere.

Few triumphs can have been better timed. The Springbok selectors were in the process of planning the kind of new dawn that had successfully revived the national squad in 1965 and 1975, and the entire panel had watched Transvaal's victory from the opulent President's Suite at Ellis Park. They had noted the verve and self-assured presence of the young Vaal captain.

Ian McIntosh had already been appointed to replace John Williams as the Springbok coach, although it was difficult to understand how the professor could have been held solely culpable for the results in 1992 when he had been allowed neither to plan his team's schedule nor even to appoint his own assistant coach. In any event, four defeats in five Tests required a public execution, and Williams was duly cuffed, shaved and marched to the guillotine.

The merry-go-round of Springbok coaches had started to revolve; it would turn, turn, turn throughout an often bewildering decade.

In elevating McIntosh, SARFU had discarded unwritten conventions of the past that the national coach needed to be a former Springbok player and be able to speak Afrikaans. The new coach was a Zimbabwean who had expertly guided Natal to Currie Cup titles in 1990 and 1992 and was, by widespread consent, the best man for the job. The clandestine influence of the Broederbond appeared to have evaporated in the heat of political and social reform.

Pienaar sensed the winds of change but, as the panel prepared to name their Springbok team to play two home Tests against France, he hoped simply to be included in the starting side. For him, as for so many of his predecessors, the captaincy appeared both an honour and a burden.

Twenty-one names were announced on a Saturday evening in June, but the flanker heard only his own. Now he was a Springbok. He recalls: "In that one moment, the fear of failing to achieve my goal disappeared. It was a tremendous relief. All the sacrifices suddenly seemed worthwhile."

The introduction of the Super 10 so crowded the calendar that there had been no time for national trials or a training camp. McIntosh would have only four training sessions to prepare his side for the

French. Not for the first time nor the last, basic planning and management had been inadequate.

Media and officials were milling around the players' tunnel at King's Park in Durban, and the first Springbok practice was ready to begin when, out of the blue, the new national coach called Pienaar and the popular Western Province captain, Tiaan Strauss, to one side.

McIntosh began: "Chaps, I have had a very difficult decision to make but, François, I would like you to captain the team on Saturday."

The gallant Strauss swallowed hard, congratulated his rival, and returned to the other players, most of whom had peered over to see what was happening. "My head was spinning for the rest of the session," Pienaar recalls. "The media interviews took almost an hour afterwards. Strangers were shaking my hand like old friends. Everything happened so quickly."

He had already arranged for his parents to fly to Durban and watch his Test debut, and he had resolved to spend some time with them on the Thursday evening before the match. As a SARFU sponsor, Mercedes-Benz had loaned a trio of their saloons for the team's use in Durban. To his wide-eyed delight, the new young captain was entitled to take one of these cars to visit his parents at their accommodation on the opposite side of the city.

Now he was driving a Mercedes-Benz, just like Uncle Kobus.

Pienaar led his new-look Springbok team out to play France at King's Park more in hope than in expectation. The public's boastful arrogance of 1992 had been dramatically replaced by a new realism, an acceptance that the side lacked Test experience, and a common understanding that know-how may have to be bought by a few defeats. As a capacity crowd assembled, the stadium hummed with talk of learning curves and green shoots of recovery.

An entertaining match was eventually drawn 20-20, although the French considered they should have won. The Springboks had chased and harassed all afternoon, with Uli Schmidt proving an influential and defiant presence. The feisty hooker, a veteran of the 1986 Cavaliers series, appeared to have gone out of his way to support and assist the new captain. "Some older players could have made life difficult for me," Pienaar recalls. "Uli made life very easy."

The second Test of the series was overshadowed when news reached the players on the morning of the match that two Transvaal players, Cameron Oliver and Stef Nel, had died in a car accident. Pienaar was so upset and distracted that he arrived at Ellis Park to discover he had left his boots back at the hotel. The flying squad was detailed to fetch them, and crisis was averted.

Once again his team played with passion and commitment, withstanding dangerous French attacks and hanging in the game. The floodlit contest reached its last stop when Theo van Rensburg carefully lined up a 40-metre penalty in the 81st minute. France was leading 18-17. If he kicked the penalty, the Springboks would win the match and the series. There was nothing wrong with the direction, but the ball fell infinitesimally short, bouncing back infield from the crossbar. The French raised their arms in relief, and the series was theirs.

Pienaar's captaincy was commonly praised. Broad and upright, alternately fierce and smiling, he had looked the part, overcome his own nerves, and held an inexperienced team together through two tight matches.

Provincialism within the side seemed to have been temporarily quelled by the spirit of the new dawn, but it still streamed in the stands. Throughout Pretoria, for example, Pienaar was generally regarded not as the inspiring leader of a new Springbok squad but as a flashy big deal who lacked the genuine quality to thrive for long in international rugby. He may only have been 26, but he quickly learned the "c" in captain stands for criticism. He would live with it.

Six days after their frustrating defeat by France, the Springboks were flying east to undertake a full tour of Australia, including three Tests against the world champion Wallabies. Once upon a time, before isolation, Springboks would have thought themselves lucky to tour three times in their entire career. In the modern era, players would often tour three times in one season.

SARFU attempted to improve the grim, unsmiling image of the Springboks overseas by appointing the personable and entertaining former Springbok wing, Jannie Engelbrecht, as team manager, but the Australian media focused most of their attention on the open, courteous Springbok captain. At media conferences, he would usually remember the journalists' first names. In hotel foyers, he would greet them. He smiled, listened, heard. People liked him. Cynics accused him of being superficial, others insisted he was sincere: in any event, the Pienaar smile unveiled in 1993 would soon charm the entire rugby world.

The young captain enjoyed Australia, the relaxed atmosphere, the warm weather, the hospitable people, and the fact that his team was only seriously tested in five of their 13 matches on tour. The first of these major fixtures, against New South Wales in Sydney, was lost a week before the first Test, and few observers gave the raw tourists any chance against the Wallabies.

"We were underdogs," Pienaar recalls, "but, on the Sunday after losing to New South Wales, we went on a boat trip around Sydney harbour, and it seemed to me as though the squad came together. It was a truly beautiful setting, and the guys started singing. We carried that spirit through the week before the Test, and by the time we arrived at the stadium, the team was on fire."

Early in the match, Pienaar impeccably executed a planned move where he took a reverse pass from the scrumhalf on the blind side, drew the eighthman and then popped the ball to the right wing at speed. James Small galloped clear to score an opening try, the hyped-up Springboks sustained the momentum, and surged to a stunning 19-12 victory over the world champions.

The captain sought his coach amid the jubilant changing room. Thrown in at the deep end of international rugby in the same splash, Pienaar and McIntosh were developing a strong relationship, and the captain wanted to congratulate a man who was driven not by status and glory but by an all-consuming passion for the game. "Mac deserved the victory in Sydney more than anybody," he reflects. "The origins of his entire philosophy lay in the tactics of the 1984 Wallabies, and I knew the result would mean a lot to him. He had worked incredibly hard."

Australia recovered from the setback and, as Nick Farr-Jones's hardened team ruthlessly imposed themselves upon the second and third Tests, the young South Africans lost focus and concentration, and the series.

In the second Test at Brisbane, James Small answered back to referee Ed Morrison in the manner in which leading footballers backchat their officials each week, and the gifted, feisty wing became the first Springbok to be sent off during a Test match. Pienaar felt the sentence outweighed the crime, but the tourists could not hope to resist world-class opposition with 14 men. Joel Stransky's breakaway try gave the 28-20 defeat a gloss of respectability, but the captain knew his side had been outplayed. There were bumps on the learning curve.

The Wallabies also won the third Test in Sydney more decisively than the 19-12 result suggests. Pienaar attributes what was a jaded team performance to homesickness among his squad. "Most of us had never spent so long away from home," he recalls. "We were not used to touring, and after six weeks our minds were fixed on the trip home and seeing our families again. We had even packed our suitcases and checked out of the hotel before the Test."

Within three hours of the final whistle, the Springboks were buckling their seatbelts and flying home. The captain asked for a cold can of beer, and, setting aside the disappointment of a series defeat, reflected happily upon what he now rates as the most enjoyable tour of his career. "We did not win, but there was no doubt our performances had improved significantly since the first Test of the year against France in Durban," he remembers. "We were moving in the right direction, and that was good enough for me. I told the guys on the plane that they should hold their heads high. We were on the right track."

The squad dispersed to the battlefields of provincial rugby, and Pienaar's Transvaal team continued to sweep all before them, adding the Lion and Currie Cup titles to their successes in the Nite Series and Super 10. Scarcely a month passed without the captain being splashed over newspaper front pages, smiling broadly as he raised another trophy above his head. The cumulative effect was to establish him as a winner in the minds of the rugby public.

In many ways, the success of his provincial side contributed significantly to Pienaar's success as Springbok captain. The flow of trophies not only provided regular and welcome boosts to his own self-confidence, but also ensured that as many as 12 or even 13 of his Transvaal team-mates would eventually find their way into the national squad. When he looked around the changing room before a Test, he would see more close friends than virtual strangers.

"We wanted to develop within the Springbok squad the kind of spirit and camaraderie that existed within the provincial teams," Pienaar recalls. "That was very important to me. It clearly helped to have a core of Transvaal players in the national side, but we had to make sure nobody was excluded."

The end-of-season tour to Argentina, including two Test matches against the Pumas, seemed an ideal opportunity to develop morale, and the captain took upon himself the role of breaking up provincial cliques: if he found three Northern Transvalers sitting together at breakfast, he would light-heartedly insist one take his bowl of cereal and move to eat with the Free Staters.

Time and again, he prompted players to mix, and share experiences, and understand one another. When it emerged that the pop star Madonna was staying in a hotel across the road in Buenos Aires, groups of players would from time to time join a crowd of 6 000 people gathered in the street below her suite, chanting her name every time a curtain twitched. Capetonians laughed with Natalians, and the provincial barriers within the squad started to crumble.

Pienaar recognised that nothing bonds as effectively as adversity, and his squad's reaction to a harrowing midweek match in Tucumán utterly delighted the captain. Confronted by blatantly violent opponents and an aggressive crowd, the South Africans had stood together and fought together.

The match was peppered with mass brawls, and at one stage incensed Springbok substitutes were leaping from the bench to defend their colleagues on the field. Even non-playing members of the touring squad, sitting blazered in the stand, found themselves involved in angry confrontation when spectators pelted them with cans. Everywhere, it was one for all, all for one.

"What happened at Tucumán was terrible for rugby," Pienaar recalls, "but it was a tremendous day for our team. We had been challenged as a squad, and we had responded as a squad. In many relaxed moments over the coming years, we would sit back and be exhilarated by the tales of Tucumán."

There was also some rugby in Argentina.

South Africa proved too strong for the Pumas, anxiously winning the first Test 29-26 after leading 29-10 at half time, then surging to a more decisive 52-23 victory in the second Test at the same venue seven days later. After enduring so many defeats, the Springboks thoroughly enjoyed the experience of winning two successive Test matches and securing a first series triumph.

"We had made genuine progress," the captain says, "but the international calendar is so fragmented that, for the next six months, we would not assemble as a squad; worse than that, we would be set against each other again in the Currie Cup and Super 10. Friends became rivals, the walls went back up, and it was only two hours after we had gathered before the Test against England in June 1994 that I realised we had gone back to square one."

Never mind, the captain consoled himself, even if bitter provincialism did seem to return every year like a perennial weed, it surely wouldn't matter. As the Free Staters sipped their coffee together, and the Natalians kept to themselves, the Springboks were at least united in the belief that they would destroy an England side that had lost four of their first five matches on tour.

Loftus Versfeld was bedecked for a festival on 4 June 1994, reflecting an upbeat and positive mood throughout the country. The new South Africa had survived an anxious roller coaster ride through negotiations, patiently queued for hours on 27 April to elect the new government and, on 10 May, celebrated the joyful inauguration of Nelson Mandela as president.

Where most of the world had anticipated bloody civil war and chaos, this extraordinary country had produced a negotiated revolution, the peaceful transfer of power from white minority rule to full democracy. Applause for the outstanding political miracle of the century was ringing around the globe.

Pienaar had been anxious, he had queued, voted and celebrated. Now, on 4 June, it was time for his Springbok rugby side to sustain the party by defeating the apparently hapless English in the first Test at Loftus.

He led his team into a deafening roar, his expression fixed with the resolve of a Roman general leading his triumphant legions in a tribute through the streets of Rome, and with the singular pride of a captain leading the first Springbok team to represent a genuinely democratic and accepted country.

The playing of the national anthems ("God Save the Queen" for the English, "Nkosi Sikelel' iAfrika" and "Die Stem", back to back, for the home side), followed by the presentation of both squads to President Mandela amid a disorderly mass of photographers and sundry officials, took exactly 18 minutes.

Kick-off was delayed. No-one cared. Celebrate!

After 18 minutes of the Test, England led 20-0. The festival had become a funeral, and 54 000 gaping mouths hung open in wonder. Pienaar's team was as shocked as their supporters. The captain had twice gathered his players beneath their own posts, and urged calm, but to no avail. Amid frantic confusion, the Test match had bolted and run. Everybody was talking; nobody was listening. The day was disappearing in a ghoulish, horrifying and baffling blur.

A second-half recovery restricted the rampant tourists to a 32-15 victory, but if any pins had dropped in the Springbok changing room for 30 minutes after the game, everybody would have heard them fall. Joost van der Westhuizen had looked forward to his home Test debut, but would reflect upon the worst day of his career. Broad, powerful forwards tried, and failed, to prevent tears welling in their eyes. Pienaar stared straight ahead, blank, silent and dazed.

"We were complacent," he recalls. "That was all. We had been taught that you never take anything for granted in international rugby.

We felt humiliated and I could not stop thinking of the disappointed boys across South Africa wondering what had gone wrong. We had let everyone down."

Throughout his career, Pienaar would react to a major defeat by behaving not merely like a bear with a sore head. As his family and his friends confirm, he more accurately resembled Daddy Bear, Mummy Bear and Baby Bear combined, all with splitting migraines. Throughout his career, defeat would leave him unable to sleep, short-tempered, snappy and distracted. The only cure would be passing days; by Tuesday night, he would generally be all right.

On the Tuesday following the catastrophe at Loftus, however, he was still so grumpy that he thundered into a tackle bag during training with such force that he broke his nose. For 30 minutes, he didn't bother to seek medical attention. He had been hurt at Loftus and he hungered for revenge.

The Springbok selectors made five changes for the second Test, much to the frustration of the captain, who would have preferred to take the same team to Newlands and decisively prove the first Test had been a freak. "We all felt cross and bloody-minded," Pienaar remembers. "There were not many jokes during the week before the second Test. We felt very serious."

McIntosh laid the plans for a colossal forward onslaught, and South Africa never looked like losing from the moment a planned move sent flyhalf Hennie le Roux ecstatically bursting through to score. The 27-9 victory squared the series, and went some way towards healing the wounds of Pretoria.

Pienaar was relieved, but an incident midway through the second half had left him unsettled and unable to derive pleasure from the occasion. James Small conceded a penalty for obstructing an England 22-metre drop-out, and the South African captain implored him to stay behind the line.

"**** off!" replied the emotional, motivated wing.

Scarcely able to believe his ears, the captain glowered across the field at Small. He would later be accused of overreacting, but Pienaar was adamant his authority had been seriously undermined by one of his senior players. He raged through the remaining minutes of the Test and, at the final whistle, ran straight to the changing room where he planned to confront the wing.

A feature of Pienaar's tenure as Springbok captain was that his outwardly calm and civilised style of leadership often seemed to be underlined by a plainly physical presence. Only McIntosh's timely intervention in the corridor outside the changing room at Newlands dissuaded the incensed captain from expressing his opinion with a clenched fist. Instead, Small was firmly informed that he would not swear at the Springbok captain again. Case closed.

The episode conveyed a clear message to the players that, while he was open and approachable to suggestions about the way the team functioned on or off the field, Pienaar would not tolerate comments that he saw as a challenge to his authority. In times to come, his eyes would focus, his upper lip would tighten, and the player would fall back into line. Respect comprised 80% admiration, 15% envy and the salt in the pot, 5% fear.

If the captain seemed unusually tense and sensitive, there was a reason: he was preparing to lead his squad on tour to New Zealand, a trip that seemed to loom as the moment of reckoning for everyone involved.

Officials and supporters had grown weary of "learning curves" and every other excuse. In 12 months since the new-look side had been unleashed against France, the Springboks had won one of four series. For McIntosh as coach, even for Pienaar as the captain, for many individual players, the time had arrived when they would either swim and produce consistent results at Test level, or they would sink quietly into oblivion as a bold experiment that failed.

It was time to shape up, or slip away.

The pressure was mounting.

Thirteen years after Wynand Claassen's team had left, François Pienaar's Springbok squad arrived in New Zealand to resume the most compelling rivalry in international rugby. Only the 1937 Springboks had won a series in New Zealand, and no All Black team had ever won a series in South Africa. If history so heavily favoured the home team, the South African captain was not daunted: he believed his team could win in New Zealand, and said so.

The tourists' early form was promising, and their prospects seemed bright as they took an impressive lead into the last 10 minutes against Wellington. Then Pienaar dipped to tackle and was knocked out by an accidental knee to the head. Under management instructions to disguise any possible concussion, since that condition demanded a mandatory three-week rest, the Springbok physiotherapist and doctor propped the staggering captain from the field.

Insofar as it was functioning, his brain told him not to take risks with head injuries, but Pienaar had set his heart upon leading the Springboks against New Zealand, and he willed himself to continue as if nothing was wrong.

That same evening he spoke coherently at a banquet in Wellington, but he was alarmed to wake on the Sunday morning and realise he could recall nothing about the function. Never mind, he insisted, he would be OK. At 10 o'clock on the Monday, he was changed and prepared for training. As usual, he sprinted to the front of the warm-up group, but reeled away in agony. "It felt as if my entire head was going to explode," he reflects. "I was being so stupid. I had been concussed and there was no way I would be able to play in the first Test."

Suddenly in search of a captain, team manager Engelbrecht and coach McIntosh completed the practice and, upon their return to the hotel, called Tiaan Strauss to a meeting. There was both good news and bad news for the Western Province captain: first, he was asked to captain South Africa in the first Test, but he was then told to move from his preferred position as eighthman to play as the No. 6 flanker and fill in for the injured Pienaar.

"I was thrilled and dismayed at the same time," Strauss recalls. "I thanked them for giving me the honour of leading the side, but said I believed the captain should always be entitled to play in his best position."

So far as his grandchildren will be concerned, Strauss was in the proudest position of all, leading the South African team onto the field as only the 42nd man able to say that he, too, was once the Springbok captain.

The youngest of five children, the son of a former Griqualand West rugby stalwart, Strauss was reared on a farm set among the harsh, dry scrubland to the north of Upington, in the Northern Cape. Barefoot, resourceful, mischievous and hard, he lived most of his childhood beneath an unremitting sun.

As he grew older, more clever and stronger, his favourite chore on the farm was catching a wildebeest to sell at the local game market. The animals would move in herds, and Strauss and his friend devised an odd routine whereby, riding motorbikes, they would manage to separate a beast from the rest and ride along either side of the running animal.

The rugby player would then cut the engine and launch himself into the air towards the heaving shoulders, beating hooves and razor-sharp horns, executing a perfect tackle to bring the beast to the ground.

"Timing was everything," Strauss recalls. "You had to concentrate only on how you were going to grab the horns and then on digging your feet in and twisting the wildebeest's neck into the tackle. If you got any stage wrong, he could flick you off his back like a sack of potatoes. It happened a few times."

Moving to the University of Stellenbosch, he swiftly reaped the benefits of this most abnormal training routine, emerging as a skilful, strong and courageous eighthman both for Maties and for Western Province. Initially rated behind Jannie Breedt in 1992, Strauss emerged as one of the few major successes of the tour to France and Britain, and was mooted as a future captain.

However, he manfully accepted Pienaar's appointment in 1993 and, with the trademark white band around his head, set about establishing himself as one of the leading loose forwards in the world. Dedicated, a qualified solicitor, hearty, he loved his ice cream, enjoyed a beer, and was evidently thriving.

Now, five days away from the first Test at Carisbrook in Dunedin, he found himself charged with the responsibility of captaincy. Pienaar honourably stepped into the scenery. "That week," he recalls, "was Tiaan's show."

Amid the suffocating nerves, the Springboks grew in confidence: they had retained their 100% record on tour and watched Sean Fitzpatrick's team slide to a modest 2-0 series defeat at home to France. Perhaps they would catch the All Blacks at the right time, and carve their own names in history.

Strauss prepared the team conscientiously through the week and, tending to lead with stirring deeds rather than fine words, came within inches of providing the perfect inspiration by scoring a try inside the first five minutes. As the tackles thudded, two evenly matched teams wrestled for advantage. It became clear that the Test would be decided by an error here or a penalty goal there.

It was the South African goal kickers who faltered in the swelling pressure, missing several goalable penalties. The New Zealanders kicked much better and, to Strauss's intense frustration, the game slowly ebbed away. A Test that might so easily have been won somehow meandered to a 22-14 defeat. "We had felt very comfortable at half time," Strauss recalls. "We were in control, but we missed our chances in the second half, and suddenly it was all over."

Defeat fractured the touring squad, and distinctive camps started to form around its two dominant personalities. Through no fault or plan of either individual, the substantial Transvaal contingent tended to gather around Pienaar while many of the rest looked towards Strauss. Early in the tour, each of the Springboks had publicly signed a code of conduct in which they pledged not to speak badly about one another. As nerves frayed in the wake of Dunedin, the code of conduct metaphorically flew out of the window.

Injuries, players leaving and replacements arriving all added to an invasive sense of disruption, but, now returned to fitness, Pienaar worked frantically to pull his team together ahead of the second Test in Wellington. The 1981 Springboks had needed to win at Athletic Park to keep the series alive, and had done so. Now the 1994 team, with the benefit of sleeping in a hotel rather than the grandstand, and with no protesters in sight, were similarly challenged.

The captain enlisted the help of David van der Sandt, the SABC television reporter, to produce a motivational video combining visu-

al images of the tour with the lyrics of Something Inside So Strong
– Hannes Strydom, the sympathetic lock forward at home, had dispatched the CD to Pienaar in New Zealand with a note that read
simply, "Listen to Track 12". The captain listened, produced, then sat by
while his players watched; their emotions stirred and soared.

> *When they insist we're not good enough*
> *Well, we know better.*
> *Just look 'em in the eyes and say*
> *"We're gonna do it anyway … we're gonna do it anyway."*

Pienaar reflects: "If anything, we were too hyped up for the second Test
in Wellington. Maybe we wasted too much energy in the changing
room before the game. There is such a fine balance in getting the preparation right. We competed strongly, but perhaps we were too psyched
to take our chances when they came along. We were bold, but we
needed to be clinical as well."

Once again, an evenly contested, ferocious match tilted in favour
of the All Blacks, who led 10-6 at half time and held on to win 13-9.
What might have been if the South Africans had converted a series of
scoring chances remained nothing more relevant or cheering than that
… what might have been.

The series had been lost and, as disappointment prompted recriminations back home, the entire tour suddenly plunged into an alarming
downward spiral of confusion and controversy. Early on Sunday, the
tour management was locked in a meeting to discuss television footage
from the Test that showed Johan le Roux, the Springbok prop, biting
Fitzpatrick's ear. He had been wearing a mouthguard, and there was
scarcely a mark on the All Black captain, but the TV footage gave the
sensational impression that Hannibal Lecter played rugby.

South African rugby suddenly found itself plastered across general
news pages and nightly TV bulletins around the globe, a target for
mockery and disdain from CNN to the *Straits Times*, from *The Star* to
The Age.

Unprecedented waves of outrage panicked the tour officials, who promptly sent Le Roux home, denied him the right to wear a Springbok blazer on the flight, and left him to arrange his own legal defence. Eventually, the hapless scapegoat prop was handed a ludicrous, overblown 17-month ban.

To his enduring dismay, Pienaar had allowed himself to be swayed by the tide of public emotion. "We should have supported Johan and allowed the proper disciplinary procedures to run their course," he recalls. "Instead we deserted him and left him to the wolves. I made the worst decision of my career on the Sunday after the second Test, when the squad went on a boat trip and I allowed Johan to be left at the hotel. I should have insisted that he come along. It was the one and only occasion, I hope, that I failed to support my player.

"Everything was blown out of proportion, but I will never forget the sight of him leaving the team hotel on his way to the airport. He was wearing a navy blue and orange checked jersey. It was a terrible moment."

The ear-biting saga and seething criticism at home had combined to knock the stuffing out of the tour; and most of the squad was looking forward to nothing so much as the flight home when Louis Luyt, the recently appointed president of SARFU, told journalists in New Zealand that, in his view, Engelbrecht and McIntosh, manager and coach, were both "history".

Pienaar was also starting to contemplate his own mortality as captain but, in the depths of despair, he called a players' meeting, without management, and emotionally galvanised a new teeth-grinding resolve to dig deep and charge over the parapets one more time, in the third Test at Eden Park.

For the third time in the series, the Springboks took enough possession to have won the match and, leading 18-12 into the closing stages, they seemed set to end the tour on a high note. Yet the astute Fitzpatrick won one penalty through gamesmanship, tugging at an opponent's jersey and then profiting from the slight retaliation, and a further penalty squared the Test at 18-18. "Most of the All Black supporters said we deserved to win," Pienaar reflects. "Any of the Tests might so easily have turned our way. The margins were tiny."

In years to come, like Dawie de Villiers before him in 1965, the Springbok captain would unremittingly insist that his 1994 tour to New Zealand was judged harshly at home, arguing that the consensus view of the trip as a disaster in no way reflected the closeness of the series, noting how only three matches (two Tests and the Otago game) were lost. Yet in South African rugby, winners are heroes, losers are not. Usually, no further evidence is required.

The Springboks' return home prompted the resumption of another ancient tradition after so many years in isolation: the bout of blood-letting that follows any defeat in New Zealand. Amid trumpeting officials and screaming headlines, an amazing soap opera dominated the news for three weeks. The luckless, abused McIntosh read in a newspaper that he had been sacked, but Engelbrecht decided to confront president Luyt and daringly to defend his position.

Two bull-elephants charged and counter-charged across the media and, at one stage, a resolute group of Stellenbosch students bearing placards took to the streets to demonstrate support for the manager. Day after day, bulletin upon bulletin, Springbok rugby was demeaned and casually disgraced as it had rarely been demeaned and disgraced through 103 seasons.

Pienaar felt desperately sorry for McIntosh, with whom he had worked so hard and so effectively, but managed to avoid the crossfire and calmly await his own fate. When the dust settled, Engelbrecht had notably retained his position as manager, at least for the time being, and the third Springbok coach in two years was named as ... Kitch Christie. The captain-coach combination that had inspired Transvaal to domestic triumph moved into the national side.

The 1995 Rugby World Cup was nine months away.

"So, cappie, do you think we have the players?" the excited coach asked his captain. "Can we win the World Cup? We have to be super fit, and we need a game plan. This is an ambulance job, cappie." Pienaar nodded.

The new coach demanded, and was given, more authority over selection than any of his predecessors. Where Williams and McIntosh had only expressed their preference as one of six national selectors, and had to make the best of the side they were given, Christie essentially chose his own team.

Handed the axe, he wielded the axe and, in naming a Springbok squad to play two home Tests against Argentina, he dropped 18 of the 36 players who had played in New Zealand. When André Joubert and James Small arrived late for a training session, the coach dropped them as well.

Even Pienaar gasped. "I don't think Kitch appreciated what the squad had achieved in New Zealand, particularly in the third Test, but I had learned never to question his judgement. I trusted him," the captain says. "He wanted to make his mark and to impose discipline immediately, and he did that."

Emphatic home victories over Argentina, by 42-22 and 46-26, settled the reshaped squad, and Pienaar was reassured to see methods that had worked so well for Transvaal being deployed in his Springbok squad. The players would be run into the ground to ensure optimum fitness, instructed never to be late, not for the bus, not for a meeting and not for training; and, often, they would find lists of telling phrases slipped under their doors in the team hotel.

We need players who can take on the opposition physically ... We have a captain who we all know did an excellent job in New Zealand ... The Springbok jersey must become very difficult to earn ... We must show complete loyalty to each other ... We owe success to the entire country.

These were the tools of Christie's trade, homilies not for discussion but for implementation, and by the time the Springboks embarked on their 13-match tour of Britain, the coach had established his authority. Every evening before a game, the coach would sit with his captain in a hotel bar, sipping at pints of Guinness as they discussed players and game plans. Everything achieved by this team would be founded upon the total trust between coach and captain.

On the morning after a narrow opening win over Cardiff, Christie seized upon an opportunity to destroy any semblance of two camps within his squad. He had heard about divisions in New Zealand, and decided to act. This was a simple man using simple logic to make a simple decision, regardless of emotion, political considerations or any need to be liked. In his determination to confirm Pienaar as the un-equivocal captain, he would have to sacrifice Strauss.

The players had been instructed to gather outside the hotel at 10 o'clock on the Sunday morning, ready to set off on the ritual "Doc's run" to shake out any aches from the previous day's match, or hang-overs from the previous night. The coach stood alone, checking his watch anxiously. It was past ten. Finally, at five past the hour, Strauss emerged bleary-eyed from the foyer.

"You're late," snapped the coach.

"What?"

"Come on, then, bend over."

"What?"

Strauss looked at Christie with a combination of shock and dis-gust. It was a seminal moment. The coach returned the gaze. Would his discipline hold? After several seconds had passed like minutes, the respected loose forward bent over and put his hands on his knees as each member of the Springbok squad, in turn, walked up and delivered a powerful slap to his backside. The ritual punishment would have been hard for a senior player to accept under any circumstances. In a hotel car park on a Sunday in Wales, it had been degrading.

The message was made crystal clear: Pienaar was captain, and the harsh discipline applied equally to every member of the squad, regard-less of status and reputation. Strauss never played another Test for South Africa and, to his lasting disappointment, was omitted from the Spring-bok World Cup squad.

At the end of 1995, having played 158 matches for Western Prov-ince and 15 Tests for South Africa, he accepted an offer to play rugby league in Australia with Cronulla. "I knew I would not play for South Africa again so long as Kitch and François were in place," he recalls. "So I found a new challenge."

Indomitable and resolved, Strauss would play a further five seasons at the highest level, first emerging as an explosive force with Cronulla, then signing to play professional rugby union for New South Wales in 1998, accepting Australian citizenship, and finally earning selection in the Wallabies squad.

He scored four tries in 35 minutes during his Wallaby debut versus Ireland, and in July 1999 he became the first former Springbok captain to line up against South Africa in a Test, pulling on the famous gold jersey of Australia to play in the Tri-Nations matches at Brisbane and Cape Town. "My new team-mates made me learn the Australian anthem," Strauss recalls, with an audible Sydney twang, "but it felt strange to be playing against my old team-mates. That was where my career took me, and I was grateful to Australia for the opportunity."

The symmetry was complete when Strauss won a place in the Australian squad for the 1999 World Cup, and although he did not play in the final he had won 11 Test caps for the Wallabies before he retired at the end of 2000.

In times to come, Pienaar would also demonstrate the mental strength to strike out and embrace a new challenge, but amid the cold winds and persistent drizzle of autumn 1994 in Britain, he was focused upon developing a team and a spirit that would carry South Africa to the 1995 World Cup.

Having edged past a serious of tough, muscular challenges in Wales, the tourists celebrated the first sunshine of the tour when they dismantled Swansea 78-7 at the St Helen's Ground. Trailing 7-5 after 32 minutes, players like Chester Williams, André Joubert and Hennie le Roux detonated an explosion of ruthless, powerful, enterprising rugby. Every pass did go to hand, every bounce did find a green jersey and, as the standing ovation echoed in his ears, Pienaar began to believe his team might yet take on the world, and win.

Morale seemed strong, and exceptional players were emerging in all parts of the field. Van der Westhuizen produced a devastating display at Murrayfield, a constant threat around the scrum as he darted over to score two excellent tries in the 34-10 victory over Scotland; and Chester Williams confirmed his strength and pace as a quality finisher on the left wing in racing away from the Wales defence to score the clinching try in the 20-12 victory in Cardiff.

The Springboks had suddenly won four Tests in a row, maybe not against the strongest opposition, but four wins is four wins, and a fresh confidence could be seen in every smile, and heard in every joke on the bus.

Christie was satisfied, and he responded by allowing the players to take control of the schedule during the last week of the tour in Ireland. The result was an extravagant 54-19 victory over Irish Combined Provinces in Belfast, when the Springboks indulged in the "Brains Game", playing at double speed, tapping each penalty, running every ball, and earning a standing ovation.

The tourists adopted a similar approach against the Barbarians in Dublin, but found the invitation team playing percentage rugby to boost the reputation of their club with a prized scalp. South Africa were defeated 23-15, but Christie and Pienaar laughed their way through the post-match press conference, sure in the knowledge that the tour had put their World Cup plans on track.

"We were far from the finished article," the captain says, "and nobody was being cocky or arrogant, but there was a quiet, even unspoken conviction that we could mount a reasonable challenge for the World Cup."

This cautious optimism was certainly not shared in the pubs and clubs of Pretoria, Durban, Cape Town, Bloemfontein and Port Elizabeth, where a resentful consensus grew that Transvaal had taken over the national side. Louis Luyt ruled as a dominant president of both the Transvaal Rugby Union and SARFU, Christie and Pienaar, together with 12 members of the squad, hailed from Transvaal, and even the team doctor and physiotherapist were from Transvaal.

When that province was eliminated from the Nite Series early in the 1995 season, the former Springbok captain Naas Botha neatly echoed a general view when he enquired on his television show, "If Transvaal can't win the Nite Series, how do they think they are going to win the World Cup?"

Pienaar brushed aside the criticism from his predecessor: he insisted that in each case the best man had been chosen for the job, and he asked that his squad should be judged on its results rather than its origins. Shortly afterwards, he was alarmed to learn that Christie, concerned by a lack of direction at flyhalf, had sent scouts to a club match in Pretoria to discover whether the selfsame Botha should be considered for the World Cup squad at the age of 37.

The legendary flyhalf performed well, and flirted with a comeback when he played for a top-quality President's XV at Ellis Park but, amid general scepticism, the retired icon decided that he should remain firmly retired.

With each passing week, the pressure was mounting. Pienaar had grown concerned when he took much longer than he hoped to recover from pre-season surgery on his knee, missing the entire Super 10, including Transvaal's defeat in the final to Queensland at Ellis Park. He was then upset when he attracted bitter criticism for taking part in a TV advertisement of dubious taste.

The greatest challenge of his life drew closer and closer. His daily routine had become a dizzy whirl of gym training, repetitive media interviews, long chats with Christie and his players, sold-out public appearances, tough rugby practices, arranging tickets for friends, fulfilling his commercial obligations, rushing to catch flights, checking into hotels, signing autographs, greeting his girlfriend, speaking to his parents and brothers, staying calm and focused.

Every previous Springbok captain had experienced pressure, and many had faced extreme strain, but it is unlikely that any lived through the unremitting demands and frequently unreasonable expectations that confronted Pienaar in the days before, during and after the 1995 World Cup. Hours out of the relentless spotlight were rare; days out of the spotlight were unknown.

Yet the captain was not grumbling. He disciplined himself to prioritise the rugby, rather than what Christie dubbed "the sideshows", and he began to surf on the tide as events assumed an inexorable momentum.

His Springbok side clicked impressively in thrashing Western Samoa 60-8 at Ellis Park, and then squeezed narrow victories from two highly charged games against the Western Province and Natal provincial teams. "Kitch wanted us to be battled-hardened," Pienaar recalls, "but they were tough occasions as the crowds at Newlands and King's Park supported their provincial teams against us. As we travelled around the country, it soon became clear nobody gave us much chance of winning the World Cup. The fashionable view was we would do well to reach a semifinal. That was seen as a decent performance."

In trying times, the captain drew confidence and support from the array of talented players and strong personalities in the squad around him. This excellent captain was served by an equally excellent management team.

Morné du Plessis had been appointed team manager, bringing his unique presence to the squad, setting the highest standards of integrity and honour, and working tirelessly to ensure smooth logistics and to set the correct tone. Christie was at hand, watching his videos, hatching his plans, running the team, assisted by Gysie Pienaar, the Springbok hero in victory over the 1980 Lions.

And the captain was able to glance around the changing room or down the aisle of the team bus, and to see people he trusted: fullbacks André Joubert and Gavin Johnson, the cherished Chester Williams on the left wing, the courageous and mercurial James Small on the right wing, his smiling former housemate Japie Mulder, Christiaan Scholtz and Brendan Venter at centre, skilled playmakers Joel Stransky and Hennie le Roux at flyhalf, match-breaker Joost van der Westhuizen and the remarkably reliable Johan Roux at scrumhalf.

Among the larger frames and ruptured ears, he could find men of genuine character in the tight five: props Os du Randt, Marius Hurter, Garry Pagel and the estimable Balie Swart, "Bullet" James Dalton and Chris Rossouw as hookers, and locks Mark Andrews, Kobus Wiese, Krynauw Otto and Hannes Strydom; beside him in the back row stood the quietly brilliant Ruben Kruger, the decent and loyal Rudolf Straeuli, Adriaan Richter and the rookie Robby Brink.

The flying wing Pieter Hendriks and Naka Drotské, the all-purpose hooker, would join their ranks in due course and, while there were many men desperately unfortunate to miss selection, none more so than Strauss, Gary Teichmann and Henry Honiball, the fates had decreed that this was the group of 28 who would soon be transformed from mere rugby players into national heroes.

Their captain was François Pienaar.

They respected him for many reasons, partly because he was prepared to earn rather than demand their esteem. He would run at the front of the group, lift the largest weights in the gym, and complete the most press-ups. "François was ready to take the physical battering," one player recalls. "Over and over again, in the vital stages of the most important matches, he never hesitated to put himself in the firing line. I have never played for a braver captain."

They also respected him because he was able to take decisions, to lift his head from a scrum, assess the game situation and move forward. He could play his full part as the No. 6 flanker, but also take responsibility for 14 other players in the team, offering a word of advice here, chastising there.

In every situation, at training, at breakfast, on the bus, in the hotel foyer, in the changing room, during injury breaks, at half time, after the final whistle, at the post-match function, on television and in the newspapers, Pienaar appeared able to make the right remark at the right time, and to smile.

Well dressed and well mannered, intelligent and sincere, he had started to look every inch the ideal Springbok captain. His stature was perhaps most keenly measured in the wide-eyed awe that he inspired among new young players when they joined the Springbok squad. He led, and they followed.

During the World Cup and ever since, Pienaar's excellent reputation would spread far beyond the municipal boundaries of Johannesburg into every crowded city and rural district, into towns and townships alike, across the nation. He would soar above the petty spite of provincialism into legend.

Suddenly it was Saturday 20 May 1995, and the steelworker's son waited to have a photograph taken in a room at the Groot Constantia estate, near Cape Town ... not just any photograph. Fifteen national rugby captains either sat beside or stood behind him. Sean Fitzpatrick of New Zealand, Will Carling of England, Michael Lynagh of Australia and Philippe Saint-André of France all believed they could win the golden Webb Ellis Cup resting on a table before them, while eleven others were happy to be leading their teams at the third World Cup.

"I have often looked at pictures of that day," Pienaar says, "and wondered how I managed to look so relaxed and in control. It was nerve-wracking to meet the other captains. I can recall being tongue-tied as I left that room with Michael Lynagh, who has become a close friend. I didn't know what to say."

During the lunch that followed, the Springboks sat at three tables, but they didn't speak much because they were too busy peering across at players in rival squads, like Jonah Lomu, the man-mountain All Black. The weather was terrible outside, but the occasion was not diminished. South Africans had looked forward to participating in a Rugby World Cup for so long and finally, as the slogan in the SA Airways advertising declared, the waiting was over.

Through all their exhaustive debates and projections, Christie and Pienaar had always agreed South Africa's opening match against Australia was crucial to the entire campaign, since victory would most likely propel them, as the winners of Group A, into the same half of the knock-out draw as Samoa and France, whereas defeat would probably leave them with the huge task of having to overcome both England and New Zealand to reach the final at Ellis Park.

Cape Town dawned beautiful, blue and magnificent, and 52 000 people at Newlands congratulated themselves on taking this special Thursday afternoon off work as they relished every nuance of a world-class opening ceremony.

Pienaar habitually sat at the back of the team bus, but on this occasion he took a place in the middle from where he could more accurately judge the mood. He was relieved to find no grim, nervous faces; instead, his side seemed excited and animated, enjoying the crowds and vibe that surrounded them.

The captain was lacing his boots in the changing room when he looked up and was startled to see the usually stoic Christie with tears in his eyes. He asked what was wrong, and was told it was just the wind. In fact, the coach had walked up the tunnel to the field and been standing discreetly on the touchline when the manically impassioned Newlands crowd started to chant his name. These people had booed his team three weeks earlier. He was moved.

Years of division were being cast aside as Transvalers and Cape-tonians, English-speakers and Afrikaners, blacks and whites all wrapped themselves in the new South African flag and urged the team representing this young, hopeful country to victory over Australia, the defending champions.

Hindsight has cast the 1995 Wallabies as past their best, but the plain fact is that Bob Dwyer's team arrived in Cape Town as clear favourites to retain their title, and the Wallabies appeared to be too experienced for the World Cup novices as they established a 13-9 lead after 35 tense minutes. Then Hendriks took the ball on the left wing, somehow found an extra gear to surge around a grasping Campese and, shaking his fist, scored the defining try of his life.

Pienaar, eyes ablaze with concentration, calmed his team during half time, urging them to focus on the game plan. Stransky added a penalty and a drop goal soon after the break, and a planned move from a set scrum sent the flyhalf clean through to score from close range. The Australians battled manfully, but the new South Africa was in no mood to lose on this day at Newlands.

The 27-18 victory represented an ideal start to the campaign. "Enjoy the night, but we must be humble," Pienaar told his players afterwards. "We have a long way to go." At the final whistle, the Springbok captain had simply raised his right hand to thank the crowd and run directly from the field.

Later that night, arriving to meet his girlfriend Nerine Winter at a packed Waterfront restaurant, Pienaar was recognised and carried shoulder high to his table. "Something special was happening in our country," he reflects. "It was not normal. It was not expected." He stood at the apex of it all.

Christie had enhanced the outstanding morale within the squad when he declared at the outset of the tournament that all 26 players would get a game at some stage, and he remained true to his word in naming the South African team to play Romania at Newlands the following Tuesday.

With Pienaar rested, eighthman Adriaan Richter took over the Springbok captaincy. A 29-year-old insurance broker from Pretoria, he had been praised for his leadership of the midweek team during the 1993 tour to Australia, and played all three Tests against the All Blacks in 1994. Swept out of the national squad by Christie's new broom, he had worked his way back into contention by the sheer consistency of his performances for Northern Transvaal.

Tall and fair, his gentle nature belied an iron resolve. If he had nothing to say, Richter was happy to say nothing. However, if he did have something to say, he did not lack the courage or presence to make his voice heard. Resolved and brave, he had graduated from the Blue Bulls school where captains are expected to lead by sweating example rather than sparkling oratory.

The eighthman scored both tries in leading South Africa to a subdued, and yet steadfast, 21-8 victory over gallant, resolute opposition.

Pienaar strolled contentedly from his seat in the stand, but was amazed to arrive at the post-match function and discover that the Romanians, a national squad competing at the World Cup, were using plastic bags from a local supermarket to hold their kit and boots. He called a friend at Adidas and, within several minutes, had arranged for kitbags to be delivered to the Romanian hotel.

The Springboks appeared calm and settled, but results in Group A meant it was still mathematically possible for the host nation to be eliminated if they lost their last pool match to Canada in Port Elizabeth. As the tension mounted ahead of what had become a knockout game, Christie stayed calm and named the side that had played Romania. "If our second team can't beat Canada," he said amid raised eyebrows, "we don't deserve to win the World Cup."

He did, however, slightly change his thoroughly laid plans in deference to the situation, and that was to recall Pienaar as captain. "I wanted to give François a rest," the coach recalled, "but, if anything did happen to go wrong, I needed him on the field to put it right. He was my insurance policy."

Even the captain, however, was powerless to prevent the floodlights failing during the national anthems but, after enduring a 45-minute delay, the Springbok no-risk strategy of kicking deep and tackling every red jersey that moved seemed to be paying dividends at the Boet

Erasmus Stadium. After 70 minutes, the home team led 20-0 and were cruising into the quarterfinals.

The events of the next 30 seconds, and their consequences, would plunge Pienaar into one of the intense troughs of depression into which he occasionally slumped. So positive and optimistic so much of the time, the dark mists somehow seemed to scud across his brow and prompt real despair.

An intensely physical contest erupted in a mass brawl, after which the Irish referee, David McHugh, opted to send off two Canadians and Dalton. A midnight disciplinary committee imposed statutory 30-day bans on all three men, and the Springbok hooker was suddenly out of the World Cup. Pienaar had appealed to the referee to consider the effect of his decision, but in vain.

Worse followed. The next day, Sunday, the captain was told that Hendriks had been cited for his role in the fracas and, on Monday, a disciplinary hearing in Johannesburg handed the left wing a 60-day ban. His World Cup was over. Amid tears and recriminations, statements and threats, the team had decided to appeal against Dalton's ban, but his case was rejected on the Tuesday.

For three full days in the midst of their historic mission, the South Africans allowed themselves to be completely distracted. The side did not train, and rugby hardly seemed to cross anyone's mind. Angered by the severity of the bans and depressed by the desolation of Dalton and Hendriks, his friends, Pienaar became a morose, brooding and silent figure within the squad.

His mood was not helped by an incident on the Sunday night when he had been among three players who asked for permission to extend their day trip to the Fish River Sun near Port Elizabeth. Du Plessis, the manager, had agreed so long as the group returned to the team hotel by midnight. Letting off steam with friends in the casino, the captain lost track of time and only arrived at three in the morning to find Du Plessis, still awake, livid, pacing around the foyer. Pienaar said he was being treated like a child; Du Plessis protested. Trust splintered.

"I was being stupid," the captain recalls. "Morné asked me to consider the consequences if we had had a car accident on the way back, and he was right. I was confused and irrational at the time. The situation with Pieter and James had upset me so much. Everything was twisted and blurred."

A team meeting was arranged for nine o'clock on the Wednesday morning at the Sandton Holiday Inn and, as the players settled, Pienaar rose from his seat on the right-hand side of the front row and turned to address the squad: "Firstly, I want to apologise for my behaviour over the past few days and, second, I want to apologise to Morné for letting him down on Sunday night."

The captain's voice was cracking, and tears welled in his eyes as he asked the squad to set aside their anger and indignation over the bans, and once again to focus on winning the World Cup. "No other Springboks in history have had the opportunity that lies ahead of us now," he concluded. "We have no right to throw it away. Guys, please. Let's put this show back on the road."

Within moments, the players were stampeding out to the team bus on their way to training. Only three days later, Chester Williams celebrated his return from a hamstring injury by scoring four tries in an emphatic 42-14 quarterfinal win over Western Samoa at Ellis Park. The dream was alive and kicking.

Pienaar counted seven players nursing serious injuries after the game, and wondered how many would recover to play a week later, in the semifinal against France in Durban. Yet Dr Frans Verster, Evan Speechly and Ron Holder offered outstanding and dedicated medical attention; players demonstrated a raw resolve to keep their places in this adventure; Joubert spent hours sitting in a compression chamber to soothe his hand; and, amazingly, Christie was given a full squad from which to choose his team for King's Park.

"Cappie, do you think we can move Mark Andrews to eighthman?" It was breakfast. Pienaar looked up from his cereal in amazement.

"What?"

The coach continued: "Do you think Mark can play eighthman?"

Swallowing deep, Pienaar said he thought it might be asking too much of a lock forward who had not played eighthman since school to move into that role in such an important match, but he added he would support the coach's decision whatever it may be. Christie duly took the plunge, installed Wiese and Strydom at lock, and switched Andrews to the back of the scrum.

"That was typical of Kitch," the captain recalls. "Ninety-nine percent of top coaches would have kept the same side, but he wanted to keep challenging the opposition and keep trying new things. The media and most of the players were amazed, but he followed his instinct that Mark had the natural ball-playing ability to play eighthman in the semifinal against France."

By early afternoon on Saturday 17 June, however, it appeared as though nobody would be playing in the semifinal against France. The city of Durban had been pelted by incessant rain for 48 hours, large areas of King's Park were under water, and Derek Bevan, the Welsh referee, seriously contemplated declaring the field unplayable and abandoning the match. He pointed out that a player could drown if the scrum collapsed in casual water. At length, he decided to postpone kick-off by 90 minutes, and would then assess conditions again.

Pienaar approached his manager in the changing room and asked what would be the consequence of an abandoned match. Du Plessis found a rule book and read aloud a clause stipulating that, everything else being equal (and it was), the side with the least number of players dismissed during the tournament would be declared the winner. He added quietly that no Frenchmen had been sent off in this World Cup. As the enduring image of Dalton, hands on his head leaving the field, returned to haunt them, the Springboks reeled in despair.

The players waited, waited and waited, dreading the worst, but mercifully the rain abated and Bevan declared the match could start. Pienaar's side hurled themselves into the slush like men who had been desperate to play; in contrast, France resembled a team banking on a cancellation.

Kruger stormed to score an important try but, amid the spray and swamp, Stransky and Thierry Lacroix produced an amazing display of goal kicking as the contest boiled down to four of the most dramatic, heart-thumping minutes in all the history of Springbok rugby. South Africa was clinging to a 19-15 lead as the French drove forward, winning a series of attacking scrums.

Pienaar says: "Nine times out of ten, the attacking side would have scored in that situation and won the match. We were exhausted and they kept coming at us, forcing errors. I don't know how we survived. We were swearing and shouting at each other, urging and imploring, packing and pushing with every last ounce of energy. We were soaked and exhausted, but we would not lose."

Abdelatif Benazzi surged to score but fell a few centimetres short. Yet another scrum was called. Wiese screamed at his comrades: "We can go down, we can go up. We can go forward, left or right but there is no way we are going back." In this place, at this time, the Springbok scrum held firm.

When Bevan sounded his final whistle, Pienaar threw his arms in the air in relief and elation. The front row of Swart, Rossouw and Du Randt, overwhelmed by emotion but not by France, walked from the field arm-in-arm, tears streaming down their reddened faces, heroes this day and for ever more.

"The five non-playing members of the squad came to the changing room after the match," the captain recalls. "They were wearing blazers, but they looked as exhausted and drained as us. They were thrilled. There was a fantastic spirit within our squad. I could see we had become a family."

Floodlight failures, players suspended, waterlogged fields: it didn't seem to matter what happened. Players and officials within the squad started to sense the South African World Cup campaign was being propelled by some kind of friendly, irresistible force. Across the country, in every community, millions of people were rallying to their team's slogan "One Team, One Country", willing Pienaar's side to the triumphant victory that destiny seemed to hold in store.

The last remaining obstacle was an All Black side that had routed England in the semifinal at Newlands, and the Springboks lived through a fretful week of preparation for the most important game of their lives, indeed the most important game of millions of South

African lives. At one stage, Christie proposed the team should adopt the "Brains Game" for the final, only to revert to a more conventional strategy after witnessing a disastrous, error-ridden training session. Andrews had thrived against France, and was retained as eighthman.

Saturday 24 June 1995 dawned inevitably blue, and the lasting images of this unforgettable day are engraved in the opening chapter of this book and in the hearts of many million South Africans: the flag-bearing crowd, President Mandela wearing a Springbok No. 6 jersey, the deafening fly-past of an SAA Jumbo Jet, the six resolute tackles on Lomu, the thumping chords of "Hier kommie Bokke" and the rhythm of "Shosholoza", Stransky's drop goal in extra time, the squad assembled in prayer at the final whistle, the Webb Ellis trophy, the serene beauty of the team's lap of honour as 72 000 people thanked their lucky stars that they had been able to witness one of the great sporting occasions of all time.

South Africa 15 New Zealand 12: it all happened, and even the All Blacks' subsequent, totally unsubstantiated allegations of deliberate food poisoning could not spoil what for so many people remains a precious memory.

Nick Farr-Jones, the former Wallaby captain, had been commentating for Australian television and reflects upon "one of the great days of my life." Philippe Sella was sitting behind the posts at the northern end of the stadium. "We were disappointed to have lost in the semifinal," the legendary French centre reflects, "but, for me, the final was still a truly magical, uplifting experience."

Borne on Le Roux's shoulders, beaming broadly, saluting the crowd with one hand and holding the World Cup with the other, Pienaar appeared on top of the rugby world. His public profile within South Africa was exceeded only by that of his No. 1 supporter, Nelson Mandela, and his face would forever be associated with one of the happiest days in many South African lives; yet, within 15 months, he had been dropped and driven to effective exile in England.

The cause of this trauma was money.

Pienaar powerfully supported rugby's shuffle towards professionalism, and in 1993 had worked full-time to establish a successful players' fund in Transvaal, charging box holders for player appearances and ne-gotiating incentives with the union. However the enterprise turned sour when team-mates began to resent his 20% commission on income, an industry norm they had unanimously agreed at the outset, and Pienaar withdrew gloomily from the venture.

Where rugby players and money are concerned, he had learned, you find greed, division, emotional responses and unhappiness. He vowed to steer clear of the issue until, during the 1995 World Cup, he was approached by his former coach, Harry Viljoen, and informed about plans to launch TWRC, a professional, global competition out-side the official structures of the game.

On the eve of the World Cup final, the rugby unions of South Africa, New Zealand and Australia announced that they had sold their combined television rights to Rupert Murdoch's News Corporation for US$550m over ten years. Suddenly, the stakes were rising and, once his squad had won the World Cup, the captain assessed what he con-sidered to be a powerful hand.

As the world champions, the Springboks had become the most valuable property in the game, and there were now two wealthy tel-evision magnates who required their services: Murdoch through his television deal with the established unions, and Kerry Packer, through his backing of TWRC. Within hours of raising the Webb Ellis trophy, Pienaar saw his task as being to play his cards correctly and secure the best possible deal for his Springboks.

His basic strategy was to sign provisional contracts with TWRC, then wait for either a counter-offer from the unions or for TWRC to put hard money behind their grand intentions; and, a week after the World Cup final, he persuaded 26 of the 28 World Cup Springboks to sign TWRC contracts, promising he would keep the two boxes of secret documents at home until, in due course, the entire squad would assemble and finally decide which action to take.

Throughout the process, Pienaar believed the key to success lay in being able to keep the squad together, pushing the theme that they had won the World Cup together, now they could win the money game together. "People have tried to portray us as greedy," he recalls, "but rugby union was obviously going to turn professional and we wanted to secure our immediate futures. There was nothing immoral or mercenary about that. Rugby was our living."

After six nervous weeks of rumour and intrigue, during which Pienaar led 13 Transvaal Springboks in an unrelated four-day dispute with their provincial union, officials from NewsCorp made their move, through Louis Luyt, and offered to match whatever the Springboks had been offered by TWRC.

The squad met in Midrand and overwhelmingly voted to sign with SARFU, having apparently secured the best of both worlds: they had negotiated massive contracts and would keep playing within familiar structures. From the 27 players' point of view, their captain had played his hand to perfection.

However, by withdrawing from and effectively derailing TWRC, the world champions enraged two significant groups. Their provincial colleagues were left with no bargaining power to negotiate contracts with their unions, resulting in an unhealthy discrepancy between the earnings of the World Cup players and their team-mates; and the Wallabies and All Blacks felt betrayed, left to scramble, one by one, to secure contracts with their national unions.

Most of the anger and venom was directed personally towards Pienaar as the main influence among the World Cup Springboks. He was unkindly portrayed as selfish and duplicitous, as being unreliable and fickle. His insistence is that, at all times, he had been candid, up-front and honourable.

"I understood their reaction," the captain reflects. "As Springboks, we did look after ourselves, but we did not act improperly. We had found ourselves in a position where two groups wanted our services. We considered their respective offers and reached our decision. It was as simple as that.

"Of course, it would have been tremendous if everyone could have signed the same contracts, but that was not realistic. The world champions were always going to earn more than provincial players; and perhaps the Australians and New Zealanders should have thought why the Murdoch organisation decided to break TWRC by matching our contracts rather than theirs. It might have been because we were organised and disciplined as one unit with one voice."

In due course, fresh disclosures that Pienaar had been paid a commission of US$300 000 angered some of his own Springbok teammates, but Luyt's words had been that he would "match" the TWRC offer, and this additional sum was later paid over by News Corporation via Transvaal. The money had been offered with no implications at all for any other party. There was no reason for Pienaar to say "no, thanks", no reason why anybody should have said "no, thanks".

It was, naturally, preposterous for any World Cup Springbok to resent the commission paid to Pienaar, for it was he who was responsible for their success in the tightrope negotiations. Gratitude should have been their only response but, as the captain said so often in 1995, money breeds envy.

The advent of open professionalism, subsequently confirmed by the IRB, did not significantly affect the appearance of Springbok rugby because top South African players had been paid for the past nine years, and nobody disputed that men who dedicated their best years to the game should secure a market-related living from that game. The transition appeared seamless.

It was business as usual, above rather than under the table, and Pienaar led his Springboks to an emphatic 40-11 victory over Wales in a one-off Test at Ellis Park on 2 September, and two months later flew north to play against Italy in Rome and England in London. Du Plessis and Christie had agreed to remain in their places for one more season, attracted by the challenge of discovering how strong their relatively young squad could yet become.

"We were not arrogant in any way," the captain recalls, "but we knew we had won the World Cup largely because of our outstanding defensive pattern, and we felt we had not scraped the surface of our attacking potential. We all believed the best form of this Springbok team lay in the future."

Italy provided the tourists with a rigorous warm-up, the home team actually leading with 15 minutes left before subsiding to a 40-21 defeat; and the world champions moved on to produce a compelling display at Twickenham, defeating England with much greater comfort than the 24-10 final score suggested.

Pienaar and Christie both celebrated Christmas in the Cape, able to reflect upon a year when their Springboks had played 10 Tests and won 10 Tests, when they had won the World Cup at the first attempt, and proved their world champion status by travelling to beat England, the Five Nations winners. Captain and coach toasted 1995 in the hope that 1996 would be even better.

It very soon wasn't.

Christie had fought bravely against lymphatic cancer since locating lumps in his neck on his wedding day in 1979, but lapses in his health did occasionally force him to recuperate at the Pretoria General hospital. Early in 1996, one such lapse, combined with persistent 'flu, confined him to a hotel bed in New Zealand, where he was assisting Transvaal in their Super 12 campaign.

Upon his return home in the middle of April, the coach was cajoled by the SARFU and Transvaal president, Louis Luyt, to conclude his role with Transvaal and to resign as Springbok coach. Pienaar was surprised by the announcement, not least because the national team was not scheduled to assemble for another two months. Christie would certainly have recovered by then.

Something felt wrong. The captain shivered.

A general consensus emerged that the omnipotent Luyt, still smarting from the contract disputes of 1995, had determined to break up the World Cup-winning squad as soon as possible, and the instrument of his campaign seemed to be an emerging coach from Kimberley named André Markgraaff.

This tall, lugubrious man, who also happened to be president of his union, an influential member of the SARFU Executive Committee, and a keen supporter of Luyt's bid to become president in 1994, had already been nominated to coach with Christie during 1996 with the intention that he would take sole control for the end-of-year tour to Europe; however, with the world champion coach now out of the way, Markgraaff's bizarre promotion from guiding Griquas in the B section to coaching a leading international side was accelerated.

Pienaar was bemused by the speed of events, and further confused when his first meeting with the new Springbok coach dwelled almost exclusively on the issue of money. "I didn't know him at all," the captain recalls, "but he told me how I could make millions out of the game. It was odd. I wanted to talk about how we would win the next three Tests, but we seemed to get along."

The South African team looked forward to a frantic season: the inaugural Tri-Nations series, comprising home and away Tests against Australia and New Zealand, followed by a further three home Tests versus the All Blacks. In spite of his deteriorating relationship with Luyt, in spite of the constant, draining haggling over the SARFU contracts, Pienaar resolved to be positive.

He assured Markgraaff of his complete support, and expressed the hope that the two men could be honest with each other at all times. That had been the foundation of his partnership with Christie, and the captain desperately wanted to develop the same kind of relationship with the new coach.

History offered a precedent.

Nelie Smith had been named as the new Springbok coach in 1980, and he joined the national squad to discover Morné du Plessis absolutely established as an admired and dominant captain. Shrewd and experienced, Smith set himself to complement and not confront Du Plessis, to add value where he could, and softly and gently, slowly and calmly, to soak his influence into the team.

Sixteen years later, Markgraaff walked into the Springbok team hotel and found Pienaar similarly established as a natural, respected leader at the peak of his powers; and yet this inexperienced coach lacked the self-confidence to defer to an infinitely more qualified captain. Instead, he resolved to launch his own era in his own image in his own way. Conflict was inevitable.

The captain had hoped to build on the success of 1995, but Markgraaff signalled his intentions when he dropped Stransky, the ultimate World Cup hero, for the warm-up Test against Fiji. The Springboks won 43-18, but the mood had changed from the previous year, the family had fractured.

Still the captain resolved to be positive, to work through the problems and settle the team. When players told him the coach was a complete novice out of his depth in Test rugby, he replied that they should listen to what he was saying and work harder, even though, privately, he feared they were right.

When the Springboks flew to start their Tri-Nations campaign against the Wallabies in Sydney, Markgraaff boasted to the media that his team would play rugby "like the world has never seen", then instructed the players to tap and run penalties, take short lineouts, and kick for touch rather than the posts.

The captain suggested discreetly that the team was not ready to adopt a new strategy on the eve of a major Test, but the coach was insistent. The result was a disorderly, scrappy display, and a 21-16 defeat. South Africa's unbeaten run of 16 Tests had come to a wretched, ignominious end.

Pienaar was devastated, moved to share his fears with Du Plessis, but the manager felt unable to exert any influence. Markgraaff would not accept advice. If Christie had taken nine months to build a champion squad, his successor took scarcely nine days to drag the team back into rank mediocrity.

The squad moved on to play New Zealand in Christchurch, and spent three days listening to their innocent coach wonder aloud how anyone would be able to stop Lomu. Leading sides focus on their own performance, not on the opposition. The Springbok captain knew that, his players knew that, but Markgraaff appeared blissfully unaware of how to prepare for a major Test.

Pienaar had had enough. Two years earlier, he had reacted to a crisis in New Zealand by holding a meeting of his players without coaches and managers in attendance; now, in Christchurch, he did so again. Before the door had closed, angry players started to ask what on earth was going on. The captain worked to calm the team, reassure them of their capacity to beat the All Blacks just as they had done a year earlier at Ellis Park, sooth their anxiety.

The Springboks charged out at Lancaster Park bursting veins to assert their dominance and, even without a coherent game plan and ordered motivation, they were desperately unlucky to lose 15-11. Sean Fitzpatrick even apologised to Pienaar about the referee's poor performance, but the Springbok captain was in no doubt where to apportion blame for another wretched defeat.

"It's all his fault! It's all Markgraaff's fault," Pienaar screamed at Du Plessis when he returned to the changing room. "We should never be losing matches like this. He doesn't know what he's doing." The manager put his arm around Pienaar and guided him to a quiet corner. The coach had heard nothing.

Since April, the captain had sincerely tried to establish a relationship with the new Springbok coach. He felt he had been patient and loyal, constructive and dedicated but, on the flight home to South Africa, Pienaar resolved that he would not stand by and watch his champion team be destroyed.

He ignored rumours that he was being targeted by Luyt and Markgraaff for his role in "winning" the acrimonious contract negotiations in 1995, and reached a clear decision that, if he was to go down, he would go down fighting.

When he was told Markgraaff had stood in a Christchurch bar and blamed the captain for the defeat in New Zealand, Pienaar calmly confronted the coach. Markgraaff denied everything. Pienaar didn't believe him.

When South Africa prepared to play Australia in Bloemfontein, the captain resolutely requested the recalled Stransky to kick for touch rather than into space and to establish field position. The strategy worked, propelling the team to a 16-3 lead and a 25-19 victory, their first in the Tri-Nations series. Markgraaff sat quiet in the changing room afterwards: even he was able to recognise that the players had won essentially because they had ignored his instructions.

Pienaar effectively seized the reins. The All Blacks had already taken the Tri-Nations title, but the Springbok captain believed they could be defeated in the last match of the series at Newlands if South Africa kicked the ball into the space behind Christian Cullen, the raw young fullback. His game plan reaped dividends again, and his revived Springboks surged into an 18-6 lead.

The captain had reached the edge of the abyss.

Since Bennie Osler's ignominious exit in the fifth-Test defeat against the Wallabies in 1933, Springbok history is disappointingly punctuated by wretched episodes of genuinely great players being treated badly. Invariably cut down by small-minded contemporary envy, these legends have had to slink away from a side to which they dedicated the prime years of their lives.

However, it is doubtful whether any Springbok hero has been so ruthlessly and cruelly abused as François Pienaar at Newlands in 1996.

Shortly after half time, he accidentally collided with Fitzpatrick's knee and was knocked cold. Determined to see his side through to victory, to guarantee his team's resurgence, he recovered and told the medical staff he would play on. He wanted to demonstrate his commitment and finish the job; yet the captain started to suffer brief blackouts, blurred vision, dizziness and nausea.

In serious distress, with 15 minutes to play, Pienaar collapsed to the turf. As Newlands respectfully hushed, he was carried off the field on a stretcher, his eyes closed, his head concealed by a red protective brace.

Having been treated in the medical facility, he eventually returned to his players to be told they had lost the Test 29-18. Disappointed and still dazed, the Springbok captain arrived in the changing room to find a cheerful Luyt sitting with his arm around the shoulders of Gary Teichmann, who had led the team during the closing stages. Pienaar sat in his place, and began to change.

The captain was brutally ignored by the SARFU and Transvaal president, whose trophy cabinet he had filled for the past three seasons. Players started to shrink away from this horrendous, inexcusable scene.

Through the frozen minutes that followed, South Africa's deputy president Thabo Mbeki, New Zealand's prime minister Jim Bolger, and the decent All Black coach John Hart all specifically approached the Springbok captain and enquired how he was feeling, but Luyt and Markgraaff said nothing at all.

Pienaar's initial reaction was that he wanted to make himself available for the first Test of the All Black series the following Saturday in Durban, but doctors told him he had been concussed and should rest. He offered to sign a statement indemnifying them against any consequences. They said more emphatically that he could suffer serious and permanent damage if he played.

So the captain withdrew, and raged at his television as South Africa lost narrowly to the All Blacks in Durban and again in Pretoria. On the Monday before the third Test in Johannesburg, sitting quietly at home, he was told the coach had been telling people that he had faked the injury at Newlands.

That was the final straw. He immediately walked to his car and, seething, arrived at the Sunnyside Park hotel to find the Springboks gathered for their team photograph. Again, he confronted Markgraaff with the story. The coach denied it. Pienaar did not believe him and, stopping only to shake Teichmann by the hand, drove home. He has not spoken to Markgraaff since that day.

Pienaar returned to full fitness and, motivated beyond words, he produced outstanding form in leading Transvaal to the Currie Cup final, but his international fate had already been sealed. He was formally omitted from the Springbok squad to tour Europe at the end of the season, denied even the courtesy of a telephone call from the coach who so casually discarded this national asset.

Fifteen months after raising the World Cup, aged only 29, Pienaar was left to buy a Sunday newspaper on the street corner and read that he was not part of Markgraaff's "vision for the future". In fact, his simple presence, his stature in the team was perceived as a threat by an insecure coach, and the decision appeared to have been reached with the sanction of the ruthless Luyt.

Public outrage reverberated for weeks, with one newspaper phone-in poll suggesting 96% of the public wanted Markgraaff, not Pienaar, to be sacked from the squad; yet the deed was done and, like every sporting controversy, the issue eventually dissolved in the irrepressible stream of events.

"I was terribly disappointed," Pienaar recalls, "and I still feel an empty pain whenever I see South Africa play. My greatest regret is that

I was unable to leave Springbok rugby on my own terms, rather than on a stretcher. In any case, as the years pass, it is the happy times that I remember most clearly."

At the end of 1996, Pienaar wholeheartedly embraced a fresh challenge, agreeing to assist English millionaire Nigel Wray in turning Saracens RFC from a public park club in north London into a dynamic, trend-setting powerhouse within the growing professional game in Europe. As player, captain and then coach, he established the club among the elite and served as the club's full-time chief executive and coach.

Still turning heads, still holding audiences of strangers in the palm of his hand, he became a leading rugby analyst on British television, and is widely admired and respected as a global statesman of the game.

Through his years in a kind of exile, Pienaar received many offers to return home, from provincial unions seeking a new coach to leading companies, but he remained fiercely committed to Saracens. Characteristically, he never signed a written contract with Wray. For two decent and determined men, their shared ambition has proved a more than adequate bond.

Of course, he returned home incessantly, most poignantly in early May 1998 when he broke down several times while delivering the eulogy at the funeral of Kitch Christie; and the consistently overwhelming response to his public appearances in South Africa showed he retains a special place in the lives of many of his compatriots. Where he speaks, every table is sold. On his permanent return to South Africa, he headed his country's bid to host the 2011 World Cup.

In July 2000, he played his final game before retirement when leading a reunited Springbok 1995 team against the Golden Lions. Ellis Park officials had sullenly predicted a crowd of 2 000, but more than 57 000 spectators packed the stands to wipe the treasured, teary memories away from their eyes.

Perhaps Pienaar has become the Elvis Presley of Springbok rugby, taken in his prime, remembered in his prime, treasured in his prime.

The man in the green jersey, grinning so wide that his eyes closed, raising the golden trophy as Mandela punched the air and his country united in unbridled and unprecedented joy ... that man has been immortalised by his central role in a moment that South Africans will forever recall with enormous pride.

In spirit, in mansions and shacks, in every nook and cranny of a vast land, François Pienaar, the world champion Springbok, will never die.

13 THE STORM BREAKER

Gary Teichmann assumed the Springbok captaincy amid controversy, retained it through three coaches and three different visions, and successfully led South Africa to 17 consecutive Test wins; and yet his greatest triumph was to emerge from three hectic, often harrowing years with his dignity intact.

When he captained the first Springbok team to lose a home series against the All Blacks, in 1996, he took the criticism and worked harder.

When his Springboks were beaten by the Lions in 1997, he congratulated the victors without referring to the injuries and bad luck.

When he guided the team to the Tri-Nations triumph of 1998, he accepted the praise with humility, and shied away from the spotlight.

When coaches arrived and acted as if they had been up the mountain and discovered the hitherto concealed secrets of the game, he listened to what they had to say, implemented their requests, and gave everything.

When South African rugby veered from administrative crisis to threatened commissions of enquiry, he shrugged his shoulders, sustained his own standard on the field, and kept leading his team with rare distinction.

It seems almost inconceivable that anyone could stand in the middle of so much pressure and tension, such feral emotions and deep crisis, and manage to conduct himself in such a manner that he would remain untainted by controversy, respected by his peers, admired by millions, universally popular.

Yet this was the measure of Teichmann's achievement. He found himself in storm after storm. Decent and relaxed, he broke them all.

Backstabbing, rumour-mongering and personality assassination are not unknown phenomena in and around South African rugby yet, from 1996 to 1999, who had a bad word to say about the Springbok captain?

No-one.

Following Des van Jaarsveldt and Piet Greyling, Teichmann became the third South African captain to emerge from the country once known as Rhodesia, renamed Zimbabwe in 1980. He was born in Gwelo, now Gweru, on 9 January 1967, precisely one week after François Pienaar was born.

The pioneer Teichmanns arrived in Africa from Germany during the 19th Century, resolute Protestants fleeing declining moral standards in Europe, but by 1955 many of the family had settled in Natal and become so anglicised that they enthusiastically stood to sing God Save the Queen.

Jack Teichmann was born and bred in Ladysmith. He trained to be a stock auctioneer, married Mickey Lund, whose family farmed not far from Howick, and took the decision to leave the cheerful, close-knit farming communities of the Natal midlands and travel in search of a new life in Rhodesia. The couple initially settled in Umtali, then Gwelo, and finally in Bulawayo, working and thriving among like-minded farming families, raising five children of their own.

Their fourth child was christened Gary, and he spent most of his formative years scampering among the rock outcrops near home, usually with his pet bushbaby, Stinks. At agricultural shows, at tennis courts, at sports grounds, at friends' houses, on any available piece of veld, the Teichmann children created their own fun. They learned to get on with life, without fuss or fanfare.

Gary gradually devoted more and more time to sport, and was excited to win a place in the Partridges, the Rhodesian primary schools cricket XI that each year travelled south to compete at a festival week in South Africa. The captain of the team was a prolific young batsman from Banket named Graeme Hick, and no lesser man than the

Rhodesian prime minister, Ian Smith, arrived to present the combed, chattering, pristine boys with their Partridge caps.

As the Rhodesian war rumbled through the 1970s, and travelling in rural areas became unsafe, Jack Teichmann found it almost impossible to thrive as a stock auctioneer, and in 1979 he reluctantly decided his family should return to South Africa. Gary Teichmann reflects: "We all grew up as proud Rhodesians. It was a small country with a big heart, motivated by the heroics of its courageous sportsmen. My hero was Bucky Buchanan, the bearded scrumhalf in our Currie Cup rugby side. He epitomised that special national spirit."

Teichmann arrived in South Africa at the age of 12, and after one year at Howick Primary School where his cricket coach was Digby Rhodes (whose young son Jonty usually appeared at nets), he followed his brother, Ross, to one of the Republic's most prestigious schools, Hilton College.

These years were not years of luxury, as his parents made huge sacrifices to pay the school fees and cheerfully parked their yellow Datsun 120Y among the rows of German saloons, but they were years of quality: a quality home life was enhanced by high-quality teachers, obeyed dutifully, and high-quality coaches on the sports fields, obeyed with breathless enthusiasm.

Named as captain of the under-14 cricket side, he was replaced after one match because he kept himself on to bowl too long, but he grew to relish rugby, and eventually fell under the wise guidance of the Hilton 1st XV coaches, Klein Strydom and former Springbok wing Andy van der Watt.

"I was coasting along as an average centre," Teichmann recalls, "until one day the coaches called me over and said I was too slow for a back. They thought I should play as a forward. It is probably not an exaggeration to say that if Klein and Andy had not switched my position, I would have drifted away from rugby not long after leaving school. I owe my entire career to their decision."

The loose forward thrived in Hilton's white jersey with black trim, enjoying the prestige of representing a school team that usually attracted crowds of up to 15 000 for the annual derby with their traditional rivals, Michaelhouse. A tall and talented ball-player, he excelled in the 1984 Hilton team that would have enjoyed an unbeaten season but for an exasperating defeat against a Maritzburg College side directed by an influential flyhalf, Joel Stransky.

Teichmann enjoyed every minute at Hilton, maturing among the brilliant white buildings perched atop the lush green hills that roll past Pietermaritzburg, pursuing the Umgeni River on towards the city of Durban and the Indian Ocean 90 kilometres away. Indeed, the noble school he attended could claim much of the credit for the highly distinguished man he became.

He may have blinked into the world with a clear idea of how to behave, but he had no clear idea of what he wanted to do with his life. His bog-standard pass in Afrikaans ruled out instant university entry, so he opted to get his compulsory two years of military service out of the way. Despite not knowing the words of "Die Stem", he survived month upon month by playing rugby for the Section 20 XV and minding an SADF office in Rundu on the border between South West Africa and Angola. Amid relentless relaxation, the only gunfire he heard in two years was a staccato burst of noise down the radio from further north.

Upon his return to Natal, he worked with his brother, Ross, establishing a business selling diamond-mesh fencing but, after two punishing years, their main supplier withdrew and the venture closed. Teichmann remembers: "I was almost 23 and people were starting to feel sorry for me because I had worked hard since leaving school, but I didn't seem to be going anywhere fast."

Diffidence loomed, but he followed his genes and signed up for a two-year course in farm management at the Cedara agricultural college. He had been told the social life was spectacular and resolved that, even if he turned out not to take farming as a career, he would at least have had some fun.

He continued to play rugby for Maritzburg University, an open club, and he was selected in the Natal under-20 team, and occasionally even saw his name in club reports in the Natal Witness, but there was no-one standing on the touchline, nodding sagely and saying: "That boy will be a Springbok."

Teichmann was just a kindly face in the crowd, figuratively and literally, at the end of 1990 when, complete with banana tree branches, he joined a group of friends in roaring Natal to their stunning, historic, first-ever Currie Cup-final victory over Northern Transvaal at Loftus Versfeld. He relished the occasion, and for the first time started to wonder if he could one day play top-class rugby. The concept had never been a burning ambition in his stress-free world.

When, however, he read in the newspaper that Andrew Aitken, the Natal eighthman, had decided to move to Cape Town, Teichmann sensed that, at last, a door was opening for him. He started to train with purpose, and the results were immediate. Swiftly transformed in attitude and ambition, the eighthman made his debut for Natal in 1991, and sprang free from his cocoon.

Firmly established in a competitive Currie Cup team, admired as a gifted and creative link between the forwards and backs, he earned nationwide praise as a major factor in Natal's Currie Cup champion team of 1992.

His name started to appear in newspaper articles speculating about the national squad but, to his increasing frustration, that is precisely where he would remain for the next two years: on the fringes of Springbok selection, seemingly always in contention, seemingly never quite in the team.

One Saturday evening in October 1993, amid the festivities of the famous post-match braais on the rugby fields around King's Park, Teichmann was sitting in his parents' car when the Springbok squad to tour Argentina was announced on the radio. He reflects: "My father and I were in the front seats, my mother and Nicky, my girlfriend, were hovering around outside. I will never forget the way my father smiled when he heard my name announced on the radio.

"In fact, I derived more pleasure from making my parents so proud than I did from my selection. My father shook my hand. In that moment, I felt that, after all, I had not let them down. I had made something of my life."

However, initial excitement gave way to frustration when it became clear that Tiaan Strauss was secure as eighthman in the Test team.

Teichmann played midweek matches in Argentina, but the following year missed out on the home Tests against England and the tour to New Zealand. The young man who people said was just too light to play top international rugby was customarily to be found drowning his sorrows at the renowned Nottingham Road pub.

Kitch Christie's dramatic overhaul at the end of 1994 did bring the Natalian back into the squad, but the tour to Wales, Scotland and Ireland also unfolded as a disappointment when he was compelled to play out of position on the flank and, as a result, never threatened to win a place in the Test side.

Still playing consistently well for Natal, he prospered through various trial matches leading up to the 1995 Rugby World Cup, but only six hours before the announcement of the Springbok squad he was called to a meeting with Christie and Morné du Plessis, and gently told he would be omitted. Into his 29th year, he was starting to believe his Test chances had come and gone.

He was wrong. Appointed to succeed Wahl Bartmann as Natal captain a week after watching the World Cup final on television, he was suddenly named in the Springbok side to play a one-off Test against Wales in September. He shone in a convincing win but then, in the largest disappointment of these nearly years, was dropped for the November Tests against Italy and England.

André Markgraaff's appointment as Springbok coach brought Teichmann back into the eighthman position for the 1996 warm-up international against Fiji in Pretoria on 2 July 1996, and there, astonishingly, he would remain through 39 consecutive Test matches until 12 June 1999.

His first impressions of Markgraaff were negative, sharing his teammates' frustration at the coach's old-school dogma and inflexibility, and their excitement when Pienaar took control of the side before the Tri-Nations Test in Christchurch; but his paramount concern through these troubled times was simply to establish himself as an automatic selection in the Test team.

Even when he perceived the tension between Markgraaff and Pienaar, the prospect of captaincy did not occur to him. Even when

Pienaar was stretchered off the field during the Test against the All Blacks at Newlands, his instinct was to recoil when he realised he was now captain.

"I really did not want to be captain," he recalls. "I wanted to concentrate on securing my place in the team, without any additional concerns. I was very happy to play under François. He was an outstanding leader.

"On the Sunday after we lost at Newlands, however, I was outlining these sentiments to my father, and he responded by saying that everybody should take their opportunities when they come, however inconvenient they may seem at the time, because there is always the chance they won't come again. I instantly knew he was right, and started to accept the idea of the captaincy."

There was scarcely any time for reflection. With the inaugural Tri-Nations series completed, the Springboks and All Blacks regrouped for what may prove to have been the last conventional series between the rival countries: three Tests to be played on successive Saturdays during August 1996.

Teichmann took over, initially as the caretaker captain, during one of the endemic mismanaged crises that dominated the media and distracted the team during 1996. The soap opera started with SARFU refusing to support Morné du Plessis's condemnation of supporters waving the old South African flag during the Test in Bloemfontein, but James Small had now become the focus of furore, having been dropped for the second Test because he was seen drinking Coca Cola in a nightclub two days before the Test in Cape Town.

The new captain adopted a plan to deal with these issues.

He ignored them.

"They were not my problems," Teichmann says. "I remember sitting down at one stage and focusing on my responsibilities: they were to motivate the team as selected, to implement the game plan as outlined by the coach, and to sustain my personal performance. I could not worry about the public relations disasters, selection and the Union. They were not my areas of control."

Head down, his mind focused between the four white lines, the eighthman prepared to lead South Africa for the first time, against the All Blacks at his home ground, King's Park in Durban. He had often led Natal into the impressive arena, most memorably before the 1995 Currie Cup-final victory over Western Province, but nothing had re- motely prepared him for the stupefying roar that enveloped him as he high-stepped into view. He closed his eyes, breathed deep.

His players could not have tried harder that day, running and tack- ling to a standstill, but the underlying melody of the 1996 season lin- gered on: a committed All Black team, inspired by Sean Fitzpatrick, organised by coach John Hart, and comfortable with their professional status and contracts, proved too clinical for an unsettled Springbok squad that lacked discipline and direction under the hapless Mark- graaff, and seemed constantly at war with SARFU.

The All Blacks were happy and focused; the Springboks looked harassed and distracted. The All Blacks had retained the nucleus of their 1995 team, only adding the gifted Christian Cullen to the side; the Springboks had systematically broken up their world champions of the previous year.

The scale of the stunning, completely unnecessary purge was re- flected in the fact that only six members of the team that won the World Cup were included in Markgraaff's team to play the All Blacks in Durban 12 months later. Rarely has such a successful squad been so swiftly and ruthlessly dismantled.

New Zealand bulldozed into a 15-9 lead by half time at King's Park, and despite being hauled back to 23-19 stood their ground dur- ing a scoreless fourth quarter to seize a 1-0 lead in the series. Teich- mann was left to look back upon a sequence of missed penalties that might have ... but didn't.

While the Springboks appeared consistently on the back foot, chasing the game, the All Blacks had arrived in the country inspired by the twin propellers of avenging their 1995 World Cup-final defeat, and becoming the first New Zealand side to win a Test series on South African soil. Where Brownlie, Allen, Whineray, Lochore and Leslie had failed, Fitzpatrick resolved to succeed.

"It was very hard," the All Black captain recalls. "We had beaten the

South Africans three times in a row, but two of those were in the Tri-Nations and we still needed one more victory to win that elusive Test series.

"Our preparation for the second Test in Pretoria was very emotional. John Hart spoke to the players about the great All Blacks who had come to Africa and been beaten. It was important that some of the young players should understand what had happened before. It was a bit of a history lesson but, as a side, we took a decision to win the series for the heritage of the black jersey."

Teichmann sensed his side was teetering on the brink of special ignominy in Springbok history and, in his quiet and authoritative manner, worked to bolster self-confidence by stressing over and over again that the squad had proved their ability to beat New Zealand. "Please think about it," he implored his players. "We were robbed by the referee in Christchurch, we threw away a match-winning lead at Newlands, and we were just two penalties away from winning at King's Park. If you think we are an inferior team, I tell you we are not."

And his side responded. Few people believed the strongest South African team had been selected for the decisive Test in Pretoria (just as few thought the best side was assembled for the third Test against the Lions in 1974), but nobody faulted the courage of the 15 South Africans on the field.

Each time the All Blacks surged ahead, the Springboks fought back. Each time the All Blacks started to move their scrum forward, Teichmann's team found something extra and heaved back. "They were bashing the hell out of us and we were bashing the hell out of them," Fitzpatrick reflects. "I suppose that's the way it has always been between the two countries. Nobody ever got a chance to relax in the entire 80 minutes. The drama was intense. Every scrum, no matter where it was set, felt like it had the pressure of a five-metre scrum."

After Hannes Strydom scored an early try, the All Blacks rampaged into a 24-11 lead, but the Springboks bravely battled back to trail 24-23 with 15 minutes remaining. Zinzan Brooke produced an extraordinary drop goal, and New Zealand had extended their advantage to 33-26 with five minutes left. Fitzpatrick suddenly dreaded the seven-point difference, fearing South Africa would score a converted try, draw the Test, and take the series to a decider at Ellis Park.

"Come on! They're finished!" Teichmann was screaming at his forwards as they charged forward in search of the equalising score, of salvation. He kept one eye on the electronic digital clock at Loftus, flickering to 0, then −1, then −2, kept hearing the All Blacks ask Didier Méné, the French referee, how much time was left to play. "They're finished! Come on guys," the captain yelled.

The Springboks won a lineout deep inside the All Black half, swept the ball right, then swept the ball left again, searching for a gap through which they could escape the disaster of a series defeat. Ruben Kruger was halted by Walter Little; Olo Brown buried Os du Randt's charge; Joost van der Westhuizen was heaved into touch. Approaching seven o'clock on a crisp Saturday evening, panting New Zealanders lay their bodies on the line, their own try line.

And they prevailed; and, at the final whistle, Fitzpatrick seemed overcome by emotion as he knelt and pummelled the turf with both fists. For this legendary All Black captain, nothing would ever compensate for the fact that, in a distinguished 92-Test career, he never raised the World Cup; but the historic 1996 series win in South Africa seemed to provide some kind of consolation.

Teichmann slipped quietly away to the changing room, aching with sheer exhaustion, sore with disappointment, but he chivalrously congratulated the All Blacks, and accepted defeat with dignity and style. "Someone slapped me on the back and said 'Bad luck', but that was hardly an adequate response," the captain recalls. "We lost because poor administration, bad feeling around the World Cup players' contracts, a sapping climate of controversy, and inexperienced coaching all combined to sow doubt and confusion among the players.

"Man-for-man we were as strong as the All Blacks, but we did not believe we could win, and they did. That was the difference."

The Springboks restored some confidence with a 32-22 victory in the third Test at Ellis Park, a solid performance that Teichmann sympathetically dedicated to Morné du Plessis who had wearily decided to step down as team manager, but the New Zealanders hardly raised a sweat. They had already realised their goal and, within days, the triumphant side was being cheered by 250 000 compatriots in a ticker-tape parade down Queen's Street, Auckland.

Teichmann returned to Natal, uncertain whether he would be confirmed as captain for the Springbok tour to Argentina, France and Wales at the end of the year. "There were clearly problems between Pienaar and Markgraaff," he recalls, "but I was sure they would be resolved. In my mind, I had only been a temporary captain against New Zealand, and I would have been happy for François to lead the team to Europe. I wasn't obsessed by the captaincy at all."

In the event, the Natalian was surprised when George Davids, president of the Eastern Province Rugby Union, announced the touring squad after a match in Port Elizabeth. A sigh crept around the hall when the alphabetical list passed "P" with no Pienaar; broken applause greeted "Teichmann, captain".

With hindsight, Teichmann is unequivocal. He reflects: "It was a mistake to drop François. He had proved his form in the Currie Cup, and still had so much to offer South African rugby. It was a waste. André Markgraaff said later that he had made the decision because François would not have secured a place in his Test side, but one solution might have been for François to be named as tour captain and, if necessary, for me to lead the team in the Tests. We had always got along extremely well and I am sure that would have worked."

It would not have worked for Markgraaff. Threatened by the status and the mere presence of the world champion, the coach had decided to impose himself by naming a new captain, *his* captain, *his* man, Teichmann.

While fury raged around the country, the new captain tried to draw a line beneath the dismissal of the world champion by arranging a team meeting before the tour squad left South Africa. He stated bluntly that it was the responsibility of the coach to select the squad, and it was the responsibility of the players to bond together and perform to the best of their ability. It was as simple as that. He finished theatrically, if not realistically, by asking: "If there is any player in this room who is not happy with me as captain, please raise your hand."

No hands were raised.

For better or for worse, his era had been launched.

And Teichmann was soon delighted to discover a hitherto unseen side of the Springbok coach. Where he had been tense, obstinate and dictatorial during the series against the All Blacks, Markgraaff seemed to relax on tour. Removed from a critical media and the ruthless scrutiny of millions, he began empathising with the players, meeting their needs, even learning from them.

"Team spirit was transformed within two days," the captain recalls. "André was a different person. He seemed to realise that, as experienced professionals, it is the players who understand best what kind of training and preparation helps us to perform on the Saturday afternoon. He listened to our views, seemed to be on our side, and started to inspire affection among the squad.

"In many respects, we had all been imprisoned by the intense pressure of the Tri-Nations and All Black series. We felt liberated on tour."

Since isolation, Argentina had emerged as a kind of health farm for weary, washed-out Springboks. Just as Pienaar's 1993 side had revelled in the climate, the hospitality and the vigorous, though not intense, rugby, so Teichmann's team would be refreshed and revitalised by their two-week tour.

His team defeated Los Pumas 46-15 in the first Test in Buenos Aires, and almost duplicated the score in the second Test at the same stadium a week later, emerging with a 44-21 victory. Rugby seemed fun again.

Two Test matches in France represented the premier challenge of the tour for the Springbok globetrotters, and Markgraaff's intelligently revamped coaching and management structure ensured a happier tour than in 1992. Placing himself in a kind of manager/head coach supremo position, he had recruited Nick Mallett to coach the forwards, Hugh Reece-Edwards to guide the backline, and Carel du Plessis as a technical director. Certain administrative matters still fell through the net but, as captain, Teichmann felt supported and protected.

The awe-inspiring sight of Kobus Wiese on the charge characterised the compelling Springbok display in the first Test at the Parc

Lescure, Bordeaux. As the lock forward thundered into every maul, gleefully demanding the ball, South Africa stormed into a 19-6 half time lead, and eventually cantered to a 22-12 win over a French team brutally shaken out of its stride.

"I could hardly believe the contrast between our changing room after the victory in Bordeaux and at Loftus eleven weeks before," Teichmann recalls. "The difference was confidence. In top-level sport, where natural ability is more-or-less equal, it is confidence that separates winners from losers. The teams that attain sustained success are teams that retain a fundamental self-confidence through good days and bad days alike. We needed to be like that."

France's determination to square the series was powerfully conveyed to the Springbok captain within the opening seconds of the second Test at the Parc des Princes in Paris, when he was picked off the side of a maul and bulldozed to the ground, but the tourists' defence held its shape and authority.

Once James Dalton had scored the signature try of his career, charging to the line with four Frenchmen clinging to his jersey and shorts, the South Africans steeled themselves to defend a precarious 13-12 lead in the closing stages. The team's new-found resolve manifested itself not only in their physical courage, but also in their concentration and discipline under pressure.

Teichmann was beginning to emerge as a Test captain of stature. He held his team together by uncompromising example, battling at the core of each ruck and maul, willing to sweat the hard yards. He did not indulge in any extravagant gestures during play, being more concerned that his efforts should be felt by his team-mates than be noticed by anyone sitting in the press box.

It was perhaps for this reason that he tended to be underestimated as a captain until the unreserved admiration of his players eventually permeated into the press and the public domain. To paraphrase his predecessor, Teichmann captained the side not for 42 million, but for his 14 players.

So the French flooded forward, and the eighthman stood firm at the heart of his team. Once Ruben Kruger had finger-tipped an ominous drop goal attempt by Christophe Lamaison wide of the posts, the final whistle brought relief; and 15 exhausted Springboks sank to their knees, in victory, in joy.

As he sat in the visitors' changing room at the Parc des Princes, savouring the hard-fought 2-0 series win, the captain could have been forgiven for believing the worst was over. The traumas of July and August seemed a distant memory, a settled, happy team had emerged on tour, and he was now able to look across at three coaches who seemed to hold the future in their hands: Markgraaff, relaxed and respected; Mallett, overflowing with energy and enthusiasm; and Du Plessis, cerebral and innovative. Teichmann felt the glow of a new dawn.

The players wanted to fly home from Paris, but the bold new professional era had transformed the Springboks from a merry band of men into the "product" of an increasingly hard-nosed business. With seven-figure salaries and bonuses to be paid, the team needed to perform as often as possible, to generate as much income from television rights and gate takings as possible, so the squad headed to Cardiff for a week on the golf course and a Test match against Wales.

Acknowledging the lethargy of his squad ahead of what was the 13th Test of a gruelling season, the newly sensitised coach cancelled all training and was rewarded with a bright performance and a 37-20 victory.

Markgraaff had left South Africa as a public enemy, but he returned home on the wave of six successive Test victories, and the captain who had run across the field specifically to congratulate his coach at the end of the Test in Paris led the praise. "Whatever anyone had said about his selections, André knew where he wanted to take the team," Teichmann reflects. "The players responded to him during the tour and, by the day we beat Wales, he seemed to have come into his own as an international coach. He appeared in control."

Appearances can be deceiving.

The Springbok coach resigned seven weeks later, forced to relinquish his career following the publication of a recorded telephone conversation in which he used racist language to describe black members of the SARFU Executive. A vast majority of white rugby supporters clearly sympathised with Markgraaff, who had been treacherously entrapped by an embittered Griqualand West player, but his language caused offence among black and coloured communities, and would not be condoned within the rainbow nation. So he sank.

Teichmann was bitterly disappointed by the unexpected turn of events. He had initially hoped a public apology would save the coach's job, and he had been on the point of declaring his support for Markgraaff when he was firmly instructed to remain silent by SARFU. In the end, he could do nothing.

"It was a personal tragedy for André," the captain remembers, "and it was a massive disappointment for the Springboks because his resignation was going to take us back to square one. The confidence we had gained on tour was based around André's presence and structures. Now, we would have to spend another season becoming accustomed to somebody else in charge."

In searching for a fifth national coach in six seasons, SARFU appeared to face a clear choice between Nick Mallett and Carel du Plessis. Mallett had years of experience coaching in France and with Boland, but was renowned as a blunt, strong-minded, often unpredictable character; Du Plessis presented a clean-cut, eloquent, more considered personality, but his coaching experience amounted to no more than a few months helping a minor student team.

One candidate presented obvious coaching credentials; the other offered an eye-catching public profile. Both men had contributed to the Springbok tour to Europe at the end of the previous season, but Teichmann and his players were astonished when Du Plessis was given the job in the fragile hope that the "Prince of Wings" could somehow evolve into a "Prince of Coaches".

The captain recalls: "Carel was an extremely civilised person with a deep understanding of the game, but in appointing him as coach the Union essentially put public relations ahead of coaching experience. It was disappointing, but not surprising, that the players had not been consulted at all."

Within several days of his appointment, Du Plessis and his assistant,

Gert Smal, took the trouble to travel to Durban and meet Teichmann over breakfast at a beachfront hotel, and the captain was pleased when the new coach asked him to continue leading the team. They discussed strategy and logistics and, as fresh fruit was followed by toast, the captain grew in confidence.

Ah well, he concluded, at least Du Plessis would be able to settle into the job with a series against the Lions rather than be plunged into the cauldron of the Tri-Nations. The Home Unions had generally been happy to restrict the southern powers to victory margins of fewer than 30 points during the frantic early years of professionalism, and South Africa awaited its first Lions tour for 23 seasons, hoping only that the visitors would offer some resistance.

Amid the traditionally held conviction that the pallid chaps from the north would be physically overwhelmed by the tanned brutes on the veld, defeat was not even contemplated. Du Plessis's side hammered Tonga 74-10 in a warm-up Test, and prepared to swarm all over the Lions.

Meanwhile at an army camp near London, two veterans of the 1974 Lions, reunited as the driving force of the 1997 squad, were subjecting their players to a rigorous training and fitness programme with the Royal Marines. Fran Cotton, as manager, and Ian McGeechan, as coach, understood the nature of the challenge ahead. Led by Martin Johnson, the Lions prepared for a rugby war.

Teichmann had prospered through another creditable Super 12 campaign, leading Natal to the semifinals, and he was not overly concerned when the Lions started to squeeze victory after victory from an intimidating schedule of provincial matches, losing only to Northern Transvaal. His Springboks mustered for the first Test in Cape Town as overwhelming favourites to win.

The home team started powerfully, dominated for long periods, but failed to seize a series of scoring chances and found themselves involved in a dogfight as rain began to fall and the match hurtled into the closing minutes. Teichmann had excelled in the loose, at one stage majestically bouncing out of a tackle to create space for substitute Russell Bennett to score, yet his team appeared to freeze as they crept into the last eight minutes with a 16-15 lead.

In a frenetic blur of red jerseys and raised British voices, Matt Dawson and Alan Tait jubilantly scored late tries; and, before the Springboks knew what had hit them, they were back in their Newlands changing room reduced to astonished silence by a 27-16 defeat. The captain reflects. "It was much worse than losing to Australia or the All Blacks because we knew we were the stronger side, but what really upset me was the sense that we were right back in the same cycle of crisis and chaos that we suffered in 1996. It was like Groundhog Day. After all our hard work on tour to Europe, we were starting all over again."

The captain did not escape criticism, specifically for allowing Japie Mulder to stay on the field with an injured shoulder, a handicap that perhaps contributed to the late breaches in the Springbok defence, and the muttering classes began to suggest Teichmann was "a nice guy, but not a captain".

He responded with a characteristic shrug and a determination to square the series in the second Test at King's Park in Durban. Yet the Springbok captain was starting to feel vulnerable again: Du Plessis and Smal lacked the experience to take control and restore morale, and the new team manager, Arthob Petersen, was plainly not able to address and galvanise the players. He started to wonder how François Pienaar would have fared without the support of Morné du Plessis and Kitch Christie. As the pressure multiplied, Teichmann sensed the burden of responsibility was thudding down on his shoulders, alone.

In desperation, he looked to his more experienced players, such as Joost van der Westhuizen and Mark Andrews, to develop confidence within the side by making a positive comment at breakfast or setting a bold example at training. He yearned for the players to strut again, to show the same self-assurance, even the arrogance, they had started to develop on tour in France.

Instead, he saw only fear in their wide eyes, a dread fear of becoming only the second Springbok team to lose against the Lions. After one practice at King's Park, Teichmann happened to see Ian McIntosh and he shared his concerns with his Natal coach. "Keep going, Gary," he said. "Just keep going."

The second Test in Durban unfolded as the most disappointing match of the captain's entire career. His players carried the fight to the Lions, monopolised possession in every phase, scored three tries without reply, and might very easily have scored another three, and yet still lost 15-18 to a late drop goal that seemed almost embarrassed to squirt over the crossbar.

At the final whistle, Teichmann stood with his hands on his knees, doubled forward, staring at the turf, unable to believe what had taken place. Overcome by exhaustion and disappointment, he roused himself to shake hands with the wildly celebrating Lions and began to trudge disconsolately from the field. His team had aimed six place kicks between the uprights, none particularly difficult, and missed all six. There was no explanation, no consolation, no deliverance.

The scene he found in the home changing room had become frustratingly familiar over the past two seasons: large men slumped in the seats, tears welling in their eyes, suffering the dishonour of becoming the second South African team to lose a series against the Lions, distraught in the belief they had let down their families, their friends, their coaches and team-mates, let their country down. Amid silence, the captain said nothing, showered, dressed and left.

Perhaps only Hannes Marais, who had suffered similar agony 23 seasons earlier, fully understood the depths of Teichmann's despair.

His instinct was to accept responsibility for the defeat and, manfully facing the media an hour after the final whistle, he blamed himself for failing to nominate a designated goal kicker before the match. With three proven kickers in the side, he had not thought it necessary. He assumed that, even if two were firing blanks, the other would find form. On this awful day, Henry Honiball, Percy Montgomery and André Joubert had each missed two out of two.

The captain reflects: "Just two successful kicks would probably have made the difference between winning and losing the series."

Loyalty prevented him from expressing any reservations about Du Plessis as an international coach. The former Springbok wing had worked hard, always been honest and earnest, but his tenure was characterised by a series of lengthy meetings when the players were invited to discuss the coach's vision of how the game should be played. Intense eyes darting around the room, Du Plessis would speak passionately about the importance of skills, and movement, and versatility, of releasing players from restrictions, freeing them to play their natural game. He spoke with conviction and belief, but, before long, players were stealing glances at their watches, staring at the floor, playing with their fingers.

Teichmann recalls: "Carel was excited about what he believed our squad could achieve, but his message was not getting through. Even for me, his vision seemed fuzzy and difficult to implement. Perhaps there was too much pressure around for us to absorb his ideas, but I have always believed the game is about winning and retaining the ball and then converting that possession into points. In general, I think we needed to keep things simple."

As the series against the Lions progressed, increasingly frustrated players asked the captain to intervene and suggest to the coach that the team meetings should be kept shorter, and that any time should be spent discussing the detail of set moves and defensive patterns rather than the "vision".

Teichmann felt uncomfortable. His inclination had usually been to smooth rather than to confront difficult situations, yet he felt compelled to act on behalf of his disgruntled players. He duly raised the issues with the coach, but came away with the unsettling impression that Du Plessis was disappointed in him for failing to understand, and defend, what he was trying to convey.

In defeat, under pressure, relationships were fraying. When the captain overheard a group of players angrily blaming one another for the defeat in Durban, he intervened to soothe tempers and change the subject. Provincial divisions had started to emerge. Rugby seemed like a day-job again.

Ellis Park staged an essentially meaningless Test for the second season in succession and, with the series already lost, the Springbok captain derived no more pleasure from the 35-16 win in the third Test against the Lions than he had in defeating the demob-happy New Zealanders in 1996. He was, however, sorely disappointed to miss the concluding seven minutes of the match because he had been in the medical centre receiving stitches in a head wound.

"It was a personal thing," he reflects. "So many things had gone wrong, I had this idea in my head that I must be on the field to see the series right through to the finish. I wanted to be known as somebody who did not shirk responsibility, especially in tough times. If people wanted to blame me for losing, that was fine. I could take the criticism. Nine times out of ten, we would have won the series with plenty to spare, but we had lost. I congratulated the Lions for their fantastic spirit and exceptional planning. They maximised their resources."

Teichmann was named as the outstanding Springbok of the series, but the award felt meaningless in the context of a series defeat.

The second Tri-Nations series was starting to loom as a daunting prospect for the South Africans but, to his great credit, when other coaches may have cut their losses and launched a damage-limitation exercise to save their position, Du Plessis persisted with his expansive, skills-orientated strategy. Even in losing to the Lions, he had effectively blooded bright young talents like Percy Montgomery, Pieter Rossouw, André Snyman and Danie van Schalkwyk; and, under pressure to recall more experienced players, he kept faith with his idealistic principles and courageously invested his future in the future of his players.

After 30 minutes of his team's opening match of the series, against the All Blacks at Ellis Park, it seemed as if Du Plessis's vision had sprung to life. Dramatically raising their game, Teichmann's team produced an outstanding spell of compelling rugby, with the forwards dominating as a unit and the back line showing power and class. The young coach's pulse quickened as his Springboks powered into an extraordinary, wholly deserved 23-7 lead.

Sadly this period proved to be nothing more than a tantalising glimpse of the paradise where Du Plessis hoped to guide his team. South Africa conceded two soft tries in the space of three minutes before half time and, for all their guts, eventually yielded a late penalty to lose a titanic match 35-32.

Teichmann recalls: "We were praised for our performance but, in a sense, it was even more disappointing to have played so well and still finished with yet another defeat. Carel's bold tactics deserved much better, but I could sense the last remnants of confidence draining away from our side."

The captain desperately wanted to feel optimistic as the squad prepared to fly east to play Tests in Brisbane and Auckland, wanted to be professional and positive, but he found it hard to overlook the fact that his team appeared painfully vulnerable in so many areas; and he knew the slightest signal of weakness would be ruthlessly exploited by the Wallabies and All Blacks.

He feared the worst, and his worst fears were realised.

The Springboks produced a truly wretched performance against Australia in Brisbane, appearing lethargic, almost uninterested, and the team was relieved to escape with nothing more severe than a 33-22 defeat. Teichmann struggled to sleep that night and, in the lonely small hours, arrived at a decision that he would resign as captain at the end of the Tri-Nations series. He felt powerless to rescue the situation; he no longer felt able to motivate the team.

The captain's mood had not been improved when the Brisbane hotel staff brought a pile of facsimile messages from South Africa, all written since the end of the Test, to his room. The captain proceeded to read every one, ranging from a succinct one-word model ("Resign!") to the foulest abuse.

The team travelled to New Zealand, and began to disintegrate: the players were sniping at one another, the coaches appeared hesitant and uncertain, and the level of management plunged to standards that would have embarrassed a social XV. Teichmann sensed his team had become a laughing stock.

It was almost dark when the team arrived to practise at Eden Park on the Thursday evening before the Test, so the captain asked if the floodlights could be switched on. He was told there were no floodlights. He enquired why training had been booked at that time. The local official smirked as he said the South African management had requested that time. After 15 rushed minutes of lineout calls in twilight, the bewildered players returned to their hotel.

Worse was to follow. Management miscalculated the journey time from the team hotel to Eden Park on the day of the match, and the Springboks were left to battle through a heavy traffic jam before arriving, harassed and distracted, just 25 minutes before kick-off. "We were meant to be world champions," Teichmann recalls, "and we couldn't even arrive at the stadium on time."

Bloody-minded and downright angry, the South Africans trailed only 21-23 at half time, but they had lost both flankers, with Ruben Kruger breaking his ankle and André Venter being sent off for stamping on Fitzpatrick; and the second half unfolded as a one-sided rout. No Springbok side had ever conceded 50 points in a Test match ... until this most dismal afternoon in Auckland.

Fitzpatrick savoured the record-breaking 55-35 victory, and the All Black captain hardly attempted to suppress a smile when he told the media afterwards that he was disappointed not to have won by a larger margin.

The Springbok squad was summoned to a crisis meeting with Louis Luyt at their hotel later that same night, and it was James Small who plucked up the courage to tell the SARFU president that the players had been let down by their management. When Luyt warned the wing to be careful what he said about the people who paid his mortgage, Teichmann stepped forward.

"Dr Luyt, you should know that James is not expressing a personal view," the captain said. "That is the opinion of the entire squad."

Luyt stared at the captain, and the captain stared back. He may not be the type of man who seeks confrontation, might be the type of man who tries to avoid confrontation. Yet, once confronted, Teichmann stands.

The meeting ended amid indignation and antipathy, and the captain strode directly to his hotel room where he immediately telephoned his wife, Nicky, to tell her what had happened. "That's it," he declared. "I have had enough. I will resign after the Test against Australia. I have made up my mind."

Neither the captain nor anyone else could have predicted what happened at Loftus Versfeld when, with New Zealand celebrating a second Tri-Nations title, Australia and South Africa played out the last fixture of the series. The Wallabies edged into a 15-13 lead moments before half time but were then overwhelmed by a Springbok exhibition of irrepressible attacking rugby. The home team ran in no fewer than eight tries and posted a stunning 61-22 victory.

Two weeks after conceding the record score, South Africa was handing out a record defeat. The captain was delighted, and somewhat surprised. Indeed, as the stream of smiling officials flowed through the changing room, offering their warm congratulations, he decided this was probably not an appropriate moment to offer his resignation. The triumph was hailed as the realisation of Du Plessis's vision, and Teichmann opted to remain in the saddle.

"It had been a hectic period," he recalls. "One week, you think things can't get any worse; a fortnight later, you reckon things can't get any better. I believed my own form was pretty consistent, and that gave me the confidence to hang in there as captain. The general view was that the win at Loftus eased the pressure on Carel, and he appeared to be settling down as coach."

Once again, appearances were deceiving.

Several weeks later, the Springbok captain turned on a television to watch the evening news, and saw Du Plessis had been sacked.

"I felt sympathy for Carel," Teichmann reflects. "The Union knew about his inexperience when they appointed him to coach the side, and I think he deserved more than four months to start producing consistent results. It was hard to blame Carel because he was on the right track. It was SARFU's impatience for a quick-fix that meant every new season brought a new coach."

Du Plessis and Smal, his assistant, contested the terms of their dismissal, taking SARFU to court. During the course of these proceedings, the captain was requested by representatives of the Union to provide evidence in support of their reasons for cancelling the contracts of the two coaches.

He refused.

"Whatever happened, I had still been Carel's captain," he remembers. "He had stood by me, and he deserved my loyalty in return."

Nick Mallett was bitterly disappointed when his application to be

Springbok coach was rejected in February 1997 but, within six months, SARFU was virtually applying to him. With no other serious candidate in sight, this rugged rugby man arrived at the Union offices with a list of requirements, essentially interviewed the panel and, in his own time, agreed to accept the challenge.

It is perhaps worth noting that the two post-isolation Springbok coaches to be given total control, Christie and Mallett, enjoyed the most success.

Teichmann welcomed the appointment, but started to doubt whether his magic carpet would remain airborne. In years gone by, it would have been quite inconceivable for a Springbok captain to retain his position after a home defeat against the All Blacks, and completely unimaginable that the same man should carry on after losing to the Lions a year later, yet he did survive because, rightly, a general consensus did not hold him responsible for the defeats.

Captains such as Johan Claassen and Avril Malan may have been ritually blamed for defeats, but their modern successors invariably tucked in behind their coaches in the unforgiving line for public execution.

In a sense, Teichmann had started to assume the status of a life jacket for Springbok rugby in the heaving oceans of defeat and controversy, something for the game to cling on to during times of trouble and change.

Mallett saw no reason to make a change, and swiftly invited the eighthman to remain as captain. In years to come, Teichmann would reflect with pleasure on his unprecedented and genuinely remarkable distinction of being the nominated choice as captain of a third successive Springbok coach.

In the middle of October 1997, however, his spirits sank at the prospect of listening to yet another coach outline his strategy and vision. The process felt like moving house for the third time in 15 months: he liked the look of the destination, it was the process that he found exhausting and depressing.

As the national squad gathered for another marathon end-of-year tour to Italy, France, England and Scotland, the captain appeared sullen and quiet. This was not his nature. Mallett, more sensitive than his reputation suggests, noticed the problem and, not long after his squad's arrival in Bologna, selected a suitable moment to engage the morose leader in conversation.

"Gary, what's the matter?"

"How do you mean?"

"Well, you're not yourself."

Teichmann explained the reasons for his fatigue, outlining how he craved stability, how he wanted to settle down with one coach and play at a consistently high level. As he unloaded, the captain half-expected the new coach would stand up, smash a glass, tell him to stop moaning, remind him of his salary, and instruct him to improve his attitude or catch the next flight home.

"I completely understand," Mallett replied.

"What?"

"I understand what you are saying. If I had been in your position, I believe I would be feeling exactly the same kind of frustrations."

The two men began to find common ground: they shared a similar heritage as talented sportsmen from established English-speaking schools, Teichmann at Hilton and Mallett at St Andrew's; they both approached the game in determined, whole-hearted fashion, both played hard on and off the field, enjoyed a beer now and then, in their youth had enjoyed several beers now and then.

Animated and intelligent, Mallett outlined his coaching and management structures, explaining why he had appointed the studious Alan Solomons as his assistant coach and Rob van der Valk, a Cape Town businessman, as a highly competent administrative, logistic and commercial manager.

Teichmann felt inspired and invigorated. After two years of confusion, he sensed the professionals had finally taken control.

He started to revel in the bloke-ish atmosphere within the squad, the ethos of decency and responsibility, the accurate planning and easy laughter. Several Afrikaans-speaking players did seem ill-at-ease when the profoundly passionate coach laid into a prop who missed a tackle, but they grew to respect a man who was direct and logical, who was quick to anger and quick to forgive, who wanted nothing more than for his Springboks to be successful.

When Mallett outlined his game plan in two words – score tries – even the tight forwards showed glimmers of understanding. Communication is the art that oils the spirit of every group, in any area of life, and this coach initially showed a rare ability to communicate his ideas as simple logic.

"We have to score four tries to win a Test match," Mallett would declare, round eyes alive with zeal, his voice racing with gusto. "On the basis that we will convert half our chances, then we must create eight opportunities in every match. If we are sure we can kick a penalty, then we'll take the three points, but if there is any doubt, then we kick for touch near the corner and aim to drive through the lineout for the try. Seven points is always better than three."

The utterly professional manner in which Mallett and his team organised the squad completely transformed Teichmann's life as captain.

Surrounded by direct, capable people, deriving energy and direction from an infectious coach, he felt able to concentrate purely on his players and his own performance. Niggling issues were resolved before they became full-blown crises, and heavy responsibilities shared ceased to feel like a burden.

Mallett would bound into breakfast every morning, speaking to his players, outlining a new idea, telling an old story, listening, inspiring; and the captain and coach spoke often and easily, sharing concerns and thoughts, developing mutual respect and trust. Gary called him Nick; Nick called him Gary. They got along, no problems, no secrets, a couple of mates sharing a beer.

The new coach had demanded tries, and his appetite was sated during an enterprising 62-31 victory over Italy in Bologna. Confidence was flooding through an unchanged team and, moving on to Lyon, the Springboks swiftly established a commanding 36-15 lead in the first Test against France. Despite losing Van der Westhuizen with a serious groin injury, the team withstood a passionate French revival in the second half and were relieved to win 36-32.

South Africa was cast in the supporting role at the second Test, the last rugby international to be played at the Parc des Princes, as a powerfully patriotic capacity crowd demanded a triumphant adieu to the famous stadium constructed above the motorway speeding around the Bois de Boulogne.

A few moments before two o'clock, banks of French supporters sang their national anthem with heaving lungs and moist eyes, as they prepared to roar the royal blue jerseys to victory. Within 70 minutes, an unprecedented transformation had taken place. The hometown crowd had started to scream out "Ole!" in unison every time yet another Springbok pass went to hand; their emotional fervour had been converted into the most gracious and enthusiastic appreciation of what was a truly momentous performance by the touring side.

Teichmann recalls: "I had never seen the Springboks play better. There were so many great performances, but the image of the game that endures in my mind is of Rassie Erasmus intercepting deep inside our half and sprinting upfield before unloading for Pieter Rossouw to score the try."

France 10, South Africa 52: Mallett told his side afterwards how, in years to come, they would gather and recall the events of this incredible day.

An exceptional team had risen from the ashes of Eden Park: Montgomery at fullback, Small and Rossouw on the wings, Snyman and the veteran Dick Muir at centre, Honiball and Werner Swanepoel as the halfback partners; props Os du Randt and Adrian Garvey, James Dalton as hooker; Mark Andrews and Krynauw Otto at lock; André Venter, Erasmus and Teichmann in the back row.

The captain wondered how on earth this side had lost a series against the Lions, and he used the painful memories of that defeat to motivate the players for the tour's concluding internationals, against England at Twickenham and against Scotland at Murrayfield. Both teams would be packed with Lions in their national jerseys, and both matches presented an opportunity for revenge.

England's forwards competed effectively during the first half, but the Test turned when André Snyman scored a memorable try, zigging in, zagging out from 30 metres, and the Springboks glided to an impressive 29-11 victory. When they had every right to be mentally and physically exhausted at the end of yet another long season, the South Africans were smiling and thriving.

This was indeed their day-job, but it was fun as well.

Mallett and Teichmann played golf together around the Old Course at St Andrews, discussed the progress made on tour, mulled over selections, enjoyed each other's company. As they primed their touring team to be rigorous, a willing Scotland side found itself in the wrong place at the wrong time.

The 1951/52 Springboks had left a permanent mark on Scottish rugby with a 44-0 victory at Murrayfield. Forty-six seasons later, another South African team ran amok in Edinburgh, engraving a 68-10 triumph in the history books. Inspired and organised, Teichmann's team appeared unstoppable.

A season that had started with humiliation against the Lions ended with a reception at the Presidential Guesthouse in Pretoria. Nelson Mandela might not have found the time to attend a rugby Test match since the 1995 World Cup final, but the President seemed eager to congratulate a side that had not only excelled on the field, but had also emerged as smiling ambassadors.

Captain and coach kept in contact throughout the Christmas holidays, and they met several times during the 1998 Super 12 campaign, sharing ideas and opinions, unaffected and open, transparent, in harmony. They spoke even when there seemed nothing much to say, just to stay in touch; and they quietly agreed that 1998 would be the season when South Africa set aside a "played eight, won two" record in the event and won the Tri-Nations series.

Four home Tests against northern hemisphere opposition represented an ideal preparation for sterner challenges ahead, but these matches failed to excite an increasingly selective rugby public grown fat on the surplus of top-class rugby, and the once-unimagined spectacle of a Springbok team running out to play in a half-empty stadium became a feature of the professional era.

Teichmann took change in his stride. "Test rugby was not devalued," he insists. "When the Springboks played one series every few years, each Test did seem like a massive event and many supporters would be able to remember the result for the rest of their lives. But the pace and structure of the modern game is different, and the fact that we play six or seven home Tests each year is bound to leave some matches seeming more significant than others."

So the Springboks prepared through four successive Saturdays of official warm-up matches. Ireland adopted a bar-brawl approach but were overwhelmed 37-12 in Bloemfontein and 33-0 in Pretoria. England arrived from a thrashing in Australia, and seemed satisfied to lose only 18-0 in the rain at Newlands. Wales ran out at Loftus Versfeld with a virtual second team and a caretaker coach, and were annihilated 96-3 before a plainly uninterested crowd.

Almost unnoticed amid media moaning about sub-standard opposition, the team had now won ten Tests in succession and, for the first time, approached the Tri-Nations series with confidence. The 1998 schedule took the Springboks east to play their away matches before returning for the home games. "We felt like we were a reasonable side," the captain recalls, "but we knew we were nothing until we had won in Australia and New Zealand. It was all very well crushing northern hemisphere teams, but the real challenge still lay ahead."

The match against the Wallabies was played in Perth, and neither team managed to rise above the drenched conditions. Amid unforced errors and much slipping and sliding, Van der Westhuizen's instinctive tapped penalty and twist for the try line carried South Africa to a 13-12 victory.

On the Monday evening at the hotel, Mallett launched into a meticulous video examination of the performance. The coach was brisk, business-like, gruff and evidently not happy as he criticised his team for showing Australia too much respect. It had become routine for each player to receive a personalised, typed report after every Test, detailing what he had done right and what he had done wrong. In Perth, the players read in silence, and felt chastened.

"And by the way," the coach said, shuffling his notes together at the end of an intense hour and a half," you have just become the first Springbok team to win away in the Tri-Nations. Congratulations!" Mallett smiled, all teeth and heart. His players smiled back. The All Blacks awaited in Wellington.

Teichmann's side had developed order and discipline through the previous eleven Tests, and the captain needed his team to maintain these qualities under relentless pressure from the home side. He recognised New Zealand would take their share of possession, but would his players be able to defend?

Soon after half time, the Springbok captain suffered the indignity of being brushed aside by Jonah Lomu on the charge, but his teammates halted the giant in his tracks, kept concentrating, and kept tackling. With eight minutes remaining of a typically close-fought contest, South Africa held an 8-3 lead.

"Keep tackling, guys," he urged. "Keep concentrating."

On an increasingly rare sortie upfield, the Springboks took a lineout on the All Black 22-metre line. Clean ball was whipped to flyhalf Henry Honiball who shaped to feed his line but neatly popped an inside pass into the hands of Pieter Rossouw, bursting on the loop at pace. The lanky left wing strode through a gap in the defence, burst clear, scored without being touched by a defender, and was soon smothered by the embrace of his ecstatic captain.

"It was a wonderful moment," Teichmann recalls, "and I remember looking up to see the All Blacks standing beneath their own posts arguing about who had missed the tackle. I enjoyed that. We had spent our fair share of time behind a try line in the past two years, so it felt good to be on the other side."

The Springboks celebrated their 13-3 victory in the same plain, chipboard-and-paint Athletic Park changing room where Wynand Claassen and Naas Botha had sipped champagne after an equally momentous triumph 17 years earlier. As Teichmann, Honiball, Van der Westhuizen and others linked arms to pose for the historic photographs, it was possible to blur the eyes and consider how the more things change, the more they seem to stay the same.

For South African rugby players, whether they sleep in the grandstand or a five-star hotel, whether they are paid R20 a week or R20 000 a week, a victory over New Zealand in New Zealand remains a lifetime experience.

Teichmann's team returned home amid scenes of overblown excitement, but their bubble seemed to have burst dramatically when the wounded All Blacks seized a 17-5 lead by half time at King's Park. A capacity crowd had assembled in confidence, but now stared at the scoreboard in disbelief.

Mallett walked into the Springbok changing room during the interval and told his players that, while he certainly did not expect them to win every Test, he did expect them never to lose without putting up a struggle. His words had some effect but New Zealand still extended their lead to 23-5 and, with 15 minutes left to play, the match seemed to be drifting quietly into history.

Teichmann was reconciling himself to nothing more significant than just a bad day at the office, consoled by the knowledge that victory over Australia in the final match of the series would still install his team as champions. As the minutes ticked by in near silence, several hundred spectators decided to leave early and miss the traffic congestion. They would never forgive themselves.

Van der Westhuizen lit the spark, scampering through a gap on the fringes of a maul and dashing 30 metres to the line; substitute Bobby Skinstad rounded off a move that recycled possession seven times; and, amid thunderous mayhem in the stands, Dalton crashed over from a lineout.

Three late tries, two of which were converted, had propelled South Africa from certain defeat into a 24-23 lead. The final whistle sent the All Black captain, Taine Randell, collapsing to the turf like a boxer to the canvas. Fireworks ignited the night sky above Durban, and his South African counterpart cited the freakish comeback as further evidence of his team's spirit. Just like the habit of losing in 1996, the habit of winning was hard to break in 1998.

The next day, Teichmann and Mallett emerged victorious again, on a golf course, winning their four-ball in a mini "Ryder Cup" between the Springboks and the All Blacks. However, the New Zealanders won the overall match, just about their only taste of victory in a catastrophic losing season.

As old-fashioned rugby fever rippled through the Republic once again, the South Africans prepared to play the Wallabies at Ellis Park in a game that boiled down as a kind of Tri-Nations final. The winners would be champions.

Teichmann told the entire country about his team's resolve to win, but he told nobody about the debilitating neck injury he had sustained in Wellington and exacerbated at King's Park. He knew that any doctor would tell him not to play at Ellis Park, so he didn't ask any doctor. "After all the defeats and disappointments, I was desperate to be part of a big occasion," he recalls. "It was foolish, but I took an injection to numb the pain for the duration of the match."

On a warm, hazy Saturday evening in Johannesburg, galvanised by Pieter Muller's early tackle on Tim Horan, South Africa produced a neat and disciplined performance straight from their coach's textbook. Victory was never seriously in doubt, and a 29-15 win was decorated late in the match when Skinstad burst off the reserves bench, dashed clear and swallow-dived over the line.

"It was never easy," the captain recalls, "but we kept our discipline, stayed close to the game plan, and strangled them out of the Test."

Teichmann stepped forward and yelled for Van der Westhuizen to join him on the podium and, together, as the Ellis Park crowd roared its approval, the two heroes raised the silver Tri-Nations trophy into a perfect blue sky.

This particular Springbok captain had worked tirelessly for the moment of triumph, and proved as dedicated as any, but he appeared almost indifferent to the spotlight and the glory. He was not driven in the sense that Naas Botha was driven by an insatiable hunger for such moments of self-affirmation. Teichmann's way was to work hard, accept victory or defeat with equanimity and, howsoever, to move on the next day. "Teich" was the antithesis of intense.

Van der Westhuizen told journalists afterwards that the Tri-Nations victory ranked alongside the 1995 World Cup triumph. Asked his view, the captain said he had not played in a World Cup but added that he hoped to be able to answer the question after the tournament in Wales, only 13 months away.

It was with that campaign in mind that SARFU had arranged for the South Africans to undertake a traditional Grand Slam tour at the end of 1998, enabling them to familiarise themselves with all the major venues to be used in the World Cup the following year. Their forebears had played Tests against Wales, Ireland, Scotland and England during the course of a leisurely six-month tour. The 1998 squad would meet the same challenge on successive Saturdays.

There is no doubt which team generated more profit, and there is equally no doubt which team was truly able to enjoy the experience.

For Teichmann and his squad, the tour of Britain represented the last four steps of a long journey into rugby history. Victory in each of the four Tests would extend their run of consecutive Test victories to a remarkable 18, finally eclipsing the mark set by the All Blacks during the late 1960s.

The players assembled with the flush of Tri-Nations glory visible in every smile, but the captain was startled and surprised when the coach called the Test team to a meeting and abruptly warned they would have to fight for their places because "youngsters like Skinstad are knocking at the door".

Skinstad was a richly gifted loose forward whose boyish good looks and bright personality had combined with several outstanding per- formances, both for Western Province and as an "impact" substitute for the Springboks, to provoke a nationwide outbreak of what could be called "Bobbymania".

Within sight of his 32nd birthday, Teichmann was left under no il- lusion on whose door Skinstad was knocking, but he welcomed such competition and liked the youngster. Nonetheless, he did wonder why the coach had sought to threaten a side that had just won the Tri- Nations. In any case, "Skinstad" was a name that would not often pass him by in the months that lay ahead.

As a Springbok back row, Erasmus, Venter and Teichmann were be- ing compared to Greyling, Ellis and Bedford of the late 1960s, and, despite his veiled remarks, Mallett seemed content to retain the trio for the opening Test of the tour, against Wales at their temporary home in Wembley.

In the event, it was the admired loose forwards who rescued victory from a mediocre performance: Wales were leading the tourists with barely three minutes left when Teichmann and Erasmus combined to put Venter away. This late, late try enabled South Africa to escape with a fortunate 28-20 win.

Yet Mallett sensed staleness in the team, and decided the time was ripe to introduce his trump card. In announcing the Springbok team to play Scotland, the coach stunned his players by replacing Venter with Skinstad.

Senior Springboks would later reflect on this decision as the turning point in the team's fortunes, setting in train a process that unhappily divided the squad, undermined South Africa's bid to defend the World Cup in 1999, and would even lead towards the unsatisfactory conclusion of the Mallett era.

Teichmann recalls: "I fulfilled my responsibility to support Nick's decision in public and among the team, but privately I was afraid we would seriously miss André's work rate and physical presence; and, again, I could not understand why Nick felt an overpowering need to break up the loose forward trio that helped win the Tri-Nations title. It didn't seem to make any sense."

The team was suffering a kind of division recognised since the days of the Old Testament: the established group is disrupted by a glamorous youngster who is perceived as the leader's favourite and, though no fault of his own, becomes the target of resentment. Mallett was cast as Jacob, prime Springboks took the parts of the older brothers, and Skinstad assumed the title role.

However, South African rugby's production of Bobby and his Technicolour Dreamcoat was not destined for success on the world stage.

The situation bubbled closer to the boil when the tourists produced wholly uninspired displays against both Scotland and Ireland, yet on both occasions it was the undeniably talented Skinstad who caught the eye and the headlines. He sealed the 35-10 victory at

Murrayfield with an exhilarating solo try in the closing stages, and he produced two moments of genius to break a spirited Irish effort in Dublin, galloping clear from a lineout to score soon after half time, and then, two minutes later, dashing through a gap, creating mayhem in the Irish defence, and setting up the score to secure South Africa's 27-13 win.

Mallett celebrated these heroics as vindication of his selection, but senior players blamed the coach for the poor performances because he had disrupted a successful pack of forwards. Even as the team continued to win, the atmosphere within the camp had started to sour. The structures and discipline remained tight and generally effective, but the players so recently so close to the coach seemed to become suspicious, unsettled by the knocking at their door.

The respected positions became entrenched and, piteously, old fault lines started to emerge when players from the north regarded Skinstad's selection as evidence of a Western Province bias among a coaching staff ruled by Mallett and Solomons, two dyed-in-the-wool, devoted Capetonians.

And yet, even as the green-eyed monster of provincialism reared its head again, the Springboks had kept winning, and they approached the match against England at Twickenham knowing that victory would give them a remarkable 18th consecutive Test win and the new world record.

Teichmann firmly told his players they would have to improve their form on tour by 50% to have any chance of success. "We had lost momentum since the Tri-Nations series," the captain reflects, "and had started to rely far too much on individuals to pull us clear from tight situations. We should have been riding high in so many ways, but it had been an uncomfortable tour."

On a cold and gloomy day in London, the South African forwards lacked the unitary power to subdue the England pack, and the match deteriorated into an anxious wrestling bout with neither side able to seize control. Reaching half time at 7-7, Mallett tried to break the deadlock by introducing Venter as a substitute in the second row, but the contest remained grim and tight.

Even when England edged ahead with one penalty, and then another, the thousands of expatriate South Africans in the stands believed one single moment of inspiration would carry the Springboks to victory. Yet there was to be no repeat of the tingling late heroics of King's Park or Wembley, and referee Paddy O'Brien eventually blew the final whistle on a 13-7 England victory.

Teichmann's team would have to settle for a place in history alongside the 1960s All Blacks. "I was more upset afterwards than I had ever expected to be," the captain reflects. "It was disappointing to have travelled so far and to fall at the last obstacle, but we had achieved something extraordinary. Given the speed and competitive intensity of modern rugby, I doubt whether any international side will be able to match that record of 17 successive Test wins."

Records come and records go, but if anybody had stood up in the visitors' changing room at Eden Park, Auckland, after the Springboks had conceded more than 50 points for the first time, and proclaimed the team was about to start a run of 17 wins in a row, they would have been certified insane.

That is what happened, and the record stands as a monument not only to the coaches and players who secured this success, but also to the captain who proved that, through his quiet authority, he was able not only to break the storms of 1996 and 1997 but also to make the sun shine in 1998.

And the best, he hoped, was yet to come.

For Teichmann, the 1999 Rugby World Cup had for some time loomed on the horizon as the perfect final destination of his international career. He naturally took nothing for granted, but he could surely have been forgiven for indulging just a little in dreams of an October day in Cardiff, a World Cup final at the Millennium Stadium, his hands reaching to receive the Webb Ellis trophy ...

This was no pipe dream. South Africa remained the bookmakers' favourite to win the tournament, despite losing to England; and, as captain during the past 33 Tests, Teichmann seemed certain to lead the Springbok challenge.

As he committed himself enthusiastically to pre-season training, he looked forward to proving his form and securing his place. His career had never been a shopping list of goals that he crossed off as he played along, but the 1999 World Cup seemed somehow different. It seemed like his destiny.

In the event, the eighthman was destined not to captain his country at the showpiece occasion but to become the profoundly disappointed victim of another high-profile and controversial selection dispute. Almost impossibly, and almost by definition unfairly, his long and distinguished international career was destined to fall, almost to the day, between two World Cup tournaments.

He played his debut in the first international after the 1995 World Cup, and he would play his final international barely nine weeks before the opening match in 1999. In between, he missed only one Test, through injury, won 42 caps, and led South Africa onto the field in no fewer than 36 Test matches, more often than any other man before or since, ever. And yet, this sincere, honest and dedicated man was destined never to compete at a Rugby World Cup.

The story of his painful, slow, drawn-out rejection spanned a period of four months from March until the end of July 1999, and provoked public indignation to match that aroused by the rejection of his predecessor. Great Springbok captains of the 1990s, it seemed, would only go down in a blaze of fury.

As ever, there were two sides to the saga.

Nick Mallett had sensed his side was turning stale on tour to Europe at the end of 1998, and seems to have reached a conclusion that Bobby Skinstad would become a pivotal player within his team for the World Cup. This decision led him to the unfortunate, but clear, conclusion that there was no longer any room in the Test side for his long-standing captain and eighthman.

The coach had never been a man to shrink from the tough decisions and, emboldened by his growing status within the game, secure in his own conviction, he remained steadfast in this view and wielded the axe.

Rising in his own defence, Teichmann believed his form in leading Natal to the Super 12 semifinal once again, and then in the early international matches of the season, deserved to earn him his place at the World Cup; and yet he understands that selection is the prerogative of the coach, and the coach alone.

The captain reflects: "The decision to drop me before the World Cup was neither the right decision nor the wrong decision. Some will say it was right and others say it was wrong. Those are opinions. All that really matters is that it was Nick Mallett's job to make such decisions, right or wrong.

"However, I only wish that he and I could have sat down together at some stage and discussed the situation with mutual respect and civility. I wish the issue could have been handled in a more decent manner."

The national captain and coach had been so close for the past 18 months that Teichmann became concerned when he heard and saw nothing of the coach during the early weeks of the season. When Mallett did eventually telephone, he seemed curt and defensive, crotchety and short-tempered.

"Hi, Nick, is everything OK?" the captain asked innocently.

"Look, Gary, I am sorry," darted the reply. "I can't give you any guarantee at all. The squad will be chosen on form. It's the only way."

"Er, fine. No problem."

Teichmann was perplexed. His casual greeting had been misunderstood as a direct enquiry about his place in the team. For so long, he had been on the same wavelength as the coach. Now, he seemed to be on FM while Mallett was on medium wave. Something had changed, something felt wrong.

Barely two weeks later, the coach called again, to explain that Jake White, the Springbok technical adviser, was leaving the squad. The captain was worried because, apart from his significant contribution, White came from Johannesburg and, for many of the players from the north, represented an important influence in an otherwise Western Province-oriented coaching staff.

"Some of the players will be disappointed," Teichmann replied.

Mallett barked back: "Look, Gary, I do not need approval from the players to make a decision. It is my job to select the staff."

"Er, fine."

The tone of two telephone calls suggested the chemistry, mutual trust and understanding had evaporated, but there had been no meeting or explanation. At the time, the captain wondered if he was being paranoid. With hindsight, he looks back and suspects he would have been omitted from the national squad for three warm-up Tests ahead of the 1999 Tri-Nations series if Skinstad had driven home safely after the Stormers' match against Canterbury at Newlands.

Instead, the hugely talented youngster suffered a serious knee injury when he crashed his car, and Mallett's plans were thrown into confusion. Assured that Skinstad would recover before the World Cup, the coach seems to have decided he would retain Teichmann as captain in the meantime.

Thus, a semblance of normality was retained when the Springbok squad assembled to play two home Tests against Italy in June. Teichmann was named as captain and he kept his head down, concentrated on his own form, resolved to convey an impression of business as usual. So far as he knew for certain, it was business as usual. The coach seemed cordial, if not warm.

He led the side to an emphatic 74-0 victory in Port Elizabeth, but was later frustrated to find that, against such modest opposition, he had managed to strain a hamstring and would not be able to play in the second Test seven days later in Durban, missing an international for the first time in almost three years.

In the reshuffle that followed, Corné Krige, the gifted 24-year-old Western Province flanker, was chosen to win a first Test cap against the Italians at King's Park, and then nominated to captain South Africa on his debut.

Educated at Paarl Boys' High, he had emerged through Craven Week and the South African Schools XV before making his provincial debut at the age of 20. Persistent injury slowed his progress but he repeatedly and bravely regained full fitness until, modelling his rugby on New Zealand's Josh Kronfeld, he started to attract attention as a courageous and effective ball-fetcher.

Krige could hardly be faulted on his debut in Durban, leading South Africa to a 101-0 romp over the wretched Italians, but Teichmann swiftly recovered and was recalled without fuss to captain his team in the third Test of the year, against Wales in Cardiff. As world champions, the Springboks had been invited to play in the one-off Test to mark the opening of the Millennium Stadium.

The seven-day excursion to Wales unfolded as an unmitigated disaster for Springbok rugby. Simmering fears among the players that the team had become subject to unspoken racial quotas, whereby each side selected needed to include black or coloured players, erupted in an acrimonious meeting at the team hotel, where a Union official was openly booed when he warned the Springboks should either accept transformation or make a living somewhere else.

Two days later, quite unsurprisingly, the players produced a disillusioned performance in becoming the first South African team ever to lose against Wales. In the wake of a humiliating 29-19 defeat, the triumphs of 1998 suddenly started to seem a long, long time ago. Teichmann, at least, had performed well and was desperately striving to hang tough, and hope for the best.

As the unforgiving Tri-Nations series approached, Mallett found himself in an increasingly desperate situation. Skinstad's recovery was taking much longer than anyone had expected, although he appeared on course to play in the World Cup, and it had become evident that neither Joost van der Westhuizen nor Henry Honiball was fit to play away in Australia or New Zealand.

So, almost by default, Teichmann led an inexperienced Springbok team to play the All Blacks in Dunedin. Again the captain produced a resolved individual display at the heart of his side, and was nominated as the Springbok Man of the Match, but South Africa had failed to score in a 28-0 defeat.

Mallett appeared strangely detached from the team. He had thrown a pair of talented young halfbacks in at the deep end of Tri-Nations rugby but, after the Test, lambasted them in the media as "evidently not up to international standard". Teichmann was dismayed by the remark and then dismayed to discover that, in a round of pre-Test predictions among the Springbok management, the coach had actually given his projection as a 32-25 All Black victory.

Players started to feel as if Mallett had disowned the side, at least until the first-choice players returned to full fitness. The captain recalls: "This was not the same man that we had known and admired so much in 1998. It was strange. The empathy and humility seem to have temporarily disappeared, and the vibe from his management group left me, personally, feeling as though, after three years, I had become surplus to requirements. It wasn't much fun."

The endgame was drawing near.

Teichmann had suffered a knock on his thigh during the match against the All Blacks and, as a haematoma developed, the team doctor soon ruled him out of the team to play the Wallabies in Brisbane a week later. Resolved to stand by his side in such difficult times, the eighthman declined a chance to fly home, and remained to assist and advise his successor as captain.

Krige would have been the palpable choice to move into the breach as he had done so capably against Italy, but the luckless loose forward had suffered another serious injury in Dunedin, and Mallett imposed the captaincy on Rassie Erasmus, the gifted 26-year-old loose forward who had notably recoiled from the chance to lead the national side when the post became available against Italy.

An absolutely dedicated player, he gave the impression of preferring life as one of the young Turks in the squad, enjoying the spirit and the good times, sitting in the back row of the bus. Where some saw authority and responsibility as an honour, he regarded it as an unnecessary burden.

Erasmus was born and bred in Despatch, the same passionate Eastern Cape rugby town that gave Danie Gerber to a grateful nation, but he enrolled at university in Bloemfontein and eventually emerged in the Free State team as a formidable, wonderfully mobile and effective loose forward. He played his Test debut in 1996 and soon earned a golden global reputation.

In Brisbane, in crisis, he finally agreed to captain the side against Australia and was grateful for the presence of Teichmann, his long-time back row comrade and friend, through several meetings before the match. Erasmus tried valiantly to rally his side through an uncomfortable afternoon, but his efforts were in vain, and South Africa slipped to another demoralising defeat, by 32-6.

Teichmann recalls: "I sat in the stands, watching us lose to the Wallabies, and I realised it was necessary to bring the situation to a conclusion, one way or the other. Everything was drifting. So I approached Nick and we agreed to meet in his hotel room at nine o'clock the next morning."

The captain knocked firmly on the door.

"Come in."

Mallett was sitting on a sofa, with assistant coach Alan Solomons faithfully at his side. The mood seemed business-like and clinical.

"OK, Gary, what's the problem?" the coach asked bluntly.

"Well, there is clearly some sort of problem. You don't communicate with me any more. I would just like to know where I stand."

There was a pause. Then, Mallett blurted: "Look, I must tell you Bobby is definitely going to the World Cup as eighthman."

"OK, that is your decision."

"Yes, it is."

The split was becoming muddled and unpleasant. The captain had asked what was the problem, and the coach had incongruously replied by declaring his plans for a player who had been injured for three months. There was no logic, no clear communication, no plain speaking, no decency.

Three days after the squad's return to South Africa, Teichmann was told by a journalist that he was going to be dropped for the rest of the Tri-Nations. He sought clarification from Mallett, left two voice messages on the coach's mobile phone, and happened to be at King's Park, receiving physiotherapy treatment on his injured thigh, when the coach finally returned his call.

"Gary?"

"Yes."

"I have decided to change the captain for the rest of the Tri-Nations series. I don't believe you can hold down your place in the side anymore, and I think you should go back to the Natal team and play in the Currie Cup."

"But, Nick, if I may say so, I played pretty well in the second half against Wales and I was man of the match against the All Blacks."

"Look, Gary, that's my decision."

Mallett, an inherently decent man, accepts that the matter could have been handled more effectively, but insists he was not able formally to tell Teichmann of the decision until it had been cleared by SARFU. The coach reflects: "The problem arose when a member of the SAR-FU Executive leaked the information to a journalist in Durban, who then telephoned Gary. When he contacted me, I was in a difficult situation because I had still not received any clearance from SARFU. It was very unfortunate."

Teichmann switched off his telephone and drove directly home to share the heart-rending news with his wife, Nicky. This inherently calm man, apparently so even-tempered and controlled in every situation, privately came to terms with the fact that his Springbok career was over, with the fact that, after all, he would not have the opportunity to lead his country at the World Cup.

The history of the tournament is the poorer without him.

He would retain his dignity throughout the days and weeks that followed, as both he and Mallett resisted the temptation to enter into any public slanging match. The captain was content to set down his perspective on the matter calmly in his best-selling autobiography published in June 2000.

From the day he relinquished the Springbok captaincy, his path followed an eerily similar path to that taken by Pienaar three years earlier.

Like the world champion, Teichmann responded to the disappointment by producing a series of outstanding performances in leading his provincial side to the Currie Cup final. Like the world champion, he was denied the fairy-tale finale when his team were defeated in that final. Like the world champion, he soon left South Africa to take up a brand-new challenge in Britain.

"Nicky and I decided the time was right to spend a couple of years away from all the fuss and controversy," he recalls. "I was sad to leave Natal after 15 years with the province, particularly because we had received such unbelievable support from the Natal public, but I was given an unforgettable send-off, beside Ian McIntosh and André Joubert, after the Currie Cup final."

He joined Newport, a fallen club in South Wales being revived by Tony Brown, a wealthy businessman, and was soon joined by fellow South Africans Andy Marinos, Franco Smith and Adrian Garvey in the amber-and-gold-striped jerseys. He grew to loathe the weather, but to love the club.

Through two years, Teichmann inspired Newport back to the top of Welsh rugby and into the European Cup, finally ending his association and retiring from the game with victory in the final of the Principality Cup on 13 May 2001.

The club had begged him to extend his contract by another year, but the eighthman longed to return home to Natal, to start work for his earth-moving and construction company, Teichmann Civils, and to sink quietly back into the stable family life that he had known as a child, and sought as a father.

Gary Teichmann captained South Africa in more Tests than anyone else, and led the team to more consecutive Test wins than anyone else; yet, through this success, he remained the same humble, decent, likeable man.

His ultimate reward was not the Webb Ellis trophy, as he had hoped, but a much greater prize: the enduring affection of millions of South Africans.

14 THE PROFESSIONALS

For Springbok captains, more money meant less responsibility.

Until the early 1980s, the amateur captain of the South African rugby side acted like a CEO. He was accountable both to the convenor of selectors and the Board, but in essence he took the decisions and accepted ultimate responsibility for the discipline, image, training and strategy of the team.

Management groups started to play a greater role through the 1980s and into the 1990s, with a coach handling matters on the field and a manager taking charge of administrative and logistical issues, but the captain still retained major influence and standing as a significant director in the side.

Perversely, the advent of professional rugby in 1995 enriched the captain with a substantial monthly salary, but it also diminished him to the status of mere employee, subject to instruction by the Union and the coach. As the hundreds of thousands of rands flew in, so his authority and power fled.

The first professional Springbok captain, François Pienaar, largely carried his standing from the 1995 World Cup, and Gary Teichmann developed influence through longevity as national coaches passed through a revolving door, but their successors would exist at the whim of omnipotent coaches.

Where once the captain had written the music, polished the instruments, prepared the hall and conducted the orchestra, now he was expected to stand in the front row, follow instructions and sing the chorus.

Rugby's inevitable evolution into full professionalism had started a process whereby a series of basically artistic instincts was replaced by carefully planned and rehearsed scientific reactions. The game became so structured and strongly organised that, in almost any given situation or position, robotic players from 1 to 15 knew where they should stand and what they must do.

The leading international Test squads began to operate with as many as 20 support staff, all absolutely qualified to deal with issues that ranged from diet, medicine and psychology, to media relations and logistics, to technical skills such as kicking, lineout work, scrumming, defensive patterns, et cetera; and it was the coach who presided over the pyramid, inspiring, hiring and firing.

Within this modern structure, the captain started to look, if not quite like a quaint anachronism, then certainly a figure with far fewer decisions to make and a substantially diminished role in the running of the side.

The Test captain's essential job description now boiled down to de-livering appropriate, short speeches at various functions, reflecting the policy and goals of the Union; and, second, being able to motivate and direct the team during the actual 80 minutes, the only period when the coach was out of earshot, faithfully implementing the instructions as laid down in interminable meetings. The captain became less of an officer, more of a staff sergeant major.

Midway through the 1999 Tri-Nations series, Nick Mallett needed to find a new Springbok captain. Bitterly criticised following three successive Test defeats, and just eight weeks before the start of the World Cup, the coach found himself under increasing pressure with fast-diminishing options.

He had discarded Teichmann with Skinstad in mind, but the heir apparent was still not fully recovered from injury and, as July turned to August, seemed an impractical choice to lead the squad to the World Cup. Corné Krige was another potential captain ruled out by long-term injury, and Rassie Erasmus had said he wanted to concentrate on his own personal performance.

Mallett turned to a senior player, a tempestuous character who had once appeared too erratic to be considered for captaincy but had since matured to the point where he led the Blue Bulls to the Currie Cup title in 1998. In crisis, Joost van der Westhuizen seemed to be the man for the job.

The world-renowned scrumhalf was preparing for another training session at Loftus Versfeld when his cellphone rang, flashing the name "Nick" across the liquid crystal display. Far less self-assured than his strutting persona suggested, he was suddenly anxious. What could the coach want now?

"Hello?"

Mallett typically came straight to the point, inviting Van der Westhuizen to captain the Springboks in the Tri-Nations match against New Zealand in Pretoria, his home town, the following Saturday.

"What about Gary?" the scrumhalf enquired.

"No, I would like you to captain the side."

"OK. Is this just a short-term thing?"

"No, no, I want you to lead the team through the World Cup."

"OK."

Van der Westhuizen had not immediately warmed to Mallett. The pair had clashed during the 1996 tour to Europe when the then assistant coach repeatedly told the scrumhalf to improve his communication, and again when the scrumhalf adhered to the absurd notion that the coach disliked Afrikaners.

Yet the team's success in 1998 had spawned mutual respect and, even if his instinct told him Teichmann should captain the side, Van der Westhuizen was realistic enough to accept the invitation with enthusiasm.

"It was the chance of a lifetime," the scrumhalf recalls. "As a boy, I always dreamed of playing for South Africa, but I never dared hope I would one day be a Springbok captain. I felt really sorry for Gary, and I telephoned him to tell him so, but I had to accept Nick's offer. It was an incredible honour."

Joost van der Westhuizen was born in Pretoria, the second of three sons in a hard-working Afrikaner family living in East Lynne, a neat suburb close to the frontier with Mamelodi, the vast, sprawling black township. His father and mother, Gustav and Mariana, both worked many years at the city council, and brought up their boys to work hard, worship hard and play rugby.

In 1980, the entire family secured tickets to watch Morné du Plessis lead the Springboks against the Lions at Loftus Versfeld, and a year later they rose at four in the morning, prepared coffee and sandwiches, and watched on television as the Boks lost the third Test in New Zealand. "We were cheated," says Van der Westhuizen, eyes burning with anger. He was only 10, but the fierce commitment that would become his trademark was already in full flow.

He had torn his blazer fighting on his first day at primary school, but began playing rugby at the age of nine and soon relished the game more than anything else in his life. That would never change. Years later, he would run out to play for Northerns and South Africa with the selfsame boyish enthusiasm that he showed working his way into the 1st XV at Hoërskool F.H. Odendaal.

It didn't matter whether he was messing around with friends on a piece of waste ground or being paid many millions of rands to play in packed stadiums. For the scrumhalf, rugby would always be a passion, never a job.

His name first surfaced in 1987 when he inspired his unfashionable high school team, Odies, on a fairy-tale surge to the final of the exalted Administrator's Cup, and he continued to attract praise as he worked through the rugby ranks at the University of Pretoria. Tall and quick, brave and bold, he was emerging as a game-breaker, able to turn matches in a moment of brilliance.

Van der Westhuizen's ticket to fame and fortune, however, was bought in hardship and sweat. From 1989 until 1992, the student worked four night shifts each week, from six in the evening until six in the morning, as a security guard at an office block in downtown Pretoria, earning R2 000 per month; and he practised incessantly, kicking with his right foot, passing, sprinting.

His career took off during 1992, when he rose from the Pretoria University third team to the Junior Springboks in the space of five months. It was, of course, his excellent good fortune to emerge in the year of South Africa's readmission to international rugby, but he seized every opportunity, thriving in the national team that reached the last eight at the Sevens World Cup in 1993.

He was eventually named in the Springbok side to play against Argentina in October 1993, and scored a try after 11 minutes of his Test debut. Still only 22, he battled the following year, was dropped after an inauspicious home Test debut against England at Loftus, struggled in New Zealand, and only secured his place with two memorable tries against Scotland later in 1994.

Dedicated and intense, a constant threat to the opposition, a magnificent defensive force, he developed consistency and excelled in the 1995 World Cup-winning squad, curbing occasional petulance and becoming one of South Africa's most popular and most marketable sportsmen.

Professionalism transformed his life, taking him from a city flat to the large house he built for himself and his wife, Marlene, near the Roodeplaat Dam, east of Pretoria; from a bakkie (pick-up truck) into a garage full of fast cars; and into various business projects such as a golf shop, a landscape gardening business, and the J9 clothing brand. Rugby catapulted the security guard to superstardom.

Yet, for all his new riches, Van der Westhuizen remained a straightforward boereseun (farm lad) at heart, never happier than when pottering around in the veld or at the dam, working with his hands, mending something, feeding his animals, just another ordinary guy wearing an old T-shirt and khaki shorts.

He became established as one of the very finest scrumhalves in the world, representing an important focal point of quality and consistency in the Springbok roller coaster ride through 1996, 1997 and 1998. He survived through successive coaches and controversies by keeping his head down, usually keeping his mouth shut, and maintaining his exceptional level of performance.

For Van der Westhuizen, nothing mattered so much as keeping his place in the Springbok team. He would say or do whatever was required. It was his life, his being, his existence, his ambition. It was everything.

Thus, in the first week of August 1999, aged 28, the scrumhalf prepared to play his 54th Test for South Africa, and his first as captain. "Morale was low after three consecutive Test defeats," he reflects, "but I have never known a Springbok side that didn't expect to win at home, and we felt we could surprise the All Blacks at Loftus Versfeld.

I enjoyed leading the side. I had learned a lot from François Pienaar and Gary Teichmann, and I knew the strengths and weaknesses of the players pretty well, but it was not an easy job. The media attention makes life difficult, because you have to be endlessly diplomatic in everything you say."

The passionate new captain scored an early try, after Erasmus had drawn three defenders, but the pressure applied by the All Black forwards slowly started to force errors out of the Springboks, and Andrew Mehrtens clinically diverted the stream of penalties into points on the scoreboard.

With Van der Westhuizen trying desperately to survive on scraps of clean possession, eagerly clapping encouragement around the edges of the scrum, the New Zealanders led 20-11 at half time and ultimately secured an emphatic 34-18 victory. The Springbok captain's sense of disappointment had been compounded when his close friend, centre André Snyman, suffered a broken ankle and, in one unfortunate instant, was ruled out of the World Cup.

Victory over Australia at Newlands, in the last Tri-Nations fixture, seemed imperative for a Springbok team urgently in need of some encouragement before setting off to defend their world title, and the scrumhalf spearheaded a resolute, valiant defensive performance to eke out a tense 10-9 win. "We tackled all day long," he recalls. "Conditions were difficult, but the guys showed great guts. I was relieved and felt we could now move forward to the World Cup."

In 1995, the Springboks were generally written off during the weeks before the World Cup yet, within Pienaar's squad, self-confidence was built on the solid foundations of five successive wins. Four years on, it was not only the supporters but also the players themselves who seemed to lack confidence.

The bewildering succession of major injuries and the change in captaincy had contributed to the destabilisation of a squad that, only 12 months before, had appeared fixed in a winning groove at the top of world rugby.

After the early conclusion of the domestic programme, Mallett gathered his squad at a training camp in Plettenberg Bay, and tried to draw a line beneath the disappointing Tri-Nations campaign. He redefined tactics and strategy, identified and resolved problems, and worked to rediscover that elusive winning mood that had been evident during 1995 and, indeed, throughout 1998.

The coach seemed happy with his captain. "It had been a difficult year for the team, and Joost offered uncontested leadership," Mallett reflects. "The senior players such as Mark Andrews and Os du Randt respected him, and I sensed the captaincy had a positive effect on his performance. He was fantastically resolved and brave, and this spirit rubbed off on the entire squad. Our most recent results had been disappointing, but there was nobody in the team who didn't believe we had at least a decent chance of retaining the World Cup."

Van der Westhuizen worked hard to talk to every member of the squad, to understand each individual's needs. For somebody who had for so long been happy to confine his social interaction to a few close friends, such glad-handing may not have come naturally, but he embraced the task. The new captain also negotiated with SARFU to secure the squad's win bonuses, and people who had thought he was too much of a loner to be captain began to revise their view.

Fuelled by excitement as the tournament drew near, confidence began to seep through the squad. Coach and captain seemed satisfied.

When the Springbok 1999 World Cup squad arrived in Scotland, the base for their three group matches, the players could have been forgiven for believing they had arrived in the wrong place at the wrong time.

South African perceptions of the World Cup were based on the experience in 1995, of bunting and billboards in the streets, of front- and back-page headlines every day, of the vibe and the buzz. Four years on, the Springboks arrived in the Scots capital and found Edinburgh going about its daily business: no fanfare, no mood, no visible sign of a great impending event, no nothing.

For young men who had worked tirelessly to reach this point, the downer was profound, and may have contributed significantly to three mediocre displays as the defending champions advanced through their group.

Scotland had conceded no fewer than 147 points in their last three games against South Africa at Murrayfield, but the home team competed with resolve in the opening match of the group and were actually leading 19-18 after almost an hour before the Springboks stretched away to a 46-29 victory. Mindful of peaking too early with, hopefully, the final more than a month away, Van der Westhuizen was generally content with his team's winning start.

The scrumhalf enjoyed Murrayfield, recalling happy days at the Sevens World Cup in 1993 and his two tries against Scotland the following year, but he had been amazed to be preparing for a lineout in the first half of the World Cup match and to hear the sound of artificial crowd cheering being piped into the stadium by small black speakers placed around the touchline.

"It was unreal," he recalls. "Their own side was playing a World Cup game against the defending champions in one of the greatest rugby stadiums, and they had to generate the cheering off tape. That was disappointing."

It soon got worse, much worse.

South Africa's remaining group matches were to be played against Spain and Uruguay. In their planning, the tournament organisers had scheduled these matches respectively at the 62 000-capacity Murrayfield and the 54 000-capacity Hampden Park in Glasgow, clearly convinced thousands upon thousands would pay R250 each to witness hopelessly one-sided contests.

They were wrong. Scarcely four thousand people watched the Springboks play Spain, and fewer arrived to see the game against Uruguay. For a pitiful lack of atmosphere and purpose, for demeaning the jersey, these wretched occasions almost exceeded the 1980 Tests on tour versus the South American Jaguars and the United States Eagles during the dark days of isolation

When the final whistle echoed around a cavernous, empty stadium, and the players returned to the changing room saying they felt as if they had sweated through an average training session, even the coaches struggled to perform and cogently criticise two poor, ineffective Springbok performances.

André Vos, an emerging talent from East London, had been selected to lead South Africa against Spain, and it was the eighthman who mercifully scored the first try after 29 eerie, scoreless minutes when the Springboks looked almost unable to come to terms with their ludicrous environment. The match wandered listlessly down a path strewn with errors to a 47-3 Springbok win.

Five days later, Mallett recalled Van der Westhuizen to captain a stronger side against Uruguay, but the outcome was even more depressing. Once again, the Springboks were humiliated by an inability to score in the first half hour. They did manage to jog across the opposition line several times, securing a 27-3 lead by half time, prompting expectations of an avalanche of points in the second half, boosting the side's confidence ahead of a quarterfinal. In the event, South Africa managed to add only 12 points in a pitiable 39-3 victory.

These low-key occasions would have been instantly, gratefully consigned to history and never mentioned again, but for the fact they left damaging scars on the entire Springbok campaign: Henry Honiball was injured against Scotland, and Brendan Venter, the experienced and influential centre, was distinctly unlucky to be sent off for stamping in injury time at the end of the first half against Uruguay. When an appeal against Venter's 30-day ban was cast aside, Mallett was forced to face the knockout stages without two key players.

"Our initial strategy at the World Cup was to play with the ball in hand," the coach reflects. "Henry and Brendan were to be instrumental in laying the midfield platform, from which we would use players like Bobby Skinstad to exploit second-phase possession. Everything had to change when they became unavailable, and we needed to play to the strengths of their replacements: Jannie de Beer, one of the finest drop-kickers in the world, and Pieter Muller, a strong centre who could carry the ball. It was 1995-style rugby, and it was our best option."

The Springboks left Scotland without a backward glance, and headed for what they regarded as the start of the tournament proper, a colossal quarterfinal against a powerful England team at the Stade de France, Paris.

Van der Westhuizen was approaching what he hoped would be the most exhilarating and memorable three weeks of his distinguished career, yet he was not sleeping soundly. The captain was growing anxious.

He was primarily concerned whether his team would be able to rise above their unimpressive form in the group matches and then adapt to the new strategy enforced by the absence of Honiball and Venter. Late on the Sunday night, soon after arriving in Paris, the captain arranged to see the coach.

They discussed the strategy and reflected upon the performances, but the pivotal captain-coach relationship was not maturing to a point where it compared with Pienaar-Christie in 1995 or even Mallett-Teichmann in 1998.

Mallett and Van der Westhuizen were both strong-willed, physically brave South Africans, but they did not click like adjacent pieces in a jigsaw puzzle, often failing to communicate clearly and unequivocally with each other. It was nobody's fault: sometimes the pieces fit, sometimes they don't.

So the captain reflects upon that late-night meeting in Paris as a moment when he persuaded the coach to alter the strategy, while Mallett reflects blankly that Van der Westhuizen required a clear game plan that he could implement on the field. The captain believed he had won a debate, whereas the coach thought he was only outlining what had already been decided.

Enterprising South African journalists crawled into this communication gap and produced headlines suggesting Van der Westhuizen had effectively informed the coach that the players would take control of the tactics and "play it their way". Such twisted fiction served only to unsettle the squad.

Aside from his team's poor form and his brittle relationship with Mallett, the captain was also troubled by something he could not discuss in public. A handful of people realised the scrumhalf had seriously damaged his knee during the last Tri-Nations match against Australia at Newlands, but had courageously decided to play through the instability and throbbing agony.

The coach was aware. "People often say it is wrong to include any player who is injured," Mallett reflects, "but there is no absolute law. Some players have the ability to play through pain and instability. Joost is one of them. He is one of the bravest people I have ever known. There are many players who would have withdrawn with his injury, but he wanted to play. He didn't tell anyone, played his guts out, and was voted one of the top two scrumhalves at the tournament. In my mind, his performance justified his selection, injured or not."

Skinstad was another leading Springbok resolved to perform on the World Cup stage. Medical opinion maintained his knee had healed, but the young talent seemed hesitant in the group games, rusty after a long absence, perhaps wary of taking another blow on the knee. Coach and captain were united in the hope that he would rediscover his best form against England in Paris.

South Africa started as marginal underdogs at the Stade de France, but the Springbok forwards magnificently raised their tempo in the scrums, lineouts and mauls, faithfully implemented the tactics devised by their army of coaches, nullified the influence of Lawrence Dallaglio, and won the possession from which an inspired De Beer kicked five drop goals out of five attempts.

Van der Westhuizen's 29th Test try gave the Springboks a 16-12 lead at the interval, and they retained this advantage throughout the second half, never looking like losers, resembling champions again, winning 44-21. "We thrashed them at front," the captain reflects, with sabre-toothed vigour.

The Springbok campaign suddenly sparked into life as the team travelled to London to prepare for a semifinal against Australia at Twickenham. Skinstad had made 26 tackles against England, and appeared returned to full fitness; Van der Westhuizen had threatened regularly:

472

the game-breakers were beginning to sparkle, and the forwards were starting to rumble. After two depressing weeks of trying to convince themselves they were playing in a World Cup, the defending champions found themselves two wins away from immortality.

Mallett considered a dilemma. Instinct told him the original game plan with Honiball, recovered from injury, at flyhalf presented the best chance of defeating the Wallabies, yet, battered by unremitting, harsh and often nauseating criticism from home, the coach felt unable to drop De Beer, the hero of Paris. He needed to make up his mind quickly, and retained both team and tactics.

The excited, flag-waving, face-painted emigrant South African community in London, supplemented by many thousands travelling from home, remarkably turned Twickenham into Ellis Park or Newlands on Saturday 30 October 1999. A tumultuous capacity crowd witnessed a semifinal of gut-wrenching tension in which the galloping science of professional rugby appeared to have created two defences through which no side would be able to score a try.

Penalty by penalty, amid remarkable pressure, Australia and South Africa wrestled for a place in the World Cup final. The gloom and persistent rain echoed King's Park four years earlier, but neither Skinstad nor Van der Westhuizen could find the gap to glory, and their dream appeared to have died when the Wallabies led 18-15 into injury time, deeper into injury time, deeper still.

Referee Derek Bevan, who ironically had handled that 1995 semifinal in Durban, blew his whistle six minutes into injury time, not to end the match but to award South Africa a penalty 40 metres from the posts, close to the touchline. In this minute, at this time, De Beer simply needed to kick this penalty to keep his country in the World Cup. If he missed, the game was lost.

Perhaps only Jack van der Schyff, the Springbok fullback who lined up the conversion to defeat the 1955 Lions at Ellis Park, fully understood the magnitude of the moment, that brief silence on the edge of the precipice.

Van der Westhuizen lay down on the sodden Twickenham turf to hold the ball upright with an outstretched finger, as De Beer steadied.

"Just keep the ball still," the soft-spoken flyhalf murmured.

"Don't worry, I don't mind if you kick my hand off, just make sure you kick the bloody thing over," responded the Springbok captain.

De Beer kicked, followed through ... and celebrated. It was 18-18, and the flyhalf had bravely pulled his side back from the brink. The final whistle followed soon afterwards, and Van der Westhuizen sensed the tide had turned. "I could see it in the Australians' eyes," he recalls. "They were finished. I was convinced we would win. Destiny seemed to be carrying us through."

Three minutes into the first half of extra time, South Africa won yet another penalty and De Beer confidently stroked his team into a 21-18 lead. The flyhalf had missed four out of five drop goal attempts during the semifinal, enduring the mocking jeers of Australians in the crowd, but he seemed to be making dramatic amends by kicking the late penalties that really mattered.

Van der Westhuizen, convulsed with adrenalin and enthusiasm, gathered his team into a huddle back inside their own half. "OK, boys, now we're going to get stuck into these Aussies," urged the captain, as emotion flooded his common sense. When others might have calmly demanded discipline and concentration, the scrumhalf's instinct was to reach for the jugular.

The contest rolled on, but on this afternoon when the line between triumph and failure had never seemed finer, it was Australia who drew level with another penalty, moved ahead through Larkham's freakish 40-metre drop goal, and edged six points clear when Matt Burke calmly kicked another penalty.

South Africa's captain had gestured angrily at what looked a forward pass in the move that led to the Wallabies' equalising penalty, but the day that seemed to have turned decisively in his side's favour now started to drift away. There was no further twist, no late escape, no try, and the final whistle brutally confirmed the Springboks' first defeat ever in a World Cup match, by 21-27.

"Of course, we were very disappointed," Van der Westhuizen recalls, "but I felt proud of the way the team had competed. The Wallabies knew the semifinal could so easily have gone our way. It went their way. Sometimes you just have to accept that. I told the guys we could hold our heads high."

The following day at the same stadium, France produced the shock of the tournament by defeating New Zealand in the second semifinal, taking them into a final against Australia. Thus, the Springboks and All Blacks were left to contest the innately meaningless and soulless match for third place.

However, adjectives such as "meaningless" and "soulless" just do not exist in Van der Westhuizen's dictionary, and his competitive spirit ignited the occasion on a floodlit Thursday night at the Millennium Stadium in Cardiff. On the beach, in the back yard or at the World Cup – it didn't matter: give the scrumhalf a ball and this bristling, bustling No. 9 always gave the fabled 110% in return.

While others were contemplating their flight home, he hurled himself into every challenge, suffered a broken nose at the bottom of one maul, staggered off to receive stitches, returned, and led his side to a 22-18 victory. Whatever he may have lacked in cunning, he more than compensated with courage.

Consoled by third place, the Springbok players were scheduled to remain for several days in their Cardiff hotel, not more than a drop goal from the stadium, and they were provided with prime seats to attend and enjoy the World Cup final, the showpiece event of their sport. Professionals to the core, all but three of the South African players declined the opportunity to watch Australia defeat France, and chose instead to sell their match tickets for pounds sterling.

Van der Westhuizen eventually limped into the international arrivals hall at Johannesburg airport and, gratified to discover public opinion credited his side for an honourable defence of the title, swiftly arranged an operation on his knee. The troublesome joint was carved open and efficiently patched up, but the four-month recovery ruled him out until the latter stages of the 2000 Super 12.

Mallett telephoned the captain immediately after surgery, but there was no further contact as the weeks passed. The scrumhalf sensed a problem, began to feel marginalized. History was starting to suggest that any Springbok captain who does not hear from his coach during the Super 12 stands on thin ice.

As the opening Tests of the 2000 season beckoned, Van der Westhuizen was invited to a meeting in Cape Town. In deciding to change his captain again, the coach was resolved not to repeat the fiasco of Teichmann's dismissal. All the necessary clearances had been timeously secured, there were no prior leaks to the media, and the fellow selectors flanking the coach presented a sense of unity as the captain finally arrived for the meeting at Newlands.

It will have been no consolation to the fiercely proud Van der Westhuizen, but it may be accurate to state that, in 110 years, no Springbok captain has ever been sacked with such dignity and proper process.

Mallett opened the meeting, explained his plans for 2000, how he wanted to adopt a much more expansive game and how he felt the team required fresh leadership at the start of what would be a rebuilding phase.

He added: "And we have asked André Vos to be captain."

"That's fine," the scrumhalf said, slipping smoothly into self-preservation mode. "I am still recovering from my knee operation and I would appreciate the chance to step down as captain and regain full fitness."

"OK."

"Can I ask a question?"

"Sure."

"If I prove I am still the best scrumhalf, will I still be selected?"

"Of course."

Van der Westhuizen was relieved. His greatest fear had been that, at the age of 29, he would follow the precedents of Pienaar and Teichmann, and be sacked as captain and effectively eliminated from the game, driven into exile. Captaincy was always a bonus for the scrumhalf – they could give it or take it away – but he desperately wanted to keep playing for South Africa.

He recalls: "I wanted to stay in the squad, so we agreed to issue a media release stating that I had resigned the captaincy to regain my fitness, but would still be available for selection. I didn't want to be history.

"With hindsight, I am proud to have captained the Springboks seven times and lost only twice. It was a positive experience for me, and certainly one of the major highlights of my career. Of course, I would like to have developed a much closer relationship with Nick Mallett, but that didn't work out."

The former captain endured an uncomfortable season, losing his place in the side during the Tri-Nations series, enduring a spell on the substitutes' bench, but fighting back to regain his berth towards the end of the year.

He remains as wonderfully dedicated and enthusiastic as ever, and will be forever recalled as one of the truly great Springbok players who stepped forward to captain the side in a time of need. Just a couple of penalties either way on that grey October semifinal day in London, and Van der Westhuizen may easily have joined the select band of men to have raised the World Cup.

Yet the wheels of destiny continued to grind.

By the turn of the millennium, the leading South African players had grown used to visiting Australia and New Zealand twice, maybe even three times, every season. As they worked the treadmill for the News Corporation schedules, places like Sydney and Auckland became as familiar as Cape Town and Durban.

It was therefore not surprising that, in striving to contact his new captain, Mallett should have had to prefix his telephone call with the digits 09 61 ... André Vos happened to be in Canberra, Australia, preparing to play for the Cats against the ACT Brumbies in the Super 12 semifinal. He was surprised to receive a call from the Springbok coach. They had not spoken in weeks.

Mallett posed the question, the eighthman replied by asking if the coach was 100% sure. The coach said he was certain. The eighthman responded that, in that case, he would be honoured to become Springbok captain.

The coach reflects: "In a sense, André was being thrown in the deep end as captain of a new team, but he had shown genuine leadership qualities and he had also become an automatic selection as eighthman."

There was another, largely unspoken factor in the appointment of Vos as the new captain, specifically that he projected an enlightened, progressive image in tune not only with SARFU's declared policy of transformation but also with the broader ambitions of the ruling African National Congress.

It was, of course, nothing new that chiefly political considerations should have influenced the choice of Springbok captain, and it would be totally wrong to suggest that Vos needed to be a card-carrying member of the ANC in the same way that so many Springbok captains during the 1950s, 1960s and 1970s had to be approved by clandestine leaders of the Broederbond.

However, following various clashes with the ANC government during the late 1990s, including a damaging court battle against Nelson Mandela, the Union was resolved to smooth relations and establish its credentials in the vanguard of the new political elite. It was considered crucial that the captain, as a spokesman and emblem of the sport, should strike the "correct" tone.

Polite, well spoken, intelligent, brave and a Bible-reading Methodist, Vos appeared the very model of a modern Springbok captain.

Born on 9 January 1975, curiously sharing a birthday with Teichmann, he was reared in the quiet, cosy Eastern Cape city of East London. Both his parents were employed by Nestlé, the confectioner; and, together with his solitary sibling, Judy, he grew up within an unwavering, happy family environment. His education started at Stirling Primary and advanced to Selborne College.

Like so many of his predecessors, this Springbok captain owed a debt of thanks, and petrol, to parents who selflessly drove him up and down the region to play his sport. Freezing five o'clock calls were the norm as the boy was driven to Queenstown or King William's Town for an 08h00 kick-off.

Physically small for his age, he relied on his eyes and hands to thrive in a wide variety of sports and, having started on the wing, he eventually secured the eighthman berth in the Selborne team to play the traditional "derby" against Dale College. Playing before crowds of up to 8 000, another youngster reaped the full benefit of South Africa's impassioned schools sport structure

He represented Border schools at Craven Week, moved on to enrol at the University of Port Elizabeth in 1993, and confidently attended pre-season trials for the Varsity under-21 team. Under-21 A and B sides were named at the end of the day, and Vos was devastated to be omitted altogether, left among four players loitering on the touchline, ignored and unwanted.

Dogged and persistent, he kept plugging away.

In June 1993, he sat in the main grandstand at the Basil Kenyon Stadium in East London to watch the South Africa B side play against France. "I suppose I was feeling quite low at the time," he vividly recalls, "but there was one incident when a Transvaal flank, Ian Macdonald, made a great break down the touchline. For some reason, that move left a deep impression on me."

The flanker on the charge, the crowd on its feet: the images remained with him, inspired him, motivated him to train harder. By the end of the 1993 season, he was established as eighthman in the UPE under-21 side; within two years, he was named to play his provincial debut for Eastern Province.

Alex Wyllie, the famous former All Black coach, was guiding EP at the time, and many observers questioned his judgement in plucking the lightweight student from obscurity and throwing him into the Currie Cup cauldron, but Vos prospered in the big league. He was bright, brave and evidently gifted.

The eighthman played 35 matches for Eastern Province during 1995 and 1996 before opting to follow the well-trodden path from the impoverished Eastern Cape to the richer opportunities in Johannesburg. He signed for the Golden Lions and, through 1997, started every match for his adopted province.

Out of the blue, on a Friday night before a Currie Cup game against South Western Districts, he received an intriguing invitation to move to Australia, live in Brisbane and play for the Queensland Reds in the following year's Super 12. The offer was almost unique:

South African players often played overseas at the end of their careers, not at the start. "I am cautious by nature," he says, "but I was not sure of getting a start for the Cats, and I thought I might learn something with the Reds. It seemed like an adventure, so I booked the flight."

The 23-year-old enjoyed Australia. He ate five meals a day, sweated and lifted relentlessly in the gym, played impressively for Queensland, and bulked out into a physically imposing, 104-kilogram professional rugby player. "I was a bit of a nerd at school," he says. After Brisbane, a nerd no more.

He was invited to spend a second year with Queensland, but Vos had set his heart on becoming a Springbok and, after a word with Mallett, thought it was necessary to be playing in South Africa. So he returned home and, mercifully avoiding injuries, maintained an enviable momentum: selected to lead the Golden Lions for the rest of 1998, chosen to captain the midweek side on the Springbok Grand Slam tour at the end of that season, making his Test debut as a late substitute against Italy in Port Elizabeth, June 1999.

"Friends of mine were watching that match on television," he recalls, "and they said I ran onto the field with a broad smile on my face. My folks had driven down from East London, so it was a special day for all of us."

There was no shortage of talented loose forwards in the Springbok squad during 1999, and Vos was content to seize his chances where he could find them in a disrupted and injury-hit squad. He appeared as a substitute after five minutes of the Tri-Nations match against the All Blacks in Dunedin and, despite the heavy defeat, breathlessly telephoned his parents after the game to tell them: "If this is what Test rugby is all about, then I want a whole lot more."

His ambition was sparked by the power and the glory.

Safely named in the 1999 World Cup squad, the eighthman captained the team against Spain, started the matches against Uruguay and New Zealand, and appeared as a substitute in all of the other games, strongly impressing observers within and beyond the squad; yet his immediate prospects of securing a regular place in the Springbok team seemed resolutely blocked by the world-class loose forward combination of Erasmus, Venter and Skinstad.

Once again, one man's terrible misfortune proved to be another's window of opportunity. It soon emerged that Skinstad, while fully recovered from the knee injury resulting from his motor accident, had suffered a second, separate injury in the World Cup semifinal and would miss the 2000 season. His absence created an obvious vacancy in the green-and-gold No. 8 jersey.

When Van der Westhuizen fell out of favour and Erasmus affirmed he was happy to keep leading the Cats in the Super 12, but not to captain the Springbok side, the captain's berth also seemed to be available.

The cards had fallen spectacularly in his favour and, aged only 25, a year younger than Pienaar when he was elevated, Vos took the call from Mallett in an Australian hotel, and agreed to become the Springbok captain.

One moment he was cast as a steady, reliable substitute in the shadows; the next moment, he was presented with an opportunity to establish himself as a long-term captain following respectfully in the footsteps of De Villiers, Du Plessis, Botha, Pienaar and Teichmann. Now, Vos seized the torch.

For South African rugby, the millennium season unfolded as a year of not just one overblown, extravagant "vision", but two. Week upon week, the respectful and dutiful captain toiled quietly in the shadow of his coach.

Mallett had bounced back from the 1999 World Cup resolved to lead a sea change in the way South Africans played rugby, replacing what many perceived as the traditional forwards-oriented strategy with a more open approach. Bursting with enthusiasm and ideas, he reeked of missionary zeal.

In effect, the progressive-thinking coach was designing a sleek, modern yacht to dominate the stormy oceans of international rugby. Unfortunately, the structure would be battered and beaten by the gales of a relentless Test schedule, and was destined to flounder on the rocks of official impatience.

"When I saw our international programme for 2000, I wrote a formal letter of protest to SARFU," Mallett recalls. "A home series versus England followed by an additional match against Australia before the Tri-Nations series was obviously not the ideal schedule in which to develop a completely new pattern of play, but I was convinced we needed to move on after the World Cup."

The squad was imbued with their coach's sense of adventure, and a bold, right team was chosen for the warm-up Test against Canada. In the sort of neat coincidence that somehow suggested everything was on track, Vos found himself preparing to captain South Africa for the first time in his home town.

"We didn't have many big sporting events in East London," he reflects. "It felt as though the whole town was going crazy. On the Tuesday afternoon before the Test, more than 4 000 people came to watch us train at Selborne College, my old school. Mark Andrews was also at Selborne, and the next day we both went back to address the boys. It was just a fantastic week."

The Hollywood scriptwriter was not finished. As another Springbok dawn gashed gold-vermilion across the horizon, Vos captained his new-look side into a 27-3 lead after only 30 minutes. Breyton Paulse, the quickfire wing, enhanced his billowing status with a thrilling 75-metre dash to score, and the team appeared to move with the fluency and skill of their coach's dreams. The day was sealed, with a degree of fairy-tale inevitability, when Vos lunged to score the last of eight tries, setting seal on an encouraging 51-18 victory, and a happy day.

In an ideal world, these Springboks would have been able to advance at a steady pace across the stepping stones of a home series against, say, Wales or Scotland; but in 2000 they were soon confronted by the formidable brick wall of a physical, confident and well-drilled England touring team.

"South Africans always underestimate English sides," Mallett reflects, "but we knew the Tests would be tough. Clive Woodward had intelligently put a series of professional elements in place, and they looked very strong."

The Springbok coach maintained his expansive strategy for the first Test in Pretoria, but his team was relentlessly disrupted by a series of injuries, and any hope of smooth continuity was lost amid the hectic blur of substitutions. No fewer than six South African players, including the captain, at one stage or another had temporarily to leave the field to receive medical attention.

Under such circumstances, Vos was exhilarated when his team withstood a ferocious physical challenge and emerged with an 18-13 win, even if England did indignantly claim they were denied a fair try. In adversity and under enormous pressure, gritty pragmatism prevailed over the new idealism: the Springboks kept their champagne rugby on ice and relied on flyhalf Braam van Straaten to kick six penalties, scoring all 18 points, and secure the victory.

A week later in Bloemfontein, however, there was no escape from the path of the turbo-charged England bulldozer. The touring tight five set about their task like an expert demolition crew, offering ball and space for flyhalf Jonny Wilkinson to score all his side's points in a 27-22 win, and level the series.

South Africa would probably have moved the ball around, if they had won enough of the ball, but it was only Van der Westhuizen's late try that gave a false gloss of respectability to an emphatic defeat. In time-honoured tradition, both the media and the public proceeded to savage the home side.

The broad-shouldered coach accepted most of the blame, but the young captain also suffered censure. One reporter suggested Vos resembled a child in the second half, being told what to do by the senior players.

"That was unfair," the captain retorts. "As a captain, I have always liked to hear the views of senior players during the game. That was my style. Leading a team is not about imposing your opinions on everyone else. It was unfortunate if some people thought that was a sign of weakness."

To sustain the seafaring analogy for the 2000 season, Mallett's sleek and modern yacht had been battered by the English storms but it remained afloat as the crew peered uneasily at a series of lighthouses flashing on the horizon. When it would ideally have been heading for calmer waters of Europe, their brand-new expansive strategy headed west, to be rigorously examined by the All Blacks and the Wallabies on the stormiest, tallest seas of world rugby.

It would be facile to reflect with hindsight upon the sheer inevitability of the shipwreck that followed, but Mallett resolutely believed in the logic of his strategy, and the coach retained the confidence of Vos and his players.

The standard annual Tri-Nations challenge of away Tests versus Australia and New Zealand had been rendered more daunting in 2000 by the addition of a prior match against the Wallabies to contest the Mandela Challenge.

There seemed no limit to the demands on the players. Every Saturday on the schedule had to be filled with another bone-crunching Test against top-class opposition, but there was no point complaining. The southern hemisphere rugby powers had sold their souls to the television broadcasters with no thought of player burn-out or fatigue; and, in return for their healthy salaries, leading players were expected to play, and play, and play to fill the TV schedules.

Vos did not flinch from the challenge. The young captain had certainly not enjoyed the criticism, but he believed in what the team was trying to achieve, and learned to withstand the incessant media barrage with distinction. "It was a tough period for everyone," Mallett reflects, "but André stuck it out and showed himself to be an outstanding young man in many respects. He faced the pressure, stood by his principles, by his team-mates and by his coach."

The apprehensive Springboks braced themselves for the storm.

In Melbourne for the Mandela Challenge against Australia, they were told by their coach to "throw caution to the wind", and for 40 exhilarating minutes the expansive approach yielded ringing applause and a 23-17 half time lead. Reality kicked in thereafter: the world champions squeezed their grip on possession, and ruthlessly cruised to an ultimately decisive 44-23 victory.

Moving on to Lancaster Park, Christchurch, the South Africans prepared to face a resurgent All Black side, revitalised by the appointment of Wayne Smith as coach and emboldened by a spectacular 39-35

Tri-Nations triumph in Sydney the previous week. Vos and his un-daunted team again planned to swing the ball but, although their pack won enough possession, backline handling errors ceded momentum and New Zealand eked out a 25-12 win.

"We had three outstanding scoring chances in Christchurch," Vos recalls, "but we failed to convert them all. It was frustrating because we all knew what we were trying to achieve, and we all believed we were close to getting things right, but each defeat increased the pressure on everyone."

Within a week, it was Saturday again and the Springboks were lining up to sing the anthems at the Stadium Australia, the newly con-structed main venue for the summer Olympic Games to be staged six weeks later. The Wallabies joined 108000 compatriots in thundering through the words of Advance Australia Fair and, on a night of soaring emotions, the visitors were overwhelmed by the home team's desire to christen the new temple in triumph.

Vos was still chasing and tackling in the 79th minute, but his side subsided to a demoralising 26-6 defeat and, perhaps yet more signifi-cantly, had now failed to score a single try in more than 200 minutes of Test rugby. The bright optimism of the new dawn had evaporated in the burning mid-season Tri-Nations sun, and all talk of an "expansive revolution" floundered in the acrimony of four successive defeats. Mal-lett's yacht was heaving on the swell, shipping water.

Vos remained steady at his post, standing on the bridge, maintain-ing the team's course was correct and pleading for public patience.

Unfortunately, patience is not recognised as legal tender in South African rugby, and the squad returned home to unrestrained criticism. Mallett was widely condemned as the arrogant, stubborn coach who had lost his way, and Vos was blithely dismissed as weak, ineffectual and out of his depth.

The Springbok captain approached the next match, against New Zealand at Ellis Park, with a real concern that his side would be booed, but these fears were instantly dispelled when he emerged at the head of his team. Clearly, the crowd had come to raise the Springboks, not to bury them. As the national anthem rose in 68 000 voices, Vos glanced along the line of players to see tears rolling down the cheeks of both Ollie le Roux and Corné Krige.

This was the time-honoured gees, the indomitable spirit that so frequently surfaced in the darkest hours, the same spirit that once inspired the pioneers and the gentlemen, the same spirit that motivated the giants, the great totems and the besieged, that still stirred the senses of these professionals.

Vos lit the spark, gathering the ball at the back of a scrum and launching a rampaging move that enabled veteran Chester Williams to slip through and score an opening try. As counter-attack swung into counter-attack, the contest became a classic exhibition of enterprising rugby. This was basketball with "big hits" as try answered try. The score mounted, and the lead shifted.

With eight minutes remaining, New Zealand was clinging to a 40-39 lead but the wide-eyed Springboks hurled themselves forward. Van Straaten stormed through a gap, John Smit bulldozed into the resulting maul, and scrumhalf Werner Swanepoel took the ball and twisted over to score his second try of the day. The conversion soared safely, time ebbed away, and before long Ellis Park roared in exhausted celebration of another famous victory, by 46-40.

Vos was touched by the occasion. "It was very special," he reflects, the gentle face relaxing into a grin. "We were under huge pressure, but the guys responded brilliantly and the Ellis Park crowd pulled us through."

The captain trusted the victory would silence increasing calls for Mallett's resignation. He appreciated the coach's direct approach, agreed with the strategy he had chosen to follow, and believed success was not far away. In private and in public, the eighthman enthusiastically endorsed his coach. He motivated his side for the last Tri-Nations match of the season, against Australia in Durban, with the thought that victory would safeguard the coach's position.

Once again, the Springboks played with searing commitment, even if they could not recreate the attacking fluency of Ellis Park; and once again, the match edged towards a nail-biting, perilously tight conclusion.

The Wallabies led 16-15 as the King's Park clock reached full time but the day seemed to have turned decisively when, seven minutes into injury time, Van Straaten calmly kicked a penalty to give South Africa an 18-16 lead. Amid almost unbearable nerves, the referee waved play on. More tackles were required; more tackles were executed. Another loud whistle pierced the drama. Full time? No, it was a penalty to Australia. Springboks sank behind their line as Stirling Mortlock snatched a 19-18 victory, fully ten minutes into added time.

Compelled by injury to leave the field at the interval, Vos had delegated his authority to his team-mate, Krige, but the harsh disappointment of defeat proved difficult to bear. "We had carried an ambitious fresh strategy into the Tri-Nations series, and the players hoped victory in Durban would keep the squad intact and ensure this process, which we all supported, moved forward to the next stage. In that context, defeat was a massive disappointment."

In truth, whether his team had won or lost at King's Park, Mallett appeared to recognise his period as Springbok coach was drawing to a close. His relations with the Union had deteriorated as this frank, profoundly decent man started to despair of the small-minded politics at the heart of the game.

This age-honoured fatal flaw was rarely more apparent than in the farcical manner of his dismissal. Mallett was not effectively sacked as coach because the Union Executive believed he had run out of ideas, or because the players did not respond to him, or even because his team had been thrashed.

No, in this ostensibly professional game, in the year 2000, the Springbok coach had happened to express a view that had crossed the mind of hundreds of thousands of South Africans during the season, specifically that the price of Test tickets seemed to have become inordinately high.

His remark was blown into a front-page headline, and thinskinned officials indignantly summoned the coach to a disciplinary hearing. The issue rumbled on for several weeks, before SARFU eventually confirmed the dismissal of the man who had guided South Africa to more Test wins than any other coach. However, perhaps the most accurate measure of Mallett's achievement was the degree to which, over three years, he retained the respect of his players.

Vos was bitterly disappointed by the news. The voyage so boldly, bravely launched against Canada had come to a sudden end; and, as a young Springbok captain identified, nurtured and encouraged by Mallett, he also started to wonder whether he would imminently be condemned by association.

Harry Viljoen, an impassioned self-made millionaire, was soon appointed as the new Springbok coach. Brimming with moves and enthusiasm, the former provincial scrumhalf had paid his coaching dues with periods at Transvaal, Natal and Western Province, and he inevitably arrived with his own "vision", at first sight a variation of Mallett's ball-in-hand, expansive, open strategy.

Players were starting to weary of "visions", being challenged to implement one strategy at provincial level, a different style of play in the Super 12, and then a third tactical approach at Test level; and yet, it was ever thus.

"Manne, it is goodbye to dullness and safety-first methods. Our aim on this tour is to rid our game of the cloak of dullness it has worn for so long." These fine words belonged not to Viljoen when he assembled his team before the 2000 tour to Argentina, Ireland, Wales and England. No. In fact, this was the bold sentiment of Philip Nel, the Springbok captain to New Zealand in 1937.

The more things change, the more they stay the same. Through 110 years of Springbok history, captains and coaches have frequently proclaimed the vision of spinning the ball wide at every opportunity ... at least, until victory has become so imperative, until the fear of failure has so dampened their initial idealism, that they eagerly revert to a more conservative approach.

Still Vos waited for his telephone to ring, waited and waited. Viljoen seized control and started to contemplate the composition of his squad, but the captain's telephone was still not ringing. As the days passed, speculation spawned that the new national coach would once again appoint a new captain.

Yet Viljoen was nothing if not calm and measured and, when he ultimately telephoned the eighthman on the eve of the squad's formal announcement and asked him to remain as captain, he did so with the assured air of a man who had not given serious consideration to any other option.

"I was relieved," Vos recalls, "but I realised I would have to prove myself to Harry Viljoen. He didn't know me, and he needed time to get a feel for the guys. I did not expect him to guarantee my place as captain. It was up to me, as the guy in possession. I simply had to make sure my form was right."

Earlier in the year, Mallett had implored his players to "throw caution to the wind" against Australia in Melbourne; now Viljoen launched his reign as coach by taking this open strategy one step further: preparing to play Argentina in Buenos Aires, the new coach forbade his players to kick the ball.

A crowd of more than 45 000 spectators in the River Plate Stadium was exhilarated by the spectacle of the Springboks attempting to pass their way clear from pressure situations inside their own half, but handling errors were inevitable and the contest became closer than it should have been. Focused on holding the ball at all times, South Africa scrambled to a 37-33 win.

Vos was enthused by the innovative approach. He had liked and admired Mallett, and he quickly began to like and admire Viljoen as well. The new coach had been variously derided as over-emotional and unpredictable, prone to return to his five-star lifestyle whenever the going got tough, but he managed to instil a fresh sense of purpose and energy to the Springbok squad.

He had raised eyebrows by appointing André Markgraaff as his assistant, but the former national coach had been forgiven for past errors and returned to the fold an older and wiser man. The chemistry seemed to work. Vos adapted to the new structures, and was already starting to feel comfortable when the South Africans arrived to play three Test matches in Europe.

Overcoming the discomfort of an eye-socket injury, the captain emerged as an outstanding performer on the tour. One moment dropping back to field the ball in cover defence, the next storming from the back of the scrum, forever tackling, he began to attract praise as the epitome of a modern eighthman.

The Vos factor stood out boldly in what materialised as otherwise average, disjointed performances. In Dublin, only André Venter's late lunge for the line enabled the tourists to break clear of an 18-18 deadlock, eventually to defeat the competitive Ireland team by 28-18. A week later in Cardiff, the Springboks sighed with relief when Wales missed a series of straightforward penalties. Locked level at 13-13 after 80 minutes, Vos's side conjured their second daring escape act of the tour, scoring ten points during added time to win 23-13.

"We were not playing well," the captain reflects, "but we were still settling under the new structures. I worried that my captaincy was at fault and, at stages of the tour, I found it hard to sleep through the night. It was not enough for me to play well as eighthman. The whole side needed to function.

"At least, we had emerged from two tight situations with victories. That sort of experience builds confidence in the team. South Africans always like to fight all the way, but we wanted to cultivate the right mood. If the guys were not a well-knit unit, then we would have failed under pressure during the final minutes in Dublin and Cardiff, but we held our ground. The spirit was fantastic."

England presented a major challenge in the last match of the tour and, to their dismay, the Springboks were again overwhelmed by superior forwards and dispatched to a third defeat in five matches against Martin Johnson's side. Amid the plainly physical approach of both teams, England briskly built a 19-9 half time lead, and then contained a second-half fightback to win 25-17.

For the mentally and physically drained South Africans, another long year ended with a spirited 41-31 victory over the Barbarians in Cardiff. Falling behind in the first half, the team displayed admirable courage and resolution by blanking the Barbarians after the interval, and ending the tour with a win.

Vos had evidently grown in stature and confidence on tour. As somebody who reflects that he only speaks when he has something to say, he had begun to wield tangible, quiet authority within the squad.

He rarely shouted or proclaimed, and he closely resembled Teichmann insofar as his influential performances and modest presence earned the respect and affection of his players.

"I tried to treat the guys as individuals," he says. "Some of them needed a quiet word of encouragement, others only responded to a rocket, but I really enjoyed the challenge of captaincy. I was lucky to play alongside a fantastic bunch of guys with the talent and the potential to become very successful.

"The worst part of the job was dealing with the media, because I constantly had to be on my guard to avoid saying the wrong thing. Eventually I stopped reading the newspapers altogether, and I still don't read them now. A captain has to fulfil his responsibilities with the media, but it's not much fun."

As the 2000 Springbok year drew to a close, the fearless and widely respected Springbok captain, still only 25 years old, seemed a symbol of hope in an otherwise uncertain future.

"The season had gone reasonably well," Vos recalls, "but as players we all knew we would have to prove ourselves in the next year's Super 12 to keep our places in the Springbok team. Like all professional rugby players, you have to keep earning your keep."

As the southern hemisphere's inter-provincial tournament unfolded, the captain led by example, excelling at eighthman in the Cats' progress to the semi-final. Brave, physical and effective, Vos was emerging as a star of the tournament.

Yet an insipid whispering campaign had begun. Some asked if he was worth his place in the Springbok team, in the company of loose forwards such as Erasmus, Krige and Skinstad. Some officials – not players – cited his stammer as a symptom of weak leadership. Similar nonsense had been held against another Springbok captain, Theuns Stofberg, 16 years earlier.

Now, as then, some mud may have stuck. Towards the end of May, Vos was named as Springbok captain not for the forthcoming 2001 season but, pointedly, just for the first two Tests of the year, against an inexperienced French touring team.

He might have been young, but he wasn't stupid. Nobody said

anything to his face, but something was afoot. Vos saw no point in fretting about machinations beyond his control, so he put his head down, worked hard and planned to lead his team to victory over the French. There was nothing else to be done.

Not for the first time, nor the last, a decent man striving at the heart of South African rugby became aware of a campaign against him, sighed at the institution's ongoing capacity for undermining its own, and carried on regardless for the cause.

The Ellis Park crowd gathered, debating not if the Boks would beat France, but by how much. Against such high expectations, the final score felt like a complete catastrophe.

South Africa 23, France 32.

"Our lineout fell apart," Vos recalls. "The whole strategy was based on a four-man lineout, but the referee's interpretation of the latest amendment to the lineout law meant that, on our throw, the French could put six jumpers in their 'box' to mark our four. It was technical and complicated, but it was the first we had heard of the ruling, and it totally disrupted our performance."

Vos' team headed to Durban for the second Test, intent upon regaining pride and squaring the series. They won more first phase possession and, showing plenty of passion in defence, emerged with an uplifting 20-15 win. It may not have been too pretty, but victory offered a base from which the team could advance.

The crisis had passed, or so it seemed. Not one of the Sunday newspaper match reports questioned the captain's performance and his leadership, or so much as suggested he would do anything other than lead his team into the third Test match of the year, versus the Italians in Port Elizabeth the following Saturday.

Harry Viljoen had other plans. Once the team had settled into their Port Elizabeth hotel, the coach called his captain to a meeting in his room. "André," he said. "We've had a chat and we're going to prefer Bob Skinstad to play at eighthman."

That was that.

With Skinstad installed at No. 8, and Erasmus and Krige secure on the flanks, there was now no room for Vos in the team, and the former captain was relegated to the bench against Italy. The brave new era launched amid such optimism after the 1999 Rugby World Cup had come to an abrupt and premature end.

"Of course, I was disappointed,"Vos reflects, 'but there was a measure of relief as well. I felt as if a burden had been lifted. I was now able to focus solely on my own performance."

In circumstances where many would have drifted away from international rugby, quietly bemoaning their harsh treatment,Vos said nothing, resolved to train even harder, and win back his place in the side by the sheer quality of his performance.

When Krige hurt his thigh against Italy, the focussed former captain bounced back into the green and gold for the Tri-Nations match against New Zealand at Newlands.

CoachViljoen then decreed that, when Krige recovered his fitness, the two loose forwards would each play half of the following match, against the Wallabies at Loftus Versfeld.Vos was given the first half, and his performance was impressive enough to secure his place in the Bok team for the rest of the season.

Quiet, deliberate, courageous, successful … each adjective sits comfortably beside the name of the man who was relieved of the Springbok captaincy in June 2001, who took the blow on the chin, and who, at a lavish gala banquet in November 2001, was officially voted as South Africa's Rugby Player of the Year.

Then, in the immortal words of Morné du Plessis when Danie Craven begged him to continue his international career and lead the Springboks to New Zealand in 1981, the 27-year-old Vos abruptly "turned the engines off" and retired from Test rugby. He arranged to meet Rian Oberholzer, CEO of SA Rugby, and asked to be released from the last year of his Springbok contract. He would continue to play for the Cats and the Golden Lions.

"It was a personal decision," he reflects. "At the time, I told the media that my body was knackered from playing so many high-intensity matches, and that was partly true, but the real reason for retiring from international rugby lay closer to home.

"The reality was that I had been married to Caroline for three and a half years but I had hardly been involved in the relationship. I couldn't keep spending six and a half months of every year away playing rugby, and I had to get my priorities right. In leading South Africa in 15 Tests, I had exceeded my boyhood dreams and it was time to direct my energy in a different direction.

"Looking back, perhaps I should have been completely honest at the time and explained my personal situation to everybody, but I really didn't think people would believe me."

The following year, Vos played a prominent role in a powerful Lions surge to the Currie Cup final, where they lost to the Bulls at Loftus Versfeld, and, in October 2002, he accepted an opportunity to move to England and play for Harlequins.

The sterling salary was welcome, and he maintained the good name of South Africans playing in the English Premiership by giving everything on the field – the typically bandaged figure striving in the Quins cause swiftly became a crowd favourite at the Stoop. He also resolved to enjoy the adventure in London.

He and his wife found many of their closest friends from home were also spending a few years in England and on free weekends they seized every opportunity to travel together, visiting Spain and Italy, Portugal and France and between seasons one year, even flying to Canada rather than returning to South Africa.

The adventure appeared to turn sour in May 2005, at the end of Vos' third season in England, when Harlequins finished bottom of the Premiership, and were humiliatingly relegated.

Just as when he was called to see Harry Viljoen to be relieved of the Springbok captaincy four years earlier, Vos found himself in a disappointing position where many players would have drifted away, finding others to blame for his misfortune.

That was not his way.

He accepted a salary cut, redoubled his efforts on the field and played a central role in Harlequins' steady march to promotion back into the Premiership. "We, the players, got the club into that mess," he reflects, "and it was up to us to put Quins back where they belong as quickly as possible."

At some stage, he will return home to South Africa, with his wife Caroline and their son, Luke, born on 18 August 2005. A new career in finance may beckon, and he may become involved in coaching rugby, unseen, at a lower level.

As the years drift by, from time to time, in quiet moments, he may look back on the best of times, on the simple pride he felt when he became a Springbok, on the sense of honour he felt when he was appointed to captain his country's rugby team.

One image will endure.

"It is the Test against New Zealand at Ellis Park in 2000," he recalls, eyes aflame again. "We had just arrived beck from Australia and someone piped up at the Press conference and said that one of his mates, a farmer in the Free State, thought we had no pride and were not worthy to play in green and gold.

"It's not my nature to lose control, but I completely let rip at that journalist. I told him what the jersey meant to my Springbok team. We might have been professionals, but we cared as much as anyone who had ever worn the green and gold before.

"Six days later, we had to match my words with deeds, in the Test against the All Blacks. It was an incredible occasion. Ellis Park is a fantastic place when it's full. Everybody seems to go nuts, and it felt to most of the guys that this was the first occasion when the entire crowd sung the whole national anthem, the Xhosa and Sotho verses as well as the Afrikaans and English.

"I'll never forget the moment when our anthem finished, and I looked down the line at my Springboks. There were tears rolling down almost every cheek. That's how much it meant to each of us, and we showed real guts, and we beat New Zealand."

The team played in the image of its captain.

André Vos, the professional who had proved himself as proud, brave and decent as any of his amateur predecessors, shines in the annals of Springbok rugby captains.

One day, no doubt, Luke will be proud.

15 THE COMET

As the Springbok players and their coaching staff made their way from the changing room to the field at the Boet Erasmus Stadium in Port Elizabeth, only a handful of the group were aware of the news that coach Harry Viljoen was about to give his squad.

The players formed a loose circle. On the back of the second Test win over France, five days ahead of an ostensibly easier match against Italy, the mood seemed positive.

Viljoen announced: "André is not going to captain the team on Saturday, guys. Bob will be captain."

One of the most gifted and charismatic South African rugby players of his generation had suddenly reached the pinnacle of his profession. It was almost 10 o'clock on the morning of Monday 25 June 2001, the young icon's date with destiny.

Bobby Skinstad first saw the light of day in Bulawayo, capital of Matabeleland in the west of Zimbabwe, on 3 July 1976. His father, a medical doctor, had settled in southern Africa, at the opposite end of the globe from his parents and roots in Norway. His mother, born and bred in County Louth, Ireland, was also enthused by the prospect of living in a region of opportunity.

The family moved to Cape Town five years later, and then on to Durban where Dr Skinstad opened his own practice. Alvin worked exceptionally hard and, a strong believer in the benefits of private education, made many sacrifices to be able to send his three sons first to Highbury Prep and then to Hilton College, the admired and renowned boarding school for boys.

Bob, the oldest, soon settled amid the beautiful whitewashed build-ings perched on the green hills of the Natal midlands, where a certain Gary Teichmann had completed his education just two years earlier, and seized every chance to play sport.

Bob excelled at basketball and swimming, but the boy's main focus rarely strayed from rugby. He adored the game ... from his first memories of watching his father play at Queen's Club in Bulawayo, to a sunny day in May 1986 when he sat with his dad in the open stands at King's Park, Durban, and cheered as Jaco Reinach sprinted to score a try for South Africa against the Cavaliers.

Through the mid-1980s, when the sporting boycott meant South African television was denied the rights to many international events, friends of the family used to smuggle video tapes into the country and the Skinstad boys would excitedly watch recordings of Five Nations rugby and the Hong Kong Sevens.

And, when the tapes ended, the boys would rush outside and play rugby, running and passing and tackling, with Bob dreaming he was one of his heroes: Liaan Kirkham, the fair-haired fullback who played for Transvaal in the 1986 Currie Cup final, or Christie Noble, the swift Western Province winger, or later Andrew Aitken, a pillar of thinking courage in the Natal back row.

South African rugby was emerging from isolation and, with the impeccable sense of timing that was to become his trademark, the youngster started to establish a reputation ... Hilton first team, Natal Schools in 1993, vice-captain to scrumhalf Joggie Viljoen in the South African Schools team of 1994.

In May 1995, enrolled as a student at the University of Stellen-bosch, near Cape Town, he was named as vice-captain of the South African under-19 team to tour Romania. His opportunities in the professional game seemed limitless but, first, there were plates to be cleared and drinks to be served.

South Africa was hosting the Rugby World Cup and, on the eve of the tournament, a dinner was held at Stellenbosch in honour of the legendary Dr Danie Craven, who had passed away two years earlier. Local students were roped in as waiters and, among them, the 18-year-old Bobby Skinstad gaped at the assembly of admired rugby players from around the world and made it his private ambition that, one day, he would take his place among them.

"Everybody was excited," he recalls. "To earn some pocket money, I was working in a pub at the time, and I managed to save just about enough to buy my dad an air ticket from Durban to Cape Town so he could come to the opening match with me.

"Some of us had queued through the night outside Newlands to get tickets for the opening match. We arrived on the Monday evening, camped on the pavement and, at 9am the next morning, I managed to buy four tickets for the standing enclosure in front of the main grandstand. That was all I could afford.

"We had a fantastic day, watching the opening ceremony, with President Mandela as guest of honour, and then the match. My dad and I were standing right in front of the Australian coaches, and nobody was more delighted than us when the Springboks beat the Wallabies."

That face in the crowd became increasingly recognised as the smiling, upbeat face of a flanker bursting clear, dummying, passing and running among the backs. Skinstad stood out at under-21 level, and made his full Western Province debut in 1996. The boyish grin began to illuminate Newlands week after week, and the young tyro excelled in WP's Currie Cup champion team of 1997.

He seemed to settle into an irrepressible momentum: on the field as a sumptuously gifted player; off the field as a handsome, eloquent, optimistic standard-bearer of "new South African" youth. A stylish culture soon started to develop around him, not only in Cape Town but also across the country.

With every flamboyant try, every glossy magazine cover, his popularity reached far beyond the touchline, and SA Rugby started to contemplate the reality of its newest rock star. Inevitably, not everybody pinned his picture on their bedroom wall.

Some traditionalists were less than impressed, calling him a scrum inspector who pranced with the backs rather than getting his hands dirty in the tight phases. They muttered about the dangers of elevating an individual above the rest in a team game.

Skinstad, aged 21, was having a ball.

He made his Test debut in November 1997, as a replacement against England at Twickenham, and revelled in his role as the Springbok "supersub" throughout the 1998 season. He came on as a replacement against Wales, and scored a try, and then repeated the feat against the All Blacks, and again against Australia. More headlines and praise followed.

Coach Nick Mallett gave him his first start against Scotland in November 1998, controversially dropping the stalwart André Venter to launch the Skinstad era in earnest. The fresh-faced flanker just played. He excelled and scored a try at Murrayfield, and scored another against Ireland in Dublin a week later.

The Bobby bandwagon was rolling at speed. There appeared no limit to its capacity. Yet within three months, his career had literally crashed into the brick wall beside the Claremont Bridge near the Newlands cricket stadium.

Together with his girlfriend, Debbie, later to become his wife, Skinstad was enjoying a quiet Saturday evening at a pub not far from Newlands. He had captained the Stormers in a Super 12 match against the Crusaders that day, and had let Todd Blackadder and the rest of his team know that this particular pub, usually closed on a Sunday, would be open. He believed that, even in the professional era, opposing teams should still socialise together.

Approaching midnight, Justin Marshall, the Crusaders scrumhalf, made a remark that Skinstad considered offensive to his girlfriend. He was young, impetuous and emotional, and, after enduring a few more childish insults, he arranged a lift home for Debbie before driving into the night, alone.

Accelerating over the Claremont Bridge, he lost control as the road swung left towards the famous cricket ground. The car skidded straight ahead and crashed into the wall. He suffered injuries to both knees, but it might easily have been worse.

Skinstad recalls: "Justin Marshall wrote in his autobiography that he thought I held him responsible for the incident. That's not true. It was an accident. I was upset that night, but the crash was not his fault. I have never blamed anyone but me."

Rehabilitation dragged frustratingly through the year. Early reports suggested he would be fit by May, then they said he would be right by July. In fact, he only just recovered by September, in time to take his place in the Springbok squad at the 1999 Rugby World Cup.

He performed well at the tournament, albeit often playing with a heavily bandaged left knee, ultimately heading the team stats for the most tackles and carries … and yet a general consensus developed that this exceptional young talent had not illuminated the event as anticipated.

There is no doubt that Skinstad was highly rated and respected by his peers. Beyond the celebrity status, the teen adulation and the sultry photo shoots, he was genuinely admired throughout the rugby world as one of those rare players with the skills, the intellect and the ability to change a match in an instant. He earned a global reputation as a genius "gamebreaker", the key to unlock the tightest defence.

He was also widely regarded as a pioneer, a key figure in a Stormers team that effectively changed the way the back row functioned at the highest levels of the game. Suddenly, here was a loose forward prepared to stand in the midfield, to wait for the ball and, combining strength and skill, to run at the opposing backline.

This comet may have blazed across the rugby sky, but he left a permanent mark on the evolution of the game.

However, he needed to be fit to play and, as 1999 drew to a close, the tough reality emerged that his left knee would require further surgery and that his subsequent convalescence would keep him out of the game for the entire 2000 season, from start to finish. He used the downtime profitably, exploring opportunities away from the game, but people began to wonder whether he would ever be the same again.

A deep-seated urge to prove the doubters wrong kept his recovery plan on course. He worked hard, aimed to regain full fitness by the start of 2001 and, from February until May, he successfully played in all but one of the Stormers' Super 12 matches.

He continued his comeback when he returned to the Springbok side as a substitute in the two home Tests against France, and he set his sights on regaining his place in the starting XV. It would not be easy

1. John Smit, the most successful Springbok captain in history, holds the Webb Ellis Cup aloft after the 2007 Rugby World Cup final. *(Tertius Pickard/Gallo Images)* | **2.** John Smit fends off Andrew Sheridan in the third Test of the British and Irish Lions' tour of South Africa in 2009. *(Duif du Toit/Gallo Images)* | **3.** Bob Skinstad led the Springboks on 12 occasions, including this nerve-wracking match against Tonga in Lens at the 2007 Rugby World Cup. *(Tertius Pickard/Gallo Images)*

1. Victor Matfield was still a dominant force in the lineouts when, in 2015, he finally quit international rugby, aged 38. *(Phil Walter/Gallo Images)* | **2.** Jean de Villiers accelerates towards the tryline in his first match as Springbok captain, against England in Durban in 2012. *(Steve Haag/Gallo Images)* | **3.** Johann Muller (right), who captained a weakened Springbok side against the All Blacks in 2007, lines up for the national anthem next to CJ van der Linde. *(Lee Warren/Gallo Images)*

4. Schalk Burger shares a moment with All Black star Kieran Read after leading the Springboks in a hard-fought match against New Zealand in Johannesburg in 2015. *(Ashley Vlotman/Gallo Images)* | **5.** Mahlatse 'Chiliboy' Ralepelle (left) became the first black Springbok captain when he led the side in a non-Test against a World XV in Leicester in 2006. *(Tertius Pickard/Gallo Images)* **6.** Jean de Villiers goes down under Dan Lydiate's challenge in that fateful Test against Wales in Cardiff on 29 November 2014. *(Steve Haag/Gallo Images)*

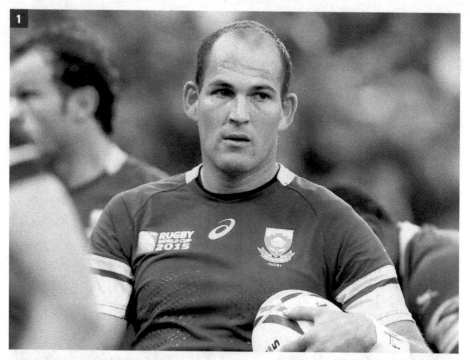

1. As is his way, Fourie du Preez led by deeds rather than words at the 2015 Rugby World Cup. *(Steve Haag/Gallo Images)* | **2.** Schalk Burger's cameo as captain was all the more remarkable given his recovery from life-threatening bacterial meningitis. *(Matt Lewis – World Rugby/World Rugby via Getty Images)*

because Vos, the incumbent captain, held the No. 8 berth, but that was the extent of his ambition as he joined his team-mates on the flight to Port Elizabeth, where they would prepare to play Italy the following Saturday.

"Bob!"

He looked up. It was a Monday morning and Harry Viljoen, the Springbok coach, was leaning across the breakfast table. Skinstad wondered what he might have done wrong.

"Yeah," he replied, uncertainly.

Viljoen continued: "I'm going to make you captain, and you're going to play eighthman on Saturday. I've spoken to André. Everything is arranged."

Skinstad was stunned. He seemed completely nonplussed.

Like everyone else, he was aware of the muttering about Vos, and he knew that one or two senior players in tandem with one or two senior administrators had been seeking to undermine the captain. He didn't like such talk, partly because he believed Vos was an outstanding captain, but also because such machinations represented the side of South African rugby that he loathed. So now he was to be captain? Right from the start, from the moment the coach spoke to him at breakfast, Skinstad felt like a compromised candidate.

Informed observers shared this view, and identified a covert group that, even in 2001, seemed obsessed with the concept that, in a democracy where all power was vested in the hands of the majority, rugby could and would remain the last area of South African life still under Afrikaner control. It was said that this powerful caucus had hounded Viljoen to get rid of Vos, and replace him with either Rassie Erasmus or Corné Krige, and that the coach had yielded on Vos but staunchly dug his heels in and insisted on Skinstad.

Much had changed in South African rugby since 1951, when the Broederbond began to exert control over who became Springbok captain, and who didn't ... but not that much.

Skinstad left the breakfast table soon afterwards and, still in shock, sought out Vos. He made a point of sitting next to him on the team bus journey to morning practice at the Boet Erasmus Stadium.

He asked: "What's the story?"

"It's all right," Vos replied. "They want you at No. 8 on Saturday, and you're going to be captain as well. I'm trying for No. 6. Don't worry, it's fine."

Skinstad could see the profound disappointment in his predecessor's eyes. It was ever thus. For the joy of every new Springbok captain, there is the despair of the deposed one. When the two men involved are friends who like and respect each other, the transition becomes even more raw and poignant.

The rest of the players were informed of the change in captaincy as they gathered in a circle on the field just before the practice began. At such momentous moments, the convention demands that everybody immediately move to shake hands with the new leader, and Skinstad was duly inundated with congratulations. It would have been unnatural for Krige and Erasmus, each a strong candidate for the job in his own right, not to feel a measure of disappointment, but both pledged their full support to the new captain.

"I was genuinely stunned," Skinstad recalls. "Captaincy was always something I really enjoyed, because I tend to talk a lot on the field and I liked the challenge of motivating the guys. I also enjoyed the responsibility, but it wasn't something I really sought. In any case, I had assumed André Vos would be captain for years.

"When Harry told me he wanted me to take over, I was keen to make the best of it. The South African public like having someone to chase, and I was prepared to be that person."

From his first press conference as captain, Skinstad broke the mould. Instead of scowling suspiciously at the journalists gathered around him, he disarmed them with a smile. Instead of avoiding issues beyond rugby, he spoke easily about his team's desire to be standard-bearers of the new democracy.

His beaming confidence may have been misinterpreted by some as a kind of superficial arrogance, but the overwhelming impression, in June 2001, was that when this son of a good Irish woman smiled, the whole world of South African rugby seemed to be smiling with him.

Italy were swept aside 60-14 at the Boet Erasmus Stadium, and

Viljoen's squad turned optimistically towards the 2001 Tri-Nations. All of a sudden the team lining up beside the 25-year-old captain appeared to be brimming with promise and potential. So it goes, so it has always gone on the Springbok rugby roller coaster. The team are either hailed as all-conquering heroes or derided as a disgrace to the jersey, rarely anything in between; and the difference between such triumph or disaster is usually the most recent result.

An appetising Tri-Nations match against the All Blacks at Newlands shaped as a providential first major test for the new captain in front of his sympathetic home crowd, but the Cape Town hero's big day turned out to be as grim and damp as the grey skies and heavy rain that descended upon the old ground.

Springbok spirits soared when the Bok forwards heaved the New Zealanders into reverse at the very first scrum. His animated head rising out of the scrum, Skinstad clapped enthusiastically. The Newlands crowd roared its approval. For all the world, it seemed if the "new era" had been launched.

Or maybe not: these high hopes were dashed by harsh reality when the conditions reduced the match to a soaked wrestling bout bereft of inspiration, running rugby and tries. Five times the Springboks kicked for goal; Percy Montgomery succeeded with just one out of four, and Butch James missed late in the game. Four times the All Blacks kicked for goal, and Tony Brown sent each penalty between the uprights. Everybody played their guts out, but superior goalkicking earned a 12-3 victory for New Zealand.

Characteristically, Skinstad was eager to seize the positives from defeat, praising his team's efforts in the scrums and lineouts, and making the point that Dean Hall's powerful surge for the tryline had come within inches of changing the course of the match.

The kicking problems were addressed by Viljoen, who set his best intentions aside and selected Braam van Straaten, a specialist goalkicker, at flyhalf for the match against Australia in Pretoria a week later. The coach, who early in his reign had famously instructed the Springbok team not to kick the ball at all, had resigned himself to the timeless reality that winning teams kick their penalties.

Van Straaten duly delivered at Loftus, kicking five of his six penalty attempts, but the match turned on what became a signature moment for the captain, just two minutes before half time ...

The Springboks are pressing on the Wallaby 22-metre line, running through the phases, picking, bursting, carrying, recycling, moves endlessly drilled in training, performing on the grand stage as 49 000 spectators watch from the stands and millions more stare critically at their television screens.

Joost van der Westhuizen takes the ball, and flips a pass into the path of the captain, running at speed, slicing clean through the Australian defence, sprinting clear, diving to score in the corner at the north-west corner. Loftus erupts. Skinstad smiles, all teeth, tongue and delight ...

The captain's try gave South Africa a 14-0 lead at half time and, amid great excitement, the home team ran out more comfortable winners than the final score of 20-15 suggested. The brave new era, stuttering at Newlands, had apparently been launched in glory at Loftus. This was Skinstad in excelsis.

When the Wallabies surprised everyone by beating the All Blacks in Dunedin two weeks later, each of the three teams stood with one win from their first two Tri-Nations matches. The upbeat Springboks were regarded as genuine title contenders as they flew east for their two away matches.

Their first destination was the Subiaco Oval in Perth. Skinstad's team excelled again, but eventually had to be satisfied with a draw when they felt their performance had merited a win. The referee, the self-assured Steve Walsh from New Zealand, was held responsible for the South Africans' frustration.

"Walsh hammered us," Skinstad recalls. "He seemed to treat us like the poor cousins of the Tri-Nations that afternoon." The perception of inferiority was not helped by the fact that, as the saga unfolded, the Springbok team management behaved in an absurdly self-critical and insecure manner ... like poor cousins.

The problems began early in the second half when Springbok centre Robbie Fleck appeared to launch himself at his opposite number. Walsh waded in and flourished his yellow card not at Fleck but at

Butch James, the flyhalf whose reputation as a physical player often preceded him.

"It wasn't him," Skinstad protested to the referee. "It was Robbie."

"He didn't use his arms in the tackle."

"You've got the wrong guy!"

The referee waved the captain away, James wandered to the sin bin and the Springboks played without their flyhalf for the next 10 minutes. Tempers started to fray. Skinstad, frenetically working on the fringes of the scrum, was struggling to hold the 14 men together under a relentless Wallaby onslaught.

Moments after James was allowed to rejoin the fray, Walsh blew hard on his whistle once again.

"You!" the Kiwi referee declared, producing his yellow card once again and pointing at Skinstad. "Sin bin for persistent infringement at the breakdown."

The young Springbok captain was exhausted and now exasperated. In the heat of the moment, in absolute frustration and disappointment, he started to clap his hands in mock applause at the referee's decision as he made his way to the touchline. The gesture was inappropriate, but understandable.

Even deprived of their captain for 10 minutes, the South Africans held firm. Matt Burke and Van Straaten traded penalties during the closing 10 minutes and, when Stephen Larkham's last gasp attempted drop goal slipped past the right-hand post, a tense, fraught contest concluded as a 14–14 draw.

That should have been that.

Instead, it was announced that a 10-man committee, comprising Springbok officials and senior players, was going to meet and discuss their captain's reaction to his yellow card. Self-flagellation was popular among medieval monks, but it hardly seemed required behaviour for a 21st-century professional rugby team.

This group assembled and took a decision that Skinstad should be fined for his derisive applause of the Kiwi referee. "We looked at the case," Viljoen pronounced to the media afterwards, "and the clinching argument was that John Eales would never have done such a thing."

Perhaps only South African officials would have so embarrassingly and unnecessarily undermined their own national captain in public. Would the All Blacks have put their captain on trial? Never. Would a Wallaby coach have said his captain was guilty because he didn't measure up to his Bok counterpart? Never.

Only the poor cousins, pathetically desperate for the approval of their rivals, hopelessly over-sensitive to any perceived criticism, felt obliged to grovel when private censure would have sufficed.

As the squad flew to Auckland, the captain worked hard to restore authority and morale within his squad, but his team were comprehensively outplayed at Eden Park. The All Blacks, under great pressure after losing at home to the Wallabies, improved dramatically, won 26-15 and thus condemned the Springboks to last place on the final Tri-Nations table for the third year in succession.

This seemed a poor return on the team's effort and endeavour, and the Springbok captain was left to watch on television as Toutai Kefu's sensational injury-time try took the Wallabies to victory over New Zealand in Sydney and enabled Eales to conclude his fine career with another major trophy in his hands.

Skinstad took time to reflect and, recognising the paramount importance of a seamless working partnership between captain and coach in all successful teams, began to wonder.

"I respected Harry Viljoen," he recalls. "He was forward-thinking, he had a bold vision and he was prepared to weather the storms and build something worthwhile. We had always had a good relationship but, towards the end of the Tri-Nations, he seemed to be getting frustrated. It looked as though his whole aim had been to change Springbok rugby, and he was starting to think that might be impossible.

"Perhaps I was just newer to a leadership position, and less aware of the realities than he was, but I seemed to see more potential in everything. There is no criticism in this, but it may be accurate to say that, by the time he appointed me as captain, some of the sparkle had gone from Harry's eyes."

The end-of-season tour to Europe would prove a test for both men, not least because another demanding schedule had been arranged for a group of Springboks that, as usual, was both physically and mentally running on empty almost 11 relentless months after they had reported for Super 12 training.

There was no respite on the professional treadmill. Year after year, season after season, the leading stars of South Africa's professional rugby sweatshop would quite literally be played into the ground at Stade de France, Twickenham, Millennium Stadium, Murrayfield and Lansdowne Road.

Disappointment was almost inevitable.

Against France in Paris, South Africa led 10-9 early in the second half, but conceded a rash of penalties and subsided to a 20-10 defeat. Skinstad sat in the changing room, rueing what he considered to be serious errors in selection. As captain, he was not once consulted on such matters, even informally.

Next, against Italy in Genoa, showing seven changes, including the introduction of Louis Koen at flyhalf and the shifting of Braam van Straaten into the midfield, the team's core strength secured a 54-26 victory, but hardly anybody was impressed and even fewer were encouraged.

The ship was rocking. Too many players had lost faith ... lost faith in selection that seemed to favour a small and protected inner circle, lost faith in a training regime that appeared to be organised on a whim, and lost faith in a team management that seemed ill-equipped to organise and motivate.

Skinstad was aware of the complaints, and decided to act.

On the Monday before the Test at Twickenham, he sat down with Viljoen and issued an ultimatum. "Either these issues are resolved quickly," he said, "or I am not prepared to be captain."

The exchange was open and honest, and concluded with Viljoen's sincere pledge that he would address the problems once he returned to South Africa after the tour.

Five days later, England did not play well against South Africa at Twickenham: they didn't have to. Their forwards stuttered, they relied heavily on Jonny Wilkinson to kick penalty goals, and they couldn't score a try until Dan Luger sprinted the length of the field in injury time; and yet, such was the hapless form of their traditionally formidable opponents that the home team still eased to a regulation 29-9 victory.

For Springbok supporters, defeat was rarely more depressing. Skinstad's personal sense of disappointment was compounded by a dislocated shoulder, which ruled him out of the Test against the United States Eagles to be played at the Robertson Stadium in Houston a week later. When some would have been tempted to head straight home, the captain flew to Texas with his team and, wearing a neck brace, supported the side as they did enough to secure a 43-20 victory. André Vos stepped in to lead the team on the field.

A long season was simmering to an end and, as South Africa's finest rugby players wandered anonymously through Houston airport, that sunny, glorious day at Loftus, when the young captain burst through the Australian defence to score in the corner, suddenly seemed a long, long time ago.

Viljoen had arranged to spend a few days in America after the tour, so the coach and captain courteously bade farewell to each other in Houston. They have never spoken since.

For the third time in five years, a Springbok captain-coach relationship had dissolved in rancour. Just as Pienaar and Markgraaff would not speak for years after 1996, and Teichmann and Mallett avoided each other after 1999, so Skinstad and Viljoen made a complete break in 2001.

The increasingly disillusioned coach reflected on his position and, despite the ongoing support of SA Rugby officials, announced his decision to resign on 19 January 2002. "I'm not enjoying the job," Viljoen said. "The pressures have become unbearable and it is impacting negatively on my family."

Serious applications for the vacant position hardly flooded the SA Rugby offices and, following an urgent appeal to South Africa's four Super 12 coaches to put themselves forward, the process boiled down to a choice between Rudy Joubert, technical advisor to the 1995 Springboks and recently coach of Cardiff RFC in Wales, and Rudolf Straeuli, a popular member of the world champion South African squad who had established himself as a respected provincial coach, initially with Border and latterly with the Sharks.

The incumbent captain followed events with interest – even though he was acutely aware that, in recent Springbok history, the arrival of a new coach had almost always heralded the appointment of a new captain – and he shared the overwhelmingly positive reaction when Straeuli was given the job.

"Rudolf and I got along well," he recalls, "but, to be honest, I never got the impression that he wanted me to remain captain. There were no hard feelings. That was his prerogative."

However, the new coach was not going to be rushed into an appointment. He began a drawn-out process by announcing four candidates for the captaincy – Skinstad, Krige, John Smit and Van der Westhuizen, and explaining that he would monitor their performances before making a final decision.

The procedure could not be faulted for transparency, but this quartet of proven senior players did not enjoy being drawn into what amounted to a beauty pageant, with one winner and three losers.

In any event, in practice, the relentless physical demands of professional rugby suggested the contest was as likely to be won by the last man standing as the strongest candidate. John Smit, probably Straeuli's preferred choice, suffered a long-term shoulder injury, and Krige was sidelined with sore ribs.

So, almost by default, Skinstad was named captain for the first two Tests of the season at home to Wales, but he suffered no illusions: "I was just keeping a seat warm," he recalls. "It was obvious to everybody that Rudolf had decided Corné was going to be the captain as soon as he was fit."

The Welsh were defeated without undue alarm, 34-19 at Vodacom Park (now Free State Stadium) in Bloemfontein and 19-8 a week later at Newlands, and Corné Krige was duly named as Springbok captain for the Test against Argentina, to be played at the PAM Brink Stadium in Springs on 29 June 2002.

Almost a year after his appointment as an upbeat 25-year-old captain with an apparently boundless future ahead of him, Skinstad had joined the ranks of former Springbok captains. The demotion of the most gifted and charismatic player of his generation might have been expected to prompt a public outcry, but it didn't, largely because South Africans have never been averse to decapitating the tallest poppy.

A nodding consensus held that Skinstad had become a shadow of the superstar who had generated such excitement in 1998, and two reasons were usually given: first, they said he had become increasingly distracted by off-the-field activities ("Bob has become an industry," ran the refrain); second, they said he had never completely recovered from his accident in 1999 ("Bob has lost a metre of pace," pundits agreed).

So, quietly, he returned to the ranks.

Like Vos before him, but few of his other predecessors, Skinstad managed to retain his Springbok place after losing the captaincy, and he played No. 8 against Argentina and Samoa, and through the Tri-Nations championship that followed. He even resumed the duties of captain on several occasions when Krige was forced by injury to leave the field. An injury of his own ruled him out of the tour to Europe at the end of 2002, but he returned to the team in 2003, appearing as a substitute in his 34th Test, against Argentina at Port Elizabeth.

Then, a fortnight before his 27th birthday, he decided he had had enough. His flame had started to wane towards the end of 2001. He did produce strong, prominent performances after that time, but he rarely seemed to show the sense of sheer enjoyment and youthful energy so symptomatic of his glory days.

Skinstad turned the key in the ignition twice more, gamely trying to fire the engine again: first, at the start of 2003, when he left the Cape to play for the Cats in Johannesburg; and, second, in January 2004, when he agreed to follow Teichmann, Montgomery and other Springboks to play for Newport in Wales.

There he played only nine matches in the second half of the northern hemisphere season, though significantly he also represented the Barbarians against a Scotland XV, England XV and Portugal that year. The Barbarians, which brought together players from different nationalities, celebrated rugby that was played the Skinstad way – with energy, style and enthusiasm.

Yet Skinstad's enthusiasm had by then sufficiently been doused and he temporarily retired from first-class rugby at the age of 28. "My heart wasn't in it any more," he recalls, honestly. "I was just going through the motions, and that wasn't a good enough reason. Debs, my wife, was amazingly supportive and neither one of us felt I should be playing the game just for a salary.

"When I started playing for Western Province and the Springboks, I had this romantic dream of playing the game in a natural way, entertaining the crowds. I also loved the idea of mixing with the great players, the kind of people who made rugby what it was, becoming friends with opponents and just making the most of the opportunity. Everything seemed such fun.

"The dream didn't last long. I suppose I woke up to the reality that playing professional rugby is a job like any other. You just did it. Some guys are happy with that, and that's fine, but I had a more idealistic view of what playing top-level rugby would be like, and the reality seemed a bit of a letdown. The game turned out to be much colder and more clinical than I imagined. Players are just a product."

In plain language, he lost interest in professional rugby, and in 2005, by then married and based in London, he turned his energies to another of his great passions: advertising and the media. "I enjoy the industry," he says. "I like the concept of developing a story to sell a product, and I enjoy the process of working out what elements can sell a brand, and what can't. That sort of thought process intrigues me."

Still short of his 29th birthday, the former Springbok captain started work for Saatchi & Saatchi, a leading advertising agency, from their office in the West End of London. He had moved 9 600 kilometres from his comfort zone in Cape Town and successfully reinvented himself in a completely new arena. This shift was successful and led to work across Europe and USA for the famous group over three years.

The gladiator inside him nevertheless felt unfulfilled, and the spark to the flame was the Barbarians. Skinstad found the sense of camaraderie appealing and it brought him back in touch with what had made him fall in love with the game.

There were six more Baa Baa caps, starting with a 48-17 win

over East Midlands on 16 March 2005 and concluding with a 28-19 win over Georgia on 4 June 2006. The venues – Bedford's Goldington Road and the Mikheil Meskhi Stadium in Tbilisi – were hardly among the great rugby stadia. Sandwiched in between were fixtures against the Combined Services, another against East Midlands, the Royal Navy and a Scotland XV.

"I was in heaven, it was fantastic," he says of his experiences with the Barbarians. "We had coaches such as Zinzan Brooke and Bob Dwyer, while on occasion I had Brian O'Driscoll as one of my centres and Christian Cullen as fullback."

It was fitting company for Skinstad, who suddenly had an itch he needed to scratch. Aware that he would not be considered for Springbok selection if he played overseas, Skinstad sat down and plotted the route that could lead him to the 2007 Rugby World Cup in France.

To many, a return to the Stormers might have seemed a logical choice, but it would have been based more on sentiment than common sense. The Cape side had descended into mediocrity, and in 2006 finished eleventh in the Super 14 tournament. Apart from Jean de Villiers and Schalk Burger (Jnr), there were no players in their ranks who could be considered world class. By contrast, the Sharks had finished fifth, equal on log points with the Bulls, but inferior by the narrowest of margins on points for and against.

Those were the pick of the South African teams, and the choice was obvious, as Skinstad would not have been comfortable in the Bulls culture, which espoused execution over innovation.

A conversation with John Smit, the Springbok and Sharks captain, then paved the way for Skinstad's return.

There had been no promises from Bok coach Jake White, but at worst Skinstad was going to have a soft landing in a decent Sharks team.

One thing Skinstad would not have to concern himself with was that he might, through no fault of his own, be considered divisive. White had by then established a team with a strong leadership core that included Smit, Os du Randt, Victor Matfield, Schalk Burger, Juan Smith, Fourie du Preez, Jean de Villiers and Percy Montgomery.

"The team was very settled and confident, so I was always going to be less of a threat. If a player who came in wasn't contributing they would tell him very quickly. If they saw a contribution, they would be happy," Skinstad said. "As you get older you're also more at peace with who you are and comfortable in your skin."

While no longer the X-factor player of years gone by, Skinstad was impressive enough for White to believe that he was capable of making a significant contribution.

His recall to the international scene came in the second Test against England in 2007, after Danie Rossouw contracted flu. Pierre Spies was consequently elevated to the starting line-up and Skinstad included on the bench. He was a blood replacement for Juan Smith from the 10th to the 16th minutes before being sent on again during the closing stages of South Africa's 55-22 victory in Pretoria, but was elated. Then, the following week, he started in the 35-8 thumping of Samoa at Ellis Park in Johannesburg. His selection in the run-on team for the 21-26 defeat to the All Blacks in Durban two weeks later confirmed that White had a significant role in mind for the former captain.

However, there was a twist in the tale. On the advice of sports scientist Professor Tim Noakes, the South African Rugby Union (SARU) made a decision with White to send a so-called B-team on the away leg of South Africa's Tri-Nations campaign. White had to find a new leadership core, and Skinstad was an obvious choice as captain for what were considered missions impossible in Australia and New Zealand.

His return to the role, against a full-strength Wallaby side in Sydney, almost yielded a spectacular upset. The makeshift Springboks wreaked havoc, with two tries inside the first 10 minutes, but were ultimately outclassed 25-17. Skinstad's ability to inspire his men was still evident, but there was yet another character test around the corner.

"Unfortunately I broke my rib in that match. I thought that was it and the journey would be over for the year," he said. "It was a nice experience in the sense that I could say that at least there was some galvanising of young players to perform beyond what the expectations of the public and team management had been."

Johann Muller would take over the captaincy for the following match against the All Blacks, but Skinstad's leadership journey was far from over. Jake White had planned a World Cup warm-up phase that would include matches against Namibia, Irish team Connacht and Scotland. The match against Connacht, in Galway, masqueraded as a dress rehearsal for the pool match that would be played against Tonga in Lens at the World Cup. In both instances White looked to Skinstad to lead under circumstances where his troops might be either hesitant or complacent.

Against Connacht, the players were clearly petrified of injury before the start of the World Cup journey. Having been up just 3-0 at half time, the Springboks lifted their intensity to win 18-3. But it was the pool match against Tonga that almost produced the biggest shock of the World Cup, with the Springboks saved by the bounce of the ball in the closing stages to win 30-25. It would probably have been much different had flyhalf André Pretorius succeeded with three first-half penalties, but the job was done.

White also used Skinstad to close out pool matches against England and the USA, as well as in the semifinal against Argentina.

But it was in the wake of the Argentina clash that Skinstad's career took another cruel turn. He would be replaced by Wikus van Heerden as bench cover for the World Cup final. Skinstad knew it was coming, as a rejuvenated England would be the opponents. It was a match that demanded a grafter like Van Heerden.

"I understood that Wikus would be picked, but it was still a terrible thing to hear. It was about five minutes past eight when Jake came up to me before breakfast and brought the bad news. I was upset, but at nine o'clock I received a phone call that my son had been born. That just put it all in perspective," Skinstad recalled.

While he shed a tear in the company of team psychologist Henning Gericke, it didn't take Skinstad long to get over what for men of lesser character would have been a devastating blow. What made it easier to digest was that Van Heerden was a friend as well as a colleague. "I still went out and did the wrong thing by having too many beers. There was the disappointment of having been dropped, but on the other hand I could celebrate the birth of my son. It was probably a way of dealing with the fact that Jake had done the right thing," Skinstad recalled.

He was spot-on, as Van Heerden secured a crucial turnover ball after replacing Danie Rossouw in the final 10 minutes.

On an individual level, Skinstad's career ended on an unspectacular note. His role as captain after the comeback had been functional rather than pivotal. Skinstad, however, reflects fondly on the relationships that were born out of the World Cup experience. "There were quality players that are still very good friends of mine. We were the dirt-trackers, the guys that were neither here nor there. Yet we had a fantastic work ethic and horsed around together. I loved the fact that we were able to be a happy little team that was very much functional."

Skinstad was undoubtedly one of the most talented players of his generation and those who watched him blaze onto the scene will feel his career should have spanned many more than 42 Tests. On sheer ability he belonged up there with the rugby gods.

However, he has a more mature view.

"I look at things in context. Remember, I smashed my car into a bridge and in the process hurt both my knees, the left one badly. It gave me perspective to realise that rugby wasn't everything. That crash was coming because I was deified by some people and a villain to others. I polarised people around the country – and still do, until they meet me. I just thank God it wasn't a worse accident," he said.

"I can now reflect that I wouldn't have gone into business had I not hit the brakes. I could have been a 31-year-old rugby player thinking he was the bee's knees, gone into business and lost all his money. It happens to others."

Strangely, Skinstad's biggest regret is that he pulled out of university as a 19-year-old to pursue a rugby career earlier than he should have. He was neither as confident nor as grounded as he should have been at the height of his career, when he was in his early twenties. If he had another go, he might also have closed off his career in a foreign country, which would have given him the opportunity of experiencing a different culture or another language.

There might also have been more captaincy highlights had Skinstad fitted the mould of a leader that the country and fellow South African players mostly respect: the grafter, of which Corné Krige was a good example. They were played off against one another in the media, and what had earlier been a good relationship suffered.

"We were very comfortable on the field, but there was a cloud around us off it. I was disappointed about some of the things that happened in that relationship, whether from his side or mine. Today we are good friends," said Skinstad.

"People didn't realise that we were a very complementary pair of players. I might have a few flashes of brilliance and he would work the full 80 minutes."

Skinstad never derived any pleasure from proving anyone wrong.

"It's a terrible thing to prove yourself to the detriment of others," he said.

"As South Africans we have unfortunately grown up with that: Do the stoic, hard work because we have been told to shut up and graft. The things that really change the world in terms of our sport are then appreciated later."

Skinstad subsequently became a happy family man, and his entrepreneurial spirit has made him successful in business. The corporate world is a fitting match for this business entrepreneur. He is a director of a listed company and has a strong acumen for venture capital investments and new business opportunities. Skinstad has also forged a successful career as a rugby commentator for SuperSport.

A wasted talent he was certainly not.

Perhaps Skinstad attracted criticism because Skinstad was different.

As such, of course, he should be celebrated. James Dean appeared in only three films, but he made a lasting impact on the film industry. Skinstad captained South Africa in just 12 Tests, but his rare talent, his optimism and his smiling face remain permanently engraved in the annals of Springbok rugby.

16 THE WARRIOR

Each Springbok captain is perhaps most accurately and perceptively assessed by his predecessors, the men who have played under the same pressure, the same burden of expectation.

Of Corné Krige, the revered former Springbok captain Morné du Plessis was moved to write: "He gave real meaning to the concept of 'leading from the front', as his physical commitment was at times frightening to behold. Has anybody ever shed so much blood on a rugby field?"

The answer to this question may well be no. The man chosen by Rudolf Straeuli to succeed Bob Skinstad as Springbok captain was, in every imaginable sense, a true rugby warrior.

Krige was inherently decent, unquestionably brave and physically strong. Indeed, he seemed the epitome of all the qualities that had served generations of Springbok captains so well in the past. It was his misfortune that, through two turbulent and traumatic years at the helm, the job would require other skills: the diplomatic talents of the Secretary General of the United Nations, the vision of Martin Luther King *et cetera*.

Challenged on the field, he fought back. Challenged off the field, he closed ranks. Yet raw courage and pure loyalty was not enough. The bloodied warrior was to be left exposed and disappointed.

When he eventually sat down to write his autobiography, Krige selected as his title *The Right Place at the Wrong Time*, providing perhaps the most telling, accurate and poignant insight to his experiences as Springbok captain during a troubled period in South African rugby history.

The robust back row forward famously captained the team in 1999, on his debut, standing in for Gary Teichmann and leading South Africa to a 101-0 victory over Italy. Three years later, in June 2002, newly appointed coach Rudolf Straeuli offered him the job in his own right.

As ever, the accession was far from straightforward. Krige had heard rumours that leading officials within SA Rugby preferred Skinstad to be retained as captain and, having been summoned to a meeting with the new coach, he bluntly asked if this was the case. "It's true," Straeuli replied, candidly, "there are people who don't want you to lead the team, but it's my decision, and I want you to be the captain."

An immediate bond seemed to have been forged between coach and captain and, as the 2002 season began to unfold, Straeuli and Krige planned another new dawn for Springbok rugby.

Corné Krige was born in Lusaka, Zambia, in the same hospital where George Gregan, the Australian scrumhalf and captain, had been born two years earlier. The co-incidence was remarkable, but it could not be said that the two contemporary international rugby stars shared the same heritage.

Krige's paternal grandfather, Pieter-Daniel, had been one of a group of Afrikaners who, soon after the end of the Second World War, had left the Free State, headed north and started to farm near the town of Fort Jameson, in what was then called northern Rhodesia. The family settled and, into the 1970s, his son Corrie was living with his wife Cecilia, known as "Babsie", on a 3 000-hectare farm, just 45 kilometres from Lusaka.

They grew maize and a bit of tobacco, and raised several hundred head of cattle, and, on 21 March 1975, the couple celebrated the birth of their third and last son, Corné.

The boy was raised in the bush. He learned the local Nyanja language from Sampson, his parents' chef and cleaner. He slept under the stars, fought with his brothers, fished and hunted. In those happy formative years, his entire family – his mother, father, brothers, uncle Ouboet and aunt Bennie – used to embark on two-week hunting trips to the Luangwa Valley, armed with rifles and a licence to hunt 12 animals.

Organised sport was, literally and figuratively, a thousand kilometres away.

This idyllic childhood was interrupted when, at the age of seven, young Krige was sent away to school near Cape Town. The well-intentioned plan was that he would attend Paarl Boys Primary School and stay with family friends nearby, but the boy was consumed with homesickness. He used to cry himself to sleep, burying his head deep in the pillow so his hosts would not be able to hear him sob.

He struggled to settle at school and, in 1986, his life became even more difficult when he returned home for Christmas to be informed that his parents had decided to divorce. "I was 11, my brothers Bennie and Pierre were 14 and 17," he recalls in his autobiography. "Three strong lads? Yes, sure, until we were confronted by the news. I vividly remember the three of us sitting down and crying our eyes out."

Krige found some solace in his growing passion for sport. He thrived at athletics and swimming, but he was beginning to shine on the rugby field, where he represented his school and then earned selection for the Western Province primary schools team at the annual Craven Week festival. Individual sports were all right, but it was the camaraderie and bonding of team sports that he relished above all else.

Rugby shaped him: it taught him to be brave as, from an early age, he would selflessly put his body on the line for his team, and it taught him to be loyal, to support his mates at all times. He performed adequately in the classroom and duly progressed to Paarl Boys High, where he played in two of the furious, traditional school derby matches against Paarl Gymnasium, losing in 1992 and winning in 1993. "To this day, that victory over Paarl Gym remains one of my proudest moments on a rugby field," he recalls.

One particular incident from his school days, related in his autobiography, provides a useful insight into the basic nature of this straightforward and tough man, who was destined to lead his country's rugby team through a bewildering series of unprecedented controversy, crisis and hullabaloo.

Krige recalls:

"One of the players in the opposing team was a kid called Tertius Hickman. He was a year younger than me, but we'd played trials against each other for the Under-19s, and he was quite good. In this match, he was playing quite well, and I thought he was being far too cocky for his own good. I ended up punishing him, laying it on the line, in effect putting him in his place. By the end of the game, he was black and blue.

"After the final whistle, a short, stocky man I didn't know came up to me. He introduced himself as Thomas Hickman, Tertius' father. My heart sank, but he put out his hand for me to shake and said, 'I want to thank you for sorting out my son. He needed someone to give him a hiding, or he'd get too big for his boots.'

"I was unsure of what to say but that was the start of a long friendship with the Hickman family. To this day, we're still very good friends and I often visit them at their home."

Such tales of "battering the youngster and becoming friends for life" are well known and well received within the global brotherhood of rugby union. It's a man's game, the members will say in rugby clubs from Aberdeen to Auckland, from Penzance to Potchefstroom, and opposing players will continue to exchange brutally clenched fists on the field as freely as they exchange pints of beer in the bar afterwards.

These ethics sit at the heart of the game. They are understood and completely accepted by the likes of Krige and the Hickmans and yet, during 2002 and 2003, as controversy swirled around South African rugby, they would appear bizarre and barbarous to people looking in from outside the game.

It would be the fate of the warrior captain to find himself caught between the culture of the brotherhood and the judgement of the outside world, and to suffer the consequences.

Upon leaving school, the loose forward continued to make swift progress. In 1994, he was named as captain of the South African team to compete at the under-19 World Championships in Lyon, France, where he led his side to victory over Italy in the final. It was no surprise when, two years later, he made his debut for Western Province and earned widespread acclaim as a new force for the Stormers in the Super 12.

In October 1997, aged only 22, he was included in Nick Mallett's first Springbok squad for the tour to Italy, France, England and Scotland. Krige appeared to have the game at his feet.

Not for long.

Days after the announcement of the squad, playing in the Currie Cup final, he damaged the anterior cruciate ligament in his right knee and was ruled out of rugby for nine months. Soon after he recovered, he was involved in a car accident near Malmesbury, when his pick-up truck rolled six times and he might easily have been killed. Only expert surgery prevented the loss of the middle finger on his right hand.

He finally toured with the Springboks at the end of 1998, but had to wait until 1999 to play his Test debut, as captain in the romp over Italy. Just two months later, playing against New Zealand in Dunedin, he ruptured the anterior cruciate ligament in his left knee and was ruled out for the rest of the season. He recovered fitness again, but then, playing a warm-up match in February 2000, suffered a broken jaw.

Four serious injuries within 28 months put a question mark over a career, broken on the relentless treadmill of professional rugby and withering in the treatment rooms of Cape Town.

Krige fought back once again, captaining Western Province to the Currie Cup title in 2000, but his Springbok career seemed to be stalled by the appointment of Harry Viljoen as Springbok coach. He was made to feel surplus to requirements, cast as a tight phase expert out of place in a team aiming to play expansive rugby. At the end of 2001, he almost left South Africa to play for Bath in the English Premiership.

He decided to stay at home ... and, six months later, he became Springbok captain.

"It was a tremendous privilege," he recalls, "and I decided to give my utmost, all I had, to make a success of the job. I thought Rudolf Straeuli had started very well as Springbok coach. He wanted to go back to the basics of South African rugby, and to play to our traditional strengths. He brought back Springbok trials and organised our first training camp at the South African Police Training College in Pretoria.

"We got on from the word go. I think Rudi enjoyed the way I played and liked me as a person. Both times when Western Province beat his Sharks team to win the Currie Cup in 2000 and 2001, we had been quite far behind. I was captain in both matches: perhaps he respected me for that."

When Straeuli and Krige took over, they had two years and 16 Tests to prepare the Springbok challenge for the IRB Rugby World Cup in 2003, and their plans started well. The Pumas were defeated 49-29 at the PAM Brink stadium in Springs and, a week later, the Samoans were beaten 60-18 at Loftus Versfeld.

Optimism rippled through the country. The 2002 Springboks were neither the first South African team to fly east with real hope of success in their two Tri-Nations away matches, and nor were they the first to return home with a sense of deflation and two defeats. The All Blacks had proved too powerful in Wellington, winning 41-20, and the Wallabies had won a much closer match in Brisbane, by 38-27.

All was not lost for South Africa with the two home matches to come, but a narrow defeat to New Zealand in Durban, by 23-30, effectively ended Springbok hopes. A measure of pride was restored against the Australians at Ellis Park, when fullback Werner Greeff scored a thrilling try after the hooter had sounded and then picked himself up to kick the decisive conversion and secure a famous 33-31 victory.

Something like the golfer who finishes a generally average round by holing a long putt on the 18th green, the South Africans ended the Tri-Nations with a smile, and another wooden spoon.

Krige had characteristically led the team from the front, literally hurling himself into every contest, refusing to step back from any challenge and, occasionally, playing on the edge of legality.

During the match in Brisbane, Ben Tune had thrown a punch that opened a cut above Krige's eye, and the Australian winger seemed to boast about the feat in the media afterwards. The Springbok captain, who frequently spoke to his players about "being clever" in physical confrontations, made a mental note.

The Tune punch was still being talked about prior to the return match at Ellis Park and the referee, Paddy O'Brien, of New Zealand, not only warned Krige not to do anything stupid but also asked both his touch judges to keep their eyes wide open whenever Tune was caught in a ruck.

Early in the game, Tune was caught in possession and a ruck formed. O'Brien blew quickly, but the Wallaby wing emerged bleeding. Neither the referee nor his assistants had seen anything but Krige, as he later confirmed to O'Brien, had successfully got his man and settled his score from Brisbane.

He had proved himself a true rugby warrior, a man who could take rough treatment without complaint and could give it without being caught. At rugby clubs all around the world, legions of Thomas Hickmans would have nodded in admiration. Beyond the brotherhood, others recoiled at the brutality.

Nonetheless, the team appeared to have found some direction under Straeuli's firm hand and, by the end of the Tri-Nations, the mood within the squad was overwhelmingly positive.

These good vibrations were to be nullified and obliterated by the relentless demands of professional rugby, where the leading players were required to play at least 40 intensely physical, bone-crunching matches each year. Injuries and burnout were inevitable and, in November 2002, an exposed Springbok coach was compelled to take what amounted to a second-string team on tour to France, Scotland and England.

Straeuli had been dealt an impossible hand. Even Krige had initially been unavailable for the tour, having dislocated his thumb while playing for Western Province and been advised to have an operation. However, when Skinstad, Van der Westhuizen and Victor Matfield all withdrew, Straeuli called his captain again. "I need you to come to Europe," the coach pleaded. "We just don't have enough experience."

Others would have made their excuses. Krige agreed.

Disaster loomed, and disaster happened.

First, the desperately inexperienced South African team suffered a 30-10 defeat in Marseille, a record defeat against France that might, in truth, have been even heavier. August's bright optimism evaporated and, through no fault of their own, the coach and captain found themselves plunged into crisis. SA Rugby officials openly expressed their displeasure at the performance, and the tour went from bad to worse.

Straeuli accurately identified his team's tackling at Marseille as inadequate, and prescribed a tough contact practice session ahead of the Test in Edinburgh. Within minutes, centre Marius Joubert went down with a shoulder injury that ruled him out. Every expression darkened once again, as if management and players alike appeared to realise this was fated to be the Springbok tour when everything went wrong.

As dusk settled upon Murrayfield the following Saturday evening, the Springboks sat in their changing room, silent, stunned and shocked by a poor performance and a 21-6 defeat against a Scotland side that even a depleted South African team would have expected to overcome with something to spare.

Yes, the weather had been foul. Yes, the Scots had been awarded a doubtful try. Yes, another record margin of defeat was embarrassing.

Surely the tour couldn't get worse.

Yes, it could.

The South African squad flew south to London, where they would play England on Saturday 23 November 2002. "It was," Krige recalls, painfully, "a day I wish had never happened."

What did happen? In simple terms, a fiercely competitive Springbok captain saw his team being overrun and humiliated, completely lost control and indulged in an orgy of violence.

The contest had been relatively even for 23 minutes, but the tone changed when a hot-headed Springbok swore at the referee, Paddy O'Brien. The New Zealander responded by saying he would not tolerate any more indiscipline, and the unfortunate player to "catch the bullet" was lock Jannes Labuschagne, who was promptly sent off for a late tackle on Jonny Wilkinson. Reduced to 14 men against powerful opponents, the South Africans proceeded to subside. The Springbok captain lost his head. "I knew we were going to lose," Krige later confessed in his autobiography, "but I made up my mind to take a few people down with me. I committed some appalling fouls, hitting people in possession and smashing others off the ball."

Of course, there is no doubt that, in a century of Test rugby, other Springbok captains have been guilty of similarly severe foul play. Unfortunately, it is also the case that Krige's misdemeanours were laid out before millions of appalled television viewers around the world. The damage inflicted upon the good name of South African rugby by the pandemonium at Twickenham in 2002 can scarcely be underestimated.

Krige punched Jason Robinson, head-butted Matt Dawson, elbowed Martin Johnson after a tussle with the England captain and then, most embarrassingly, knocked out his own flyhalf André Pretorius because Dawson, the primary target of his stiff-arm challenge, had managed to duck in time.

Amid chaos and acrimony, England won the match by 53-3.

"It was the worst beating a Springbok side has ever suffered," Krige wrote. "And you can imagine how I felt as the team's captain. You can choose whichever words you wish: hurt, pain, anger, resentment, fury. All of them applied to my state of mind that afternoon as we trudged off Twickenham. When I sat down in the dressing room after the final whistle, I just cried my eyes out. I was mentally shattered."

Such humiliation claimed its victims. Seven members of that team never played for South Africa again, one won only two more caps, and two others secured three more caps. Krige escaped further disciplinary action by the International Rugby Board, following a plea on his behalf by Rian Oberholzer, the CEO of SA Rugby, and, upon his return home, the captain issued a public apology for his lack of discipline.

Passing time has hardly eased his sense of shame. "Today, I struggle to believe that it was really me who had been involved," he wrote. "I have a wife and child, friends and family. I live a decent, ordinary life; I am not a hit man, an assassin. But I regret that day more than any in my entire rugby career.

"I let down the Springbok team and its emblem and image, the South African people, myself. Even today, I am still deeply embarrassed whenever I see any of that footage on television. But my philosophy in life has always been 'if you are in the wrong, front up, accept the criticism, take it on the chin and then move on. Do not complain if you are responsible for your own misfortunes' – which I was."

A record defeat against France, a record defeat against Scotland and a record defeat against England: all in the space of 15 days. There were extenuating circumstances, specifically the understrength squad, yet the results stood stark in the record book, and a sense of shock reverberated through the game.

Straeuli had been wounded too, with the result that, in the eyes of his captain, the relaxed, assured, people-friendly coach of 2002 became more cautious in 2003. Sustained public criticism, unrealistic expectations and intense pressure seemed to transform the perception of this light-hearted, bright and sympathetic man.

In 1994, as a member of the Springbok squad touring Wales, Scotland and Ireland, Straeuli emerged as the practical joker of the tour, setting off fireworks in his Swansea hotel room, ceaselessly smiling, at one stage being pinned to ground by police after disconnecting the electricity supply to the marquee where HRH Princess Anne was attending the official banquet following the Test at Murrayfield.

Nine years on, the carefree player had become a hunted coach and, week-by-week, through 2003, a small group of players began to undermine the coach's standing within the squad.

When SA Rugby employed a security consultant, Adriaan Heijns, some of these players whined that the coach had hired Heijns to spy on them. When the coach tried to impose discipline, some of these players complained he was heavy-handed.

When the coach tried to toughen up his players by switching their team accommodation from their normal five-star luxury hotel to less familiar surroundings, some of these players resented the imposition. When the coach tried to instil uniformity and professionalism, asking the players to wear the same colour T-shirt and to shave on a regular basis, some of these players pouted like children.

In such situations, it is often the captain who steps forward and acts as an intermediary between the coach and increasingly disgruntled players but, as the 2003 season unfolded, Krige felt variously unable and unwilling to bring management and players together and to restore harmony.

Again, his reflections are almost painfully honest. "I felt intimidated," he wrote later, "and this prevented me from fully airing the players' concerns. I somehow felt it was too dangerous, that Rudi would take it personally. I thought I would say so much and be dropped and perhaps not get back into the side. I suppose the bottom line is that I wasn't brave enough to state my case. Today, I deeply regret my inability to speak up, because that aspect of my captaincy failed. I let the players down by not standing up to the coach."

Krige's fears of retribution seem to have been exaggerated. In truth, SA Rugby and Straeuli had gone to extraordinary lengths to support and protect the captain, and to involve him in every discussion relating to the team. If the captain subsequently felt unable to support the decisions taken jointly, that is nobody else's fault.

Key relationships within the squad became strained and it was amid this atmosphere that the 2003 Springboks tried to win some rugby matches.

Two home Test matches against Scotland seemed a digestible start to a season that would lead towards the Rugby World Cup in Australia, particularly since the series offered an opportunity for the Springboks to exact swift revenge for their embarrassing defeat in Edinburgh the previous season.

That was the plan but, with Joost van der Westhuizen standing in as captain for the injured Krige, the South Africans struggled. They trailed 12-25 after an hour of the first Test in Durban, fought back to lead 29-25 and then breathed a communal sigh of relief when Nathan Hines, the Scottish lock forward, inexplicably dropped the ball as he seemed ready to score a match-winning try in the dying seconds. A week later at Ellis Park, the Springboks had to come from behind once again, scrambling to a 28-19 victory.

"A win is a win," ran the general consensus but, two weeks later, even with Krige recovered to lead the team, the lethargic Springboks proved unable to subdue the spirited Argentine forwards in Port Elizabeth and relied upon flyhalf Louis Koen to kick a last-minute penalty and scrape a 26-25 victory.

Another unforgiving Tri-Nations series loomed ominously and yet, even under bitter criticism, even apparently unaware of their strongest team, even lacking confidence, the Springboks somehow managed to dig deep into that time-honoured well of tradition, spirit and courage that has served the team so well through the generations … and Krige's team managed to defeat the Wallabies at Newlands.

The hero was Brent Russell, the lively Sharks utility back who had come on as a replacement and promptly skipped around the Australian defence to score a memorable try. South Africa led 20-10 at the break and, with heroic defence, notably in the midfield, they closed out a 26-22 victory.

"Can this team win the World Cup?" the question was asked.

"Of course," came the reply.

As ever, the Springbok team was only ever one glorious victory from being hailed as the next world champions … and one disappointing defeat away from being lambasted as a disgrace to the jersey.

The squad prepared to play the All Blacks in Pretoria, and the Springbok forwards, by now almost the Blue Bulls in green and gold, held their own for an hour. Then the All Black wingers Doug Howlett and Joe Rokocoko each scored a couple of tries, and the home team disintegrated in the closing quarter. A typically close-fought Tri-Nations match quickly became a rout. Try followed try and, when the final whistle eventually sounded, the Loftus crowd gazed in disbelief at the electronic scoreboard and surveyed the proof of another record defeat against a traditional rival.

South Africa 16 New Zealand 52.

The humiliation struck at the heart of Springbok rugby.

Krige appeared on the point of mental and physical exhaustion as he desolately left the field. He was also furious because, in his view, certain of his team-mates had ducked out of tackles, even turned their backs on play and, unthinkably, effectively stopped trying while wearing a Springbok jersey. "I'm disgusted," he shouted at the post-match huddle in the changing room. "You should be ashamed."

From the historic low of Twickenham 2002, morale seemed to have plunged even lower, and the away leg of the Tri-Nations series seemed a daunting prospect for a Springbok team riddled with failing relationships, bereft of self-confidence, and the target of vitriolic criticism on all sides. Three months before the Rugby World Cup, hardly a single player seemed certain of his place in the South African team.

In the event, the team lost 29-9 to the Wallabies in Brisbane, and had two players sent to the sin bin, thus affirming global perceptions of a dirty team, but then managed to produce a more courageous display in Dunedin, battling hard and restricting the All Blacks to a close-fought 19-11 victory.

Perhaps, optimists suggested, if the team could just be allowed a little peace, some time to rebuild morale and confidence, South Africa could still mount a serious challenge at the World Cup.

These beleaguered Springboks were denied even that because, through plain mismanagement, a relatively minor spark was allowed to escalate into a blazing inferno that dominated the headlines and once again dragged the team into controversy and disrepute at home and around the world.

Ever since the late 1990s, SA Rugby had responded to political pressure that the national team should be more representative of South Africa's demography by imposing a gentlemen's agreement that black and coloured players would be given proper opportunities in the Springbok team. "Quota" was the word that dared not speak its name, but successive national coaches understood the reality and quietly complied.

The arrangement succeeded insofar as it kept the politicians at bay, but it created unwelcome tension within the squad. Divisions occasionally appeared between white players, who privately doubted whether some of their black and coloured team-mates deserved to wear the green and gold, and an increasingly protective group of black and coloured players who, by and large, preferred each other's company.

The situation amounted to a tinderbox of racial tension.

A spark was ignited on the very first day of a pre-Rugby World Cup training camp in Pretoria when Geo Cronjé, a towering, bearded and essentially conservative Afrikaner lock forward from Pretoria, declined to share a room with Quinton Davids, his coloured team-mate from Cape Town.

Management dithered, the story leaked into the media, SA Rugby set up an investigation, banner headlines proclaiming racism within the Springbok camp flashed around the world and, most damaging of all, the hitherto unspoken tensions within the national squad exploded into the open.

Krige watched aghast as his squad polarised before his eyes. The captain tried to be even-handed and keep the group together. On the one hand, he attended a meeting with just the black and coloured players to hear their grievances. On the other hand, he refused to tell the SA Rugby investigators Cronjé was a racist because he knew such a statement would probably have ended the lock forward's career.

The Springbok squad to challenge for the Webb Ellis Cup was announced on Saturday 30 August 2003, live on the SuperSport television channel – neither Cronjé nor Davids was included – and, as thirty excited players posed for photographs and sang the national anthem, Krige allowed himself the hope that he and his squad would finally be able to focus on their preparations for the career-defining tournament.

The captain's hope was in vain.

Instead there followed one of the most notorious episodes in the history of Springbok rugby. What had been planned as a pseudo-military team-building camp unfolded as four days of some sensible, proven and carefully planned team-building exercises interspersed with incidents that bordered on abuse and seemed singularly inappropriate to a professional sports team.

Various South African provincial teams had embarked upon similar ventures with varying levels of success, but even those who planned this camp would later concede some aspects were excessive.

"Welcome to Kamp Staaldraad," announced Adriaan Heijns, SA Rugby's security consultant who, much to the players' surprise, appeared to be running the entire exercise.

Over the four days that followed, amid the many worthwhile exercises, these professional athletes were stripped and searched, instructed to drag logs and tyres through the bush, marched through the night, ordered to inflate rugby balls in a lake with icy water up to their neck, ordered to put on headgear and boxing gloves and fight each other, compelled to kill chickens with their bare hands, and made to huddle together in a pit naked in the middle of the night while the chanting of the All Black haka was blasted from speakers.

The players did as they were told. So did the captain. At stages, Krige felt the urge to speak out, notably when the cold water took its toll on his senses. He wanted to lead his players out of that freezing lake. In his autobiography he recalls wanting to say: "That's it. I'm leaving. Do what you like, but I'm leading my players off this camp."

In fact, he stayed and he obeyed and completed the camp.

When details of what had happened were eventually made public, Krige's innate sense of loyalty meant he initially seemed to defend what had taken place in the bush, explaining it had been an emotional, bonding experience for the players. This was right and proper since the captain had been involved in the overview planning of the exercise, if not in all the detail. It is true that, when the team bus headed into the bush north of Pretoria that night, he had known where the bus was going.

Writing in his autobiography some months of public outrage later, Krige reflects: "I know today I should have stood up for my players. I should have done it, but I didn't. Rugby players have rights, like anyone else. They have their dignity, and they should be able to retain it while training to represent their country. Deliberately degrading and dehumanising athletes should have no place in any sporting team's preparations."

Anybody is entitled to change their mind about anything, but it seems certain that if Krige had expressed such strong views when Kamp Staaldraad was mooted and discussed with him, the exercise would not have unfolded as it did.

With the benefit of 20/20 hindsight, almost everybody agrees that Kamp Staaldraad went too far, and it will never be repeated. It was a well-intentioned aberration that subsequently caused embarrassment to South African rugby when photographs of Springboks huddling naked in a pit were published in various newspapers around the world.

The camp had been conceived three months in advance to engender morale and team spirit before the World Cup. If there is any blame to be apportioned for errors of judgement, it should be laid at the door of everyone who was consulted and signed off on the plans: officials of SA Rugby, the team manager, the coach and the captain.

The Springbok players, admirably, put the experience behind them and headed for Australia, to contest the fifth Rugby World Cup tournament. They travelled more in hope than expectation, because their recent form was poor and, as a result, there was no sign of a settled and confident team. Any sense of optimism was based solely on a deep-rooted conviction that any Springbok team always has a puncher's chance.

It never looked like being enough.

South African ambitions appeared to hinge on the outcome of their pool match against England in Perth, where victory would secure a relatively straightforward route to the semi-finals. Defeat, on the other hand, would put them in the quarterfinal path of the All Black juggernaut. Krige inadvertently provided the English team with their pre-match motivation by carelessly describing his opposite number, Martin Johnson, as "one of the dirtiest captains in world rugby". The off-hand remark may have been fair comment, but it was fanned into global headlines and appeared faintly ironic in the light of the Springbok captain's recent antics at Twickenham.

The Boks opened their campaign with a 72-6 canter over Uruguay and prepared to face a powerful, settled English team, already installed as the tournament favourites. Straeuli tried everything, even arranging for England jerseys to be pulled over tackle bags at his squad's training sessions.

Krige rallied his players and, for almost an hour, they matched England. Victor Matfield was imperious in the lineout and South Africa suddenly seemed capable of a surprise triumph. Straeuli was encouraged to hear Johnson calling lineout ball almost exclusively on himself, trying to slow the game down.

Then, the match turned. Flyhalf Louis Koen missed a couple of potentially decisive penalties and, when his clearance was charged down for Greenwood to sprint through and score a priceless try, the English machine was able to relax, crank up a gear and ultimately ease to a 25-6 victory.

The Springboks regained some momentum with a 46-19 win over Georgia and an impressive 60-10 victory over a Samoan team that had given England a genuine scare ... still a puncher's chance.

And yet, as the Springboks prepared for their quarterfinal against New Zealand in Melbourne, a general lack of self-belief seemed to permeate through the squad. Six consecutive defeats against the All Blacks, suffered since August 2000, had left this particular group of South African players, however talented, struggling to understand, and even to imagine, quite how it felt to overcome their oldest rivals.

They sang their national anthem before the game, puffed out their cheeks and prepared to play maybe the biggest match of their careers ... but Springbok spirits appeared to drain away when the New Zealanders efficiently dominated possession for the first 25 minutes and, once the All Blacks scored their opening try, the South Africans stood beneath their posts, heads bowed, thinking "here we go again".

The result was never in doubt, and New Zealand won 29-9.

Krige sat sombre in the changing room afterwards.

"What are you going to do now?" Matfield asked.

"Retire," the captain replied.

"I'm sorry," the lock said. "I feel that some of us have let you down."

"It's OK," Krige responded. "You tried your best."

The disappointed Springboks faced up to the reality of elimination, and the wrath of their compatriots. South Africans have never been world class in the art of accepting defeat, but the squad's return home coincided with revelations of what had taken place at Kamp Staaldraad prior to the tournament. Photographs of Springbok rugby players, the pride of the nation, huddled together in a dark pit, naked and dishevelled, were splashed across front pages, and the understandable uproar that followed began to claim victims.

Krige, it seemed, might survive. To his surprise, he had been asked by Straeuli to remain as captain for one more year. He was told to visit the SA Rugby office and sign a new Springbok contract.

But events were gathering pace. Rian Oberholzer resigned as CEO and Rudolf Straeuli resigned as coach. In circumstances when others might have sprinted to Newlands, signed their contract extension and secured another full year's salary, Krige reflected for a moment and decided to step down as well.

After 39 Tests, he retired from Springbok rugby with his honour intact.

"I have given this a lot of thought and discussed things with my wife and family," the captain said in a media statement. "I have thoroughly enjoyed playing for the Springboks and it has been a dream come true to captain the team. I appeal to all involved at SA Rugby to realise the potential and value of the players we have in this country. I believe we have a squad that can be world-beaters, if utilised correctly."

Seven months later, on 21 August 2004, a crowd of some 12 000 spectators arrived at Newlands to watch Western Province thrash Griqualand West. The spectators had also turned up to bid farewell to Corné Krige, who, at the age of 29, had decided to conclude his playing career with Northampton in England.

The departing hero marked the occasion by kicking a drop goal in the closing minutes. At the final whistle, he was carried around Newlands on the shoulders of his team-mates before disappearing from view. A reception was held in his honour, to which officials of the Western Province Rugby Union had taken the trouble of inviting each of the surgeons who had operated on Krige during a career punctuated by injuries.

He had signed to join his former Stormers coach Alan Solomons at Northampton, leading a group of six South African players at the midlands club. When results suffered, the imports were blamed. Solomons was fired after a series of defeats, and, on 10 February 2005, Krige announced his own retirement.

In difficult circumstances, typically, he remained at his post until the end of the English season, playing a major role in helping the club avoid relegation from the Premiership. Then, together with his wife Justine and their young daughter, Sophia, the former Springbok captain flew back to Cape Town, back home.

Still short of his 30th birthday, his career was over.

"I was still quite young," he reflects, "but the birth of our child made me think differently about bashing my body about for a few more years. The thing that has always underpinned my rugby was my total commitment and my fear was that I would not be able to give that same commitment for another year."

The warrior, scarred and exhausted, laid down his weapons ... soon to be reincarnated as a quiet family man, working hard to establish his outdoor advertising business in Cape Town, spending his weekends at home, relieved to escape the endless turmoil that seemed to have enveloped his life for so long.

How will Corné Krige be remembered?

As the Springbok captain who lost his head at Twickenham? Or as the Springbok captain identified with the controversy of Kamp Staaldraad? Or even as the Springbok captain who led the team to record defeats against four different countries within the space of ten months?

Each of these verdicts would be extremely harsh.

He made mistakes, there is no doubt. Everyone makes mistakes.

Yet Krige's errors were born not of cunning or malice, but of passion and loyalty: he hated seeing his team embarrassed by England, so he went berserk; he felt such a strong sense of duty to Springbok rugby and all that it represented that he baulked at challenging the team's authorities; and his individual levels of performance and commitment never flagged through a sequence of disappointing results.

No, far from being condemned, Krige deserves to be remembered as a true rugby warrior who led the South African rugby team with guts and honour through a notably turbulent period.

He should be recalled, above all, as the man who faced the most challenging and difficult situations, as a strong man who never stopped trying.

17 THE HEALER

The Mugg & Bean at Sandton City is a coffee shop typical of that vast, affluent, polished shopping complex north of central Johannesburg. It's smart and clean, invariably busy with shoppers, tourists and office workers, the sort of place where it's possible to sit and watch a bright, dynamic and positive country passing by.

One morning in March 2004, the newly appointed Springbok rugby coach is sitting quietly at a table, waiting patiently. Then he stands to greet the player he has arranged to meet, and the two men shake each other warmly by the hand. They have known each other for a decade, and they get along.

Jake White, the coach, talks about his challenge to revive the Springbok rugby team, and outlines his plans to develop a united, happy and successful squad from the ashes of race rows, a disappointing World Cup and the shame of Kamp Staaldraad. The player, all 1.88 metres and 116 kilograms of him, listens with interest.

After a while, White clears his throat and says: "And I want you to be the Springbok captain."

"OK ..." replies John Smit, the Sharks hooker, cautiously.

"Is that a 'yes'?" the coach presses.

"So long as I am your first choice hooker, it's a yes," Smit replies. "I'll be captain if you are one hundred per cent sure that I'm worth my place in the team. If you have doubts, choose somebody else."

The coach smiles, and adds: "You're my first choice hooker."

"Then I'll be your captain."

The two men shake hands again. The core partnership that would, within just seven months, heal Springbok rugby, guiding the team from despair to triumph, has been firmly established.

His two elder brothers called him "twins" because they reckoned he got a double share of everything. Basil Smit, a mechanical engineer, and his wife, Valerie, a primary school teacher, probably did dote on their youngest son John, and in 1992 they took a decision that would shape the rest of his life.

The family was living in Pietersburg, now Polokwane, and sons Brian and David had been educated at the renowned local high school, Capricorn Hoërskool. However, when the family moved to Rustenburg, after some debate it was agreed that, at the age of 13, young John would be sent away to board at Pretoria Boys High School.

"At that time, I wasn't too interested in rugby," he recalls. "Tennis was my favourite sport, but that quickly changed. As soon as I arrived, I realised that if you played sport at Boys High, then the No. 1 sport to play would be rugby. The school had outstanding coaches, like Paul Anthony and Jannie Biddulph, and I never looked back. The fact is, if I hadn't been sent to Boys High, I would never have become a Springbok."

The game came quickly to him. Broad and strong, he was picked to make his debut as a prop for the PBHS first XV when he was still only 16 years old. Their opponents that afternoon in 1994 were Jeppe High School for Boys, one of the strongest schools in Johannesburg, a team guided by a renowned schools coach named … Jake White.

It was not a happy day for the young prop: he found himself scrumming against a super-sized 19-year-old and spent most of the afternoon having his eager face rubbed into the turf. He trooped away at the final whistle, chastened and disheartened. The idea that this deflated 16-year-old would one day combine with the Jeppe coach and lead the Springbok rugby team seemed unimaginable.

The schoolboy continued to mature and the following year, alongside millions of his compatriots, he found himself caught up in the euphoria that swept across the country during the 1995 Rugby World Cup. He sat among his mates at school, watching South Africa's semi-final victory over France on television, and, for the first time in his young life, started to feel the power of sport to unite.

"Do you want to come to the final?"

Smit looked at David Tubb, his school friend, in disbelief, and asked: "Are you serious?"

"My dad's got two tickets, and he said I could bring a friend. Do you want to come?"

The invitation was immediately accepted and so, on 24 June 1995, the two teenagers were driven down the M1 from Pretoria to Johannesburg to watch South Africa play New Zealand in the World Cup final. They had seats in the south stand, which turned out to be ideal on the day because, just before kick-off, they were thrilled by the sight of the jumbo jet seeming to fly directly at them and, two hours later, they were in an ideal position to watch Stransky's winning drop goal soar between the uprights, into history.

Smit remembers: "It took us four hours to drive home to Pretoria that night. Everyone seemed to be out in the streets, celebrating, singing, dancing and blowing their horns. I loved every minute. That was one of the best days of my life. It was incredible to see rugby making so many people so happy."

His rugby career meandered along. He held his place in the Boys High first XV for a second and third successive season. There were highs, such as being chosen for the Northern Transvaal High Schools team to play at Craven Week, and there were lows, such as being thrashed 62-13 by PBHS's traditional rivals, Afrikaanse Hoër Seunskool. As he recalls, he "never dreamed" of becoming a pro rugby player.

"I was keen to be a physiotherapist," he says, "and everything was arranged for me to study at Tukkies, the University of Pretoria. That was what I would be. Then, out of the blue, the Sharks contacted me and offered me an academy contract. I was surprised, but it was tempting and my parents were very supportive. So I decided to take the chance, and headed down to Durban to take my BCom in rugby."

The initial plan was for him to pursue his degree in physiotherapy at the University of Natal in Pietermaritzburg, but he shelved the course within six months. From 1997, it was rugby, rugby, rugby.

He rose through the Sharks ranks, made his Super 12 debut against the Waratahs in 1999 and, later that year, was named captain of the South African team to play in the SANZAR under-21 championships in Argentina. The assistant coach of that talented side, putting his faith in John Smit, was Jake White.

"Even then, Smittie stood out as a natural leader," White recalls. "There was a media conference at the start of the tournament and he was asked to attend alongside the Australian and New Zealand captains. He went along, but was then completely ignored because the journalists only directed questions at the captains of the teams who everyone expected to reach the final. As soon as he got back to our hotel, John called a team meeting and told his players about the disrespect shown to South African rugby. He was eloquent and passionate. From that moment, every South African was motivated to do whatever was required to win."

White continues: "The thing that impressed me most, though, was that he came to me after that meeting and told me emotion would get his team only so far. He said intelligence and skill would win the day, and he sat with us for hours as we analysed the opposition and devised ways of beating them."

Against expectations, Smit's under-21 team defeated both the Australian and the New Zealand teams within the space of four days, and famously claimed the title. The chances of the former Jeppe coach and the Boys High rookie one day leading the Springboks seemed to be improving.

The hooker established himself in the Sharks team and, in June 2000, was selected by Nick Mallett to make his Springbok debut against Canada. His future appeared green and golden.

Instead, there followed three years of intermittent injury, dashed hopes and frustration. He did win a further 25 Test caps during this period, and yet he tended to bounce in and out of the Springbok squad, on the bench, off the bench. Advocates praised his strength;

critics complained about his lack of mobility. Then, in 2002, just when Rudolf Straeuli was poised to name him captain, he suffered a serious shoulder injury.

Intelligent, serious and committed, he took time to serve on the Executive Committee of the South African Rugby Players Association (SARPA), and made a genuine contribution to the body created to protect the working environment and conditions of the country's 450 professional rugby players.

On the field, he kept plugging away, training hard, playing well, enduring Kamp Staaldraad and then being appointed to captain the Springboks in their 2003 World Cup pool match against Georgia.

He surveyed the mass resignations at the end of that year with interest, and monitored the process of finding a new Springbok coach: the release of a four-man shortlist, the withdrawal of two of those four, the introduction of a new list with eight names and, eventually, the formal appointment of Jake White.

Soon afterwards, he was phoned and invited for coffee at the Mugg & Bean in Sandton, and on 25 March 2004 John Smit was unveiled to the media as the new Springbok rugby captain.

It is said, in business and sport, that the best time to take over a company, or a team, is when things seem so bad they can't get any worse. If this is true, then White and Smit could not have chosen a better time to take control of Springbok rugby. Ranked sixth in the world after the World Cup quarterfinal defeat, in the wake of race rows, Kamp Staaldraad and an exodus of top players to Europe, expectations were low.

Their first challenge, in June 2004, was a two-Test home series against an upbeat Ireland team, ranked fifth in the world, ahead of South Africa. When Irish journalists called their team "favourites" ahead of the first Test in Bloemfontein, they successfully pricked South African pride. "No Springbok team has ever lost a series against this bunch," Smit told his team, "and we're not about to become the first."

White's broom had swept clean, to the extent that his first team included only five members of the side selected for the previous Test, the World Cup quarterfinal against New Zealand, but one of the most inexperienced South African teams ever to take the field responded to the call, and prevailed. A two-try burst early in the second half secured a 31-17 victory, leaving both the coach and captain with a strong sense of relief.

Progress continued seven days later at Newlands, when South Africa burst into a 23-7 lead before half time and secured the series win over Ireland with a final score of 26-17. The following Saturday in Pretoria, the revitalised Boks impressively overwhelmed a touring Wales team, posting a 53-18 victory.

"Not bad," chorused the cautious critics, "but the Tri-Nations will be the real test."

A new team was taking shape: Percy Montgomery had been recalled as a principal goalkicker and fullback, the talented Jaco van der West-huyzen was thriving at flyhalf, young Schalk Burger was being acclaimed as a world-class flanker, Victor Matfield and Bakkies Botha looked a world-class pair of locks, and the developing unit was held together by the quiet, effective and respected leadership of the hooker, John Smit.

The captain's contribution was appreciated by Jean de Villiers, fast emerging as an incisive, dynamic centre, who reflected the general view when he told journalists: "John toughens up our mental approach. He knows what makes the players tick, and you only hear perfect sense coming from his mouth. He's not the type of captain who rants and raves, but he has a great sense of timing. When he talks, we listen."

They did. They listened when Smit supported a suggestion that the squad should publicly protest about the stalling of their contract nego-tiations. Talks between SARPA, the players' union, and SA Rugby had collapsed and it was mooted that the players should make their feelings clear by wearing armbands during their next match, against a Pacific Islands team in Gosford, ahead of the away leg of the Tri-Nations.

Such action had been proposed several times before, but had always been dismissed because players seemed incapable of standing together. Historically, they had been divided and ruled. However, in 2004, for the first time, emboldened and empowered by Smit's calm, resolved leadership, the Springboks united in their own cause. "It was a big thing for the players," the captain says. "We wanted to make a point, and together we decided to wear the armbands, whatever the conse-quences. The spirit of solidarity was very strong."

The contract issues were resolved, and Smit's standing among his players soared. Bonding off the field prompted success on the field. The Springboks surged to an impressive 33-0 lead over the Fijians, Samoans and Tongans, cruising to a 38-24 victory. White remembers a "great vibe" in the South African changing room after the match.

The team opened their 2004 Tri-Nations campaign against the All Blacks in Christchurch, taking the lead after only 23 seconds. After Smit had snatched a loose ball at the base of a ruck, centre De Wet Barry ran clear and offloaded to De Villiers, who dashed through to score a stunning try. Montgomery converted, and the South Africans looked up at the scoreboard and dared to think victory was possible.

It soon got better. Tries by Jacques Cronjé and Fourie du Preez gave the visitors a 21-12 half-time lead and an unexpected win suddenly seemed probable. The All Blacks fought back, dominating possession and territory, but the Springbok tackling was nothing less than heroic. Smit implored his players on, at the heart of every scrum and maul, and, as the final hooter sounded, his team were still clinging to a 21-18 lead.

Job done, it seemed …

Not quite. Heartbreak followed.

Aware the match would end as soon as the ball went dead, the New Zealanders mounted one last attack, poured forward, and sent winger Doug Howlett over to score in the right-hand corner. South African players sunk to their knees, dejected, deflated, lucklessly defeated by 23-21.

White tried to raise his side's spirits. "We've lost today," he told them, "but the All Blacks beat us by 50 points last year, so we're moving in the right direction."

The Springboks regrouped and headed to play Australia in Perth with real optimism, but, for the second time in eight days, they found themselves on the wrong end of an epic Tri-Nations match.

Again they started well, playing committed and positive rugby. Van der Westhuyzen rounded off a fine move, De Villiers scored an intercept try and again the Springboks led at half time, by 16-15. Montgomery kicked magnificently, and, again, gallant defence seemed to have secured victory.

Again they conceded a try in the dying minutes when Clyde Rathbone, the former South African under-21 winger who had defected to Australia, burst through to score and seize a 30-26 win for his adopted nation. Again, coach White praised his team, salvaged the many positives and moved on.

"We can still win this tournament," the coach ventured.

Eyebrows rose. Two losses hardly suggested glory ahead, but other results and two bonus points by virtue of the narrow away defeats, by just two and four points, meant the Springboks could yet secure the title with two home victories, over New Zealand in Johannesburg and a week later over Australia in Durban.

"It's in our hands," Smit told his players, quietly. "It's ours to win."

Such lofty ambitions seemed distant when the All Blacks arrived at Ellis Park and leapt into a 10-0 lead after only six minutes. Smit gathered his team behind their posts and told them to relax, concentrate and play the kind of high-tempo, fast, physical rugby for which they were becoming admired. Marius Joubert launched the fightback, breaking Tana Umaga's tackle to score. Another thumping big hit created a chance for Breyton Paulse to cross the All Black line, and Barry's brilliant break created a second try for Joubert.

South Africa led 19-13 at half time, and the buoyant Ellis Park crowd began to sense a first victory in nine painful matches against New Zealand. The visitors bounced back to lead 23-22, but the home team maintained the momentum. Joubert seized the day, creating a try for De Villiers, then taking an inside pass from flanker Jacques Cronjé and scampering over to complete a memorable hat-trick of tries.

The stadium roared at the final whistle, saluting a famous 40-26 victory, giving Smit what he vividly recalls, smiling, as "the most incredible feeling I have experienced on a rugby field".

White recognised the significance of the win and, during the private team meeting later that night, the coach proposed a toast to all the players among them who had never before defeated the All Blacks. He asked them to stand, and no fewer than 22 of the 26-man squad rose to their feet. "Guys like Marius Joubert and Joe van Niekerk had played 30 Tests and never beaten New Zealand," the coach reflects.

Another super Springbok Saturday beckoned, because victory over the Wallabies at King's Park the following weekend was going to secure the glory of a Tri-Nations title. Excitement billowed through South African rugby, as the disappointment, despair and trauma of 2003 receded into the history books.

The home team seemed propelled by a national surge of pure adrenaline and, although the Wallabies led 7-3 at half time, the Springboks produced a decisive burst of scoring early in the second half. Paulse tapped back his own high ball, enabling Matfield to collect and score. Van Niekerk then powered his way over on the left and, with Montgomery adding the conversions, the home team constructed a 23-7 lead.

The Australians fought back, scoring two tries in the last nine minutes and fraying nerves among the capacity crowd, but the final whistle confirmed a 23-19 victory and prompted scenes of delight as Springboks fell into each other's arms. Smit, a key factor in his team's decisive domination of the scrum and lineouts, stepped up to a podium on the field and, his eyes glazed with happiness, lifted the Tri-Nations trophy.

In the aftermath of triumph, amid the backslapping, the captain regularly recognised the contribution of his coach to success. White had paid his coaching dues at school level, at provincial and international under-21 level, as a Springbok technical advisor to Nick Mallett, and as assistant coach to the Sharks … yet he had never played even provincial rugby, had never coached any senior provincial team and was far from unanimously hailed as the correct choice when he was announced as the new national coach.

Critics dismissed him as a jumped-up teacher.

Smit, at least, had never doubted White.

"People quickly began to understand Jake's strengths," the captain reflects. "First, he has a great talent for dealing with players, and an unbelievable ability to assess people and make good decisions. Second, he works hard, combining knowledge of the game with really thorough preparation."

Following the Tri-Nations success, with White being hailed as a genius, South African supporters started to speculate about the prospect of a Grand Slam at the end of the year. Could the 2004 team match the triumphant feats of the 1912/13, 1931/2, 1951/52 and 1960/61 Springbok squads who had headed to the frozen north and defeated Wales, Ireland, England and Scotland on the same tour?

Any knowledge of history should have prompted caution in making such a prediction, but expectations tend to fly fast and loose around the heads of winning teams in green and gold.

In the event, it soon became clear the Springboks were running on empty at the end of a long and arduous season. June's energy and accuracy became November's fatigue and errors.

Starting the tour at the Millennium Stadium in Cardiff, South Africa defeated Wales rather more comfortably than the 38-36 scoreline suggested. Two late tries flattered the Welsh, but Springbok feathers were ruffled when Burger, the increasingly celebrated young flanker, was sent to the sin bin for "diving over the top".

Smit was surprised, and asked for clarification from the referee. The response was unclear, and experienced observers detected ulterior motives in the harsh discipline meted out to one of the touring team's most influential players in the opening match of the tour. It had been done before. Whether or not Burger was being deliberately inhibited, a Grand Slam would clearly not be yielded without a struggle.

The squad moved to Dublin, where it was the Springbok coach's turn to suffer at the eye of what appeared to be another contrived controversy. Asked by a journalist how many Ireland players would get into his Bok team, White took a moment to consider and replied honestly, too honestly. "Three," he said.

Outrage ensued. The Irish were quick to take offence. With coach Eddie O'Sullivan and the local press cleverly feeding off each other, an innocent remark was whipped into an international incident, and a bunch of rent-a-quote Irishmen lined up to express their deep hurt.

The ploy was a demeaning sideshow, yet it succeeded because the Ireland players found a useful vehicle for their pre-match motivation, and the innocent South Africans were distracted.

On the field, a close and hard-fought international before a capacity crowd at Lansdowne Road turned on an extraordinary incident midway through the first half.

Paul Honiss, the New Zealand referee, had picked up the familiar melody from Cardiff and heavily penalised the Springboks, most notably Burger, during the opening 20 minutes of the match. In the 21st minute, he blew his whistle again, and awarded a penalty against Van Niekerk for going off his feet.

"No more of that, John," the referee shouted across at the Springbok captain. "Next time somebody is going to get sent off. It won't be just a penalty. Go and talk to your players!"

Smit turned to address his team, precisely as Honiss had instructed him to do, but, in that instant, Ireland's flyhalf Ronan O'Gara tapped the penalty and scampered 10 metres to score in the corner. The Springboks, most of whom had been paying attention to their captain, looked towards the referee, expecting him to ask for the penalty to be retaken. Instead, to their amazement, they saw Honiss awarding the try.

Already fatigued and below par, now intensely frustrated, the South Africans failed to recover and, despite a late rally, subsided to a 17-12 defeat. Their Grand Slam ambitions had been shattered at the end of a taxing week in Ireland, and the disappointed squad travelled solemnly to London.

There were no external factors in England, no staged media ambushes or bizarre refereeing. As Smit recalls, his team were well beaten by the world champions. In cold and wet conditions, the home forwards provided a solid platform for flyhalf Charlie Hodgson to score 27 points and dominate the game.

Bryan Habana, who was making his Test debut as a substitute for De Villiers, was sent clear by Van der Westhuyzen late in the game for a try that gave a veneer of credibility to a final score of 32-16. It could scarcely conceal the uncompromising reality that South Africa's fifth – yes, fifth – successive defeat against England at Twickenham had been as emphatic as any of the previous four.

For Smit and White, the Springbok honeymoon was over.

"We were tired," White notes, "and we were playing teams when they were fresh and hungry at the start of their season. The reverse had been true when teams like Ireland and Wales visited us in June. That's just how it is."

Next stop, Edinburgh, and Smit worked hard to rebuild his team's morale after two successive defeats. His efforts were rewarded by a significant, morale-boosting 45-10 victory over Scotland.

There was still one last appointment in the Springbok diary for 2004, a Test match against an Argentine side missing several top players who were not released by their European clubs. South Africa won 39-7 and the players flew home for a five-week holiday, before they were due to report for pre-season training.

Smit and White deservedly finished the year with smiles on their faces, holding more silverware. They took the honours at the annual International Rugby Board Awards function, with Smit accepting the Team of the Year award on behalf of his Springboks, and White being named Coach of the Year. Completing a notable clean sweep, Schalk Burger was announced as the IRB Player of the Year.

However, perhaps the most significant and important achievement of this captain, supported by this coach, was being secured, largely unseen, inside the Springbok camp.

Smit's success was to heal the racial unease within his squad.

Racial unease? In the rainbow nation? Indeed. Since the country's transition to democracy in 1994, South African rugby had tended to give the impression of desperately trying to keep up with the times. Winning the World Cup in 1995 sparked a dazzling burst of nation-building, but this spirit was not sustained and, through the years that followed, South African rugby resorted to artificial methods to demonstrate its credentials as a sporting body in tune with the new South Africa, and in step with the ANC government.

Then, just before the 2003 Rugby World Cup, Geo Cronjé baulked at the idea of sharing a room and bathroom with his coloured team-mate and designated room-mate, Quinton Davids. All the anger and antipathy suddenly erupted, inside the team, in the media.

Tempers did calm – and Ashwin Willemse emotionally explained to his white team-mates how it felt to be a black Springbok while the squad was huddled together, shivering in a damp pit, naked and cold, in the middle of the night during Kamp Staaldraad – and yet a sense of unease remained.

This was the landscape inherited by John Smit when he was appointed Springbok captain in 2004.

He addressed the situation with resolve and sensitivity, taking care to ensure the black players felt properly involved in every aspect of the side, taking care to notice if any member of the squad was feeling excluded and taking care to bring them back into the fold.

Smit made no great speeches and issued no thunderous edicts. In a thousand tiny and unreported gestures of kindness, thoughtfulness and generosity – with a glance or a smile, or an encouraging pat on the back, or even a quick SMS message to wish somebody well after an operation – he eliminated the sense of "them" and "us", healed the anger and antipathy, and effectively united his Springbok team.

Another long, gruelling season beckoned. In 2005, the Springboks were scheduled to jump on the treadmill and play a dozen internationals, including four matches against the Wallabies, three against France, two against New Zealand and further matches against Wales, the champions of Europe, and Argentina.

First, Uruguay were welcomed as the season's aperitif in East London, and ruthlessly dispatched 134-3. The mismatch enthused few beyond the ardent statisticians, who eagerly noted that 134 was the highest points total ever scored by South Africa in a Test and that the achievement of Tonderai Chavhanga, who scored six tries on his international debut, was unprecedented and unlikely to be repeated.

Everybody knew the talented touring French team would provide very much tougher opposition a week later in Durban. The South Africans prepared carefully but, moments before kick-off at King's Park, White looked around the changing room and thought he had never seen Springboks look so nervous. "France do that to you," the coach says. "They are so unpredictable, you never know what to expect. They can blow you away."

In their apprehension, the home side seemed to be sucked into playing the kind of expansive, broken game that played into France's hands. This suited Habana, whose speed was rewarded with two more tries, but a frenetic and full-blooded contest reached its conclusion when Julien Candelon, the French wing, scored on his debut five minutes from full time to bring the delighted tourists level at 30-30.

Home draws tend to be received like defeats in South Africa, but the Springboks responded to criticism with a more physical, more disciplined performance in the second Test in Port Elizabeth. Outmuscling and outthinking their opponents, they stuck to the game plan, stifled French flair and claimed a 27-13 victory.

The battle for the Nelson Mandela Challenge Plate followed, and the home and away matches against the Wallabies put the Springboks on a roller coaster ride ... from complacency, defeat and despair in Sydney, where they were outscored by five tries to nil and emphatically beaten 30-12 ... to delight, victory and jubilation at Ellis Park, where they overran the Australians with an all-action, fast and wonderfully committed performance, winning 33-20.

The former President himself attended the Test match in Johannesburg, played for the trophy named in his honour, and the occasion was organised as a joyful public celebration of Madiba's 87th birthday. The beloved icon smiled broadly as Smit's team fizzed, buzzed and won. All seemed well. Nine members of the victorious Springbok squad were black or coloured, and scarcely anybody seemed to notice.

"It felt like 1995 without the cup," somebody said afterwards.

A jubilant Ellis Park awash with national flags and unity, Mandela beaming, Springboks winning: these were images that tickled the emotions of South Africans but, in fact, there were similarities between 1995 and 2005 that reached beyond the visible and the obvious.

An important element of the World Cup-winning campaign was the team management's ability to construct a cocoon around the coaches and players, efficiently insulating the team from the infighting, instability and tantrums typical of South African rugby administration over the years. Union officials might have been constantly squabbling and threatening, but the cocoon meant that the Springbok coaches and players were able to ignore such shenanigans, stay focused and concentrate entirely on the business of winning rugby matches.

Ten years on, Jake White was managing to build a very similar cocoon around his squad. With energy, perception, intelligence and a few loyal staff, the coach-turned-administrator succeeded in creating what amounted almost to a separate unit within the organisation. As a result, while leading officials of SA Rugby waged a civil war throughout 2005, Smit and his players remained blissfully removed from the turmoil.

White was almost superhuman. He soaked up the stress, dealt with pressure from the media, handled those meddling administrators who wanted to impose their will on team selection, faced down threats that he would be sacked unless he toed the line, and courageously passed none of this hassle and pressure on to his squad.

So, in good heart after their showing at Ellis Park, and the praise that followed, the Springboks were able to address the challenge of defending their Tri-Nations title, starting with home Tests, against Australia in Pretoria and then against the in-form All Blacks in Cape Town.

The campaign didn't start well. By half time at Loftus Versfeld, the capacity crowd was hushed and agitated. The Wallabies, without a win in five visits to South Africa, had produced a strong performance against a Springbok team that seemed strangely off the pace. The visitors deserved more than their 13-11 lead.

Smit was also agitated, and he was angry.

"Come on, guys," the captain urged, gathering his players around. "We're throwing away everything that we have worked so hard for. This is the Tri-Nations, and we've forgotten who we are."

Every player was listening intently, focused on the captain.

Smit was in full flow.

"We need to think about what we are doing here today, wearing this jersey," he said. "Each one of us knows what this jersey means. Do you think we have done justice to that jersey in the first half? All the supporters sitting out there expect better from players wearing the Springbok jersey, and they are entitled to expect better. Imagine you never play for South Africa after today. Will you be happy that you were worthy of the jersey? Will you be able to pass the jersey on to the next player with a happy conscience?

"Come on, we have 40 minutes to put things right."

Evidently, the jersey did mean something. The Springboks were revived. Paulse dashed clear to round off an incisive attack and scored in the right-hand corner, and a late drop goal by André Pretorius nailed down the 22-16 victory.

A much better display would be required in Cape Town a week later if the South Africans were going to beat a confident All Blacks side, flying after their 3-0 series romp against the Lions. The British rugby media were hailing Tana Umaga's team as unbeatable, coach Graham Henry as unequalled in his tactical planning and the new flyhalf Dan Carter as a genius likely to dominate the sport for years to come.

The upbeat New Zealanders high-stepped onto the Newlands turf, where the determined Springbok captain personally delivered a formal welcome to South Africa. Early in the Test, Smit lined up Mils Muliaina and executed a thunderous, crunching tackle on the nimble All Blacks fullback. Every player in green and gold appeared to grow, while the men in black took a step back. Thus the tone was set.

Every Springbok followed his captain's example, repeatedly knocking the visitors back behind the advantage line, harassing Carter into errors, getting in the All Blacks' faces. A Montgomery penalty, an opportunist 70-metre dash to score by De Villiers, a Pretorius drop goal … and South Africa led 13-0, but nothing was going to come easy and the New Zealanders battled back to reach half time trailing just 13-16.

Smit's team braced themselves for the second half, returned the physical challenge with interest, selflessly hurled their bodies into every contest, concentrated, kept errors to a minimum and won 22-16.

"It was a huge win for us," Smit reflects. "I don't think I have ever played in such a brutal, bruising game of rugby, and I was so proud that the guys had come out on top."

His team had prevailed, and so had he, the Springbok captain who, according to one TV contributor before the start of the Tri-Nations, rated as only the fourth most effective hooker in the country.

Under attack at various stages of 2004 and 2005, his position was eased by the unwavering support of the only man whose opinion really mattered, the Springbok coach. White often explained that he favoured Smit as a hooker because his scrummaging and throwing-in to the lineout were world class, and because his effective work in the tight phases complemented a team full of forwards who thrive in the loose.

Armed with two wins from two, Smit led his squad on the away leg of the Tri-Nations, aware that two tough matches lay ahead, but now the players travelled more in expectation than hope.

This precious self-belief was amply demonstrated at the Subiaco Oval in Perth, where the Springboks gave nothing more than a competent performance, and yet still emerged as winners, thanks mainly to the devastating speed and finishing ability of Habana. Twice the young winger received the ball on a counter-attack deep inside his own half; twice he sprinted clear of the Australian defence; twice he scored a try.

The South Africans defended their lead with assurance and, while the Wallabies remained in contention until the end, the visitors secured a solid 22-19 victory. It was the Springboks' first win in 20 Test matches against the major rugby nations away from home, and also their first win in Australia since 1998.

Just two wins in four matches had been sufficient for South Africa to win the Tri-Nations in 2004, but, as the series unfolded the following year, with the struggling Australians losing each of their games, it became clear that South Africa would need to win all four out of four to finish on top. So, the team travelled to play New Zealand in Dunedin, aware that only a victory would enable them to retain their title.

The All Blacks launched a momentous evening by performing a new version of their haka, which included an alarming cut-throat gesture and had apparently been revised to reflect "Samoan and Fijian culture".

Umaga, out of Samoa, captaining New Zealand, won the toss, and yet another spectacular and magnificently close-fought contest ensued. Like two great heavyweight boxers, both in peak physical condition, the rivals stood toe to toe, neither giving nor asking an inch, slugging each other with skill and strength.

Montgomery kicked an early penalty; the All Blacks replied when Joe Rokocoko scored after André Pretorius' clearance had been charged down; the Springboks responded when the irrepressible Habana collected a loose ball 25 metres out and disappeared in a green and gold blur streaking across the tryline. The home team appeared to have seized control when tries by Leon MacDonald and Rokocoko, his second, established a 21-10 lead, but South African scrumhalf

Ricky Januarie voraciously charged down an attempted clearance by MacDonald and the visitors reached half time, trailing just 17-21, with everything still in the balance.

Both teams sustained the remarkable tempo into the second half, alternately surging forward in attack and falling back in desperate defence. After Montgomery had kicked another penalty, the alert Januarie took his team into the lead, intercepting an All Black pass and sending Jaque Fourie over beneath the posts.

Time ebbed away and the South Africans were defending a 27-24 lead with conviction, making every tackle, giving nothing away. "Stay focused," Smit implored his players. "Stay focused."

Three minutes remained ... barely three minutes between the Springboks and a first victory in Dunedin since 1921; only three minutes between them and an unprecedented third successive triumph over the All Blacks; three minutes between them and a victory that would put them No. 1 in the world rankings.

New Zealand won a lineout 10 metres from the South African line. The ball was thrown to the back where Keven Mealamu claimed it and, all power at the apex of an All Black drive, the hooker somehow managed to burrow over the line, score a last-gasp try and deny the Springboks yet again.

There was no time for a Springbok response, and the capacity crowd at Carisbrook roared in salute of their victorious team, which duly went on to defeat Australia and win the Tri-Nations.

"To come within three minutes of making history and then to have everything taken away was hard to accept," Smit recalls. "I started to wonder if we were making a habit of conceding so many late tries in big matches, but there was nothing fundamentally wrong with our strategy. We needed to keep plugging away and, sooner rather than later, our fortunes would change."

In spite of their disappointment in Dunedin, the Springboks looked forward to the end-of-season tour with confidence. Why? Because, through the previous 15 months, this group of players had developed the key attribute of every winning team ... the m-word.

Momentum.

That made all the difference.

Momentum incorporated belief, confidence and trust in each other. Momentum kept the team developing, moving forward and dreaming. Momentum meant players had unconditional confidence in their coach to select the right teams and make the right decisions. Momentum meant the coach believed in his players. Momentum meant every player looked to the captain with total respect, and vice versa.

By November 2005, after a great deal of hard work and planning, the Springbok rugby squad had developed true momentum, and they pre-pared for the tour, including Tests against Argentina, Wales and France, with the air of a team that had identified its goals and understood what was required to achieve them. Credit for this enviable clarity of purpose was entirely due to the diligent coach and his captain.

Arriving in Buenos Aires, the South Africans found a full-strength Argentine team itching to claim a prized scalp. With a 32 000 capacity crowd at the José Amalfitani Stadium, including football legend Diego Maradona, Los Pumas looked capable of causing a real upset when they scored three tries in the first half and claimed a 20-16 half-time lead.

Smit calmed his players amid the brewing bedlam. "OK, guys," the captain said. "We know what we have to do. Let's keep concentrating. Let's keep hold of the ball and get control of this game."

Clinically and efficiently, the pumped-up home team was con-tained. The Springboks applied themselves to the task of squeezing what had been a perilously loose contest: they dominated possession, kept the scoreboard ticking over, restricted the Pumas to a solitary penalty in the second half and ultimately ran out more convincing winners than the final score of 34-23 might suggest. Smit sealed the victory, charging through to score a try with eight minutes remaining. His team's momentum had been maintained.

The players were rewarded by a four-day break at an Argentine mountain resort, a welcome breather from the usually frenetic tour schedule of Test matches on successive Saturdays. Relaxed and almost rested, the squad flew to Europe and settled in Cardiff, where they prepared to play Wales. The reigning Six Nations champions were strug-gling. Missing several key players through injury, on the two previous weekends they had been overrun 41-3 by the All Blacks and nervously squeaked to a single-point victory over Fiji.

Most observers anticipated a Springbok rout, but the home team produced an improved performance and, while the visitors were never in danger of losing, they had to work hard to secure their 33-16 victory. Once again, Habana scored two tries and seized the post-match headlines, but the young wing would have quickly recognised another solid, efficient contribution by Smit's solid and efficient pack of forwards.

The green-and-gold caravan moved on to Paris for the last international of the year. Of the previous 11 Tests, the Springboks had won eight, drawn one and lost only in Sydney and Dunedin. White had already started to declare the 2005 season a marked improvement on the 2004 campaign.

Victory over the French on a snowy, wintry night at the Stade de France would have set the seal on a fine season, but the Springboks soon seemed to be playing a match too far against an eager, talented, in-form home team. Once again, their efficiency and sharpness faded into fatigue and error.

France raced into a 15-0 lead after only 10 minutes, and never looked like losing a Test that too frequently seemed to stray across the thin line between "hard-fought" and "plain dirty".

Smit's Springboks had earned a worldwide reputation as a brave, physical team, able to withstand the blunt force of any opponent, and had established a respectable record on foul play. For these reasons, on this icy night in Paris, the incident that sent Jérôme Thion, the French captain, to hospital disappointed the South African captain almost as much as his team's eventual defeat, by 26-20.

In the 13th minute, Smit accidentally raised his forearm to protect his face in a collision, and his elbow thudded directly into Thion's throat. The independent citing commissioner disagreed with Smit that it was an accident and he was suspended for six weeks. It was an eerie precursor to the most trying season of Smit's Springbok career.

The first challenge of 2006 seemed modest enough: a series against Scotland, to whom the Springboks had never lost on home soil. They duly dispatched the Scots with victories of 36-16 in Durban and 29-15 in Port Elizabeth.

As it happened, however, the latter match signalled the start of a dramatic decline. Schalk Burger, the flank who White would later describe as the best player he had coached, suffered a career-threatening neck injury. The all-action openside flanker had continually defied belief by sticking his head into rucks where his peers would not dare to venture, and at last it seemed he had tempted fate one too many times.

Burger, with adrenaline pumping, played through the match, blissfully unaware of the injury. He would later have to undergo a fusion of his sixth and seventh vertebrae.

However, even the Incredible Schalk, as he had been dubbed by Springbok supporters, is a mere mortal. There were pins and needles down one side of an aching body. A scan revealed the worst. White was rattled, declaring that it was the equivalent of losing three players and that Burger might never play again.

"Jake drew a lot of confidence from picking Schalk and suddenly had to make other plans. The loss was a big blow to the team, and Jake lost confidence. He drew comfort from picking guys like Schalk, Percy Montgomery, Os du Randt and myself," Smit recalls.

The headline-grabbing injury to Burger meant that the absence of bruising lock John Philip "Bakkies" Botha, who had an Achilles injury, was glossed over. Jean de Villiers, who was the Springboks' first-choice inside centre, had sustained a rib injury in the opening Test against Scotland and would next do duty during the home leg of the Tri-Nations tournament.

All of this spelt danger for the showdown with France in Cape Town, though the Springboks appeared to be headed for a victory after turning a 12-11 half-time lead into a 12-point cushion with half an hour left. Brent Russell had added a try to Montgomery's two penalties early in the second half and the Springboks were cruising.

Or so it seemed.

France found an immediate response through the first of right wing Vincent Clerc's two tries. Four minutes later, the match was turned on its head when Damien Traille touched down. He added a drop goal and the 17 unanswered points gave Les Bleus a 28-23 lead as the match headed into the final 15 minutes. Montgomery struck his seventh penalty not long after that to give the Springboks hope, but they lost their way in the last 10 minutes. Clerc scored his second try and Dimitri Yachvili added a late penalty to seal France's 36-26 victory.

White, who had restored respectability to South African rugby, had hit turbulence.

The defeat to France was taken on the chin, but neither coach nor captain could foresee the calamity that was to follow as the Springboks embarked on their Tri-Nations tour.

Brisbane's Suncorp Stadium was the stage for the second-highest defeat in Springbok history. The 0-49 drubbing was eclipsed only by a 3-53 humiliation at the hands of England in November 2002. However, this was a far more competent Springbok team than the one that was put to the sword at Twickenham.

"I recall the Aussies being unbelievably pumped," says Smit.

"There was an up-and-under on Pierre Spies, who was making his Test debut, and I recall him being chased down and the Wallaby screams of 'f**k him up, kill him', and how wide-eyed he was. He had the fright of his life.

"On top being highly motivated, the Wallabies were a very good team. The more we tried to patch things up, the more tries we leaked. We came close to beating them in our next match in Sydney. It just didn't make any sense and was like a bad movie that wouldn't end."

If that was a bad movie there were a number of sequels that proved box office flops. Smit's team was beaten 35-17 by a Dan Carter-inspired All Black team in Wellington.

Even when the Springboks played well, fate conspired against them. In their next assignment against the Wallabies, in Sydney, they came within a whisker of spectacularly overturning their humiliation in Brisbane. However, a late converted try by Mat Rogers secured a fortuitous 20-18 win for the Wallabies. The Springboks, with their morale sapped, then had the stuffing knocked out of them by a below-strength New Zealand in Pretoria. It was South Africa's fifth defeat on the trot and, at 45-26, another humiliating one.

The margin of defeat suggested the Springboks had little chance in the following week's match against their great rivals in Rustenburg. On top of it all, the All Blacks were beefed up with their first-choice tight five. A newspaper billboard captured the magnitude of the challenge facing the Springboks: "Now for the All Blacks' A-team".

White was still soldiering on without Burger and Botha, while flank Juan Smith had been added to the injury list. On the credit side De Villiers had returned by then.

The South African Rugby Union (SARU) arranged a think-tank for White with, among other "experts", former Springbok coaches. There were no great technical insights, but White was hopeful that it would bring his bosses some perspective on the difficulties he faced. He also attempted to negate the All Blacks' pace out wide by requesting that the playing field be narrowed, but his pleas fell on deaf ears. It was common cause that White's job was on the line in Rustenburg.

The Springboks were cornered, but, as has been the case throughout history, it is precisely in such desperate situations that they thrive.

Victor Matfield, who by then had established himself as the world's premier No. 5 lock and a valuable wingman to Smit, was outstanding in disrupting the All Blacks' possession. Spies by then had found his feet in the Test arena, Bryan Habana was his opportunistic self in intercepting a pass by So'oialo, and Pretorius held his nerve on the kicking front.

However, no one played a bigger part in deciding the outcome than So'oialo, who foolishly stormed into the side of a ruck to concede a late penalty.

"Rather you than me, Petoors," Smit said to flyhalf André Pretorius, who smiled, placed the ball, took aim and executed a sweet strike. Pretorius' inclusion, in place of Butch James, had been part of a reshuffle that would not stand the test of time. Jaque Fourie had also been moved to fullback in place of the out-of-sorts Montgomery, which meant Wynand Olivier partnered De Villiers in midfield.

However, it was this awkwardly arranged backline that somehow ensured that White would hang on to his job, courtesy of a 21-20 victory. The following week's 24-16 victory over Australia at Ellis Park confirmed that the status quo would remain.

It was amid all this drama that Smit had to stand tall, with his captaincy credentials being tested to the utmost. Had Smit been under the impression that White's position was safe until the 2007 World Cup in France, he was mistaken.

An end-of-season tour to Ireland and England loomed, and White made the bold decision to rest key players with a view to having them in peak physical condition for the following year's World Cup. He had buy-in from SARU without having to worry that he would spend that November desperately clinging to his job should resting the likes of Matfield, Montgomery, scrumhalf Fourie du Preez and loosehead prop Os du Randt result in defeats.

The plan was also to rest Habana, but he was called up to play out of position at outside centre in the opening match against Ireland at Lansdowne Road because of an injury to Jaque Fourie.

White had an outside centre available in Jaco Pretorius, who, alongside Frans Steyn and Bevin Fortuin, was among the experimental selections. However, it was thought prudent to have an experienced player in the No. 13 jersey because of the defensive demands, so Pretorius and Steyn were on the wings, with Fortuin at fullback. Steyn, 19 at the time, would ultimately be at the heart of the Springboks' success under Smit's leadership.

A 15-32 defeat to Ireland meant that White's back was exposed again. The daggers came from the amateur arm of the Blue Bulls Rugby Union, who tabled a motion of no confidence in White during the build-up to the first of two Tests against England at Twickenham. It would be voted on at the next meeting of SARU's Presidents Council on 29 November, which plunged White into another survival battle.

The Springboks firmly believed they were a better side than the English, but let a 21-13 lead slip in the last quarter. A penalty by Andy Goode, followed by Phil Vickery's converted try, gave England a somewhat undeserved 23-21 victory.

Sensing the writing was on the wall for the coach, respected sports scientist Professor Tim Noakes drafted a letter to SARU president Oregan Hoskins on the eve of the second Test. Noakes had been appointed as a medical consultant to South African rugby in 2004, which gave his letter the required clout. He argued that the team was performing poorly because it lacked key players. To have taken them on tour would have been trading away the Springboks' chances of success at the World Cup for the sake of a few victories.

The letter might not have been enough had the Springboks lost the second Test, and their situation looked dire when they were down 3-14 after half an hour. By half time, however, they were 16-14 up, and after the break Pretorius added three drop goals to his one in the first half. South Africa won 25-14, emboldening White for his next big challenge: a meeting with South Africa's leading rugby administrators.

Leaving the preparation of the team for their next match, against a World XV in Leicester, in the hands of his assistants, Gert Smal and Allister Coetzee, White flew back to answer the questions. Among other things, he was questioned about Smit's captaincy credentials, which just showed how badly out of touch some rugby officials were. However, sanity prevailed in a very roundabout way, with 14 votes in favour of White's retention and 5 against.

"Everyone who could was trying to make the leadership believe it was just a bad season and the team was still on track to be able to compete in the World Cup," Smit recalls.

Smit and other senior players never for a moment lost faith in their coach. "The belief was firm that Jake had put us on the right path and that circumstances had put us in a situation where we lost a few games. But what we were doing, when we did it well, was still a recipe to win a World Cup," Smit says.

While it was a miserable year, Smit believes it was crucial in shaping the team that won the World Cup. "It probably galvanised us as a group because Jake took some serious shots."

South Africa's route to World Cup glory had meanwhile been carefully crafted. The team would be at full strength for the home leg of the Tri-Nations before boosting the conditioning of senior players by standing them down from the away leg. Thereafter the Springboks would face modest opposition in Namibia, followed by a short overseas tour where they would play Irish side Connacht and Scotland.

Smit, however, would play very little part in these matches after suffering a hamstring tear early in South Africa's opening Tri-Nations match against Australia. A scrum collapsed in the 11th minute and the unfortunate captain's right boot hooked into the Newlands turf.

The media speculated feverishly that the dream might be over for Smit, and at one stage he himself became despondent. Such fears were unfounded, though, and it was a heavily strapped Smit who led the Springboks out for their opening World Cup pool match against Samoa at the Parc des Princes in Paris on 9 September 2007.

It was a comfortable 59-7 victory, but costly. Jean de Villiers was ruled out of the rest of the tournament after tearing a bicep early in the second half, while Burger was cited for tackling Samoan scrumhalf Junior Polu in the air. A ban of four weeks was brought down to two on appeal. By then, however, the Springboks were such a well-oiled machine that they could take anything on the chin.

As it happened, De Villiers' injury proved Frans Steyn's date with destiny. He had served notice of his precocious talent with two match-winning drop goals against the Wallabies at Newlands. At just 20 years of age, his impact at the global showpiece would be profound and, ultimately, decisive.

South Africa's defining group match would always be the one against England on 14 September at St Denis on the outskirts of Paris. The contrasting looks in the captains' eyes as they walked down the Stade de France's tunnel gave a hint of what was to come. Smit was a picture of focus and confidence, whereas Martin Corry appeared wide-eyed and scared.

Corry had every reason to be concerned. Apart from the Springboks having been harnessed into a very good side, England's first-choice flyhalf, Jonny Wilkinson, as well as his deputy, Olly Barkley, were injured. Mike Catt was consequently picked as Shaun Perry's halfback partner, a combination that was badly exposed by the Springbok pairing of Fourie du Preez and Butch James.

England's fans were in full voice with "Swing Low, Sweet Chariot" immediately after the kick-off, but their spirits were quickly doused as South Africa mauled their way upfield from the first lineout.

The Springboks then landed a savage blow with a surge down the blind side by right wing JP Pietersen. He passed to Du Preez, who stumbled on his way to the tryline but managed to offload to supporting flank Juan Smith. It was a try that owed much to Du Preez's vision, as would be the case when Pietersen scored in the second half.

Steyn split the uprights not long after the early score and the Springboks led 10-0 with just 11 minutes played.

Du Preez very nearly crafted a try for Jaque Fourie with a judicious kick downfield, but the outside centre lost control of the ball as he stretched for the tryline.

The Springboks kept piling on the pressure, with superbly executed kicks downfield by Du Preez and James. Left wing Bryan Habana, in particular, revelled in chasing Du Preez's pinpoint high kicks.

There were three missed drop goal attempts – two by fullback Percy Montgomery and the other by Steyn – before the Springboks struck viciously in the last five minutes of the first half. Montgomery increased the lead to 13-0 with a penalty in the 36th minute, and three minutes later the Springboks made their turnover possession count. Du Preez beat the England defence with a superb show of pace and drew the fullback before passing to Pietersen on his outside. The conversion made it 20-0 and left England reeling just before half time.

The relentless pressure continued into the second half. Montgomery increased the lead to 26-0 with another two penalties before Du Preez changed direction smartly after spotting space on the blind side. He again found Pietersen with his final pass and Montgomery added the conversion for a 33-0 lead. There were still 17 minutes left to rub it in, but the Springboks did no more than contain the English before a final Montgomery penalty made it 36-0.

It would be the defining match of their campaign and indeed also of White's tenure as Springbok coach.

"Jake always spoke about playing a game that was the equivalent of shooting a 59 in golf. It was just the best strategic and tactical game that we ever played together. There was complete control," Smit recalls.

"While the scoreline suggests otherwise, it was a very calculated and conservative performance. We took every kick and stuck to a recipe that we knew was going to win us the World Cup.

"We didn't expect that performance to come so early, but I think it was aided by the fact that England were badly affected at flyhalf. It was easy for us to overwhelm them tactically because they couldn't combat Fourie and Butch. Their tactical kicking was unbelievable throughout the tournament."

The victories over Samoa and England paved the way for an easy route to the quarterfinals, though the Springboks' second string very nearly came unstuck against Tonga in Lens. They led 27-10 with 15 minutes remaining, but were ultimately saved from embarrassment by the bounce of the ball when it rolled into touch from a kick rather than bouncing favourably for wing Tevita Hemilitoni Tu'ifua. The Springboks won 30-25.

White picked a strong side for the final pool match against the USA. Burger had returned, but the gloss was wiped off the 64-15 victory by tighthead prop BJ Botha's serious knee injury.

Smit's troops marched on to Marseille for a quarterfinal against Fiji, but certainly could not have foreseen the events on the eve of their match at the Stade Velodrome. Host nation France, awful in going down 12-17 to Argentina in their opening game and forced into playing their quarterfinal in Cardiff, somehow found it in themselves to beat the All Blacks 20-18. A revived England had also scrummed the Wallabies into submission to win their quarterfinal 12-10. The Springboks needed only to beat Fiji for a semifinal against either Argentina or Scotland.

There was a brief scare when the islanders wiped out a 14-point deficit to draw level at 20-20, but the Springboks played with great control in the last 20 minutes and added 17 unanswered points.

A 37-13 victory over Argentina in the semifinals was never in doubt, while England unexpectedly advanced to the final by beating France 14-9. It was almost unthinkable that the final would be a repeat fixture of the one the Springboks had won so convincingly. They knew they had the measure of the English, but it was not quite that simple.

"We knew it was a different team that had stood up against its coaching staff and taken matters into its own hands. They had beaten Australia and France, while Jonny Wilkinson had also returned. We were facing a different monster," Smit says.

Apart from an improved halfback pairing in Andy Gomarsall and Wilkinson, England were now captained by the vastly experienced tighthead prop Phil Vickery. He had been suspended for the previous encounter against the Springboks. Nevertheless, the Springboks were in no doubt they had England's measure. The only question was whether Smit's men could handle the pressure.

Smit admits that he was nervous as he led his team out of the tunnel at the Stade de France. The excitement of the 80 000 in attendance was palpable and the pressure was amplified by a global television audience of nearly 17 million. Smit's men were mindful that they carried the dreams of the Rainbow Nation, desperate for a repeat of the World Cup win of 1995. However, the steely resolve in Smit's eyes spoke of a man with little, if any, doubt. He had come too far to fail.

Smit's team talk was to the point. It was about finishing a journey and getting their other hand on the trophy. If ever there was a match where he didn't have to motivate his team, this was it.

The final turned out to be a kicking duel, with Springbok hearts fluttering just once early in the second half when English centre Mathew Tait scythed through their defence. Left wing Mark Cueto went over in the corner after the ball had been recycled, but a desperate tackle from the outstanding Springbok No. 8, Danie Rossouw, prompted a discussion between referee Alain Rolland and touch judge Joël Jutge. The matter was referred to television match official Stuart Dickinson, who found that Cueto's left boot had been on the touchline before he grounded the ball.

England were trailing 3-9 at the time and a converted try would have edged them ahead. However, they had to make do with three points through Wilkinson's boot as Rolland was playing a penalty advantage at the time.

Even if England had led 10-9, there would not have been panic in the Springbok ranks. "The talk while waiting for the TMO to make a call was to revert back to our tactical policy of getting into England's half and holding on to the ball until we scored. We wanted to build a lead of eight points to get out of reach of a single score and then play the game in England's half," Smit recalls.

England were held at bay by a great defensive display that extended to the lineouts, where Springbok lock Victor Matfield was commanding. Montgomery's fourth penalty in the 49th minute restored South Africa's six-point lead. The chance to extend the lead beyond seven points arrived on the hour, when Ben Kay was penalised for blocking Os du Randt's attempted tackle on Danny Hipkiss.

It was just inside England's half, 20 metres from the right-hand touchline. This was out of Montgomery's reach, but set the stage for Steyn to immortalise himself in Springbok annals. "I think the fact that he was 20 and carefree helped," Smit says of his instruction to Steyn to aim for goal. "My message to him was 'Hey, get it over and we're eight points ahead'. I was acting blasé. If it wasn't over, England would probably restart with a 22-metre drop, which was good territory for us. Frans was 'Ja, OK, no problem.'"

Steyn's kick sailed majestically through the posts. It was a decisive blow, as England would have to score at least twice to eclipse South Africa's nine-point lead. "Frans's kick gave us the comfort zone to be able to play a tactical game that smothered England," recalls Smit.

Appropriately it was Du Preez who booted the ball into touch for Rolland to sound his final whistle after the Boks ran down the clock off the back of the final scrum: South Africa 15, England 6.

In his autobiography, *Captain in the Cauldron*, Smit would liken the emotion of lifting the Webb Ellis Cup to when his daughter, Emma, was born. He had a deep sense of satisfaction, happiness and relief that his roller-coaster journey had ended at the pinnacle of the game. Or, at least, he thought it had ended.

Smit was 29 at the time and thought his international swan song would be the Test against Wales on a short tour to the northern hemisphere just over a month after the final.

But unbeknown to the man who was by then the most decorated Springbok captain in history, there would be 36 more Tests and many more glory days to come.

It was nevertheless time for a mental break and Smit found it at French club Clermont. And just when he thought he had slipped into a comfort zone, White's successor, Peter de Villiers, came knocking.

The new Springbok coach had been a controversial appointment, with his pedigree hardly measuring up to that of Bulls coach Heyneke Meyer or one of White's assistants in Allister Coetzee. SARU's president, Oregan Hoskins, confirmed that the issue of transformation had been taken very seriously in arriving at De Villiers' appointment. It was an unfair statement and immediately put the new coach under immense pressure. De Villiers had nonetheless preached a revolutionary gospel, but changed tack when confronted with the realities of the job.

"The manner in which Peter was announced didn't help his entrance as the first non-white Springbok coach," Smit recalls.

"My relationship with Peter was always good and he was always upfront. He came to see me in France to ask that I return. I was delighted that he was interested and did whatever I could to get out of my contract in France."

De Villiers was sometimes like a deer in headlights in the face of the global media, and he gained a reputation for making silly statements. Yet the public image masked his abilities as a coach. "There was never a dull moment. He was an interesting coach and a good one for us. He understood where we were. I don't know how many other coaches would have come in and not wanted to change the blueprint or wipe out the legacy. He saw within two weeks that his original plan would have been a disaster," Smit says.

"Peter had the intelligence to be able to manage people. There were lots of strong characters and he connected with them as human beings first. That was his best move and for a lot of guys it was some of their most enjoyable times. He was caring and hard when he needed to be."

Smit led the Springboks to a series victory over Wales to kick off De Villiers' reign, but his Tri-Nations was rudely interrupted by injury before his career took another turn on the end-of-season tour.

Bismarck du Plessis was increasingly flexing his muscles as a hooker, to a point where De Villiers and Smit both felt he could add significant value in the starting line-up. The only problem was that it was Smit who would have to make way.

Smit, however, had experience of playing prop early in his career, and in the absence of serious contenders a positional switch to tighthead was proposed. It is arguably the most specialist position in the game, and the good ones command huge salaries. Not only was Smit being challenged to make a switch at age 30, he also had to continue captaining the side.

The issue of Du Plessis supposedly being a better hooker than him was a constant theme from 2008 onwards, and Smit's handling of the situation highlights his quality as a leader and human being. Not once did insecurity dictate Smit's behaviour. "I knew we would be a better team if Bismarck was in it," he says. "My thinking was that if I could reach a level where we were able to hold our own in the scrums, we would have an unbelievably big and mobile pack with Bismarck in it.

"I was given a choice and embraced the challenge. The selfish thing would have been to stay at hooker, but I could see the potential of how much better we could become if it worked."

Smit coped on a tour that was also important in cementing De Villiers in the job. South Africa's Tri-Nations campaign included the high of a historic victory over the All Blacks in Dunedin and a runaway win over the Wallabies in Johannesburg, but over the course of the tournament they were still the weakest side.

A 20-15 victory over Wales in Cardiff was followed by an iffy 14-10 win over Scotland at Murrayfield. It hardly inspired confidence ahead of a match against England at Twickenham.

Yet the Springboks always enjoy a match against the big-talking English, and it never required Smit to conjure up his powers of motivation. In this instance, however, he took charge aggressively and addressed every team-mate personally about what was pertinent to his role.

Bryan Habana, the reigning world player of the year, was going through a poor run of form at the time, but drew inspiration from Smit and sealed the emphatic 42-6 victory with a try on the stroke of full time. There was a marvellous touchdown by Jaque Fourie from long distance, a barge through a posse of defenders by Danie Rossouw, and a delightful offload by JP Pietersen to Adrian Jacobs – tries that all carried the seal of a world-champion side.

The Springboks seemed to have found their feet under De Villiers and the denouement set the stage for a wonderful 2009 in which they would play the British and Irish Lions, as well as the All Blacks, on three occasions.

Smit, who had moved back to hooker for the rout of England due to an injury to Du Plessis, had again been earmarked to anchor the Springboks' scrum when the season got under way with the first Test against the Lions in Durban. Realising that the Lions held the belief that they would have the upper hand in the scrums, the Springboks prepared exhaustively. There were live scrumming sessions in training, with team management deciding to call up forwards from the ranks of the Emerging Springboks, who were training for a midweek match.

It would ultimately be largely on the back of a dominant scrum that South Africa would power to victory in the first Test. However, it was loosehead prop Tendai "Beast" Mtawarira rather than Smit who sowed the havoc. Mtawarira gave Phil Vickery a memorable working over before the Englishman was substituted out of his misery by Adam Jones early in the second half. That did nothing to stem the flow, and the Springboks used their lineout drive to telling effect to set up a try for flank Heinrich Brüssow to give them a decisive 26-7 lead.

The Springboks still came uncomfortably close to losing the match in the coach's box through a flurry of substitutions. They were under the mistaken impression that the match was in the bag. Smit was among those substituted before flank Tom Croft and scrumhalf Mike Phillips' converted tries in the 68th and 76th minutes gave the Lions a sniff.

Sensing that things were falling apart, the Springboks hatched a plan whereby Smit's replacement, Deon Carstens, would fake an injury to get the captain back on. Smit's cool head helped steady the ship in those anxious last minutes and the Springboks held on to win 26-21.

From there it was on to the Highveld where the second Test would be played at Loftus Versfeld in Pretoria.

The Springboks' plan for clinching the series was simple: they would speed the game up at every opportunity so that the Lions' lungs would start burning early from playing at altitude.

However, it didn't quite work out that way, as flank Schalk Burger was yellow-carded in the first minute for making contact with Lions left wing Luke Fitzgerald's left eye.

With that, the Springbok plan had been blown out of the water.

"We were forced into doing the exact opposite of what we had wanted to. With a man down, we had to slow the game down at every opportunity," Smit recalls. "Once Schalk returned we went back to Plan A. We were horrendous in that first half."

The Lions carried a 16-8 lead into half time, and that was further increased with a penalty by flyhalf Stephen Jones on the hour mark. South Africa were staring down the barrel.

However, another twist of fate conspired in the Springboks' favour as both the Lions' starting props – Jenkins and Jones – were injured early in the second half. This resulted in uncontested scrums, which came as a relief for the Springboks as they were under pressure at set piece.

It also served as the base to set up a delightful Habana touchdown that sparked the fightback. Morné Steyn added a penalty in the 68th minute and the Springboks had reduced the deficit to one point.

By now the match had turned into a wild ride. Stephen Jones added another penalty, but six minutes before full time the Springboks took the lead for the first time through a sensational try by Jaque Fourie.

The Springbok outside centre smashed through Ronan O'Gara and then beat Mike Phillips on his way to the right-hand corner. Steyn converted splendidly and it was 25-22 to the Springboks.

Jones levelled the score with a penalty three minutes before the end, but a moment of madness by O'Gara gave the Springboks the chance they needed to clinch the series. O'Gara, who was an injury replacement for inside centre Jamie Roberts, played Bok scrumhalf Fourie du Preez in the air and was penalised just inside the Springboks' half.

It would require a sweet strike but on the Highveld was inside Steyn's range. The rest is history. One of the most brutally physical Tests in the annals of Springbok rugby was settled 28-25 in their favour.

"We really got our confidence back when Jaque pulled the cat out of the bag and, in fairness, benefited from a large amount of stupidity," says Smit.

With that Smit had achieved everything he possibly could at the highest level. He had captained South Africa to a Tri-Nations title, a World Cup and a series victory over the Lions. There was little more left to achieve. However, the Tri-Nations beckoned and included were home Tests against the All Blacks in Bloemfontein and Durban. South Africa's campaign would end against the All Blacks in Hamilton.

The matches in Bloemfontein and Durban were remarkably one-sided. Notwithstanding four missed kicks by flyhalf Ruan Pienaar in the first half in Bloemfontein, the Springboks led 14-3 at the break. Steyn, an injury replacement for Pienaar in the second half, held his nerve to strike three important penalties to steer South Africa to a 28-19 win. With that he had also set himself up for selection for the Durban show-down against an All Black side in which Stephen Donald was doing an erratic job of standing in for the injured Dan Carter at flyhalf.

The Springbok game plan, with which they trumped the All Blacks, was beautiful in its simplicity. It often involved high kicks by Du Preez that would be relentlessly chased. They were accused of winning ugly, but were doing it by big margins. Steyn achieved a remarkable personal feat by scoring every one of the Springboks' 31 points as they comfortably won the second Test 31-19. It was followed by a 29-17 win over the Wallabies at Newlands, which included seven penalties and a drop goal by Steyn, who was writing his name into Springbok folklore.

However, the Springboks still had work to do to secure the Tri-Nations title and would have to do so in Australasia. There was little doubt in the camp that they would achieve that. "We weren't stressed about playing the All Blacks. Everyone was going to be in trouble against us that year. The team was extremely confident after the series win over the Lions and we couldn't wait for the Tri-Nations. It was ours to take," Smit recalls.

He captained the Springboks to an impressive 32-25 win over the Wallabies in Perth before they came down to earth with a 6-21 defeat in Brisbane the following weekend. It meant the Springboks needed to beat the All Blacks in Hamilton to be crowned tournament win-ners. They were on the cusp of a remarkable third successive win over the All Blacks. The last time South Africa had managed that inside a calendar year was in 1949, and it didn't seem plausible that they could do it again 60 years later.

However, the Springboks seized the day against an All Black side bolstered by Carter's return. Welshman Nigel Owens would referee the game, but Smit still realised he had to prepare his team for the possibility of marginal calls going against them in the cauldron of the Waikato Stadium. They would lose if they allowed it to weigh down their spirits.

"True as Bob, we were penalised for obstruction from the first kick-off," Smit recalls of a harsh early penalty meted out to his side by Owens. "I told the guys he's done us a favour because it was exactly what I had spoken about and these were the challenges we would face. Nothing works better than making a South African think someone is out to get him."

The precocious talent of Frans Steyn made a decisive difference as he had the All Blacks reeling with three long-range penalties in the first half. It played on the mind of All Black captain Richie McCaw, who was no doubt reluctant to test the limits at the breakdown.

"Richie took fewer risks because he knew just about every penalty would be within range. The All Blacks stopped getting turnover ball because we had a monster boot."

It was an epic match in which the All Blacks came very close to transforming an apparently hopeless scenario of being 12-29 down into a victory. However, the Springboks held on and Smit led his team to glory yet again.

When reflecting on Smit's career, many people reckon that should have been that. He was 31 and the opportunity was there to bow out on a high as captain of one of the greatest Springbok teams in history.

"I had the conversation with Peter and he said that I should stay. I said that I would stay for a year and he could then decide on the way forward. However, they insisted on a two-year contract," Smit recalls. "In 2009 I played some of my best rugby and the same applies to my form at the World Cup in 2011."

Smit's stint at tighthead prop ended on an unhappy end-of-season tour that kicked off with a 13-20 defeat to France in Toulouse. He would play one more match in the No. 3 jersey in a 32-10 win over Italy in Udine before being restored to hooker for a 10-15 defeat to Ireland at Croke Park in Dublin that brought the curtain down on the season.

It was a decline that extended into 2010 with Smit being weighed down by a neck injury that ultimately required surgery and saw him miss the end-of-season tour.

Notwithstanding his form, Smit's career came to a painful end in 2011. The Springboks had again been well conditioned heading into the Rugby World Cup in New Zealand, but nothing could prepare them for what they would face in the quarterfinals.

It was not so much the Wallabies as it was Bryce Lawrence.

South Africa had Australia pinned down for much of the match, but the New Zealand referee failed to spot a myriad of breakdown infringements. A rare foray into Springbok territory resulted in a penalty against Danie Rossouw at a lineout and Wallaby flyhalf James O'Connor held his nerve to bring up the final scoreline of 11-9.

"It really hurt. I would rather have been beaten after performing badly, but it wasn't the case," Smit says.

"It's a very difficult topic to discuss because anything I say sounds as if I'm shifting the blame, which isn't in my nature. I haven't watched that game again because I know I will get angry all over again if I have to hear myself repeatedly asking the referee to keep David Pocock [the Wallaby openside flank] on his feet, and him continually saying he's got it under control. I can only remember shouting about it all game long."

Lawrence's off day with the whistle meant that the All Blacks were spared a semifinal showdown with the Springboks, who many experts rated as the one side capable of beating the host nation.

In fairness, the Springboks had also contributed greatly to their own demise through lost opportunities. Of course, captain and coach did not escape blame. De Villiers was criticised for picking Smit when he had a better hooker in Du Plessis. It was an analysis that failed to take cognisance of Smit's form at the time as well as leadership dynamics. For much of Smit's latter years those noises were a clamour, but he assisted Du Plessis's development rather than becoming insecure.

"I'd like to think that I invested a lot of myself in Bismarck. I passed on everything I knew and helped him with everything. It was enjoyable watching him become such a good player. I feel I had a little part in it," Smit says.

"In the end he was pushing and was a better rugby player. The balancing act was how much better he was against the leadership change it would have required."

Smit had already confirmed it would be the end of his Springbok career when English club Saracens came calling and convinced him not to hang up his boots for good. After a successful stint in England, Smit signed a contract with Toulon, the ambitious French club bankrolled by billionaire Mourad Boudjellal. However, Smit never made it to the south of France, as the Sharks came knocking with an offer to pack down in the toughest scrum of his life: to be their chief executive.

It's been a bumpy ride, but Smit has been able to draw on the skills honed by his eight-year reign as Springbok captain. Posters of the famous 'Rumble in the Jungle' between Muhammad Ali and George Foreman, as well as of other sporting greats such as Pete Sampras, Ernie Els, Kelly Slater, Gary Player and Ayrton Senna adorn his office walls in King's Park. It is fitting company for Smit, who has strong claims to be considered the greatest Springbok captain. He led South Africa in 83 of his 111 Tests, delivered the World Cup, a series victory over the Lions and two Tri-Nations trophies. Perhaps his time as captain ended in heartache, but his legacy will endure. He restored pride to the Springbok jersey when South African rugby was swimming in the depths of despair, and his tenure was marked by unprecedented success.

To some he was not South Africa's best hooker, but to those with deeper understanding he was a giant among the giants.

18 THE SPECIALIST

Victor Matfield cannot recall how he received the news from his coach, Jake White, that he would, for the first time, captain the Springboks in a Test match against the All Blacks at the Absa Stadium in Durban on 23 June 2007.

It was an honour, but never Matfield's *raison d'être*. Rather, he reflects fondly on the task of fulfilling critical supporting roles for both John Smit and Jean de Villiers.

Matfield's leadership emanates from a strong personality cultivated by his parents, Fai and Hettie, in their home in Pietersburg (now Polokwane). Both were educators, and Fai Matfield also had the pleasure of coaching his son, born on 11 May 1977, in both rugby and cricket.

The Matfield household was a conservative one, but Fai realised the importance of giving young Victor a voice. "My dad would listen to my opinion and then we would debate the issue. When I captained the cricket team, I didn't want a teacher to prescribe the bowling changes. I wanted to make the decisions," Matfield recalls.

In later years Matfield's voice would charm and irritate coaches in equal measure. Swys de Bruin, the Griquas coach who lured Matfield to Kimberley when he was surplus to requirements at the Blue Bulls, gave him carte blanche to run the lineouts. Heyneke Meyer, who later re-signed Matfield for the Pretoria-based union and eventually made him his captain, would lean heavily on him from provincial to international level. Jake White, by contrast, felt it necessary to cut Matfield down to size, to the point of demanding that he have a haircut.

Initially there was little love lost in the relationship, but Matfield would play his best rugby under White, culminating in a man-of-the-match performance against England in the 2007 Rugby World Cup final at the Stade de France in St Denis on the outskirts of Paris. Time and again, the English would be thwarted by a man whose legacy will undoubtedly be his leadership in an aspect of the game – the lineout – rather than as the figurehead of a team.

Matfield's talent in that regard was already evident at age group level. So much so that De Bruin, as coach of the Natal under-21 team, put his stamp of approval on underhanded tactics to deal with the annoyingly good lock of the Blue Bulls.

"Even when you played against Victor at under-19 and under-21 level, you really had to be good in the lineouts. Our tactic to eliminate Victor was to strike him in the ribs when he landed after jumping for the ball," De Bruin recalls. "Initially it angered and pacified him, but he grew as a player and had an amazing temperament. That is when I got to like him. He was a very robust player at the time, but came to realise that intelligence was more important than brute strength."

It's an intelligence that De Bruin would tap into after luring Matfield to Kimberley from the Blue Bulls in 1999. For most it would be unfathomable that the Blue Bulls would allow the young Matfield to leave, but at the time Krynauw Otto was their senior No. 5 lock. There was not a sufficient appreciation of his talent at a rugby union then on a downward spiral. Matfield would have to bide his time.

All that would change very quickly in Kimberley.

"It was 42 degrees Celsius the day Victor arrived in Kimberley. I recall seeing this giant stepping out of an Uno while I was busy preparing for a training session," De Bruin says.

The Griquas coach had a good understanding of the importance of the lineout. The scrum could pave the way for physical dominance, but often there might be less than 10 scrums in a match. There were significantly more lineouts, however, and it was an obvious route to both gaining momentum and stopping it.

"I realised very quickly that Victor was special when it came to the lineouts. Halfway into the season I told him that I wanted him to become a master at the lineouts and that he should analyse opponents. He did it exceptionally well," De Bruin recalls.

The Griquas coach had found more than just a clever lock. He suddenly had an assistant, having previously to divide his attention between the backs and forwards on the training field.

Matfield took to his task with aplomb. As time passed, he would learn the art of getting into the heads of rival locks when they made lineout calls. He would pore over hours of video footage to study the calls they made in specific areas of the field, to develop a feel for opponents' body language and somehow to know how to outfox the best lineout defences.

"I hadn't seen anything like it before," De Bruin says.

In truth, neither had the rest of the rugby world.

Matfield came to the attention of the national selectors in his second season in Kimberley, and at age 23 would officially become a Springbok in 2000 as he toured along to Argentina, the United Kingdom and Ireland. He would be no more than a second-stringer on a tour that was a logistical nightmare. By way of example, for the meeting with Ireland A in Limerick seven of the Springboks arrived only on the eve of the match, following a flight from Argentina. Among them was the skipper, Ollie le Roux. Not surprisingly, the Springboks were beaten 28-11.

Just the week before, Matfield had made his debut as a substitute for Quinton Davids in a 32-21 victory over Argentina A at Tucumán. After the Limerick disaster, Matfield started again in a 34-15 victory over Wales A in Cardiff before he had the honour of captaining the second-stringers in their 30-35 defeat to an England Divisional XV in Worcester. The circumstances surrounding the preparation for this match were nevertheless the antithesis of everything Matfield stood for as a professional. Four players from a touring South Africa under-23 team – De Wet Barry, Marius Joubert, Adri Badenhorst and Pieter Dixon – had to be flown in from Amsterdam to make up numbers following call-ups to the Test squad in London.

However, Matfield's career had gained liftoff and he was among a handful of second-stringers that impressed under trying conditions.

After two years with Griquas, in which he played every Currie Cup match as well as contributing to the Cats' cause in Super Rugby, he returned to the Blue Bulls. The union, however, had hit turbulence and it would be a bumpy ride to the summit of Super Rugby under the coaching of Heyneke Meyer.

It took a good few years for what would be a defining partnership in South African rugby to develop.

Meyer, having done an impressive job as an assistant coach with the Stormers in Super Rugby and with the Springboks during their 1999 Rugby World Cup campaign, was appointed for the first time as head coach of the Northern Bulls in 2000. The Super Rugby campaign under the future Springbok coach, sans Matfield, yielded only one victory and a second-from-bottom finish. However, the rot ran much deeper. Later in the year, under Eugene van Wyk, the Blue Bulls were not even among the top eight finishers in the 14-team Currie Cup.

A predictable reshuffle followed, and Phil Pretorius was grabbed from the ranks of the Falcons to coach the Bulls in 2001. This time their campaign yielded just two victories, and a rock-bottom finish. For Matfield, this was a school of hard knocks as he started in every one of the Bulls' matches. However, he stood tall and was rewarded by Springbok coach Harry Viljoen with his first Test cap as a second-half replacement for Johan Ackermann in the 60-14 victory over Italy in Port Elizabeth on 30 June.

In the meantime, Meyer quietly went about his work as coach of the Blue Bulls. While the Super Rugby team fell from one calamitous defeat to the next, Meyer's Vodacom Cup team powered to the title on the back of 11 wins from 12 matches. Of the 36 players used, Meyer had awarded first caps to 26, an indication that he was building the union from the bottom up.

While the Blue Bulls drew another blank in the Currie Cup after struggling with their goalkicking, the Meyer-Matfield partnership was developing at senior level. Matfield, having established himself as Mark Andrews' lock partner in an unhappy Tri-Nations campaign for the Springboks, returned to the Blue Bulls for a run of six Currie Cup matches.

Viljoen remained a firm believer and had him down as a No. 4 lock in each of the Springboks' four end-of-season Tests against France, Italy, England and the United States. Matfield had three different lock partners in Andrews, A.J. Venter and Albert van den Berg on a tour that yielded comprehensive defeats to France and England. Viljoen, frustrated at the pressures of the job, decided to walk away. By then he had lost the plot, but significantly in Matfield he had developed a lock that would become the envy of the rugby world.

Meyer, meanwhile, had done enough to earn another crack at coaching Super Rugby in 2002, but his fortunes went from bad to worse as the Bulls lost all 11 of their matches. Matfield was ever-present in the starting line-up and even earned a go at captaincy in the 24-53 defeat to the Chiefs in Hamilton. Unbeknown to those baying for his blood, Meyer had been working tirelessly in the background on recruitment. Significantly, he had swooped for the gifted young flyhalf Derick Hougaard in the back yard of bitter rivals Western Province. The investment yielded a spectacular dividend as Hougaard, a scholar at Boland Landbou the previous year, scored a remarkable 26 points in the 31-7 victory over the Lions in the 2002 Currie Cup final.

Another shrewd acquisition was an unheralded lock-flank from the Falcons, John Philip Botha. The man who would enter rugby folklore as "Bakkies" contributed to the Blue Bulls' resurgence in the winning of the Vodacom Cup in 2001. His partnership with Matfield, which would serve the Bulls and South Africa for many years, was born out of the ashes of the failed Currie Cup campaign that same year.

It was also with Botha and Matfield at lock that the Blue Bulls confirmed their revival by winning the Currie Cup in 2002. The Springbok coach at the time, Rudolf Straeuli, would then give Botha his international break against France in Marseille. Matfield enjoyed a run of five internationals earlier in the season, but did not tour to France, Scotland and England because of an ankle injury. Even so, Straeuli was still unconvinced of his merits.

Things changed after a run of defeats, including a 53-3 humiliation to England at Twickenham, marked by a red card to lock Jannes Labuschagne. It would be the last time he played for South Africa.

When the 2003 season kicked off with a match against Scotland in Durban, it was Botha and Matfield at the coalface in a modest 29-25 win for the Springboks. The Meyer-Matfield partnership had earlier in the year been stymied by another change of coach at the Bulls. This time Rudy Joubert took charge and the Bulls side was the best of the South African bunch, finishing sixth and only a single log point behind the last-placed semifinalists. Joost van der Westhuizen, the great former Springbok scrumhalf, had captained the Bulls, while Matfield was paired with both Botha and Geo Cronjé during the campaign.

The Blue Bulls then confirmed their rebirth with a second successive Currie Cup final win under Meyer – this time by 40-19 over the Natal Sharks. Matfield and Botha, both picked to represent the Springboks for their disastrous 2003 Rugby World Cup campaign, were absent.

Joubert remained in charge for the 2004 Super Rugby campaign and, with Van der Westhuizen having moved on, the coach decided it was time to entrust the leadership duties to Matfield. Again the Bulls finished sixth, but careers were being shaped: Botha, Matfield, Hougaard and a future great scrumhalf in Fourie du Preez. While Matfield's leadership credentials were enhanced, he might well have gone on to captain the Springboks ahead of John Smit had Meyer not been overlooked as Straeuli's replacement in the wake of the 2003 World Cup disaster.

As it happened, the choice of Jake White for the Springbok coaching job proved inspired. He appointed John Smit as captain without hesitation, and, while he recognised Matfield's merits as a player, he picked him reluctantly.

Notwithstanding his conservative upbringing, Matfield was a fiercely independent thinker and strong-willed. White was an old-school coach who felt Matfield wanted everything his own way and needed to be "managed". The coach wanted his players cut from similar cloth, to the point of the length of Matfield's hair becoming an issue. The irritation was mutual. It was fertile ground for a personality clash.

Matfield started the White era as No. 5 lock in the two-Test series against Ireland and a match against Wales. All were won comfortably after initial pessimism that South Africa might even lose to the Irish on home soil.

All seemed fine, but simmering in the background was the White-Matfield situation, which boiled over in Australia in July 2004. The Springboks were based in the coastal suburb of Terrigal, north of Sydney, in preparation for a showdown in Gosford against a combined Pacific Islands team, and Matfield took a knock to his knee during training. Having injured the knee four weeks earlier, Matfield sat out the rest of the session as a precaution. By evening, however, he was running comfortably on the hotel treadmill.

To his great irritation, the Springbok medical staff decreed he be sent home. "I told the doctor I was fine and he said I wasn't. My response was 'How can you say that? I just ran and was OK'. They still sent me back," Matfield recalls.

Matfield believed the episode was aimed at teaching him a lesson, and he demonstrated his defiance by playing for the Blue Bulls on the same weekend that the Springboks, with Albert van den Berg as their No. 5 lock, lost 21-23 to the All Blacks in Christchurch. Van den Berg, called up after Gerrie Britz suffered a minor injury in the 38-24 win over the Pacific Islands, made a modest contribution. Britz was even less convincing in the Test against Australia in Perth. The Springboks were routed in the lineouts as they went down 26-30.

White was not stubborn to the point of lacking appreciation for Matfield's talent, while the man increasingly seen as the world's foremost No. 5 lock had John Smit fighting in his corner. The Springbok captain was not the least bit insecure that Matfield might have designs on his position. Smit considered Matfield a great leader in his own right and felt it of crucial importance that he run the Springbok lineouts.

Like Matfield, Smit thought the episode in Terrigal was about teaching the lock a lesson rather than an injury. Either way, White had got his point across and knew deep down that Matfield was without equal among South Africa's No. 5 locks.

Matfield reflects on it all with a smile and concedes that there might also have been immaturity on his part. "Jake had called me to Johannesburg to tell me he wouldn't pick me if I didn't cut my hair. My attitude was pick me or don't. Jake and I clashed until I was sent back and then Heyneke called us to a meeting," Matfield recalls.

To Matfield's surprise, Meyer did not stick up for him.

"He said in front of Jake, 'Victor, you are always different'. Then he said to Jake, 'Listen, he's still got work ethic and discipline'. I realised then for the first time that I needed to go with the flow a little more if that was what would be required to be a Springbok. It's not the end of the world to trim one's hair a little!

"I have a lot of respect for Jake as a coach. We clashed, but I think he's a lot like me. He's his own man. When I retired, he called and asked that I come and play for the Brumbies and said that he'd like to use me in a coaching role."

If there was a match where White realised Matfield was irreplaceable, it was probably the showdown against Australia in Durban on 21 August. Having beaten the All Blacks 40-26 in Johannesburg the previous week, the Springboks were in a position to clinch the Tri-Nations. That they managed to do so owed much to Matfield's lineout prowess and ball skills. Wallaby hooker Brendan Cannon was unnerved by Matfield's sheer presence and conceded possession three times by delaying his throw-ins. On top of that, the towering Springbok No. 5 scored South Africa's try of the year to edge South Africa ahead early in the second half. Matfield, on his charge to the goal line, beat the great Wallaby scrumhalf George Gregan by feigning a pass to Botha before cutting inside to score. He also made the final pass for eighthman Joe van Niekerk's try not long after that.

And so a match in which the Springboks trailed 3-7 at half time was turned on its head. They prevailed 23-19 to signal emphatically the birth of a great era in South African rugby.

In Pretoria, Meyer was being primed for a third crack at coaching the Bulls. Anton Leonard would be the captain with Matfield second in command. The Meyer era was now gaining momentum, with the likes of Bryan Habana, Danie Rossouw, Fourie du Preez and Morné Steyn also flexing their muscles. Matfield played all but one match in a campaign that ended with a semifinal defeat to the Waratahs in Sydney. However, it was his character as much as his talent that impressed Meyer. "The thing that struck me about Victor was that he spoke well of my predecessor as Bulls coach, Rudy Joubert," Meyer recalls.

"In situations like that most players will tell you how useless the other guy was. I really liked Victor's integrity."

And then there was Matfield's remarkable work ethic, which was demonstrated after his return to the Bulls camp following participation in a charity match to help raise money for victims of the 2004 Indian Ocean tsunami. The match, on 5 March 2005, required Matfield to miss the Bulls' first match of their Australasian tour against the ACT Brumbies in Canberra. He would then link up with them again prior to the following Friday's match against the Highlanders at Carisbrook in Dunedin, six days after the charity match.

Having done his duty in the southern hemisphere's 54-19 victory over the North at Twickenham, Matfield took on the arduous journey from London to New Zealand's South Island. "Victor had to fly halfway around the world to join up with us and only landed on the Tuesday morning before our next game. I told him upon his arrival that he didn't have to train as he was clearly exhausted. Victor not only trained, he led the lineouts," Meyer recalls.

The Matfield-Meyer relationship was cemented in 2006 when Matfield was appointed Bulls captain. As in 2005, the Bulls' campaign ended on foreign shores at the semifinal stage – this time through a defeat to the Crusaders. The Bulls had not yet cracked the code to touring successfully, while home defeats to the Brumbies, Hurricanes and Crusaders showed that they were far from the complete team. They finished fourth, which set up a lost-cause play-off match. Nonetheless, a special generation of players was growing in stature.

That same year Matfield played a significant part in saving Jake White's job when the great Springbok revival of the previous two seasons went pear-shaped under the strain of rugby politics and injuries.

Coming off a run of five consecutive defeats, White's job was on the line as the Springboks geared up to play the All Blacks in Rustenburg on 2 September 2006. New Zealand, having just beaten South Africa 45-26 at Loftus the previous weekend, appeared to strengthen their side through a number of changes.

All it did, however, was to spark a typical backs-to-the-wall job by the Springboks. Few fought harder than Matfield, who was dominant in the lineouts and the victim of the foul play that handed Springbok flyhalf André Pretorius an opportunity to secure a narrow 21-20 victory with a pressure penalty.

However, it was the following season that would be Matfield's pathway to greatness. To kick it off, he was at the helm of the Bulls side that clinched the Super Rugby title with a stunning yet fortuitous 20-19 victory over the Sharks in Durban. John Smit, for whom Matfield was his trustiest lieutenant at Springbok level, had captained the Sharks. The potential was there for some ill feeling between the camps to spill over into the Springbok set-up, but Matfield's leadership helped turn it into a positive.

"The Bulls' feet were firmly on the ground when they came into the camp and they went out of their way to mingle with the Sharks players. When that happened, we started to become a family," recalls Gert Smal, the Springboks' forwards coach at the time.

Come the 2007 Rugby World Cup in France, Matfield had already captained the Springboks on three occasions in Smit's injury-enforced absence, starting with the 21-26 defeat to New Zealand in Durban on 23 June. Thereafter he skippered the Springboks in their World Cup warm-up wins over Namibia (105-13) and Scotland (27-3).

Matfield's finest hour would be the World Cup final. Having beaten England 36-0 in the pool stages, the Springboks would now unexpectedly meet a rejuvenated version of the Red Rose Army. As is so often the case with such matches, it was an arm wrestle rather than a great spectacle. England did most of the playing, but the Springboks were seldom troubled in their 15-6 victory.

Much of the reason for that was South Africa's success in disrupting the defending champions' lineout. By the third minute, the Springboks had already stolen two lineout balls through Botha and Matfield. By full time England had lost seven of their throw-ins. Even the balls they won back were not always of good quality due to South Africa's smart contesting policy. By contrast, South Africa could rely on Matfield, Bakkies Botha and flank Juan Smith to deliver crisp possession.

Matfield, however, was so much more than the ultimate lineout forward. There was even a brilliantly executed kick that forced England wing Mark Cueto to carry the ball into touch deep in his own territory. England attacked aggressively in the final quarter, but were snuffed out by great defence, including a crucial lineout steal by Matfield 10 minutes from full time. "You need big players for big moments in big games," Smal says of Matfield's contribution. "What made Victor so dangerous is that he could cover a wide space on the ground and in the air because of his speed of movement and agility."

On the captaincy front, Matfield enjoyed big moments when called upon to do the job in Smit's absence. In 2008 there was a first win over the All Blacks in Dunedin (30-28) and a thumping 53-8 rout of Australia in Johannesburg. He also captained the Springboks in their 18-5 win over the All Blacks in Port Elizabeth prior to the 2011 Rugby World Cup after coach Peter de Villiers had selected Smit on the bench to give Bismarck du Plessis a run at hooker.

Nonetheless, Matfield seldom thought of himself as being anything but a support act. "Except for the end-of-season tour in 2010, when John was injured, it never felt to me as if I was the Springbok captain. I took the reins when required to do so, but in that case you're leading someone else's team. At the Bulls I could say I was captain," he says.

"I enjoyed the support role because I know what Fourie du Preez meant to me at the Bulls. I told people that we were dual captains. I consulted with him on all the big decisions that I made and he was always involved in my planning.

"John was very good with matters off the field and it was good to be able to assist him with things on it. He trusted me with lineout calls and it was much the same under Jean de Villiers as Springbok captain.

"I never had a strong drive to become captain. As long as I could provide input into how we played and had a voice, I was very happy."

Smit reckons their roles could easily have been reversed. "Victor was a bona fide Springbok captain. He had all the qualities. The nice thing is he never made a big thing about it. He stepped in when he needed to and didn't shy away from the job. We were close during our times together," Smit says.

Together they would scale even greater heights in 2009.

Matfield was at the helm of a Bulls side that thumped the Chiefs

61-17 in the Super Rugby final at Loftus on 30 May. Four weeks later he would celebrate a series victory over the British and Irish Lions at the same venue. A hat-trick of victories over the All Blacks followed in the Springboks' march to the Tri-Nations title.

The team that White built had reached maturity under Peter de Villiers, who also freshened things up with some new faces, including flyhalf Morné Steyn and openside flank Heinrich Brüssow. A positional shift for Smit to tighthead prop also ensured that South Africa could benefit from Du Plessis's presence as starting hooker.

South Africa's game plan was very difficult to combat. The Springboks had a fearsome lineout defence led by Matfield, while Du Preez's pinpoint high kicks were ferociously chased down by wings Bryan Habana and JP Pietersen. Brüssow and Du Plessis were also superb at the defensive breakdowns and ensured turnover possession at vital stages, while Frans Steyn tortured the All Blacks with his fearsome boot.

"It must have been the greatest rugby year South Africa ever had. We were at a place where we had a lot of experience, the Bulls' influence was strong and Peter empowered the players," Matfield recalls.

"Heyneke always said you need guys who work hard and think the same, and then you need three or four special players who do special things. That team had it."

But the Springboks lost their way in 2010. Matfield puts it down to contrasting philosophies taking hold in the squad after the Stormers reached an all-South African Super Rugby final with the Bulls. "There were two schools of thought rather than one specific way. The moment you try to integrate and don't have a single vision, you have problems."

While emphasising unity of purpose, Matfield is a firm believer in debate. He would challenge his coaches, but behind closed doors. "If you have the same dream and vision, you can argue with one another. It's not about who is wrong or right. Rather, it's about strengthening one another through exchanging ideas. A coach, captain and leadership group has to be able to debate things. Once you've decided on the way forward, everyone has to buy in one hundred per cent," Matfield says.

Meyer had a deep appreciation for Matfield's tact in that regard. "I like a player who challenges me. Where I have immense respect for

Victor is that he would never do it in front of the team. Nor would he do it in an ugly way. He will make suggestions, but one thing I can say beyond any doubt is that he'll back the coach one hundred per cent. If something has been decided, he will back it to the death," Meyer says.

"Many people are afraid of his knowledge. He'll be a successful coach because he's a thinker and student of the game."

What separated Matfield from others was more than just his exceptional talent. He was a hard worker, be it on the training field or in aiding with preparations behind the scenes. At the core of his genius was a willingness to put in the hours and an exceptional level of fitness. "Victor would always be first on the training field and never missed sessions. He's super fit and always runs in front at training," says Meyer. Smal, having armed players with information to prepare them for looming Test matches, would always find that Matfield had done his own homework.

De Villiers' policy of empowering players brought the best out of Matfield at Springbok level and he was still world class when he retired at age 34 in the wake of the controversial Rugby World Cup quarter-final defeat to Australia in Wellington in 2011.

Having bade rugby farewell as a player, Matfield naturally became a sought-after pundit and he indeed did a stint with SuperSport. Meyer, however, had other plans following his appointment as Springbok coach in January 2012. The job should probably have been his in 2008, but had instead gone to Peter de Villiers, denying Meyer the opportunity to coach at international level the players he had shaped in their prime.

By the time Meyer was appointed as coach, it was time for a rebuilding exercise, as a number of senior players decided either to retire or explore overseas opportunities. Realising that he would embark on a journey without an obvious leadership core, Meyer was swift in calling Matfield after his appointment. Four months after announcing his retirement, the great lock was asked to make an about turn.

"Heyneke wanted me to help with the transitional phase – to play for two years so that the players could get a feel for how he did things. I could then retire to allow the other guys to come through," Matfield recalls of the original plan.

However, the International Rugby Board's regulations stipulated that Matfield would have to wait six months before making his comeback, which put a spoke in the wheels.

With his stock at No. 5 lock threadbare, Meyer called again at the end of 2012. However, Matfield was by then negotiating a coaching contract with the Blue Bulls. He would change course if Meyer could organise a Springbok contract, but it couldn't be done quickly enough.

When the coach called for a third time the following year, the paperwork was done and Matfield would be available for South Africa's June internationals. That was if he could negotiate his way through the rough and tumble of Super Rugby following a two-year absence.

Initially Matfield was in no condition for rugby. He had taken to cycling and his weight had dipped under 100 kg. He bulked up in the gym, but remained insecure. Meyer, however, had no doubt about Matfield's ability to continue adding value. "He's one of the fittest guys I coached. That is why I knew he would be successful," Meyer recalls.

It turned out to be a necessary step. Pieter-Steph du Toit, the young No. 5 lock rated by Meyer as a potential future great, was bedevilled by injuries. The other contender for the No. 5 jersey, Andries Bekker, had put his Springbok career on hold to play in Japan.

As time passed in the Super Rugby tournament, Matfield took on a more assured demeanour. "I knew that if I had to pick between myself, Pieter-Steph and Andries to carry the ball up, it would be one of them. But I believed I could organise the lineouts better and offer a higher work rate," Matfield says.

It was just as well that Meyer was so persistent, as disaster struck two weeks prior to the Springboks' first match of their international season, against a World XV at Newlands on 7 June 2014. Jean de Villiers, who had captained South Africa so impressively from the outset of Meyer's reign, had suffered a knee injury with the Stormers and would miss the June internationals. With a Test series against Wales looming, Meyer had to appoint a caretaker captain. While the coach thought long and hard about it, there really was only one choice: Matfield.

The friendly against the World XV gave Matfield an opportunity to reacquaint himself with the demands of international rugby. A week later, on 14 June, he would officially make his return to Test rugby as captain, aged 37, against Wales in Durban. A comfortable 38-16 victory over the Dragons saw Matfield equal two Springbok records: first, there was Smit's 111 Test caps and, second, Johan Ackermann's milestone of being the oldest Springbok at 37 years and 34 days. He would eclipse both in the following week's fortuitous victory of 31-30 over the Welsh in Nelspruit (Mbombela).

The statistics regularly showed that Matfield, in spite of his age, was among the hardest workers in the team. He did not contest the lineouts as fiercely as he once did, but this probably had something to do with the opposition throwing the ball into spaces he could not occupy. Matfield, no doubt, was still a formidable opponent. More importantly, his value as senior player was immense. The horrific knee injury suffered by De Villiers against Wales at the end of 2014, coupled with a fractured jaw in his first Test back against Argentina in Durban, meant that Matfield would again fulfil a vital stand-in role in a World Cup year.

Come the showpiece in England, Matfield was still operating at a high level, if not as good as during the peak of his career. He sustained a hamstring injury in the Springboks' second pool match, against Samoa, the same day that De Villiers' Test career was ended by another jaw injury.

Lood de Jager performed impressively after replacing Matfield during the second half against Samoa and followed it up with strong performances in pool matches against Scotland and the USA.

As the quarterfinal against Wales loomed, with Matfield expected to be back to full fitness, there was a sense of anticipation among media and public as Meyer pondered his team selection: Matfield or De Jager?

It was taken out of hands with a diagnosis that Matfield was still not ready, but Meyer confirmed that the great man would have been on the bench had he been fit. De Jager was in pole position, though Matfield was all but discarded and could ultimately reflect positively on his contribution as player and leader.

Matfield's captaincy style was a reflection of his intellect. "I've never been an emotional captain. I'm not a guy for big speeches and nor do they motivate me. I figure out what needs to be done and arm myself with the detail," he says.

And, of course, there are values by which he operates. "I believe a champion trains while the others rest. If you are willing to push yourself to places where others don't want to go, you enter the realm of the special players. They are the ones who stand up when others disappear. It's a quality that I look for and try to foster in myself."

Notwithstanding a Springbok career that spanned well over a decade, Matfield may still hang up his boots as a misunderstood player and person. "In my experience Victor was always humble," Smal recalls. "There was a different perception about him, which reminds me of the criticism that Naas Botha had to endure years ago. Players like that are exceptional and there will be criticism from people who don't support the teams they play for."

Meyer believes Matfield's legacy may even be greater outside than in South Africa. "Our people don't like someone who is a little different. Victor was the first modern lock. He was criticised a lot, but everyone plays that way now. It's testimony to Victor that every other country has copied our lineout systems."

Matfield does not feel in need of the love of those who fail to grasp that rugby is played beyond a single phase and forwards are required to handle the ball. "What always stood out for me is that the moment we landed in New Zealand, there were headlines about how they would counter Matfield and what the plans for the lineouts would be. That is the best testimony you can hope for," he says.

Rather than as a Springbok captain, the international rugby community will probably consider Matfield's legacy as that of a lineout pioneer. He instilled fear at set piece and with it took the game to another level. "I will probably always be remembered for the lineouts, but the time and analysis that goes into preparation for them is hugely significant. I don't wait for coaches. Before I even go into a meeting, I already have a clear picture in my mind of how we should approach the game," Matfield says.

"It's analysis from a player's side and when it comes to a legacy people will hopefully see that you spent time thinking about the game and worked harder than others."

19 THE UNDAUNTED

Louise de Villiers was just about driven to distraction by the constant thudding noise while her youngest son, Jean, studied for his matric exams. Jean invariably had a ball in his hand, and a mark on the ceiling of their home in Paarl was testimony to his ability to give expression to his passion while simultaneously having his nose in his books.

"How he passed matric – and he did it with flying colours – heaven only knows," Louise says with a laugh.

But that was Jean de Villiers. A bright lad with a twinkle in his eye and a passion for ball sport.

When Louise returned home after a day's teaching at La Rochelle Girls' High School, she would have to pass, tackle or bowl to Jean and his older brother, André-Louis. Unlike many rugby players, she learned to pass to both sides.

Their dad, André, was a former Western Province lock who owned a sports equipment business. Notwithstanding his passion for the game, André allowed the boys to pursue their own passions rather than consciously forcing them into the rugby environment.

Rugby was their shared passion, however. As it turned out, they both represented South Africa at under-19 level at the Junior World Championships in Wales in 1999. André-Louis's career as a prop would be cut short by neck and shoulder injuries sustained in a car accident not long after that. Injury would also be a determining factor in the shaping of Jean's destiny, but in an altogether different manner.

Jean would have to navigate his path with enormous strength and depth of character, which was shaped by his education at Paarl Gymnasium and a solid upbringing. Louise was a disciplinarian who allowed her boys certain liberties and encouraged debate. There were, however, certain non-negotiables. Among those was that they develop their God-given talents and finish whatever they started, something Jean did particularly well.

In terms of rugby education, the great former Springbok centre John Gainsford played his part when he visited the De Villiers family for a braai. Spotting young Jean kicking the ball in a game with his brother and friends, Gainsford called a halt to proceedings and beckoned the future Springbok captain towards him.

"Do you want to become a Springbok?" Gainsford asked.

"Yes," Jean replied.

"Then ..." said Gainsford, "... you don't kick the ball, you pass it."

Coupled with a liberal upbringing – André was at the forefront of racial integration in Western Cape club rugby – this advice provided fertile ground for the shaping of a young man with a positive rugby philosophy and an ability to see the bigger picture.

Jean, born on 24 February 1981, displayed a maturity beyond his years from an early age. It may well have played a part in team-mates' voting against him for the captaincy at under-15 level. His coach at the time, Pine Pienaar, took his protégé aside and gave him this assurance: "You are the best rugby player that has ever passed through my hands. Don't let this get you down because you are destined for bigger things."

The maturity came packaged with a wicked sense of humour. Jean had the gift of the gab and the loudest laughs in the team bus usually came from near where he sat. However, the chirpy demeanour masked the depth of his thinking. De Villiers quickly gained an appreciation for the gentle art of diplomacy and inspired his team-mates with positivity. One example was when he captained an under-15 side from Paarl Gymnasium at a sevens tournament where a defeat against weaker opponents meant their only hope to qualify for the quarterfinals was as "best loser". It would require 10 tries, but, drawing on an inspirational speech from Paralympian Fanie Lombard, Jean rallied his troops.

"Remember that Fanie Lombard said we should meet our challenges head-on. We need 10 tries to make the quarterfinals and we're going to do it." De Villiers' speech helped them to win the tournament.

Having been taken up in Western Province's structures from primary school level, it was inevitable that De Villiers would eventually graduate to the senior side. His first-class debut for Western Province came on his 20th birthday, 24 February 2001, in a Vodacom Cup match against the Leopards in Potchefstroom.

Less than two years later, De Villiers would make his Springbok debut. Rudolf Straeuli, then the Springbok coach, boldly decided to pair De Villiers with Adrian Jacobs in midfield for his Test debut against France at the Stade Velodrome in Marseille on 9 November 2002.

It hadn't even been five months since De Villiers played on the right wing for the South African under-21 team that scooped the Junior World Cup with a 24-21 victory over Australia at Ellis Park. It was turning out to be a dream season for a young man so highly regarded for his potential that he could become a Springbok having played in only one Currie Cup match for Western Province.

He seemingly had the world at his feet. However, in the seventh minute after running on in Marseille he suffered the first of several injuries that would reduce him to tears. De Villiers, having just got up to contest possession at the breakdown after bringing down French fullback Nicolas Brusque, felt his left knee twist as he got cleaned out at the ruck with his foot stuck in the grass. With that, a dream debut turned into a nightmare on a stretcher. It wouldn't be the last either.

"There was a lot of heartbreak, but I believe that had it not been for that injury on my Test debut, I wouldn't have played 109 Tests for South Africa," De Villiers reflects. "I learnt a lot about myself and life during that period. I realised how hard I could push myself, how hard one had to work to get back, what it was all about, where your strength comes from and what your support base is.

"I always talk about your pillars as a human being and the support structure of your faith, family and friends. I think it's them that carried me through all the years. Those nine months after my first injury taught me to fight for what I wanted."

De Villiers' spirit would again be tested less than a year later. He had returned to first-class action on 2 August 2003 in a thumping 59-16 victory over the Golden Lions and impressed in another handful of matches in the Currie Cup. It was too late for a meaningful role in South Africa's Tri-Nations campaign, but an injury to Gcobani Bobo opened the door for selection to South Africa's squad for the Rugby World Cup in Australia.

Sadly, it was slammed shut almost immediately. De Villiers was picked on the bench for the Springboks' warm-up game against the Falcons in Springs. However, not long after his introduction disaster struck when he was brought to ground as he stretched out his left arm in trying to offload in the tackle near the Falcons' goal-line. De Villiers' shoulder ligaments were gone, with the Springboks' opening World Cup match against Uruguay less than three weeks away. The surgeon tasked with fixing the damage, Joe de Beer, equated the injury to that usually seen in motorcycle accidents.

On reflection, De Villiers was fortunate to miss the 2003 Rugby World Cup campaign and its accompanying dramas, including revelations of racism within the team and the infamous Kamp Staaldraad.

In keeping with his positive personality, De Villiers could not find fault with Straeuli. "I'd never be able to say anything bad about him because he handed me my Springbok debut. At that stage I hadn't played a single match for the Stormers and only one Currie Cup match for Western Province," he says.

"I was picked based on what I had produced in sevens rugby, at under-21 level and one match for Western Province. To this day, when I see Rudolf, I'm grateful for what he did. Sure, he got a few things wrong, but I have nothing but gratitude. He was good to me."

The South African Rugby Union (SARU) had no such sentiment and Straeuli got the bullet with a terse statement paying scant regard for his contribution.

Straeuli had fallen prey to the inevitable paranoia that accompanies the Springbok coaching job. His sense of insecurity was fed by a former police task force commander who acted as security consultant and as an unnecessary bodyguard for the coach. The Staaldraad revelations such as nude leopard-crawling, machine gun fire and singing of the national anthem while snaked in a cave, added to the sense of scandal after the failed World Cup campaign in 2003.

The man who restored a sense of purpose to South African rugby, and to De Villiers' career, was Jake White. In July 2004, he also chose a pragmatic path by picking De Villiers on the left wing for the Springboks' match against a combined Pacific Islands side in Gosford.

The more physical and experienced De Wet Barry would be tasked with manning up to Seru Rabeni at inside centre, where De Villiers would ultimately establish himself as one of the world's leading players.

That blueprint remained in place for most of 2004, during which the Springboks captured the Tri-Nations title by beating New Zealand 40-26 and Australia 23-19 at home, following agonisingly close defeats in Christchurch and Perth.

The 23-year-old De Villiers stamped his authority on proceedings with a try-scoring spree, which kicked off with a finish in the left-hand corner during the 38-24 win over the Pacific Islands.

But it was De Villiers' next try, in New Zealand, that will be particularly fondly remembered, as it came just 23 seconds into the clash with the All Blacks in Christchurch. The All Blacks, still pumped up after laying down the challenge with their haka, carelessly left the ball unprotected at the back of the first ruck. Springbok captain John Smit pounced and passed to his left to flyhalf Jaco van der Westhuyzen, who in turn shifted the ball to Barry. The inside centre then found De Villiers with a switch pass to set up the try.

De Villiers' momentum carried him over for a memorable moment of glory. The man who would later become his best friend, Schalk Burger, was the first to offer congratulations by deliriously throwing his arms around the chest of the future Springbok captain.

Sadly, the Springboks were to be denied a famous victory. They carried a 21-18 lead into the dying embers, but All Black wing Doug Howlett touched down to secure a 23-21 win. De Villiers and his mates were mortified, but the honour in their defeat made the rugby world sit up and take notice.

Next on the radar of a rejuvenated Springbok side was a showdown with the Wallabies at the Subiaco Oval in Perth. De Villiers scored the first of many intercept tries in his career when he latched onto an injudicious pass by Wallaby flyhalf Stephen Larkham from 60 metres out. Earlier in the first half, De Villiers had also set up Van der Westhuyzen for a try with a grubber kick. However, the lead of 16-7 that was created by these exploits would eventually dissipate, with the youthful Springbok side going down 26-30.

De Villiers had nevertheless played a crucial role in the Springboks' securing a second losing bonus point, which would ultimately be decisive in their tournament triumph. To keep the Springbok dream alive, however, the Wallabies would have to beat the All Blacks in Sydney. They obliged with a narrow 23-18 victory, which set South African minds racing.

The return fixture against New Zealand at Ellis Park would offer De Villiers's first taste of victory in 23 Tests against the All Blacks. His value for South Africa is also highlighted by an impressive win ratio. Up until 2011, he was on the winning side in eight of 17 matches against the traditional foe. In the wake of the 2011 Rugby World Cup, newly-appointed coach Heyneke Meyer would have to embark on a rebuilding exercise, which saw the De Villiers-led Springboks lose five times against the All Blacks before finally cracking the code in Johannesburg in October 2015.

The test against New Zealand at Ellis Park in 2004 would also be the first time that De Villiers represented South Africa on home soil. The remarkable 40-26 victory will be particularly fondly remembered for a hat-trick of tries by Marius Joubert, which equalled Ray Mordt's record against the All Blacks from 1981.

De Villiers was again on the left wing as South Africa clinched the title with a 23-19 win over Australia in Durban the following week. Springbok rugby, after the trauma of 2003, had been reborn.

With Barry performing outstandingly in the Tri-Nations, there would be no justification for De Villiers to supplant him. In fact, De Villiers found himself relegated to bench duty when the Springboks embarked on a gruelling tour of the Home Nations and Argentina.

White persisted with the centre combination of Barry and Joubert for the first three matches against Wales, Ireland and England. De Villiers would replace the injured Ashwin Willemse on the left wing for the Twickenham clash, but was keeping the No. 11 jersey warm for Bryan Habana, who came on as a substitute and scored with a 20-metre dash from his first touch. In doing so, Habana had hijacked the No. 11 jersey, of which he became the custodian for over a decade.

Nevertheless, De Villiers was still foremost in White's plans and the coach used the opening Test of 2005, against Uruguay in East London, to give him his first taste as an inside centre at the highest level.

Barry would be restored for a series against France and a defeat in a Nelson Mandela Challenge Plate clash with Australia in Sydney. However, opportunity came knocking in an Ellis Park showdown against the Wallabies that the Springboks had to win to retain the Plate. The match would double as a celebration of Nelson Mandela's 87th birthday and White used the occasion for experimentation. Apart from picking nine players of colour in the match-day squad, he also selected De Villiers and Jaque Fourie as a centre pairing for the first time. The combination would eventually serve South Africa in 29 Tests.

De Villiers seized the opportunity and, as at Perth in 2004, intercepted a Larkham pass for a 60-metre sprint to the tryline. He also broke through the Wallabies' defensive line to deliver a scoring pass to Fourie.

The midfield also served the Boks well in three of their four Tri-Nations fixtures, including De Villiers' first Test at Newlands on 6 August – against the All Blacks. There was again the trademark intercept – this time from Kiwi scrumhalf Byron Kelleher's pass – in the first half, securing the Springboks an early 13-0 lead. They held on for a thrilling 22-16 win against an All Black side that included future greats Dan Carter and Richie McCaw.

South Africa came within a whisker of retaining their Tri-Nations crown, but fell agonisingly short at the final hurdle in Dunedin, where New Zealand beat them 31-27 with a late try by Keven Mealamu off the back of a maul.

Nonetheless, White's dream team was taking shape and it included the centre pairing of De Villiers and Fourie. By the time White's grand plan came together for the 2007 Rugby World Cup, De Villiers and Fourie were firmly established as one of the world's leading centre pairings.

However, disaster again struck early in the second half of the Springboks' opening pool game against Samoa at the Parc des Princes. This time it was a torn bicep after a tackle on Samoan fullback David Lemi, whose head struck De Villiers on the arm. The captain, John Smit, put his arm around a tearful De Villiers in the dressing room after the final whistle. The dream was over.

De Villiers would nonetheless have many career highlights in the ensuing seasons. In 2009 he was a member of the Springbok team that toppled the All Blacks in three matches in Bloemfontein, Durban and Hamilton. The crowning glory, however, was a series victory over the British and Irish Lions, with De Villiers partnering Adrian Jacobs in the first Test in Durban and the series-clinching second in Pretoria.

Peter de Villiers, who had been appointed as Springbok coach in 2008, initially shelved the White blueprint and chose Jacobs ahead of Fourie. The eccentric coach was eventually credited with having a significant role in the team's achievements.

"There was an element of Jake's team reaching maturity, but Peter also deserves credit for the manner in which he created an environment in which everyone was happy," De Villiers says.

"All the coaches who I played under had their strengths and weaknesses, and it was no different with him. The players had freedom to express their opinions and everything came together nicely on the field. There were young guys coming through that year who complemented the experienced ones, so we had just the right blend."

With a series victory over the Lions added to his honours list, De Villiers decided it was time to experience something new and signed to play for Irish province Munster. The move would also offer him an opportunity for a physical and mental break. "It was great for me, but I decided to return to have another go at a World Cup because I thought at the time it would be my last chance," he recalls.

De Villiers was in the fortunate position of being able to return to Cape Town as a kingpin in a Stormers side where a winning culture had been cultivated in his absence during the Super Rugby campaign of 2010. He would be reunited in midfield with Fourie only briefly for two home internationals against the Wallabies during an unhappy 2010 for Springbok rugby. Significantly, however, they were together as South Africa closed out the 2011 Tri-Nations with an 18-5 victory over the All Blacks in Port Elizabeth.

Up until that point there hadn't been much to celebrate since the heady days of 2009, but this win engendered optimism in the run-up to the Rugby World Cup in New Zealand. De Villiers took a blow to the ribs in South Africa's opening game against Wales – a narrow 17-16 victory – but his fate would not be as cruel as four years previously. He returned as a substitute in the 13-5 victory over Samoa as the Springboks trotted through the pool stages.

The quarterfinal demise against the Wallabies has been well documented, in particular for the performance of Kiwi referee Bryce Lawrence, whose mistakes are said to have condemned South Africa to their 9-11 defeat. However, the Springboks also had their opportunities, and among the lost ones was a forward pass from De Villiers to fullback Patrick Lambie with the tryline beckoning. Had it been on the money, and De Villiers believes it was, South Africa would have squared the game at 8-8.

Nonetheless, De Villiers' frustration was not directed at Lawrence.

"For us it was just disappointing to lose, irrespective of how it happened. I blamed us, not him. Maybe also myself for that pass. You think back and wonder what you could have done differently. Could you have given more? The reality sunk in that there was no way of changing the outcome."

De Villiers, who was 30 at the time, thought that was that for his Springbok career. He would play another season for the Stormers, but was beginning to look at overseas options.

Elsewhere there was the retirement of Victor Matfield (110 caps), while Springbok captain John Smit (111) and Jaque Fourie (69) had also called time on their international careers. The likes of Fourie du

Preez (62), Danie Rossouw (63) and Bakkies Botha (76) had also placed question marks over their future involvement by taking up lucrative offers from overseas clubs.

SARU would next have to shift its agenda to the appointment of a new Springbok coach, which of course could also play a big role in determining the identity of the new captain. Perhaps not since the 1990s did a Springbok coach face such a tough job in his first year as Heyneke Meyer, who unlike White and Peter de Villiers did not commit to a captain prior to the international season.

Instead he set about travelling through South Africa to acquaint himself with franchise players and promising juniors. By that time the speculation of who the new captain would be had begun in earnest, particularly since White and De Villiers had both made their respective captaincy announcements long before the start of the international seasons in 2004 and 2008.

It was a decision Meyer would only make in the build-up to his first Test in charge against England in Durban later in the year. It might have been a case of his first wanting to check on the availability of Du Preez, who at the time was playing for Suntory Sungoliath in Japan.

Meyer nevertheless dropped a clear hint about his liking of De Villiers after meeting players in Cape Town early in May 2012, saying he had been "really impressed" by him in their brief interaction. The Springbok coach added that he rated De Villiers' ability to organise a backline and also suggested a positional change from inside to outside centre could be on the cards.

Fast forward a month to the Beverly Hills Hotel at Umhlanga Rocks, outside Durban, and the decision was formally made. "We got together the Sunday ahead of our match against England that coming Saturday. We had meetings the entire day, the squad was kitted and we did all the standard things for a first day," recalls De Villiers. "After going to my room in the evening, I got a call from Ian Schwartz [the team manager], who asked me to come to his room. When I walked in, he and Heyneke were sitting there.

"We chatted about this and that before he suddenly came out saying that he would like me to captain the side. He set the Monday night as deadline for me to make a decision. I didn't need the time to think about it.

"I phoned my wife first, then my parents and my brother. When I woke up on Monday, there was an overwhelming feeling of 'Gosh, it's a reality'. Heyneke then announced it to the team in our first meeting on the Monday morning."

De Villiers would lead a Springbok side with an uncapped lock pairing of Eben Etzebeth and Juandré Kruger, as well as a debutant flank in Marcell Coetzee. "If I look back now, I realise it was crisis management from the outset. To have five days to build a team with a new coach and captain is a tough ask," De Villiers reflects.

"We emerged unbeaten from three tough Tests against England and then went straight into the Rugby Championship [the four-nation successor to the Tri-Nations]. Then you have the end-of-season tour directly after the Currie Cup.

"It's a tough first year and we got through it relatively successfully. We lost three games and drew two, but I think it was acceptable even if it hadn't been quite what we wanted. We laid a foundation for the future."

Meyer admits he took the decision on De Villiers with reluctance. However, the Springbok coach had little room for manoeuvre. He would probably have preferred to have Matfield at his disposal to lead the Springboks into the new era, and indeed tried to coax him out of retirement. However, International Rugby Board (IRB) rules meant that Matfield would have to wait six months to make a comeback after his retirement. It was too late.

"The difficult thing with the Springboks is that you seldom have meaningful time with the team. If I had picked a captain who had worked with me for several seasons, it would have been easier to get things through to the team," Meyer says.

"I was initially worried about the way I thought Jean would want to play. I thought he would want to move the ball at every opportunity. You can't beat the All Blacks that way because you would be playing to their strengths."

De Villiers was also the perfect captain for a regenerating Springbok team. "What impressed me from the outset is how he looked after the young guys. He really took them under his wing. Sometimes a captain comes across as untouchable to the young guys, but he was accessible and someone from whom they could draw strength," Meyer says.

Surprisingly for the coach, he had also found a captain who shared his philosophy of the game. "I believe the captain has to be an extension of the coach's personality and he has to communicate your message on the field," Meyer says.

"We think very much alike about the game and he's technically very good. Jean always makes good contributions when he talks about the game and our plan.

"He was very good friends with Victor Matfield and Fourie du Preez. The fact that he enjoyed support in the north and south made it easy.

"You seldom get someone who is a great guy, has his team's respect by leading from the front and is technically good. Sometimes you get players who are technically superb, but don't always lead by example. Jean is one of those extremely rare guys with both qualities.

"As I grew into the job, I realised it was one of the best decisions I had ever made. Jean is close to being the best captain I've worked with."

The De Villiers era would kick off with a three-match series against England in which the new captain shared the midfield with Frans Steyn for the first two Tests and with Wynand Olivier for the third. While the press and public weren't overly impressed by two victories and a draw, Meyer considers the series victory one of the biggest triumphs of his coaching career, given that he had no meaningful time in which to prepare his side.

However, frustration would follow in the Rugby Championship, in part due to Meyer's loyalty to out-of-sorts flyhalf Morné Steyn and some poor discipline.

South Africa had a gilt-edged opportunity to beat the All Blacks in Dunedin's Forsyth Barr Stadium on 15 September, and remained in the running in spite of seven missed kicks between Morné Steyn, Frans Steyn and Johan Goosen. However, Dean Greyling, a replacement for loosehead prop Tendai Mtawarira, put paid to any hopes by flying in from the side of a ruck to elbow All Black captain Richie

McCaw with 15 minutes left. With Greyling's yellow card, together with a string of penalties conceded by the prop, went any momentum the Boks might have been able to achieve in the last quarter and they lost 11-21.

It could have been the breakthrough victory that the new coach-and-captain partnership craved. Instead, a 31-8 win over the Wallabies in Pretoria on 29 September proved the highlight of the campaign. The return match against the All Blacks, at the FNB Stadium in Johannesburg, yielded a comprehensive 16-32 defeat.

A crucial end-of-season tour loomed, which would ultimately lay the platform for bigger things. De Villiers' commitment to the cause was highlighted by his playing through the 21-10 victory over Scotland at Murrayfield with a cold. This followed on a narrow 16-12 win over Ireland in Dublin.

As always, however, the success or failure of a November tour is determined by the result against England. At Twickenham on 24 November, a freak try by flank Willem Alberts proved crucial in determining the outcome, with the Springboks clinging on desperately at the end to win 16-15.

They were helped in no small part by a captaincy blunder by England's Chris Robshaw, who with two minutes left asked flyhalf Owen Farrell to kick for posts rather than set up an attacking lineout from which a maul try could have clinched a victory. There would be one more kick-off as a result, which allowed the Springboks to score one of the most crucial victories of De Villiers' captaincy career. He had played his usual captain's innings, while No. 8 Duane Vermeulen had signalled what was to come from his career with an enormous tackle count that secured the man-of-the-match accolade.

De Villiers' Boks were now set for a run of matches that would provide a significant boost to their confidence. The period also included one of the greatest anticlimaxes in the history of the rivalry between the Springboks and All Blacks.

South Africa had signalled their arrival as a team with a remarkable 38-12 win over the Wallabies in Brisbane on 7 September 2013, setting up an eagerly anticipated clash in Auckland between the game's greatest rivals the following Saturday. What hadn't been bargained on was a hapless performance by French referee Romain Poite, who wrongly yellow-carded Springbok hooker Bismarck du Plessis in the first quarter for what was deemed a late tackle on Dan Carter. The All Black flyhalf suffered a shoulder injury in the process.

Du Plessis was then legitimately carded early in the second half for leading with his elbow and striking All Black flank Liam Messam on the throat, but the events of the first half meant his dismissal would be for the rest of the match. The All Blacks led 17-10 at half time, and Du Plessis's dismissal effectively ensured their 29-15 victory. Crucially, they scored four tries for a bonus point.

"It was tough, but one accepts that kind of thing in the hope that no one will ever deliberately make mistakes. He [Poite] made the decision that he at the time thought was the right one and I accept it," De Villiers says.

South Africa remained in the running after defeating Australia 28-8 at Newlands on 28 September and could still win the Rugby Championship by achieving the improbable: a bonus-point victory over the All Blacks while also denying their scoring four tries or coming within seven points. Even if they failed to capture the Rugby Championship title, a Springbok victory at Ellis Park on 5 October would temper New Zealand's Rugby Championship triumph.

De Villiers and Meyer, however, decided to go for broke with a running rather than a low-risk game. "I didn't make that decision alone. We decided we would rather endeavour to win the Championship than just the match. If we didn't go actively seeking the four tries, we would have effectively been settling for second best," De Villiers says.

The manner in which the Springboks lost and were ultimately reduced to second best in the competition won them many friends rather than bringing about despair. De Villiers himself scored South Africa's fourth try shortly before the hour mark and the Springboks led 27-24. However, the high hopes dissipated a few minutes later when the All Black replacement flyhalf, Beauden Barrett, slipped the Bok skipper's tackle to score the try that put the Championship out of South Africa's reach. Another converted try by All Black No. 8 Kieran

Read, who had been involved in an almighty one-on-one battle with Vermeulen, made it 38-27. South Africa were on the wrong end of what had been an epic match. Had it not been for a remarkable piece of sportsmanship by De Villiers, the result might have been different.

The All Blacks led 21-15 at half time and early in the second half replaced hooker Andrew Hore with Dane Coles, who played for about 20 minutes before referee Nigel Owens realised his name hadn't appeared on the team sheet. Instead, team manager Darren Shand had typed Keven Mealamu's name. Strictly speaking, the Springbok camp could have insisted that Coles leave the field. Instead, De Villiers cracked a joke about deducting log points from the All Blacks later and play continued to the Springboks' detriment.

However, De Villiers' gesture, coupled with the free-flowing nature of the match, changed perceptions about the Springboks. Not just about the way they played, but also about how they accepted their fate without whingeing.

"Jean made great friends worldwide because of that show of sportsmanship," Meyer says.

"South Africa didn't have a great relationship with referees and I think Jean put that right with his sportsmanship. We said from the outset that we'll never make excuses. My position is that we have to be good enough to win even if the referee's decisions go against us.

"There were times when we were unreasonably penalised, as was the case with Bismarck, but we don't want to look for excuses."

South Africa's impressive try-scoring record in the Rugby Championship did much for Meyer's hitherto dour image. Having coached the Bulls and being an Afrikaner, there were preconceived notions about Meyer. These proved unfounded. De Villiers' reputation was also enhanced and he was increasingly referred to as "Captain Fantastic".

The Springboks built on this foundation with an unbeaten end-of-season tour, including a 19-10 victory over France in Paris. South Africa's last victory there had been in 1997. By the time the Springboks beat Argentina 33-31 in Salta on 23 August 2014, they had managed a run of 18 victories from 20 matches. Their only defeats had been to New Zealand, and De Villiers felt they had the number of their great rivals. He declared as much at the launch of the new Springbok jersey at Cape Town's V&A Waterfront on 24 April 2014.

Those would prove prophetic words.

Meyer's tactical approach also continued to evolve. He had already added an attacking fullback to the mix in Willie le Roux in 2013 and now decided it was time for the prodigiously gifted flyhalf Handré Pollard to step into the limelight. Morné Steyn was restored as pivot when South Africa kicked off the year with a Test series victory over Wales, but Pollard got his opportunity in the 55-6 victory over Scotland in Port Elizabeth on 28 June.

Pollard also started the Rugby Championship as flyhalf, though after two victories over Argentina there was another ill-fated flirtation with Morné Steyn against the Wallabies in Perth on 6 September.

As if to press home the point that Pollard was the way forward, Steyn failed to find touch from a penalty that would have brought relief late in the match, and Wallaby wing Rob Horne scored from the resultant counter-attack. Flyhalf Bernard Foley's conversion condemned the Springboks to a 23-24 defeat after they had looked comfortable early in the match.

From Perth it was off to Wellington, where Pollard was restored to the flyhalf role for the Test against the All Blacks on 13 September. He executed a delightful switch move with wing Cornal Hendricks in the first half for a try that saw South Africa lead 7-6 at half time. However, a brilliantly crafted try from flyhalf Aaron Cruden's cross-kick, with Read beating De Villiers in the air before offloading to skipper Richie McCaw, gave the All Blacks the advantage early in the second half. A drop goal by Pollard brought the Springboks within a point before Barrett struck a penalty that would give the All Blacks a 14-10 lead that they would desperately cling to.

The Springboks attacked relentlessly in the closing stages, but lock Lood de Jager was ushered into touch to end their hopes of a match-clinching try. Nonetheless, the outcome strengthened the perception that the Springboks were closing the gap on the world's best side.

With the Springboks beating the Wallabies 28-10 at Newlands on 27 September, the stage was set for the return match against the All

Blacks at Ellis Park the following Saturday. It was another epic struggle in which New Zealand overturned a 13-24 deficit with tries by wing Ben Smith and substitute hooker Dane Coles in the 65th and 70th minutes. Crucially, Barrett had failed to convert Coles' try, which left the door ajar. The Springboks seized their opportunity when Liam Messam fouled Schalk Burger with a stiff arm just inside the All Blacks' half. Patrick Lambie, who had come on for Pollard after the latter had scored two tries, assured De Villiers that he was up to the kick that brought joy to a passionate rugby nation.

"It was a huge opportunity and I feel blessed that it was handed to me. I only had two thoughts in my head: the one was to trust that it would go over and the other to make sure that I strike the ball well. It's when you start thinking about a hundred different things that everything goes wrong. I had trained hard," Lambie recalls.

"We overcame a barrier. Having done it once, we knew it was possible to do it again."

De Villiers had been correct in his summation of where his team stood in relation to the All Blacks. Pundits were now of the opinion that the second-best team in the world had beaten the best. In addition, the Springbok captain's performances belied the fact that he had celebrated his 33rd birthday in February.

With the Boks having closed the gap on New Zealand, not many experts could predict the disappointment that would follow on South Africa's end-of-season tour. The opening match against Ireland, on 8 November, which resulted in a 15-29 defeat in Dublin's Aviva Stadium, exposed De Villiers' team as being far from the complete article.

A persistent downpour before kick-off signalled that the Springboks would be tested in ways that they were not used to. Francois Hougaard, so assured at scrumhalf in the victory over the All Blacks, fumbled behind the base as the combination of clever breakdown tactics and a wet ball exposed his and indeed the Springboks' weaknesses. They attacked relentlessly, but were repeatedly repelled, with Irish flyhalf Jonathan Sexton giving a masterclass in tactical kicking.

De Villiers was probably also too cavalier in his decision-making by foregoing goalkicking opportunities and instead opting for the ball to be put into touch. In truth, the Springboks were dominant at set piece, and there was every reason to believe that their superiority would be rewarded. They played themselves back into the match as the final quarter loomed, but the yellow-carding of hooker Adriaan Strauss for challenging Ireland fullback Rob Kearney in the air put paid to any hopes.

As has so often been the case in the past, Twickenham would provide the opportunity for redemption. The end-of-season showdown against England plays a big part in shaping the public's view on the success or failure of a season, and the Springboks always enjoy a match against the boastful Red Rose Army. The 31-28 scoreline belied the extent of South Africa's dominance, and when they followed it up with a 22-6 win over Italy in Padua, their season was over as far as World Rugby (the IRB changed its name on 19 November) was concerned. However, the South African and Welsh rugby unions had arranged a match outside the Test window. It would offer a boost in excess of R15 million to SARU's bottom line.

Sadly, on the playing side South Africa were led into an ambush. With the match falling outside the international window, there was no obligation on northern hemisphere clubs to release players for international duty. While there were no concessions for the Springboks, the Welsh and French rugby unions had agreed to allow the home side to pick a centre pairing of Jamie Roberts (Racing Métro) and Jonathan Davies (Clermont), as well as Toulon's Leigh Halfpenny at fullback. A further two France-based players, lock Luke Charteris and scrumhalf Mike Phillips, both from Racing Métro, were included on the substitutes' bench.

Absurdly, Springbok wing Bryan Habana, who like Halfpenny was contracted to Toulon, could not play. There were other high-profile Springbok absentees in wing JP Pietersen, scrumhalves Fourie du Preez and Ruan Pienaar, centre Frans Steyn, flankers Francois Louw and Schalk Burger, and tighthead prop Jannie du Plessis.

It was a game too far, and fertile ground for the Springboks' first loss to Wales since the debacle at the opening of the Millennium Stadium in 1999, when they lost 19-29 in the wake of a political storm about the racial composition of the team.

Defeat might have been bearable had it not been for the sickening injury suffered by De Villiers close to the hour mark.

The replay is not for the squeamish. De Villiers was part of the chasing pack as flyhalf Patrick Lambie kicked off, and the ensuing ruck changed his destiny for ever. His left boot got stuck in the turf, and as the Welsh pushed him over his knee twisted as his leg bent in the wrong direction. De Villiers' agonised scream could even be clearly heard on television sets, and prompted referee John Lacey to call an immediate halt to proceedings. Play was suspended for several minutes, with paramedics tending to the seriously injured Springbok captain.

Watching the replay, it was difficult to see a way back for De Villiers. "My first thought was that this wasn't the way in which I wanted my rugby career to end. Our forwards coach, Johann van Graan, was with me and said 'Don't worry. It will all work out'," he recalls.

True to form, De Villiers still attended the so-called kontiki, the traditional post-match tongue-in-cheek team meeting, that same night. "It was tough to attend that kontiki, but I didn't want everyone to feel sorry for me," he remembers. "I tried to be positive by making the guys laugh and told them it wasn't about me. It's about South Africa and the team. It was tough to be there with the realisation that it could be the last time that I talk to the team."

De Villiers also put on a brave face after meeting his mother in the lobby of Cardiff's Hilton Hotel. "His first words to me were 'Please don't tell me you're feeling sorry for me, because I'm not feeling sorry for myself'. It was his way of getting over his feelings. He was being strong and had decided he was going to put up a fight," recalls Louise de Villiers.

Such is Jean's strength of character and sense of humour that he inquired on his stretcher whether a penalty had been awarded in the Springboks' favour.

As if the injury wasn't enough, De Villiers had other stress that week with his wife, Marlie, close to giving birth to their third child.

"We had spoken to Jean in the lead-up about whether he wanted to go home, but being the captain he is, he put his country before his personal life," recalls Meyer.

"It was incredibly bad for me to see how he went off. I didn't want his last game to be like that. Once I had gotten over my fears for his safety, my concern about the knock-on effect for the World Cup kicked in.

"I'm not an emotional guy, but I burst into tears when he phoned his wife to tell her that he was OK. You could see he was smashed."

Marlie had not seen the incident live due to electricity load shedding, and messages of support poured in while she was still oblivious to what had happened.

Five days later, De Villiers underwent surgery after which the extent of the injury was made public. The Springbok captain had a full reconstruction of the anterior and posterior cruciate ligaments with an artificial graft, as well as a repair of the medial collateral ligament. His hamstring was also torn. Craig Roberts, the Springboks' team doctor, estimated a recovery period of eight months. That was if, indeed, he recovered. De Villiers would turn 34 in February 2015 and had already entered the twilight of his decorated career.

But life was better than it appeared. Two days after the successful surgery, he hobbled out of the maternity theatre in the Louis Leipoldt Mediclinic with his son Luca. Jean de Villiers was on crutches, but as always could see life in perspective.

However, he was not prepared to die with the World Cup dream inside him. His rehabilitation was overseen by Roberts and the highly regarded duo of Springbok physiotherapist Rene Naylor and Western Province Rugby Union strength and conditioning coach Steph du Toit.

"The important thing in such a situation is that you need the player's buy-in, which we had from the outset. Jean was so determined that nothing would stop him. The easiest part was to get him to train," Du Toit recalls.

With surgery behind him, De Villiers' next step was to strengthen his knee so that he could meet everyday demands. The synergy of the muscles had to be repaired and normal range of movement established. However, there is a big difference between being medically fit and rugby fit. The most important thing for someone in De Villiers' position was achieving a good range of movement and explosiveness.

His first step towards that was in the swimming pool before he moved on to low-impact exercise such as rowing and cycling.

"When you work with certain players, you realise why they are Springboks. Jean's attitude was awesome. We had to pull him back a few times and say 'Listen, Jean, go and spend time with your family'," Du Toit recalls.

On 11 July 2015, De Villiers made an emotional return as a substitute for the Springboks in a warm-up match against the World XV at Newlands. Rather than remain with the Springboks, De Villiers took his next significant steps in a Western Province jersey in friendly matches against the Pumas at the Drakenstein Correctional Centre near Paarl and the Eastern Province Kings in Port Elizabeth.

While he met those challenges, the Springboks stumbled over their first two big hurdles of the season against the Wallabies in Brisbane (24-20) and the All Blacks in Johannesburg (20-27).

His great friend Schalk Burger got his opportunity to lead South Africa in the latter encounter on 25 July 2015 after Victor Matfield was injured against the Wallabies. Burger had knocked on death's door after contracting bacterial meningitis in hospital following surgery to reduce pressure on a nerve causing discomfort in a calf muscle. Burger fought his way back to health and defied medical opinion that he would never be the same as before by excelling for the Stormers in their 2014 Super Rugby campaign and making an emotional return to the Test arena in the 38-16 victory over Wales in Durban on 14 June that year.

It was fitting that Burger, born in Port Elizabeth on 13 April 1983 and like De Villiers a product of Paarl Gymnasium, would captain the Springboks at least once. In what was increasingly becoming a money game, Burger still embraced the amateur ethos. He was a professional in every sense, but played the game with a smile and revelled in the sense of camaraderie and friendship it engendered.

De Villiers' long-awaited return to the Test arena came on 8 August 2015 against Argentina in Durban, but it proved an anticlimax. Not only was the Springboks' 25-37 defeat their first ever against Argentina, but De Villiers suffered yet another injury after being tackled by Juan

Martín Hernández. The Argentine flyhalf's head struck De Villiers on the jaw and put the Springbok captain under renewed pressure in his relentless quest to make it to the World Cup.

The diagnosis was that he would be sidelined for between four and six weeks, with South Africa's first pool match, against Japan, scheduled for 19 September. In De Villiers' initial absence, Meyer had also fostered an exciting new centre pairing of Damian de Allende and Jesse Kriel. These youngsters more than held their own against the Wallabies and All Blacks and, inevitably, public and media increasingly questioned whether De Villiers still belonged in the side.

Meyer, however, stood by his captain and had him pencilled in at inside centre for the Japan clash in Brighton, which will for a long time be regarded as one of the biggest embarrassments in the history of South African rugby. A decorated Springbok side was on the wrong end of a spectacular World Cup upset, with the Cherry Blossoms sealing a late win after a sustained spell of pressure. Blame had to be apportioned and inevitably public opinion was firmly against veterans like De Villiers and Victor Matfield, though neither had played badly.

The De Villiers-led Springboks regained their composure to thrash Samoa 46-6 in Birmingham on 26 September, but it would be his last hurrah. An attempted tackle on Tim Nanai-Williams resulted in a collision between De Villiers' jaw and the shoulder of the Samoan fullback, who was in the motion of passing the ball.

For a minute De Villiers was in denial before the reality sank in that the dream was over.

De Villiers could do no more than console himself with the fact that his Test career stretched for over a decade. Most importantly, he made it to the 2015 Rugby World Cup, a remarkable achievement even if it didn't produce a fairy-tale finish.

Matfield, his deputy in that match, also suffered a hamstring strain, leaving Meyer in a position where he had to select a new captain. The honour fell to Fourie du Preez, who up until the World Cup had featured in only eight Tests in the Meyer era.

Meyer would ideally have included him at every available opportunity, but Du Preez was based in Japan, which raises the conflict between club and country. Du Preez himself had not even been confident that he would recover in time from a knee injury in the run-up to the World Cup.

"Life is funny. A few weeks before the World Cup I didn't think I was going to be there and a few months before that I didn't think I was still going to play rugby. To have become captain is unbelievable for me," he says.

In doing so, he belatedly, at 33 years of age, fulfilled a prophecy by Meyer that he would one day become Springbok captain.

Du Preez, born in Pretoria on 24 March 1982, and a product of Afrikaanse Hoër Seunskool (Affies) in the capital city, was an example of the so-called once-in-a-generation player. South Africa hadn't seen his like before in the professional era and probably wouldn't again.

As a scrumhalf, he had it all. He was an exceptional decision-maker, brilliantly creative, quick, highly intelligent, and he executed his superb passing and kicking game with precision. On top of that, Du Preez was driven to the point of wanting to win at all costs.

Rugby ran in the family, with his father, Fourie Snr, a stalwart as eighthman for the Northern Transvaal between 1963 and 1972. Fourie Jnr's precision-passing was honed by an exercise in which he would thread passes from all angles through the middle of a hanging tyre. Malome Mahlangu, the trusted family gardener with whom Fourie Jnr had a close relationship, would throw the balls back at him. Du Preez would also work exhaustively on his kicking – up-and-unders with both feet to refine a skill in which he would be a cut above the rest.

Du Preez excelled at Affies and was signed to the Blue Bulls Rugby Union, at the time a troubled rugby body that Heyneke Meyer would rebuild from the bottom up to produce a golden generation of players.

"Heyneke told me in the first year that he worked with Fourie that he would one day become a Springbok captain. It was apparent in team meetings that he saw things others didn't and at the time he was only 19. He would point out potential weaknesses in moves and had a much greater vision about the game," Fourie Snr recalls of his genius son.

Du Preez's ability to handle pressure was never more evident than in the week he was appointed captain. A defeat to Scotland in Newcastle on 3 October would have been the Springboks' death knell. But cometh the hour, cometh the captain: South Africa 34, Scotland 16.

Meyer offered this assessment: "I've said before that in times of peace the leaders are not always needed, but that true leaders step up to the plate in times of war and that is what Fourie did for us. He took over from Jean and Victor at a very difficult time for the Springboks, but turned things around for us and the players followed his lead.

"He came through when his team needed him the most and that underlined what an unbelievable captain and player he is."

Having restored the sense of calm to their campaign with the win over Scotland, the Du Preez-led Boks topped the group with a 64-0 thrashing of the USA to set up a quarterfinal against Wales at Twickenham on 17 October. It was a nerve-wracking affair, but Du Preez's try five minutes from full time after a play off the back of a scrum was decisive in securing the 23-19 victory. The Springboks, losers to Japan just under a month earlier, were suddenly poised for glory.

"The loss to Japan was obviously a massive shock, but after that game it could have gone much worse. We could have lost three times in a row and been the worst Springbok team of all time. We had a decision to make – we could lie down or stand up, and we stood up," Du Preez says.

The World Cup didn't run according to script for Jean de Villiers, but much like Du Preez he was a man who elevated the team above himself. He had rejoined the squad and deservedly shared in their joy. It would also help him gain a sense of perspective.

"I played 109 Tests, 37 as captain and never thought I'd get there. If I had to write down goals at the beginning of my career, it would have been to play 50 Tests. I was privileged and look back with fond memories. When it comes to World Cup tournaments, the reality is that I was just very unlucky," he says.

Indeed, it felt almost inevitable that De Villiers would eventually be beaten by injury, but even so he retired from international rugby unbowed.

STATISTICS

(In date order)

Tests played	Tests captained	Opponents	Year	Venue	Result	Score
Castens, HH						
1	1	British Isles & Ireland	1891	Port Elizabeth Cricket Ground	Lost	4-0
Snedden, RCD						
1	1	British Isles & Ireland	1891	Eclectic Cricket Ground, Kimberley	Lost	3-0
Richards, AR						
3	1	British Isles & Ireland	1891	Newlands, Cape Town	Lost	4-0
Aston, F						
4	3	British Isles & Ireland	1896	Crusader Ground, Port Elizabeth	Lost	8-0
				Wanderers, Johannesburg	Lost	17-8
				Kimberley	Lost	9-3
Heatlie, BH						
6	2	British Isles & Ireland	1896	Newlands, Cape Town	Won	5-0
			1903	Newlands, Cape Town	Won	8-0
Frew, A						
1	1	British Isles & Ireland	1903	Wanderers, Johannesburg	Drew	10-10
Powell, JM						
4	1	British Isles & Ireland	1903	KAC Ground, Kimberley	Drew	0-0
Carolin, HW						
3	1	Scotland	1906	Hamden Park, Glasgow	Lost	6-0
Roos, PJ						
4	3	Ireland	1906	Balmoral Ground, Belfast	Won	15-12
		Wales	1906	St Helen's Ground, Swansea	Won	11-0

Tests played	Tests captained	Opponents	Year	Venue	Result	Score
(Roos, PJ , continued)						
		England	1907	Crystal Palace, London	Drew	3-3
Morkel, DFT						
9	2	British Isles & Ireland	1910	Wanderers, Johannesburg	Won	14-10
		England	1913	Twickenham, London	Won	9-3
Millar, WA						
6	5	British Isles & Ireland	1910	Crusader Ground, Port Elizabeth	Won	8-3
				Newlands, Cape Town	Won	21-5
		Ireland	1912	Lansdowne Road, Dublin	Won	38-0
		Wales	1912	Cardiff Arms Park	Won	3-0
		France	1913	Route du Médoc, Le Bouscat, Bordeaux	Won	38-5
Dobbin, FJ						
9	1	Scotland	1912	Inverleith, Edinburgh	Won	16-0

Pienaar, TB

He did not play in any tests. At that stage Queensland rugby was in abeyance and the game was best played in New South Wales, who often played in test matches. Pienaar played against New South Wales. The Springboks won the three encounters. Later in 1921 New South Wales beat New Zealand 17-0.

Morkel, WH						
9	3	New Zealand	1921	Carisbrook, Dunedin	Lost	13-5
				Eden Park, Auckland	Won	9-5
				Athletic Park, Wellington	Drew	0-0
Albertyn, PK						
4	4	British Isles & Ireland	1924	Kingsmead, Durban	Won	7-3
				Wanderers, Johannesburg	Won	17-0
				Crusader Ground, Port Elizabeth	Drew	3-3
				Newlands, Cape Town	Won	16-9
Mostert, PJ						
14	4	New Zealand	1928	Kingsmead, Durban	Won	17-0
				Ellis Park, Johannesburg	Lost	7-6
				Crusader Ground, Port Elizabeth	Won	11-6
				Newlands, Cape Town	Lost	13-5

Tests played	Tests captained	Opponents	Year	Venue	Result	Score

Osler, BL

17	5	Wales	1931	St Helens Ground, Swansea	Won	8-3
		Ireland	1931	Lansdowne Road, Dublin	Won	8-3
		England	1932	Twickenham, London	Won	7-0
		Scotland	1932	Murrayfield, Edinburgh	Won	6-3
		Australia	1933	Kingsmead, Durban	Lost	21-6

Nel, PJ

16	8	Australia	1933	Newlands, Cape Town	Won	17-3
				Ellis Park, Johannesburg	Won	12-3
				Crusader Ground, Port Elizabeth	Won	11-0
				Springbok Park, Bloemfontein	Lost	15-4
			1937	Sydney Cricket Ground	Won	9-5
				Sydney Cricket Ground	Won	26-17
		New Zealand	1937	Lancaster Park, Christchurch	Won	13-6
				Eden Park, Auckland	Won	17-6

Craven, DH

16	4	New Zealand	1937	Athletic Park, Wellington	Lost	13-7
		British Isles & Ireland	1938	Ellis Park, Johannesburg	Won	26-12
				Crusader Ground, Port Elizabeth	Won	19-3
				Newlands, Cape Town	Lost	21-16

Du Plessis, F

3	3	New Zealand	1949	Newlands, Cape Town	Won	15-11
				Ellis Park, Johannesburg	Won	12-6
				Kingsmead, Durban	Won	9-3

Kenyon, BJ

| 1 | 1 | New Zealand | 1949 | Crusader Ground, Port Elizabeth | Won | 11-8 |

Muller, HSV

13	9	Scotland	1951	Murrayfield, Edinburgh	Won	44-0
		Ireland	1951	Lansdowne Road, Dublin	Won	17-5
		Wales	1951	Cardiff Arms Park	Won	6-3
		England	1952	Twickenham, London	Won	8-3
		France	1952	Stade Yves du Manoir, Colombes, Paris	Won	25-3
		Australia	1953	Ellis Park, Johannesburg	Won	25-3
				Newlands, Cape Town	Lost	18-14
				Kingsmead, Durban	Won	18-8
				Crusader Ground, Port Elizabeth	Won	22-9

Tests played	Tests captained	Opponents	Year	Venue	Result	Score
Fry, SP						
13	4	British Isles & Ireland	1955	Ellis Park, Johannesburg	Lost	23-22
				Newlands, Cape Town	Won	25-9
				Loftus Versfeld, Pretoria	Lost	9-6
				Crusader Ground, Port Elizabeth	Won	22-8
Vivier, SS (Also known as Viviers)						
5	5	Australia	1956	Sydney Cricket Ground	Won	9-3
				Exhibition Ground, Melbourne	Won	9-3
		New Zealand	1956	Athletic Park, Wellington	Won	8-3
				Lancaster Park, Christchurch	Lost	17-10
				Eden Park, Auckland	Lost	11-5
Du Rand, JA						
21	1	New Zealand	1956	Carisbrook, Dunedin	Lost	10-6
Claassen, JT						
28	9	France	1958	Newlands, Cape Town	Drew	3-3
				Ellis Park, Johannesburg	Lost	9-5
		Ireland	1961	Newlands, Cape Town	Won	24-8
		Australia	1961	Ellis Park, Johannesburg	Won	28-3
				Boet Erasmus Stadium, Port Elizabeth	Won	23-11
		British Isles & Ireland	1962	Ellis Park, Johannesburg	Drew	3-3
				King's Park, Durban	Won	3-0
				Newlands, Cape Town	Won	8-3
				Free State Stadium, Bloemfontein	Won	34-14
Van Jaarsveldt, DC						
1	1	Scotland	1960	Boet Erasmus Stadium, Port Elizabeth	Won	18-10
Dryburgh, RG						
8	2	New Zealand	1960	Ellis Park, Johannesburg	Won	13-0
				Newlands, Cape Town	Lost	11-3
Malan, AS						
16	10	New Zealand	1960	Free State Stadium, Bloemfontein	Drew	11-11
				Boet Erasmus Stadium, Port Elizabeth	Won	8-3
		Wales	1960	Cardiff Arms Park	Won	3-0

Tests played	Tests captained	Opponents	Year	Venue	Result	Score

(Malan, AS, continued)

		Ireland	1960	Lansdowne Road, Dublin	Won	8-3
		England	1961	Twickenham, London	Won	5-0
		Scotland	1961	Murrayfield, Edinburgh	Won	12-5
		France	1961	Stade Yves du Manoir, Colombes, Paris	Drew	0-0
		Australia	1963	Ellis Park, Johannesburg	Lost	11-9
		Ireland	1965	Lansdowne Road, Dublin	Lost	9-6
		Scotland	1965	Murrayfield, Edinburgh	Lost	8-5

Malan, GF

18	4	Australia	1963	Loftus Versfeld, Pretoria	Won	14-3
				Newlands, Cape Town	Lost	9-5
				Boet Erasmus Stadium, Port Elizabeth	Won	22-6
		Wales	1964	King's Park, Durban	Won	24-3

Smith, CM

7	4	France	1964	PAM Brink Stadium, Springs	Lost	8-6
		Australia	1965	Sydney Cricket Ground	Lost	18-11
				Lang Park, Brisbane	Lost	12-8
		New Zealand	1965	Carisbrook, Dunedin	Lost	13-0
25	22	New Zealand	1965	Athletics Park, Wellington	Lost	6-3

De Villiers, DJ

				Lancaster Park, Christchurch	Won	19-16
				Eden Park, Auckland	Lost	20-3
		France	1967	King's Park, Durban	Won	26-3
				Free State Stadium, Bloemfontein	Won	16-3
				Ellis Park, Johannesburg	Won	19-14
				Newlands, Cape Town	Drew	6-6
		British Isles & Ireland	1968	Loftus Versfeld, Pretoria	Won	25-20
				Boet Erasmus Stadium, Port Elizabeth	Drew	6-6
				Newlands, Cape Town	Won	11-6
				Ellis Park, Johannesburg	Won	19-6
		France	1968	Stade Municipal, Parc Lescure, Bordeaux	Won	12-9
				Stade Yves du Manoir, Colombes, Paris	Won	16-11
		Australia	1969	Ellis Park, Johannesburg	Won	30-11
				Free State Stadium, Bloemfontein	Won	19-8
		England	1969	Twickenham, London	Lost	11-8
		Ireland	1970	Lansdowne Road, Dublin	Drew	8-8
		Wales	1970	Cardiff Arms Park	Drew	6-6
		New Zealand	1970	Loftus Versfeld, Pretoria	Won	17-6
				Newlands, Cape Town	Lost	9-8

Tests played	Tests captained	Opponents	Year	Venue	Result	Score
(De Villiers, DJ, continued)						
				Boet Erasmus Stadium, Port Elizabeth	Won	14-3
				Ellis Park, Johannesburg	Won	20-17
Bedford, TP						
25	3	Australia	1969	King's Park, Durban	Won	16-9
				Newlands, Cape Town	Won	11-3
		Scotland	1969	Murrayfield, Edinburgh	Lost	6-3
Marais, JFK						
35	11	France	1971	Free State Stadium, Bloemfontein	Won	22-9
				King's Park, Durban	Drew	8-8
		Australia	1971	Sydney Cricket Ground	Won	19-11
				Exhibition Ground, Brisbane	Won	14-6
				Sydney Cricket Ground	Won	18-6
		British Isles & Ireland	1974	Newlands, Cape Town	Lost	12-3
				Loftus Versfeld, Pretoria	Lost	28-9
				Boet Erasmus Stadium, Port Elizabeth	Lost	26-9
				Ellis Park, Johannesburg	Drew	13-13
		France	1974	Stadium Municipal, Toulouse	Won	13-4
				Parc des Princes, Paris	Won	10-8
Greyling, PJF						
25	1	England	1972	Ellis Park, Johannesburg	Lost	18-9
Du Plessis, M						
22	15	France	1975	Free State Stadium, Bloemfontein	Won	38-25
				Loftus Versfeld, Pretoria	Won	33-18
		New Zealand	1976	King's Park, Durban	Won	16-7
				Free State Stadium, Bloemfontein	Lost	15-9
				Newlands, Cape Town	Won	15-10
				Ellis Park, Johannesburg	Won	15-14
		World XV	1977	Loftus Versfeld, Pretoria	Won	45-24
		Jaguars	1980	Wanderers, Joahnnesburg	Won	24-9
				King's Park, Durban	Won	18-9
		British Isles & Ireland	1980	Newlands, Cape Town	Won	26-22
				Free State Stadium, Bloemfontein	Won	26-19
				Boet Erasmus Stadium, Port Elizabeth	Won	12-10
				Loftus Versfeld, Pretoria	Lost	17-13
		Jaguars	1980	Prince of Wales Country Club, Santiago	Won	30-16
		France	1980	Loftus Versfeld, Pretoria	Won	37-15

Tests played	Tests captained	Opponents	Year	Venue	Result	Score
Stofberg, MTS						
21	4	Jaguars	1980	Wanderers, Montevideo	Won	22-13
		New Zealand	1981	Lancaster Park, Christchurch	Lost	14-9
		England	1984	Boet Erasmus Stadium, Port Elizabeth	Won	33-15
				Ellis Park, Johannesburg	Won	35-9
Claassen, W						
7	7	Ireland	1981	Newlands, Cape Town	Won	23-15
				King's Park, Durban	Won	12-10
		New Zealand	1981	Athletics Park, Wellington	Won	24-12
				Eden Park, Auckland	Lost	25-22
		USA	1981	Owl Creek Polo Field, Glenville, New York	Won	38-7
		Jaguars	1982	Loftus Versfeld, Pretoria	Won	50-18
				Free State Stadium, Bloemfontein	Lost	21-12
Serfontein, DJ						
19	2	Jaguars	1984	Loftus Versfeld, Pretoria	Won	32-15
				Newlands, Cape Town	Won	22-13
Botha, HE						
23	9	New Zealand Cavaliers	1986	Newlands, Cape Town	Won	21-15
				King's Park, Durban	Lost	19-18
				Loftus Versfeld, Pretoria	Won	33-18
				Ellis Park, Johannesburg	Won	24-10
		New Zealand	1992	Ellis Park, Johannesburg	Lost	27-24
		Australia	1992	Newlands, Cape Town	Lost	26-3
		France	1992	Stade der Gerland, Lyons	Won	20-15
				Parc des Princes, Paris	Lost	29-16
		England	1992	Twickenham, London	Lost	33-16
Breedt, JC						
6	2	World XV	1989	Newlands, Cape Town	Won	20-19
				Ellis Park, Johannesburg	Won	22-16
Pienaar, JF						
29	29	France	1993	King's Park, Durban	Drew	20-20
				Ellis Park, Johannesburg	Lost	18-17
		Australia	1993	Sydney	Won	18-12
				Brisbane	Lost	28-20

Tests played	Tests captained	Opponents	Year	Venue	Result	Score
(Pienaar, JF, continued)						
				Sydney	Lost	19-12
		Argentina	1993	Estadio Ferro Carril Oeste, Buenos Aires	Won	29-26
				Estadio Ferro Carril Oeste, Buenos Aires	Won	52-23
		England	1994	Loftus Versfeld, Pretoria	Lost	32-15
				Newlands, Cape Town	Won	27-9
		New Zealand	1994	Athletics Park, Wellington	Lost	13-9
				Eden Park, Auckland	Drew	18-18
		Argentina	1994	Boet Erasmus Stadium, Port Elizabeth	Won	42-22
				Ellis Park, Johannesburg	Won	46-26
		Scotland	1994	Murrayfield, Edinburgh	Won	34-10
		Wales	1994	National Stadium, Cardiff	Won	20-12
		Western Samoa	1995	Ellis Park, Johannesburg	Won	60-8
		Australia	1995	Newlands, Cape Town	Won	27-18
		Canada	1995	Boet Erasmus, Stadium, Port Elizabeth	Won	20-0
		Western Samoa	1995	Ellis Park, Johannesburg	Won	42-14
		France	1995	King's Park, Durban	Won	19-15
		New Zealand	1995	Ellis Park, Johannesburg	Won	15-12
		Wales	1995	Ellis Park, Johannesburg	Won	40-11
		Italy	1995	Stadio Olimpico, Rome	Won	40-21
		England	1995	Twickenham, London	Won	24-14
		Fiji	1996	Loftus Versfeld, Pretoria	Won	43-18
		Australia	1996	Sydney	Lost	21-16
				Free State Stadium, Bloemfontein	Won	25-19
		New Zealand	1996	Lancaster Park, Christchurch	Lost	15-11
				Newlands, Cape Town	Lost	29-18
Strauss, CP						
15	1	New Zealand	1994	Carisbrook, Dunedin	Lost	22-14
Richter, AH						
10	1	Romania	1995	Newlands, Cape Town	Won	21-8
Teichmann, GH						
42	36	New Zealand	1996	King's Park, Durban	Lost	23-19
				Loftus Versfeld, Pretoria	Lost	23-19
				Ellis Park, Johannesburg	Won	32-22
		Argentina	1996	Estadio Ferro Carril Oeste, Buenos Aires	Won	46-15
				Estadio Ferro Carril Oeste, Buenos Aires	Won	44-21
		France	1996	Stade Municipal, Parc Lescure, Bordeaux	Won	22-12
				Parc des Princes, Paris	Won	13-12
		Wales	1996	National Stadium, Cardiff	Won	37-20

Tests played	Tests captained	Opponents	Year	Venue	Result	Score
(Teichmann, GH, continued)						
		Tonga	1997	Newlands, Cape Town	Won	74-10
		Lions	1997	Newlands, Cape Town	Lost	25-16
				King's Park, Durban	Lost	18-15
				Ellis Park, Johannesburg	Won	35-16
		New Zealand	1997	Ellis Park, Johannesburg	Lost	35-32
		Australia	1997	Suncorp Stadium, Brisbane	Lost	32-20
		New Zealand	1997	Eden Park, Auckland	Lost	55-35
		Australia	1997	Loftus Versfeld, Pretoria	Won	61-22
		Italy	1997	Stadio Dall'Ara, Bologna	Won	62-31
		France	1997	Stade der Gerland, Lyon	Won	36-32
				Parc des Princes, Paris	Won	52-10
		England	1997	Twickenham, London	Won	29-11
		Scotland	1997	Murrayfield, Edinburgh	Won	68-10
		Ireland	1998	Free State Stadium, Bloemfontein	Won	37-13
				Loftus Versfeld, Pretoria	Won	33-0
		Wales	1998	Loftus Versfeld, Pretoria	Won	96-13
		England	1998	Newlands, Cape Town	Won	18-0
		Australia	1998	Subiaco Oval, Perth	Won	14-13
		New Zealand	1998	Athletics Park, Wellington	Won	13-3
				King's Park, Durban	Won	24-23
		Australia	1998	Ellis Park, Johannesburg	Won	29-15
		Wales	1998	Wembley Stadium, London	Won	28-20
		Scotland	1998	Murrayfield, Edinburgh	Won	35-10
		Ireland	1998	Lansdowne Road, Dublin	Won	27-13
		England	1998	Twickenham, London	Lost	13-7
		Italy	1999	Boet Erasmus Stadium, Port Elizabeth	Won	74-3
		Wales	1999	Millennium Stadium, Cardiff	Lost	29-19
		New Zealand	1999	Carisbrook, Dunedin	Lost	28-0
Erasmus, J						
34	1	Australia	1999	Suncorp Stadium, Brisbane	Lost	32-6
Van der Westhuizen, JH						
68	7	New Zealand	1999	Loftus Versfeld, Pretoria	Lost	34-18
		Australia	1999	Newlands, Cape Town	Won	10-9
		Scotland	1999	Murrayfield, Edinburgh	Won	46-29
		Uruguay	1999	Hampden Park, Glasgow	Won	39-3
		England	1999	Stade de France, Paris	Won	44-21
		Australia	1999	Twickenham, London	Lost	27-21
		New Zealand	1999	Millennium Stadium, Cardiff	Won	22-18

Tests played	Tests captained	Opponents	Year	Venue	Result	Score
Vos, AN						
22	13	Spain	1999	Murrayfield, Edinburgh	Won	48-0
		Canada	2000	Basil Kenyon Stadium, East London	Won	51-18
		England	2000	Loftus Versfeld, Pretoria	Won	18-13
				Free State Stadium, Bloemfontein	Lost	27-22
		Australia	2000	Colonial Stadium, Queensland	Lost	44-23
		New Zealand	2000	Lancaster Park, Christchurch	Lost	25-12
		Australia	2000	Stadium Australia, Sydney	Lost	26-6
		New Zealand	2000	Ellis Park, Johannesburg	Won	46-40
		Australia	2000	King's Park, Durban	Lost	19-18
		Argentina	2000	River Plate Stadium, Buenos Aires	Won	37-33
		Ireland	2000	Lansdowne Road, Dublin	Won	28-18
		Wales	2000	Millennium Stadium, Cardiff	Won	23-13
		England	2000	Twickenham, London	Lost	25-17
		France	2001	Ellis Park, Johannesburg	Lost	32-23
		France	2001	Absa Stadium, Durban	Won	20-15
Skinstad, RB						
42	12	Italy	2001	Telkom Park, Port Elizabeth	Won	60-14
		New Zealand	2001	Fedsure Park Newlands, Cape Town	Lost	12-3
		Australia	2001	Minolta Loftus, Pretoria	Won	20-15
				Subiaco Oval, Perth	Drew	14-14
		New Zealand	2001	Eden Park, Auckland	Lost	26-15
		France	2001	Stade de France, Paris	Lost	20-10
		Italy	2001	Stadio Luigi Ferraris, Genoa	Won	54-26
		England	2001	Twickenham, London	Lost	29-9
		Wales	2002	Vodacom Park, Bloemfontein	Won	34-19
				Newlands, Cape Town	Won	19-8
		Australia	2007	Telstra Stadium, Sydney	Lost	25-17
		Tonga	2007	Stade Felix Bollaert, Lens	Won	30-25
Krige, CP						
39	18	Italy	1999	King's Park, Durban	Won	101-0
		Argentina	2002	PAM Brink Stadium, Springs	Won	49-29
		Samoa	2002	Loftus Versfeld, Pretoria	Won	60-18
		New Zealand	2002	Westpac Trust Stadium, Wellington	Lost	41-20
		Australia	2002	The Gabba, Brisbane	Lost	38-27
		New Zealand	2002	Absa Stadium, Durban	Lost	30-23
		Australia	2002	Ellis Park, Johannesburg	Won	33-31
		France	2002	Stade Velodrome, Marseilles	Lost	30-10
		Scotland	2002	Murrayfield, Edinburgh	Lost	21-6
		England	2002	Twickenham, London	Lost	53-3
		Argentina	2003	EPRFU Stadium, Port Elizabeth	Won	26-25
		Australia	2003	Newlands, Cape Town	Won	26-22

Tests played	Tests captained	Opponents	Year	Venue	Result	Score
(Krige, CP, continued)						
		New Zealand	2003	Loftus Versfeld, Pretoria	Lost	52-16
		Australia	2003	Suncorp Stadium, Brisbane	Lost	29-9
		New Zealand	2003	Carisbrook, Dunedin	Lost	19-11
		England	2003	Subiaco Oval, Perth	Lost	25-6
		Samoa	2003	Suncorp Stadium, Brisbane	Won	60-10
		New Zealand	2003	Telstra Dome, Melbourne	Lost	29-9
Smit, JW						
111	83	Georgia	2003	Stadium Australia, Sydney	Won	46-19
		Ireland	2004	Vodacom Park, Bloemfontein	Won	31-17
				Newlands, Cape Town	Won	26-17
		Wales	2004	Securicor Loftus, Pretoria	Won	53-18
		Pacific Islands	2004	Express Advocate Stadium, Gosford	Won	38-24
		New Zealand	2004	Jade Stadium, Christchurch	Lost	23-21
		Australia	2004	Subiaco Oval, Perth	Lost	30-26
		New Zealand	2004	Ellis Park, Johannesburg	Won	40-26
		Australia	2004	Absa Stadium, Durban	Won	23-19
		Wales	2004	Millennium Stadium, Cardiff	Won	38-36
		Ireland	2004	Lansdowne Road, Dublin	Lost	17-12
		England	2004	Twickenham, London	Lost	32-16
		Scotland	2004	Murrayfield, Edinburgh	Won	45-10
		Argentina	2004	José Amalfitani Stadium, Buenos Aires	Won	39-7
		Uruguay	2005	Absa Stadium, East London	Won	134-3
		France	2005	Absa Stadium, Durban	Drew	30-30
				EPRFU Stadium, Port Elizabeth	Won	27-13
		Australia	2005	Telstra Stadium, Sydney	Lost	30-12
				Ellis Park, Johannesburg	Won	33-20
				Securicor Loftus, Pretoria	Won	22-16
		New Zealand	2005	Newlands, Cape Town	Won	22-16
		Australia	2005	Subiaco Oval, Perth	Won	22-19
		New Zealand	2005	Carisbrook, Dunedin	Lost	31-27
		Argentina	2005	José Amalfitani Stadium, Buenos Aires	Won	34-23
		Wales	2005	Millennium Stadium, Cardiff	Won	33-16
		France	2005	Stade de France, Paris	Lost	26-20
		Scotland	2006	Absa Stadium, Durban	Won	36-16
				EPRFU Stadium, Port Elizabeth	Won	29-15
		France	2006	Newlands, Cape Town	Lost	36-26
		Australia	2006	Suncorp Stadium, Brisbane	Lost	49-0
		New Zealand	2006	Westpac Stadium, Wellington	Lost	35-17
		Australia	2006	Telstra Stadium, Sydney	Lost	20-18
		New Zealand	2006	Loftus Versfeld, Pretoria	Lost	45-26
				Royal Bafokeng Sports Palace	Won	21-20
		Australia	2006	Ellis Park, Johannesburg	Won	24-16
		Ireland	2006	Lansdowne Road, Dublin	Lost	32-15

Tests played	Tests captained	Opponents	Year	Venue	Result	Score
(Smit, JW, continued)						
		England	2006	Twickenham, London	Lost	23-21
				Twickenham, London	Won	25-14
		England	2007	Vodacom Park, Bloemfontein	Won	58-10
				Loftus Versfeld, Pretoria	Won	55-22
		Samoa	2007	Ellis Park, Johannesburg	Won	35-8
		Australia	2007	Newlands, Cape Town	Won	22-19
		Samoa	2007	Parc des Princes, Paris	Won	59-7
		England	2007	Stade de France, Paris	Won	36-0
		USA	2007	Stade de la Mosson, Montpellier	Won	64-15
		Fiji	2007	Stade Velodrome, Marseille	Won	37-20
		Argentina	2007	Stade de France, Paris	Won	37-13
		England	2007	Stade de France, Paris	Won	15-6
		Wales	2007	Millennium Stadium, Cardiff	Won	34-12
		Wales	2008	Vodacom Park, Bloemfontein	Won	43-17
				Loftus Versfeld, Pretoria	Won	37-21
		New Zealand	2008	Westpac Stadium, Wellington	Lost	19-8
		Wales	2008	Millennium Stadium, Cardiff	Won	20-15
		Scotland	2008	Murrayfield, Edinburgh	Won	14-10
		England	2008	Twickenham, London	Won	42-6
		Lions	2009	Absa Stadium, Durban	Won	26-21
				Loftus Versfeld, Pretoria	Won	28-25
				Coca-Cola Park, Johannesburg	Lost	28-9
		New Zealand	2009	Vodacom Park, Bloemfontein	Won	28-19
				Absa Stadium, Durban	Won	31-19
		Australia	2009	Newlands, Cape Town	Won	29-17
		Australia	2009	Subiaco Oval, Perth	Won	32-25
				Suncorp Stadium, Brisbane	Lost	21-6
		New Zealand	2009	Waikato Stadium, Hamilton	Won	32-29
		France	2009	Stadium Municipal, Toulouse	Lost	20-13
		Italy	2009	Stadio Friuli, Udine	Won	32-10
		Ireland	2009	Croke Park, Dublin	Lost	15-10
		Wales	2010	Millennium Stadium, Cardiff	Won	34-31
		France	2010	Newlands, Cape Town	Won	42-17
		Italy	2010	Buffalo City Stadium, East London	Won	55-11
		New Zealand	2010	Eden Park, Auckland	Lost	32-12
				Westpac Stadium, Wellington	Lost	31-17
		Australia	2010	Suncorp Stadium, Brisbane	Lost	30-13
		New Zealand	2010	FNB Stadium, Soweto	Lost	29-22
		Australia	2010	Loftus Versfeld, Pretoria	Won	44-31
				Vodacom Park, Bloemfontein	Lost	41-39
		Australia	2011	ANZ Stadium, Sydney	Lost	39-20
		New Zealand	2011	Westpac Stadium, Wellington	Lost	40-7
		Australia	2011	Mr Price Kings Park, Durban	Lost	14-9
		Wales	2011	Wellington Regional Stadium	Won	17-16
		Fiji	2011	Wellington Regional Stadium	Won	49-3

Tests played	Tests captained	Opponents	Year	Venue	Result	Score
(Smit, JW, continued)						
		Namibia	2011	North Harbour Stadium, Albany	Won	87-0
		Australia	2011	Wellington Regional Stadium	Lost	11-9
Muller, GJ						
24	1	New Zealand	2007	Jade Stadium, Christchurch	Lost	33-6
Matfield, V						
125	22	New Zealand	2007	Absa Stadium, Durban	Lost	26-21
		Namibia	2007	Newlands, Cape Town	Won	105-13
		Scotland	2007	Murrayfield, Edinburgh	Won	27-3
		Italy	2008	Newlands, Cape Town	Won	26-0
		Argentina	2008	Coca-Cola Park, Johannesburg	Won	63-9
		New Zealand	2008	Carisbrook, Dunedin	Won	30-28
		Australia	2008	Subiaco Oval, Perth	Lost	16-9
		New Zealand	2008	Newlands, Cape Town	Lost	19-0
		Australia	2008	Absa Stadium, Durban	Lost	27-15
				Coca-Cola Park, Johannesburg	Won	53-8
		Italy	2010	Puma Stadium, Witbank	Won	29-13
		Ireland	2010	Aviva Stadium, Dublin	Won	23-21
		Wales	2010	Millennium Stadium, Cardiff	Won	29-25
		Scotland	2010	Murrayfield, Edinburgh	Lost	21-17
		England	2010	Twickenham, London	Won	21-11
		New Zealand	2011	Nelson Mandela Bay Stadium, PE	Won	18-5
		Samoa	2011	North Harbour Stadium, Albany	Won	13-5
		Wales	2014	Growthpoint Kings Park, Durban	Won	38-16
				Mbombela Stadium, Nelspruit	Won	31-30
		Scotland	2014	Nelson Mandela Bay Stadium, PE	Won	55-6
		Australia	2015	Suncorp Stadium, Brisbane	Lost	24-20
		Argentina	2015	Estadio José Amalfitani, Buenos Aires	Won	26-12
De Villiers, J						
109	37	England	2012	Mr Price Kings Park, Durban	Won	22-17
				Coca-Cola Park, Johannesburg	Won	36-27
				Nelson Mandela Bay Stadium, PE	Drew	14-14
		Argentina	2012	DHL Newlands, Cape Town	Won	27-6
		Argentina	2012	Malvinas Argentinas Stadium, Mendoza	Drew	16-16
		Australia	2012	Patersons Stadium, Perth	Lost	26-19
		New Zealand	2012	Forsyth Barr Stadium, Dunedin	Lost	21-11
		Australia	2012	Loftus Versfeld, Pretoria	Won	31-8
		New Zealand	2012	FNB Stadium, Soweto	Lost	32-16
		Ireland	2012	Aviva Stadium, Dublin	Won	16-12
		Scotland	2012	Murrayfield, Edinburgh	Won	21-10

Tests played	Tests captained	Opponents	Year	Venue	Result	Score
(De Villiers, J, continued)						
		England	2012	Twickenham, London	Won	16-15
		Italy	2013	Growthpoint Kings Park, Durban	Won	44-10
		Scotland	2013	Mbombela Stadium, Nelspruit	Won	30-17
		Samoa	2013	Loftus Versfeld, Pretoria	Won	56-23
		Argentina	2013	FNB Stadium, Soweto	Won	73-13
		Argentina	2013	Malvinas Argentinas Stadium, Mendoza	Won	22-17
		Australia	2013	Suncorp Stadium, Brisbane	Won	38-12
		New Zealand	2013	Eden Park, Auckland	Lost	29-15
		Australia	2013	DHL Newlands, Cape Town	Won	28-8
		New Zealand	2013	Ellis Park, Johannesburg	Lost	38-27
		Wales	2013	Millennium Stadium, Cardiff	Won	24-15
		Scotland	2013	Murrayfield, Edinburgh	Won	28-0
		France	2013	Stade de France, Paris	Won	19-10
		Argentina	2014	Loftus Versfeld, Pretoria	Won	13-6
		Argentina	2014	Estadio Padre Ernesto Martearena, Salta	Won	33-31
		Australia	2014	Patersons Stadium, Perth	Lost	24-23
		New Zealand	2014	Westpac Stadium, Wellington	Lost	14-10
		Australia	2014	DHL Newlands, Cape Town	Won	28-10
		New Zealand	2014	Ellis Park, Johannesburg	Won	27-25
		Ireland	2014	Aviva Stadium, Dublin	Lost	29-15
		England	2014	Twickenham, London	Won	31-28
		Italy	2014	Stadio Euganeo, Padua	Won	22-6
		Wales	2014	Millennium Stadium, Cardiff	Lost	12-6
		Argentina	2015	Growthpoint Kings Park, Durban	Lost	37-25
		Japan	2015	Brighton Community Centre, Brighton	Lost	34-32
		Samoa	2015	Villa Park, Birmingham	Won	46-6
Burger, SWP						
84	1	New Zealand	2015	Emirates Airline Park, Johannesburg	Lost	27-20
Du Preez, PF						
75	3	Scotland	2015	St James' Park, Newcastle	Won	34-16
		USA	2015	Olympic Stadium, London	Won	64-0
		Wales	2015	Twickenham, London	Won	23-19

INDEX

CPSIA information can be obtained
at www.ICGtesting.com
Printed in the USA
LVHW020041240120
644556LV00001B/2